PUNISHMENT AND PRIVATE LAW

The role of punishment in private law is controversial, and the dominance of the compensatory paradigm has tended to deflect attention away from difficult questions that arise in this regard. This volume aims to redress this imbalance. It examines instances or potential instances of punishment in private law. In doing so, it engages with complex debates such as whether private law ought to be an engine of punishment and, if so, how and when punishment should be dispensed. The chapters span the full width of private law, and are written by leading scholars drawn from a range of jurisdictions.

Volume 38 in the series Hart Studies in Private Law

Punishment and Private Law

Edited by
Elise Bant
Wayne Courtney
James Goudkamp
and
Jeannie Marie Paterson

•HART•
OXFORD • LONDON • NEW YORK • NEW DELHI • SYDNEY

HART PUBLISHING
Bloomsbury Publishing Plc
Kemp House, Chawley Park, Cumnor Hill, Oxford, OX2 9PH, UK
1385 Broadway, New York, NY 10018, USA
29 Earlsfort Terrace, Dublin 2, Ireland

First published in Great Britain 2021

A catalogue record for this book is available from the British Library.

Library of Congress Cataloging-in-Publication data

Names: Bant, Elise, editor. | Goudkamp, James, 1980- editor. | Paterson, Jeannie Marie, editor. | Courtney, Wayne, editor.

Title: Punishment and private law / edited by Elise Bant, James Goudkamp, Jeannie Marie Paterson and Wayne Courtney.

Description: Oxford, UK ; New York, NY : Hart Publishing, an imprint of Bloomsbury Publishing, 2021. | Series: Hart studies in private law ; volume 38 | Includes bibliographical references and index.

Identifiers: LCCN 2021004150 (print) | LCCN 202100415 (ebook) | ISBN 9781509939152 (hardback) | ISBN 9781509949465 (paperback) | ISBN 9781509939176 (pdf) | ISBN 9781509939169 (Epub)

Subjects: LCSH: Exemplary damages—English-speaking countries. | Punishment—Philosophy.

Classification: LCC K923 .P859 2021 (print) | LCC K923 (ebook) | DDC 346.03—dc23

LC record available at https://lccn.loc.gov/2021004150

LC ebook record available at https://lccn.loc.gov/2021004151

ISBN: HB: 978-1-50993-915-2
ePDF: 978-1-50993-917-6
ePub: 978-1-50993-916-9

Typeset by Compuscript Ltd, Shannon

To find out more about our authors and books visit www.hartpublishing.co.uk. Here you will find extracts, author information, details of forthcoming events and the option to sign up for our newsletters.

FOREWORD

When I was a student more than four decades ago, the received wisdom was clear: punishment (as part of the criminal law) stood in sharp contrast to private law, and never the twain shall meet. Well, they might meet once in a blue moon in the form of a truly exceptional award of punitive damages in the law of tort. Even that rare exception baffled me as a student because the legal criteria laid down in the seminal House of Lords decision of *Rookes v Barnard* [1964] AC 1129 (commonly referred to as the categories test) seemed, with respect, odd (I shall return to this point briefly later). Indeed, this strict dichotomy – as is pointed out right at the outset of the very first chapter in this book – stood for a great many years.

However, the common law never stands still. Indeed, the ability to – as well the attainment of actual – change is part of its genius. That an ostensibly cumbersome 'creature' can suddenly turn sharply agile has always fascinated me – and even more so after leaving legal academia and joining the Bench. Watching and even harnessing as well as applying it in practical action, so to speak, has made me marvel at this unique quality all the more. The manner in which the concept of punishment has found its way into the warp and woof of private law is an excellent illustration of this. That it has done so in different ways in different jurisdictions points to another (admittedly more recent) phenomenon – the concept of 'comparative common law' (as contrasted with the traditional dichotomy in comparative law between the common law on the one hand and civil law on the other). Indeed, a striking example of this can be seen, in fact, in relation to the issue concerning the award of punitive damages in the law of tort to which I have already referred. Shortly after the decision in *Rookes v Barnard* was issued, the High Court of Australia famously declined to follow the categories test laid down in that decision in *Uren v John Fairfax & Sons Pty Ltd* (1966) 117 CLR 118. Indeed, the categories test was also rejected by the New Zealand Court of Appeal in *Taylor v Beere* [1982] 1 NZLR 81 and by the Appellate Division of the Alberta Supreme Court in *Paragon Properties Ltd v Magna Envestments Ltd* (1972) 24 DLR(3d) 156 (which was, in turn, subsequently endorsed by the Supreme Court of Canada in *Vorvis v Insurance Corporation of British Columbia* [1989] 1 SCR 1085). However, the Hong Kong courts have consistently endorsed the categories test in *Rookes v Barnard*, although the situation in Malaysia appears somewhat less clear. All these decisions were considered by the Singapore Court of Appeal in *ACB v Thomson Medical Pte Ltd* [2017] 1 SLR 918, which ultimately declined to follow the categories test and held that that test (hitherto applicable in Singapore) should be departed from.

The present book brings both the aforementioned threads together in a seamless fashion. It is a landmark in assembling together under one legal roof the latest scholarship on what is – in terms of legal age – the relatively 'young' development of punishment in the context of private law. It also accomplishes this in a manner that maximises the comparative impact. It bears emphasising that such an impact cannot be underestimated, particularly in the context of increased (and increasing) globalisation and internationalisation. Indeed, the resultant opportunity for jurisdictions to learn from each other is, in my view, of inestimable value (as, for example, was the case in Singapore in relation to the legal test governing the award of punitive damages in the law of tort as described briefly in the preceding paragraph). Looked at in this light, the present book is, in every sense, an accomplishment of the first rank.

Turning to this work proper, the various chapters are bookended by two excellent chapters, the authorship of which has been shared between the editors. The first is an overview of the book itself whilst the second looks to the future of the law in this particular (and developing) area. Indeed, the former chapter is so comprehensive that it would be an exercise in futility for me to even attempt to describe the various chapters in any detail. What I would like to state is that I was deeply impressed by each and every chapter and learnt much from them. I will endeavour to describe briefly only the highlights of this experience in the remaining part of this Foreword.

The first chapter (by Wayne Courtney and James Goudkamp, entitled 'Punishment and Private Law') comprises Part I of the book (aptly described as 'Introduction'). As already mentioned, it summarises the various chapters that follow – if I may say so – brilliantly. This constitutes, in fact, the second part of the chapter; the first part is an equally brilliant introduction (and response) to the various issues that arise in the form of various conceptual objections to discourse about punishment in the context of private law.

Part II of the book encompasses subject matter within its very title – 'History, Theory and Concepts'. I found the foundational chapter by Kit Barker (Chapter 2, intriguingly entitled 'Punishment in Private Law – No Such Thing (Any More)') most interesting and instructive as he explores the meaning and function of punishment in private law from historical as well as theoretical perspectives. Chapter 3, entitled 'Punishment and Private Law: Some Comparative Observations' by Solène Rowan, underscores what I have always felt to be important – comparative insights (here, from French law). I found the next chapter (Chapter 4, entitled 'Privacy, Punishment and Private Law') by Andrew Roberts and Megan Richardson particularly interesting because of their utilisation of theories of *criminalisation* as a basis for justifying the use of *private* law in the context of the punishment of breaches of privacy. Chapter 5, entitled 'Punishments and Penalties in Private Law' by James Penner, seeks to escape the concept of 'punishment' by focusing, instead, on that of 'penalties'; this is a very interesting idea which the author skilfully applies to the law governing fiduciaries (itself a category which had not occurred to me in this particular context). The final chapter in this Part is Chapter 6 and is entitled 'The Ultimate Sanction: The Purpose and Role of Contempt in Private Law Litigation' by David Rolph. Once again, I found this chapter of great interest, focusing as it does on the specific topic of contempt of court which, as the author correctly points out, has both criminal as well as civil aspects – the relationship between which is not necessarily coherent and/or clear-cut.

Part III of the book is devoted entirely to the important topic of 'Punitive Damages'. Chapter 7, entitled 'Punitive Damages Transformed into Societal Damages' by Catherine M Sharkey, is the first chapter in this Part. I found it interesting not only because it was written from a US law perspective but also because the author attempts to resolve the perennial tension between retribution and deterrence by arguing for a transformation of punitive damages into what she terms 'societal damages'. The following chapter (Chapter 8, entitled 'Punitive Damages: Ten Misconceptions' by James Goudkamp and Eleni Katsampouka) is the equivalent of an excellent collection of short stories that have been woven around a common theme. Put simply, each of the ten misconceptions is self-contained but each is also an example of what solid legal reasoning ought to be. Chapter 9, entitled 'Exemplary Damages in Contract Law' by Katy Barnett, deals with the vexed question as to whether or not punitive damages ought to be awarded in a *contractual* context. The author's survey is an excellent example of comparative common law and her arguments in favour of the award of such damages will give much legal food for thought. I found the next chapter (Chapter 10, entitled 'Effecting Deterrence through Proportionate Punishment' by Elise Bant and Jeannie Marie Paterson), a fascinating legal tapestry woven from both the common law as well as statute, and which presents a compelling case for the concept of proportionality in punishment in the private law context. The final chapter in this Part (Chapter 11, entitled 'Vicarious Punishment: Vicarious Liability for Exemplary Damages' by Phillip Morgan) raised, once again, a topic which had not occurred to me but which is of the first importance in the practical context and which therefore generated much legal food for thought. It puts forward a particularly persuasive case, in my view, with regard to the vicarious liability of the State.

Part IV of the book is entitled 'Limiting Punishment' – more accurately, in the context of the law of *contract*. The first chapter in this Part (Chapter 12, entitled 'Agreed Punishment' by Wayne Courtney) serves a dual-function inasmuch as it not only furnished me with an excellent overview of developments in three significant areas of law (*viz*, the Penalty Rule, relief against forfeiture and the control of contractual powers consequent upon a breach of contract) but also proffered an interesting argument that these doctrines were not really about preventing punishment and that, to the limited extent that they did, were circumscribed by the concept of proportionality. The following chapter (Chapter 13, entitled 'Controlling Private Punishment in Three Dimensions: Penalties and Forfeiture in England and Australia' by Nicholas A Tiverios and Ben McFarlane) is, as its title suggests, a highly interesting comparative analysis of two very topical areas of the law by authors who are recognised specialists in both the areas of law concerned. The final chapter (Chapter 14, entitled 'Penalty in the Contract of Employment: The Good, the Bad (Leavers) and the Ugly' by Mimi Zou and Hin Liu) raised another topic that I was not familiar with – the operation of the Penalty Rule in the employment context. In this chapter, the authors argue persuasively that the Penalty Rule is an inadequate legal response and suggest that there should be statutory reform instead.

Part V is the concluding Part and is aptly entitled 'Conclusion'. It comprises, as in Part I, one chapter (Chapter 15, entitled 'Punishment and Private Law: Future Themes and Perspectives' by Elise Bant and Jeannie Marie Paterson). It is yet another excellent chapter by the other editors of this fine work. As the title of the Chapter itself suggests, the authors deal with broad themes that would require to be considered in the future – the role of punishment in achieving private law aims, managing the fluid and interlocking boundaries (particularly between the criminal law on the one hand and the civil law on the other), the importance of testing deterrence (via more empirical research and the more traditional legal analysis of the 'fit' between punishment measures as well as awards on the one hand and deterrent objectives on the other), and the role that statute can play in the future development of the law in this area. In the authors' view, 'the way forward' is one that integrates insights not only across the criminal and civil spheres but also 'the considerable insights offered from theoretical, economic, political, historic, comparative and broader perspectives' (p 408). Indeed, they demonstrate, in fact, how this integration might look like in very skilfully weaving together the many insights in the various chapters into the aforementioned broad themes themselves.

This is a fine work of scholarship that will surely be one of the leading texts in this important and developing area of the law. As I have sought to demonstrate within the brief compass of this Foreword, there is an incredible amount of insights that one can glean from all the chapters. The authors and editors are to be warmly congratulated on this excellent work. I commend this book to all who are interested in the law in the highest possible terms.

Andrew Phang
Justice of the Court of Appeal
Supreme Court of Singapore
February 2021

PREFACE

This volume was conceived during a chance conversation in July 2018 at the Obligations IX conference at Melbourne Law School. Following this initial discussion, it quickly became clear that the four of us had a common interest in the role of punishment in private law and plans for a project on this theme progressed rapidly. A workshop was arranged at which drafts of the chapters that comprise this volume were presented. It was generously hosted by the National University of Singapore over the course of three days in December 2019. We particularly thank Finna Wong for her diligent work in relation to the administrative arrangements. We also wish gratefully to acknowledge financial support provided by the Allan Myers Oxford-Melbourne Research Partnership and the EW Barker Centre for Law and Business at the National University of Singapore. Without these sources of funding neither the workshop nor this volume would have been possible. In addition, we thank Justice of the Court of Appeal Andrew Phang for kindly agreeing to write the foreword. As a leading contributor to Singapore's important and highly respected jurisprudence in this field, we are delighted that he has introduced the volume. Harry Bithell, Sophie Hepburn and Titiksha Mohanty provided valuable research assistance in connection with our own editorial work on the chapters. Finally, we express our gratitude to Hart Publishing and its copyeditor Catherine Minahan. Hart Publishing immediately and enthusiastically backed the project. It is undoubtedly the best in the business in facilitating research of this kind.

Elise Bant
Wayne Courtney
James Goudkamp
Jeannie Marie Paterson
7 January 2021

CONTENTS

Foreword ... v
Preface ... ix
Contributors ... xiii
Table of Cases ... xv
Table of Legislation ... xxxvii

PART I
INTRODUCTION

1. *Punishment and Private Law* ... 3
Wayne Courtney and James Goudkamp

PART II
HISTORY, THEORY AND CONCEPTS

2. *Punishment in Private Law – No Such Thing (Any More)* ... 35
Kit Barker

3. *Punishment and Private Law: Some Comparative Observations* ... 63
Solène Rowan

4. *Privacy, Punishment and Private Law* ... 83
Andrew Roberts and Megan Richardson

5. *Punishments and Penalties in Private Law, with Particular Reference to the Law Governing Fiduciaries* ... 105
James Penner

6. *The Ultimate Sanction: The Purpose and Role of Contempt in Private Law Litigation* ... 131
David Rolph

PART III
PUNITIVE DAMAGES

7. *Punitive Damages Transformed into Societal Damages* ... 155
Catherine M Sharkey

8. *Punitive Damages: Ten Misconceptions* 187
James Goudkamp and Eleni Katsampouka

9. *Exemplary Damages in Contract Law* 225
Katy Barnett

10. *Effecting Deterrence through Proportionate Punishment: An Assessment of Statutory and General Law Principles* 255
Elise Bant and Jeannie Marie Paterson

11. *Vicarious Punishment: Vicarious Liability for Exemplary Damages?* 287
Phillip Morgan

PART IV
LIMITING PUNISHMENT

12. *Agreed Punishment* 321
Wayne Courtney

13. *Controlling Private Punishment in Three Dimensions: Penalties and Forfeiture in England and Australia* 351
Nicholas A Tiverios and Ben McFarlane

14. *Penalty in the Contract of Employment: The Good, the Bad (Leavers) and the Ugly* 375
Mimi Zou and Hin Liu

PART V
CONCLUSION

15. *Punishment and Private Law: Future Themes and Perspectives* 397
Elise Bant and Jeannie Marie Paterson

Index 409

CONTRIBUTORS

Elise Bant is Professor of Private Law and Commercial Regulation at the University of Western Australia and a Professorial Fellow at Melbourne Law School.

Kit Barker is Professor of Private Law at the TC Beirne School of Law, University of Queensland.

Katy Barnett is Professor of Law at Melbourne Law School.

Wayne Courtney is Professor at the National University of Singapore.

James Goudkamp is Professor of the Law of Obligations at Oxford University and a Fellow of Keble College, Oxford.

Eleni Katsampouka is a Stipendiary Lecturer in Private Law at St Anne's College, Oxford.

Hin Liu is Lecturer in Private Law at St Hugh's College, Oxford.

Ben McFarlane is Professor of English Law at Oxford University and a Fellow of St John's College, Oxford.

Phillip Morgan is Senior Lecturer in Law at the University of York.

Jeannie Marie Paterson is Professor of Law at Melbourne Law School.

James Penner is Kwa Geok Choo Professor of Property Law at the National University of Singapore.

Megan Richardson is Professor of Law at Melbourne Law School.

Andrew Roberts is Professor of Law at Melbourne Law School.

David Rolph is Professor at Sydney Law School.

Solène Rowan is an Associate Professor and Futures Scheme Award holder at the Australian National University.

Catherine Sharkey is the Crystal Eastman Professor of Law at New York University School of Law.

Nicholas A Tiverios is Senior Lecturer in Private Law at the University of Western Australia.

Mimi Zou is an Associate Professor at the University of Reading.

TABLE OF CASES

Australia

10th Cantanae Pty Ltd v Shoshana Pty Ltd (1987) 79 ALR 299 (FCAFC)..........256
Ali v Hartley Poynton Ltd [2002] VSC 113, [2002] Aust Torts Reports 81-665......222
Amaca Pty Ltd v Banton [2007] NSWCA 336..........230
AMEV-UDC Finance Ltd v Austin (1986) 162 CLR 170 (HCA)...........346–47, 373
Ancient Order of Foresters in Victoria Friendly Society Ltd v Lifeplan Australia Friendly Society Ltd [2018] HCA 43, (2018) 92 ALJR 918..........244, 250, 257, 266, 276–85, 398, 400, 402, 404
Andrews v Australia and New Zealand Banking Group Ltd [2012] HCA 30, (2012) 247 CLR 205................ 15, 22, 30, 330–31, 360–61, 382
Androvitsaneas v Members First Broker Network [2013] VSCA 212..................347
Arab Bank Australia Ltd v Sayde Developments Pty Ltd [2016] NSWCA 328, (2016) 93 NSWLR 231..........367
Aristocrat Technologies Australia Pty Ltd v DAP Services (Kempsey) Pty Limited (in liq) [2007] FCAFC 40, (2007) 157 FCR 564..........267
Asia Television Ltd v Yau's Entertainment Pty Ltd [2000] FCA 254, (2000) 48 IPR 283..........348
Auburn Shopping Village Pty Ltd v Nelmeer Hoteliers Pty Ltd [2018] NSWCA 114, 19 BPR 38569..........354, 358, 362
Australasian Meat Industry Employees' Union v Mudginberri Station Pty Ltd (1986) 161 CLR 98 (HCA).................. 132–36, 139–41, 144–46
Australia Capital Financial Management Pty Ltd v Linfield Developments Pty Ltd [2017] NSWCA 99, (2017) 18 BPR 36683.......... 357, 366, 370–71
Australian Building and Construction Commissioner v Construction, Forestry, Mining and Energy Union [2018] HCA 3, (2018) 262 CLR 157........... 271, 273
Australian Competition and Consumer Commission v Acquire Learning & Careers Pty Ltd [2017] FCA 602, [2017] ATPR 42-543..............273
Australian Competition and Consumer Commission v CG Berbatis Holdings Pty Ltd [2003] HCA 18, (2003) 214 CLR 51............ 358, 360
Australian Competition and Consumer Commission v Chrisco Hampers Australia Ltd (No 2) [2016] FCA 144..........272
Australian Competition and Consumer Commission v Coles Supermarkets Australia Pty Ltd [2015] FCA 330, (2015) 327 ALR 540..........273

Australian Competition and Consumer Commission v Cotton On Kids Pty Ltd [2012] FCA 1428, [2012] ATPR 42-427 274
Australian Competition and Consumer Commission v Reckitt Benckiser (Australia) Pty Ltd (No 7) [2016] FCA 424, (2016) 343 ALR 327 .... 275–76, 278, 280
Australian Competition and Consumer Commission v Reckitt Benckiser (Australia) Pty Ltd [2016] FCAFC 181 .... 271, 273, 275, 278, 280
Australian Competition and Consumer Commission v Singtel Optus Pty Ltd [No 4] [2011] FCA 761, (2011) 282 ALR 246 272
Australian Competition and Consumer Commission v Thermomix in Australia Pty Ltd [2018] FCA 556....274
Australian Competition and Consumer Commission v TPG Internet Pty Ltd (No 2) [2012] FCA 629, [2012] ATPR 42-402....273
Australian Competition and Consumer Commission v TPG Internet Pty Ltd [2013] HCA 54, (2013) 250 CLR 640 .... 271, 273–74, 276
Australian Competition and Consumer Commission v Woolworths Limited [2016] FCA 44, [2016] ATPR 42-521 ....272, 274–75
Australian Consolidated Press Ltd v Morgan (1965) 112 CLR 483 (HCA) 132, 139, 141
Australian Consolidated Press Ltd v Uren (1967) 117 CLR 221 (HCA) 36, 227–28, 291
Australian Postal Corporation v Lutak (1991) 21 NSWLR 584 (SC)....277
Australian Securities and Investments Commission v Sigalla (No 4) [2011] NSWSC 62, (2011) 80 NSWLR 113....151
Autodesk Inc v Yee (1996) 68 FCR 391 (FCA)....267
Ayers Rock SkyShip Pty Ltd v Voyages Indigenous Tourism Australia Pty Ltd [2019] NSWSC 828, (2019) 19 BPR 39541.... 354, 362
Backwell v AAA [1997] 1 VR 182 (CA) 230
Bailey v Namol Pty Ltd (1994) 53 FCR 102 (FCAFC)....267
Baltic Shipping Co Ltd v Dillon (The Mikhail Lermontov) (1993) 176 CLR 344 (HCA).... 17, 241
Barton v Armstrong [1976] AC 104 (PC) 278
Briginshaw v Briginshaw (1938) 60 CLR 336 (HCA)....146
Broken Hill Proprietary Co Pty Ltd v Dagi [1996] 2 VR 117 (SC)....151
Bundanoon Sandstone Pty Ltd v Cenric Group Pty Ltd [2019] NSWCA 87 347
Burger King Corp v Hungry Jack's Pty Ltd [2001] NSWCA 187, (2001) 69 NSWLR 558....346
Butler v Fairclough (1917) 23 CLR 78 (HCA).... 236–37
Carson v John Fairfax & Sons Ltd (1993) 178 CLR 44 (HCA)....267
Clark v Macourt [2013] HCA 56, (2013) 253 CLR 1....364
Coates v Sarich [1964] WAR 2 (FC) 330
Commonwealth v Amann Aviation Pty Ltd (1991) 174 CLR 64 .... 244, 364

Commonwealth v Director, Fair Work Building Industry Inspectorate [2015] HCA 46, (2015) 258 CLR 482 .... 271, 273
ConAgra Inc v McCain Foods (Aust) Pty Ltd (1992) 33 FCR 302 (FCAFC) 256
Consul Development Pty Ltd v DPC Estates Pty Ltd (1975) 132 CLR 373 (HCA) 277
Crescendo Management Pty Ltd v Westpac Banking Corporation (1988) 19 NSWLR 40 (CA) 355
Dart Industries Inc v Decor Corporation Pty Ltd (1993) 179 CLR 101 (HCA) 279
Dea v Allstates Leasing System (WA) Pty Ltd (1983) 152 CLR 359 (HCA) 335
Director of Public Prosecutions v Jones (1985) 65 ACTR 11 (SC) 148
Dynamic Supplies Pty Limited v Tonnex International Pty Limited (No 3) [2014] FCA 909, (2014) 312 ALR 705 267
Egan v South Australian Railway Commissioner (1979) 25 SASR 5 (SC) 366
Esanda Finance Corp Ltd v Plessnig (1989) 166 CLR 131 (HCA) 321, 331, 346–47
Evans v Health Administration Corporation [2019] NSWSC 1781 94
Facton Ltd v Rifai Fashions Pty Ltd [2012] FCAFC 9, (2012) 199 FCR 569 267
Fiorelli Properties Pty Ltd v Professional Fencemakers Pty Ltd [2011] VSC 661, (2011) 34 VR 257 330
Forestry Commission of NSW v Stefanetto (1975) 133 CLR 507 (HCA) 329, 359, 366
Freedom v AHR Constructions Pty Ltd [1987] 1 Qd R 59 (SC) 330
Giller v Procopets [2008] VSCA 236, (2008) 24 VR 1 277
Gould v Vaggelas (1984) 157 CLR 215 (HCA) 278, 398
Gray v Motor Accident Commission [1998] HCA 70, (1998) 196 CLR 1 .... 13, 20, 36, 85, 91–93, 100–101, 212–13, 220, 228, 230–31, 236, 268, 298, 327, 399
Grimaldi v Chameleon Mining NL (No 2) [2012] FCAFC 6, (2012) 200 FCR 296 279
Guan v Linfield Developments Pty Ltd [2017] NSWCA 99 366
Gunns Ltd v Alishah (No 4) [2010] TASSC 24 .... 49, 53
Hamilton v Lethbridge (1912) 14 CLR 236 (HCA) 366
Harkianakis v Skalkos (1997) 42 NSWLR 22 (CA) 133
Harris v Digital Pulse Pty Ltd [2003] NSWCA 10, (2003) 56 NSWLR 298 .... 13, 18, 51, 56, 230, 233, 236, 242–43, 246, 250, 276–77, 281
Hearne v Street [2008] HCA 36, (2008) 235 CLR 125 .... 135, 148–50
Henjo Investments Pty Ltd v Collins Marrickville Pty Ltd (No 2) (1989) 40 FCR 76 (FCAFC) 399
Henville v Walker [2001] HCA 52, (2001) 206 CLR 459 .... 278, 398
Hinch v Attorney-General for the State of Victoria (1987) 164 CLR 15 (HCA) 150

Hoobin (decd), Re [1957] VR 341 (SC) 330
Hospital Products Ltd v United States Surgical Corporation (1984) 156 CLR 41 (HCA).................... 277, 281
Hospitality Group Pty Ltd v Australian Rugby Union Ltd (2001) 110 FCR 157 (FCAFC) 236, 249
Jendell Australia Pty Ltd v Kesby [1983] 1 NSWLR 127 (SC)....................136
JPA Finance Pty Ltd v Gordon Nominees Pty Ltd [2019] VSCA 159, (2019) 58 VR 393 354
Kay v Playup Australia Pty Ltd [2020] NSWCA 33 354
Lamb v Cotogno (1987) 164 CLR 1 (HCA)........ 54, 56, 232–33, 267, 269, 291, 405
Lamson Store Service Co Ltd v Russell Wilkins & Sons Ltd (1906) 4 CLR 672 (HCA)....................366
Legione v Hateley (1983) 152 CLR 406 (HCA)...... 21, 330–31, 335, 343–44, 357–58
Lexane Pty Ltd v Highfern Pty Ltd [1985] 1 Qd R 446 (SC) 344
McDonald v Dennys Lascelles Ltd (1933) 48 CLR 457 (HCA).................... 344–45
McRae v Commonwealth Disposals Commission (1951) 84 CLR 377....................244
Mangrove Mountain Quarries Pty Ltd v Barlow [2007] NSWSC 492, (2007) 23 BCL 448 348
Mann v Paterson Constructions Pty Ltd [2019] HCA 32, (2019) 373 ALR 1 347
Masters v Cameron (1954) 91 CLR 353 (HCA)....................329
Matthews v Seamen's Union of Australia (1957) 1 FLR 185 (Commonwealth Industrial Court) 148
Midalco Pty Ltd v Rabenalt [1989] VR 461 (SC) 230
Mineralogy Pty Ltd v Sino Iron Pty Ltd (No 6) [2015] FCA 825, (2015) 329 ALR 1 .... 353–54, 358, 362
Moore v Scenic Tours Pty Ltd [2020] HCA 17, (2020) 377 ALR 209........... 17, 241
Musca v Astle Corporation Pty Ltd (1988) 80 ALR 251 (FCA).................. 256, 399
New South Wales Bar Association v Evatt (1968) 117 CLR 177 (HCA)..............348
New South Wales Egg Corporation v Peek (1987) 10 NSWLR 72 (CA)..............146
New South Wales v Ibbett [2006] HCA 57, (2006) 229 CLR 638 ....204, 248, 311
NLS Pty Ltd v Hughes (1966) 120 CLR 583 (HCA) 330
O'Dea v Allstates Leasing System (WA) Pty Ltd (1983) 152 CLR 359 (HCA) 335, 366
Pacific Brands Sport & Leisure Pty Ltd v Underworks Pty Ltd [2005] FCA 288, (2005) Aust Contract R 90-213 347
Paciocco v Australia and New Zealand Banking Group Ltd [2016] HCA 28, (2016) 258 CLR 525 ....21, 242, 324–25, 331–35, 338, 365, 367, 371
Palmer Bruyn & Parker Pty Limited v Parsons [2001] HCA 69, (2001) 208 CLR 388.................... 256, 282, 398–99
PC Developments Pty Ltd v Revell (1991) 22 NSWLR 615 (CA)....................344
Perkins; Mesto v Gilpin, Re [1998] 4 VR 505 (SC) 133

Pitt v Curotta (1931) 31 SR (NSW) 477 (Eq Div) 330, 345
Plan B Trustees Ltd v Parker (No 2) [2013] WASC 216 281
Queensland Nickel Sales Pty Ltd v Mount Isa Mines Ltd [2019] QCA 32 346
R v Fletcher, ex parte Kisch (1935) 52 CLR 248 (HCA)..148
R v Hoar (1981) 148 CLR 32 (HCA)...92
R v Metal Trades Employees' Association, ex parte Amalgamated Engineering Union, Australian Section (1951) 82 CLR 208 (HCA) 132
Raben Footwear Pty Ltd v Polygram Records Inc (1997) 75 FCR 88 (FCAFC) 267
Renard Constructions (ME) Pty Ltd v Minister for Public Works (1992) 26 NSWLR 234 (CA) 346
Rich v Australian Securities and Investment Commission [2003] NSWCA 342, (2003) 203 ALR 671 61
Ringrow Pty Ltd v BP Australia Pty Ltd [2005] HCA 71, (2005) 224 CLR 656..329, 333, 366
San Sebastian Pty Ltd v Minister Administering Environmental Planning and Assessment Act 1979 (NSW) (1986) 162 CLR 340 (HCA).....................278
Shevill v Builders Licensing Board (1982) 149 CLR 620 (HCA) 347
Singtel Optus Pty Ltd v Australian Competition and Consumer Commission [2012] FCAFC 20, (2012) 287 ALR 249.......................271–72, 274
Smyth v Jessep [1956] VLR 230 (SC)...330, 344–45
Stern v McArthur (1988) 165 CLR 489 (HCA)..................... 343, 345, 353, 358, 372
Tabcorp Holdings Ltd v Bowen Investments Pty Ltd [2009] HCA 8, (2009) 236 CLR 272..238–39, 243, 248, 252
Tanwar Enterprises Pty Ltd v Cauchi [2003] HCA 57, (2003) 217 CLR 315...341, 353, 358, 360
Thompson v British Medical Association (NSW Branch) [1924] AC 764 (PC)...348
Trade Practices Commission v CSR Ltd (1991) ATPR 41-076 (FCA) 271–73
United States Surgical Corp v Hospital Products International Pty Ltd [1983] 2 NSWLR 157 (CA)..18
Uren v John Fairfax & Sons Pty Ltd (1966) 117 CLR 118 (HCA) 45, 100, 214–15, 226–28, 268, 292, 405
Warman International Ltd v Dwyer (1995) 182 CLR 544 (HCA) 18, 60, 277, 279, 281
Whitfield v De Lauret & Co Ltd (1920) 29 CLR 71 (HCA)..................228, 243, 268
Witham v Holloway (1995) 183 CLR 525 (HCA)... 132–33, 136, 139, 142, 146–48, 150–51
XL Petroleum (NSW) Pty Ltd v Caltex Oil (Australia) Pty Ltd [1985] HCA 12, (1985) 155 CLR 448 ....228, 248, 268
Yardley v Saunders [1982] WAR 231 (SC) 330
Zhu v The Treasurer of the State of New South Wales [2004] HCA 56, (2004) 218 CLR 530 243

Canada

Airbus Helicopters SAS v Bell Helicopter Textron Canada Ltd 2019 FCA 29, (2019) 163 CPR (4th) 197
Amartek Inc v Canadian Commercial Corp (2003) 229 DLR (4th) 419 (ONSC) 249
Amartek Inc v Canadian Commercial Corp (2005) 256 DLR (4th) 287 (ONCA) 249
Atlantic Lottery Corp Inc v Babstock 2020 SCC 19 .... 6, 235–36, 247–49, 251–52
Bazley v Curry [1999] 2 SCR 534 (SCC) 289, 304, 307–8
Blackwater v Plint 2005 SCC 58, [2005] 3 SCR 3 310
Brickles v Snell [1916] 2 AC 599 (PC) 343–44
Canada, Vancouver (City of) v Ward 2010 SCC 27, [2010] 2 SCR 28 57
de Montigny v Brossard (Succession) 2010 SCC 51, [2010] 3 SCR 64 .... 54, 57–58
Elsley v JG Collins Insurance Agencies Ltd [1978] 2 SCR 916 (SCC) 321
Fidler v Sun Life Assurance Co of Canada 2006 SCC 30, [2006] 2 SCR 3 .... 17, 45, 76
Hall v Hebert [1993] 2 SCR 159 (SCC) 6
HF Clarke Ltd v Thermidaire Corp Ltd [1976] 1 SCR 319 (SCC) 22
Honda Canada Inc v Keys 2008 SCC 39, [2008] 2 SCR 362 17
Jacobi v Griffiths [1999] 2 SCR 570 (SCC) 309
Jane Doe 72511 v Morgan 2018 ONSC 6607 102
Keays v Honda Canada Inc 2008 SCC 39, [2008] 2 SCR 362 228
Kilmer v British Columbia Orchard Lands Ltd [1913] AC 319 (PC) 342–43, 345
M(K) v M(H) [1992] 3 SCR 6 (SCC) 277
Norberg v Wynrib [1992] 2 SCR 226 (SCC) 13
NTI v Canada (Attorney-General) [2012] NUCJ 11 249
Paragon Properties Ltd v Magna Envestments Ltd (1972) 24 DLR (3d) 156 (ABSC) 227
Pate Estate v Galway-Cavendish and Harvey (Township) 2013 ONCA 669, (2013) 368 DLR (4th) 193 197
Performance Industries Ltd v Sylvan Lake Golf & Tennis Club Ltd [2002] SCR 678 (SCC) 235, 246, 250–51
Poje v Attorney-General of British Columbia [1953] 1 SCR 516 (SCC) 132
Royal Bank of Canada v W Got Associates Electrical Ltd [1999] 3 SCR 408 (SCC) 76, 235, 246
Smith v Landstar Properties Inc [2011] BCCA 44 249
Steedman v Drinkle [1916] 1 AC 275 (PC) 343–44
Vorvis v Insurance Corp of British Columbia (1989) 1 SCR 1085 (SCC) 214, 227, 235, 244, 246
Whiten v Pilot Insurance Co 2002 SCC 18, [2002] 1 SCR 595 .... 7, 12–14, 17, 45, 76, 197–98, 235–36, 246, 250–51, 253, 291, 327

European Court of Human Rights

Holy Monasteries v Greece (1994) 20 EHRR 1 316
Miloslavsky v UK [1996] EMLR 152 205

France

Civ 1
20 October 1959, Bull civ I no 419....................67
20 March 1989, Bull civ I no 122....................67
Civ 3, 25 Feb 2004, Bull civ III no 41 74
Com 23 January 1979, Bull civ IV no 30 65
Com 29 January 1991, Bull civ IV no 43 65
Paris 15 December 1993, No 19930474....................69
Paris 20 June 1995, D 1995.IR.187 65
TGI Paris 31 January 1984, D 1984.283 67

Hong Kong

Allan v Ng & Co [2012] HKCA 119, [2012] 2 HKLRD 160 (CA) 215, 228
China Light & Power Co Ltd v Ford [1996] 2 HKC 23 (CA) 228
Pao On v Lau Yiu Long [1980] AC 614 (PC)....................355
Union Eagle Ltd v Golden Achievement Ltd
[1997] AC 514 (PC) 343–44, 351
Yuen Kun Yeu v Attorney-General of Hong Kong
[1988] AC 175 (PC) 298

Ireland

Conway v Irish National Teachers Organisation (1991) 2 IR 305 (SC) 214

Malaysia

Cheong Fatt Tze Mansion Sdn Bhd v Hotel Continental Sdn Bhd [2011]
4 MLJ 354 (HC)....................227
Linggi Plantations v Jagatheesan [1972] 1 MLJ 89 (PC) 329, 345
Sistem Televisyen Malaysia Bhd v Nurullah bt Zawawi [2015]
6 MLJ 703 (CA) 227
Zulkiply bin Taib v Prabakar a/l Bala Krishna [2015] 2 MLJ 607 227

New Zealand

127 Hobson Street Ltd v Honey Bees Preschool Ltd [2019] NZCA 122, [2019] 2 NZLR...790 326, 330, 338
127 Hobson Street Ltd v Honey Bees Preschool Ltd [2020] NZSC 53.................365
Aquaculture Corp v New Zealand Green Mussel Co Ltd [1990] 3 NZLR 299 (CA)...13, 263, 276
Attorney-General for England and Wales v R [2002] 2 NZLR 91 (CA) 249
Bottrill v A [2002] UKPC 44, [2003] 2 NZLR 721...... 16, 188, 191, 208, 221–22, 225, 230, 263, 291
Cook v Evatt (No 2) [1992] 1 NZLR 676 (HC) 263
Couch v Attorney-General (No 2) [2010] NZSC 27, [2010] 3 NZLR 149 .... 14, 222, 230, 234, 263, 399
Daniels v Thompson [1998] 3 NZLR 22 (CA)..95
Donselaar v Donselaar [1982] 1 NZLR 97 (CA) 263
Dunlea v Attorney-General [2000] 3 NZLR 136 (CA).................................. 36, 228
Eden Refuge Trust v Hohepa [2011] NZHC 730, [2011] 3 NZLR 273 263
Monroe v Attorney-General (High Court, 27 March 1985).................................311
Paper Reclaim Ltd v Aotearoa International [2006] NZCA 27, [2006] 3 NZLR 188 ....236, 241, 247–48, 251, 263
Premium Real Estate Ltd v Stevens [2009] NZSC 15, [2009] 2 NZLR 384..........263
S v Attorney-General [2003] NZCA 149, [2003] 3 NZLR 450...............300, 309–11
Siemer v Solicitor-General [2009] NZCA 62, [2009] 2 NZLR 556........132, 146–47
Skids Programme Management Ltd v McNeill [2012] NZCA 314, [2013] 1 NZLR 1.. 263, 265
Taunoa v Attorney General [2007] NZSC 70, [2008] 1 NZLR 429.........................57
Taylor v Beere (1982) 1 NZLR 81 (CA).. 214, 227–28, 263
TK (Hong Kong) Ltd v Diamond Milk Formulas Ltd [2016] NZHC 2642...352
Universal Management, Re [1983] NZLR 462 (CA)..368
W v W [1999] 4 LRC 260 (PC)..9, 16, 188, 297, 314
Wilaci Pty Ltd v Torchlight Fund No 1 LP (in receivership) [2017] NZCA 152, [2017] 3 NZLR 293..352

Singapore

ACB v Thomson Medical Pte Ltd [2017] SGCA 20, [2017] 1 SLR 918........ 41, 215, 227–28, 262
ACES System Development Pte Ltd v Yenty Lily (trading as Access International Services) [2013] SGCA 53, [2013] 4 SLR 1317.............249
Denka Advantech Pte Ltd v Seraya Energy Pte Ltd [2020] SGCA 119...22, 326, 330, 332, 351, 365, 373

Main-Line Corporate Holdings Ltd v United Overseas Bank Ltd [2009] SGHC 232, [2010] 1 SLR 189 256
Mayson v Clouet [1924] AC 980 (PC) 345
MFM Restaurants Pte Ltd v Fish & Co Restaurants Pte Ltd [2010] SGCA 36, [2011] 1 SLR 150 249
PH Hydraulics & Engineering Pte Ltd v Airtrust (Hong Kong) Ltd [2017] SGCA 26, [2017] 2 SLR 129 ....14, 225, 236, 241–42, 247–48, 251, 262
PH Hydraulics & Engineering Pte Ltd v Intrepid Offshore Construction Pte Ltd [2012] SGHC 133, [2012] 4 SLR 36 261
Turf Club Auto Emporium Pte Ltd v Yeo Boong Hua [2018] SGCA 44, [2018] 2 SLR 655 249

United Kingdom

20:20 London Ltd v Riley [2012] EWHC 1912 (Ch D) 388
AB v South West Water Services Ltd [1993] QB 507 (CA) 13, 189, 292
Addis v Gramophone Co Ltd [1909] AC 488 (HL) 13, 75, 216–18, 236, 348
Akhtar v Ball (Walsall County Court, 10 July 2015) 6
Aldington v Watts (High Court, 30 November 1989) 205
Alexander v Rayson [1936] 1 KB 169 (KBD) 20
Allen v The Chief Constable of the Hampshire Constabulary [2013] EWCA Civ 967 288
Amble Assets LLP (in Administration) v Longbenton Foods Ltd (in Administration) [2011] EWHC 1943, [2012] 1 All ER (Comm) 764 ....329–30, 345
AMP v Persons Unknown [2011] EWHC 3454 95
Angelic Star, The [1988] 1 Lloyd's Rep 122 (CA) 363
Anonymous (1602) Cary 2; 21 ER 1 368
Antaios Compania Naviera SA v Salen Rederierna AB (The Antaios) [1985] AC 191 (HL) 347
Anufrijeva v Southwark LBC [2003] EWCA Civ 1406, [2004] QB 1124 192
Archer v Brown [1985] QB 401 (CA) 193, 209–10, 298
Aribisala v St James' Homes (Grosvenor Dock) Ltd [2008] EWHC 456, [2009] 1 WLR 1089 329
Armes v Nottinghamshire County Council [2017] UKSC 60, [2018] AC 355 ....288–89, 304, 308
Armstrong, ex parte Lindsay, In re [1892] 1 QB 327 (QBD) 136, 145
Arpad (No 2), The [1934] P 189 (CA) 324
Ashby v White (1703) 2 Ld Raym 938; 92 ER 126 292
Ashley v Chief Constable Sussex Police [2008] UKHL 25, [2008] 1 AC 962 57
Ashmore, Benson, Pease & Co Ltd v AV Dawson Ltd [1973] 1 WLR 828 (CA) 20

Askey v Golden Wine Co [1948] 2 All ER 35 (CA)....................15
Aston Cantlow and Wilmcote with Billesley Parochial Church Council v
Wallbank [2003] UKHL 37, [2004] 1 AC 546....................316
Astro Exito Navegacion SA v Hsu (The 'Messiniaki Tolmi') [1983]
1 Lloyd's Rep 666 (QBD)....................143
AT v Dulghieru (2009) EWHC 225 (QB)....................209–12
Attorney-General v Blake [2001] 1 AC 268 (HL)....................18, 75–76, 206, 239–40, 245, 248–49, 364
Attorney-General v Butterworth [1963] 1 QB 696 (CA)....................142
Attorney-General v Newspaper Publishing Plc [1988] Ch 333 (CA)....................138
Attorney-General v Times Newspapers Ltd [1974] AC 273 (HL)....................133
Axa Insurance UK Plc v Financial Claims Solutions Ltd [2018]
EWCA Civ 1330, [2019] RTR 1....................191–92, 201, 208, 210, 212, 298
Axa Insurance UK Plc v Thwaites (Norwich County Court,
8 February 2008)....................193
Bell v Midland Railway Co (1861) 10 CBNS 287; 142 ER 462....................215–16
Bellman v Northampton Recruitment Ltd [2018] EWCA Civ 2214,
[2019] 1 All ER 1133....................288
Benson v Frederick (1766) 3 Burr 1845; 97 ER 1130....................215
Berg v Sadler & Moore [1937] 2 KB 158 (CA)....................20
BICC Plc v Burndy Corp [1985] Ch 232 (CA)....................343, 357
Black v North British Railway Co 1908 SC 444 (IH)....................188
Blyth v Birmingham Waterworks Co (1856) 11 Ex 781; 156 ER 1047....................220
Boardman v Phipps [1967] 2 AC 46 (HL)....................25, 121–26, 129, 207
Borders (UK) Ltd v Commissioner of Police for the Metropolis [2005]
EWCA Civ 197, [2005] Po LR 1....................48, 193, 209–11, 298
Bradford City Council v Arora [1991] 2 QB 507 (CA)....................189
Bramblevale Ltd, In re [1970] Ch 128 (CA)....................146, 151
Brayshaw v The Partners of Apsley Surgery [2018] EWHC 3286,
[2019] 2 All ER 997....................289
Bridge v Campbell Discount Co Ltd [1962] AC 600 (HL)....................21, 332–33, 336, 373
Bristow v City Petroleum Ltd [1987] 1 WLR 529 (HL)....................340–41
British Broadcasting Corp v Beckett [1983] IRLR 43 (EAT)....................349
Broome v Cassell & Co [1972] AC 1027 (HL)....................4, 6, 9, 36, 46, 52–53, 70, 74, 79–80, 188–89, 191, 208, 215, 227, 230–31, 290–95, 297–98, 324
Buxton Lime Firms Co Ltd v Howe [1900] 2 QB 232 (Div Ct)....................340–41
Cadogan Petroleum Holdings Ltd v Global Process Systems LLC
[2013] EWHC 214, [2013] 2 Lloyd's Rep 26....................344
Catmur v Knatchbull (1797) 7 TR 448; 101 ER 1069....................145
Cattle v Stockton Waterworks Co (1874–75) LR 10 QB 453 (QBD)....................368

Cavendish Square Holding BV v Makdessi [2015] UKSC 67, [2016] AC 1172 ....21–22, 30, 242, 321, 324–25, 328–33, 335, 337–40, 343, 345, 347, 349, 352, 354–56, 360–61, 363–67, 369–71, 376, 382, 385–86, 400
Cawley v South Wales Electricity Board [1985] IRLR 89 (EAT) 349
Celestial Aviation Trading 71 Ltd v Paramount Airways Private Ltd [2010] EWHC 185, [2011] 1 All ER (Comm) 343
Cellulose Acetate Silk Co Ltd v Widnes Foundry (1925) Ltd [1933] AC 20 (HL) 336
Chapman v Honig [1963] 2 QB 502 (CA) 142
Cine Bes Filmcilik Ve Yapimcilik AS v United International Pictures [2003] EWCA Civ 1669, [2004] 1 CLC 401 ....337, 365
Clark v Watkins (1863) 1 New Rep 227 359
Clydebank Engineering and Shipbuilding Co Ltd v Don Jose Ramos Yzquierdo y Castaneda [1905] AC 6 (HL) 321, 339–40, 365–66
Connor v Chief Constable of Cambridgeshire, The Times, 11 April 1984 (QBD) 293
Cooden Engineering Co Ltd v Stanford [1953] 1 QB 86 (CA) 360
Co-operative Group (CWS) Ltd v Pritchard [2011] EWCA Civ 329, [2012] QB 320 222
Co-operative Insurance Society Ltd v Argyll Stores (Holdings) Ltd [1998] AC 1 (HL) 13, 75, 324
Copeland v Commissioner of Police of the Metropolis (EWHC, 2 May 2013) 189
Corcoran v Corcoran [1950] 1 All ER 495 (PDA) 140
Couling v Coxe (1848) 6 CB 703; 136 ER 1424 142
Cox v Ministry of Justice [2016] UKSC 10, [2016] AC 660 .... 288–89, 306, 308
Crawfordsburn Inn Ltd v Graham [2013] NIQB 79 189
Crosby's Case (1771) 3 Wils KB 188; 95 ER 100 148
Crouch v Great Northern Railway Co (1856) 11 Exch 742; 156 ER 1031 216
Crown Dilmun v Sutton (2004) EWHC 52 (Ch), [2004] 1 BCLC 468 207
Cumber v Chief Constable of Hampshire (Portsmouth County Court, 21 May 1993) 6
Customs and Excise Commissioners v Barclays Bank Plc [2006] UKHL 28, [2007] 1 AC 181 143
Dagenham (Thames) Dock Co, ex parte Hulse, Re (1873) LR 8 Ch App 1022 342–43
Daley v Mahmood (Central London County Court, 12 August 2005) 190
Dawoodi v Zafrani [2015] EWHC 3168 (TCC) 190
De Francesco v Barnum (1890) 45 Ch D 430 379

Derbyshire v Lancashire CC (1983) 133 NLJ 65 6
Devenish Nutrition Ltd v Sanofi Aventis SA [2007] EWHC 2394 (Ch), [2008] All ER 249 ...... 193, 207
Dies v British and International Mining and Finance Corp Ltd [1939] 1 KB 724 (KBD)......345
Dingwall v Burnett 1912 SC 1097 (IH) 336
Director of the Serious Fraud Office v O'Brien [2014] UKSC 23, [2014] AC 1246......132–34, 144
Doyle v Olby (Ironmongers) Ltd [1969] 2 QB 158 (CA) 202, 256, 398
Drane v Evangelou [1978] 1 WLR 455 (CA) 73
Dubai Aluminium Co Ltd v Salaam [2002] UKHL 48, [2003] 2 AC 366......289
Duke of Brunswick v Slowman (1849) 8 CB 317; 137 ER 532 215
Dunlop Pneumatic Tyre Co Ltd v New Garage and Motor Ltd [1915] AC 79 (HL) 22, 321, 332–33, 335–36, 338–40, 365–67, 371, 386
Edgington v Fitzmaurice (1885) 29 Ch D 459 (CA)......278
Else (1982) Ltd v Parkland Holdings Ltd [1994] 1 BCLC 130 (CA)......330, 370–71
Elliot v Flanagan [2016] NIQB 8 205
Emeh v Kensington and Chelsea and Westminster AHA [1985] QB 1012 (CA)......399
ENE Kos 1 Ltd v Petroleo Brasileiro SA (The Kos) (No 2) [2012] UKSC 17, [2012] 2 AC 164......346
Essa v Laing Ltd [2004] EWCA Civ 2, [2004] ICR 746 203
Esso Petroleum Co Ltd v Niad Ltd (High Court, 22 November 2011) 76
Experience Hendrix LLC v PPX Enterprises Inc [2003] EWCA Civ 323, [2003] 1 All ER (Comm) 830......76
Export Credits Guarantee Department v Universal Oil Products Co [1983] 1 WLR 399 (HL)......352
Fairclough & Sons v Manchester Ship Canal Co (No 2) (1897) 41 Sol Jo 225 (CA)......142
Farley v Skinner [2001] UKHL 49, [2002] 2 AC 732......17
FHR European Ventures LLP v Cedar Capital Partners LLC [2014] UKSC 45, [2015] AC 250......201
Fielding v Variety Inc [1967] 2 QB 841 (CA) 206
Financings Ltd v Baldock [1963] 2 QB 104 (CA)...... 346–47
Finch v Finch in DEC Yale (ed), Lord Nottingham's Chancery Cases, vol 1......358
Flynn v Chief Constable of the Police Service of Northern Ireland [2016] NIQB 24......293
Freston, In re (1883) 11 QBD 545 (CA) 132–33, 139
Galbraith v Mitchenall Estates Ltd [1965] 2 QB 473 (QBD) 344
G&C Kreglinger v New Patagonia Meat and Cold Storage Co Ltd [1914] AC 25 (HL)......357
General Trading Co (Holdings) Ltd v Richmond Corp Ltd [2008] EWHC 1479 (Comm), [2008] 2 Lloyd's Rep 475......364

Gilbert-Ash (Northern) Ltd v Modern Engineering (Bristol) Ltd [1974] AC 689 (HL) 329
Giraud UK Ltd v Smith [2000] IRLR 763 (EAT) 339–40
Gogay v Hertfordshire County Council [2000] EWCA Civ 228, [2000] IRLR 703 349
Grantham Wholesale Fruit, Vegetable and Potato Merchants Ltd, In re [1972] 1 WLR 559 (Ch D) 139
Gray v Braid Group (Holdings) Ltd [2016] CSIH 68, 2017 SC 409 387
Great Peace Shipping v Tsavliris Salvage (International) Ltd [2002] EWCA Civ 1407, [2003] QB 679 356
Griffon Shipping LLC v Firodi Shipping Ltd (The Griffon) [2013] EWCA Civ 1567, [2014] 1 Lloyd's Rep 471 328
Guinness Plc v Saunders [1990] 2 AC 663 (HL) 281
Gulati v MGN Ltd [2015] EWHC 1482, [2016] FSR 12 91
Gulati v MGN Ltd [2015] EWCA Civ 1291, [2017] QB 149 94
H (Minors) (Sexual Abuse: Standard of Proof), In re [1996] AC 563 (HL) 11
Hadley v Baxendale (1854) 9 Ex 341; 156 ER 145 202
Hall v Higham (1663) Ch Rep 5; 21 ER 711 358
Hanley v Pease & Partners Ltd [1915] 1 KB 698 (KBD) 348
Harris v Evans [1998] 1 WLR 1285 (CA) 298
Hart v Riversdale Mill Co Ltd [1928] 1 KB 176 (CA) 340
Henderson v Dorset Healthcare University NHS Foundation Trust [2020] UKSC 43, [2020] 3 WLR 1124 20–21
Herbert Clayton & Jack Waller Ltd v Oliver [1930] AC 209 (HL) 17
Heywood v Wellers [1976] QB 446 (CA) 17
Hicks v Chief Constable of South Yorkshire [1992] 2 All ER 65 (HL) 219
HIH Casualty and General Insurance Ltd v Chase Manhattan Bank [2003] UKHL 6, [2003] 2 Lloyd's Rep 61 19
Hill v Chief Constable of West Yorkshire [1989] AC 53 (HL) 298
Hinton v Sparkes (1868) LR 3 CP 161 (Court of Common Pleas) 329
Holden v Chief Constable of Lancashire [1987] QB 380 (CA) 189
Hollister Inc v Medik Ostomy Supplies Ltd [2012] EWCA Civ 1419, [2013] Bus LR 428 206
Holman v Johnson (1775) 1 Cowp 341; 98 ER 1120 19
Holyoake v Candy [2017] EWHC 3397 (Ch) 352
Home Office v Harman [1983] 1 AC 280 (HL) 145, 148
Huckle v Money (1763) 2 Wils KB 206; 95 ER 768 ......48, 215, 290
Hudson, Re [1966] Ch 209 (Ch D) 143
Hughes v Lord Advocate [1963] AC 837 (HL) 202
IBM United Kingdom Holdings Ltd v Dalgleish [2015] EWHC 389 (Ch), [2015] Pens LR 99 201
Imam-Sadeque v Bluebay Asset Management (Services) Ltd [2012] EWHC 3511, [2013] IRLR 344 ......339, 386

Imperial Chemical Industries Ltd v Shatwell [1965] AC 656 (HL) 299
Industrial Development Consultants Ltd v Cooley [1972] 1 WLR 443 (Fam) 119
Jennison v Baker [1972] 2 QB 52 (CA) 135, 145
JGE v Portsmouth Roman Catholic Diocesan Trust [2012] EWCA
Civ 938, [2013] QB 722 .... 289, 308
Jobson v Johnson [1989] 1 WLR 1026 (CA)..329, 357, 363
John v MGN [1997] QB 586 (CA) 79, 189, 197
Johnson v Unisys Ltd [2001] UKHL 13, [2003] 1 AC 518 348
Jones v Ruth [2011] EWCA Civ 804, [2012] 1 WLR 1495..................................203
JSC BTA Bank v Ablyazov (No 14) [2018] UKSC 19, [2020] AC 727..................143
KD v Chief Constable of Hampshire [2005] EWHC 2550 (QB),
[2005] Po LR 253 .... 193, 204
Keech v Sandford (1726) Sel Cas Ch 61; 25 ER 223..122
Kenny v Preen [1963] 1 QB 499 (CA) 364
Kent & Sussex Sawmills, Re [1947] Ch 177 (Ch D)..369
Kreglinger (G & C) v New Patagonia Meat and Cold Storage Co Ltd [1914]
AC 25 (HL)...342, 359, 361
Kuddus v Chief Constable of Leicestershire Constabulary [2001]
UKHL 29, [2002] 2 AC 122... 12–13, 28, 46, 56, 70, 74,
187–88, 191–92, 218–19, 256, 259, 290–93,
295, 299–301, 303, 307, 310, 399
Kuwait Airways Corp v Iraqi Airways Co (No 6) [2002] UKHL 19,
[2002] 2 AC 883... 202–3
Lancashire County Council v Municipal Mutual Insurance Ltd
[1996] 3 WLR 493 (CA) 81, 305
Lancore Services Ltd v Barclays Bank plc [2008] EWHC 1264 (Ch),
[2008] 1 CLC 1039 366
Leigh & Sillivan Ltd v Aliakmon Shipping Co Ltd [1986] AC 785 (HL) 368
Lister v Hesley Hall Ltd [2001] UKHL 22, [2002] 1 AC 215 289
Livingstone v Rawyards Coal Co (1880) 5 App Cas 25 (HL) 202–3
Lloyd v Google LLC [2019] EWCA Civ 1599, [2020] QB 747 .... 90, 94
Lock v Bell [1931] 1 Ch 35 (Ch D)..329
Lomas v JFB Firth Rixson Inc [2012] EWCA Civ 419,
[2012] 2 Lloyd's Rep 548...346
Lombard North Central Plc v Butterworth [1987] QB 527 (CA)............... 346, 363
London Borough of Lambeth v Agoreyo [2019] EWCA Civ 322,
[2019] ICR 1572 349
Lordsvale Finance plc v Bank of Zambia [1996] QB 752 (QBD).................. 22, 365
Loudon v Ryder (No 1) [1953] 2 QB 202 (CA) 193–95, 214
Lowe v Peers (1768) 4 Burr 2225; 98 ER 160 359
Lucas (T) & Co Ltd v Mitchell [1972] 3 WLR 934 (CA).......................................389
Lumley v Wagner (1852) 5 De G & Sm 485; 64 ER 1209 379
McCall v Abelesz [1976] QB 585 (CA)...17
Mafo v Adams [1970] 1 QB 548 (CA) 297

Makanjuola v Commissioner of Police of the Metropolis (1990) 2 Admin LR 214 (QB)....299
Makdessi v Cavendish Square Holding BV [2013] EWCA Civ 1539, [2014] 2 All ER (Comm)....366
Manley v Commissioner of Police of the Metropolis [2006] EWCA Civ 879, [2006] Po LR 117....293
Marion White Ltd v Francis [1972] 1 WLR 1423 (CA)....389
Marks v Marks (1718) Prec Ch 486; 24 ER 218....359
Mattis v Pollock [2003] EWCA Civ 887, [2003] 1 WLR 2158....307
Mcmillan v Singh (1984) 17 HLR 120 (CA)....210
Mehta v Royal Bank of Scotland (2000) 32 HLR 45 (QB)....313
Merest v Harvey (1815) 5 Taunt 442; 128 ER 761....234
Mezey v South West London and St George's Mental Health NHS Trust [2007] EWCA Civ 106, [2007] IRLR 244....349
Mileage Conference Group of the Tyre Manufacturers' Conference Ltd's Agreement, In re [1966] 1 WLR 1137 (Ch D)....142
Ministry of Defence v Fletcher [2010] IRLR 25 (EAT)....191, 204, 292
Mitchell v Glasgow City Council [2009] UKHL 11, [2009] 1 AC 874....299
Mohamud v WM Morrison Supermarkets plc [2016] UKSC 11, [2016] AC 677....288–89
Mohidin v Commissioner of Police of the Metropolis [2015] EWHC 2740 (QB)....191, 294
Morris-Garner v One Step (Support) Ltd [2018] UKSC 20, [2019] AC 649....76, 209, 249, 363–64
Moschi v Lep Air Services Ltd [1973] AC 331 (HL)....363
Mosley v News Group Newspapers Ltd [2008] EWHC 1777 (QB), [2008] EMLR 20....138, 192, 260, 300
MSC Mediterranean Shipping Co SA v Cottonex Anstalt [2016] EWCA Civ 789, [2016] 2 Lloyd's Rep 494....346
Murad v Al-Saraj [2005] EWCA Civ 959....126
Murray v Leisureplay Plc [2005] EWCA Civ 963, [2005] IRLR 946....333, 364, 366
Mussen v Van Diemen's Land Co [1938] Ch 253 (Ch D)....344
Muuse v Secretary of State for the Home Department [2010] EWCA Civ 453....189, 191, 219
Nosworthy v Instinctif Partners Ltd [2019] UKEAT/0100/18....383–84, 388–90, 393
Nottinghamshire Healthcare NHS Trust v News Group Newspapers Ltd [2002] EWHC 409 (Ch), [2002] EMLR 33....260
NT1 & NT2 v Google LLC [2018] EWHC 799, [2019] QB 344....99
OBG Ltd v Allan [2007] UKHL 21, [2008] 1 AC 1....368
O'Mara Books v Express Newspapers [1999] FSR 49 (Ch D)....260
OOO Abbott v Design & Display Ltd [2016] EWCA Civ 98, [2016] FSR 27....18, 206

Organ Retention Group Litigation, In Re [2004] EWHC 644 (QB), [2005] QB 506 ... 218
Overstone Ltd v Shipway [1962] 1 WLR 117 (CA) ... 347
Parabola Investments Ltd v Browallia Cal Ltd [2009] EWHC 901, [2009] 2 All ER (Comm) 589 ... 300
Parker v McKenna (1874) LR 10 Ch App 96 ... 18
ParkingEye Ltd v Somerfield Stores Ltd [2012] EWCA Civ 1338, [2013] QB 840 ... 20
Parkinson v College of Ambulance Ltd [1925] 2 KB 1 (KBD) ... 20
Patel v Mirza [2016] UKSC 41, [2017] AC 467 ... 4, 20–21, 203–4, 324
Peachy v Duke of Somerset (1720) 1 Str 447; 93 ER 626 ... 342, 357–61
Pell v Express Newspapers [2009] EWHC 118 ... 300
Penarth Dock Engineering Co Ltd v Pounds [1963] 1 Lloyd's Rep 359 (QBD) ... 325
Perera v Vandiyar [1953] 1 WLR 672 (CA) ... 192, 364
Peter Pan Manufacturing Corp v Corsets Silhouette Ltd [1964] 1 WLR 96 (Ch D) ... 207
Phillips v Britannia Hygienic Laundry Co Ltd [1923] 2 KB 832 (CA) ... 142
Phipps v Boardman [1965] Ch 992 (CA) ... 18, 122–25
Phonographic Performance Ltd v Amusement Caterers (Peckham) Ltd [1964] 1 Ch 195 (Ch D) ... 132, 141
Phonographic Performance Ltd v Ellis [2018] EWCA Civ 2812, [2019] Bus LR 542 ... 190, 202, 260
Photo Production Ltd v Securicor Transport Ltd [1980] AC 827 (HL) ... 321, 363
PJS v News Group Newspapers Ltd [2016] UKSC 26, [2016] AC 1081 ... 90
Pooley v Whetham (1880) 15 Ch D 435 (CA) ... 133, 144
Potton Ltd v Yorkclose Ltd [1990] FSR 11 (Ch D) ... 280
Protector Endowment Loan and Annuity Co v Grice (1880) 5 QBD 592 (CA) ... 360
Pye v British Automobile Commercial Syndicate Ltd [1906] 1 KB 425 (KBD) ... 329
Quinn v Leatham [1901] AC 495 (HL) ... 202
Quinn v Ministry of Defence [2018] NIQB 82 ... 314
R (ex parte Lamari) v Secretary of State for the Home Department [2013] EWHC 3130 (QB) ... 191
R (Jalloh) v Secretary of State for the Home Department [2020] UKSC 4, [2020] 2 WLR 418 ... 293
R (Lumba) v Secretary of State for the Home Department [2011] UKSC 12, [2012] 1 AC 245 ... 191, 297
R (National Council for Civil Liberties) v Secretary of State for the Home Department [2019] EWHC 2057, [2020] 1 WLR 243 ... 94
R v Adomako [1995] 1 AC 171 (HL) ... 100
R v Barnardo (1889) 23 QBD 305 (CA) ... 140
R v Barnes [2004] EWCA Crim 3246, [2005] 1 WLR 910 ... 339
R v Bateman (Percy) (1927) 19 Cr App R 8 (CA) ... 221

R v Brown [1994] 1 AC 212 (HL)....327
R v Hopley (1860) 2 F & F 202; 175 ER 1024....327
R v Parke [1903] 2 KB 432 (KBD)....148
Ramzan v Brookwide Ltd [2010] EWHC 2453 (Ch), [2011] 2 All ER 38....75, 190
Rank Film Distributors Ltd v Video Information Centre [1982] AC 380 (CA)....260
Redgrave v Kelly (1889) 5 TLR 477 (QBD)....340
Rees v Commissioner of Police for the Metropolis [2019] EWHC 2339 (QB)....193
Rice v Great Yarmouth BC (2001) 3 LGLR 4 (CA)....347
Richards v IP Solutions Group Ltd [2016] EWHC 1835, [2017] IRLR 133....339, 385–88
Riches v News Group Newspapers Ltd [1986] QB 256 (CA)....189, 193, 297
Robinson v Chief Constable of West Yorkshire Police [2014] EWCA Civ 15, [2014] PIQR P14....299
Robinson v Harman (1848) 1 Ex 850; 154 ER 363....364
Robophone Facilities Ltd v Blank [1966] 1 WLR 1428 (CA)....333, 335, 340, 363–64
Rookes v Barnard [1964] AC 1129 (HL)....4–5, 12–13, 16, 28–29, 48, 53, 57, 70, 73–74, 79, 163, 188–92, 194, 198–201, 204, 208–9, 212–16, 219, 227, 231, 256, 259–60, 262–63, 287, 290–92, 294–95, 297, 313, 315, 327
Rose, Rose v IRC, Re [1952] Ch 499 (CA)....118
Rowlands v Chief Constable of Merseyside Police [2006] EWCA Civ 1773, [2007] 1 WLR 1065....46, 208, 293, 297, 300, 306–7
Roy v Duke of Beaufort (1741) 2 Atk 190; 26 ER 519....359
Ruxley Electronics & Constructions Ltd v Forsyth [1996] AC 344 (HL)....238–39, 252
S Pearson & Son Ltd v Dublin Corp [1907] AC 351 (HL)....19
Sagar v H Ridehalgh and Son Ltd [1931] 1 Ch 310 (CA)....340
Sanders v Pope (1806) 12 Ves Jun 282; 33 ER 108....343
Scandinavian Trading Tanker Co AB v Flota Petrolera Ecuatoriana (The Scaptrade) [1983] 2 AC 694 (HL)....342, 346, 357, 362, 371
Seager v Copydex Ltd (No 2) [1969] 1 WLR 809 (CA)....18, 207
Sealand Petroleum Co Ltd v Barratt [1986] 1 WLR 700 (QBD)....340
Seaward v Paterson [1897] 1 Ch 545 (CA)....140–41
Seddon v North Eastern Salt Co [1905] 1 Ch 326 (Ch D)....19
Sharma v Noon Products Ltd (High Court, 7 April 2011)....218
Shaw v Holland [1900] 2 Ch 305 (CA)....207
Shelbourne v Cancer Research UK [2019] EWHC 842, [2019] PIQR P16....289
Shepherd (FC) & Co Ltd v Jerrom [1987] QB 301 (CA)....361
Shiloh Spinners Ltd v Harding [1973] AC 691 (HL)....341–43, 353, 357–59
Signia Wealth Ltd v Vector Trustees Ltd [2018] EWHC 1040 (Ch)....369, 377, 383, 388
Sloman v Walter (1783) 1 Bro CC 418; 28 ER 1213....342, 358–59

Smith New Court Securities Ltd v Citibank NA [1997]
AC 254 (HL) 203, 256, 398
Socony Mobil Oil Co Inc v West of England Ship Owners
Mutual Insurance Association Ltd (The Padre Island)
(No 2) [1989] 1 Lloyd's Rep 239 (CA) 329
Solle v Butcher [1950] 1 KB 671 (CA) 356
South Australia Asset Management Co v York Montague Ltd [1997]
AC 191 (HL) 203
Sport Internationaal Bussum BV v Inter-Footwear Ltd [1984]
1 WLR 776 (HL) 342, 346, 357
Squire v Bayer & Co [1901] 2 KB 299 (Div Ct) 340
St John Shipping Corp v Joseph Rank Ltd [1957] 1 QB 267 (QBD) 20
Standard Chartered Bank v Pakistan National Shipping Corp
(Nos 2 and 4) [2002] UKHL 43, [2003] 1 AC 959 .... 222, 278, 398
Stanley Cole (Wainfleet) Ltd v Sheridan [2003] ICR 297 (EAT) 349
Staveley Iron and Chemical Co v Jones [1956] AC 627 (HL) 299
Stockloser v Johnson [1954] 1 QB 476 (CA) 330, 344–45
Stoffel & Co v Grondona [2020] UKSC 42, [2020] 3 WLR 1156 20–21
Stourton v Stourton [1963] P 302 (PDA) 140, 145
Street v Mountford [1985] AC 809 (HL) 368
Theedom v British Railways Board [1976] IRLR 137
(Industrial Tribunal) 348–49
Thompson v Hudson (1869) LR 4 HL 1 (HL) 359–60
Thompson v Metropolitan Police Commissioner [1998]
QB 498 (CA) 10, 12, 191, 193, 199, 204, 293–94, 297, 299, 302, 338
TPKN v Ministry of Defence [2019] EWHC 1488 289
Treadaway v Chief Constable of the West Midlands, The Times,
25 October 1994 (QBD) 292
Tribe v Tribe [1996] Ch 107 (CA) 20
Tuke v Hood [2020] EWHC 2843 (Comm) 206
Tullett Prebon Group Ltd v El-Hajjali [2008] EWHC 1924,
[2008] IRLR 760 .... 336, 339–40
UK Housing Alliance (North West) Ltd v Francis [2010]
EWCA Civ 117, [2010] 3 All ER 519 359
Van Colle v Chief Constable of Hertfordshire [2008] UKHL 50,
[2009] 1 AC 225 298
Various Claimants v Barclays Bank plc [2020] UKSC 13,
[2020] 2 WLR 960 288–89
Various Claimants v Catholic Child Welfare Society
[2012] UKSC 56, [2013] 2 AC 1 .... 288–89, 306, 308
Various Claimants v WM Morrison Supermarkets plc [2020]
UKSC 12, [2020] AC 989 .... 94, 288–89
Vauxhall Motors Ltd v Manchester Ship Canal Co Ltd [2019]
UKSC 46, [2020] AC 1161 .... 30, 342, 346, 353–54, 356–57, 362, 368–69, 371

Versloot Dredging BV v HDI Gerling Industrie Versicherung AG [2016] UKSC 45, [2017] AC 1 .... 19, 202
Vidal-Hall v Google Inc [2015] EWCA Civ 311, [2016] QB 1003 93
Walker v Earl of Grosvenor (1797) 7 TR 171; 101 ER 915 145
Wall v Rederiaktiebolaget Luggude [1915] 3 KB 66 (KBD) 336
Wallis v Smith (1882) 21 Ch D 243 (CA) 329
Walton v Walton (CA, 14 April 1994) 371
Walumba Lumba v Secretary of State for the Home Department [2011] UKSC 12, [2012] 1 AC 245 57
Watkins v Secretary of State for the Home Department [2006] UKHL 17, [2006] 2 AC 395 6
Watts, Watts & Co Ltd v Mitsui Co Ltd [1917] AC 227 (HL) 21
Wellesley v Duke of Beaufort (1831) 2 Russ & M 639; 39 ER 538 .... 132, 135, 137, 140, 145
Welsh Development Agency v Export Finance Co Ltd [1992] BCC 270 (CA) 368
Wilde v Gibson (1848) 1 HLC 605; 9 ER 897 19
Wilkes v Wood (1763) Lofft 1; 98 ER 489 .... 52, 56, 100, 215, 228–29, 290
Williams Bros v Ed T Agius Ltd [1914] AC 510 (HL) 364
Williams v Currie (1845) 1 CB 841; 135 ER 774 215–16
Williams v Settle [1960] 1 WLR 1072 (CA) 260
Wilson v Barton (1671) Nels 148; 21 ER 812 358
Wright v Prudential Assurance Co Ltd [2018] EWHC 402 (Ch), [2018] Bus LR 1173 360
Wrotham Park Estate Co v Parkside Homes Ltd [1974] 1 WLR 798 (Ch) 249
X (Minors) v Bedfordshire CC [1995] 2 AC 633 (HL) 298

United States

3G Fishing Charters LLC and others v Kirby Inland Marine LP and others, No 3:14CV00107 Class Action Complaint 181
Alyeska Pipeline Service Co v Wilderness Society 421 US 240 (1975) 6
Anhold v Daniels 614 P 2d 184 (Wash 1980) 170
Bessette v WB Conkey Co 194 US 324 (1904) 132–33, 135–36, 139, 148, 152
Blakeman v Schneider 864 SW 2d 903 (Ky 1993) 138
BMW of North America, Inc v Gore 517 US 559 (1996) 47, 159–60, 162, 166–67, 290
Charity, In re 2017 WL 3580173 (Bankruptcy ED Va 15 August 2017) 177–78
Cisson v CR Bard 810 F 3d 913 (4th Cir 2016) 178
City of Newport v Fact Concerts Inc 453 US 247 (1981) 312
Collins, In re 233 F 3d 809 (3rd Cir 2000) 174
Cooper Industries Inc v Leatherman Tool Group Inc 532 US 424 (2001) 47–48

Dardinger v Anthem Blue Cross & Blue Shield 781 NE 2d 121 (Ohio 2002) 173, 175–77
EEOC v Dial Corp 259 F Supp 2d 710 (ND Ill 2003) 179
Exxon Shipping Co v Baker 554 US 471 (2008) 157, 196
Facebook Inc Consumer Privacy User Profile Litigation, Re Case 402 F Supp 3d 767 (Northern District of California 2019) 97–98
Fay v Parker 53 NH 342, 382 (1873) 74
Frank Music Corp v Metro-Goldwyn-Mayer Inc 886 F 2d 1545 (9th Cir 1989) 282
Fust v AG 947 SW 2d 424 (Mo 1997) 182
Gompers v Buck's Stove & Range Co 221 US 418 (1911) 133–34, 137–38, 147
Green v United States 356 US 165 (1958) 138
Grimshaw v Ford Motor Company 119 Cal App 3d 757 (1981) 54, 265
Harleysville Group Ins v Heritage Communities Inc 803 SE 2d 288 (SC 2017) 158
Heller v Silverbranch Construction Corporation 382 NE 2d 1065 (Mass 1978) 266
Hicks v Feiock 485 US 632 (1988) 132, 137–38
Hilao v Estate of Marcos 103 F 3d 767 (9th Cir 1996) 180
International Fidelity Insurance Co v Wilson 387 Mass 841 (1983) 265
International Union, United Mine Workers of America v Bagwell 512 US 821 (1994) 132, 137
Iorio v Allianz Life Ins Co of North America 2009 WL 3415703 (SD Cal 21 October 2009) 179
Johnson v Ford Motor Co 113 P 3d 82 (Cal 2005) 160–61, 167
Kemezy v Peters 79 F 3d 33 (7th Cir 1996) 157
Kokkonen v Guardian Life Ins Co of Am 511 US 375 (1994) 183
Lake River Corp v Carborundum Co 769 F 2d 1284 (7th Cir 1985) 8
Lutheran Bhd Variable Ins Prod Co Sales Practices Litig 2004 WL 909741 (D Minn 28 April 2004) 168
Mac Tools v Griffin 879 P 2d 1126 (Idaho 1994) 169
McCandless v State 166 NYS 2d 272 (1997) (Court of Claims) 313
McKee v AT&T Corporation 191 P 3d 845 (Wash 2008) 169
Mathias v Accor Econ Lodging Inc 347 F3d 672 (7th Cir 2003) 165
May Department Stores Co v State ex rel Woodard 863 P 2d 967 (Colo 1993) 168
Metcoff v NCT Group Inc 50 A 3d 1004 (Conn Super 2011) 172
Miller v Blanton 210 SW 2d 293 (1948) (Ark) 311
Mosing v Domas 830 So 2d 967 (La 2002) 171
Motorola Credit Co v Uzan 338 F 3d 39 (2nd Cir 2004) 196
Motorola Credit Co v Uzan 509 F 3d 74 (2nd Cir 2007) 196
Nami Res Co LLC v Asher Land & Mineral Ltd 554 SW 3d 323 (Ky 2018) 171
Nevitt, In re 117 Fed Rep 448 (8th Cir 1902) 132, 136–37
Oklahoma ex rel Hunter v Purdue Pharmaceuticals LP and others No CJ-2017-816 (Okla Dist Ct 2019) 173, 180–81

Osborne v Keeney 399 SW 3d 1 (Ky 2012) 158
Palmer v Combined Insurance 217 FRD 430 (ND Ill 2003)........................... 178–80
Patton v Mid-Continent Systems Inc 841 F 2d 742 (7th Cir 1988) 7
Patton v Target Corp 242 P 3d 611 (Or 2010) 182
Payne v Jones 711 F 3d 85 (2d Cir 2012).. 173–74
Pencil Hill Ltd v US Citta Di Palermo SpA (HC, 19 January 2016) 352
People ex rel Dunbar v Gym of America Inc 493 P 2d 660 (Colo 1972) 168
Personna Noble v Northland Invest Corp
No X10-UWY-CV-16-6033559-S 179–80
Philip Morris USA v Williams 549 US 346 (2007) 159–60, 179
Polar Bear Productions Inc v Timex Corp 384 F 3d 700 (9th Cir 2004) 282
Priebe & Sons Inc v United States 332 US 407 (1947)..............................21, 326–27
Saunders v Branch Banking & Trust Co of Va 526 F 3d 142 (4th Cir 2008) 177
Saunders v Equifax Info Servs 469 F Supp 2d 343 (ED Va 2007) 177
Seltzer v Morton 154 P 3d 561 (Mont 2007)...171
Sheldon v Metro-Goldwyn Pictures Corp 309 US 390 (1940) 18
Shillitani v United States 384 US 364 (1966) 132, 137–38
Simon II Litigation, In re 211 FRD 86 (EDNY 2002);
407 F 3d 125 (2nd Cir 2005)..158
State ex rel Wilson v Ortho-McNeil-Janssen Pharmaceuticals Inc
777 SE 2d 176 (SC 2015) 169
State Farm Mut Auto Ins Co v Campbell 538 US 408 (2003)...........45, 159–60, 162
Sundquist, In re 580 BR 536 (Bankruptcy ED Cal 2018)..................173–74, 176–77, 183–84
Sundquist v Bank of America 566 BR 563 (Bankruptcy ED Cal 2017)........ 173–74, 176–78, 183–84
Tawney v Columbia Natural Resources, LLC 2007 WL 5539870
(Cir Ct W Va 27 June 2007) 179
Thyssen Inc v SS Fortune Star 777 F 2d 57 (2nd Cir 1985)..................236, 242, 244
Times Mirror Magazines, Inc v Field & Stream Licenses Co 103
F Supp 2d 711 (SDNY 2000)..183
Turner v Rogers 564 US 444 (2011) 151
Tylenol (Acetaminophen) Mktg Sales Practices & Prods Liab Litig,
In re 144 F Supp 3d 680 (ED Pa 2015) 170
Weinberger v Estate of Barnes 2 NE 3d 43 (Ind 2013) 182
Wilson v Houston Funeral Home 42 Cal App 4th 1124 (1996) 17
Wischer v Mitsubishi Heavy Indus Am Inc 673 NW 2d 303
(Wis Ct App 2003) 176

Other Jurisdictions

Attorney General of St Helena v AB [2020] UKPC 1 204
Attorney General of St Christopher, Nevis and Anguilla v John Joseph Reynolds
[1980] AC 637 (PC) 57

Attorney General of Trinidad and Tobago v Ramanoop [2005] UKPC 15, [2006] 1 AC 328 57
British Guiana Credit Corp v da Silva [1965] 1 WLR 248 (PC) 17
Commissioner of Public Works v Hills [1906] AC 368 (PC) 329
Cukurova Finance International Ltd v Alfa Telecom Turkey Ltd [2013] UKPC 25, [2016] AC 923 .... 30, 342–43, 357, 360–61
Merson v Cartwright and Attorney General [2005] UKPC 38 57
Webster v Bosanquet [1912] AC 394 (PC) 340
Workers Trust & Merchant Bank Ltd v Dojap Investments Ltd [1993] AC 573 (PC) 328, 330, 345

TABLE OF LEGISLATION

Australia

Australian Securities and Investments Commission
Act 2001 (Cth) 28, 268, 270, 275
s 12GBA....................270
s 12GBCA....................275
s 12GBCA(1)....................275
s 12GBCA(2)(b) 275
s 12GBCC....................276
s 12GLB 270
Circuit Layouts Act 1989 (Cth), s 27(4) 267
Civil Law (Wrongs) Act 2002 (ACT), s 45 406
Civil Liability Act 1936 (SA), s 34....................406
Civil Liability Act 2002 (NSW), s 5D....................406
Civil Liability Act 2002 (Tas), s 13 406
Civil Liability Act 2002 (WA), s 5C....................406
Competition and Consumer Act 2010 (Cth)
sch 2 (Australian Consumer Law) 28, 75, 170, 234, 268–70, 273, 275, 278, 280
s 224 270
s 224(1) 271
s 224(2) 271
s 224(3) 275
s 224(3A) 170, 275
s 236 271
s 237 271
ss 237-238....................170
s 246(2)(d)....................270
s 247 270
Copyright Act 1968 (Cth)
s 115(4) 267
s 115(4)(b) (ia)....................267
Corporations Act 2001 (Cth)....................268
Crimes Act 1914 (Cth), s 16A....................61
Defamation Act 2005 (Vic), s 37 267
Designs Act 2003 (Cth), s 75(3)....................267
Domestic Building Contracts Act 1995 (Vic), s 53(2)(b)(ii) 236

Environment Protection and Biodiversity Conservation
Act 1999 (Cth), s 481 271
Evidence (National Uniform Legislation) Act 2011 (NT)
s 140(1) 150
s 141(1) 150
Evidence Act 1995 (Cth)
s 140(1) 150
s 141(1) 150
Evidence Act 1995 (NSW)
s 140(1) 150
s 141(1) 150
Evidence Act 2001 (Tas)
s 140(1) 150
s 141(1) 150
Evidence Act 2008 (Vic)
s 140(1) 150
s 141(1) 150
Evidence Act 2011 (ACT)
s 140(1) 150
s 141(1) 150
Fair Work Act 2009 (Cth), s 546....................271
Law Reform (Vicarious Liability) Act 1983 (NSW), ss 6–8....................311
Luna Park Site Act 1990 (NSW)....................149
Motor Accident Insurance Act 1994 (Qld)
s 55(1) 232
s 55(2) 232
Motor Accidents Act 1988 (NSW), s 81A 232
National Consumer Credit Protection Act 2009 (Cth) 275
s 167 271
Patents Act 1990 (Cth), s 122(1A)....................267
Penalties and Sentencing Act 1992 (Qld), s 9 61
Police Legislation Amendment (Civil Liability) Act 2003 (NSW)....................311
Securities and Investment Commission Act 2001 (Cth)....................28
Supreme Court Act 1970 (NSW)
s 101(5) 150
s 101(6) 150
Trade Marks Act 1995 (Cth), s 126(2) 267
Trade Practices Act 1974 (Cth)....................273
s 76....................271
Transport Accident Act 1986 (Vic), s 93(7) 232
Treasury Laws Amendment (2018 Measures No 3) Act 2018 (Cth) 275
Treasury Laws Amendment (Strengthening Corporate and Financial
Sector Penalties) Act 2019 (Cth) 275

Wrongs Act 1958 (Vic), s 51 406

Canada

Quebec Charter of Human Rights and Freedoms 54
Quebec Civil Code 58

European Union

General Data Protection Regulation 92
Art 83(2)(a), (b), (c) and (e) 92
Art 83(5) 92

France

Civil Code 36, 50, 64, 70
Art 50 72
Art 395 72
Art 412 72
Art 413 72
Art 1112 77
Art 1112-1 77
Art 1150 66
Art 1221 77
Art 1231-3 66
Art 1231-5 65
Art 1240 63
Art 1241 63
Art 1266-1 (draft) 36, 50, 63, 71–73, 76–82, 174–75, 402
Art 1382 63
Art 1383 63
Code of Civil Procedure
Art 32-1 72
Art 207 72
Code of Commerce, arts L442-1–L442-8 72
Code on Contract Law 63
Construction and Habitation Code, arts L631-7 and L651-2 72
Urban Code, arts L430-2 and L430-9 72

New Zealand

Accident Compensation Act 2001, s 319 263
Bill of Rights Act 1990, s 24(e) 147
Commerce Act 1986, s 81A 264
Credit Contracts and Consumer Finance Act 2003 264
 s 94(1)(c) 264
Fair Trading Act 1986
 s 9 264
 ss 41-43 264
Financial Markets Conduct Act 2013
 s 19 264
 s 489 264
Plant Variety Rights Act 1987, s 17(c)(4) 264
Residential Tenancies Act 1986, s 77(2)(o) 264

Singapore

Consumer Protection (Fair Trading) Act 260–61
Copyright Act 2006
 s 119 261
 s 119(2)(d) 261–62
 s 119(5) 261
Trade Marks Act 2005
 s 31(5)–(6) 261
 s 31(5)(c) 262

United Kingdom

Children Act 2004, s 58 327
Civil Evidence Act 1995, s 1 11
Civil Procedure Rules
 16.4(1)(c) 188
 33.2 11
 36.17 24
 40.13 330
 44.2(2)(a) 312
 54.5(1) 293
Companies Act 2006, s 994 391
Competition Act 1998
 s 47C 190
 sch 8A, para 36 190

Consumer Protection Act 1987 .... 192, 199
Consumer Rights Act 2015
s 63 330
sch 2 330
Contempt of Court Act 1981 146
Copyright, Designs and Patents Act 1988 260
s 97(2) 190, 202, 260
s 229(3) 260
s 296(2) 260
s 296ZD(2) 260
s 298(2) 260
Copyright Act 1956, s 17(3) 260
Copyright and Related Rights Regulations 1966 (SI 1996/2967), reg 17 260
Copyright and Rights in Database Regulations 1997 (SI 1997/3032), reg 23 260
County Courts Act 1984, s 138 342
Crime and Courts Act 2013
s 33 133
s 34 .... 190, 192
s 34(5) 188
ss 34–38 291
s 35(2) 210
s 39(2) 204
s 42(4)(c) 192
Criminal Injuries Compensation Act 1995 3
Criminal Justice Act 2003 195
pt 11, ch 2 11
Criminal Justice and Courts Act 2015, s 33 95
Crown Proceedings Act 1947, s 2(1)(a) 289
Employment Rights Act 1996 31
pt II 339
pt X 346
s 27 390
s 27(2)(e) 390
s 113 379
Extradition Act 2003, s 151A 144
High Speed Rail (London – West Midlands) Act 2017, s 51(10) 190
Housing Act 1988 73
Human Rights Act 1998 .... 40, 192, 292–93, 314
Law of Property Act 1925
s 49(2) 330
s 146(2) 342
Law Reform (Miscellaneous Provisions) Act (Northern Ireland) 1937, s 14(2)(a) 190

Law Reform (Miscellaneous Provisions) Act 1934
s 1(1) 208
s 1(2)(a).... 190, 296
Law Reform Contributory Negligence Act 1945....222
Merchant Shipping Act 1995 190
Misrepresentation Act 1967....399
s 1(b) 19
s 2(2) 19
Modern Slavery Act 2015.... 31, 390
Official Secrets Act 1911, s 1(1)(c) 239
Patents Act 1977, sch A1, para 12(4) 260
Police Act 1996, s 88(1)....289
Proceeds of Crime Act 2002, s 412....144
Protection from Eviction Act 1977 73
Protection from Harassment Act 1997.... 95, 204
Reserve and Auxiliary Forces (Protection of Civil Interests) Act 1951.... 190, 291
s 13(2) 190
Rules of the Court of Judicature (Northern Ireland), r 8(3)....188
Senior Courts Act 1981
s 38....342
s 69(1) 316
Sexual Offences Act 2003
s 1(1) 220
s 67(3) 94
Theft Act 1968, s 21 95
Torts (Interference with Goods) Act 1977, s 11(1) 222
Trade Union Act 1992, s 236....379
Truck Act 1896....339
Wages Act 1986....339

United States

17 USC, § 504(c)(1)....266
Alaska Statutes, § 45.50.531 (2016)....266
California Civil Code
§ 1780....265
§ 1793.2, (d)(2) 166
California Constitution 97
Colorado Revised Statutes, § 13-21-102....170
Connecticut Unfair Trade Practices Act 180
False Claims Act, 31 USC....41
Fed R Bank P, § 9019(a)....183
Fed R Civ P, § 60(b) 184

Federal Tort Claims Act 1946, 28 US Code, § 2674 312
Georgia Code
§ 10-1-399 265
§ 51-12-5.1(e)(2) 183
Kentucky Revised Statutes Annotated, § 367.120 168
Maryland Code Annotated Commercial Law, § 13-102 169
Massachusetts General Law, ch 93A, § 3 265
Missouri Annotated Statutes, § 537.675(3) 182
North Dakota Century Code, § 32-03.2-11 171
Oregon Revised Statutes Annotated, § 31.735 182
Stored Communications Act 97

PART I

Introduction

1

Punishment and Private Law

WAYNE COURTNEY AND JAMES GOUDKAMP

I. The Controversy

A. Introduction

A sharp contrast is often drawn between the criminal law and private law, and this contrast frequently provides a platform for the claim that punishment rather than compensation is the province of the criminal law whereas the reverse is true for the private law. This understanding has long enjoyed substantial support. As Glanville Williams observed almost 75 years ago, '[i]t is commonly said that the civil action for damages aims at compensation, as opposed to the criminal prosecution which aims at punishment'.[1] A remarkable feature of this claim is its mutual exclusivity. It denies that either field pursues both ends. Given this book's purpose we do not need to evaluate the proposition that the criminal law's purpose is punishment rather than compensation.[2] We merely note that it misses an important part of the truth in view of, for example, the power of the criminal courts to make compensation orders.[3] Although the goal of compensation is admittedly generally less significant than that of punishment, it is a function of the criminal law nevertheless.

As for the other half of the claim – that private law is about compensation rather than punishment – it too is a half-truth. On the one hand, it is undoubtedly the case that compensation is central to at least parts of private law. Consistently with this, compensatory damages is the only remedy for torts that is available as of right.[4] On the other hand, private law recognises several remedies that are

[1] G Williams, 'The Aims of the Law of Tort' (1951) 4 *Current Legal Problems* 137, 137.

[2] For discussion, see A Ashworth, 'Punishment and Compensation: Victims, Offenders and the State' (1986) 6 *OJLS* 86.

[3] See, eg, the Powers of Criminal Courts (Sentencing) Act 2000 (UK), s 130. Consider also the provision in many jurisdictions for criminal injuries compensation schemes: see, eg, the Criminal Injuries Compensation Act 1995 (UK).

[4] This led John Gardner to argue that 'tort law cannot be understood without understanding the primacy of the reparative … in its remedial doctrines': J Gardner, *Torts and Other Wrongs* (Oxford,

avowedly non-compensatory, such as punitive (or exemplary) damages and restitutionary damages. The claim is also mired in controversy, especially in so far as it suggests that punishment does not have, or should not have, a place in private law. Those who oppose private law operating as an engine of punishment[5] draw upon several well-rehearsed arguments. It is these arguments that render punishment in private law controversial, and we begin this chapter by exploring them with reference to the chapters that comprise this collection. Many of these arguments are advanced in the context of punitive damages, which is private law's most explicit manifestation of a concern with retribution. But they can be (and sometimes expressly are) extended so as to constitute objections to punishment in private law more generally, and it is clear that the debate about whether punishment has a place in private law goes far beyond the institution of punitive damages.

B. Punishment is Inconsistent with the Nature of Private Law

It is often claimed that punishment is incompatible with the nature of private law. Ernst Weinrib's influential theory of corrective justice[6] supplies a well-known example of the idea that is in play here.[7] A key strand in his account is the proposition that private law is correlative in that it focuses on neither just the perpetrator of the wrong nor just the victim, nor even on both the perpetrator and victim independently. Instead, it is asserted that private law is concerned with both the perpetrator and victim as an interacting pair. Weinrib contends that, by virtue of private law's bilateral structure, which he claims is its 'most striking feature',[8] private law cannot be adequately explained by considerations that relate to only one of those parties, or even by considerations that concern both parties seen separately. Punishment, because it focuses on the wrongdoer, is a one-sided consideration and hence, in Weinrib's view, inconsistent with the nature of private law. Thus, he writes that 'under corrective justice damages are compensatory not punitive'.[9]

Oxford University Press, 2019) 22. cf R Stevens, *Torts and Rights* (Oxford, Oxford University Press, 2007) who rejects the proposition that tort law aims at compensation and maintains that supposed 'compensatory' damages are in fact damages that are awarded in substitution of the right that the defendant violated.

[5] Judicial statements opposed to punishment having a place in private law include *Rookes v Barnard* [1964] AC 1129 (HL) 1221; *Broome v Cassell & Co* [1972] AC 1027 (HL) 1086–87; *Patel v Mirza* [2016] UKSC 41, [2017] AC 467 [108].

[6] E Weinrib, *The Idea of Private Law* (Harvard University Press, 1995); E Weinrib, *Corrective Justice* (Oxford, Oxford University Press, 2012).

[7] See also A Beever, 'The Structure of Aggravated and Exemplary Damages' (2003) 23 *OJLS* 87, 105–10.

[8] Weinrib, *The Idea of Private Law* (n 6) 1.

[9] ibid, 135, fn 25 (arguing that damages under corrective justice are not punitive). cf P-W Lee, 'Contract Damages, Corrective Justice and Punishment' (2007) 70 *MLR* 887 (arguing that punitive damages can be reconciled with corrective justice).

Weinrib's important account of private law has been extensively debated.[10] Space precludes detailed consideration of it in this chapter and it is necessary to confine ourselves to making two basic points. The first is that while there is undoubtedly considerable truth in the proposition that private law is bilaterally structured, Weinrib arguably overplays his hand. Thus, there are numerous well-documented respects in which private law deviates significantly from the paradigm of correlativity. Of particular relevance for present purposes is the fact that private law is sometimes explicitly concerned with punishment. The most obvious (but certainly not the only) instance of this concerns punitive damages, which, as their name implies, are expressly aimed at retribution. Seeking to explain away this difficulty for his account of private law, Weinrib is driven to say that punitive damages are in reality sometimes another species of award. Thus, he argues that when punitive damages are granted on account of the defendant's having acted with a profit motive, which is one of the three situations in which they are available in England,[11] they are masquerading as restitutionary damages.[12] In their chapter in this volume, Goudkamp and Katsampouka argue that this account of punitive damages is as implausible as it is imaginative.[13] They observe that it cannot explain, among other things, the fact that punitive damages are calibrated not by reference to the gain made by the defendant (that being how restitutionary damages are quantified) but in view of (or at least principally in view of) the defendant's culpability. In any event, Weinrib's argument does nothing to account for the two other situations in which punitive damages can be awarded in Engalnd, and it does not cater for other jurisdictions where punitive damages can be awarded in cases that do not fall within the three categories in which English law is prepared to grant the remedy.

Our second and more fundamental point is that even if one accepts the premise that private law is bilaterally structured, the conclusion that private law should not accommodate unilateral concerns such as punishment, which conclusion Weinrib apparently invites his reader to accept, is a *non sequitur*. In other words, the fact that a particular model may explain the law or a good portion of it as it presently stands does not mean that the law should be changed so as to bring it into increased conformity with that model. Just as no one would think that it follows from feminist accounts of the law that the law should be developed so as to further entrench gender inequalities, simply pointing to respects in which private law is bilaterally orientated identifies no reason in support of its being so structured.

[10] See, eg, P Cane, 'Corrective Justice and Correlativity in Private Law' (1996) 16 *OJLS* 471; J Goudkamp and J Murphy, 'The Failure of Universal Theories of Tort Law' (2015) 21 *Legal Theory* 47.

[11] *Rookes* (n 5).

[12] For another attempt to recast punitive damages as being, in reality, a different species of award, see Stevens (n 4) 85 (arguing that punitive damages are in fact damages awarded as a substitute for the claimant's right that the defendant violated).

[13] See Goudkamp and Katsampouka, ch 8, section III.E.

C. Punishment of the Defendant Involves a Windfall to the Claimant

Where a claimant suffers loss as a consequence of the defendant's wrong, the claimant will be entitled to compensatory damages. Although the claimant is in principle entitled to be fully compensated for their loss, there are compelling reasons to think that most claimants are undercompensated, sometimes significantly. For example, the claimant may not choose to pursue each and every item of loss suffered because certain items may be thought to be too minor or too expensive or too difficult to justify proving. Similarly, it is a notorious fact that where the claimant seeks redress in respect of future losses, the process of reducing those losses to a present-day capital sum may leave the claimant shortchanged because of unrealistic assumptions about the rate of return that the claimant can safely achieve on the award.[14] In the United States, there is an added procedural issue: a successful litigant ordinarily cannot recover their legal costs incurred in the suit from the losing party.[15] The result is that these costs will be paid from the claimant's compensation, often leaving the claimant very far from fully compensated. Even in other parts of the common law world where costs shifting is permitted, the successful party in litigation is not indemnified in respect of their costs and, typically, only around two-thirds of the costs are recoverable.

Where the compensatory damages awarded leave the claimant undercompensated, any punitive award that is made can indirectly serve to compensate the claimant. The purpose of such an award is not, of course, compensation but compensation will be among its effects. To this extent, punitive awards are compensatory and it is awkward to characterise them as involving a windfall to the claimant. However, in certain situations punitive awards will be extra-compensatory, as where the compensatory damages fully compensate the claimant, or where the claimant has suffered no loss,[16] or where the punitive award is sufficiently large that it goes beyond any shortfall in the compensatory award. Where a punitive award is extra-compensatory, it will, by definition, place the claimant into a better economic position than they would have been in had they not been wronged.[17] This is sometimes thought to be objectionable.[18] It is asserted that not only has

[14] For discussion, see P Cane and J Goudkamp, *Atiyah's Accidents, Compensation and the Law*, 9th edn (Cambridge, Cambridge University Press, 2018) 145–49.

[15] *Alyeska Pipeline Service Co v Wilderness Society* 421 US 240, 243 (1975) (the so-called 'American Rule').

[16] In England, it seems that punitive damages may be unavailable in the absence of loss: see the obiter dicta in *Watkins v Secretary of State for the Home Department* [2006] UKHL 17, [2006] 2 AC 395 [26], [32]. cf *Derbyshire v Lancashire CC* (1983) 133 NLJ 65; *Cumber v Chief Constable of Hampshire* (Portsmouth County Court, 21 May 1993); *Akhtar v Ball* (Walsall County Court, 10 July 2015). It appears that there is no such limitation in Canada: *Atlantic Lottery Corp Inc v Babstock* 2020 SCC 19 [130], [163], [169].

[17] This is acutely drawn out in *Hall v Hebert* [1993] 2 SCR 159 (SCC) 175.

[18] eg, Lord Reid in *Broome* (n 5) 1086 refers to awards of punitive damages as involving 'a pure and undeserved windfall at the expense of the defendant'. Similarly, Allan Beever (Beever (n 7)

the claimant not done anything to justify being made the beneficiary of such munificence but, from the claimant's perspective, whether or not their economic situation is improved in this way is generally a matter of luck. It is certainly true that it may be a matter of chance from the claimant's viewpoint whether they are 'fortunate' enough to be wronged by a defendant who deserves punishment, and a given claimant may, as a consequence of a punitive award being made, recover more than another claimant who suffers identical or even more extensive damage.

One response to the windfall objection involves emphasising that its gripe is not, in fact, with the defendant being punished but with the claimant benefiting from the punishment. The complaint would fall away if the sums extracted from the defendant were paid to the state or, indeed, if the punishment effected a setback to the defendant's interests without any other person realising a corresponding gain.[19] As such, the windfall argument is not, in fact, an argument against punishment in private law but an argument against punishing the defendant in a manner that enriches the claimant. Another reply to the windfall complaint takes issue with the notion that the claimant has not done anything to merit having their position improved. For example, it is sometimes suggested that the claimant, in activating the machinery of the legal system in order to see that punishment is imposed where it is deserved, is providing a valuable public service (or, as Sharkey puts it in her chapter, 'acting as a private attorney-general'[20]) and that they should be remunerated for that work (or at least have some incentive to undertake it).[21] As against this it may be replied that the receipt enjoyed by the claimant is unlikely to correspond to the amount of work done by the claimant given that that is not the basis on which punitive awards are assessed.

D. Punishment is Inefficient

Some law-and-economics scholars oppose punishment in private law on efficiency grounds. The criticism is often advanced in the context of the law of contract as part of the efficient breach thesis, which has achieved greatest credence in the United States.[22] On this view, the spectre of a punitive award being made would impede the parties' ability to act or renegotiate (with certainty) and

107 (footnote omitted)) writes that 'a claimant cannot justly demand to be put in a better position than she would have been in had she not been wronged. She cannot be owed a windfall. This is even clearer in contract. A claimant cannot be owed to be placed in a better position than she would have been had the contract been performed'.

[19] Several jurisdictions in the United States have provided for 'split-recovery' statutes pursuant to which punitive damages will be diverted to the state or a public fund. Some states have achieved the same end as a matter of common law. For discussion, see Sharkey, ch 7 of this volume. See also the reform proposal in France considered by Rowan, ch 3, section V.A.

[20] Sharkey, ch 7, section IV.A.

[21] *Whiten v Pilot Insurance Co* 2002 SCC 18, [2002] 1 SCR 595 [37].

[22] See, eg, *Patton v Mid-Continent Systems Inc* 841 F 2d 742, 750–51 (7th Cir, 1988). cf W Dodge, 'The Case for Punitive Damages in Contract' (1999) 48 *Duke Law Journal* 629.

would hinder the efficient reallocation of resources through breach. A typical illustration is as follows. A seller refuses to honour its contract with the buyer to supply goods at a price of £1,000 and instead seizes upon a lucrative opportunity to sell the same goods to a third party for £1,500. The buyer can obtain equivalent goods in the market for £1,300. Pursuing these alternative arrangements leads to a Kaldor-Hicks efficient outcome.[23] The outcome becomes Pareto efficient[24] if, as the law requires, the seller also pays the conventional measure of £300 compensatory damages (being the difference between market and contract prices) to the buyer. Imposing a punitive award on top of this sum does not increase efficiency; on the contrary, a punitive award of more than £200 is counterproductive as it deters the seller from taking up the alternative transaction. Further, the seller's ability to evaluate the alternative transaction is impaired if it cannot predict what sum (if any) it might have to pay the buyer by way of punitive damages.[25]

Contracting parties can achieve greater certainty by agreeing in advance the sum payable for a breach of contract (liquidated damages). Such agreements are regulated by the rule against penalties. Richard Posner once described the rule as a 'major unexplained puzzle in the economic theory of the common law'.[26] The rule was not, of course, crafted with efficiency in mind and economic arguments about its merits can (and do) go either way.[27] Much depends upon the underlying assumptions and complexity of the economic model used. Suppose in the example above that the parties agreed in advance that the seller would pay £600 damages for non-delivery. Looking only at the matter *ex post*, such an agreement deters efficient breach, but this is far from the whole story. A full analysis entails consideration of the parties' pre-contractual and pre-breach conduct, including how parties arrive at particular figures as liquidated damages and the function of the clause in signalling reliability in performance or assigning to one or the other party the burden of 'insuring' against the risk of non-performance.[28] Adding the rule against penalties into the mix raises questions about the level at which the rule cuts in, whether the rule should apply only to certain breaches (eg, 'opportunistic' breaches as opposed to 'efficient' ones), and how the existence of the rule might

[23] A reallocation is Kaldor-Hicks efficient when it produces a net benefit.

[24] A reallocation is Pareto efficient when at least one person is made better off and no one is made worse off.

[25] For doubts regarding the claim that punitive damages awards are unpredictable at least in relation to England, see Goudkamp and Katsampouka, ch 8, section III.B.

[26] R Posner, 'Some Uses and Abuses of Economics in Law' (1979) 46 *University of Chicago Law Review* 281, 290.

[27] There is a substantial literature. For an overview, see G De Geest and F Wuyts, 'Penalty Clauses and Liquidated Damages' in B Bouckaert and G De Geest (eds), *Encyclopaedia of Law and Economics*, vol 3 (Cheltenham, Edward Elgar, 2000).

[28] See, eg, *Lake River Corp v Carborundum Co* 769 F 2d 1284, 1289 (7th Cir, 1985) (Posner J) ('the parties … will, in deciding whether to include a penalty clause in their contract, weigh the gains against the costs – costs that include the possibility of discouraging an efficient breach somewhere down the road – and will include the clause only if the benefits exceed those costs').

increase transaction costs and affect the parties' negotiations for a release from liability after breach or in anticipation of breach.[29]

Debates about whether punishment is efficient have also arisen in the tort context.[30] Typically, the focus here is on the problem of under-detection.[31] Suppose that D, a driver, injures C in a hit-and-run accident and escapes detection. The law cannot charge the consequences of D's behaviour to him because he cannot be identified. There is hence a concern about under-deterrence. However, the law can address this by extracting from other negligent drivers sums in respect of the loss that they cause plus, where appropriate, an extra amount – a punitive award – that reflects the fact that some motorists, such as D, will avoid detection. The sum falls, on this account, to be calculated in view of the probability of detection. It should be observed that this efficiency-based justification for punitive damages, while it might be normatively defensible, does not clearly comport with the law as it presently stands. For example, although it is true that punitive damages are calculated with deterrence in view, the primary criterion according to which the award is assessed is the defendant's culpability.[32]

E. Insufficient Procedural Safeguards

Another prominent objection to punishment in private law is that private law lacks the procedural safeguards for which the criminal law provides.[33] One premise of this argument is that the imposition of punishment is qualitatively more onerous than an obligation to pay compensation and other non-punitive awards, and the conclusion is that the conditions for imposing punishment in private law ought to be, but are not, as robust as those applied in the criminal law. As to the premise, while it is certainly the case that state-imposed punishment is draconian, it is less clear that the obligation to pay (for example) compensation in the sum of £100 is qualitatively less burdensome than a fine of the same amount.[34] For one thing, an order to pay compensation may be paired (especially in the tort context) with a public determination that the defendant behaved defectively in some way. In other words, a finding of civil liability has the potential to be stigmatic in the same way as a criminal conviction and sentence.[35] Further, defendants, especially when

[29] See also the discussion in Courtney, ch 12, section II.B.ii.

[30] For discussion, see J Coleman, *Markets, Morals, and the Law* (Oxford, Oxford University Press, 1998) ch 6; AM Polinsky and S Shavell, 'Punitive Damages: An Economic Analysis' (1998) 111 *Harvard Law Review* 869.

[31] See Sharkey, ch 7, section III.A.i.

[32] In *W v W* [1999] 4 LRC 260 (PC) 263 Lord Hoffmann said that '[t]he main purpose' of punitive damages 'is to punish the defendant'.

[33] *Broome* (n 5) 1087 (Lord Reid) ('palm tree justice').

[34] For further discussion of this point, see AM Honoré, 'The Morality of Tort Law – Questions and Answers' in D Owen (ed), *Philosophical Foundations of Tort Law* (Clarendon Press, 1997) 73, 88–90.

[35] This theme is powerfully developed in P Cane, 'Retribution, Proportionality, and Moral Luck in Tort Law' in P Cane and J Stapleton (eds), *The Law of Obligations: Essays in Celebration of John Fleming* (Oxford, Clarendon Press, 1998) 141.

uninsured, may regard the obligation to pay compensation as indistinguishable from a penalty. It was for this reason that Peter Birks claimed that 'every award of damages has a penal … function'.[36] We observe in passing that whereas awards of even compensatory damages may well be perceived by defendants as punitive, Birks clearly went too far in contending that punishment is a purpose of every damages award. It does not follow from the fact that a given damages award may be perceived as punitive that punishment is a function of the award. We return to this theme in section II.

As to the conclusion that private law should not countenance punishment on account of the lack of procedural safeguards, it is true that, in general, the protections that apply in private law are much less robust than those that exist in the criminal law. Focusing on the position in England, consider the following illustrations:

1. In principle, the criminal law places the burden of proof on all issues on the prosecution and requires that the prosecution establish liability beyond reasonable doubt. By contrast, the civil law requires defendants to bear the burden of proof on various issues, most notably so-called 'affirmative defences',[37] and requires liability to be established on the balance of probabilities.
2. The criminal law is committed to the idea that conduct that is proscribed should be defined as precisely as is reasonably possible.[38] Conversely, private law does not place the same premium on certainty. Thus, it has often been claimed that, compared with the position in the criminal law, conduct that attracts civil liability is sometimes defined in fairly vague terms.[39] The tort of negligence is typically cited as an illustration of this[40] on account of the tort's simply imposing an obligation to take reasonable care but without stipulating specifically that which must be done in any given situation.
3. In the criminal law, it is thought important that maximum sentences be fixed, and that the sentence imposed be no higher than the maximum prevailing at the time that the offence concerned was committed.[41] It is doubtful that the civil law contains similar protections. Thus, the jurisdiction to award punitive damages, which is the clearest illustration of punishment in private law, is not subject to a definite ceiling.[42]

[36] P Birks, *Civil Wrongs: A New World* (London, Butterworths, 1992) 79. Consider also Peter Cane's remark that 'even compensatory damages may have a punitive element': Cane (n 35) 170.

[37] See J Goudkamp, *Tort Law Defences* (Oxford, Hart Publishing, 2013) 138–39.

[38] For discussion, see, eg, J Horder, *Ashworth's Principles of Criminal Law* (Oxford, Oxford University Press, 2019) 81–84.

[39] See, eg, Gardner (n 4) 181–82.

[40] ibid.

[41] Art 7(1) of the European Convention on Human Rights states in relevant part: 'Nor shall a heavier penalty be imposed than the one that was applicable at the time the criminal offence was committed.'

[42] However, awards of punitive damages in claims against the police in malicious prosecution are confined to particular brackets based on the rank of the police office involved: *Thompson v Metropolitan Police Commissioner* [1998] QB 498 (CA). Consider also the federal constitutional restrictions in the United States, which are discussed by Sharkey in ch 7, section II.A.

4. The admissibility of hearsay evidence is subject to various restrictions in criminal proceedings[43] whereas the hearsay rule does not apply in civil litigation.[44]

Although there clearly are major differences between the criminal law and private law in terms of the procedural safeguards on the imposition of punishment, the significance of these differences can be, and often is, seriously overstated. Consider the following points:

1. It is well known that, in criminal proceedings, the burden of proof on various issues is regularly placed on the defendant and, further, that there are widespread departures from the principle that the prosecution must establish the elements of offences beyond reasonable doubt.[45] Reality and rhetoric in the criminal law routinely diverge from each other radically in these respects. Further, although the standard of proof in the civil law is always the balance of probabilities, that standard is more difficult to meet where serious wrongdoing is alleged. The logic underpinning this rule is that it is inherently less likely that a defendant will have acted, for example, fraudulently than negligently, with the result that, before a finding of fraud is made, clear and convincing evidence will be required, and greater evidence than would be needed to justify a finding of negligence.[46] While this is certainly not the same thing as requiring proof according to the criminal law standard, in view of this rule the bald remark that the civil law dispenses punishment according to a lower standard of proof than the criminal law oversimplifies matters.

   The point can be carried further. Although the standard of proof in private law is formally the balance of probabilities, it is arguable that the courts sometimes informally apply a more demanding standard because it is thought unfair that D should liable for 100 per cent of C's loss simply upon C establishing that it is marginally more probable than not that D acted as alleged. Thus, Peter Cane writes:

   > while in theory a person might be liable in tort on a bare balance of probabilities, in practice the test operates in an imprecise way and actually depends on the court being *satisfied* that the tort more probably than not caused the harm. An adjudicator is unlikely to feel such satisfaction unless the probability that the tort cause the harm is not just greater than even, but considerably greater than even.[47]

[43] Criminal Justice Act 2003 (UK), pt 11, ch 2.

[44] Civil Evidence Act 1995 (UK), s 1. But see CPR 33.2.

[45] See A Ashworth and M Blake, 'The Presumption of Innocence in English Criminal Law' [1996] Crim LR 306.

[46] 'When assessing the probabilities the court will have in mind as a factor, to whatever extent is appropriate in the particular case, that the more serious the allegation the less likely it is that the event occurred and, hence, the stronger should be the evidence before the court concludes that the allegation is established on the balance of probability. Fraud is usually less likely than negligence. Deliberate physical injury is usually less likely than accidental physical injury': *In re H (Minors) (Sexual Abuse: Standard of Proof)* [1996] AC 563 (HL) 586 (Lord Nicholls).

[47] Cane (n 35) 166 (emphasis in original).

2. The criminal law often scores particularly poorly in terms of the precision with which it defines prohibited conduct. For example, it is notorious that the criminal law provides extensively for negligence-based liability,[48] which form of liability is often thought, as we have observed, to offer relatively little guidance to defendants as to how, specifically, they should proceed. It follows that the claim that criminal law provides enhanced safeguards by virtue of its insisting that offences be precisely defined is, at least unless it is heavily qualified, overstated.
3. A key idea in sentencing offenders, which has been prominent ever since Bentham's writings on the subject, is what Andrew Ashworth dubs the principle of parsimony, that is, the notion that punishment should be minimised as far as possible.[49] The same idea has clearly taken root in private law.[50] Thus, it is well established that awards of punitive damages are subject to an 'if but only if test'. According to this test, punitive damages can be granted only if the compensatory damages (and, presumably, any other remedies) awarded do not sufficiently punish and deter.[51] This restriction is reflected in Lord Nicholls' remark in *Kuddus v Chief Constable of Leicestershire Constabulary* that punitive damages are 'a remedy of last resort'.[52] Further, if punitive damages are awarded it is clear law that they should be kept to the bare minimum necessary to fulfil their goals. Thus, in *Thompson v Metropolitan Police Commissioner*, Lord Woolf MR stressed that punitive damages 'should be no more than is required' by their purpose of 'marking … disapproval' of the defendant's conduct.[53]

F. Second-order Disputes

The arguments considered in the foregoing subsections address whether punishment has a place in private law at all. Yet even those who oppose punishment in principle usually concede that private law is sometimes in the business of punishing, as when, for example, it awards punitive damages. Assuming (or conceding)

[48] HLA Hart claimed that 'English law is rather sparing in its punishment of negligence in the sense of unintentional neglect to take reasonable precautions against harm to others, and apart from a few isolated situations, it can be said that negligence is only punishable as a crime if it results in death (where it constitutes one species of manslaughter) or if it is shown in driving motor vehicles on the road: not only is there the offence of driving without due care and attention but there is also the more severely punished offence of causing death by dangerous driving': HLA Hart, *Punishment and Responsibility*, 2nd edn (Oxford, Oxford University Press, 2008) 132. This may or not may not have been true in Hart's time but it is certainly not the case today: see Goudkamp and Katsampouka, ch 8, section III.I.

[49] A Ashworth, *Sentencing and Criminal Justice*, 6th edn (Cambridge, Cambridge University Press, 2015) 103.

[50] See also Bant and Paterson, ch 10 of this volume, on the concept of proportionate punishment.

[51] *Rookes* (n 5) 1128; *Whiten* (n 21) [74].

[52] *Kuddus v Chief Constable of Leicestershire Constabulary* [2001] UKHL 29, [2002] 2 AC 122 [63].

[53] *Thompson v Metropolitan Police Commissioner* [1998] QB 498 (CA) 517.

that punishment plays some role in private law opens up numerous further controversies. Although the disputes in this regard are, in a sense, secondary in nature, this should in no way distract attention from the fact that at least several of them are major debates in their own right and are, accordingly, considered extensively in the various contributions to this book. We single out five for special mention.

The first concerns the perennial controversy as to why punishment in the form of punitive damages is permitted in tort (or at least in relation to certain torts) and yet, in the case of at least some jurisdictions, regarded as anathema to contract[54] and equity.[55] As a matter of principle, the differential treatment is justified only if tort law can be sufficiently distinguished from contract and equity. Arguments for or against punitive damages in contract and equity often proceed in two steps. By induction from tort cases or from theory, they identify essential conditions for the award of punitive damages. Next, they consider whether the same conditions exist for a breach of contract or breach of equitable duty.[56] These arguments are sometimes supplemented by reference to considerations specific to each field. In contract, for example, certainty and efficiency are often touted as particularly important objectives,[57] and the claim is sometimes made that it follows that punitive damages should, in view of these goals, be unavailable for breach of contract (although the implication that the values of certainty and efficiency are less important in other parts of private law is highly contestable, as is the assumption that making punitive damages available in the law of contract would undermine them). In chapter 9 Barnett contends that punitive damages in contract can be justified in certain circumstances.

The second flashpoint is whether, within tort law, punitive damages should be available across the board or withheld in relation to certain causes of action, such as that in negligence. In England, the availability of punitive damages was previously restricted by the notorious 'cause of action' (or 'pre-1964') test.[58] Pursuant to that rule, punitive damages were available only in causes of action in which they had been awarded prior to 1964, that being the year in which *Rookes v Barnard*[59] was decided. The House of Lords abolished this much maligned rule in *Kuddus*.[60]

[54] This position is often traced to *Addis v Gramophone Co Ltd* [1909] AC 488 (HL). More recently, Lord Hoffmann said that 'the purpose of the law of contract is not to punish wrongdoing': *Co-operative Insurance Society Ltd v Argyll Stores (Holdings) Ltd* [1998] AC 1 (HL) 15. See also *Gray v Motor Accident Commission* (1998) 196 CLR 1 [13]. cf *Whiten* (n 21).

[55] *Harris v Digital Pulse Pty Ltd* [2003] NSWCA 10, (2003) 56 NSWLR 298. cf *Aquaculture Corp v New Zealand Green Mussel Co Ltd* [1990] 3 NZLR 299 (CA); *Norberg v Wynrib* [1992] 2 SCR 226 (SCC) 299–300.

[56] See, eg, N McBride, 'A Case for Awarding Punitive Damages in Response to Deliberate Breaches of Contract' (1995) 24 *Anglo-American Law Review* 369.

[57] See English Law Commission, *Aggravated, Exemplary and Restitutionary Damages* (Law Com No 247, 1997) pt V para 1.72.

[58] *AB v South West Water Services Ltd* [1993] QB 507 (CA).

[59] *Rookes* (n 5).

[60] *Kuddus* (n 52) [63].

Despite this development major doubts remain as to whether punitive damages can be awarded for, in particular, the tort of negligence. Goudkamp and Katsampouka observe that there are no cases in England in which punitive damages have been awarded for that wrong.[61] Even in other jurisdictions where punitive damages can be awarded for negligence, argument has broken out as to whether the award should be made only where certain conditions are satisfied. In New Zealand, for example, punitive damages can be awarded in a claim in negligence only where the defendant intended to injure the claimant or was subjectively reckless with respect to the risk of injury.[62]

A third debate concerns the circumstances in which, if punishment in private law is justified, the defendant's conduct merits a retributive response. For example, those who support the availability of punitive damages in contract must specify the types of breach that qualify for an award. Adjectives like 'deliberate' are too vague and almost certainly set the bar too low. The concept of 'wilful' breach has gained more traction in the United States but there is no clear consensus about its meaning.[63] Corbin caustically remarked that 'its use indicates a childlike faith in the existence of a plain and obvious line between the good and the bad, between unfortunate virtue and unforgivable sin'.[64] In *Whiten v Pilot Insurance Co*[65] the Supreme Court of Canada referred to 'egregious' or 'outrageous' conduct[66] – terms familiar to tort lawyers in Commonwealth jurisdictions – but then tacked on the puzzling requirement of an independently actionable wrong before punitive damages can be awarded. The main difficulty with this prerequisite is it will be a matter of happenstance whether or not there is an independently actionable wrong and it conflates the remedy for *this* breach of contract with the other wrong (which, curiously, can be another breach of contract).[67] Barnett's contribution in chapter 9 proposes a different set of criteria to determine when punitive damages ought to be available in claims for breach of contract.

[61] Goudkamp and Katsampouka, ch 8, section III.I.

[62] *Couch v Attorney-General (No 2)* [2010] NZSC 27, [2010] 3 NZLR 149.

[63] R Craswell, 'When is a Willful Breach "Willful"? The Link between Definitions and Damages' (2009) 107 *Michigan Law Review* 1501; O Ben-Shahar and O Bar-Gill, 'An Information Theory of Willful Breach' (2009) 107 *Michigan Law Review* 1479; S Thel and P Siegelman, 'Willfulness Versus Expectation: A Promisor-Based Defense of the Willful Breach Doctrine' (2009) 107 *Michigan Law Review* 1517.

[64] AL Corbin, *Corbin on Contracts*, vol 5 (St Paul, MN, West Publishing Co, 1951) 545.

[65] *Whiten* (n 21) [68], [70], [72].

[66] See also *PH Hydraulics & Engineering Pte Ltd v Airtrust (Hong Kong) Ltd* [2017] SGCA 26, [2017] 2 SLR 129 [135]–[136] (rejecting punitive damages for breach of contract as a general rule but not excluding the possibility of such damages for a 'particularly outrageous type of breach').

[67] See also J Swan, 'Punitive Damages for Breach of Contract: A Remedy in Search of a Justification' (2004) 29 *Queen's Law Journal* 596; J McCamus, 'Prometheus Bound or Loose Cannon? Punitive Damages for Pure Breach of Contract in Canada' (2004) 41 *San Diego Law Review* 1491.

A fourth battleground concerns the relationship between punitive remedies and other responses. Punitive damages are explicitly aimed at punishment. But certain other remedies are also concerned, or are arguably concerned, at least in some circumstances, with punishment. Rowan discusses this in her chapter,[68] and gives several illustrations, including principles that disapply or attenuate the doctrine of remoteness of damage.[69] Whether or not these and certain other rules are indeed infused with a punitive agenda is controversial. Beyond this major dispute questions also arise as to whether the law should provide for several punitive mechanisms[70] (is there not a concern of double or disproportionate punishment?) and whether certain devices for meting out punishment are better suited for the task than others. Arguably, punishment should be dispensed by and only by punitive damages on the basis that principle requires that their award be fixed by reference to (principally) the defendant's culpability, in contrast to at least certain of the other rules in question that instead tether the amount of punishment imposed to some other criterion, such as the claimant's loss.

A fifth issue that has generated significant debate is whether punitive damages should be insurable.[71] On the one hand, if punitive damages are awarded in order to punish, one may think that, consistently with the position that obtains in relation to criminal law sanctions,[72] contracts of liability insurance in respect of them should be pro tanto unenforceable. On the other hand, it has been suggested that if punitive damages are not insurable claimants may have little or no incentive to claim them and the realisation of certain of their stated goals, such as public denunciation of the defendant and appeasement, may, in turn, be impeded. The issue of insurability is touched upon by Sharkey in her chapter.[73] Her thesis (which we describe in further detail in section III.C) is that punitive damages should be reinvented as damages awarded in respect of societal harm. Reimagined in this way, she argues that they should be insurable and that there is no legitimate basis for sequestering them from other species of compensatory damages in relation to which no issue regarding insurability arises.

[68] Rowan, ch 3, section II.B. See also Goudkamp and Katsampouka, ch 8, section III.D and Bant and Paterson, ch 10, sections I and IV.

[69] In English law the orthodox view is that the 'reasonable contemplation' remoteness rule applies irrespective of the nature of the breach, but some scholars argue that it ought to be relaxed for deliberate breaches (see, eg, J Gordley, 'Responsibility in Crime, Tort and Contract for the Unforeseeable Consequences of an Intentional Wrong: A Once and Future Role?' in P Cane and J Stapleton (eds), *The Law of Obligations: Essays in Celebration of John Fleming* (Oxford, Clarendon Press, 1998) 175, 198–200) or where the loss is deliberately caused (see, eg, N Andrews et al, *Contractual Duties: Performance, Breach, Termination and Remedies*, 3rd edn (London, Sweet & Maxwell, 2020) para 23.055). Consider also *Principles of European Contract Law*, Art 9:503, comment B and note 5 (exception for 'intentional' or 'grossly negligent' breaches).

[70] Roberts and Richardson address this issue in ch 4 of this volume.

[71] See, generally, Law Commission of England and Wales (n 57), pt V, paras 1.234–1.248.

[72] *Askey v Golden Wine Co* [1948] 2 All ER 35 (CA) 38.

[73] Sharkey, ch 7, section V. See also Rowan, ch 3, section V.C (observing that a proposed provision to permit punitive awards barred the awards from being insurable).

II. Punishment

A. Terminology

The term 'punishment' does not have an accepted or stable definition in private law, which is a theme with which Kit Barker engages in his chapter. One meaning (and probably the core meaning) looks to the purpose of a given rule. When used in this sense, a particular rule is punitive when it pursues a retributive agenda. Its aim is to inflict some sort of sanction on the wrongdoer on the grounds of desert. The sanction may take a variety of forms, punitive damages being the most obvious example. Another sense of the term 'punishment', as identified by Barker, concerns a rule's effects. The consequences of a rule may be perceived as punitive even if they are not imposed with the aim of punishing the wrongdoer.

B. Overt and Covert Punishment

Some private law rules are overtly punitive in terms of their aim. For example, it is beyond serious argument that punitive damages are awarded with the aim of punishing the defendant given the repeated judicial pronouncements to that effect at the ultimate appellate level, the fact that the defendant must behave outrageously before the jurisdiction to award them will be available and the fact that they are assessed, first and foremost, with the defendant's culpability in view. It is true that punitive damages are often said to discharge other functions, such as deterrence,[74] appeasement[75] and vindication,[76] and that the various functions of a punitive award may compete or conflict with each other.[77] The diversity of functions that punitive damages serve is reflected in the range of names by which the award is known. Thus, beyond punitive damages, the remedy is in certain jurisdictions regularly referred to as exemplary damages,[78] which usage perhaps emphasises the goal of deterrence. But none of this changes the fact that punitive damages are explicitly awarded for the purposes of punishment.

Certain rules in private law, although not expressly aimed at punishment, are perhaps nevertheless concerned with punishment and, as such, dispense punishment covertly or informally.[79] We touched on this possibility in section I.F,[80] but it is worth deepening the discussion.[81] Consider mental distress damages

[74] *Rookes* (n 5) 1221.
[75] *W v W* (n 32) 264.
[76] *A v Bottrill* [2002] UKPC 44, [2003] 1 AC 449 [29].
[77] For discussion, see B Chapman and M Trebilcock, 'Punitive Damages: Divergence in Search of a Rationale' (1989) 40 *Alabama Law Review* 741.
[78] This appears to be the dominant terminology in Australia.
[79] This theme is developed by Rowan as regards French law: see Rowan, ch 3, section II.
[80] See the text accompanying n 69.
[81] See, further, Goudkamp and Katsampouka, ch 8, section III D.

awarded for breach of contract. Formally, the purpose of this form of damages is to compensate the claimant for distress and inconvenience. However, one leading commentator has suggested that a distinction between damages for mental distress and punitive damages is often hard to draw.[82] Consistently with this, judges have sometimes perceived awards of mental distress damages as allied with punitive damages. For example, in *Herbert Clayton & Jack Waller Ltd v Oliver* Lord Buckmaster remarked that '[w]hat are known as … exemplary damages in tort find no place in contract *nor accordingly can injury to the feelings or vanity*'.[83] Lord Buckmaster was writing before mental distress damages were vouchsafed their present position in contract law, but this has no bearing on the affinity that he perceived between damages awarded in respect of such loss and punitive damages.

While mental distress damages may sometimes be awarded with the end of punishment in view, damages for mental distress are an awkward way to smuggle punishment into contract, and questions thus arise as to whether it is sensible to mete out punishment in this way. The treatment of mental distress damages varies among the major common law jurisdictions. In Australia and England, such damages are confined to breaches causing physical injury or inconvenience, and to breaches of contracts that have as an important object the provision of pleasure, relaxation or peace of mind.[84] However, it is not obvious why the latter class of contracts calls for special treatment and it would appear to rule out claims for such damages by corporate claimants. This rule also shifts the focus onto the nature of the claimant's injury and away from the defendant's culpability. In many cases involving claims for non-pecuniary damages the breach is not egregious[85] and it may involve mere carelessness.[86] Smuggling might seem to be unnecessary (or less necessary) in Canada, where punitive damages can exceptionally be awarded for breach of contract.[87] In any event, the Canadian law on the recovery of mental distress damages is more generous to claimants than that in Australia and England. Recovery is determined by foreseeability, with the object of the contract being a significant factor.[88] Unsurprisingly, such damages are regarded as compensatory and are awarded in a wider range of situations than punitive damages.[89]

[82] E Peel, *Treitel: The Law of Contract*, 15th edn (London, Sweet & Maxwell, 2020) para 20.022. cf para 20.088.

[83] *Herbert Clayton & Jack Waller Ltd v Oliver* [1930] AC 209 (HL) 230 (emphasis added). Consider also *British Guiana Credit Corp v da Silva* [1965] 1 WLR 248 (PC) 259; *McCall v Abelesz* [1976] QB 585 (CA) 594.

[84] *Baltic Shipping Co Ltd v Dillon (The Mikhail Lermontov)* (1993) 176 CLR 344 (HCA); *Farley v Skinner* [2001] UKHL 49, [2002] 2 AC 732; *Moore v Scenic Tours Pty Ltd* [2020] HCA 17, (2020) 377 ALR 209 [68]–[69].

[85] A striking counter-example from the United States is *Wilson v Houston Funeral Home* 42 Cal App 4th 1124 (1996), where the court countenanced damages for emotional distress and punitive damages.

[86] See, eg, *Heywood v Wellers* [1976] QB 446 (CA); *Baltic Shipping* (n 84); *Farley* (n 84).

[87] *Whiten* (n 21).

[88] *Fidler v Sun Life Assurance Co of Canada* 2006 SCC 30, [2006] 2 SCR 3 [44]–[49].

[89] ibid [61]–[63]; *Honda Canada Inc v Keys* 2008 SCC 39, [2008] 2 SCR 362 [56]–[60]. There is no requirement of an independently actionable wrong. Nor is high-handed or oppressive conduct always essential.

The position in the United States is unsettled, with opinion divided over whether emphasis should be placed on the nature of the contract, the nature of the breach or both.[90] Looking to the nature of the breach arguably facilitates punishment disguised as damages for mental distress. Yet almost all US jurisdictions have held firm against awarding punitive damages solely on the basis of a 'wilful', 'wanton' or 'bad faith' breach of contract.[91]

Another illustration of a rule that may involve covert punishment is an account of profits.[92] An account of profits is usually not regarded as being punitive in nature.[93] Supporters of this view may concede that the remedy can operate harshly upon the defendant – either by comparison with other remedies or by reference to the sum calculated as the profits – but say that this establishes, at most, that the remedy may involve punishment in the 'effects' sense of the term. And since the remedy can be granted for unwitting or well-intentioned breaches,[94] even that characterisation is doubtful. On some occasions, however, an account of profits may be impledly aimed at punishment[95] and, consistently with this, the defendant's culpability is sometimes taken into account in deciding whether to grant the remedy[96] or in denying an allowance for skill and effort.[97] Consider *Attorney-General v Blake*,[98] where a majority of the House of Lords awarded an account of profits as an extraordinary remedy for breach of contract. It is impossible to discount the egregious and criminal quality of Blake's conduct as a significant factor,[99] notwithstanding Lord Nicholls' analogies with breach of fiduciary duty and breach of confidence. As Lord Hobhouse observed in dissent, the claim had an 'essentially punitive nature'.[100] It seems that in ordering the account the House had punitive purposes in view, although it is perhaps debatable whether these were explicit or implicit, at least in the case of the majority judgments.

[90] The *Restatement (Second) of Contracts* (American Law Institute, 1981) §353 refers to both, whereas the *Restatement (First) of Contracts* (American Law Institute, 1932) §341 stressed the nature of breach. See also D Hoffman and A Radus, 'Instructing Juries on Noneconomic Contract Damages' (2012) 81 *Fordham Law Review* 1221, 1226–29.

[91] For a detailed account, see J Sebert, 'Punitive and Nonpecuniary Damages in Actions Based upon Contract: Toward Achieving the Objective of Full Compensation' (1986) 33 *UCLA Law Review* 1565, 1629–47; W Dodge, 'The Case for Punitive Damages in Contract' (1999) 48 *Duke Law Journal* 629, 635, 646–51. The *Restatement (Second) of Contracts* (n 90) §355 only permits punitive damages when the conduct constituting breach also constitutes a tort for which punitive damages are recoverable.

[92] See the discussions by Penner, ch 5, section VI.B–VI.E and by Bant and Paterson, ch 10, section IV.

[93] *Warman International Ltd v Dwyer* (1995) 182 CLR 544 (HCA) 557; *Harris* (n 55) [306]–[310]; *OOO Abbott v Design & Display Ltd* [2016] EWCA Civ 98, [2016] FSR 27 [7]. See also *Sheldon v Metro-Goldwyn Pictures Corp* 309 US 390, 399 (1940).

[94] *Parker v McKenna* (1874) LR 10 Ch App 96, 124–25.

[95] See further, Goudkamp and Katsampouka, ch 8, section III.D.

[96] See, eg, *Seager v Copydex Ltd (No 2)* [1969] 1 WLR 809 (CA) (breach of confidence).

[97] *Phipps v Boardman* [1965] Ch 992 (CA) 1021; *United States Surgical Corp v Hospital Products International Pty Ltd* [1983] 2 NSWLR 157 (CA) 242 (revd on appeal on other grounds: (1984) 156 CLR 41 (HCA)); *Harris* (n 55) [48]–[49].

[98] *Attorney-General v Blake* [2001] 1 AC 268 (HL).

[99] ibid 275.

[100] ibid 295.

Finally, consider the rules regarding fraud by a contracting party. A party cannot exclude liability for its own fraud.[101] There has been greater flexibility in English law to rescind contracts for fraud than for non-fraudulent misrepresentation[102] and the right to rescind for fraud is exempt from the 'inequity' qualification under statute.[103] And in insurance law, an insurer can refuse outright to pay a claim fraudulently made, even though part of the claim is justified.[104] Lord Sumption recently rationalised this rule on the basis that 'the law of insurance is concerned more with controlling the impact of a breach of good faith on the risk than with the punishment of misconduct'.[105] But it could equally be argued that an implicit purpose of this and the other rules just mentioned is to punish fraud.

C. Liability and Remedies

Discussions regarding punishment in private law tend to focus on remedies. This may be an artefact of punitive damages being the most explicit manifestation of private law pursuing a retributive agenda. However, the fact that debates about punishment in private law are often centred on remedies should not be permitted to deflect attention from the possibility that private law is also concerned with punishment in connection with the decision to impose liability.[106] Consider, for example, the doctrine of illegality. Although the doctrine sometimes operates only to diminish the quantum of the claimant's recovery,[107] its major role is to preclude the claimant from establishing liability against the defendant.

According to the classic exegesis in *Holman v Johnson*,[108] the doctrine's purpose is to prevent the court from sullying its hands by aiding a party who had transgressed the law. So understood, if the doctrine was punitive, it was only in the 'effects' sense of that term. However, during the twentieth century the law in (at least) the UK developed such that punishment was, or was arguably, among the doctrine's aims. Consistently with this, the parties' respective knowledge of, and extent of participation in, the illegal activity became relevant considerations

[101] *S Pearson & Son Ltd v Dublin Corp* [1907] AC 351 (HL); *HIH Casualty and General Insurance Ltd v Chase Manhattan Bank* [2003] UKHL 6, [2003] 2 Lloyd's Rep 61.

[102] eg, the rule barring rescission of an executed contract of sale for non-fraudulent misrepresentation: *Wilde v Gibson* (1848) 1 HLC 605, 9 ER 897; *Seddon v North Eastern Salt Co* [1905] 1 Ch 326 (Ch D), now abrogated by the Misrepresentation Act 1967 (UK), s 1(b). Courts may also, in practice, be slower to find that the party misled affirmed the contract.

[103] Misrepresentation Act 1967 (UK), s 2(2).

[104] *Versloot Dredging BV v HDI Gerling Industrie Versicherung AG* [2016] UKSC 45, [2017] AC 1 [1]; Insurance Act 2015 (UK), s 12.

[105] *Versloot Dredging* (n 104) [36].

[106] For illuminating treatment, see Cane (n 35).

[107] When the illegality doctrine functions in this way, the head of damages affected is often a future loss of earnings. For discussion, see J Goudkamp and L König, 'Illegal Earnings' (2018) 9 *Journal of European Tort Law* 54.

[108] *Holman v Johnson* (1775) 1 Cowp 341, 98 ER 1120.

in some categories of case, such as contracts that were apparently lawful but were entered into with the purpose of committing an unlawful act[109] or were performed in an unlawful manner.[110] Similarly, courts sometimes took account of the severity of any criminal punishment already imposed on the claimant for the conduct in issue.[111] This reflected a concern with proportionality and, perhaps, also the avoidance of 'double' punishment, and it is noteworthy that the same considerations may inform the award and assessment of punitive damages.[112] In the field of unjust enrichment the plea of illegality could be countered by the *locus poenitentiae* principle. In so far as that principle demanded genuine repentance by the claimant in withdrawing from the transaction,[113] it might be seen as concerned with whether the claimant had engaged in punishment-worthy conduct.[114]

As to the position in the twenty-first century, the English Law Commission in its 2009 Consultation Paper, *The Illegality Defence*,[115] discounted punishment as 'an aim underlying the illegality doctrine' but acknowledged that a successful defence might have 'exactly this effect'. In *Patel v Mirza*[116] the UK Supreme Court likewise eschewed punishment as a function of the illegality doctrine and instead identified the doctrine's principal rationales as being to prevent wrongful profiting and ensuring that the law's coherence was not undermined.[117] At the same time, however, the majority in *Patel*, in holding that the illegality doctrine should be governed by a test that balances a range of salient factors, identified as material several considerations that seem to be, or are arguably, sensitive to retributive justice. For example, Lord Toulson, delivering the principal majority judgment, considered that it was material to enquire as to the seriousness of the claimant's conduct and whether there was a marked disparity in the parties' culpability.[118] His Lordship also referred to the imperative of not imposing 'what would amount

[109] See, eg, *St John Shipping Corp v Joseph Rank Ltd* [1957] 1 QB 267 (QBD) 283.

[110] *Ashmore, Benson, Pease & Co Ltd v AV Dawson Ltd* [1973] 1 WLR 828 (CA); *ParkingEye Ltd v Somerfield Stores Ltd* [2012] EWCA Civ 1338, [2013] QB 840.

[111] See, eg, *St John Shipping* (n 109) 279–80, 292.

[112] See, eg, *Gray* (n 54) [40]–[43]. The position in English law has become muddled: see Goudkamp and Katsampouka, ch 8, section III.F.

[113] *Parkinson v College of Ambulance Ltd* [1925] 2 KB 1 (KBD) 16; *Alexander v Rayson* [1936] 1 KB 169 (KBD) 190; *Berg v Sadler & Moore* [1937] 2 KB 158 (CA) 165.

[114] cf Millett LJ's remark that 'genuine repentance is not required. Justice is not a reward for merit; restitution should not be confined to the penitent': *Tribe v Tribe* [1996] Ch 107 (CA) 135. Regarding the present status of this principle see G Virgo, 'Illegality and Unjust Enrichment' in S Green and A Bogg (eds), *Illegality after Patel v Mirza* (Oxford, Hart Publishing, 2018) 213, 229–30.

[115] English Law Commission, *The Illegality Defence: A Consultative Report* (CP No 189, 2009) paras 2.28–2.29.

[116] *Patel v Mirza* (n 5) [108], [155], [184], [192], [213]–[214], [230]. The approach in *Patel* was recently affirmed by the UK Supreme Court in *Stoffel & Co v Grondona* [2020] UKSC 42, [2020] 3 WLR 1156; *Henderson v Dorset Healthcare University NHS Foundation Trust* [2020] UKSC 43, [2020] 3 WLR 1124, and it is now clear, if it was not clear before, that the *ratio* of *Patel* applies not only in claims in unjust enrichment (that being the relevant context in *Patel*) but in claims brought in all branches of private law.

[117] ibid, esp at [99]. cf English Law Commission (n 115) paras 2.5–2.27.

[118] *Patel* (n 5) [107].

in substance to an additional penalty disproportionate to the nature and seriousness of any wrongdoing'.[119] Thus, although punishment was not formally identified as purpose of the illegality doctrine, the doctrine is, or is arguably, nevertheless sensitive to the issue of retributive justice as evidenced by the test that controls its application. *Patel* has recently been followed by the UK Supreme Court in *Stoffel & Co v Grondona*[120] and *Henderson v Dorset Healthcare University NHS Foundation Trust*.[121] Those cases suggest that Lord Toulson's remarks in *Patel* regarding disproportionality should be understood as establishing a disproportionality check on the doctrine's application rather than a proportionality requirement that must be satisfied before the doctrine will be engaged.

D. Limiting Punishment

Private law's concern with punishment is sometimes negatively orientated, in that it seeks to limit it. In view of the way in which the illegality doctrine has been developed in the UK in *Patel*, *Stoffel* and *Henderson*, the doctrine is perhaps such a limiting device. However, other, clearer illustrations of rules that restrict punishment concern consensual punishment, especially the principles regarding penalties and forfeitures. A rationale offered for the rule against penalties, and occasionally for relief against forfeiture, is that they manifest the general proscription of punishment by contracting parties.[122] Since a court will not award punitive damages for breach, the parties should not be able to achieve the same ends by private agreement. Although superficially plausible, this justification is contestable. Consider the rule against penalties. The rule has been used to invalidate clauses that did not have any obvious punitive purpose.[123] Recent developments in Australia and the United Kingdom herald greater deference to party autonomy in evaluating penalties.[124] Rather than asking whether the agreed sum is out of proportion to the claimant's loss occasioned by the breach as predicted at the time of contract – the traditional approach – the law in both jurisdictions now involves some form of 'legitimate interest' test. That is, the agreed sanction may protect some legitimate interest of the injured party in performance of the associated

[119] ibid [108].

[120] *Stoffel & Co v Grondona* (n 116).

[121] *Henderson v Dorset Healthcare University NHS Foundation Trust* (n 116).

[122] *Priebe & Sons Inc v United States* 332 US 407, 418 (1947); *Legione v Hateley* (1983) 152 CLR 406 (HCA) 425, 445; *Cavendish Square Holding BV v Makdessi* [2015] UKSC 67, [2016] AC 1172 [31], [148], [254]; *Paciocco v Australia and New Zealand Banking Group Ltd* [2016] HCA 28, (2016) 258 CLR 525 [21], [253]. Some aspects of relief against forfeiture are plainly not concerned with punishment: see Courtney, ch 12, section IV.A and Tiverios and McFarlane, ch 13, section II.

[123] See, eg, *Watts, Watts & Co Ltd v Mitsui Co Ltd* [1917] AC 227 (HL); *Bridge v Campbell Discount Co Ltd* [1962] AC 600 (HL) (on the assumption that the penalty rule applied in the circumstances). See also E Peel, *Treitel: The Law of Contract*, 14th edn (London, Sweet & Maxwell, 2015) para 20–131(c) (this point is not found in the 15th edn, which focuses upon *Cavendish*).

[124] The leading decisions are, respectively, *Paciocco* (n 122) and *Cavendish* (n 122).

primary obligation, going beyond mere compensation for non-performance. But it is hard to see how preventing punishment, as a supposed rationale, is the exact obverse of the legitimate interests permitted under the new test. It is also doubtful that the punishment rationale explains why sanctions agreed in advance are subject to restrictions (eg, the rule against penalties) that are not applied to an equivalent agreement by the parties, post-breach, to compromise a damages liability.

Unsurprisingly, rival explanations for the rule against penalties exist. These include that it: (i) curtails unjustified attempts to deter breach or practically to compel specific performance;[125] (ii) regulates substantive unfairness in a particular type of contract term;[126] and (iii) addresses limits in contracting parties' cognition, which are especially salient in forecasting loss from breach.[127] Zou and Liu pick up on the first explanation in chapter 14 in connection with employment contracts. They lament English law's willingness to embrace deterrence as a legitimate objective of an agreed damages clause, and regard it as incompatible with a worker's fundamental right to quit. In Australia, the rule against penalties extends to sanctions that are triggered by events other than breach of contract.[128] Courts there have adopted another perspective, which is to consider the function of the clause, in particular whether it was intended to operate as a security for the fulfilment of another stipulation in the contract.[129] Again, it is far from clear that this perspective tallies with the punishment rationale.[130]

III. Outline of the Book

A. Structure

Devising a structure for the book proved to be challenging. A split between theoretical analysis on the one hand and doctrinal analysis on the other suggested itself though a few chapters straddle that divide. As to the predominantly doctrinal

[125] *Dunlop Pneumatic Tyre Co Ltd v New Garage and Motor Ltd* [1915] AC 79 (HL) 86 (Lord Dunedin); *Lordsvale Finance plc v Bank of Zambia* [1996] QB 752 (QBD) 762–63. This view was rejected in *Cavendish* (n 122).

[126] M Chen-Wishart, 'Controlling the Power to Agree Damages' in P Birks (ed), *Wrongs and Remedies in the Twenty-First Century* (Oxford, Clarendon Press, 1996) 271; *HF Clarke Ltd v Thermidaire Corp Ltd* [1976] 1 SCR 319 (SCC) 331; *Denka Advantech Pte Ltd v Seraya Energy Pte Ltd* [2020] SGCA 119 [90]. cf *Cavendish* (n 122) [13]; C Goetz and R Scott, 'Liquidated Damages, Penalties and the Just Compensation Principle: Some Notes on an Enforcement Model and a Theory of Efficient Breach' (1977) 77 *Columbia Law Review* 554, 592 ('no reason to presume that liquidated damages provisions are more susceptible to duress or other bargaining aberrations').

[127] MA Eisenberg, 'The Limits of Cognition and the Limits of Contract' (1995) 47 *Stanford Law Review* 211, 225–36. cf RA Hillman, 'The Limits of Behavioural Decision Theory in Legal Analysis: The Case of Liquidated Damages' (2000) 85 *Cornell Law Review* 717.

[128] *Andrews v Australia and New Zealand Banking Group Ltd* [2012] HCA 30, (2012) 247 CLR 205 [10].

[129] ibid.

[130] See Courtney, ch 12, section III.B.i.

chapters, we further contemplated grouping them within a single compendious part and, alternatively, creating parts for each of the traditional categories of tort, contract and equity. Neither of these alternatives was appealing. The former would have treated diverse chapters as an undifferentiated mass, which is unsatisfactory. The latter approach would not have easily accommodated the chapters concerned with contempt and statute.

We ultimately chose a structure comprising five parts, which we feel avoids the difficulties with the alternative arrangements just mentioned. Part I contains this introduction. Part II covers historical, theoretical and comparative aspects of punishment in private law. Part III discusses various aspects of punitive damages at common law and under statute. Punitive damages are such a central issue in discussions about punishment in private law that it seemed sensible to bracket these chapters together. Part IV examines limits placed upon the parties' freedom to agree punitive terms. We deal with this area separately as it raises distinct questions about punishment by private individuals (rather than by the state) and the boundaries of freedom of contract and party autonomy. Part V contains the conclusion, with suggestions for future development and reform. We now turn to each of the substantive chapters and address them with a view to enabling the reader to understand them in context of the debates to which they contribute.

B. Part II – History, Theory and Concepts

Part II opens with Barker's chapter on the meaning and function of punishment in private law, which lays the foundation for the rest of the book. Barker provides a historical account of the intermingling, and then gradual separation, of the civil and criminal law in the English common law. He then considers the meaning of the term punishment in private law, noting that usage is varied and that punishment can refer to judicial acts, the aims of those acts or their effects. He identifies a combination of acts and purposes as being the most common meaning.

Barker's central – and striking – argument is that there is no such thing as punishment in private law in the 'purposes' sense of that term. He justifies his position from two perspectives. If, according to one perspective, punishment means 'doing justice' then punishment might take the guise of retributive justice, corrective justice or distributive justice. None of them, Barker argues, provides a convincing fit for the structure of private law. Retributive justice is hard to square with vicarious liability and liability insurance, and it is also a morally objectionable basis for constructing a general case for punitive damages. As for corrective justice, the primary function of punitive damages is not to compensate individuals for harm done to them, nor to compensate society for harm done to public interests. Even if punitive damages did historically fill remedial gaps in private law, those gaps have closed or shrunk and there is little reason to rely upon punitive damages nowadays. Distributive justice would allocate certain defined sanctions among certain defined persons, according to their relative merit, whereas punishment generally assigns an indivisible burden to the defendant and without reference to the corresponding entitlements enjoyed by the claimant or other citizens.

Barker's other perspective canvasses pragmatic or instrumental considerations, such as protection or rehabilitation, deterrence, appeasement and social messaging (including denouncing wrongdoing and marking rights). These, too, are found wanting. There are relatively few mechanisms for protection and rehabilitation in private law and it is not evident that courts consider that use of them constitutes punishment. Punitive awards, to be (optimally) effective as deterrents, would require sophisticated calculations based on a range of economic and behavioural considerations. They are manifestly not calculated in this way, even assuming the necessary information to be available. The appeasement and social messaging functions risk collapsing back into other rationales. So far as they have a distinctive role, it is at best minor or incidental to the nature of punishment.

Turning to a comparative account, orthodoxy has it that punishment is alien to civil liability in Continental legal systems. With reference to French law, Rowan probes this conventional view in chapter 3. She points to a provision in a draft bill that would have expressly provided, had it been enacted, for the introduction of civil penalties to deter and punish. Rowan also contends that, contrary to traditional wisdom, the civil law in France already informally recognises remedies that serve these ends. In developing this claim, Rowan points to agreed punishment in the form of penalty clauses, the disapplication of remoteness restrictions where the defendant wronged the claimant deliberately or fraudulently or through gross negligence and the potential for judges to make augmented awards of damages in respect of non-pecuniary loss.[131] Rowan also addresses the *astreinte*, an enforcement device that is explicitly punitive, and which may bear some parallel to the provision for enhanced awards of interest in English law.[132]

In chapter 4, Roberts and Richardson address the privacy context. They observe that the law in this area has historically shown little concern for punishment but that, due to changing social circumstances, pressure is gradually building for punishment to play a greater role. The evolving social conditions that they identify include the growing realisation that there is a public as well as private interest in privacy, heightened concern with data protection and emerging technologies. Roberts and Richardson, in a rich analysis that draws upon political philosophy and that has implications beyond the field of privacy, start from the position that because the criminal law is the primary mechanism for dispensing punishment, scope exists for private law to play only an ancillary role in this regard. They then identify situations in which private law can usefully complement the criminal law, such as where there are lacunae in the criminal law

[131] For doubts about whether more liberal assessment of the claimant's non-pecuniary loss can properly be explained as involving punishment, see A Beever, 'Justice and Punishment in Tort: A Comparative Theoretical Analysis' in C Rickett (ed), *Justifying Private Law Remedies* (Oxford, Hart Publishing, 2008) 247, 294.

[132] CPR 36.17.

and where the criminal law is underenforced. Roberts and Richardson's chapter compels reflection on a host of fundamental questions about the relationship between private law and the criminal law, such as whether private law should be deployed to rectify shortcomings in the criminal law (as opposed to the criminal law simply being reformed), and whether and the extent to which the two areas of law should occupy some or all of the same territory (as opposed to one right tool being selected for a particular job).

In chapter 5, Penner considers the role of punishment in private law, at first generally and then with particular reference to fiduciaries. He starts his general treatment of punishment with an assurance theory of prohibition, which is that a civilised society cannot stand idly by while wrongs are committed. It is society's moral duty to take the side of the victim in some suitably public and expressive manner. Society's response is not always to punish: punishment is justified when it is the only way of assuring citizens that, in respect of the wrong, the state takes their rights and interests seriously. Penner builds on this by adopting a familiar distinction between penalties and punishments.[133] Punishment, he says, has no place in a system of private law, but sometimes the law does *penalise* civil wrongs. It imposes sanctions with the aim of regulating individuals' conduct so as to protect valuable social preferences or to coordinate behaviour in the pursuit of worthwhile activities. These activites include the practices of contracting, creating trusts, engaging in agency and so forth.

Applying this perspective to wrongful gains, Penner distinguishes between the defendant's duty to account for gains to which the claimant was already entitled, and the defendant's duty to disgorge other gains. The former duty is neither punishment nor penalty: the gain was always the claimant's. The latter may involve penalties. Because a bribe paid to induce disloyalty is not something to which the claimant was antecedently entitled, stripping the gain from the defendant is a penalty. Penner argues that *Boardman v Phipps*[134] illustrates the same idea applied to a fiduciary's breach of the no-conflict rule. So why is this windfall for the claimant accepted if it is a penalty but objected to if it is a punishment? Penner explains here that the beneficiary always has the power to approve or ratify the fiduciary's breach and so, in a broad sense, retains a form of authority over the fiduciary's conduct. He points out that since the fiduciary rules operate as a kind of regulatory penalty, they may not be, and are not designed to be, perfect deterrents.

Discussions regarding punishment in private law often centre on rules such as punitive damages and the penalty doctrine, and little attention is given to what is, in some ways, the most obvious and ultimate expression of punishment in the civil law: the jurisdiction to punish contempt of court. This power is Rolph's concern in chapter 6. Rolph concentrates on the divide between civil and criminal contempt. This distinction is often understood as that between breaches of orders

[133] See, eg, J Feinberg, 'The Expressive Function of Punishment' (1965) 49 *Monist* 397.
[134] *Boardman v Phipps* [1967] 2 AC 46 (HL).

and undertakings (civil contempt) and contempt in the face of the court and interference with the administration of justice (criminal contempt), and it has various (if relatively arcane) practical consequences. Rolph examines efforts that have been made to locate the basis of the dichotomy, such as the notion that criminal contempt is focused on punishment whereas sentences imposed for civil contempt are remedial and coercive. None of these efforts is found to be wholly successful. Rolph then considers calls to minimise or abolish the separation between the two species of contempt. His ultimate conclusion is that the distinction, although it generates anomalies and incongruities, will likely subsist for the foreseeable future. Rolph emphasises in this regard, among other things, the fact that the separation between criminal and civil contempt is entrenched in various statutes and that it has constitutional implications in some jurisdictions.

C. Part III – Punitive Damages

The stated rationales for awarding punitive damages present numerous issues that go far beyond the overarching question whether punishment should have a place in private law. For example, it is often said that the goal of awarding punitive damages is to punish and deter, but is the punishment being imposed in the interests of retribution, or in order to deter, or with both of these ends in view? And given that the aim of punishment in the sense of retribution may not always support the same award of punitive damages as the goal of deterrence, how is the tension, or conflict, between these two functions to be resolved? It is with such taxing issues that Sharkey grapples in chapter 7. Focusing on the position in the United States, her main aim is to investigate courts' claims that they are acting retributively when awarding punitive damages, and to suggest that they may in fact be concerned with making awards whose purpose is 'societal deterrence'. It is then argued, building upon her previous work in the field,[135] that developing punitive damages into 'societal damages' is normatively desirable, especially in certain contexts, such as the consumer protection setting.

In the course of her exegesis, Sharkey refers to several highly inventive schemes that have been devised in the United States, by both judges and the legislature, for dealing with the windfall objection that inevitably looms large when it is suggested that awards should take cognisance of the societal harm that the defendant caused. These schemes include, for example, arrangements pursuant to which the punitive damages award will be reduced if the defendant agrees to make payments to various bodies that are well positioned to ameliorate the societal harm caused. These arrangements are remarkable at several levels seen from the perspective of lawyers elsewhere in the common law world, where the focus of punitive damages awards is firmly on retribution, and where punitive damages

[135] Especially CM Sharkey, 'Punitive Damages as Societal Damages' (2003) 113 *Yale Law Journal* 347.

awards are at such a modest level[136] that redirecting them would have at best a *de minimis* impact in terms of addressing any societal harm.[137]

No central thesis is developed by Goudkamp and Katsampouka in chapter 8. Their concern, instead, is to expose what they argue are a series of misunderstandings regarding punitive damages. Concentrating on English law, the errors that they identify encompass confusion as to what the law actually is as well as misperceptions of how it operates in practice. As to the former, they contend, for example, that recent cases that suggest that prior punishment of the defendant is irrelevant to the decision to award punitive damages are based on a misreading of earlier authorities. As to the latter, Goudkamp and Katsampouka argue, for instance, that the frequently-made claim that punitive damages awards are often excessive is inconsistent with the empirical evidence.[138] Other mistakes that Goudkamp and Katsampouka seek to identify include the widely-held belief that punitive damages are anomalous (they argue that a range of other remedies also manifest a concern with punishment), the suggestion that punitive damages are sometimes masquerading as disgorgement damages and the idea that merely negligent conduct cannot enliven the jurisdiction to award punitive damages. By seeking to correct assorted errors regarding punitive damages – they identify 10 in total – Goudkamp and Katsampouka's ultimate aim is to clear various obstacles from the path to a better understanding of punitive damages.

Barnett tackles punitive damages in contract in chapter 9. The title of her chapter, 'Exemplary Damages in Contract', reflects the terminology that is generally preferred in Australia. She relates the opposition to punitive damages in contract to various features of the law, including the fact that contractual duties are often strict and breach is 'demoralised', that contract law is not generally aimed at deterrence in that it 'tolerates' breach subject to the obligation to pay compensation and that damages, not specific performance, is the default remedy.

In this normative conflict Barnett finds the seeds of an argument in favour of punitive damages in contract. She explains that the defendant's culpability sometimes *is* considered in the way in which the courts formulate the measure of damages. Barnett then presents four criteria to guide awards of punitive damages. First, punitive damages are a 'last resort' option, when specific relief or other measures of damages are inadequate or unavailable. Second, the breach must be egregious or malicious. Third, the injured party must have a 'legitimate interest' in performance of the contract. Fourth, allowing the particular breach to pass unsanctioned would undermine the institution of contract or some public policy. She marshals cases to support these suggested requirements.

[136] See Goudkamp and Katsampouka, ch 8, section III.A.

[137] The English Law Commission declined to recommend the enactment of legislation that would divert punitive damages awards from the claimant to the state or a public fund: Law Commission, *Aggravated, Exemplary and Restitutionary Damages* (Law Com No 247, 1997) part V, paras 1.142–1.150, 1.158.

[138] J Goudkamp and E Katsampouka, 'An Empirical Study of Punitive Damages' (2018) 38 *OJLS* 90.

In chapter 10, Bant and Paterson identify patterns of reasoning spanning the common law, equity and statute, from which principles of proportionate punishment can be distilled. They begin with a survey of several common law jurisdictions and show that deterrent and punitive measures in the civil sphere can be found in a range of statutes, especially those dealing with intellectual property and consumer protection. They then concentrate upon a key piece of Australian legislation, the Australian Consumer Law (and on equivalent provisions in the Australian Securities and Investment Commission Act 2001 (Cth)). Bant and Paterson argue that courts often emphasise the deterrent function of sanctions imposed by statute without exploring the measures that are most apt to achieve that goal. Developing principles of proportionate punishment will, they say, improve the efficacy of statutory schemes and promote consistency in deterrence across statutory and common law regulatory mechanisms. On proportionality, they draw insight from the equitable remedy of an account of profits. The argument here notes the debate about the punitive nature of that remedy and eschews any suggestion that an account ought to be the only measure for civil penalties. An account can serve a deterrent purpose, which is consistent with punishment. Another advantage of drawing guidance from the account of profits remedy is that there are well-established principles regarding the calculation of an appropriate sum, addressing matters such as causation of gains, the defendant's own skill and effort exerted in producing them and the boundaries to be placed on the defendant's liability to account.

In chapter 11, Morgan addresses vicarious liability for punitive damages. The notion that a defendant who is merely vicariously liable may be ordered to pay punitive damages has long elicited strong objections.[139] The basic point made in this regard is that it makes no sense for a defendant who is not themself a wrongdoer but is simply vicariously responsible for someone else's wrong to be punished. One possible counterargument to the foregoing seeks to undermine the notion that vicariously liable defendants are not wrongdoers. This response can be developed by reference to the master's tort theory pursuant to which the master is imputed not with the liability of the servant but with the servant's acts such that the master is themself a wrongdoer.[140] However, Morgan, observing that vicarious liability does not presently operate through the master's tort theory, approaches the problem differently.[141] Focusing on English law he argues that vicarious liability for punitive damages is unjustified where the punitive damages are awarded under the second *Rookes* category (ie, cases in which the defendant had a profit motive)

[139] See, eg, *Kuddus* (n 52) [131]; Beever (n 7) 96 ('vicarious liability for exemplary damages is an injustice of the first order'); P Giliker, *Vicarious Liability in Tort: A Comparative Perspective* (CUP, 2010) 43; A Tettenborn, 'Punitive Damages – A View From England' (2004) 41 *San Diego Law Review* 1551, 1567–68 ('it is entirely inconsistent with [the] rationale [for punitive damages] to impose a penal sanction on a given defendant independently of the blameworthiness of that defendant').

[140] For a defence of the master's tort theory, see Stevens (n 4) ch 11.

[141] For a yet further strategy, see Sharkey, ch 7, section V (arguing that if punitive damages are reinvented as societal damages there should be no bar to vicarious liability).

but is warranted in relation to punitive damages awarded under the first *Rookes* category (ie, where there is oppressive, arbitrary or unconstitutional conduct by government servants acting as such). Morgan's argument in this regard ultimately rests on the imperative that the state act lawfully. The state, he emphasises, is uniquely positioned, and allowing vicarious punishment of the state is warranted, he contends, by a concern to protect citizens from misuse of executive power and from the danger that the state may fail to deal properly with the wrongdoing of its own agents.

An important strand of the analysis focuses on the fact that in category one cases, the wrongdoing by the government's servant will almost always be criminal. Morgan points out that if one is considering the issue of punitive damages in category one cases, that is only because, given the restriction on awarding punitive damages where other forms of punishment have been imposed,[142] the state has elected not to pursue the wrongdoer, whether through the criminal justice system or otherwise. Morgan identifies this as a reason to tolerate vicarious punishment of the state and, indeed, perceives the power to do so as an important bulwark against abuse by the state of its unique powers. It is interesting to observe that looking at the *Rookes* categories through the lens of vicarious liability, as Morgan does, sketches out a possible justification for distinguishing between different categories of case in which punitive damages can be awarded. The possibility is intriguing in circumstances where the *Rookes* categories are generally regarded as being fundamentally irrational, as is apparent from the fact that courts in other jurisdictions have refused to follow *Rookes*.[143]

D. Part IV – Limiting Punishment

Part IV contains three chapters about the limits of consensual punishment in contract. Courtney's analysis on agreed punishment in chapter 12 opens this Part. He begins by distinguishing between penalties and punishment. He also concedes that the prohibition on punitive damages in contract is a formidable obstacle to permitting parties to agree punitive sanctions. That aside, there are, he argues, several reasons why the law might choose to forbid agreed punishment in contract *even if* it allowed punitive damages for breach. Some of these mirror general arguments against punishment in private law, namely, insufficient procedural safeguards, windfalls and a private citizen's lack of authority to punish. There are also concerns about the state enforcing private norms of punishment that are not necessarily compatible with those accepted by the community at large.

Courtney considers three sets of principles that limit punitive or excessive sanctions: the rule against penalties, relief against forfeiture and techniques to control the exercise of contractual powers. He argues that none of them is really

[142] For discussion of this rule, see Goudkamp and Katsampouka, ch 8, section III.F.
[143] See Goudkamp and Katsampouka, ch 8, section III.G.

concerned with preventing punishment according to the definition offered at the start of his chapter.[144] Rather, they tend to focus upon harsh treatment – penalty – and whether it is disproportionate to the breach of contract or its consequences. Courtney also points to limited instances in which contract law seems to tolerate punishment.

Tiverios and McFarlane continue the analysis of the rule against penalties and relief against forfeiture in chapter 13. They collocate the doctrines through a series of contrasts: between the purposes of each of them; between law and equity; and between Australian and English law. The law can control objectionable terms either by rendering them void (the approach of the common law) or by upholding them as valid while restricting their enforcement (the solution adopted by equity). The chapter traces the common origins of the rule against penalties and relief against forfeiture, and notes the recent divergence in Australian and English law over the breach requirement[145] and the role of equity in the former rule. The authors also note the controversy surrounding the requirement of a proprietary or possessory right as a basis for relief against forfeiture.[146] This requirement prevents relief against forfeiture from operating as a general restriction on termination of contracts; nor can it protect a claimant against losing 'mere' contractual rights.

The latter part of the chapter addresses internal consistency in the structure of the doctrines in Australia and England. Tiverios and McFarlane point out that the English rule against penalties is 'symmetrical': it only applies to clauses activated by breach and it restores the default remedy – common law damages – in the event that a penal clause is invalidated. In *Cavendish Square Holding BV v Makdessi*,[147] Lord Neuberger and Lord Sumption thought that this correspondence clearly marked the rule against penalties as being about regulation of remedies rather than substantive unfairness of terms. The requirement of a proprietary or possessory right for relief against forfeiture may be doubtful in principle but it does serve a pragmatic purpose. It prevents relief against forfeiture from spilling over into run-of-the-mill situations where an apparently harsh sanction is triggered without breach. It therefore respects the boundaries of the penalties rule as marked out in *Cavendish*. By contrast, there is no such concern for Australian law because the rule against penalties has been expanded to apply to sanctions not triggered by breach. Indeed, this development paves the way for the two doctrines to be reunified. This would not be a trivial step, as there remain some substantive differences

[144] He combines HLA Hart's well-known definition of punishment (Hart (n 48) 4–5) with Feinberg's expressive theory of punishment (Feinberg (n 133)).

[145] Compare *Andrews* (n 128) [10], [46] with *Cavendish* (n 122) [12]–[13], [41]–[42], [129]–[130], [241].

[146] *Çukurova Finance International Ltd v Alfa Telecom Turkey Ltd (Nos 3 to 5)* [2013] UKPC 2, [2016] AC 923 [94]; *Vauxhall Motors Ltd v Manchester Ship Canal Co Ltd* [2019] UKSC 46, [2019] 3 WLR 852 [49]–[50]. See further PG Turner, 'What Delimits Equitable Relief from Forfeiture?' (2019) 78 *CLJ* 276; N Tiverios, 'The Forfeiture of Contractual Rights' (2020) 79 *CLJ* 17.

[147] *Cavendish* (n 122) [13].

in the operation of the two doctrines. Tiverios and McFarlane conclude by identifying the changes necessary to accomplish it.

In chapter 14, Zou and Liu consider the application of the rule against penalties to employment contracts, in particular to 'bad leaver' clauses. The drafting of such clauses varies widely although the focus is often on the reason why the employment was terminated. An employee may be a 'bad leaver' if dismissed for misconduct. A more stringent form of clause applies to an employee who leaves voluntarily without an 'acceptable' justification, such as redundancy, retirement or illness. Alternatively or additionally, the 'bad leaver' definition may attach to the departing employee's breach of post-termination restrictions, for example non-competition and non-solicitation covenants. Sanctions for being a bad leaver commonly include a reduction in or loss of, or failure to 'earn', a monetary bonus; forfeiture of share options; or a compulsory transfer of an existing shareholding.

Zou and Liu's thesis is that the rule against penalties is manifestly inadequate to regulate bad leaver provisions. They rely upon the 'right to quit' as being a fundamental freedom of an employee in modern labour law. The right to quit is supported by normative claims about personal freedom and autonomy; control of oppressive conduct by stronger parties (employers); and utilitarian and efficiency-type arguments. The critical failing of the rule against penalties in this context is that it is too easy for an employer to evade the breach trigger by careful drafting. Further, while deterrence can be a legitimate function of a penalty clause in general, this cannot be accepted in the context of bad leaver provisions because it is incompatible with the fundamental right to quit. Zou and Liu argue that there are no other suitable controls at common law (eg, restraint of trade) or under statute (eg, the Employment Rights Act 1996 (UK) or Modern Slavery Act 2015 (UK)) to address the problem. They propose statutory reform to target clauses that 'excessively interfere' with an employee's 'freedom to exit an employment relationship'. Whether a clause is excessive is, they argue, to be decided by weighing up the employee's freedom to exit against the employer's legitimate business interests.

PART II

History, Theory and Concepts

2

Punishment in Private Law – No Such Thing (Any More)

KIT BARKER*

I. Introduction

The definition, meaning and purposes of punishment have long been the subject of detailed investigation and debate in the context of what we now, in modernity, classify as the criminal law.[1] Even in this field, where the language is well settled, there is long-standing confusion about the nature of the idea and its proper role. The stage is set with both protagonists and abolitionists. For abolitionists, punishment is generally taken to involve retribution, retribution means revenge, and revenge is uncivilised, wrong and serves no beneficial social purpose.[2] The concept (understood in that way) therefore needs to be replaced, or redefined more positively, so as to liberate it from its barbaric historical associations and set it towards more worthwhile ends that produce greater social benefits.

In modern private law, the controversy surrounding punishment is greater still. Whilst most criminal lawyers support the idea in some manifestation, in private law the concept's opponents outnumber its supporters. A popular view is hence

* My thanks to Catherine Sharkey, Jason Neyers, Lionel Smith, Heather Douglas, Warren Swain and Simon Bronitt for helpful comments upon an earlier draft of this chapter. All errors remain my own.

[1] For references to the (vast) literature, see M Tunick, *Punishment Theory and Practice* (Berkeley, CA, University of California Press, 1992); A Duff and D Garland (eds), *A Reader on Punishment* (Oxford, Oxford University Press, 1994); D Dolinko, 'Punishment' in J Deigh and D Dolinko, *The Oxford Handbook of Philosophy of Criminal Law* (Oxford, Oxford University Press, 2011) 403; T Brooks, *Punishment* (London, Routledge, 2012). It is sometimes observed that more time has been spent justifying than defining punishment. Most definitions begin with Hart's five elements: (i) the infliction of pain for (ii) an offence against legal rules (iii) of an actual offender for the offence (iv) intentionally administered (v) by an authority of the legal system in which the offence is committed: HLA Hart, *Punishment and Responsibility* (Oxford, Oxford University Press, 1968) 5. It is common to add a sixth (vi), which expresses condemnation of the offence: Dolinko (n 1) 405.

[2] For an example of the abolitionist enterprise, hostile to imprisonment regimes and detecting the root of their deficiencies in the philosophy of retribution, see K Menninger, *The Crime of Punishment* (New York, Penguin, 1968), ch 8.

the blunt, Blackstonian one that punishment has no place at all in this sphere.[3] To punish a person is to sanction the breach of her public duties to the state, not her private duties to other individuals, so that the use of the concept is inapposite in civil litigation and inconsistent with the latter's bilateral (corrective justice) form. Punishment simply cannot be a 'remedy' for a private wrong. This was the clear view of Lord Reid in *Broome v Cassell & Co*.[4] But even those who support the use of punitive damages in private law tend to consider them justified only as an exceptional, not as a standard measure, and therefore give them a strictly limited scope, confining them to specific categories of case, or to instances in which wrongdoing is proved to be cynical, deliberate and outrageous,[5] or 'contumelious'.[6] As a matter of positive law, civilian jurisdictions have generally taken the former, Blackstonian view, but some (France is a topical example[7]) have recently been flirting with the exceptionalist position. For those who see the persistence of punishment in civil actions as a hang-over of history and a genetic glitch that has been gradually working itself out as our modern categories of public and private law have emerged from their once undifferentiated state, this is awkward. It suggests that the punitive instinct is still a live force in modern private law not just in common law jurisdictions, but in some civilian systems too. Indeed, even more anomalously from their point of view, it seems to be part of a modern law reform agenda.[8]

[3] There is greater subtlety in the various positions than the bluntness of this statement implies, because some writers re-interpret the idea of punishment in such a way as to give it what is, in their view, an acceptable meaning or function. See DB Dobbs, 'Ending Punishment in "Punitive" Damages: Deterrence-Measured Remedies' (1988) 40 *Alberta Law Review* 831; RW Wright, 'The Grounds and Extent of Legal Responsibility' (2003) 40 *San Diego Law Review* 1425; AJ Sebok, 'What Did Punitive Damages Do? Why Misunderstanding the History of Punitive Damages Matters Today' (2003) 78(1) *Chicago-Kent Law Review* 101; E Weinrib, 'Punishment and Disgorgement as Contract Remedies' (2003) 78(1) *Chicago-Kent Law Review* 55; A Beever, 'The Structure of Aggravated and Exemplary Damages' (2003) 23 *OJLS* 87; A Beever, 'Justice and Punishment in Tort: A Comparative Theoretical Analysis' in CEF Rickett (ed), *Justifying Private Law Remedies* (Oxford, Hart Publishing, 2008) 249; R Stevens, *Torts and Rights* (Oxford, Oxford University Press, 2007) 85–88.

[4] *Broome v Cassell & Co* [1972] AC 1027 (HL) 1086.

[5] Law Commission, *Aggravated, Exemplary and Restitutionary Damages* (Law Comm No 247, 1997); *Dunlea v Attorney-General* [2000] 3 NZLR 136 (CA) [34].

[6] *Australian Consolidated Press Ltd v Uren* (1967) 117 CLR 221 (HCA) 232–34; *Gray v Motor Accident Commission* (1998) 196 CLR 1 (HCA) [14] (Gleeson CJ, McHugh, Gummow and Hayne JJ).

[7] There have been two, distinct proposals – for a scheme of punitive damages in which some of the award can be siphoned off to the state (Draft Art 1371 of the Code Civile) and, more recently (following governmental inaction on the first) for a civil penalties regime with the same feature (Draft Article 1266-1). On the first, see S Rowan, 'Comparative Observations on the Introduction of Punitive Damages in French Law' in J Cartwright, S Vogenauer and S Whittaker (eds), *Reforming the French Law of Obligations: Comparative Reflections on the Avant-projet de réforme du droit des obligations et de la prescription ('the Avant-projet Catala')* (London, Hart Publishing, 2009) 325; H Koziol, 'Punitive Damages – A European Perspective' (2008) 68 *Lousiana Law Journal* 741. On the second, see Rowan, ch 3 of this volume.

[8] See, eg, Law Commission (n 5) (suggesting that punitive damages be expanded); A Burrows, 'Reforming Exemplary Damages: Expansion or Abolition?' in P Birks (ed), *Wrongs and Remedies in the Twenty First Century* (Oxford, Clarendon Press, 1996) 153. Note, however, that the recent Australian trend has been for the statutory abolition of exemplary awards both in defamation cases and in cases of negligently inflicted personal injury – a political response to insurance industry lobbying, rather than any more principled objection.

In engaging with the question whether punishment belongs in modern private law, it is important to be mindful that the legal categories of public and private law – in particular tort and crime – are modern phenomena in the grander timescale.[9] Although Roman law distinguished between *delictum* and *crimen*[10] (and between *privata iudicia* and *publica iudicia*[11]), the private action of *delictum* encompassed many 'modern crimes', including theft, and 'retained until the end a punitive character',[12] so that even in those days it could not be said that punishment was solely the initiative of the state. In the Germanic world, after the fall of the Roman Empire in the West, the Roman distinction between *crimen* and *delictum* was almost completely lost (the word *crimen* often being used simply to denote 'sin') and – with some exceptions amongst learned ecclesiasts – really only reappeared in the revived academic law schools as they spread from Italy in the late eleventh century.[13] In the early days of English law, there was therefore only an undifferentiated notion of 'wrongdoing', 'offending', 'trespassing' or 'transgressing' that did not discriminate clearly between the public and private aspects of wrongdoing in the sense of wrongs to individuals and wrongs to the public as a whole. Although legal redress was often activated by victims or their families, penalties could be payable

[9] On the history of the tort/crime distinction and the practices of feud and vengeance preceding its development, see D Seipp, 'The Distinction Between Crime and Tort in the Early Common Law' (1996) 76 *Boston University Law Review* 59; J Lindgren, 'Why the Ancients May Not Have Needed a System of Criminal Law' (1996) 76 *Boston University Law Review* 29; P Hyams, 'Does it Matter When the English Began to Distinguish Between Crime and Tort?' in RW Kaeuper (ed), *Violence in Medieval Society* (Woodbridge, Boydell Press, 2000) 107; P Hyams, 'Feud and the State in Late Anglo Saxon England' (2001) 40 *Journal of British Studies* 1; P Hyams, 'Nastiness and Wrong, Rancor and Reconciliation' in WC Brown and P Górecki (eds), *Conflict in Medieval Europe: Changing Perspectives on Society and Culture* (London, Routledge, 2016) 188; C Donahue, 'The Emergence of the Crime Tort Distinction in England' in WC Brown and P Górecki (eds), *Conflict in Medieval Europe: Changing Perspectives on Society and Culture* (London, Routledge, 2016) 208; Sir Frederick Pollock and FW Maitland, *The History of English Law Before the Time of Edward I*, vol 2 (Cambridge, Cambridge University Press, 1898) ch 8; SFC Milsom, *Historical Foundations of the Common Law*, 2nd edn (London, Butterworths, 1981); J Hudson, *Formation of the English Common Law: Law and Society in England from the Norman Conquest to Magna Carta* (London, Longman, 1996) chs 3, 6; J Hudson, *The Oxford History of the Laws of England*, vol II: *871–1216* (Oxford, Oxford University Press, 2012) 709–49, 743–45.

[10] *Delictum* denoted an unlawful act causing loss or injury to the person, property, honour or reputation of another (ie, a wrong to private interests) and was prosecuted by the individual in question. *Crimen* denoted a wrong against the state or community as a whole (ie, a wrong to public interests) such as treason, murder, sacrilege or arson, and was prosecuted by state organs. The distinction between wrongs to individuals and the community was not, of course, unique to the Romans and is found in Aristotle's *Rhetoric*. See J Barnes (ed), *The Complete Works of Aristotle*, vol 2 (Princeton, NJ, Princeton University Press, 1984) (adultery and assault are private wrongs; avoiding military service is a wrong to the community).

[11] The former being actions that could be brought only by individuals in protection of their private interests and personal affairs, the latter being actions that could be brought by anyone not specifically prohibited from so doing on the infraction of rules ordained in the public interest. In the latter instance, the individual could keep the penalty.

[12] Hyams, 'Does it Matter' (n 9) 109 (citing B Nicholas, *An Introduction to Roman Law* (Oxford, Clarendon Press, 1962) 207–08).

[13] ibid 109, 10 and 115.

both to the victim and to early personifications of the state. Personal vengeance, corrective justice, tort and crime were inextricably intermingled.

Paul Hyams suggests that *Glanvill*[14] (1187–89) was 'first witness' to the common law's acceptance of the modern distinction between crime and tort in England in the late 1100s,[15] but the distinction the author of that treatise himself drew between 'civil' and 'criminal' pleas bore little resemblance to the categories that we now know.[16] Historians differ in the extent to which they attribute the development of the modern distinction in English law to the earlier Roman learning,[17] but they agree that the Assize of Clarendon of 1166 was a key date, marking as it did an important attempt by Henry II to assume greater royal control over the punishment of serious wrongs and laying the foundations of the modern system of trial by jury.[18] The exact mechanics of the process via which private actions for compensation of 'private' wrongs became separated from 'public' actions for wrongs to the King, society, or state is beyond the scope of this work. Hyams confesses soberingly that he knows of no fully satisfactory account of it,[19] but the critical phase, it is generally accepted, relates to the development in the thirteenth century of private appeals and the private action in trespass for compensation in central royal courts, on the one hand (the early forebears of tort), and, on the other hand, felony appeals and then jury presentments on indictment (the forebears of crime).[20]

Even after these threads had begun to disentangle, the functions of the different actions and the forms of justice they instantiated remained for a long while mixed. David Seipp's illuminating analysis of the yearbooks from 1290 to 1500 suggests that (with the isolated exception of Henry of Bracton) the language of 'criminal' and 'civil proceedings' disappeared again after *Glanvill*, until a penchant for Roman learning caused it to resurface in the sixteenth century.[21] Meanwhile, punishment continued to play out in private writs of trespass, which gave rise to fines payable to the king, as well as to compensation for the victim.[22] Similarly, Pollock and Maitland report that, in roughly the same period, the use of the 'public' process of jury presentment proved laborious in respect of some lesser misdemeanours, and

[14] GDG Hall (ed), *The Treatise on the Laws and Customs of the Realm of England Commonly Known as Glanvill* (Oxford, Oxford University Press, 1965).

[15] ibid 110.

[16] For a full account, see Hudson, 'Oxford History' (n 9) 710–16.

[17] Donahue (n 9) accords less significance to this than Hyams, 'Does it Matter' (n 9).

[18] Hyams, 'Does it Matter?' (n 9) 123 (the attempt was 'genuine and serious', although it 'largely failed'); Hyams, 'Nastiness and Wrong' (n 9) 195–96.

[19] Hyams, 'Does it Matter?' (n 9) 126. For some of the detail, see Pollock and Maitland (n 9) 510–11.

[20] For a clear exposition, see Seipp (n 9). Note that trespasses were such a broad category that they could be the object of either the private writ, or the public 'indictment'.

[21] Seipp (n 9) 81. Bracton (c1210–c1268) was an ecclesiast and well versed in Roman learning. See Henry de Bracton, *Bracton on the Laws and Customs of England*, vol 2 (Cambridge, Belknap Press, 1968) 290–91.

[22] Seipp (n 9) 70.

that legislators like Edward I (1239–1307) favoured using civil actions to punish wrongdoers in such instances by awarding victims the incentive of double or treble damages.[23]

Over time, punishment therefore gradually became a more public business, in part in consequence of the desire of monarchs to exercise power over the most serious types of wrongdoing, in part due to their desire to raise revenue for themselves, and in part, no doubt, due to increases in the resourcing and sophistication of the state's own enforcement processes. But the separation of punishment from private actions has nonetheless been protracted and variable. Even as late as the eighteenth century, for example, private prosecutions were still overwhelmingly the dominant mechanism used for enforcement of the criminal law and their popularity persisted well into the nineteenth century.[24]

As we shall see in the sections that follow, views as to whether punishment has any role within our modern category of private law, and precisely what role it should have, depend in great measure upon how the idea is understood, what purposes it is thought to fulfil and what conditions are attached to its operation. Punishing wrongdoers might fulfil a variety of different purposes (and therefore have a variety of different meanings), ranging from 'retribution and moral vengeance' at one end of the scale to 'deterrence', or even simply 'marking a wrong', at the other. All of these ideas featured as aims in greater or lesser measure in the undifferentiated, primordial law of wrongs that existed in England in pre-Angevin times. There has been a general shift amongst those who support punishment in modern private law, I shall suggest, to weaker and weaker ideas over time. Indeed, some of the meanings and purposes attributed to punishment in this context in the modern day are now so highly diluted that it is probably better to abandon the principal term altogether in favour of more precise, less atavistic terminology. This is what I mean to imply in the title of this chapter, when I say that there is no longer such a thing as punishment in private law.

My purpose here is not to try to resolve the debate about whether private law *should* punish (although I shall allude to some of the key arguments along the way)

[23] Pollock and Maitland (n 9) vol 2, 521, citing examples from the First Statute of Westminster (1275). The strategy of incentivising private individuals to enforce what we would now regard as public, criminal laws continued, on and off, for some 700 years through '*qui tam*' actions (most of statutory origin). These permitted private parties to enforce a variety of laws in exchange for a share of the relevant penalties. The practice gave rise to numerous abuses and was eventually discarded in England in 1951, but it survives to this day in the United States in cases of fraud upon government. See generally, JR Beck, 'The False Claims Act and the English Eradication of Qui Tam Legislation' (2000) 78 *North Carolina Law Review* 539.

[24] D Hay, 'Controlling the English Prosecutor' (1983) 21 *Osgoode Hall Law Journal* 165; D Friedman, 'Making Sense of English Law Enforcement in the 18th Century' (1995) 2 *University of Chicago Law School Roundtable* 475. According to Friedman, the persistence of private actions was in part down to profit – private prosecutors hoping to be bought off by their offenders. It was also clearly due to the lack of an organised state police force, which only started to materialise in London in the 1820s.

but to return to basics and to unpick the concept's meaning and the moral values and social purposes that might underpin it, so that we can be clear at least about what is at stake in the debate. The aim of this type of exercise is both to preserve the integrity and therefore the utility of our language conventions and, by being clear, to increase the chance of our making rational, normative choices. Unless we have a lucid idea of what punishment is, it is very hard for us to reach any stable view as to whether the law should endorse it, where in our modern scheme it belongs, or what conditions we should attach to its operation.

II. Definitions

To define the role of punishment in modern private law, we must therefore be clear about what we mean by punishment and what we now mean by private law. Punishment may be imposed by agents other than courts of law (parents punish their children, for example) but it is the legal concept of punishment that concerns us here.

A. Private Law

For current purposes, I define private *law* as the set of legal rights, duties, powers, liberties and immunities (both primary and secondary and both common law and statutory) that exist between one individual and another, as opposed to those that exist between citizens and the state (acting qua state) ('public law'). Private law usually protects private *interests*, which are the interests that you and I have as individuals (rights to the person, to property and so on), as opposed to the interests we share because we are members of the same political community ('public interests', such as the interest we all enjoy in living in a safe society). Private law is also usually *enforced privately*, in the sense that it is usually individuals that that have the powers of suit when a private law right is infringed. It is important to note, however, that, even in the modern day, these three 'privates' – private *law*, private *interests* and private *enforcement* – do not always perfectly align. There are hence cases in which public interests are taken into account by courts and legislatures in modelling the rights, duties, liberties and immunities that private law gives. The defence of absolute privilege to actions in defamation law and the defence of illegality in contract or negligence claims provide classic examples. There are also cases in which *private individuals* have powers of suit in respect of the infringement of *public rights* (for example, when a plaintiff seeks to quash a decision in administrative law on the ground that the decision-maker breached a public law rule, or when a plaintiff brings an action against the state under the Human Rights Act 1998 (UK)); and there are some cases in which public institutions are involved in enforcing private rights and duties (as, for example, where a public receiver is appointed on the bankruptcy of a defendant to ensure fair settlement of debts as between the defendant's creditors).[25] Some wrongful acts (for example, battery or fraud) are violations of both public and private rights and can trigger more than one enforcement process at the same time.

Important for our current purposes is the recognition that private individuals can be involved in the *enforcement* of *both* public and private law. As we have seen, there was a time, prior to the twelfth century, when private enforcement was – largely as a matter of practical necessity – the principal mechanism for the protection of both public and private interests. In the modern day, individual private rights to bring actions play a significant part in the enforcement of the public law rules of competition law; and there are some jurisdictions in which individuals are still allowed (indeed positively incentivised) to sue for public frauds upon the State in the United States via the '*qui tam*' action.[26] If we recognise these modern examples in which private powers of suit are used in the protection of what are now conceptualised as public rights and interests, it could be argued that the pursuit of punitive ends in private law actions through punitive damages, for example, whilst exceptional, is still a less isolated phenomenon than one might think. Such actions could be seen to form part of a pattern in which private actions play an interstitial, regulatory or enforcement role, filling in the remaining gaps in our public laws and advancing objectives which those laws are, for one reason or another, unable efficiently to effect.[27] This is an especially popular view in the United States, where private tort actions are regarded as playing an important ex post facto regulatory role. The reasons for this phenomenon are complex, but seem at the deepest level to be grounded in Americans' deep distrust of governmental regulation.[28] Private actions, brought to sanction wrongs, are a way in which a style of regulation can be kept in the hands of citizens themselves.

B. Punishment – Act, Purpose or Effect?

Turning then to the definition of punishment, a first and important question is whether the term refers to (i) a judicial act, (ii) a purpose (or purposes) judges have in mind when acting, or (iii) simply an observed effect of a judge's actions. Each appears to be a possibility. The answer that most closely reflects judicial practice

[25] For fuller modelling of the patterns of enforcement across public and private law, see K Barker, 'Modelling Public and Private Enforcement: The Rationality of Hybridity' (2018) 37(1) *University of Queensland Law Journal* 9.

[26] False Claims Act, 31 USC and generally F Lipman, *Whistleblowers: Incentives, Disincentives, and Protection Strategies* (Chichester, Wiley, 2011) ch 8; Beck (n 23).

[27] A view clearly taken in Law Commission (n 5) para 1.15 and recently by the Singapore Court of Appeal in *ACB v Thomson Medical Pte Ltd* [2017] SGCA 20 [173].

[28] S Issacharoff, 'Regulating After the Fact' (2007) 56 *De Paul Law Review* 375. On the use of tort to regulate state power, see P Cane, *Controlling Administrative Power: A Historical Comparison* (Cambridge, Cambridge University Press, 2016) 368–98.

(although there are some unfortunate divergences) is that it refers to (i) and (ii), but not (iii). An order for the payment of 'punitive damages' is hence clearly a judicial act – something judges do. The purpose of such an order is to 'punish' (although there is, as we shall see in section III, an extensive debate about what this actually means). However, as a matter of law, damages are not punitive damages simply because they have a harsh *effect* upon a defendant. We might think, for example, that requiring a negligent driver to pay $1 million in compensation for a pedestrian's injury where his negligence consisted in a moment of inattention is 'punitive' because it imposes a liability wholly out of proportion to his moral fault. In this instance, however, the word 'punishment' merely describes the order's effect on the defendant and attaches a negative connotation to it. The court's order for compensation does not become an act of punishment because it is seriously painful; and a court's purpose in making the order is not to punish.

In asking whether punishment has a role in modern private law, we are therefore concerned with judicial orders and their purposes, not their effects – a point that was recently made by Bromberg J in the Federal Court of Australia in deciding whether civil penalties are punitive. His Honour correctly observed that if one were concerned simply with an order's effects, 'all manner of civil remedies' would qualify, but that it is 'the 'purpose rather than the consequence' of the order that is relevant in making this judgment.[29] If punishment exists in private law, it is therefore a judicial act upon a wrongdoer, adversely affecting his or her rights (claim rights, liberties, immunities, etc), done in response to the latter's wrong, the *purpose* of which is to punish.

An important upshot of this approach to the definition of punishment is that, technically, an order can be punitive even where the consequences that it describes for a defendant are less serious than those of an order for compensation, restitution or disgorgement of a wrongdoer's profits. Take, for example, a case in which D has defrauded P of $2 million and invested the money profitably in real estate, now worth $4 million. If a court were simply to fine the defendant $10,000 (but do nothing else), would this count as 'punishment', having regard to the fact that the consequences of the order for D are less serious than those of an order for compensation, restitution or disgorgement? It would be hard, I suggest, *not* to classify it as such, although we would be forgiven for thinking that it was not punishing very effectively. Assuming, for example, that the purposes of punishment include retribution and/or deterrence (as to which see the next section), a fine of $10,000 would be neither proportionate to the seriousness of D's offence (and hence not 'just retribution'), nor likely to deter frauds in the future. If the aim of the order was to punish (ie, to achieve one or more of these ends), it was nonetheless still an order for punishment. It just did not punish very well.[30]

[29] *Construction, Forestry, Mining and Energy Union v Victoria (No 2)* [2013] FCA 1034 [32]–[33] (Bromberg J).

[30] We are likewise justified in saying that tort damages provide 'compensation' even when we know that they do not fully compensate the loss but are subject to significant limitations.

Defining punishment by reference to the *purpose* of an order means that it is irrelevant to the order's classification 'as punishment' whether it is made by a criminal or a civil court; whether it is available at common law or in equity; whether it responds to a crime, tort, breach of contract, breach of fiduciary duty; or whether it carries consequences that are of greater or lesser severity.[31] This will seem odd to those who perceive punishment as being wedded indissolubly to a particular area of law or set of procedural protections, but taking this approach has the advantage of avoiding all sorts of self-referential definitional reasoning, such as the conclusion that private law does not punish 'because' punishment is a response only to a crime; or 'because' its proceedings only require proof on a balance of probabilities, not the normal criminal law burden; or 'because' the consequences it can bring to bear on D are less serious than those standardly imposed by criminal courts. It separates the analytical question of what punishment *is* from normative questions about when judges should do it, in what proceedings and subject to what conditions.

The disadvantage of the approach – inevitable, I am afraid – is that, from the external point of view, it can be hard to determine the exact purpose of a judicial act (order). This was a particularly acute problem in the days when juries were exclusively responsible for determining damages awards, because nothing appeared on the face of the record to tell us their reasons for making the awards they did. But it persists to some degree even in the modern day, not just because juries continue to be involved in awarding damages in some instances, but also because the labels that courts ascribe to monetary awards do not necessarily properly advertise the aim, or aims, they are designed to achieve. It is only by knowing this aim (or aims) that we can be sure whether or not the orders made by judges in private law cases are engaged in punishment at all. That is an interpretive question and, as will become evident, there is plenty of scope for differences in view.

III. The Meanings and Aims of Punishment

A judicial order is therefore punitive where it *aims* to punish, whatever its *effects* may be and whether or not it responds to what is technically classified in the modern law as a crime. But what aim instantiates the idea of punishing? This section canvasses some of the possibilities. They include the idea that punishment does a form of justice (retributive, corrective or distributive) on the one hand, or that it achieves some instrumental, social good, on the other, such as protection of the public and the prevention of wrongdoing, deterrence, or some form of public education or symbolic social messaging in the form of 'marking' right from wrong. The general conclusion I shall reach is that the aims currently identified

[31] Although the consequences must always be unpleasant: Hart (n 1) 4–5.

with punishment by writers and courts are not one but several,[32] so that the term has a variety of different meanings. To the extent that courts endorse different aims in criminal and civil cases, the meaning of punishment will therefore differ in the two contexts. The principal question with which I am concerned is whether the meanings in those contexts are now so different that it is better to abandon the use of the concept altogether in private law and revert instead to different terminology that reflects the differences. I shall suggest that it is. I shall also suggest that it would be helpful to significantly narrow our understanding of punishment to its core, retributive ideology.

A. Retributive Justice

A popular conception of punishment in the criminal law is that it is a form of institutionalised vengeance – retributive or 'vindictive' justice.[33] Whilst some academic writers have suggested that retributive justice is not a distinct form of justice at all but simply an aspect of either corrective justice, or distributive justice or both, these views are no longer mainstream, although it would be misleading to suggest that they do not still attract their occasional supporters. The story of the relationship between corrective, distributive and 'vindictive' justice in our intellectual history is traced with extraordinary clarity and surefootedness by Izhak Englard in his book on *Corrective and Distributive Justice*.[34] Here, I take Ronen Perry's view, drawing on Englard and reflecting Pufendorf and others, that retributive justice is genuinely a third form of justice.[35]

On this view, distributive justice is the form of justice that distributes goods (or, on some views, rights and duties) between individuals or groups, in accordance with a criterion of relative merit, where the 'merit' criterion can be constructed in a wide range of different ways. It might refer to the parties' relative need, moral virtue or wealth, for example. Corrective justice restores the rightful, formal equality of the doer and the sufferer of an injustice, by requiring the former to set right the

[32] D Owen, 'A Punitive Damages Overview: Functions, Problems and Reform' (1994) 39 *Villanova Law Review* 363, 373–74 lists: (1) education, (2) retribution, (3) deterrence, (4) compensation, and (5) law enforcement.

[33] A retributive account is usually attributed to Kant, whose premise was that to punish an offender for any reason other than his desert is to treat him as a means, not an end. See A Ripstein, *Force and Freedom: Kant's Legal and Political Philosophy* (Cambridge, MA, Harvard University Press, 2009) ch 10 (although cf Tunick (n 1) 96–98). Retributive views have been resurgent in the criminal law since the late 1960s: A von Hirsch, *Doing Justice: The Choice of Punishments* (Boston, MA, Northeastern University Press, 1986); M Cotton, 'Back with a Vengeance: The Resilience of Retribution as an Articulated Purpose of Criminal Punishment' (2000) 37 *American Criminal Law Review* 1313.

[34] I Englard, *Corrective and Distributive Justice: from Aristotle to Modern Times* (Oxford, Oxford University Press, 2009).

[35] R Perry, 'The Third Form of Justice' (2010) 23 *Canadian Journal of Law and Jurisprudence* 233; R Perry, 'The Role of Retributive Justice in the Common Law of Torts: A Descriptive Theory' (2006) 73 *Tennessee Law Review* 177.

injustice he has done to the latter. In contrast to the proportionate or 'geometric' way that justice is meted out in distributive justice, the calculation in corrective justice is 'arithmetic', which is to say that its measure is simply what is necessary to restore a victim's prior entitlements. It therefore does not matter whether a rich man wrongly injures a poor man, or vice versa – the demands of corrective justice are the same, in each instance being to restore to each his own.[36] Retributive justice is a third form of justice according to which legal institutions exact reprisal upon a wrongdoer according to the principle that one who has wrongly hurt another (or society) deserves in turn to be hurt, if not in exactly equal measure[37] then in a just proportion to the wrong done. It is sometimes called the justice of 'just deserts.'

The way in which retributive justice differs in structural form from corrective justice is hence that it ignores the victim – it takes flesh from the wrongdoer without restoring the flesh of the wronged (or indeed the moral 'fabric' of society). The way in which it differs structurally from distributive justice is that what is taken from the wrongdoer is decided in proportion to the wrong he has done,[38] not by comparing his merits relative to the person wronged, or anyone else.

Retribution is an institutionalised version of the practices of personal vengeance that characterised early societies, including Medieval England.[39] It is referred to as an aim in both the criminal law and private law cases and writings on punitive damages.[40] Some modern commentators have claimed that it is a victim's

[36] For a classic statement of this conception of justice as the foundation of all private law, see E Weinrib, *The Idea of Private Law* (Cambridge, MA, Harvard University Press, 1995); E Weinrib, *Corrective Justice* (Oxford, Oxford University Press, 2012).

[37] Historically, the 'equal measure' conception of an 'eye for an eye' (*Exodus* 21:24) (itself replicating the Babylonian code of Hammurabi (1750BC)) was intended to curb the vindictive instinct and restrain more extreme forms of reprisal. By modern liberal standards, however, it is now also too extreme.

[38] According to Perry 'Third Form of Justice' (n 35) 236, the proportionality of sanction to wrong has both a cardinal and an ordinal aspect, which is to say that the appropriate sanction is decided both by reference to an idea of the absolute seriousness of the wrong, and by reference to its seriousness compared to other wrongs. It would hence be *absolutely* disproportionate to impose a death sentence for speeding, but the penalties for speeding should also be relatively more serious than for parking in the wrong place.

[39] For slightly differing accounts of vengeance and feud in the Anglo-Saxon world, see P Hyams, 'Feud and the State in Late Anglo Saxon England' (2001) 40(1) *Journal of British Studies* 1 and (taking a narrower definition of feud as open-ended reprisal between kinship groups and intimating that it really only entered England in Tudor times) JD Niles, 'The Myth of Feud in Anglo-Saxon England' (2015) 114 *Journal of English and Germanic Philology* 163. Note that some authors (eg Brooks (n 1) 16–17) maintain that retribution differs from vengeance not just in being institutionalised but in having limits that vengeance does not. In fact, however, vengeance was itself subject to significant social control: Hyams (n 39). Many others claim that the idea of retribution nowadays has nothing to do with vengeance, consisting only in the expression of institutional disapproval for the breaking of the law: see, eg, Royal Commission Report, *Capital Punishment* (HC 1955, 536) 17–18, cited in J Feinberg, *Doing and Deserving: Essays in the Theory of Responsibility* (Princeton, NJ, Princeton University Press, 1970) 101. Such views reconstruct retribution as denunciation (section III.G).

[40] On the latter, see, eg, *Whiten v Pilot Insurance Co* [2002] SCC 18, [2002] 1 SCR 595 [43], [68], [74], [94], [103] (punitive damages engage in retribution, deterrence and denunciation); *Fidler v Sun Life Assurance Co of Canada* [2006] SCC 30, [2006] 2 SCR 3 [61] (following *Whiten* ibid); *State Farm Mut Auto Ins Co v Campbell*, 538 US 408, 416 (2003) (deterrence and retribution); *Uren v John Fairfax & Sons Pty Ltd* (1966) 117 CLR 118 (HCA) 149 (Windeyer J) (moral retribution or deterrence); AJ Sebok, 'Punitive Damages: From Myth to Theory' (2007) 92 *Iowa Law Review* 957.

personal 'right (liberty and power) to be punitive' that explains not just some otherwise puzzling aspects of punitive awards,[41] but also large parts of our modern system of private law. As states emerged from civil chaos, so it has been argued, they granted powers of 'civil recourse' to victims in exchange for the surrender of the latter's private liberties to take revenge upon their offenders,[42] so that the 'right' to be retributive underpins both the modern criminal law (the right in this instance belonging to the state itself) and the law of torts (where the right that once belonged to the individual has been now been cashed in for private rights of action). Some writers suggest that retribution is not simply a right (liberty and power) but a social duty, and that it is this that makes it a true theory of justice.[43]

There are several obstacles to understanding modern private law as endorsing retributive aims. One of them is that often it allows persons other than the wrongdoer to bear the burden of a judgment through the doctrine of vicarious liability[44] and the practice of liability insurance. If retribution means anything, it clearly means making the *wrongdoer* hurt, not some third party. Such defects could presumably be cured by legislation if one wanted, and some States in the United States have taken that step by making punitive damages uninsurable as a matter of public policy.[45] But a more serious objection is simply that vengeance is a morally bankrupt practice and therefore a poor normative platform on which to build either a case for punitive damages, or a modern civil justice system.[46]

[41] B Zipursky, 'A Theory of Punitive Damages' (2005) 84 *Texas Law Review* 105, 151–53 (arguing that only the private right to be punitive can explain why punitive awards do not always raise constitutional concerns in the United States).

[42] B Zipursky, 'Rights, Wrongs and Recourse in the Law of Torts (1998) 51(1) *Vanderbilt Law Review* 1, 5, 83 (the right to recourse 'is a civilised transformation of … a quite primitive "instinct" of retributive justice', 'arguably in the same conceptual family as the retributive notion of an eye for an eye'). See also B Zipursky, 'Civil Recourse, not Corrective Justice' (2003) 91 *Georgia Law Review* 695. Note that Zipursky has never actually advocated revenge as a normative principle and has since revised the way he expresses his theory so as to remove the allusion to it, replacing it with the concept of a right to demand a 'response' from a wrongdoer so as to make him or her 'accountable': B Zipursky, 'Substantive Standing, Civil Recourse, and Corrective Justice' (2011) 39 *Florida State University Law Review* 299, 314–15, 323–26.

[43] M Moore, 'The Moral Worth of Retribution,' in FD Schoeman (ed), *Responsibility, Character, and the Emotions: New Essays in Moral Psychology* (Cambridge, Cambridge University Press, 1988) 179, 182 (although note that retribution in this account is not equated with revenge). For the view that retributive hatred is a rational and moral response to wrongdoing, see JG Murphy, 'Retributive Hatred: An Essay On Criminal Liability and the Emotions' in RG Frey and CW Morris (eds), *Liability and Responsibility* (Cambridge, Cambridge University Press, 1991) 351.

[44] See, eg, *Rowlands v Chief Constable of Merseyside Police* [2006] EWCA Civ 1773, [2007] 1 WLR 1065. Opinions on whether exemplary damages are available against one who is only vicariously liable were divided in *Kuddus v Chief Constable of Leicester* [2001] UKHL 29, [2002] 2 AC 122 (HL) (Lord Mackay being in favour and Lord Scott strongly against).

[45] C Sharkey, 'Revisiting the Noninsurable Costs of Accidents' (2005) 64 *Maryland Law Review* 409, 427–28.

[46] *Broome* (n 4) 1073 (Lord Hailsham) ('vindictiveness is not a good motive for awarding punishment'); cf contra Moore (n 43) 208–17, who suggests (forgive the crude paraphrase) that the morality of retribution lies in its connection to the morality expressed in our own virtuous feelings of guilt, that morality then correctly being applied to others who do the acts about which we ourselves would rightfully feel guilty.

No victim advances his own moral virtue by scourging his offender – as Nietzsche put it, he becomes darker, not lighter, for the exercise.[47] At best, the wrong is a reason for society to excuse the victim for taking action (purposely hurting another) that would otherwise itself be considered wrongful, and two wrongs (or, more accurately in this instance, one wrong and another prima facie but excusable wrong) do not make a right. The law should not exact retribution (revenge) because it is *excusable* to do so, even if it is. It should do so only if it is *right*.[48] This normative objection to retribution clearly applies in both private and public law, although the dangers of the practice's getting out of hand are potentially so serious that criminal law processes now seem best adapted to effecting it, if one is really minded to engage in it. It is the retributive aspect of punishment that is most closely connected to the perceived need for higher standards of proof and additional procedural protections; and therefore with the idea that punishment belongs in the criminal law only. It is no doubt also this feature that has led the US Supreme Court to bring constitutional due process protections to bear upon excessive awards of punitive damages in some instances.[49]

B. Corrective Justice

A second possibility, odd as it may sound, is that punishment aims to do corrective justice, either by requiring wrongdoers to compensate victims themselves for intangible forms of injury that are not otherwise taken into account in compensatory damages, such as litigation costs, distress and anger, injury to autonomy, dignity or reputation ('honour');[50] or by rectifying a wrongful injury done to

[47] F Nietzsche, *The Gay Science*, tr W Kaufmann (New York, Vintage Books, 1974) 254. Nor, probably, does he advance his own welfare – we are all damaged by the violence we do, whatever our reasons for doing it. For a more considered assessment of Nietzsche's attitudes to punishment, see Tunick (n 1) ch 2.

[48] A Kantian justification of punishment (my thanks to Jason Neyers for this point) is that it is a rightful hindrance to the wrongdoer's own hindrance of freedom and the affirmation and 'restoration' of the superiority of the law itself – see Ripstein (n 33) 314–24. This justification has little to do with the morally questionable practice of 'retribution as revenge' criticised in the text. Punishment simply invalidates and deters a wrongdoer's unilateral choice to exempt himself from the norms of the legal system, thereby constituting the law's systematic 'effectiveness … in space and time' (ibid 319). See also E Weinrib, 'Deterrence and Corrective Justice' (2002) 50 *University of California Los Angeles Law Review* 621, 633–34, 638–40. As in Weinrib's account, deterrence in this conception is an instantiated effect of punishment, not an instrumental aim. Another potential counter-argument to the point made in the text is that vengeance may not be virtuous, or good for the victim, but is nonetheless socially useful for deterrent reasons – see section III.E.

[49] *BMW of North America Incorporated v Gore* 517 US 559 (1996); *Cooper Industries Inc v Leatherman Tool Group Inc* 532 US 424 (2001). I am grateful to Catherine Sharkey for this point.

[50] R Wright, 'The Grounds and Extent of Legal Responsibility' (2003) 40(4) *San Diego Law Review* 1425, 1431; MH Redish and AL Mathews, 'Why Punitive Damages are Unconstitutional' (2004) 53 *Emory Law Journal* 1, 13–19; Sebok, (n 3) 195–202; *Cooper Industries Inc v Leatherman Tool Group Inc* 532 US 424 (2001) 437–38, fn 11. For the view that punitive damages rectify 'moral' injury, see P-W Lee 'Contract Damages, Corrective Justice and Punishment' (2007) 70(6) *MLR* 887.

society in the form of harm to public interests.[51] Some go so far as to maintain that the criminal law itself does corrective justice, so that there is little to distinguish it from the law of tort.[52] That idea, superficially at least, fits an ambiguous paragraph in the *Rhetoric*, identified by Allan Beever, in which Aristotle described punishment as 'curing' acts of wrongdoing,[53] and it also chimes with the idea in Hegel that punishment somehow 'annuls' or cancels the crime.[54] Rather more commonly, it is suggested that courts in common law systems in the eighteenth and nineteenth centuries used punitive damages in tort law to fill gaps in compensation for emotional distress and other intangible personal harms.[55] Some doubt has been expressed as whether this account tells the full story.[56] Nonetheless, *McGregor on Damages* cites one more recent case, *Borders (UK) v Commissioner of Police of the Metropolis*,[57] where the English Court of Appeal upheld an exemplary damages award for what was 'in reality but a second component of the claimant's actual loss', which suggests that such awards are indeed still sometimes used for compensatory purposes, even in the modern day.[58] In *Rookes v Barnard*, it was the view that punitive awards have historically been compensating aggravated losses in precisely this way that led the House of Lords to conclude that there were so few real precedents for punishment in English private law.[59]

[51] The main historical proponent of this idea was Aquinas: Perry, 'Third Form of Justice' (n 35) 239. See also H Morris, 'Persons and Punishment' (1968) 52(4) *Monist* 475, for whom punishment strips free-riders of gains wrongfully made at society's expense. For an interesting variant, in which punitive damages combine the primary objective of deterrence with the compensation of societal harm, see CM Sharkey, 'Punitive Damages as Societal Damages' (2003) 113 *Yale Law Journal* 347; CM Sharkey, 'The Future of Classwide Punitive Damages' (2013) 46 *University of Michigan Journal of Law Reform* 1127. Social compensation is achieved by distributing awards to either (i) other victims of D's wrong not before the court, or (ii) other, distinct victim groups (or the state) ('Societal Damages' 391). In (i), the model combines deterrence with corrective justice (assuming that each victim is awarded his own loss) and in (ii) with distributive justice ('fairness'). See further ch 7.

[52] RE Barnett, 'Restitution: A New Paradigm of Criminal Justice' (1977) 87(4) *Ethics* 279; RE Barnett, 'Getting Even: Restitution, Preventive Detention and the Tort/Crime Distinction' (1996) 76 *Boston University Law Review* 157, 158–60. Barnett uses the language of 'restitutive justice' but the idea is the same. Contrast Weinrib (n 3) 55 (confining punishment to the criminal law).

[53] Beever, 'Justice and Punishment' (n 3) 258. Note, however, Beever's observation that Aristotle did not clearly distinguish between corrective and retributive justice.

[54] GWF Hegel, *Philosophy of Right*, tr TM Knox (Oxford, Oxford University Press, 1952) 99 (punishment restores the status quo ante by eliminating the moral gain that the wrongdoer made and by restoring the right).

[55] Sebok (n 3) cites *Cooper Industries Inc v Leatherman Tool Group Inc* 121 S Ct 1678 (2001) as clearly (albeit in his view, wrongly) stating this view. See also *Huckle v Money* (1763) 95 ER 768.

[56] Zipursky (n 41) 37 points out – correctly, I think – that most judges, historically, have simply not conceptualised punitive damages in this way. See also Sebok (n 3) 180–95 and 205–06 (concluding that the purposes of punishment in the 19th century were much more varied than this and that, if compensating intangible harm was one of them, it was rare and directed at compensating insult, not what we now think of as mental distress).

[57] *Borders (UK) v Commissioner of Police of the Metropolis* [2005] EWCA Civ 197.

[58] J Edelman, J Varuhas and S Colton (eds), *McGregor on Damages*, 20th edn (London, Sweet & Maxwell, 2019) para 52-048.

[59] *Rookes v Barnard* [1964] AC 1129 (HL) 1229–30 (Lord Devlin).

A variation on the theme that punitive damages compensate personal loss – but one that still appears to understand them as an instrument of corrective justice – is Rob Stevens' view in *Torts and Rights* that they are 'substitutive' for private rights that a defendant has infringed – the next best thing to the rights themselves.[60] Their measure provides an index of the value of the seriousness of the infringement and thereby makes the rights of the injured party fully good. The difficulty with this view, if I interpret it correctly, is that it is hard to see how the seriousness of an infringement (the defendant's wrong) – which is measured *ex post facto* and in part by the defendant's motivations – can provide an index of the value of a plaintiff's prior, primary entitlement. If this were so then the value of rights would vary from case to case according to the way in which they are infringed, which presents a serious logical difficulty. My *wrong* may, as Stevens suggests, be greater when I kick you deliberately than when I trip you accidentally, but the value of your *right* is the same in each case.[61] It is hard, then, to see how a higher award of punitive damages in the former case could be substitutive for your right, as opposed to being retributive, deterrent or expressively denunciatory in purpose.

Even if, historically, punitive damages did contribute to doing corrective justice for individual victims, it is often pointed out that there is little reason for them to be involved in this way nowadays, given the expansion in the civil law's categories of compensable harm (to include damages for psychiatric harm, mental distress, and harm to dignity and personal autonomy) and the wide range of cases in which it will now reverse wrongdoers' unjust enrichment. The advent of class action proceedings and associated cy-près schemes for the distribution of damage fund surpluses also means that private law has mechanisms for compensating harms caused to multiple individuals injured by the same wrong, where previously it did not. This being so, punitive damages should certainly not be part of a modern law reform agenda, and it would be very odd to find law reform bodies recommending their retention, expansion or their introduction for the first time. They would, at best, be a hangover from history, awaiting retirement from the field. To this extent, it seems probable that the occasional modern reference in the case law to punitive damages as serving to do corrective justice for victims,[62] is more likely an allusion to perceived *effect* of such awards than to their actual purposes.

The other view is that punishing individuals compensates *society*, or the state, for harm to public interests – a view attributed by Perry to Thomas Aquinas and

[60] Stevens (n 3) 60 ('next best substitute for the primary right'). The account is complicated because the author also labels such damages 'retributive' of the infringement (ibid 85). They are nonetheless analysed under the heading of 'substitutive' awards.

[61] ibid 85–86. The seriousness of the wrong done (moral character of D's act in infringing) is not relevant to corrective justice, save insofar as it creates greater damaging consequences for P. It is relevant only to retributive justice, or to the importance of deterring or denouncing the conduct – see sections III.E and III.G.

[62] *Gunns Ltd v Alishah (No 4)* [2010] TASSC 24 [55], [58] (Porter J).

some other early Christian writers.[63] Whether this is so even in the criminal law is doubtful, since it is hard to see how society's own injury is made good by its becoming a killer, or imprisoner.[64] In any event, it cannot easily explain punitive damages in modern private law, for the simple reason that such damages do not go to society but to the individual victim (although it is interesting to note that, on some American models and the recent French one, a proportion of punitive awards can indeed be diverted in this way[65]). If rectification is to be made to society, whatever sanction is imposed on a wrongdoer must clearly be paid into the public coffers. But it is then, again, hard to see why the private law mechanism of punitive damages would be used to do this – first diverting money from wrongdoer to the victim and thence to the state – when this can equally and more directly be done in one move, by imposing a criminal fine upon the wrongdoer, or confiscating his profits directly.

C. Distributive Justice

It has sometimes been suggested that punishment effects distributive justice.[66] This view is described by Perry as the 'Scotist' position, after the 'Subtle Doctor' John Duns Scotus (1265–1308). Perry reports, again citing Englard, that most scholars who take this view do so either (i) because punishments are meted out to wrongdoers in some measure of *proportion* to the seriousness of the wrong they have done; or (ii) because the wrongdoer's *personal characteristics*, including merit, status, wealth and past record, are taken into account when the sanction is determined.[67] These features of punishment have a deceptive semblance of

[63] Perry, 'Third Form of Justice' (n 35) 238–39. For a modern version with key differences, see Sharkey (n 51). See also R Burgh, 'Guilt, Punishment and Desert' in Schoeman (n 43) 316.

[64] This actually probably compounds society's past injury, rather than reducing it, since it makes us all purposeful killers or deprivers of others' liberty. The argument therefore suffers from defects similar to those affecting the 'just desert' argument underpinning retribution.

[65] Draft Art 1371 (n 7) permitted part of a punitive award to be diverted to the state; similarly, penalties payable under the new Draft Art 1266-1 (n 7) are payable to a compensation fund. Sharkey, 'Punitive Damages as Societal Damages' (n 51) 373, 375–86 (writing in 2003) reported eight States in the United States where the same is possible: Alaska, Georgia, Illinois, Indiana, Iowa, Missouri, Oregon and Utah. An interesting and controversial feature of the US schemes is that they were introduced to protect insurers by reducing the incentive for plaintiffs to claim during the 'insurance crisis', and to raise revenue for the state (ibid 375–77).

[66] For a recent example, see B Kuklin, 'Public Requitals: Corrective, Retributive and Distributive Justice' (2018) 66 *Cleveland State Law Review* 245. For a view that punishment is a 'product' of distributive justice, in the sense that it is the mechanism via which first order rules of distributive justice are enforced and their violation is deterred, see Beever, 'Justice and Punishment' (n 3) 269–70. The view is attributed to civilian writers, but Beever is clearly sympathetic.

[67] Perry, 'Third Form of Justice' (n 35) 242–43. In some historical writers, there are traces of a third basis for reaching this conclusion – namely, that the relevant form of justice must be distributive because it is done in the name of society (ie to protect public interests). This falls into the error of the type of self-referential reasoning identified in section II – it assumes that the only form of justice done in the protection of public interests is distributive justice, which is clearly not the case (retributive justice is also exacted by the state for the protection of such interests).

measuring proportions and merits, which makes a distributive justice analysis superficially tempting. The fallacy of this view is revealed by Perry. If punishment did distributive justice, he points out, it would distribute certain, defined sanctions between certain, defined individuals in accordance with their relative merit, but that is not what it does – it only ever allocates a single, indivisible burden to the wrongdoer.[68] It was this feature of punishment that caused Spiegelman CJ's reluctance to accept that punitive damages have a role in equity in *Harris v Digital Pulse Pty Ltd*, it being said that equity balances the positions of both parties.[69] Of course, punishments can again have observable distributive *effects* (for example, the practice is likely to result in more sanctions being meted out to murderers than parking offenders) and this could form the basis of comparative reflection and critique in penal policy, but this does not necessarily mean that punishment is designed to achieve any of those effects.[70] There certainly seems to be little suggestion in the modern law, for example, that punitive damages are designed to do distributive justice.

D. Protection, Prevention (Prophylaxis) and Rehabilitation

A function of punishment in the criminal law is often said to be protection of public safety and the rights of others. Locking up wrongdoers – 'incapacitating them' – prevents them hurting their neighbours in the future.[71] Processes of 'civil' incarceration, in which the dangerously insane are removed to secure isolation without proof of wrongdoing, share this purpose.[72] Similarly, the rehabilitation of offenders is designed in part to lower rates of recidivism, as well (perhaps) as for the good of the offender. Protection of the public is sometimes also identified as a possible function of civil penalties, alongside the expression of moral disapproval, retribution and deterrence.[73] Although private law has its own devices for

[68] As Perry puts it (ibid 243), 'in a typical exercise of distributive justice a divisible benefit or burden is distributed among several persons in accordance with their relative merit. In a specific implementation of retributive justice nothing is distributed. The court allocates an indivisible burden to a single person.'

[69] *Harris v Digital Pulse Pty Ltd* [2003] NSWCA 10, (2003) 56 NSWLR 298 [51] (Spiegelman CJ). Also arguing against punitive damages in equity, see CEF Rickett, 'Punitive Damages: The Pulse of Equity' (2003) 77 *Australian Law Journal* 496.

[70] Perry, 'Third Form of Justice' (n 35) 244. This was apparently the conclusion reached by both Grotius and Pufendorf.

[71] Attitudes to incapacitation fluctuate and its popularity is currently on the rise. Witness the Australian Law Reform Commission's change of heart as between 1988 (Australian Law Reform Commission, *Sentencing* (Rep No 44, 1988)), when it rejected incapacitation, and 2006 (Australian Law Reform Commission, *Same Crime, Same Time: Sentencing of Federal Offenders* (Rep No 103, 2006)), when it advocated it. For a classic statement of the idea in the United States, see J Wilson, *Thinking About Crime* (New York, Basic Books, 1975).

[72] CR Williams, 'Psychopathy, Mental Illness and Preventive Detention' (1990) 16 *Monash University Law Review* 161.

[73] Australian Law Reform Commission, *Principled Regulation: Federal, Civil and Administrative Penalties in Australia* (Rep No 95, 2003) para 3.5.

preventing future rights infringements – most notably, the powerful remedy of injunctive relief – it has no equivalent device to imprisonment, and there is no evidence that it regards itself as punishing when it issues an injunction (although it clearly does think in terms of punishment if the injunction is disregarded and a contempt of court thereby committed). It also has a system of primary and secondary (remedial) rules in equity that prevents fiduciaries profiting from their positions of trust, which operate in a prophylactic, not a 'punitive' or deterrent manner.[74] My own view is that if it does not already do so, the criminal law would itself be wise to identify social protection and the prevention of future harm as an aim of judicial acts of *sentencing* and as *distinct* from punishment, rather than claiming that protection is part of the purpose (and therefore the meaning) of punishment itself. Punishment would then be something that sentencing does, alongside other things, rather than being that in which sentencing necessarily consists. We shall return to this point in the conclusions section at the end of this chapter.

E. Deterrence

A popular view in both the criminal literature and in discussions of punitive damages[75] and civil penalties is that it is a core purpose of punishment to modify conduct by deterring specifically, generally or both. That this may be the function of punitive damages is suggested by the modern preference of some judges and law reform bodies for the terminology of 'exemplary' awards, since making an example of a person is the clearest way of changing the behaviour of others.[76] Deterrence is at the heart of economic accounts of the law, which maintain that there is no purposive difference between the civil and criminal law – both are to be understood simply as pricing mechanisms incentivising efficient behaviour.[77]

From the analytical point of view, as has been indicated, it is perfectly possible for a sanction to have a deterrent *aim*, even if it imposes on the wrongdoer a liability that is less than the loss he has caused or the gain he has made from his wrong.

[74] See further L Smith, 'Deterrence, Prophylaxis and Punishment in Fiduciary Obligations' (2013) 7 *Journal of Equity* 87; Penner, ch 5 of this volume. The distinction between deterrence and prophylaxis (see Smith, 88–89) is that deterrence aims to alter the behaviour of defendants or others, whereas prophylactic rules simply *prevent* the occurrence of an undesired consequence.

[75] The story started in *Wilkes v Wood* (1763) Lofft 1, 98 ER 489 (Pratt LCJ). On the US approach, see Dobbs (n 3). For the view that punitive damages combine optimal deterrence with corrective and distributive justice aims, see Sharkey 'Societal Damages' (n 51). On the role of deterrence in tort theory generally, see GT Schwartz, 'Mixed Theories of Tort Law: Affirming Both Deterrence and Corrective Justice' (1997) 75 *Texas Law Review* 1801.

[76] See *Broome* (n 4) 1073 (Lord Hailsham); J Edelman, 'In Defence of Exemplary Damages' in Rickett (ed) (n 3) 225. Interestingly, the Law Commission of England and Wales (n 5) rec 16 preferred the term 'punitive' damages, on the basis that this better reflects their (at least partly) retributive rationale.

[77] R Posner, 'An Economic Theory of the Criminal Law' (1985) 85 *Columbia Law Review* 1193.

However, it is most unlikely that it will deter *effectively* unless it sanctions him in at least the latter measure, and it will probably, in fact, be necessary to harm the defendant in a measure greater than his net profit,[78] because a repeat offender can otherwise gamble on the chance of non-detection or non-enforcement in sufficient cases to leave him no worse off (and sometimes better off) for his offending. Whether gain-based awards are sufficient to deter wrongdoing in the standard case depends largely on the way they are calculated, and the truth of most accounts of profit – even ones that are calculated on a 'net' profit basis – is that that they are likely to leave the defendant to some degree worse as a result of the wrong, because they will not be calculated net of *all* losses that the wrongdoer incurred in committing the wrong. They are unlikely, for example, to take account of the time the wrong took, or its opportunity costs. From this point of view, there is probably much to be said for the view that accounts of profit should feature more prominently in the law's deterrent arsenal, if deterrence is the game really being played.[79]

The aim of deterrence does not as easily explain why punitive damages are often calculated in the United States as *multiples* of (twice or three times) a plaintiff's *loss*, since requiring a defendant who has made no gain from a wrong to pay only for the actual loss caused could still act as a significant smack on the wrist and a warning to others. Indeed, the cases recognise that singular, compensatory sums are often sufficient to deter. Perhaps the suspicion is that although the defendant cannot always be *proved* to have gained by his wrong, some such gain must be assumed (why else would the wrongdoer do it?), and multiples of the plaintiff's proven loss provide a convenient, if arbitrary, measure that can be used to try to ensure that the wrongdoer's liability exceeds any such personal, intangible gain. On this type of account, however, capping punitive damages by reference to any particular multiple would probably be irrational, since the cap could not be guaranteed to exceed a defendant's gain – more flexibility would be required than the 'multiples' system allowed. Nor does the deterrence rationale easily explain why punitive damages are sometimes said to be *contingent* or 'parasitic'[80] on compensatory ones, since if the objective is to incentivise defendants not to wrong others then it is immaterial whether the infringement of the plaintiff's right actually caused any loss on the facts. The better view is that, whilst it is appropriate for a court to consider whether a loss-based award is sufficient to deter,[81] exemplary awards are available even where no loss at all is provable, so that no compensation order can be made. This intuition is vindicated in Canada in the recognition of the

[78] *Broome* (n 4) 1130 (Lord Diplock).

[79] J Berryman, 'The Case for Restitutionary Damages Over Punitive Damages: Teaching the Wrongdoer that Tort Does Not Pay' (1994) 73 *Canadian Bar Review* 320. See also J Edelman, *Gain-Based Damages: Contract, Tort, Equity and Intellectual Property* (Oxford, Hart Publishing, 2002) ch 3.

[80] *Gunns* (n 62) 59. A close reading of this paragraph actually suggests that it may be interpreted consistently with the suggestion in the text – the term 'parasitic' indicating not so much that compensatory damages must also be given, but that it must first be considered whether they are enough to deter.

[81] *Rookes* (n 59) 1228 (Lord Devlin).

Supreme Court that punitive damages under the Quebec Charter of Human Rights and Freedoms operate completely independently of other heads of damages.[82]

Deterrence rationalisations of punitive damages are somewhat better able to deal with the phenomenon of vicarious liability and liability insurance than retributive theories, because imposing liability on an employer can still incentivise him to prevent his employee's wrongdoing; and higher insurance premiums and insurer involvement in an insured's activity around risk might have some tangible effect on the defendant's future behaviour.[83] However, there are undoubtedly still tensions. The insulating effect of a liability insurance policy for a particular defendant could presumably only be overcome by a court's hiking any award so high as to exceed the coverage of the policy, or by governments' legislating to prohibit the insurance of exemplary awards. The fact that insurance is still generally permitted[84] means that if specific deterrence is a judicial aim, exemplary sums will regularly be ineffective to achieve it. That has led some courts, including the High Court of Australia in *Lamb v Cotogno*, to justify exemplary awards in cases of vicarious liability either by reference to their broader, *general* deterrent effect on others, or by reference to other aims entirely.[85] Specific deterrence is clearly also unable to explain exemplary awards in cases in which the wrongdoer is deceased.[86]

Once (if) one accepts the hypothesis that the purpose of punitive damages is to deter, the correct way of calculating them becomes almost entirely speculative, beyond the guiding mandate that a wrongdoer should never be allowed to gain and should – at least to some extent – be made to lose in consequence of the wrong. Greater sophistication in quantifying the right incentive is claimed in the economic literature, with the key objective of the award being to ensure that the full social costs of the defendant's wrongdoing (but no more than this) are internalised in the damages award. Even assuming, however, that these social costs can be correctly calculated (which is unlikely), it is not clear that courts (or juries) are concerned to deter only wrongs that produce net social loss. In fact, as we know from the famous case of *Grimshaw v Ford Motor Company*,[87] economically rational wrongs are often precisely the sort of wrongs that courts and juries think *most* need to be deterred. If punishment in private law is therefore really about deterrence, it is largely a matter of guesswork as to how (in what measure) it should

[82] *de Montigny v Brossard (Succession)* 2010 SCC 51, [2010] 3 SCR 64 [38]–[46]. My thanks to Lionel Smith for drawing my attention to this authority.

[83] For a suggestion to this effect, see A Widiss, 'Liability Insurance Coverage for Punitive Damages – Discerning Answers to the Conundrum Created by Disputes Involving Conflicting Public Policies, Pragmatic Considerations and Political Actions' (1994) 39 *Villanova Law Review* 455, 501.

[84] For the exceptions in the United States, see Sharkey (n 45).

[85] *Lamb v Cotogno* (1987) 164 CLR 1 (HCA). The other aim identified in such a case was the appeasement of victims and the prevention of social violence. See section III.F.

[86] *de Montigny* (n 82) paras 50–55 (the explanation for relief in such instances lies not in deterrence but in expressive denunciation of the wrong and affirmation of the value of the victim's right – see section III.G).

[87] *Grimshaw v Ford Motor Company* 119 Cal App 3d 757 (1981).

be done, beyond the parameters described. This may ironically make retributive characterisations of punitive damages more attractive to courts and law commissions, for the simple reason that picking a figure that is in 'just proportion to the wrong' still seems easier and more publicly defensible than picking a figure that will 'effectively change behaviour', when there are simply no empirical data available to a court on an award's likely incentive effects. Awards will also always need to take account of a defendant's resources, since where economic penalties are concerned, the diminishing marginal utility of money means that a higher sanction will be required to change the behaviour of a rich person (or multinational, or government) than that of a poor one. Liability to compensate may be sufficient to deter you or me, but it is most unlikely to deter the rich and powerful.

Whilst deterrence is most commonly regarded by its proponents as an instrumental purpose and as informing the construction of both primary and secondary legal duties in private law, there is a rival view that is popular amongst deontologists. Professor Weinrib hence suggests that deterrence is in fact better understood in this context not as an aim informing the content of legal rules, but as a consequence of the instantiation and actualisation of the norms of corrective justice in a system of positive law.[88] Private law hence does not *aim* to deter, but it is positive law nonetheless, and positive law changes behaviour by enforcing the private rights that it instantiates. This approach comes close, I think, to arguing that deterrence is an *effect* of the law's doing corrective justice (something that is necessarily entailed by using the law's coercive force to do it), not an aim in its own right. It is certainly not a purpose that judges have in mind when setting damages awards or structuring primary legal rules. In so far as this account sets deterrence as amongst the effects of private law, not its purposes, it should probably not appear in a section concerning the 'aims' of punishment. Indeed, Weinrib himself makes it clear that his account is diametrically opposed to that of economists and all other instrumentalists who think of private law as having social 'aims'. It is also in tension with the purposes that judges themselves regularly proclaim for their punitive awards, which means that it may be best to understand Weinrib's thesis as an ideal, rather than an internal explanation of their current practice.

F. Appeasement Through Catharsis

Another understanding of the aim of punishment is that it helps to appease victims of wrongdoing, by cathartically relieving them of the anger they are caused by a wrong. Appeasement is sometimes also cited as a function, or effect, of awards of compensation for injury in the law of torts.

If the aim of punishment were simply to alleviate an individual victim's anger for the sake of his or her healing then it would, I suggest, be doing nothing other

[88] Weinrib (n 48).

than corrective or restorative justice.[89] There are certainly signs that the law is prepared to promote this end, as, for example, by allowing victims to provide victim impact statements in modern criminal law proceedings, but this does not identify any aim for punishment that is distinct from that we considered in section III.B. Therefore, if there is a distinct aim of appeasement, it must be that it serves the instrumental, social function of avoiding civil violence – that it prevents victims from taking the law into their own hands. There is some support for this understanding of exemplary awards in *Lamb v Cotogno*,[90] and some writers, as we have seen, suggest that the whole civil justice system can be understood as having come into being with this very aim in mind. It nonetheless seems questionable whether the prevention of social violence through acts of private vengeance is now punishment's aim. It may well be that fewer destabilising reprisals will take place when defendants are punished, but the practice of punishing wrongdoers in order to achieve this end in its own right seems morally questionable. Furthermore, in the context of private law, the ability of plaintiffs to obtain corrective justice would seem to be enough in any event to achieve catharsis and prevent them from running amuck, provided that compensation is calculated so as to account for all relevant aspects of a plaintiff's harm, including his or her righteous anger and harm to dignity.[91]

G. Social Messaging – Denouncing Wrongdoers and Marking Rights

A final aim of punishment is said to be to denounce or 'mark disapproval'[92] of a wrong, or, as Lord Camden put it in *Wilkes v Wood*, to 'prove detestation' of it,[93] but the purpose and meaning of denunciation must again itself be identified. If the aim is to change the behaviour of the wrongdoer and others by 'making an example' of him, denunciation is deterrence. If its aim is to bring shame, moral censure (stigma), and associated social and economic exclusion to him in proportion to his wrong, it is retribution. If it is supposed to help to restore the dignity of a wrongdoer's victim and to lessen his anger, it is an exercise in corrective or restorative justice and /or appeasement.

[89] The idea of restorative justice refers to particular framework of modern criminal law theory, which combines the idea of restoration of victims with rehabilitation of offenders and reconciliation between the offender and the community, using particular techniques of encounter and inclusion. In this form, it appears to combine many of the other, perceived (non-retributive) aims of punishment with particular strategies for achieving them. See generally J Braithwaite, *Restorative Justice and Responsive Regulation* (Oxford, Oxford University Press, 2002).

[90] *Lamb* (n 85) 9–10. See also *Harris* (n 69) [56] (Spiegelman CJ).

[91] This is doubted by T Frankel, 'Lessons from the Past: Revenge Yesterday' (1996) 76 *Boston University Law Review* 89, 94–96, who suggests that the personal right to seek vengeance achieves catharsis in ways that the modern tort system, with its objectivised awards of tort damages, does not, albeit that it undoubtedly creates less certainty in the system.

[92] *Kuddus* (n 44) [91] (Lord Hutton).

[93] *Wilkes* (n 75).

For denunciation to be a *distinct* aim of punishment, its rationale must therefore be understood in a different way. One view is that, rather than directly seeking to change future behaviour, the denunciation of wrongdoing *affirms and confirms* the value of our legal rights. Its purpose is then to 'announce' or 'vindicate' the right that has been infringed and the moral and social values on which it is based.[94] This 'communicative' or 'expressive' function of punishment is widely accepted in the criminal law, where it is connected to the idea that conviction of a crime conveys particular moral condemnation of a wrongdoer's acts.[95] It is also referred to in some judgments on punitive damages[96] and in a number of cases in which courts have made awards of 'vindicatory damages' for the violation of public, constitutional or human rights.[97] Many of these cases involve wrongs committed by agents of the state against important civil rights and liberties.[98] The idea of 'vindication' in such cases refers to the law's function in 'declaring' rights – something that is arguably done in private law by judicial declarations, injunctions and other monetary awards in any event, but which is done more emphatically by more substantial sums. On this theory, 'money talks', and the larger the damages award, the louder it shouts. 'Vindicatory' damages are said to be distinct from punitive ones in the detail that their aim is not to punish',[99] by which, I think, it is meant that it is no part of their function to exact retribution upon a wrongdoer, but, to the extent they are designed to 'mark' a wrong or affirm the importance of a right, they clearly share the expressive messaging function of punitive awards and the criminal law.[100]

[94] This is sometimes referred to as 'norm projection and reinforcement': M Gallanter and D Luban, 'Poetic Justice, Punitive Damages and Legal Pluralism' (1993) 42 *American University Law Review* 1393, 1429–32. See also M Harper, 'Comment on the Tort/Crime Distinction: Generation Later' (1996) 76 *Boston University Law Review* 23, 25. On vindication more generally, see K Barker, 'Private and Public: The Mixed Concept of Vindication in Torts and Private Law' in S Pitel, J Neyers and E Chamberlain (eds), *Tort Law: Challenging Orthodoxy* (Oxford, Hart Publishing, 2013) 59.

[95] On 'expressivism' as a distinct, hybrid approach to the theory of punishment, see Brooks (n 1) ch 6. On the expressive importance of criminal punishment generally, see J Feinberg, *Doing and Deserving: Essays in the Theory of Responsibility* (Princeton, NJ, Princeton University Press, 1970) 98; J Hampton, 'The Moral Education Theory of Punishment' (1984) 13(3) *Philosophy and Public Affairs* 208; J Hampton, 'Correcting Harms Versus Righting Wrongs: The Goal of Retribution' (1992) *University of California Los Angeles Law Review* 1659; R Rychlack, 'Society's Moral Right to Punish: A Further Exploration of the Denunciation Theory of Punishment' (1990) 65 *Tulane Law Review* 299. For criticism, see R Epstein, 'The Crime/Tort Distinction: A Generation Later' (1996) 76 *Boston University Law Review* 1, 18–20.

[96] *Rookes* (n 59) 1226 (exemplary awards 'vindicate the strength of the law' (Lord Devlin); *de Montigny* (n 82) para 55.

[97] *Attorney General of the St Christopher, Nevis and Anguilla v John Joseph Reynolds* [1980] AC 637 (PC); *Attorney General of Trinidad and Tobago v Ramanoop* [2005] UKPC 15, [2006] 1 AC 328; *Merson v Cartwright and Attorney General* [2005] UKPC 38; *Taunoa v Attorney General* [2007] NZSC 70, [2008] 1 NZLR 429 [109], [255], [299]; *Vancouver (City of) v Ward* 2010 SCC 27, [2010] 2 SCR 28. See also (a case in private law) *Walumba Lumba v Secretary of State for the Home Department* [2011] UKSC 12, [2012] 1 AC 245 [213], [216]–[217] (Lady Hale); [178], [180] (Lord Hope) (vindicatory damages recognise the importance of the right and the wrong done).

[98] See Morgan, ch 11 of this volume.

[99] *Ashley v Chief Constable Sussex Police* [2008] UKHL 25, [2008] 1 AC 962 [22] (Lord Scott).

[100] On the connection between vindication and punishment, see further RA Duff, 'Torts Crimes and Vindication: Whose Wrong is it?' in M Dyson (ed), *Comparing Tort and Crime: Learning from across and within Legal Systems* (Cambridge, Cambridge University Press, 2015) 146, 150–61. Whilst I here

It is telling that the vast majority of cases in which such damages have been awarded are cases involving state wrongdoing and/or the violation of public constitutional or human rights, where it might be thought that social messaging functions are especially important.

Assuming that a purpose of punishment is simply to 'affirm' or 'mark' the importance of rights in this way, we still need to know why the law would do it. One possibility is that by doing so we indirectly prevent their being disrespected in future through a process of social influencing that is more subtle than the typical sanction (threat)-based approach that is involved in theories of specific or general deterrence.[101] But this idea – that we mark right and wrong so as prevent future divergences from accepted social norms, folds back into the idea that the purpose of punishment is to prevent future harm (section III.D). The other possibility is simply that we punish in order to publicise rights, full stop, which seems a little unlikely, given the very many other ways in which rights can be announced. It is perhaps more conceivable as a function of a criminal code than of isolated civil law judgments, which so very rarely make the morning news. One view is that formally announcing rights is simply something that is conceptually entailed by any legal system that does corrective justice, or that is required for any legal system (whatever its purpose) to be either legally effective or consistent with the values of the rule of law. If these views are taken then announcing rights and denouncing wrongs through punishment is not a core aim of punishment at all, it is again just one of its effects, or an aspect of its process (transparency) that helps to legitimate it.[102]

The upshot is that if punishment aims to denounce wrongdoing or announce the importance of rights, it has the potential to collapse into one of the other theories we have already mentioned. If the purpose of denouncing is to make an example of a wrongdoer and change his or others' behaviour, it becomes a theory of deterrence, or harm prevention through social influencing. If it is designed to restore or uphold a victim's dignity, it is part of the process of setting right a wrong and restoring a person. If, on the other hand, its aim is simply to convey a message about the importance of rights and social values, this is something that is done in a very broad range of cases that apparently have nothing to do with punishment at all,[103] so that the connection between the ideas becomes weak at best. It is also

suggest that both punishment and 'vindication' serve expressive purposes, Duff suggests at 153 that, for the same reason, vindicatory awards are to be seen as 'a kind of punishment'. There is no substantive difference between us, but this illustrates the slippery nature of the language of punishment.

[101] Gallanter and Luban (n 94), 1429. There is a hint of this reasoning in *de Montigny* (n 82) [53]: 'denunciation contributes to the preventive objective' of the Quebec Civil Code. A similar, more subtle approach to behavioural modification is found in modern 'nudging' practices in the public policy context: see H Strassheim and S Beck (eds), *Handbook of Behavioural Change of Public Policy* (Cheltenham, Edward Elgar, 2019).

[102] See further Barker (n 94) 72–73.

[103] Aside from the cases involving 'vindication' in private law, there are also cases, alluded to by Dolinko (n 1) 405 in public law, where condemnation but no punishment is arguably involved: the impeachment of a president, or the disbarment of a lawyer from practice, for example.

unclear whether announcing rights is an aim of private law, or something that it inevitably does whenever judgment of any sort is pronounced. It would certainly seem to be a very expensive and inefficient public messaging system, if this is what it is. Awarding amounts of money to plaintiffs in isolated cases in order to educate us about the value of rights is not a sound educational practice. Of more value are public expressions of the reasons why rights are important, to be found in judicial reasons and public policy documents. Money may therefore talk, but it remains an inarticulate mode of expression. For this reason, it seems particularly ill-suited as a mechanism for us to express our core values.

IV. Gathering In

Gathering all of this in leaves us in a position to state some observations about the possible aims and meanings of punishment. First and rather obviously, the idea is currently understood across both public and private law to have a range of aims and meanings, not any single one. It is not uncommon for judges or law reformers, when referring to the idea, to identify more than one of these aims in the same breath and, depending on the context, they clearly do not always identify the same aim, or set of aims. What judges mean by punishment therefore varies according to the aims they list; and across the different areas of law in which they list them. A judge who says that the aims of punishment are to engage in retribution, deterrence and rehabilitation of a wrongdoer *means something different* from one who says that it is designed to deter, correct the wrong and mark the infringement of rights. The meanings of punishment therefore exist along a shifting scale and vary from one type of case to another.

Second, the strongest and perhaps the core conception of punishment is one of retributive justice or reprisal, but that aim seems to have little purchase in modern private law, even if it still (in my view wrongly but understandably) retains a hold on the imagination of penal policy makers in the criminal sphere. In such cases as it does persist in the law, one would expect to find appropriate procedural safeguards in place for the protection of wrongdoers, akin to those that the criminal law provides. Cases involving punitive damages in civil cases do not generally apply such safeguards, which immediately leads one to suspect that the aims of awards in such cases are different. Indeed, I would go so far as to suggest that no case in which the standard civil burden of proof is used is likely to be one in which a court's aim is truly retributive. Retribution as it has been defined in the previous section of this chapter is simply too risky a business to be left to the balance of probabilities, even when it is placed in the hands of judges, not juries.

Third, although there are some historical suggestions that punishment was directed at, and therefore in its terms meant, doing corrective justice for victims (and perhaps society), there is little reason for it to feature in private law for these purposes in the modern day. Corrective justice for individuals can be done through many other, modern devices, and if one believes that society needs to be compensated for damage to public interests beyond the damage caused to the private interests of particular victims, this would seem to require resource reallocation mechanisms that currently do not generally exist in private law, to channel payments from wrongdoers to the state *qua state*. Why one would now introduce such mechanisms in private law in preference to simply imposing criminal fines upon wrongdoers for their wrongs, or confiscating their profits, is a little unclear, but there are precedents for the exercise to which we should clearly be attentive before drawing any final conclusion on that matter. Catherine Sharkey's work in this volume proves an important stimulus in that debate.

Fourth, the idea that punishment is concerned with distributive justice is probably based on a false premise. It stems from an analytical confusion between the different forms of justice. Although it is always important to us to reflect upon the distributive effects that punishment has and to consider these carefully when setting sentencing rules and guidelines, punitive damages do not distribute any common benefit or burden between wrongdoer and victim, or indeed between the victim and anyone else. Other phenomena in private law (rules concerning mitigation of damage or the capping of the compensatory awards of high-earners) probably do this, but punishment as it is understood in the context of punitive damages awards very clearly does not.

This leaves what appear to be a number of social goals and meanings for punishment that are generally abhorrent and incoherent to deontologists but acceptable to instrumentalists and pragmatists, either as global aims, or as aims that private law takes up interstitially by way of default, on the hypothesis that public law does not yet do them or do them sufficiently well. These include the prevention of wrongdoing ex ante, its deterrence of specific rights violations, preservation of the peace through appeasement of the wronged, and 'denunciation'.

The fifth observation is that, of these ideas, it is deterrence and denunciation that feature most strongly in the language of punishment in private law. The association of exemplary damages in tort with deterrence is very common and connects with the language of deterrence in some cases involving the liability of fiduciaries for breaches of fiduciary duty.[104] But whether or not deterrence is an aim of the private law or simply an effect of its customary operation, the use of the language of punishment becomes increasingly strained in this association. Deterrence, like harm prevention, is an idea so remote from the core idea of retribution as to scarcely merit being tied to it. The same is true of denunciation. If denouncing a wrong meets any end that is different from those previously listed, it refers to the aim of announcing or marking the importance of rights. There are certainly some signs that private law, in common with public law, does expressively declare and affirm rights, but it is hard to tell whether this is the aim or just the effect of exemplary awards. In any event, I suggest that any such declaratory function is so far

[104] *Warman International Ltd v Dwyer* (1995) 182 CLR 544 (HCA) 198–99.

removed from the core, retributive conception that it is normatively misleading to include it within the latter's rubric.

All of this suggests that, in modernity, it may be best to follow Chief Justice Spiegelman's suggestion in the New South Wales Court of Appeal in *Rich v Australian Securities and Investment Commission*[105] that we confine the language of punishment to orders in which our aim is retribution and use different language to identify the other aims we have listed: deterrence, harm prevention, rehabilitation, corrective justice and the declaration or marking of rights. This would mean that, in the criminal law, crime is (currently)[106] largely, but by no means exclusively, tied to punishment (punishment being just one possible aim of sentencing[107]), but that private law, whilst sometimes sharing some ends and effects of the modern criminal law and civil penalty systems (deterrence, occasionally corrective justice,[108] the marking of rights), is never really about 'punishment' at all.

V. Conclusion

There is no such thing as punishment in modern private law, as I have defined it.[109] I have reached this blunt conclusion via what may well seem to the reader a long and circuitous route, in full consciousness that those who share the view reached it long before me. My own journey to this conclusion has nonetheless been a little different. It has not so much been an exercise in determining whether private law *should* punish, but rather an inquiry into what, in law, it *means* to punish and whether it *makes sense* to say that private law currently does. This requires one to take an interpretive view and to see whether the meanings of the idea that are most clearly instantiated in private law (deterring and denouncing wrongs, perhaps also sometimes historically setting them right) are sufficiently close to the ideas that instantiate it in the criminal law (where retribution is an idea that is still strong). If they are not then it is time to be clearer about the fact and to use language to discriminate properly between the different aims and ideals that historically were mixed in the common law's primordial mass. This is most effectively done, I suggest, by limiting the language of punishment to a single end (retributive justice) that currently has no place in modern private law.

[105] *Rich v Australian Securities and Investment Commission* [2003] NSWCA 342, (2003) 203 ALR 671 [89]–[90] (revd [2004] HCA 42).

[106] Since policy may change again. If the criminal law completely gave up retribution, it would, on the language convention suggested, also cease to punish.

[107] This may actually already be the understanding. Although some writers hence appear to regard all sentencing as punishing (see, eg, M Bagaric, T Alexander and R Edney, *Sentencing in Australia*, 6th edn (Sydney, Thompson Reuters 2018) 20, 'the … purpose of sentencing is … to achieve those aims which justify the infliction of punishment'), this is not reflected in sentencing guidelines, which clearly identify punishment as just one sentencing aim: Penalties and Sentencing Act 1992 (Qld), s 9; Crimes Act 1914 (Cth), s 16A. My thanks to Heather Douglas for this point.

[108] Since compensation orders are now widely available in criminal proceedings.

[109] Section II.B.

This conclusion does not dictate any other. In particular, it does not resolve the question whether private law rules *should* instantiate retributive norms, although my personal view is that there are very good reasons why they should not. Nor does it preclude the use of private actions as mechanisms for the enforcement of *public* norms – a possibility that is currently actively being pursued in a number of contexts as a bolster to existing public enforcement processes. It does, however, provide an opportunity to approach these questions with far greater clarity, and clarity is the only condition under which rational decisions about the future can be made.

3

Punishment and Private Law: Some Comparative Observations

SOLÈNE ROWAN

I. Introduction

'I want to endow the French law of civil liability with a new role, that is, to deter and sanction behaviours which, whilst not necessarily criminally punishable, are socially unacceptable.'[1] So said Jean-Jacques Urvoas, the then French Minister of Justice, in 2016 when presenting new Article 1266-1 of the Civil Code in a draft bill for the reform of civil liability.[2] This is perhaps the most controversial provision of the draft bill, providing for the introduction of civil penalties to deter and punish 'faults with a view to gain or making a saving'. These penalties will be of general application in tort law and are intended to 'moralise behaviours'.[3]

The publication of the draft bill and the proposed reform are significant events. Having reformed the section of the Code on contract law in 2016, the French Government is now turning its attention to tort law.[4] Somewhat surprisingly, only five of the 2,281 articles of the original 1804 Code related to tort liability. These articles contain high-level propositions and general statements of principle. Just as surprisingly, the two most important articles, Articles 1382 and 1383 – newly renumbered Articles 1240 and 1241 following the 2016 reform of contract law – have remained unaltered in the intervening two centuries, even as society and technology have changed beyond recognition. The courts have, however,

[1] G Marraud des Grottes, 'Interview with Jean-Jacques Urvoas' *Revue Lamy Droit Civil* (1 June 2016) 6211.

[2] J-J Urvoas, '*Projet de réforme de la responsabilité civile*' (March 2017) at www.justice.gouv.fr/publication/Projet_de_reforme_de_la_responsabilite_civile_13032017.pdf, accessed 22 March 2020.

[3] Interview with Jean-Jacques Urvoas (n 1). See also J-J Urvoas, 'Discours de présentation du projet de réforme' (Academy of Moral and Political Sciences, Paris, 13 March 2017) at www.presse.justice.gouv.fr/discours-10093/archives-des-discours-de-2017-12856/projet-de-reforme-de-la-responsabilite-civile-29780.html, accessed 22 March 2020.

[4] The draft bill also contains articles relating to aspects of liability for breach of contract, which have been left out of the 2016 contract reform.

progressively interpreted and adapted these articles. Indeed, this has become so extensive that they are almost meaningless in isolation and without explanation.

High amongst the objectives of the draft bill is to modernise tort law by augmenting the Code with new provisions to replace the original articles. Rules that have been developed in the cases over the previous 200 years will be codified and clarified, and there are also several notable innovations. This chapter will focus on one such innovation, that is, the formal recognition that punishment should have a role in the law of tort.[5] At present, nowhere is punishment stated to be an objective of French civil law.[6] Instead, in both tort and contract law, remedies are, at least on their face, concerned only with compensating loss. The victim can expect to be returned insofar as possible to the position in which they would have been had the wrong not been committed. This is measured exclusively by reference to their loss. The seriousness of the wrong and the extent of any profit accruing to the wrongdoer are irrelevant.

The proposed introduction of a punitive sanction in the draft bill follows increasing calls in academic literature over the last 70 or so years[7] for civil liability to go beyond mere compensation. These calls have intensified over the last three decades, with a high-water mark 15 years ago when a reform project gave serious consideration to the introduction of punitive damages. Whilst not ultimately obtaining legislative approval, this nonetheless laid the ground for the civil penalties that are proposed in the current draft bill. As one commentator imaginatively put it, 'like the phoenix of the Greek mythology, the idea that punishment should have a role in private law dies only to be born again'.[8]

The purposes of this chapter are twofold. First, to explore the historical controversies and reticence around the formal introduction of punishment in French civil law; second, to undertake a comparative analysis of the proposed punitive sanction in the draft bill by reference to English law. It seeks to show that remedies that are intended to deter and punish are already present in French civil law, coexisting disparately and informally with compensation as a central remedy. This has, however, proved insufficient to prevent a proliferation of 'profitable wrongs', so called because the wrongdoer aims to benefit from their wrongful conduct even after any compensatory liability is taken into account. Such wrongs are widely regarded as morally reprehensible yet can fall short of the criminal standard. It is to fill this perceived moral gap and give stronger protection to the rights of

[5] J-S Borghetti, 'L'avant-projet de réforme de la responsabilité civile (1)' D 2016.1442 [47]; E Dreyer, 'L'amende civile concurrente de l'amende pénale?' JCP No 25 Juin 2017, 1344; F Graziani, 'La généralisation de l'amende civile: entre progrès et confusions' D 2018.428.

[6] G Viney, 'Rapport de Synthèse' LPA 20 November 2002 No 232, 66.

[7] B Starck, *Essai d'une théorie générale de la responsabilité civile, considérée en sa double-fonction de garantie et de peine privée*, thesis, Paris University, 1947; S Carval, *La responsabilité civile dans sa fonction de peine privée* (Paris, LGDJ, 1995); A Jault, *La notion de peine privée* (Paris, LGDJ, 2005); Z Jacquemin, *Payer, réparer, punir. Etude des fonctions de la responsabilité contractuelle en droit français, allemand et anglais*, thesis, Paris University, 2015.

[8] Starck (n 7) 377.

individuals that the French reformers have sought to introduce the new punitive mechanism of the draft bill.

In contrast with French law, the remedies that are available for profitable wrongs in English private law have been fortified with gain-based and punitive damages. The new civil penalty of the draft bill would bring about a *rapprochement* between French and English law. However, significant differences would remain. In particular, civil penalties have the potential to be materially more severe and punitive than the equivalent remedies in England.

II. Disparate and Informal Manifestations of Punishment in French Civil Law

Although deterrence and punishment are not formal objectives in the French private law sphere, they are familiar concepts that are present in many areas.[9] The enforcement of penalty clauses, the disapplication of the remoteness rule resulting in larger awards of damages where wrongful conduct is deliberate, and the monetary sanction for non-compliance with court orders are just a few examples.

A. Punishment through Penalty Clauses

The validity of both liquidated damages clauses, which fix the amount of compensation payable for a breach of contract, and penalty clauses, which aim to deter and punish breach, is recognised in French law.[10] Penal awards were justified by the draftsmen of the 1804 Civil Code as an 'excellent expression of morality in forcing people to perform the obligations that they have undertaken'.[11] French courts have the power to reduce the amount of an agreed penalty that is 'manifestly excessive'[12] so as to curtail abuse, but without extinguishing its deterrent and punitive functions. The power is exercised only exceptionally[13] where the disproportion is extreme.[14] The agreed sum will not be capped at the amount of the actual loss[15] and commonly only the excess is removed.[16] As such, any reduction will not, as a general rule, completely deprive the award of coercive and punitive effect.

[9] Carval (n 7); Jault (n 7); Jacquemin (n 7) [258]–[348].

[10] French Civil Code 2016, Art 1231-5; Draft Parliamentary Bill 2017, Art 1284.

[11] P-A Fenet, *Recueil complet des travaux préparatoires du code civil*, vol 13 (Paris, Videcoq, 1836) 324.

[12] French Civil Code 2016, Art 1231-5.

[13] F Chabas, 'La réforme de la clause pénale' (L No 75-597 du 9 juillet 1975)' D 1976 Chron 229, 234; Y-M Laithier, 'Clause pénale et dommages et intérêts incitatifs' in C Jamin (ed), *Droit et Économie des contrats* (Paris, LGDJ, 2008) 141.

[14] G Viney and P Jourdain, *Traité de droit civil, Les effets de la responsabilité*, 3rd edn (Paris, LGDJ, 2010) [256].

[15] Com 23 January 1979, Bull civ IV no 30; Com 29 January 1991, Bull civ IV no 43.

[16] Paris 20 June 1995, D 1995.IR.187.

B. Punishment of Deliberate Wrongs: Disapplication of the Remoteness Rule and Inflated Damages Awards

The operation of the remoteness principle in contract law also reveals the latent presence of punishment in French law. Pursuant to Article 1231-3 of the Civil Code,[17] the defaulting party must compensate only those consequences of non-performance that were reasonably foreseeable when the contract was concluded. If, however, the breach is grossly negligent (*faute lourde*), deliberate or dishonest (*dol*), this rule is disapplied and liability extends to all consequences flowing from the breach. Reliance on exclusion and limitation clauses is also not permitted, and it is forbidden to seek indemnification under an insurance policy.

The approach of French courts has been to apply this exception to the remoteness principle expansively. There is no requirement to prove an intention to cause harm. It suffices for the defaulting party wilfully to refuse to perform their obligations.[18] It is therefore far from unusual for compensation to be ordered for all consequences flowing from a breach. One example is where an airline had overbooked flights and was unable to carry every passenger who had bought tickets. By reference to old Article 1150 of the Civil Code, which was the predecessor of new Article 1231-3, the airline was ordered to compensate passengers for all losses arising out of the breach and was unable to rely on a limitation clause.[19]

Additionally, in both contract and tort cases, academic writing has shown a tendency on the part of lower courts, consciously or otherwise, to vary the quantum of damages in accordance with the culpability of the defaulting party.[20] This is most evident with awards for non-pecuniary losses, which in France are compensated on a wide basis and involve putting figures to intangibles. This is possible because the assessment of damages is at the discretion of first instance and lower appeal courts. Provided that their decisions do not disclose any punitive intention, the *Cour de cassation* will not interfere. An extreme example is a hardly disguised punitive award of €100,000 that was ordered against the energy company Total to 'compensate' the non-pecuniary damage of the Bird Protection League, suffered as a result of the harm caused to sea birds by oil that spilled from the vessel, *Erika*, in 1999.[21]

[17] Its predecessor before the 2016 reforms was Art 1150 of the 1804 Civil Code.

[18] Civ 4 February 1969, D 1969.601 noted by J Mazeaud; Com 19 January 1993, JCP 1993.I.711.

[19] Paris 15 September 1992, D 1993 98 noted by P Delebecque.

[20] Viney (n 6) 66; D Fasquelle, 'L'existence de fautes lucratives en droit français' LPA 20 November 2002 No 232 27, [18]–[24]; J-S Borghetti, 'Punitive Damages in France' in H Koziol and V Wilcox (eds), *Punitive Damages: Common Law and Civil Law Perspectives* (New York, Springer, 2009) 62–66; I Vingiano-Viricel, 'La faute lucrative: une notion en construction en droit français' RTD Com 2017.19, [7]–[12].

[21] Cited by TGI Paris 16 January 2008, no 9934895010, D 2008.35q and 2681, noted by L Neyret, JCP ed G 2008.II.10053 noted by B Parance, 251; Borghetti (n 20).

C. Punishing Non-Compliance with Court Orders: The *Astreinte*

A further example of punishment is the *astreinte*.[22] This enforcement device coerces compliance with court orders[23] by applying financial pressure on the defaulting party. It takes the form of a monetary penalty payable to the victim for each additional period of default, usually in days, weeks or months, after the order is made. So as to be effective, the penalty is generally greater in amount than any advantage that the defaulting party would stand to gain from non-compliance.[24] Few fortunes are able to resist indefinitely.[25]

The *astreinte* is unequivocally punitive in nature.[26] It is granted *in terrorem* in the belief that 'it is necessary to frighten, almost terrorise, to incite performance'.[27] This is reinforced by the *astreinte* being uninsurable,[28] and by the willingness of French courts to take any abusive persistence in non-compliance and bad faith into account when assessing the final sum to be paid.[29]

III. A Step Further: The Formal and General Introduction of Punishment in Civil Law

Since punishment in the civil sphere is already known in France, a number of commentators have argued that its existence should be formalised and developed in those contexts where the existing array of civil remedies is too weak. The paradigm is profitable wrongs, against which compensatory damages and the criminal law do not adequately protect. These arguments have resulted in several proposals to introduce punitive damages, gain-based damages and, more recently, civil penalties into French law.

A. The Objection to Profitable Wrongs

A common denominator of profitable wrongs is that the 'beneficial consequences for the wrongdoer would not be undone by the simple reparation of any harm

[22] Carval (n 7) [36]–[41]; Jault (n 7); S Rowan, *Remedies for Breach of Contract: A Comparative Analysis of the Performance Interest* (Oxford, Oxford University Press, 2012) 44–45.

[23] Especially specific performance and injunctions or orders to protect the privacy rights of claimants.

[24] C Hugon, 'Regard sur le droit des voies d'exécution' RDC 2005.183, Civ 20 Oct 1959 D1959.537 noted by G Holleaux.

[25] W Jeandidier, 'L'exécution forcée des obligations contractuelles de faire' RTD civ 1976.700.

[26] Y Chartier, *La réparation du préjudice* (Dalloz Paris, 1983) [762]–[767].

[27] Hugon (n 24) 193.

[28] Civ 1, 20 March 1989, Bull civ I no 122; Viney and Jourdain (n 14) [6-5].

[29] TGI Paris 31 January 1984, D 1984.283 noted by R Lindon; Civ 1, 20 October 1959, Bull civ I no 419.

which it has caused'.[30] They occur where the wrongdoer intends that, even taking into account any liability to compensate the losses that flow from their default, they will make a profit or save money.[31] In France these wrongs have been characterised as 'morally condemnable',[32] 'morally shocking',[33] 'socially and economically harmful'[34] and 'unacceptable'.[35] Two elements are thought to be particularly objectionable. First, that one party can infringe the private rights of others, simply by paying compensation; second, that they do so intentionally with the calculation of making a gain.[36] The outrage lies in the deliberateness of the wrongdoing and the disregard of the law and the rights of others. Both are violated with impunity and to exploit a deficiency in the available remedies.

Profitable wrongs are thought to have become more problematic and frequent in the last 50 years. This has been attributed in French commentary to the development of industrial activities, mass consumption and new technologies. General factors are blamed, such as increased market competition and pressure on businesses to 'give precedence to profit over legal or moral considerations'.[37] Although no empirical study has been undertaken of the frequency and areas in which profitable wrongs occur, commentators have cited a wide variety of areas in which they are apparently recurrent. These encompass the law of privacy, defamation, unfair competition, environmental law and consumer law.[38] Commonly cited is the publication of photographs of celebrities in magazines and newspapers, intentionally infringing their rights to privacy in order to boost sales. The profit generated may well exceed the compensable loss caused to the celebrity. Another illustration is wrongfully causing pollution in the knowledge that any eventual sanction is likely to be less onerous than the cost of disposing of the pollutant lawfully.[39]

[30] G Viney, 'Exposé des motifs: Sous-titre III. De la responsabilité civile (Article 1340 a 1386)' in *Avant-projet de réforme du droit des obligations et de la prescription: Rapport remis au garde des Sceaux* (Paris, La Documentation française, 2006) 159, 168.

[31] Fasquelle (n 20) 30; G Viney, 'Projet de réforme du droit des obligations: les Éléments clés en matière de droit de la responsabilité' *Revue Lamy Droit Civil* 2005 No 22.

[32] Graziani (n 5); J Meadel, 'Faut-il introduire la faute lucrative en droit français?' LPA 17 April 2006 No 77, 6; Y-M Laithier, 'Le prononcé de dommages- intérêts punitifs en cas de faute lucrative' in N Ferrier and A Pélissier (eds), *L'entreprise face aux Évolutions de la responsabilité civile* (Paris, Economica, 2012) 117, 117–18.

[33] Fasquelle (n 20) 28; P Jourdain, 'Rapport introductif' in 'Faut-il moraliser le droit français de la réparation du dommage? (À propos des dommages et intérêts punitifs et de l'obligation de minimiser son propre dommage)' LPA 20 November 2002 No 232, 3–4; M Chagny, 'La notion de dommages et intérêts punitifs et ses repercussions sur le droit de la concurrence – Lectures plurielles de l'article 1371 de l'avant-projet de réforme du droit des obligations' JCP G 2006 I 149.

[34] Dreyer (n 5); B Javaux, 'L'amende civile, entre sanction pénale et punitive damages?' JCP Gen No 6 11 February 2019, 152.

[35] Graziani (n 5).

[36] E Dreyer, 'La sanction de la faute lucrative par l'amende civile' D 2017.1136.

[37] Fasquelle (n 20) 4.

[38] ibid 30; Jourdain (n 33) 4; Carval (n 7); Laithier (n 32) 118; M Cappelletti, 'Comparative Reflections on Punishment in Tort Law' in J-S Borghetti and S Whittaker (eds), *French Civil Liability in Comparative Perspective* (Oxford, Hart Publishing, 2019) 329.

[39] Jourdain (n 33) 4.

A well-known example is the Yves Saint Laurent case decided by the Court of Appeal of Paris in 1993.[40] Yves Saint Laurent, a luxury fashion house, launched a perfume bearing the name 'Champagne', and was promptly sued by producers of the famous sparkling wine of the same name and the Office for the Protection of Protected Appellations. It was alleged to have used the word 'Champagne' in breach of legislation that protects product names, with a view to benefiting from the global renown of the wine. The Court of Appeal found against Yves Saint Laurent and ordered that it cease using the name, withdraw the perfume from sale and pay 150,000 French Francs in compensation. However, it was a decision that had no substantive negative economic effect for Yves Saint Laurent, which boasted of having lost in the eyes of the law but won economically. Its profit was far greater than the compensation awarded and the cost of removing the perfume from the shelves. The highly publicised trial had boosted sales, which yielded 200 million French Francs in the first three months post-launch and left stocks empty anyway.

B. Punitive Damages, Gain-Based Damages or Civil Penalties as the Most Suitable Mechanism?

Commentators have therefore argued[41] that financial incentives to break the law for profit should be neutered. This is to fill a perceived moral gap and better protect private law rights that neither civil law remedies nor the criminal law adequately protect. These arguments have been met with general support from reformers but without any clear agreement on the most appropriate solution.

i. Punitive Damages

The introduction of punitive damages[42] was considered relatively recently in the 'Proposals for Reform of the Law of Obligations and the Law of Prescription', commonly referred to as the 'Catala proposals'.[43] These proposals were made

[40] Paris 15 December 1993, No 19930474.

[41] See n 7; Graziani (n 5); J Prorok, 'L'amende civile dans la réforme de la responsabilité civile. Regard critique sur la consécration d'une fonction punitive Générale' RTD Civ. 2018. 327.

[42] S Rowan, 'Comparative Observations on the Introduction of Punitive Damages in French Law' in J Cartwright, S Vogenauer and S Whittaker (eds), *Reforming the French Law of Obligations, Comparative Reflections on the Avant-projet de réforme du droit des obligations et de la prescription ('the Avant-projet Catala')* (Oxford, Hart Publishing, 2009) 325. See also the Proposal of the Beteille Law of 9 July 2010 (*proposition de loi* No 657), which provided for punitive damages to be introduced for deliberate faults with a view to gain, subject to an upper limit of twice the amount of the compensatory damages awarded.

[43] *Avant-Projet de Réforme du Droit des Obligations (Art 1101 à 1386 du Code civil) et du Droit de la Prescription (Art 2234 à 2281 du Code Civil)* under the direction of P Catala, 22 September 2005 (Documentation Française, 2006) translated into English by J Cartwright and S Whittaker: at www.justice.gouv.fr/art_pix/rapportcatatla0905-anglais.pdf, accessed 22 March 2020. See also Cartwright, Vogenauer and Whittaker (eds) (n 42).

in 2005 against the background of the bicentenary of the Civil Code. Aimed at revising the articles of the Code relating to the law of contract, civil liability, unjust enrichment and prescription, they were considered by many to be the most ambitious attempt to reform the core areas of French private law since the creation of the Civil Code in 1804.[44]

Draft Article 1371 of the Catala proposals provided that

> A person who commits a manifestly deliberate fault, and notably a fault with a view to gain, can be condemned in addition to compensatory damages to pay punitive damages, part of which the court may in its discretion allocate to the Public Treasury. A court's decision to order payment of damages of this kind must be supported with specific reasons and their amount distinguished from any other damages awarded to the victim. Punitive damages may not be the object of insurance.

The scope of the draft article was wide, encompassing contract as well as tort, going beyond profitable wrongs and applying regardless of the motives of the defaulting party. All 'manifestly deliberate faults', of which 'fault with a view to gain' was just one example, would have sounded in punitive damages. The remedy would also have been available where the wrongdoer acted not for profit but maliciously.[45]

Article 1371 generated considerable interest and extensive comment. Reactions were mixed. Many endorsed the proposed introduction of punitive damages,[46] but others were more circumspect. A recurrent concern was that there would be undeserved windfalls and the seminal principle of civil liability, that the injured party must be compensated not only fully but also commensurately with their loss (*principe de la réparation intégrale*), would be infringed.[47] There were also fears of a litigation boom, as well as of arbitrariness and excess in the quantum of damages awards similar to the practice in the United States.[48] Other criticisms included the lack of guidance as to the circumstances in which part of the punitive award should be directed to the state and in what proportion.[49]

[44] S Vogenauer, 'The Avant-projet de réforme: An Overview' in Cartwright, Vogenauer and Whittaker (eds) (n 42) 3.

[45] In this way, avoiding a criticism made by English commentators of Lord Devlin's second category in *Rookes v Barnard* [1964] AC 1129 (HL) that it does not allow punitive damages to be awarded where the wrongdoer acts not for profit but maliciously: *Broome v Cassell* [1972] AC 1027 (HL) 1088 per Lord Reid, who thought that the distinction between greed and malice could be justified only by reference to authority. See also Lord Nicholls in *Kuddus v Chief Constable of Leicestershire Constabulary* [2001] UKHL 29, [2002] 2 AC 122 [67].

[46] Borghetti (n 20).

[47] M Behar-Touchais, 'L'amende civile est-elle un substitute satisfaisant a l'absence de dommages et interest punitifs?' LPA 2002, 36; Borghetti (n 20) [47]; Prorok (n 41).

[48] S Carval 'L'amende civile' in 'Avant-projet de loi portant reforme de la responsabilite civile, Observations et propositions de modifications' JCP suppl 25 July 2016 42, [7]; Javaux (n 34); Borghetti (n 20) citing L Engel, 'Vers une nouvelle approche de la responsabilité. Le droit français face à la dérive américaine' *Esprit* 1993.

[49] 'Rapport du groupe de travail de la Cour de cassation sur l'avant-projet de réforme du droit des obligations et de la prescription' 15 June 2007. See also S Rowan, 'Reflections on the Introduction of Punitive Damages for Breach of Contract' (2010) 30 *OJLS* 495.

ii. Gain-Based Damages

Whilst the Catala proposals were never enacted, Article 1371 proved to be the trigger for wider discussion and analysis of how best to tackle profitable wrongs. The criticisms made of punitive damages led to gain-based damages being proposed as an alternative by a competing reform project led by a group of academic lawyers. In their Article 120, they proposed that 'in case of deliberate breach, the injured promisee may be awarded [instead of compensatory damages] all or some of the profit resulting from the breach'.[50]

This was met with broad approbation[51] as a less drastic and more proportionate solution, but there were also concerns that it would be too weak. As it is limited to gains accruing from the wrongful conduct, a party tempted to commit a profitable wrong might form the view that they have little to lose. The punitive and deterrent effect at the core of punitive damages would be removed.[52]

iii. The Latest Proposal: Civil Penalties

The mechanism proposed by the most recent (and likely to be enacted) reform project is the civil penalty (*amende civile*). This is seen by the draftsmen as a middle ground between punitive damages and gain-based damages.[53] Draft Article 1266-1 provides:

> In extra-contractual matters, where the author of the harm has deliberately committed a fault with a view to gain or making a saving, a court may, at the request of the victim or the *ministère public* (the state) and by specially reasoned decision, order payment of a civil penalty.
>
> This penalty is proportionate to the seriousness of the fault, the financial means of the wrongdoer, and the profit gained from the wrongful conduct.
>
> The penalty cannot be more than tenfold the amount of the profit gained.
>
> If the wrongdoer is a corporation, the penalty can be up to 5% of the amount of the highest turnover before tax made in France in the tax years since the year preceding that when the fault was committed.
>
> This penalty is directed to the financing of a compensation fund related to the nature of the harm suffered or, failing this, to the public treasury.
>
> It is not insurable.

Civil penalties already exist in various areas of French law.[54] They are intended to deter and punish acts that are reprehensible but not sufficiently serious to justify

[50] Terré Reform Project, Art 120.

[51] R Mesa, 'L'opportune consécration d'un principe de restitution intégrale des profits illicites comme sanction des fautes lucrative' D 2012.2754; Carval (n 7). See also Z Jacquemin, 'Pour une reconnaissance de la spécificité contractuelle dans les effets de la responsabilité' RDC 2016.808; Laithier (n 13); Laithier (n 32).

[52] Prorok (n 41).

[53] Urvoas (n 3).

[54] Behar-Touchais (n 47); Jault (n 7) [402]; Borghetti (n 20) [18]–[21].

criminal liability. This includes the breach by state officials of some of their public duties;[55] bringing court proceedings abusively;[56] demolishing a building without the requisite permission;[57] using a building for commercial purposes where only residential occupation is permitted;[58] and restrictive competitive practices.[59] Article 1266-1 would make these penalties generally applicable in the law of tort for profitable wrongs.

Civil penalties are proposed as a compromise between punitive and gain-based damages.[60] On the one hand, they are clearly deterrent and punitive in nature and a more potent remedy than gain-based damages. This is most evident in the quantum of the award being dependent on the gravity of the fault and potentially much higher than the profit made from the wrong, and indeed very high in absolute terms.[61] It is also obvious from the preclusion in Article 1266-1 of insurance against the risk of punitive awards so to uphold their punitive and deterrent effects.

On the other hand, civil penalties are better suited to the legal tradition of French law, and as such avoid some of the criticisms made of punitive damages.[62] Since they would be paid to a designated fund set up to counteract at a general level the negative consequences of the wrong, they would not benefit the victims directly. The cardinal principle that the victim should not be awarded more than compensation would therefore be preserved.[63] This is seen to be consistent with the main purpose of civil liability, which is the reparation of wrongs.[64]

IV. Remedies for Profitable Wrongs in English and French Civil Law

In contrast with France, English law has long grappled with the problem of profitable wrongs. It has also shown similar hesitation as to whether punitive or gain-based damages are the most suitable response.

A. Tackling Profitable Wrongs in English Tort Law

Whilst the principal purpose of damages in English civil law is to compensate loss, in certain narrowly drawn circumstances, awards that are punitive and deterrent in

[55] French Civil Code, Art 50.

[56] New Code of Civil Procedure, Art 32-1.

[57] Urban Code, Arts L430-2 and L430-9.

[58] Construction and Habitation Code, Arts L631-7 and L651-2. See also Arts 395, 412, 413 of the Civil Code, which sanction the avoidance of tutorship duties; or Art 207 of the New Code of Civil Procedure, which sanctions the avoidance of duties owed by witnesses at trials.

[59] Code of Commerce, Arts L442-1–L442-8.

[60] Urvoas (n 3).

[61] Dreyer (n 5); Prorok (n 41).

[62] Carvl (n 48); Urvoas (n 2).

[63] Borghetti (n 20) [50]; Dreyer (n 5) [13]; Prorok (n 41); Graziani (n 5); Cappelletti (n 38).

[64] Borghetti (n 20) [47]; Urvoas (n 3); Prorok (n 41); Graziani (n 5).

nature may be ordered in tort law.[65] The starting point is the classic speech of Lord Devlin in *Rookes v Barnard*,[66] in which awards of punitive damages were held to be restricted to three situations: first, where there is 'oppressive or unconstitutional action by the servants of the government', which covers the abuse of executive power; second, where the 'defendant's conduct has been calculated by him to make a profit for himself which may well exceed the compensation payable';[67] and, third, where expressly authorised by statute.[68]

Lord Devlin's second category is in substance similar to the 'fault with a view to gain or making a saving' in draft Article 1266-1. It targets the wrongdoer who 'with a cynical disregard for a plaintiff's rights has calculated that the money to be made out of his wrongdoing will probably exceed the damages at risk'.[69] The same kind of conduct is therefore considered as particularly reprehensible and deserving of punishment in both France and England. No tolerance is shown towards a person who cynically disregards the victim's rights for profit. Such behaviour brings the law into disrepute and should be deterred.

In practice, and contrary to conventional wisdom,[70] the most common type of case in which punitive damages are awarded under Lord Devlin's second category involves claims for wrongful eviction,[71] while actions in defamation and privacy invasion do not constitute an important source of punitive damages awards under the second category (or otherwise).[72] This is notable from a comparative perspective. No mention is made in the French academic literature of profitable wrongs committed by landlords wrongfully harassing and/or evicting their tenants. Indeed, the most commonly cited example is the breach of 'personality' and privacy rights for gain.

Explanations offered by commentators in England for the significance of punitive damages in landlord and tenant cases include that an important function of English tort law is to protect property interests; and that police and local authorities may be reluctant to prosecute landlords who wrongfully evict tenants, leaving a lacuna in the criminal law that effectively forces claimants to seek private law redress.[73] It may be that in France the state is more willing to protect tenants than in England, although it is hard to say whether this is indeed the case. Article 226-4 of the Penal Code enables a landlord who enters the rented property without the permission of the tenant to be fined up to €15,000 and imprisoned for up to one year. Civil liability arises under Article 1719, para 3 of the Civil Code, which

[65] For arguments that they should be available for equitable wrongs, see A Burrows, *Remedies for Torts, Breach of Contract, and Equitable Wrongs*, 4th edn (Oxford, Oxford University Press, 2019) 525 ff.

[66] *Rookes v Barnard* [1964] AC 1129 (HL) 1226–27.

[67] ibid 1226.

[68] ibid 1225.

[69] ibid 1227.

[70] See J Goudkamp and E Katsampouka, 'An Empirical Study of Punitive Damages' (2018) 38 *OJLS* 90.

[71] ibid 112–13; for a well-known example, see *Drane v Evangelou* [1978] 1 WLR 455 (CA).

[72] Goudkamp and Katsampouka (n 70) 111–12.

[73] ibid, although there are criminal sanctions against landlords for wrongful eviction under the Protection from Eviction Act 1977 (UK) (as amended by the Housing Act 1988 (UK)).

protects the right of tenants to peaceful enjoyment of the rented property, and Article 9 of the Code, which protects a right to private life.[74]

Although punitive damages have long been available in England,[75] they have nonetheless been controversial, generating similar discussions to those that have occurred in France. They have been described as anomalous,[76] as confusing the role of the civil and criminal law, and (famously) as 'out of place, irregular …, exceptional, unjust, unscientific, not to say absurd and ridiculous when classed among civil remedies, … a monstrous heresy, … an unhealthy excrescence, deforming the symmetry of the body of the law'.[77] It has been argued that gain-based damages would therefore be more acceptable in a civil law context.

At present, the gain-based remedy of an account of profits is only available for torts that involve infringements of intellectual property rights, for instance the infringement of patents, copyrights, trademarks and passing off.[78] Profitable wrongs are mainly tackled through punitive damages. Yet Harvey McGregor, for instance, has argued (when editor of *McGregor on Damages*) that the real purpose of Lord Devlin's second category is not to punish the wrongdoer but to prevent their unjust enrichment.[79] He described punitive damages as a 'somewhat makeshift and arbitrary' method of achieving this end, although 'it may be that the emergence of restitutionary damages will take away from Lord Devlin's second category and render it unnecessary'.[80] In the same vein, Lord Scott in *Kuddus v Chief Constable of Leicestershire Constabulary*[81] suggested that restitutionary damages could be a substitute for Lord Devlin's second category.[82]

Others have drawn a clear distinction between the aims of punitive and gain-based damages. While punitive damages are capable of stripping the wrongdoer of wrongfully obtained profits, this is ancillary to their intended objectives of punishment and deterrence. As Lord Diplock in *Broome v Cassell*[83] put it, '[the second category] may be a blunt instrument to prevent unjust enrichment by unlawful acts … It is only if there is a prospect that the damages may exceed the defendant's gain that the social purpose of this category is achieved – to teach a wrong-doer that tort does not pay'.[84] The view that punitive damages are not simply designed

[74] Civ 3, 25 feb 2004, Bull civ III no 41; D 2004.1631 noted by Caron.

[75] Since the 1760s: see, for their historical origins, J Edelman (ed), *McGregor on Damages*, 20th edn (London, Sweet & Maxwell, 2017) para 13-002.

[76] *Rookes* (n 66) 1221 (Lord Devlin).

[77] *Fay v Parker* 53 NH 342, 382 (1873) (Foster J).

[78] Burrows (n 65) 338–52.

[79] H McGregor, *McGregor on Damages*, 17th edn (London, Sweet & Maxwell, 2003) paras 11-028 and 11-046.

[80] ibid para 11-046; in the new edition now edited by James Edelman (n 75), it is argued that the rationale for Lord Devlin's second category is punishment or deterrence. Punitive damages are not simply designed to operate as an indirect method for extracting profits tortiously obtained by the defendant: paras 13-048–13-051.

[81] *Kuddus v Chief Constable of Leicestershire Constabulary* [2001] UKHL 29, [2002] 2 AC 122.

[82] ibid [109].

[83] *Broome v Cassell* [1972] AC 1027 (HL).

[84] ibid 1130.

to serve as an indirect means for stripping profits seems to have been accepted in recent cases.[85]

B. Tackling Profitable Wrongs in English Contract Law

The position in English contract law is quite different. Punitive awards are not available for breach of contract. This rule has been attributed to the decision in *Addis v Gramophone Company Limited*.[86] Common objections to the awarding of punitive damages for breach of contract are that it would impair commercial predictability and the concept of punishment is not easily applicable in the context of private agreements in which rights and duties are allocated by mutual consent.[87]

The unavailability of punitive damages in contract law is consistent with the relatively liberal approach that English courts have historically adopted to contractual breach and the motives of the defaulting party, including whether they act deliberately, cynically or in bad faith.[88] Contract law has no regard to blame. There is no general duty to behave honestly and in good faith. As Lord Hoffmann made clear in *Cooperative Insurance Society Ltd v Argyll Stores (Holdings) Ltd*,[89] 'the purpose of the law of contract is not to punish wrongdoing'.[90]

Profitable breaches of contract are in exceptional circumstances met with the gain-based remedy of an account of profits. In *Attorney-General v Blake*,[91] a majority of the House of Lords held that an account of profits could be awarded for a breach of contract where other remedies are inadequate and the injured party has a legitimate interest in depriving the defaulting party of their profit. The potential for gain-based awards to deter and punish has, however, been weakened by

[85] See the new edition of *McGregor* (n 75) citing Geraldine Andrews QC in *Ramzan v Brookwide Ltd* [2010] EWHC 2453 (Ch), [2011] 2 All ER 38. For a recent discussion of these issues, see J Goudkamp, 'Exemplary Damages' in G Virgo and S Worthington (eds), *Commercial Remedies: Resolving Uncertainties* (Cambridge, Cambridge University Press, 2017) 318; in the context of Australian consumer law, see E Bant and J Paterson, 'Should Specifically Deterrent or Punitive Remedies Be Made Available to Victims of Misleading Conduct under the Australian Consumer Law?' (2019) 25 *Torts Law Journal* 99.

[86] *Addis v Gramophone Company Limited* [1909] AC 488 (HL). But see Goudkamp (n 85) on *Addis v Gramophone*.

[87] For a full discussion of the objections to punitive awards for breach of contract and their counter-arguments, see N McBride, 'A Case for Awarding Punitive Damages in Response to Deliberate Breaches of Contract' (1995) 24 *Anglo-American Law Review* 369; J Edelman, 'Exemplary Damages for Breach of Contract' (2001) 117 *LQR* 539; E McKendrick, 'Breach of Contract, Restitution for Wrongs and Punishment' in A Burrows and E Peel (eds), *Commercial Remedies: Current Issues and Problems* (Oxford, Oxford University Press, 2003) 93; A Tettenborn, 'Punitive Damages – A View from England' (2004) 41 *San Diego Law Review* 1551; R Cunnington, 'Should Punitive Damages be Part of the Judicial Arsenal in Contract Cases?' (2006) 26 *Legal Studies* 369; J Edelman, 'In Defence of Exemplary Damages' in CEF Rickett (ed), *Justifying Private Law Remedies* (Oxford, Hart Publishing, 2008) 225; Rowan (n 49); Goudkamp (n 85).

[88] Rowan (n 49).

[89] *Cooperative Insurance Society Ltd v Argyll Stores (Holdings) Ltd* [1998] AC 1 (HL).

[90] ibid 15.

[91] *Attorney-General v Blake* [2001] 1 AC 268 (HL).

their exceptionality. While deterrence was central to *Blake*, the House of Lords was unequivocal that an account for profits should be ordered only in the narrowest of circumstances. It has therefore been rare for a defaulting party to be deprived of all the profits arising from their contractual default, at least in the context of commercial disputes.[92] The courts have been more willing to make awards of partial disgorgement,[93] but these have been analysed as compensatory rather than gain-based or punitive.[94]

Following the recognition in *Attorney-General v Blake* of a gain-based remedy in a contractual context, a growing number of commentators have argued that the remedial regime for breach of contract should be further reinforced by the introduction of punitive damages. The recognition in Canada that punitive damages can be available in contract claims has reinforced the view that the rule could be ripe for reconsideration.[95] Nevertheless, the courts have thus far been unmoved.[96]

The confinement in England of punitive awards to tort law matches Article 1266-1, which applies to tort but not contract law.[97] However, the rationale is different. The reasons that are cited in France include that parties can if they wish elect to have a deterrent and punitive remedy by inserting a penalty clause into their contract; and the risk that civil penalties in a contractual context may be too radical and controversial, and could deter international businesses from opting for French law as their governing law in cross-border contracts.[98] In other words, the parties are able to provide for punishment if they think it desirable, something that is not possible under English law due to the rule that penalty clauses are unenforceable.

This restriction on the scope of Article 1266-1 is surprising given that the mechanisms proposed in the Catala and Terré projects and also in an earlier draft of Article 1266-1 were intended to apply in contract law. Morally reprehensible breaches that are committed with a view to making a gain or making a saving are not unusual in a contractual context, as illustrated for instance by a series of Canadian cases on insurance companies' withholding indemnification so as to coerce the insureds into lower settlements.[99] It is all the more surprising that, as explained earlier, deterrence and punishment are already present in French

[92] eg *Esso Petroleum Co Ltd v Niad Ltd* [2001] EWHC Ch 458.

[93] eg *Experience Hendrix LLC v PPX Enterprises Inc* [2003] EWCA Civ 323, [2003] 1 All ER (Comm) 830.

[94] *Morris Garner v One Step (Support) Ltd* [2018] UKSC 20, [2019] AC 649.

[95] eg *Royal Bank of Canada v W Got Associates Electrical Ltd* [1999] 3 SCR 408; *Whiten v Pilot Insurance Co* 2002 SCC 18, [2002] 1 SCR 595; *Fidler v Sun Life Assurance Co of Canada* 2006 SCC 30, [2006] 2 SCR 3.

[96] Rowan (n 49).

[97] In an earlier published version of Art 1266-1, its scope was broader and included contract law: see Catala (n 43).

[98] S Carval, 'Le projet de réforme de la responsabilité civile', JCP 2017.401; J-S Borghetti, 'Un pas de plus vers la réforme de la responsabilité civile: présentation du projet de réforme rendu public le 13 mars 2017' D 2017 770; T d'Alès et L Terdjman, 'L'introduction envisagée de mécanismes répressifs dans le droit de la responsabilité civile: le Rubicon sera-t-il franchi ?' AJ Contrat 2017.69.

[99] See n 95.

contract law, for example in the disapplication of the remoteness rule for deliberate breaches and the enforcement of penalty clauses.[100] It is also evident in the central importance of specific performance, which is meant to deter breach and can seem almost punitive in some circumstances due to there being very few restrictions on the remedy.[101]

Only the pre-contractual period, which is governed by tort law principles, will be within the scope of Article 1266-1. Contractual negotiations are already given strong protection in French law. Article 1112 of the Civil Code provides that negotiations must satisfy the requirements of good faith, and Article 1112-1 imposes a general duty to provide information (*devoir d'information*). A party who does not disclose information with a view to gain or making a saving will therefore be faced not only with the threat of compensatory liability, but also with exposure to liability for a civil penalty.[102]

V. The Degree of Punishment in English and French Civil Law

The enactment of draft Article 1266-1 would therefore in many ways align French law more closely with English law and bring about a *rapprochement* between the two regimes. As in English law, French law would tackle profitable wrongs with a punitive sanction that would apply in tortious situations only. Nevertheless, there would remain significant differences, for example as to the beneficiary of the penalty and the level of the penal award. The strong public dimension of the proposed civil penalties is likely to cause greater stigma, as well as potentially being more severe, than any English law remedies.

A. The Beneficiary of the Punitive Sanction

An intriguing feature of Article 1266-1 is the diversion of the penalty to a compensation fund whose purpose it is to counteract the negative consequences of the wrongful conduct. Where no relevant fund exists, the penalty will be paid to the state. In contrast with England, it cannot be paid to the victim. This feature has been welcomed by many French commentators as avoiding an undesirable windfall for the victim. Where the money is paid into a compensation fund, it is put to the honourable use of repairing the harm caused. It promotes the value of 'social solidarity'.[103] This is particularly easy to imagine in respect of wrongs that cause

[100] Rowan (n 49).
[101] Rowan (n 22). New Art 1221 has introduced 'manifest proportionality' as a limitation of the remedy, but commentators have argued that the courts are unlikely to feel restrained by it.
[102] Prorok (n 41).
[103] Cappelletti (n 38).

environmental harm, which in the prevailing political climate of growing environmental awareness and concern has obvious attractions.

One significant difficulty with directing the penalty to a fund, or the state if no such fund exists, is that the victim will have no financial incentive to seek the penalty. Few would bring a claim in the knowledge that they cannot benefit thereby. Indeed, to claim this form of relief might even be regarded as burdensome and likely to increase legal fees, which will hardly appeal to prospective claimants. The current scheme is also likely to lead to the courts' being reluctant to inflate, as they currently do, the compensatory award for non-pecuniary loss to avoid the risk that the wrongdoer is punished twice. This could dilute still further the incentive of the victim to claim the relief.[104] Another potential problem is that the scheme could be vulnerable to abuse in settlement negotiations. The victim could seek to obtain an inflated amount of compensatory damages in exchange for a promise not to seek a civil penalty, thereby preventing the compensation fund or the state from receiving the award.[105] For these reasons, many commentators have argued that the court should also have been given the power to order civil penalties of its own motion, so as to improve the efficiency of the mechanism.[106]

Concern about creating such a tactical incentive was one of the reasons cited by the English Law Commission for refusing to recommend that part of punitive awards should be allocated to a person other than the victim.[107] Unlike in Article 1266-1, there is no jurisdiction in England for part of a punitive award made in civil litigation to be allocated to a compensation fund or the state. The scheme that was ultimately rejected by the Law Commission involved 33 per cent of the total punitive award's being payable to the state or a public fund. As well as the risk of abuse in settlement negotiations, the cost of administering and enforcing the scheme was thought to be disproportionate to the likely amount of punitive damages in issue.[108]

In an effort to address this problem, draft Article 1266-1 provides that the *ministère public* (the state) can claim the penalty where the victim does not. This would extend the role of the *ministère public* as the guardian of the public interest beyond its current remit of prosecuting crimes for the benefit of society into the civil sphere. Punishment in tort law would have a hybrid nature. It would be triggered by the breach of a private duty but would nevertheless see the state playing an important role. This would contrast with punishment in English tort, which is concerned only with protecting private rights and involves one individual claiming and obtaining relief from another.

[104] Dreyer (n 5) [14].
[105] Javaux (n 34).
[106] As was the case in a previous version of the draft bill.
[107] Law Commission, *Aggravated, Exemplary and Restitutionary Damages* (Law Com No 247, HMSO, 1997) pt V, para 1.150 et seq.
[108] ibid para 1.158.

B. The Level of the Penal Award

Draft Article 1266-1 also contains guidance on quantifying civil penalties. An award should be proportionate to the seriousness of the fault, the financial means of the wrongdoer and the profit gained from the wrongful conduct. These criteria resemble those in England for assessing punitive damages. English courts take into account, amongst other things, the gravity of the wrongdoer's conduct, their wealth,[109] the conduct of the parties up to the time of judgment and in particular whether the wrongdoer has expressed regret,[110] the level of compensation awarded and the extent to which that award already incidentally punishes and deters the wrong, and any criminal penalties already imposed.[111]

Where the principles in England and France differ significantly is in the severity of the penalty. In English law, while the amount of a punitive award should reflect the seriousness of the wrongdoer's conduct, it should nevertheless be moderate. Any penalty must be the minimum necessary to achieve the dual purposes of the remedy, namely punishment and deterrence. In other words, courts should keep a sense of proportionality.[112] An oft-cited instance of the courts' applying the principle of proportionality is the defamation case *John v MGN*,[113] in which the Court of Appeal substituted the jury's punitive damages award of £275,000 with the sum of £50,000. Sir Thomas Bingham MR regarded the award made by the jury as 'manifestly excessive' and 'well beyond the minimum sum needed' to punish the newspaper and deter it and others from similar behaviour.[114]

It has been shown that, in practice, punitive awards are indeed modest, or at least 'anything but excessive',[115] and there has been considerable uniformity in their amounts. An empirical study by James Goudkamp and Eleni Katsampouka, which examines every decision in which punitive damages were sought between 1 January 2000 and 31 December 2015, shows that, in relation to Lord Devlin's second category, the mean and median awards were £12,082 and £5,158 respectively, with most punitive awards (whether falling within Lord Devlin's first or second category) between £588 and £33,851. In not a single claim was the amount awarded even close to a seven-digit figure.

[109] *Broome* (n 83) 1081. The empirical study of Goudkamp and Katsampouka (n 70) 116–17 suggests that the courts apply this principle.

[110] *Rookes* (n 66) 1226–27 (Lord Devlin); *Broome* (n 83) 1071.

[111] *Rookes* (n 66) 1228 (Lord Devlin); see also the empirical study of Goudkamp and Katsampouka (n 70) 117–18, which concludes that in practice it 'appears that there is a loose positive relationship between the size of punitive damages awards on the one hand and the quantum of both aggravated damages and compensatory damages awards on the other. Accordingly, the size of the loss suffered by the claimant seems to affect the size of punitive damages awards.'

[112] *Broome* (n 83) 1081, where Lord Hailsham said that juries should be 'fully aware of the danger of an excessive award'.

[113] *John v MGN* [1997] QB 586 (CA).

[114] ibid 626.

[115] Goudkamp (n 85) 114–15.

These awards would probably seem toothless to the authors of the draft bill. While paragraph 2 of draft Article 1266-1 requires the court to assess the quantum of civil penalties in a proportionate manner, unlike in England, paragraph 3 gives considerable discretion to the court by setting the limit on the amount that can be awarded very high, at 10 times the profit resulting from the wrong.[116] In some respects this seems incoherent. If paragraph 2 requires the penalty to be proportionate to the profit resulting from the wrong, it seems odd that under paragraph 3 the profit made can be multiplied so aggressively when calculating the award. Regardless, what is clear is that the amount can be high. This has been met with ire from some commentators, who have described it as 'unacceptable' and 'verging on extravagance'.[117]

That the punishment can be severe[118] is all the more evident in paragraph 4 of Article 1266-1. This provides that where the wrongdoer is a company, the ceiling can be up to 5 per cent of its yearly turnover in France.[119] It appears that the potentially higher limit is intended to reinforce the punitive function of civil penalties; companies generally have greater financial means than individuals and it is thought appropriate to hit them harder.[120] This, however, has been criticised by some academic commentators and has been characterised as 'repressively delirious' by one.[121] It is certainly easy to see how it could lead to extreme results. Staying with the earlier example of Total, its turnover in France in 2017/2018 was US$47.716 billion[122] and 5 per cent of this amount would lead to a civil penalty of US$2.385 billion. This is in stark contrast with the modest amounts awarded in England.

The potential extreme severity of civil penalties has led many commentators to argue that some of the safeguards found in the criminal law should be applied in this context.[123] In particular, it has been noted that Article 1266-1 does not comply with the 'principle of legality of crimes and sanctions' (*principe de légalité des délits et des peines*), which is cardinal in French criminal law and provides that, without a basis in a legal text, there can be no punishment. The main problem with Article 1266-1 is that it contains no clear and precise definition of 'fault with a view to gain or making a saving', leading to calls to provide such a definition.[124]

[116] Borghetti (n 20) [49]; Dreyer (n 5) [7].
[117] Dreyer (n 5) [11].
[118] ibid [8]; Graziani (n 5).
[119] In the previous draft of the bill, the ceiling was 10% of its yearly global turnover!
[120] Borghetti (n 20) [49].
[121] Dreyer (n 5) [9].
[122] Total, Document de Référence 2018 at www.total.com/sites/default/files/atoms/files/ddr2018-fr.pdf accessed 22 March 2020.
[123] A criticism that has also been made in English law: *Broome* (n 83) 1087 (Lord Reid); Burrows (n 65) 374–78.
[124] C Jauffret-Spinosi, 'Les dommages-intérêts punitifs dans les systèmes de droit étrangers' LPA 20 Nov 2002, 8; Behar-Touchais (n 47) 41–42; Carval (n 48) [11]–[17]; Dreyer (n 5) [8]–[11]; Prorok (n 41).

C. Insurance

Article 1266-1, paragraph 5 of the draft bill would forbid insurance against the risk of being ordered to pay civil penalties. The justification is that if liability to pay a civil penalty were an insurable risk, the financial impact on the wrongdoer would be reduced. This would correspondingly dilute its retributive and deterrent effects.

In this respect, Article 1266-1 diverges from English law, which allows insurance against punitive damages awards. In *Lancashire County Council v Municipal Insurance Ltd*,[125] Simon Brown LJ said that punitive damages were still 'likely to have punitive effect'[126] despite their being insurable. A wrongdoer who makes an insurance claim in respect of liability to pay a punitive award might subsequently face higher premiums and possibly even difficulties renewing cover.[127]

This principle seems well accepted in England. In its report on *Aggravated, Exemplary and Restitutionary Damages*,[128] the Law Commission recommended that punitive damages should be insurable. It cited four main reasons: the interest in punishing and deterring the wrongdoer and appeasing the victim is futile if the wrongdoer cannot pay;[129] the insurance industry, in controlling the availability and cost of insurance, can exert significant pressure on present and future insureds;[130] the court and the legislature should not lightly interfere with commercial agreements;[131] forbidding insurance would result in conflict between the insurer and the wrongdoing insured, who would seek to maximise the size of any compensatory award if they could achieve a commensurate diminution in any punitive award, whereas the insurer would prefer the opposite outcome.[132]

These divergences across the Channel further illustrate that the new civil penalty in France could be materially more severe than punitive damages under English law. Civil penalties are clearly intended to land a direct blow on the wrongdoer's finances. Unless they are insolvent, they will always have to pay something, however moderate. Unlike in England, it also shows a preference for the court rather than the insurance industry to decide the extent of the punishment.

VI. Conclusion

The draft bill contemplates that civil penalties will become a formal weapon to deter and punish tortious wrongdoing that is committed with a view to making a

[125] *Lancashire County Council v Municipal Mutual Insurance Ltd* [1996] 3 WLR 493 (CA).
[126] ibid 503–04.
[127] ibid.
[128] Law Commission (n 107).
[129] ibid para 1.237.
[130] ibid para 1.238.
[131] ibid paras 1.242–1.246.
[132] ibid para 1.248.

gain or a saving. Since the effects of such wrongs are not neutralised by the existing arsenal of remedies, additional weaponry is needed. If enacted, Article 1266-1 would also bring French law closer to English law. Both jurisdictions would sanction profitable wrongs through punishment.

There is, however, a real risk that Article 1266-1 will not appear in the Civil Code, at least in its current form. The lack of definition of 'fault with a view to gain or making a saving', as well as the severity and potential extremity of the penalty, will no doubt attract criticism when considered by Parliament. The compromise solution of gain-based damages to target profitable wrongs might in the end be more attractive. Yet civil penalties and gain-based damages should not be seen as interchangeable, as they have different rationales and different effects. While gain-based damages deprive the wrongdoer of their ill-gotten profits and punish them indirectly, civil penalties are a much stronger remedy and would reinforce the law more significantly.

An alternative solution would be for the draftsmen to rework Article 1266-1. Its perceived failings could be addressed by defining 'fault with a view to gain or making a saving', providing more guidance as to how the quantum of civil penalties should be assessed and reducing the maximum penalty. Whilst it is doubtful that punitive damages awards that are as modest as those in English law would be adopted as a model because they are likely to be perceived as lacking teeth, more moderate penalties would increase the prospect of draft Article 1266-1 obtaining legislative approval.

4

Privacy, Punishment and Private Law

ANDREW ROBERTS AND MEGAN RICHARDSON

I. Introduction

Historically, privacy protection in Anglo-Australian law has been thought of as a subject of private law and (largely) private interests without much reference to ideas about punishment, for a range of policy, legal and practical reasons. However, the reasons seem less convincing in the current environment of radical transparency, extreme speech and seriously harmful conduct affecting not just certain individuals and groups but the public at large. Indeed, there are plenty of 'privacy' cases where public interests are prominent alongside private interests, and these are dealt with under private law or under the more public-facing provisions of a data protection regime (or under both together). In this chapter we argue that, in this changing environment, a reassessment is needed of the normative basis of the power to punish in private law, and the role that this power ought to play in securing conditions of privacy.

While private law has developed various causes of action for breach of privacy, the criminal law has seldom used the concept of privacy in defining its proscriptions. There is no recognised category of 'privacy crimes'. But new technologies are posing ever more serious threats to our privacy. On the one hand, this has led to a 'ramping up' of privacy law protections, including a tort of misuse of private information recognised by UK courts (and explicit reliance on a broadly construed doctrine of breach of confidence for the protection of privacy in Australia).[1] At the same time, there is a growing appreciation that privacy is a collective and social good, not only an individual good, and that some breaches of privacy affect large numbers of people and constitute serious public harms. In this chapter we suggest that as the law of privacy generally tilts more towards the public interest side, greater thought should be given to the benefits of including a punitive element in privacy cases that still ostensibly fit within the rubric of private law (or a data protection regime, or both together) but involve significant public harms.

[1] M Richardson, M Neave and M Rivette, 'Invasion of Privacy and Recovery for Distress' in JNE Varuhas and NA Moreham (eds), *Remedies for Breach of Privacy* (Oxford, Hart Publishing, 2018) 165.

However, there is still a need to reconcile this position with the basic tenet of criminal law that that law, along with all its traditional protections, should be employed as the primary means of dealing with cases of egregiously wrongful conduct that result in serious harm.[2] Specifically, the question we address concerns the role that private law ought to play in punishing breaches of privacy.

In section II of the chapter, we consider when the state is justified in punishing. As the criminal law provides the primary means of doing so, we look to theories of criminalisation to identify the relevant justificatory grounds, *viz* wrongful conduct that causes serious harm in respect of which there is some public interest. In section III, we consider how these conditions ought to be understood in the context with which this chapter is concerned (breaches of privacy). The normative foundation of our analysis is republican liberalism.[3] In particular, we posit that the overriding aim of a republican-liberal state (and the legal norms that it generates) should be to provide conditions in which every individual is able to pursue their own conception of the good life – and, further, that securing such conditions is a necessarily cooperative endeavour, requiring broad political participation. We argue that the concepts of harm, wrongdoing and public interest that provide the justificatory basis for punishing breaches of privacy need to be understood in light of these core normative ideas. In section IV, we consider when private law might be justified on this reasoning. In brief, we identify four broad circumstances – first, where there are blind spots in the criminal law, with the result that its proscriptions are framed in ways that fail to address serious breaches of privacy; second, where the criminal law has not yet responded to an emerging privacy problem; third, to punish breaches of privacy that warrant public condemnation but not the degree of disapprobation represented by a criminal conviction; fourth, to ensure conduct that has been criminalised is punished where the institutions of the state are either indifferent to the wrongdoing or lack the resources to respond to it.

II. Why Punish?

Any serious discussion of punishment for breach of privacy in private law needs to be prefaced with discussion of the prior question of what justifies state-imposed punishment generally. Of course, the primary means by which the state imposes punishment is the criminal law. We might reasonably suppose, therefore, that theories of criminalisation will furnish us with a set of general principles that might

[2] See P Alldridge, 'Attempted Murder of the Soul: Blackmail, Privacy and Secrets' (1993) 13 *OJLS* 368, who suggests that blackmail ought to be regarded as a crime against privacy rather than property. He also suggests that there is a range of offences that could be grouped together as 'offences against privacy'; P Alldridge, *Relocating Criminal Law* (Dartmouth, Ashgate, 2000).

[3] On liberal republicanism, see generally: CR Sunstein, 'Beyond the Republican Revival' (1988) 97 *Yale Law Journal* 1539; CE Baker, 'Republican Liberalism: Liberal Rights and Republican Politics' (1989) 41 *Florida Law Review* 491; R Dagger, *Civic Virtues: Rights, Citizenship, and Republican Liberalism* (Oxford, Oxford University Press, 1997).

usefully guide our thinking on the question of the circumstances in which punishment for breaches of privacy might be justified, before moving on to consider the question of when it might be appropriate to use private law to punish those who are involved in such conduct. Moreover, that these principles, forming part of the body of law that regulates the life of the community, ought to be shaped by a coherent set of norms understood as serving certain fundamental values. The requirements of coherence and consistency do not mean that the punishment imposed in criminal and private law must take the same form. But it must be possible, at some level of abstraction, to point to a set of norms that provide the justificatory basis for the infliction of any form of punishment, including within criminal law or within private law. So much is implied in the observation made by the High Court of Australia that 'the purposes for the awarding of exemplary damages have been wholly met if substantial punishment is exacted by the criminal law'.[4] In view of this, we might consider the justificatory foundations of criminal law to be a suitable starting point for the development of a normative account of exemplary damages for breach of privacy.

A problem with this approach is that there is considerable disagreement among criminal law theorists as to how we should understand the purpose of this body of law, and consequently about the justificatory grounds for criminalisation and imposition of punishment.[5] However, central to almost all theories of punishment are ideas about harm and wrongdoing. Here we think it is useful to take as our starting point Andrew Ashworth's observation that the criminal law has two broad aims.[6] The first, and main, aim is to protect interests that are considered central to the possibility of well-ordered life in society by proscribing conduct that is harmful to those interests and using the threat of punishment as a deterrent – while leaving less socially important interests to be protected by regulation, civil actions and social norms. The second, and corresponding, aim is to delineate the extent of the state's authority to punish moral wrongdoing.

Those who accept that prevention of harm is the primary justification for punishment indeed often argue that the role of the state is to provide conditions of security for its citizens, and that the criminal law plays a part in this by punishing those who engage in conduct that results in, or which is likely to result in, harm to these conditions.[7] This account of the function of criminal law is said to be consistent with the egalitarian liberal ideal of state neutrality. The argument is that taking the function of the criminal law to be prevention of public harm constitutes

[4] *Gray v Motor Accident Commission* (1998) 196 CLR 1 (HCA) [42] (Gleeson CJ, McHugh, Gummow and Hayne JJ).

[5] See, eg, H Gross, *Crime and Punishment: A Concise Moral Critique* (Oxford, Oxford University Press, 2012) ch 5 (identifying six different theories of crime and punishment); V Tadros, *Wrongs and Crimes* (Oxford, Oxford University Press, 2016).

[6] A Ashworth, 'Defining Criminal Offences Without Harm' in P Smith (ed), *Criminal Law: Essays in Honour of JC Smith* (London, Butterworths, 1987) 8.

[7] See, eg, A von Hirsch, 'Proportionality in the Philosophy of Punishment: From "Why Punish?" to "How Much?"' (1990) 1 *Criminal Law Forum* 259.

a constraint on the state's ability to impose a moral order that privileges certain private conceptions of harm or of the good life.[8] However, critics of this view point out that if prevention of public harm is central to the justification for punishment, that justification falls away if its preventative function can be fulfilled by other means.[9] The aim of a data protection regime, for example, is to secure compliance with principles intended to ensure that those who possess our personal data do not deal with it in ways that cause or expose people to harm. The primary means of deterrence is enforcement notices backed by powers to impose civil penalties that, in the most serious cases of non-compliance, can run to millions in the relevant currency.

If it is possible to prevent public harm by penalising rather than punishing, why punish? What is it about certain forms of conduct that justifies punishment rather than some other form of response? Douglas Husak observes that, whatever else it does, punishment expresses condemnation,[10] and our condemnation will be warranted only if the person who is on the receiving end of it is to blame for their conduct and its consequences. We need to be able to say that, in light of applicable norms, what that person did was wrong. There will be some circumstances in which people do things that we consider wrong but not blameworthy. We should blame a person, Hyman Gross suggests, only if that person had the ability to control the events that resulted in (or created the risk of) harm, had a duty to exercise control to prevent harm from occurring and, in breaching, failed to discharge that duty.[11] No blame should attach to harm caused by the conduct of those who lack the capacity to foresee the consequences of their acts, or whose conduct we take to be 'involuntary' – sleepwalkers, those suffering from other forms of automatism, those acting under duress (Gross uses the language of 'intention' to denote this idea but we think 'voluntary' is preferable). Nor to conduct, involuntary or otherwise, that results in harm but in respect of which there is no duty of prevention.

We now have three conditions that we say, when present in any given circumstances, provide a strong justificatory basis – according to any theory of punishment – for state-imposed punishment, namely, conduct: (i) that is morally wrongful; (ii) that causes harm (and more particularly harm in a public not merely private sense, ie affecting the fabric of society); (iii) in respect of which there is a public interest in punishment. But the operative concepts – harm, wrongs, and public interest – are indeterminate. There is likely to be reasonable disagreement

[8] A von Hirsch and A Ashworth, *Proportionate Sentencing: Exploring the Principles* (Oxford, Oxford University Press, 2005) 14.

[9] A Ashworth and L Zedner, 'Punishment Paradigms and the Role of the Preventive State' in AP Simester, A Du Bois-Pedain and U Neumann (eds), *Liberal Criminal Theory: Essays for Andreas von Hirsch* (Oxford, Hart Publishing, 2014) 3, 4–7.

[10] D Husak, 'Limitations on Criminalization and the General Part of Criminal Law' in S Shute and A Simester (eds), *Criminal Law Theory: Doctrines of the General Part* (Oxford, Oxford University Press, 2002) 26.

[11] Gross (n 5) 72.

as to how these concepts ought to be understood. This has prompted criminal law theorists to pose important questions regarding who should determine the circumstances in which condemnation and punishment are warranted, and how such decisions ought to be made. Andrew Ashworth and Lucia Zedner, for example, ask 'who has standing to determine what constitutes a harm, by what metric, and what form and level of punishment is then justified'?[12] However, it seems to us that this claim might need some refinement. The core values of a political theory ought to give substance to some of the questions – 'What constitutes harm?', for example. But such theories will not provide us with a definitive answer to questions about the point at which it is appropriate for the state to step in and punish those who have caused it, or what level and form of punishment is appropriate in the circumstances. These are matters in respect of which there is likely to be reasonable disagreement even among those who are committed to the core values of a particular political theory. Nevertheless, we might expect a well-developed theory to have something to say about the way in which questions that are likely to give rise to reasonable disagreement ought to be addressed. This process should itself be consistent with the core values of the theory, so that its use will invest decisions that are made with a certain form of legitimacy and authority.

Likewise, it seems to us that, if it is to be coherent and substantive, our consideration of the justification for punishment for interference with privacy, and of the limits of this form of punishment, needs to be grounded in some form of political theory about privacy. We propose to take the values of republican liberalism as laid out, inter alia, by Richard Dagger, Cass Sunstein and Edwin Baker as our normative framework.[13] These seem to us accurately to reflect the nature of life in a modern political community that treats the freedom and welfare of its members as its predominant concerns. Briefly, the aim of a republican-liberal state will be to secure conditions that enable its citizens to develop and maintain autonomous ways of life. This much it has in common with liberalism. However, the main point of departure is its view of the relationship in which citizens stand with one another, and the obligations implied by that relationship. Like liberalism, the core value of republican liberalism is autonomy. However, while liberals tend to think of autonomy as a condition of independence, republican liberals recognise that the development of an autonomous way of life is a necessarily cooperative endeavour. Thus, republican liberals emphasise our interdependence and say that this gives rise duties of reciprocity. Our reliance on the assistance of others for the realisation of an autonomous life grounds a duty to ensure that others enjoy the conditions that are a prerequisite for autonomy. There is a common interest in securing these conditions, and for republican liberals this can only be guaranteed through broad political participation. As Sunstein points out, the republican-liberal preference will be for 'political institutions that promote debate and discussion, bringing to

[12] Ashworth and Zedner (n 9) 7.
[13] Sunstein (n 3); Baker (n 3); Dagger (n 3).

bear alternative perspectives and additional information'. They will be 'hostile to processes that promote law-making as deals or bargains amongst self-interested groups'.[14]

Although necessarily brief, this outline of republican-liberal ideas gives us enough to invest the justificatory conditions of state-imposed punishment with some substance. We can say that the *harm* with which we are concerned is the result of conduct that overrides the autonomous choices of the person on the receiving end, or that will tend to undermine the conditions that are prerequisites for the possibility of autonomy – and when this rises to the level of a harm that corrodes important civic bonds it is not just a private harm suffered by discrete individuals but also a *public harm* suffered by society at large. We should consider engaging in, or facilitating, conduct, knowing or intending that it will have these effects, to be a *wrong* – along with reckless or negligent conduct that pays insufficient attention to the likelihood of these effects. It is a wrong committed against the community at large – a shared wrong.[15] It breaches the duty of reciprocity that we owe one another as members of a political community committed to ensuring that each has conditions that enable them to pursue their own conception of the good, and amounts to denial of the equal status implied by this duty. While we all have an interest in ensuring this duty is discharged, punishment may not always be the most effective or desirable means of securing compliance. There remains a possibility that a wrong, even if it constitutes a shared wrong, might not warrant punishment. We have said that state-imposed punishment will be justified only if there is a *public interest* in imposing it. But how is the question of when it is the public interest to punish to be determined? A republican-liberal response to this question is that it should be for the members of the community in whose name punishment will be imposed to determine the circumstances in which this is done. As Iseult Honohan explains, the process of determining what is in the public interest 'requires the input of many in expression, discussion and action'.[16] Republican liberals will say that whether certain forms of conduct ought to be punished by the state and what form that punishment will take – a question that necessarily entails consideration of the body of law through which punishment is imposed – are questions that ought to be determined in a political process that provides broad participatory opportunities. Thus, in the ideal world of a well-functioning deliberative democracy premised on liberal values, the deliberative contributions of many will provide a sound epistemological basis for any decision about the extent of the community's shared interest (the public interest) in punishing harmful wrongdoing.

[14] Sunstein (n 3) 1549.

[15] See, eg, SE Marshall and RA Duff, 'Criminalization and Sharing Wrongs' (1998) 11 *Canadian Journal of Law & Jurisprudence* 7.

[16] I Honohan, 'Dealing with Difference: The Republican Public-Private Distinction' in M Baghramian and A Ingram (eds), *Pluralism: The Philosophy and Politics of Diversity* (London, Routledge, 2000) 156, 164.

III. Punishing Breaches of Privacy

We now have a normative foundation in which to ground our thinking about why, and in what circumstances, certain conduct ought to be punished by the state. We have said that the starting point in the search for justificatory conditions of punishment should be harm that negatively impacts on individual or group autonomy. In common with liberalism, the premise for all aspects of republican-liberal thinking is the idea that what makes life valuable is autonomy. We ought to be free to determine for ourselves what constitutes a life worth living and to pursue it in a way that is consistent with others' rights to do the same. The liberal account of the value of privacy explains why privacy, understood as freedom from intrusion, is a fundamental component of a more basic liberty.[17] At its core, liberals will often argue, privacy enables us to withdraw from public gaze.[18] Among other things, it provides us with physical, cognitive, emotional and moral space that enables us to reflect, formulate plans, to experiment with new ideas, and to take part in activities without the risk of being ridiculed, ostracised or attacked, or worse.[19]

But the fact that privacy enables an individual to withdraw from the public sphere in this way does not exhaust its value. Privacy provides us with the ability to engage with select audiences, setting boundaries on who can 'see' us and on what terms – choosing what information to disclose, when to do so, to whom and for what purposes.[20] It is the ability of an individual to withhold or selectively to disclose private information that defines the nature of the relationships that individual has with others within what might loosely be termed the private sphere (which in today's world may be closely imbricated with the public sphere but can still be understood as conceptually and practically distinct).[21] The premise of this reasoning is that realisation of almost all conceptions of the good life will depend on the development and maintenance of a diverse range of social relationships. Some of these relationships will be instrumentally valuable, a means to realising the agent's self-determined ends, others might be constitutive of their conception of the good life. There will be those (probably most of us) who take the view that life would be worthless without loyal friendship and intimacy. What marks out such relationships from other forms of social relationships – the relationship we have with our bank manager, workplace supervisor, or child's teacher – is what we

[17] B Roessler, 'Privacy as a Human Right' (2017) 117 *The Proceedings of the Aristotelian Society* 187.

[18] R Gavison, 'Privacy and the Limits of Law' (1980) 89 *Yale Law Journal* 421.

[19] B Goold, 'Surveillance and the Political Value of Privacy' (2009) 1 *Amsterdam Law Forum* 3. See also N Richards, *Intellectual Privacy: Rethinking Civil Liberties in the Digital Age* (Oxford, Oxford University Press, 2015).

[20] K Hughes, 'A Behavioural Understanding of Privacy and its Implications for Privacy Law' (2012) 75 *MLR* 806.

[21] D Boyd and A Marwick, 'Social Privacy in Networked Publics: Teens' Attitudes, Practices, and Strategies' (Oxford Internet Institute: A Decade in Internet Time: Symposium on the Dynamics of the Internet and Society, Oxford, 22 September 2011). See also A Marwick and D Boyd, 'Networked Privacy: How Teenagers Negotiate Context in Social Media' (2014) 16 *New Media & Society* 1051.

choose to disclose to the other, and the availability of that choice depends on our ability to withhold certain information. One of the hallmarks of close and intimate friendship is a reciprocal willingness to share intimate, sensitive and potentially shameful or embarrassing information with the other, and the trust that we place in that person not to disseminate it.[22] But equally fundamental to the ability to form these relationships is the decision about whom to share with and on what terms. The privacy that enables one to control whether, and when, to share and withhold information is as valuable to the development of intimate relationships on this conception of the good life as it is to the ability to enjoy the absence of such relationships for those whose idea of the good life may be more centred on other things, such as wealth and power (or simply the pleasure of solitude).

As the overriding objective for the liberal state, on a republican-liberal account, is, or ought to be, to promote autonomy and provide liberal subjects with conditions in which they are able to develop autonomous ways of life, its interest in ensuring a base level of privacy of its members is self-evident. This also helps us to understand the nature of a 'harm' associated with a breach of privacy that might (or might not) warrant punishment. In short, how much does the breach affect the autonomy of the person or persons whose privacy is violated,[23] and along with that their capacity to play a part in the cooperative endeavour of securing conditions of autonomy for all? How might a loss of privacy lead to other losses, such as opportunities forgone (or not pursued), options being withdrawn, discrimination, manipulation, identity theft, and other impediments to personal, social, professional and political flourishing?[24] What might the impacts be not only for the particular plaintiff or plaintiffs, but also for third parties and larger publics who might benefit directly or indirectly from protections of privacy; and how might these impacts be taken into account in an assessment of public interest? Consideration may also be given to specific features of the defendant's wrongful conduct, and especially to the defendant's egregious disrespect of the plaintiff's (or plaintiffs') rights, which some have suggested offers a distinct justification for punishment[25] but we think can equally be considered as especially 'harmful' conduct geared to the undermining of the right itself, and along with that the civic bonds of a republican-liberal society.[26]

[22] See, eg, C Fried, 'Privacy' (1968) 77 *Yale Law Journal* 475, 484, 'intimacy is the sharing of information about one's actions, beliefs, or emotions which one does not share with all, and which one has the right not to share with anyone. By conferring this right, privacy creates the moral capital which we spend in friendship and love.'

[23] See, eg, *Lloyd v Google LLC* [2019] EWCA Civ 1599, [2020] QB 747 [45] (Sir Geoffrey Vos C, Davis LJ and Sharp P concurring), 'the key to these claims is the characterisation of the class members' loss as the loss of control or loss of autonomy over their personal data'.

[24] See generally Varuhas and Moreham (eds) (n 1).

[25] See, eg, *PJS v News Group Newspapers Ltd* [2016] UKSC 26, [2016] AC 1081 [42] (Lord Mance), [92] (Lord Toulson dissenting); JNE Varuhas, 'Varieties of Damages for Breach of Privacy' in Varuhas and Moreham (eds) (n 1) 55.

[26] cf NA Moreham, 'Compensating for Loss of Dignity and Autonomy' in Varuhas and Moreham (eds) (n 1) 125 (although Moreham is not making the argument in quite these terms, rather emphasising the harm to dignity and autonomy inherent in all breaches of privacy, citing inter alia Mann J in

Finally, there is the question of the severity of the harm. In general, the justificatory grounds for punishing will be more compelling in cases of serious public harm that can be specifically identified and measured – affecting, for instance, the capacity and willingness of individuals and groups to participate in the political and social life of the polity (aspects of particular concern for republicans).[27] But as the above reasoning suggests, there might also be a range of more speculative 'harms' that are harder to measure but should equally be considered in assessing the question of serious public harm. In all cases, the question of whether harm is sufficiently severe and public to warrant punishment will come down to the seriousness of an interference with privacy, depending on its effect on the political and personal autonomy for everyone concerned.

IV. Punishing Breaches of Privacy using Private Law

The overriding aim of a republican-liberal democracy, we have argued (along with other republican liberals), is to establish conditions in which citizens are free to form and pursue their own conceptions of the good life, treating this as a necessarily cooperative endeavour. Because it addresses the most serious threats to this freedom, we can expect the criminal law to play a central role in the state's efforts to secure the conditions of privacy that will be required if this aim is to be realised.[28] But what role, if any, might the citizens of a republican liberal democracy envisage for the power to punish by awarding exemplary damages in private law actions for interference with privacy? Should the power to punish within private law take over where the criminal law ends? Or does it occupy some, or all, of the same ground?

The relationship between the criminal sanction and punishment in private law in the form of an award of exemplary damages was considered by the High Court of Australia in *Gray v Motor Accident Commission*.[29] Some useful principles can be distilled from the judgments. First, exemplary damages are intended to punish and deter wrongdoers.[30] It follows that where 'substantial punishment' has been exacted by the criminal law, exemplary damages should not be awarded.[31] Second, this may be seen also as a matter of right (not just practical justice).

Gulati v MGN Ltd [2015] EWHC 1482, [2016] FSR 12, upheld by the Court of Appeal in *Gulati v MGN Ltd* [2015] EWCA Civ 1291, [2017] QB 149; but what we are suggesting here is that (i) the right to privacy is also undermined; and (ii) the defendant's deliberate egregious conduct is especially instrumental in undermining the right).

[27] See, eg, A Roberts, 'A Republican Account of the Value of Privacy' (2015) 14 *European Journal of Political Theory* 320.

[28] See, eg, JL Marti, 'The Republican Democratization of Criminal Law and Justice' in S Besson and JL Marti (eds), *Legal Republicanism: National and International Perspectives* (Oxford, Oxford University Press, 2009) 123, 123–24.

[29] *Gray* (n 4).

[30] ibid [15] (Gleeson CJ, McHugh, Gummow and Hayne JJ).

[31] ibid [55].

In his concurring judgment, Kirby J described it as a fundamental principle of human rights, namely, the right of an individual 'not be liable to be tried or punished again for an offence for which he or she has already been finally convicted or acquitted in accordance with law is a fundamental principle of human rights'.[32] The majority did not go quite as far, framing it as 'a practice, if not a rule of law, that a person should not be twice punished for what is substantially the same act', including as between criminal and private law.[33] It is clear enough from these statements that the power to award exemplary damages is envisaged as one that could be exercised in respect of breaches of privacy that also constitute criminal offences. But they also suggest that the power only extends to circumstances of wrongdoing that are not addressed by criminal law.

We will turn to the question of what those circumstances might be in respect of privacy shortly. But before doing so, we want to point out that where the conduct concerned is breach or violation of privacy, we think a third body of law enters the frame. It seems to us that the power to impose penalties conferred by regulators by statutory data protection regimes is a means of punishing – in substance, if not designation – those who engage in this kind of conduct. For instance, although referred to as 'penalties', the matters that are required to be taken into account in determining the level of fines imposed for non-compliance under the EU General Data Protection Regulation (GDPR)[34] are similar to the principles that we have suggested provide the justification for punishing. The maximum fines are of a magnitude that most would consider 'punitive' in the ordinary sense of the word – up to €20 million, or 4 per cent of worldwide revenue, whichever is the greater.[35] Whether this level of financial penalty is imposed will depend – among other things – on 'the nature, gravity and duration of the infringement taking into account the nature scope or purpose of the processing concerned as well as the number of data subjects affected and the level of damage suffered by them', as well as any efforts to mitigate the damage.[36] Further, in determining the appropriate response to a failure to comply with the obligations imposed by the GDPR, account must also be taken of matters that concern the wrongfulness of the data controller's actions – whether the infringement was intentional or negligent, and any history of infringement.[37] Thus, the question of the role of exemplary damages in punishing breach of privacy might require consideration not only of the way in which private law and criminal law are related, but also of the relationship in which

[32] ibid [95], citing the International Covenant on Civil and Political Rights (UNGA 1966) Art 14(7). See also M Kirby, 'Carroll, Double Jeopardy and International Human Rights Law' (2003) 27 *Criminal Law Journal* 231.

[33] *Gray* (n 4) [43] (Gleeson CJ, McHugh, Gummow and Hayne JJ), citing *R v Hoar* (1981) 148 CLR 32 (HCA) [15].

[34] Council Regulation (EU) 2016/679 of 27 April 2016 on the protection of natural persons with regard to the processing of personal data and on the free movement of such data, and repealing Directive 95/46/EC (General Data Protection Regulation) [2016] OJ L119/1.

[35] ibid Art 83(5).

[36] ibid Art 83(2)(a) and (c).

[37] ibid Art 83(2)(b) and (e).

private law stands with data protection law. While this adds another dimension to the question with which we are concerned, it does not alter the fundamental nature of the inquiry. The issue of double punishment, for example, would require us to consider whether the power to award exemplary damages should be exercised not only in circumstances in which a person or entity has been subject to criminal proceedings, but also in the face of any action taken by a data protection regulator.

Ian Ayres and John Braithwaite suggest there is much to be said from a republican perspective for a system of legal norms that uses multiple techniques (not just criminal law) in striving to ensure that individuals and corporations, directly or indirectly, act in 'socially responsible ways'.[38] However, to simplify matters, in the remainder of this part of the chapter, we will consider only the relationship between criminal law and private law, and the role that the latter ought to play in punishing breaches of privacy. Before doing so, we want to make a brief preliminary observation. The liberal-republican commitment to self-government and participatory democracy would normally be expected to manifest a preference for punishment's being exacted through the criminal law, with all its protections for the defendant. We noted in the previous section that it ought to be for the members of the community in whose name punishment will be imposed to determine the circumstances in which this is done. Just where the community's collective interest lies in respect of punishing breaches of privacy ought to be determined collectively in a process that enables the input of many, with due regard for the rights of defendants. Second, for similar reasons it might be argued that even within private law there should be a preference for any power to award exemplary damages to be provided for by statute, for instance under the *aegis* of a statutory tort.[39] Nevertheless, we recognise that there may still be legitimate scope to consider the power to draw on a common law power to award exemplary damages, that is, for breach of a common law privacy tort, at least under certain conditions. In *Gray v Motor Accident Commission*, Kirby J suggested that (common law) '[e]xemplary damages are awarded for conduct which shocks the tribunal of fact, *representing the community*'.[40] One way to provide for a measure of community input where community interests are involved, as Kirby J has also suggested in his extra-judicial writing,[41] is to look to a range of sources for advice on matters of public policy. Indeed we already have examples of privacy cases where a range of evidence and arguments have been permitted, for instance cases where the data protection commissioner has intervened,[42] and claims brought via class action or by civil

[38] I Ayres and J Braithwaite, *Responsive Regulation: Transcending the Deregulation Debate* (Oxford, Oxford University Press, 1992) 47. See generally ch 3.

[39] See, eg Australian Law Reform Commission, *Serious Invasions of Privacy in the Digital Era* (Law Com No 123, 2014), Recommendation 12–4.

[40] *Gray* (n 4) [101] (emphasis added).

[41] M Kirby, *Judicial Activism: Authority, Principle and Policy in the Judicial Method* (London, Sweet & Maxwell, 2004) 80.

[42] See, eg, *Vidal-Hall v Google Inc* [2015] EWCA Civ 311, [2016] QB 1003.

society groups.[43] These provide useful models for community participation in cases where exemplary damages are sought for breach of privacy.

Subject to this qualification, it seems to us that a power to award exemplary damages in private law privacy cases initiated by individuals and groups serves liberal-republican aims in at least four ways. First, it might be used to address blind spots in the criminal law, imposing punishment for the kind of serious breaches of privacy that we might expect to be criminalised but have not been. Second, it provides a means of overcoming the criminal law's inertia. The criminal law is often slow to respond to emergent threats, such as those posed by the power of big data and misuse of personal information. Third, as we have already suggested, it could be used to punish breaches of privacy that warrant public condemnation but not the degree of disapprobation represented by a criminal conviction. Finally, it provides individuals with the power to ensure that conduct that has been criminalised is punished where the institutions of the state are either indifferent to the wrongdoing, or lack the resources to respond to it adequately.

A. Addressing Blind-Spots in the Criminal Law

As we have said, we might expect serious breaches of privacy to be punished under the criminal law. But for various reasons criminal law will often fail to live up to this expectation. Traditionally, it has tended not to use the concept of privacy to articulate the harm it addresses. This is not to say that the criminal law is unconcerned with privacy. But in common law jurisdictions the protection it affords privacy is often implicit, and one of the consequences of this tendency is that interference with privacy that will have a significant effect on the autonomy of those who suffer it might fall outside the scope of the criminal law. In England and Wales, for example, the offence of voyeurism is conceived as a sexual offence, concerned with observation and recording for sexual gratification.[44] English law has no equivalent of the offence of photographing or filming persons in their homes or other private spaces, found in the criminal codes of many civil law jurisdictions.[45] So, provided it is not motivated by a sexual purpose, and is not shown to others (and does not

[43] See, eg, *Various Claimants v Wm Morrison Supermarkets plc* [2020] UKSC 12, [2020] AC 989; *Gulati v MGN Ltd* [2015] EWCA Civ 1291, [2017] QB 149; *R (National Council for Civil Liberties) v Secretary of State for the Home Department* [2019] EWHC 2057, [2020] 1 WLR 243; *Evans v Health Administration Corporation* [2019] NSWSC 1781; *Lloyd* (n 23).

[44] Sexual Offences Act 2003, s 67(3): 'A person commits an offence if – (a) he records another person (B) doing a private act, (b) he does so with the intention that he or a third person will, for the purpose of obtaining sexual gratification, look at an image of B doing the act, and (c) he knows that B does not consent to his recording the act with that intention.'

[45] See, eg, BJ Koops et al, 'The Reasonableness of Remaining Unobserved: A Comparative Analysis of Visual Surveillance and Voyeurism in Criminal Law' (2018) 43 *Law & Social Inquiry* 1210. cf Australian Law Reform Commission (n 39) ch 14, which discusses surveillance device regimes in States and Territories.

fall within another criminal regime, such as that concerned with protection from harassment),[46] covert recording of a person engaged in sexual activity does not attract criminal sanction.[47] In *Daniels v Thompson*,[48] the New Zealand Court of Appeal suggested that '[e]xemplary damages may fulfil a useful role in helping to control deplorable conduct outside the reach of the criminal law'.[49] But what constitutes 'deplorable conduct'? We have argued in this chapter that it should be conduct in respect of which the imposition of punishment is justified; that is to say, a wrong that has resulted in significant harm, in respect of which there is a public interest in punishment.

Let us suppose that A has photographed or filmed B engaging in sexual activity, not for sexual gratification but because A realises that if B is aware that A has the recording, this will enable A to manipulate B's decision-making without making the explicit demands that would expose A to the risk of prosecution for blackmail.[50] Or, as in the case of *AMP v Persons Unknown*,[51] A may have come across images of B engaging in sexual activity that were stored on B's mobile phone (which was lost or stolen), and used these to try to manipulate B's decision-making in ways that might seem innocuous – in this case sending a request to A to become a 'friend' on Facebook, but with an implied threat that if she did not accept the request, A would further disseminate the images. Even if A's conduct at that point does not constitute a crime, we might think the breach of privacy to be the kind of 'deplorable' conduct that ought to be publicly condemned and punished as though it were a crime (assuming that A is amenable to the jurisdiction of the court).[52] We can expect B's awareness that A has the recording to condition their choices, pressuring them to make decisions that are unlikely to give A reason to disseminate

[46] Protection from Harassment Act 1997.

[47] At the time of writing the UK Law Commission had signalled its intention to review the law relating to the taking, making and sharing of intimate images. See, eg, Law Commission, 'Taking, Making and Sharing Intimate Images Without Consent' at www.lawcom.gov.uk/project/taking-making-and-sharing-intimate-images-without-consent/, accessed 31 January 2020. Note also that scenarios of unauthorised capturing and dissemination of intimate images are a common feature of privacy tort and other private law claims in common law jurisdictions (including England and Wales), even in the absence of formal 'image rights': see Richardson, Neave and Rivette (n 1).

[48] *Daniels v Thompson* [1998] 3 NZLR 22 (CA).

[49] ibid 52.

[50] In England and Wales, the offence of non-consensual disclosure of a private sexual photograph or film is created by Criminal Justice and Courts Act 2015, s 33. However, the offence requires that the film be disclosed with the intention of causing distress to the person depicted. Furthermore, no offence is committed if the only person to whom the image is disclosed, is the person depicted. The offence of blackmail would require the showing of the image to be accompanied by a 'demand with menaces': Theft Act 1968, s 21.

[51] *AMP v Persons Unknown* [2011] EWHC 3454.

[52] In this case (where the images had been posted on a Swedish website hosting BitTorrent file by the time the case got to courts), the also quite extreme remedy of an injunction against persons unknown was sought and granted by the court, relying on the misuse of private information tort and harassment, in an effort to limit further circulation of the images within the UK jurisdiction. For further discussion of the case, see especially A Murray, *Information Technology Law: The Law and Society*, 2nd edn (Oxford, Oxford University Press, 2013) 397.

the recording. If understood in the way described in section III of the chapter, in terms of the effect of the breach of privacy on the autonomy of those who suffer the breach, the harm caused by A's conduct is likely to be potentially significant. It constitutes a wrong because it is conduct that corrodes the civic bonds that are essential to the cooperative endeavour of securing conditions in which each can pursue their own conception of the good. Indeed, it is conduct that denies B those conditions. But that denial does not affect only B. On a republican understanding of interdependence in securing conditions of freedom, those conditions can only be secured through broad political participation.[53] And, insofar as it undermines a person's ability to play a full part in the collective enterprise of securing conditions of freedom, serious violation of individual privacy – the kind of intrusive conduct in which A has engaged, for example – will be a matter of public interest. Where the intrusion is blameworthy, the justificatory grounds for the imposition of punishment will be made out.

The use of punitive measures in private law actions for breach of privacy in the circumstances considered in this section, might be viewed as a part of a process of citizen-initiated law reform. Frequent use of exemplary damages ought to draw attention to an apparent lacuna in the criminal law. In a well-functioning republican-liberal democracy, we might expect this to prompt political deliberation on the question of whether the kind of conduct in question ought to be criminalised. If the wrongdoing is particularly serious, one would expect criminalisation to follow. Of course, this would not be the inevitable outcome in less clear-cut cases. In such circumstances, deliberation may result in a collective decision that the wrongdoing should be dealt with in other ways. The view might be taken that the level of culpability is such that a civil penalty, such as an award of exemplary damages, is an appropriate response, about which we will have more to say shortly.

B. Responding to Emerging Privacy Problems

In addition to circumstances in which there has been some, albeit incomplete or inadequate, attempt to address a privacy problem using the criminal law, there will be some in which there has – for various reasons – been no attempt at all. Digital technologies are transforming the way in which we lead our lives and the world in which we live. This, of course, has delivered significant benefits. But at the same time, the collection, retention and transmission of vast quantities of personal information pose a substantial threat to privacy as well as to other aspects of our lives, with the criminal law slow to respond.[54]

[53] See, eg, Roberts (n 27). See generally I Honohan, *Civic Republicanism* (London, Routledge, 2002).

[54] Our premise is that citizens will in due course consider criminalisation of the conduct in question to be warranted. It seems to us that when this eventually occurs, the rationale for addressing wrongdoing in the circumstances under consideration in this section will no longer exist, and it ought to be dealt with by means of criminal law.

The alleged violation of privacy that gave rise to a class action against Facebook in *Re Facebook Inc Consumer Privacy User Profile Litigation*[55] provides an example of the way in which private law might be utilised where the criminal law has yet to respond to all the problems to which new technology gives rise. The plaintiffs alleged that Facebook had, without their consent, made its users' sensitive personal data available to numerous companies. It was claimed that not only did Facebook exchange data with other companies under reciprocal data-sharing arrangements, it permitted third parties to install apps that harvested vast amounts of personal information. The plaintiffs alleged that users' interactions with the apps – which might take the form of a video game, or lifestyle quiz – enabled the app developer to access and collect information about those users. It was also able to harvest any information about their 'Facebook friends' that the users of the app would have been able to access, including information that the friends had disclosed only to the app user or a small number of people. It was said the app developers were able to access videos that users had made, videos they had watched, photographs, information about their religious preferences and political views, and the content of communications between the user and others. While claims included alleged breaches of the Stored Communications Act (an Act that combines criminal as well as civil liability) along with breach of contract, deceit and negligence, and violation of the California right of publicity, specific concerns about the privacy dimensions of the profiling activities were addressed under the privacy torts of intrusion on seclusion and public disclosure of private facts, recognised under California law, as well as breach of the right to privacy in the California Constitution (treated as a separate claim).[56]

Of the various privacy violations described in the judgment of Judge Vince Chhabria in his preliminary decision allowing most of the claims to proceed to trial,[57] the most egregious from a republican-liberal perspective concerns the use of an app developed by Cambridge University-based data scientist and psychologist Aleksandr Kogan, which asked users to answer a series of questions that it was said would help them to 'better understand themselves'. In addition to the information that users provided in their interactions with the app, the app collected information about users and their 'Facebook friends'. Although the app was downloaded by a mere 300,000 or so Facebook users, the app developer was able to compile a database containing personal information harvested from the accounts of some 87 million users. This information was made available to a political consulting firm, Cambridge Analytica, which used it to send out targeted political messaging during elections. There are good grounds for thinking that republican liberals would consider the conduct that has just been described to warrant exemplary damages. The plaintiffs in the proceedings claimed that the events gave rise

[55] *Re Facebook Inc Consumer Privacy User Profile Litigation* Case 402 F Supp 3d 767 (Northern District of California, 2019) (Granting in Part and Denying in Part Motion to Dismiss First Amended Complaint).

[56] ibid 781–82.

[57] ibid 795–96.

to three kinds of harm.[58] First, disclosure of the information was in itself a 'privacy injury'.[59] Second, the disclosure gave rise to the risk that they would become victims of identity theft. Third, the disclosure of the information deprived them of the economic value of the data insofar as it deprived them of an opportunity to trade the data themselves. While the second and third harms would be a matter of concern for republican-liberals, they do not address directly what republican-liberals would take to be the most serious form of harm occasioned by the conduct in question – namely, the power to manipulate the decision-making of the subjects of the information (including in their election choices). However, the first harms – namely, loss of privacy – could easily be seen in these terms, being a direct consequence of the fact that (in the judge's words) 'the plaintiffs' sensitive information was disseminated to third parties in violation of their privacy'. Indeed, this was the category of harm that Judge Chhabria concluded was sufficient to confer standing on the plaintiffs in this case.[60]

C. Punishing Less Culpable Forms of Wrongdoing

In an early contribution to the contemporary revival of interest in republican ideas, Philip Pettit and John Braithwaite suggested that the development of republican criminal justice policy ought to be guided by what they referred to as the 'principle of parsimony'.[61] Because the consequences of criminal conviction, and the public shaming that goes with it, are so serious, republican-liberals will tend to favour less rather than more criminal law. Those who are accused of criminal conduct will be afforded significant protections – proof beyond reasonable doubt being the prime example – that are intended to reduce the prospects of the innocent being wrongly convicted, punished, and stigmatised.

The parsimony principle is intended to operate as a constraint on the scope of the criminal law.[62] We might ask whether the thinking that it embodies ought to be extended to the imposition of punishment using other forms of law. That is to say, if the principle suggests that we should not punish certain conduct using the criminal law, does the thinking that it embodies necessarily lead to a conclusion that we should not use the law to punish at all? It seems to us that this question should be answered in the negative. As we have already explained, the parsimony principle is grounded in the idea that the imposition of criminal sanctions is the

[58] ibid 784.

[59] ibid. Specifically identifying the harm here as concerned with the dissemination and use of their private information, 'that is, injury from Facebook's widespread disclosure of their sensitive information, including their photographs, videos they made, videos they watched, religious preferences, posts, and even private one-on-one messages sent through Facebook'.

[60] ibid.

[61] J Braithwaite and P Pettit, *Not Just Deserts: A Republican Theory of Criminal Justice* (Oxford, Clarendon Press, 1990) 79–80.

[62] ibid 80.

most serious intervention by the state in an individual's life, and the effect on that person's life is likely to be profound. In some cases, it will involve loss of liberty, in others an order to undertake work that benefits the community or a fine. But in every case, the state condemns the individual in terms that ought to be reserved for the most egregious forms of wrongdoing – it is as far as the state can go in its condemnation of the person's conduct. Labelling someone a criminal has moral significance and weight that the award of exemplary damages does not carry. The stigma of being convicted of a crime – of being a criminal – will quite possibly have significant consequences for the individual concerned (as well as their friends and families). Among other things, they will be required to disclose the fact of conviction when applying for jobs and when travelling between countries, and might be denied opportunities that are open to others. Their standing in the community will be diminished, along with their prospects of employment and other opportunities that would otherwise be open to them.[63]

There are good reasons for exercising restraint when it comes to using criminal law to punish wrongdoing. But it does not follow that any wrongdoing that is not addressed by the criminal law should be left unpunished. There may well be agreement among the members of a polity that the public interest is served by using forms of law other than the criminal law to punish, or by some form of non-legal response, an educational programme for example. A relevant consideration in reaching a decision about the body of law that ought to be used might be the degree of culpability on the part of the wrongdoer. As we observed in section II, punishment is warranted only in respect of conduct that is blameworthy. But blameworthiness is not an 'all-or-nothing' state of affairs. A person might be considered more or less blameworthy depending on their motivation, foresight of the possible consequences of their actions and attitude towards those who suffer the harm. This is reflected in the retributive approach to criminal sentencing. But these factors might shape our thinking on questions concerning the form of law that the state ought to use to punish wrongdoing. There may well be circumstances in which some form of public condemnation is thought to be warranted, but not to the degree expressed in a conviction for a criminal offence.

Of course, if the issue involves dealings with personal information or data, we might see a special role for data protection law in filling the gap – indeed, in practice, data protection laws may well be pertinent (as we have discussed earlier in the chapter). But putting that option aside, there is also the prospect of using private law for an equivalent function. Moreover, privacy laws might be pertinent ways of addressing breaches of privacy that data protection standards do not reach, and again can have a role in filling gaps in the criminal law for less 'serious' breaches

[63] See, eg, *NT1 & NT2 v Google LLC* [2018] EWHC 799, [2019] QB 344 (the 'right to be forgotten' cases) for discussion of the ongoing harms associated with public criminal convictions. On the effects of even minor criminal convictions on employment decisions, see C Uggen et al, 'The Edge of Stigma: An Experimental Audit of the Effects of Low-Level Criminal Records on Employment' (2014) 52 *Criminology* 627.

that are nevertheless sufficiently publicly harmful and culpable to warrant a punitive remedy. That there is legitimate reason to use tort law to punish breaches of privacy in these circumstances seems consistent with case authority. The High Court of Australia has made it clear that the award of exemplary damages and punishment under the criminal law and private law serve the same ends, even if the laws themselves are not entirely overlapping. In *Uren v John Fairfax & Sons Pty Ltd*,[64] it was observed that the roots of criminal and tort law are intermingled,[65] and that the purpose of exemplary damages is to 'express … disapproval or "detestation"' (to use the older language of Pratt CJ in *Wilkes v Wood*).[66]

The commonality does not end there. Just as criminal conviction expresses collective moral condemnation, it was said in *Gray v Motor Accident Commission* that 'awarding exemplary damages [under tort law] is the punishment of the wrongdoer in an *emphatic* and *public* way'.[67] Further, while the High Court stated that exemplary damages 'could not properly be awarded in a case of alleged negligence in which there was no conscious wrongdoing by the defendant',[68] this assertion was not accompanied by reasoning, and the proposition that negligence is not sufficient for culpability may potentially be revisited in a case more directly on point. It is worth noting that those whose negligence results in serious harm are punished under the criminal law, some jurisdictions having an offence of manslaughter by gross negligence, for example.[69] Andrew Ashworth points out that blame and punishment in the criminal law are grounded in the idea of autonomy; that we are free to choose among various courses of action.[70] On the basis of this proposition, he suggests that it is possible to argue that 'a person who negligently causes harm could have done otherwise – he could have taken the care necessary to avoid the harm'.[71] If criminalisation and consequential punishment can be justified on this basis, so too can punishment in the form of an award of exemplary damages in private law – including not only in cases of intentional

[64] *Uren v John Fairfax & Sons Pty Ltd* (1966) 117 CLR 118 (HCA).

[65] ibid 149 (Windeyer J). cf ibid 131 (Taylor J): 'No doubt the criminal law prescribes penalties for wrongs which are also crimes but it prescribes no penalty for wrongs which are not at one and the same time crimes, and in both types of cases the courts of this country, and I venture to suggest the courts of England, had admitted the principle of exemplary damages as, in effect, a penalty for a wrong committed in such circumstances or in such manner as to warrant the court's signal disapproval of the defendant's conduct.'

[66] ibid 127 (McTiernan J), citing Pratt CJ in *Wilkes v Wood* (1763) Lofft 1, 98 ER 489.

[67] *Gray* (n 4) [97] (emphasis added).

[68] ibid [22].

[69] England and Wales, for example, has a common law offence of gross negligence manslaughter: *R v Adomako* [1995] 1 AC 171 (HL) 187 (Lord MacKay): '[I]n my opinion the ordinary principles of the law of negligence apply to ascertain whether or not the defendant has been in breach of a duty of care towards the victim who has died. If such breach of duty is established the next question is whether that breach of duty caused the death of the victim. If so, the jury must go on to consider whether that breach of duty should be characterised as gross negligence and therefore as a crime.'

[70] A Ashworth, *Principles of Criminal Law*, 6th edn (Oxford, Oxford University Press, 2009) 186.

[71] ibid. See also D Husak, 'Negligence, Belief, Blame and Criminal Liability: The Special Case of Forgetting' (2011) 5 *Criminal Law & Philosophy* 199.

harm, but potentially also in cases involving recklessness (ie conscious disregard for others' privacy and indifference to the consequences of a loss of privacy) as well as cases of negligence (ie the failure of those who have the necessary capacity, to apply due care in considering others' privacy interests and/or the consequences of a breach of privacy). The extent of the harm, or risk of harm, involved will of course also affect any assessment of the seriousness of the wrongdoing and the question of whether it ought to be met with a punitive response under private law.

D. Overcoming Prosecutorial Indifference, Corruption and Lack of Resources

The final broad set of circumstances in which we see a role for private law in punishing privacy harms comprise those in which the conduct in question constitutes a crime but the state or its agents have failed to initiate proceedings against the wrongdoer. This may well be the result of a rational decision-making process concerned with the allocation of finite resources, but it might also be a consequence of indifference – or worse, corruption – on the part of those who have power to investigate and to initiate proceedings through which the state's power to punish is exercised. In *Gray v Motor Accident Commission*, the Australian High Court thought it doubtful that a mere possibility of criminal proceedings was a sufficient reason to withhold an award of exemplary damages in a 'proper case', although, as to proceedings already concluded, it noted that

> if criminal charges, alleging the same conduct as is alleged in a civil proceeding, have been brought and proved, it would be a most unusual case in which it was open to a civil court to conclude that the outcome of those criminal proceedings did not take sufficient account of the need to punish the offender and deter others from like conduct.[72]

When it made this observation, the Court was concerned with the problem of double punishment. But, of course, for reasons such as those we have just identified, criminal proceedings might not have occurred at the time of the civil proceedings (and may not even be in prospect). Whatever the reason for that eventuality, the opportunity that the award of exemplary damages affords citizens to seek punishment for wrongdoing provides a means of circumventing unwillingness on the part of state officials to seek punishment of those suspected of wrongdoing.[73] By extension, the same might also be argued for cases where the legislature has failed to act in criminalising egregiously harmful conduct, or to provide, in respect of such conduct, sufficient penalties to act as an effective deterrent in the current social and technological environment. Indeed, clearly, already privacy law is being used

[72] *Gray* (n 4) [46].

[73] cf the role of private prosecutions. See, eg, A Prestidge, 'Private Prosecutions in New Zealand – A Public Concern?' (2019) 50 *Victoria University of Wellington Law Review* 107; New Zealand Law Commission, 'Criminal Prosecution' (Preliminary Paper No 28, 1997).

for this purpose to deal with serious social issues that on any republican-liberal (or indeed just liberal) viewpoint warrant serious punishment, and yet which are not being (adequately) addressed through the criminal law – whether through a failure of the legislator in acting expeditiously to deal with the situation, or on the part of those responsible for enforcing the law. Where these failings occur and where there are strong policy reasons for taking steps to hold a wrongdoer liable for their privacy harms – as for instance in revenge porn cases – the justification for exemplary as well as other damages seems entirely obvious.[74]

In cases such as these, it might be helpful to think about the role of a punitive response in private law actions for interference with privacy in the kind of circumstances with which we are concerned at present, in terms of empowerment. An idea that occupies a prominent position in the literature is that tort law confers power to pursue and receive a remedy – compensatory damages – in respect of loss suffered as a consequence of a tortfeasor's abuse of social power.[75] Once we consider the additional possibility of exemplary damages, this account must be extended. The availability of such damages confers on a plaintiff power to seek public condemnation of the wrong that was committed. But it also empowers plaintiffs publicly to bypass the effects of an improper and misguided use of power by state officials, or simply a failure to act on the part of state officials that impacts them directly. A decision made by a legislator, prosecutor or prosecution agency not to criminalise a certain type of behaviour or pursue a prosecution might be the result of corruption, improper influence or some misguided assessment of public interest, or a perfectly proper allocation of finite resources. But in each of these circumstances, the decision-maker exercises some form of political power, in a way that is or might be adverse to the privacy interests of the person who has suffered harm (with further possible impacts for a range of others they are connected with in the course of their lives). Moreover, to the extent that this disempowerment undermines that person's capacity to play a role in the cooperative endeavour of securing conditions that are prerequisites for autonomy, political power is exercised in a way that adversely affects the interests of all members of the community.

Attempts to challenge the exercise of this power via the 'backdoor' of bringing civil proceedings will face various obstacles; and rightly so, as we have argued in this chapter. Decisions should not be taken lightly to award exemplary damages in cases that are, after all, essentially civil cases designed to deal with civil wrongs.

[74] See, eg, *Jane Doe 72511 v Morgan* 2018 ONSC 6607 [142] (Gomery J): 'In my view, the compensatory damages already awarded are not sufficient to accomplish the objectives of punishment, deterrence and denunciation. Punitive damages are necessary here to emphasize the seriousness of Nicholas' malicious actions and to deter others from similar behaviour. Revenge porn is an assault to the victim's personal agency and sense of self-worth. Nicholas posted the video with the purpose of making Jane an "internet whore for life". This must be sanctioned.' For attempts to deploy criminal law to deal with revenge porn in Canada, see A Dodge, 'Nudes are Forever: Judicial Interpretations of Digital Technology's Impact on "Revenge Porn"' (2019) 34 *Canadian Journal of Law and Society* 121.

[75] See generally R Perry, 'Empowerment and Tort Law' (2009) 76 *Tennessee Law Review* 959; N Oman, 'A Theory of Civil Liability' (2014) *George Mason Law Review* 381; O Herstein, 'How Tort Law Empowers' (2015) 65 *University of Toronto Law Journal* 99.

Nevertheless, this option empowers a plaintiff, or plaintiffs acting in concert (for instance in a class-action scenario), to mitigate the adverse effects of problematic political decision-making. It provides individuals with an opportunity to assume responsibility for the pursuit of a punitive response to public wrongs even in the absence of deliberate state action. The idea of mitigation seems to us to be consistent with the broad position we have taken. In terms of public condemnation, the award of punitive damages in respect of conduct that might attract criminal sanction, but for some reason has not, may be a second-best outcome compared to the best option of criminal conviction (carrying the weight of strongest condemnation by the community). But it may still be the best option at hand.

V. Conclusion

Our aim in this chapter has been to provide a republican-liberal account of the part that exemplary damages might play in punishing interference with privacy. If the power to award these damages is to serve the ends that we envisage them as serving, much doctrinal work awaits. The courts have acknowledged that the roots of tort law and criminal law are intermingled, and that, insofar as both are intended to deter wrongdoing, the power to award exemplary damages and the criminal sanction serve common ends. But a detailed account of the relationship between the two bodies of law has yet to emerge from the cases. Our hope is the account that we offer here will be seen as a plausible foundation for this undertaking.

5

Punishments and Penalties in Private Law, with Particular Reference to the Law Governing Fiduciaries

JAMES PENNER*

I. Introduction

Why do we prohibit certain acts? Why do we (sometimes) punish people for committing them? These are the things we need to know if we want to see whether and, if so, where and how private law punishes anyone. Here I shall explore what I shall call an 'assurance' theory of prohibition and punishment, and set out its implications for understanding punishment within private law.[1] Although the assurance theory draws heavily upon expressivist and retributive theories, it has a different primary emphasis. After setting out the assurance account of prohibition and punishment, I shall consider the nature of penalties – setbacks to rights that do not amount to punishments. The main claim of the chapter will be that private law justifiably imposes penalties in some cases, and I shall show this by considering some examples from the law governing fiduciaries.

* Thanks to Elise Bant, Rob Chambers, Wayne Courtney, Duncan Horne and Jason Neyers for helpful comments. I owe especial thanks to Alan Brudner, Matthew Conaglen, Jeremiah Lau and Steve Smith for exacting comments, and in particular to Andrew Simester and Lionel Smith, both of whom provided extensive comments on an earlier draft and exposed some serious errors. Any that remain are down to me, of course.

[1] The account of prohibition and punishment offered here departs in significant respects (for the better, I hope) from those given in JE Penner, 'As If We Were Strangers: From Social Life to Private Law' (2019) *NUS Law Working Paper Series* 6–11; and JE Penner, 'Justifying Private Law: "Reasons Fundamentalist" Instrumentalism and the Kantian Account' in S Degeling, MJR Crawford and NA Tiverios (eds), *Justifying Private Rights* (Oxford, Hart Publishing, forthcoming).

II. Prohibition and Responding to Wrongdoers

We can begin to understand the place of prohibition and punishment in the law by noting something Green says:[2]

> In jurisprudence, we are used to distinguishing primary legal norms [Plan A norms] that aim to guide conduct from secondary, plan-B, norms that guide responses to conduct that fails to satisfy the primary norm. In areas like sexual interaction, however, it is not only the secondary enforcement but also the primary obligations imposed by law that should be seen as Plan B – as fallbacks, morally speaking. Things are not going well, sexually or legally, when men need guidance from the duty not to commit rape. The point is quite general. We also want people to avoid assault, to refrain from discrimination, and to deal fairly, not because of a lively awareness of the normative force of law, but because it would hardly occur to them to do otherwise. Law has a role to play in securing that smooth-running state of affairs, but not only by securing a duty of obedience. In some cases, law is at its best when it helps shape our social world in a way that is relatively invisible.[3]

If it is successful, Plan A is good for everyone. Tadros helpfully points out and elucidates something that anyone with moral understanding should know already – that a crime blights the life of the perpetrator as much as it blights the life of the victim, perhaps more so.[4]

Having said all this, what is the purpose of prohibition for the assurance theorist? Assurance theory trades on the following fundamental idea: when a person maliciously victimises another, a community cannot stand idly by. It must take steps to show that it *takes the side of the victim*. Indeed, for the assurance theorist, it is a moral obligation on any community to take the side of the victim over the criminal in some suitably *expressive public* way, a point the theory shares with expressivism. This is especially so in the case of serious violations, murder, assaults causing grievous bodily harm, plundering frauds and so on. A community is less of a community insofar as it fails to do this. Victims, in the absence of this 'taking their side', are treated as equal to or even less than the perpetrator who victimised them. Taking the side of the perpetrator is the clearest signal possible that the victim is isolated. Such a victim justifiably feels even more aggrieved if, at the same time, she is regarded as still a 'citizen'. We can see this in the contemporary

[2] L Green, 'Escapable Law: Gardner on Law and Morality' (2018) 18 *Oxford Legal Research Paper Series* 1, 21–22, footnotes omitted.

[3] The only qualification I would make is with regard to Green's use of 'law' in the last two sentences. It seems to me that the *state* has a role in securing that state of affairs wherein people don't commit crimes in the first place, by helping to secure a society wherein socialisation, culture, and education help to improve and certainly do not thwart our moral understanding, and social conditions are such that people are not systematically tempted to commit crimes. The law *as such*, understood in terms of statutes, cases, and the legal process may have relatively little to do in this regard. Not nothing, of course – one can legislate for the provision of social welfare, schools and so on, but these presume a prior commitment by the state to devote its, or require others to devote their, resources to that provision.

[4] V Tadros, *Wrongs and Crimes* (Oxford University Press, 2016) 1–2. It blights their lives in different ways, of course.

context most vividly, perhaps, in the Black Lives Matter movement. It simply cannot be justified that peace officers can wrongfully take the lives of citizens with no genuine criminal law repercussions, and this has nothing to do with feelings, say, of revenge.[5]

This is true of family life as well, of course. Family members, in particular parents, cannot stand idly by when, for example, one child attacks another or steals the other's things. Any normal parent or child understands this intuitively. This does not necessarily require the response of punishment,[6] but the wrong cannot be allowed to go unaddressed. A family in which a parent is *indifferent* or, worse, *encouraging* of such behaviour, is to that extent a dysfunctional family – or worse.

In short, for assurance theory the public response assures members of a community[7] that the interpersonal moral norms concerning wrongdoing are enforced, without which their community is less of a community. What particular shape this public response takes in a particular community will naturally vary. In a small, tight-knit religious community, the response might be by way of confession and repentance before a priest, who in this sense acts on behalf of the community of believers. But it is difficult for me to imagine anything but the (more or less) secular state taking on this role in modern, 'pluralistic' societies. Nevertheless, one way or another, discharging this public obligation is one of the constitutive obligations of a community. Where there is complete or systematic failure to discharge this obligation, we have a state of barbarism.

Recognising the conceptual priority of the 'taking the victim's side' over the issue of punishment itself has an immediate pay-off. It explains why those interested in 'penitential' or 'restorative' or 'reconciliatory' responses to crime, even though they may abjure punitive responses, are on the same page so far as this goes. In other words, this 'assurance' aspect of the criminal law is prior to the issue of punishment.

In view of the preceding, we can understand what a society needs to do in the way of prohibition. In the first place, the criminal law must reflect the basic moral norms of interpersonal interaction that would exist independently of the existence of any legal system. The injunctions not to murder, to respect the property of others and so on, are (to the extent they are valid, of course) morally required of every individual regardless of the behaviour of others, or of the individual's expectations of the behaviour of others. The term *mala in se*, as opposed to *mala prohibita*, is sometimes employed to describe these sorts of crime. But there are also crimes that can only arise in organised societies of a certain sophistication,

[5] cf EN Yankah, 'Crime, Freedom and Civic Bonds: Arthur Ripstein's Force and Freedom: Kant's Legal and Political Philosophy' (2012) 6 *Criminal Law and Philosophy* 255, 268: 'No theory which takes seriously our civic duties to each other can allow selfish violence to be visited on one citizen from another.' See also ibid 268–70.

[6] For example, a direction to take 'self-help'. A parent might tell the victimised sibling, 'Don't let your sister bully you that way – stand up for yourself and give as good back', which might be more effective in the circumstances.

[7] In doing so it should also reassure the individual victim, but that is *not* the primary purpose of a public criminal law sanction.

such as forgery or insider trading, which can certainly be regarded as inherently wrongful. There are also what have been categorised as 'victimless crimes', such as the crime of selling illicit drugs, which for those who favour their criminalisation must be seen as in some way inherently wrongful. In these two last cases, 'victim' in 'taking the side of the victim' needs to be understood more broadly, as in the public generally perhaps. But one of the attractive features of assurance theory is that it makes us ask the right question of criminal prohibition: in considering whether to prohibit ϕing, whom does ϕing injure, harm, or otherwise victimise to an extent so significant that a public response is required?

In prohibiting and responding to cases of ϕing, the law must solve two 'coordination problems', where the idea of a coordination problem is broadly understood. The first is the problem of indeterminacy. The exact extent, scope and justification of these norms are controversial and uncertain. Whilst the law, to be legitimate, must by and large reflect the moral considerations that underpin these moral norms, the law can and does serve as an authority that solves the problem of indeterminacy by specifying, in more or less certain terms, legal norms that reflect these moral ones. Further, the criminal law specifies more or less certain responses to, in particular punishments for, breach of these legal norms.

The second sort of coordination problem is that of organising collective action. The 'coordination' problem the criminal justice system addresses here is the problem, or goal, of coordinating a community's response to crime so as to make its response one that is genuinely on behalf of the community or public.

We can sharpen the assurance account by comparing it to the views of Gardner. First, consider the following platitude. By instituting a criminal justice system, the law creates a better way of dealing with crime, that is, dealing with criminals in a just, fair and certain manner, than would leaving it all to self-help, for example revenge, feud, vendetta. Thought about in this way, the 'coordination problem' the criminal justice system addresses is the problem or goal of coordinating a community's response to crime so as to take the side of the victim in as good a way as possible, here by displacing private retaliation.

Now one might think that this is the most important aspect of the criminal law's function, a point once strongly emphasised by Gardner:

> The blood feud, the vendetta, the duel, the revenge, the lynching: for the elimination of these modes of retaliation, more than anything else, the criminal law as we know it today came into existence.[8]

Thus, for Gardner, this 'displacement function' of the criminal law is one of its 'central pillars'.[9] In a later writing, Gardner situated this claim in the context of another consideration:

> What the paper was supposed to offer was a simple explanation of why, *assuming that the guilty wrongdoer should indeed be punished by someone*, the criminal law

[8] J Gardner, 'Crime: in Proportion and Perspective' in A Ashworth and M Wasik (eds), *Fundamentals of Sentencing Theory* (Oxford, Oxford University Press, 1998) 31, 31.

[9] ibid 32.

> (as opposed to victims or their families or their sympathizers) should be the one to exact punishment. … Already, too much academic writing about the criminal law casually runs together questions about the justification of the criminal law and questions about the justification of punishment. … [T]he criminal law should not be seen as a merely, or even mainly, punitive institution. Rather, as I explained in 'In Defence of Defences', the criminal law
>
>> … is primarily a vehicle for the public identification of wrongdoing … and for responsible agents, whose wrongs have been thus identified, to *answer for* their wrongs by offering justifications and excuses for having committed them. By calling this latter function 'primary' I do not mean to suggest that it is socially more important. I mean that the proper execution of the other functions depends upon it. Criminal law can be a proper vehicle for … punishment only because it is a vehicle for responsible agents to answer for their wrongs.[10]

The difference between the assurance account and what might be called Gardner's 'instrumentalist' account of the criminal should now be clear. However the 'displacement function' operates, in so far as it replicates or reproduces or even makes essential reference to private retaliatory motivations, it cannot be accommodated by the assurance account. The obligation to take the side of the victim is necessarily collective or communal. Not only can it not be discharged by an individual or any number of individuals, it cannot reflect their private motivations in doing so. Only some community representative *qua* community representative can discharge the obligation. This is not an empirical matter but a conceptual one.[11]

III. Punishment

In the last section we established the constitutive collective or political, that is *public*, obligation to bring malicious wrongdoers to account, and that whatever response the law provides, it must take the side of the victim in such a way as to assure citizens that it has done so. So what about the response of punishment per se?

I still think the best introduction to understanding punishment is found in Alan Brudner's 'Retributivism and the Death Penalty'.[12] In his conclusion he says:

> Somewhat surprisingly, … retributivism issues in a counsel of pragmatism with respect to the use of the death penalty. It leads to the Montesquieuian conclusion that that penal code is best which suits the 'spirit' of a people, by which is here understood the system

[10] J Gardner, *Offences and Defences: Selected Essays in the Philosophy of Criminal Law* (Oxford University Press, 2007) 282–83, footnotes omitted, original emphasis.

[11] This, to my mind, is the one case where only the 'state' can act to preserve the 'civil condition'. To this limited extent, then, I am with the Kantians when they say that we have an obligation to enter into and maintain the civil condition when we cannot avoid coming into contact with each other. Unlike Kantians, I do not think the same obligation applies when it comes to private law generally. See JE Penner, *Property Rights: A Re-Examination* (Oxford, Oxford University Press, 2020) ch 8.

[12] A Brudner, 'Retributivism and the Death Penalty' (1980) 30 *University of Toronto Law Journal* 337.

> of life-organizing beliefs regarding the foundation of human value. Not to be confused with this result is the conclusion of Beccaria, who thought that the scale of punishments ought to be relative to the level of civility of people, the more savage requiring stronger deterrents. The question legislators must ask is not how much punishment is needed to deter potential criminals in the present state of society, but how much is needed to reassure decent men in the present state of their self-knowledge.[13]

The law's response to criminal wrongdoing must be such as to assure members of the community that it does genuinely take the side of the victim, and depending upon the self-understanding, sophistication and empirical security of the community, the appropriate response will vary. In some cases and societies, only a setback to the criminal's rights, that is punishment, will do.

Let me now offer a definition, which I hope is not idiosyncratic. Punishment is

> an authoritative, and taken to be deserved, setback to the rights of an actor who has maliciously victimised another, *which neither compensates his victim nor requires him to provide a benefit owed to his victim*, a setback to his rights that expresses condemnation of the act and the community's taking the side of his victim as against the side of the victimising actor.

Each element of this definition is important, but let me focus on the italicised portion first because, obviously, it is very relevant to the discussion of punishment in private law. I take the view that all cases of compensation can be justified as civil-law responses to breaches of duty, breaches that need not involve any criminality. I also take the view that requiring a person to provide a benefit owed to his victim, as when the court enforces payment of a debt or makes a trustee account for his trusteeship, is simply enforcing primary obligations. Making someone comply with their civil obligations, however disagreeable they may find it, is not punishment.

Turning to the underlined passages of the definition, the first concerns the longstanding retributivist's concern for desert, and reflects the common, and sound, intuition that setting back someone's rights when they do not deserve it is unjustified. Of course, we can punish in error, mistaking whether someone deserved it, hence the 'taken to be' formulation. Unjust punishment is still punishment, whereas inflicting setbacks to a person's rights without any regard to desert is just violence. The second concerns the expressivist side of the equation.

The expressivist side is most famously associated with Feinberg, who frames punishment as 'condemnation'.[14] It is beyond the scope of this chapter to consider all the ways in which his subtle account underpins assurance theory, but one feature our accounts clearly agree upon is the idea that punishment expresses the state's 'disavowing' the criminal act, making emphatically clear that it does not

[13] ibid 355.
[14] J Feinberg, 'The Expressive Function of Punishment' (1965) 49(3) *Monist* 397, 401.

endorse that act as a proper act of a member of its community. Feinberg's now classic example is this:

> [S]uppose that an airplane of nation A fires on an airplane of nation B while the latter is flying over international waters. Very likely high authorities in nation B will send a note of protest to their counterparts in nation A demanding, among other things, that the transgressive pilot be punished. Punishing the pilot is an emphatic, dramatic, and well understood way of condemning and thereby disavowing his act. It tells the world that the pilot had no right to do what he did, that he was on his own in doing it, that his government does not condone that sort of thing.[15]

On this view, any just punishment must inherit its expressive/assurance character from the prior expressive/assurance function of calling offenders to account and taking the side of their victims, so as to provide the assurance I have spoken of.

It is beyond the scope of this chapter to fully explore and justify assurance theory, but one point bears noting, that of proportionate punishment, the idea that the punishment should 'fit' the crime. On the assurance account, the setback to the perpetrator's rights must bear some sort of relation to the setback to the victim's rights or interests the perpetrator caused. If it is too lenient then the state is not really taking the side of the victim; and if it is too harsh, it 'over-condemns' and thus constitutes unjust punishment.

We can now turn to the vexed issue of desert, and here later writings by Brudner are relevant, although he now makes no mention of the assurance function of punishment. Brudner brings 'desert' into his most recent account by drawing a distinction between 'moral' and 'legal' retributivism. Moral retributivism is the idea that *all* those who have acted wickedly ought to be punished with the severity they deserve because and only because they deserve it.[16] Moral retributivism seeks to give people their 'just deserts'. Legal retributivism is different:

> [L]egal retributivism nowhere argues that the reason for punishing is to give those whose actions evince moral fault their just deserts. From the broad class of evildoers, it singles out those whose actions manifest choices to which a denial of rights must be imputed, and it selects only these for retributive punishment. Thus, for legal retributivism, moral wickedness is not a sufficient condition for eligibility for judicial punishment, and so there is no need for politics or an extrinsic end to make the final selection [of what is criminalised]; legal retributivism itself determines which wrongs are criminal. Nor is moral wickedness a necessary condition of criminal liability. The physician who, from a benevolent impulse (not amounting to the vice of excessive beneficence), injects a nonconsenting friend with life-saving and riskless medication is, for legal retributivism, a right denier deserving of punishment. Accordingly, judicial punishment is the executive arm, not of legal moralism, but of equal agency rights; and the convict is subject, not to moral opinion, but to the public reason of mutual recognition.[17]

[15] ibid 404.

[16] A Brudner, *Punishment and Freedom: A Liberal Theory of Penal Justice* (Oxford, Oxford University Press, 2009) 51. This is actually what Brudner calls 'strong' moral retributivism; I can ignore the weak version for my purposes here.

[17] ibid 50.

What, on this account, then, is the 'teleology' or purpose of punishment? It is to express, or demonstrate, the invalidity of the implicit or explicit claim the criminal makes when he deliberately infringes the rights of others.[18] Desert, on this account, is not a positive reason *for* punishing but a negative restriction on who may be punished, *viz* only the deliberate infringer of rights. This reflects the Kantian idea that the maxim of a criminal's act, if universalised, amounts to the criminal's denial of his own right that his rights be respected.[19]

Wherein, then, for Brudner, lies the positive case for punishing? I have already explained this on the assurance account – punishment is justified when only punishment can do the job of assuring citizens that the state takes their rights and interests under the norms of interpersonal morality seriously. For Brudner, the positive justification is as follows:

> It might be objected that all this can take place in a philosophy seminar. If the aim of an institutional response to crime is to vindicate mutual respect as the ground of rights by showing the self-contradictoriness of claims of right to non-respectful liberty, why must the response take the form of punishment? Why not teach the truth about rights in school? If the wrongdoer's principle is a logical nullity, after all, then rights are invincible and require no conquest over a pitiful challenger to prove their strength. They can turn the other cheek. Moreover, if the application of punishment is not necessary to achieve this rarefied purpose, is it not a piece of gratuitous violence indistinguishable from the wrongdoer's?
>
> Perhaps the lesson taught by punishment could be taught in school if the intentional interloper asserted his claim in the classroom. But he did not. He interfered with someone's agency, and his interference, because of its intentionality, expressed a right-denying principle. By *actualizing* a right-denying principle, however, the wrongdoer gave that principle an appearance of worldly authority, of existential force. <u>He gave it, that is, the appearance of a law.</u> That appearance would be allowed to stand if the nemesis of his principle were demonstrated by speech alone, for what is true in logic might not be true in the world; in the world, after all, there has been a violation expressing a claim to an absolute liberty – a claim that the civil remedy did not refute. So, by visiting the self-destructive consequence of the wrongdoer's principle upon him, punishment removes the appearance of its worldly validity and vindicates the worldly authority of Law.
>
> One might further object that the authority of Law is inherently invincible and cannot be negated by logically absurd claims making pretences to existential validity. This is true. However, the invincibility of Law is a reason only for denying that the state *must* punish in all cases of intentional wrongdoing; it is not a reason for denying that <u>the state ought to punish as a general rule</u>. For if it did not, Law's authority would remain pervasively unrealized and hence no authority at all.[20]

The only concerns I have with this passage are with the underlined portions. As to the first, I think this gives greater weight to the criminal's implicit claim than is

[18] ibid 46–47.
[19] ibid 46.
[20] ibid 47, footnotes omitted, italics original, my underlining.

necessary, at least insofar as it draws upon the Kantian idea that violating someone's rights makes some kind of authority claim, of 'setting down' the law for them. As to the second, all Brudner needs to show here is that actually setting back wrongdoers' rights by punishing them is justified when it is required to vindicate the agency rights of members of a community. It does not necessarily justify responding to crime by punishing 'as a general rule'; all it requires is the general *availability* of the state's power to punish. Sometimes 'turning the other cheek' is a superior means of vindicating right, and may fully provide for the necessary assurance. And there are cases where, though deserved, it would be just wrong to punish. The state should exercise mercy.[21] McCloskey provides a telling example, of the 'criminal [who] has already suffered greatly in blinding himself in attempting to blow a safe'.[22]

IV. Punishment and Deterrence

Everyone accepts that punishment can serve a deterrent *function*, by providing a prudential reason for those who lack the virtuous character that would mean it would never occur to them to commit the crime in the first place, virtue the state can help to inculcate via Plan A, and who are not dissuaded by the moral duty not to do so, as expressed in law by making the wrong a criminal law offence (Plan B). So deterrence is Plan C.

But the fundamental point to appreciate here is that something deters A's ϕing just in so far as A takes that something as a prudential reason not to ϕ. This shows that whether or not the thing doing the deterrent is a punishment is *orthogonal* to whether it deters. Punishments and things that deter are not co-extensive.

All legal remedies of whatever kind can and do have a deterrent effect for those that take their prospect as prudential reasons for not acting in some way.[23] For the actors that economics recognises, all reasons are matters of calculated self-interest, and so economic theory and deterrence theory cannot isolate the difference between a punishment and a licence fee or price. Indeed, they do not recognise the notion of a *wrong* at all – that just is the difference between moral and prudential reasons. So take the case of tort law. I suppose that many selfishly-run businesses try not to commit torts only because of the prospect of common law damages. For them, the prospect of an award of damages deters because it is costly, not because it represents *to them* a response to a wrong.

[21] For Brudner's own discussion about the place of mercy in the criminal law, see Brudner (n 12) 352–54.

[22] HJ McCloskey, 'A Non-Utilitarian Approach to Punishment' (1965) 8 *Inquiry* 249, 261. In ch 9 of Brudner (n 16), following an excellent discussion of restorative justice, Brudner makes what I think is a different claim, which is that the state cannot wholly renounce the use of punishment. I find that claim entirely plausible, but it does not translate into the claim that punishment should be inflicted as a general rule.

[23] Smith makes the point well: see L Smith, 'Deterrence, prophylaxis, and punishment in fiduciary obligations' (2013) 7 *Journal of Equity* 87, 88–89.

But *aspects* of deterrence may enter seamlessly into the account of punishment I have given by way of contributing to the assurance punishment provides. In certain cases, the public may genuinely fear that some of their fellows may be treating prospective punishments *only* as a price, as a prudential reason, and this may be revealed as the attitude taken by a particular offender herself – repeat offenders typically face greater punishments. In such circumstances, while no punishment should be excessive, that is disproportionate to the offence, an exemplary sentence that visits the full rigour of the law, the maximum available punishment, is justified and may be instrumental in providing assurance. Such a sentence aims to speak not only to the offender herself, but to those in the community who are apt to behave likewise.[24]

Now I must address deterrence in private law. As Bant and Paterson show,[25] the literature and the cases are replete with mentions of deterrence when it comes to various remedies. It may be that this expresses some kind of deterrence theory of punishment, or that commentators and judges think that a deterrent remedy is more or less equivalent to a punishment. Alas, I do not think it is worth the candle trying to find some common thread to this loose talk. So what I shall offer here is a role for deterrent penalties in private law that both justifies the penalties themselves and justifies them as a coherent part of private law.

V. Penalties

There are various ways of characterising penalties, in particular to distinguish them from punishments. Feinberg[26] thinks punishments express condemnation[27] while penalties, such as parking fines, do not. Another way of doing so is to say that we punish 'true' crimes but only penalise 'regulatory offences'. That distinction is a controversial one, drawn in various ways, for example by distinguishing offences that are *mala in se* from those that are *mala prohibita*. In any case, the distinction is an intuitive and familiar one, which we can tease out sufficient to our purposes. Let us begin with Brudner's account.[28]

Regulatory offences, according to Brudner, are to be distinguished from true crimes because of the fact that their violation does not require the malicious

[24] For an illuminating discussion of why the law's providing sentences that reflect this sort of deterrent aim is not to violate its citizens' rights to be treated as moral agents, see JR Edwards and AP Simester, 'Prevention with a Moral Voice' in AP Simester, A du Bois-Pedain and U Neumann (eds), *Liberal Criminal Theory: Essays for Andreas von Hirsch* (Oxford, Hart Publishing, 2004) 43.

[25] Bant and Paterson, ch 10 of this volume.

[26] Feinberg (n 14). For some doubts, see AYK Lee, 'Arguing Against The Expressive Function of Punishment: Is The Standard Account That Insufficient?' (2019) 38 *Law and Philosophy* 359.

[27] For an illuminating discussion of the stigma that attends criminal conviction and punishment in relation to strict liability offences, see AP Simester, 'Is Strict Liability Always Wrong?' in A Simester (ed) *Appraising Strict Liability* (Oxford, Oxford University Press, 2005) 21.

[28] Brudner (n 16) 138–40.

infringement of another individual's rights. Offenders are therefore not (typically[29]) deserving of punishment.[30] Regulatory offences are of two broad types.[31] The first sort regulates hazardous activities, such as the production, distribution and disposal of dangerous chemicals. The second sort regulates the conduct of individuals in order to protect valuable social preferences, or to coordinate behaviour in the pursuit of otherwise valuable activities. Examples of this type are 'infractions of greenbelt and heritage laws, hunting and fishing regulations, parking ordinances, traffic rules, and laws protecting economic competition'.[32] Of course these types can overlap, traffic rules being an obvious example: these rules coordinate behaviour in the valuable activity of road travel, but also regulate the hazards that attend it.

The penalties that are imposed for regulatory offences are meant to have a deterrent effect, and so the question naturally arises whether these should be construed as merely licence fees or taxes on the relevant activity. Brudner explains why they are not:

> Viewed as a technique for shaping incentives, regulatory fines no doubt share the same genus as taxes; but they can be distinguished from taxes without reference to blame or censure by their aim of preventing undesirable, rather than pricing desirable, activity.[33]

And this point can be seen in the law itself. Someone who *intentionally* breaches a regulatory offence may indeed be liable to punishment, for example in the case of a repeat offender who may be subject to higher and higher fines. In other words, a person who *treats* the fine as a tax or a licence fee willingly disregards the deterrent ambition of a fine, which prohibits something rather than licensing it at a cost.

A. Penalties and 'Facilitative' Regimes – The Rules of Games

As will become apparent below, I am interested in whether the rules that regulate the 'facilitative' side of private law impose penalties in certain instances. By facilitative I mean that part of private law, famously investigated as a matter of general jurisprudence by HLA Hart, that confers powers upon people to organise their affairs with others. The obvious examples are the laws of contract, agency, wills and trusts. I think the idea of a penalty in this realm of rules is illuminated by a brief investigation of the nature of punishments and penalties in the realm of games, and the basic claim I shall defend is that a penalty is imposed where an individual takes an advantage outside of the rules, and the intended effect of the penalty is to strip him of that advantage, but where no judgment follows that his behaviour was

[29] See text after n 32.
[30] Brudner (n 16) 139–40.
[31] ibid 172–73. Brudner apparently thinks these types are exhaustive of the genre. It is not clear to me that that is so, but the issue need not detain us.
[32] ibid 172.
[33] ibid 178.

unsportsmanlike. Another way of putting this point is that the rules *disentitle* the wrongdoer to the gain he has acquired outside the rules.

I shall look at the rules of football (ie Association Football) and ice hockey, as they impose similar but interestingly different penalties and punishments in equivalent circumstances. In both football and ice hockey, there is a gradation of infractions of the rules resulting in penalties and punishments. We can start with punishments.

In my view, being sent off for the duration of a game, that is, getting a red card in football or a game misconduct in ice hockey, is a punishment directed to the individual player for 'malicious' or deliberate misbehaviour deserving of condemnation. These are clearly mens rea offences. Red cards or game misconducts doubtless also have a collateral penalising effect on the team, depriving the team of the player's unique skills for the duration, in the same way that imprisoning a trader for insider trading doubtless also penalises her firm, depriving it of her services. These collateral penalising effects may indeed be intended: for example, in football a player sent off cannot be replaced, so his team must carry on one player short for the duration of the game; whereas in ice hockey a player sent off may be replaced, so the penalising effect is much less.

Now, as to penalties. As I have proposed, penalties are instituted to prevent teams from getting advantages outside the rules of the game but are not condemnatory. Vigorous play often results in such infractions, in particular fouls by one player on another, but also in terms of non-foul rules, such as the offside rule in football or the icing rule in ice hockey. The typical response is for play to be halted and some advantage awarded to the other team. A free kick, a corner kick, a throw-in and so on are typical in football, whereas the standard response to a foul in ice hockey is for the player to be sent off for two or five minutes, leaving his team to play short-handed until the penalty time elapses or the opposing team scores a goal. Both games also have a 'penalty shot' rule. In football this is typically awarded when a player is fouled in the opposing team's 'penalty area', in ice hockey when a player is deprived of a clear scoring opportunity by being fouled. Interestingly, in ice hockey the player fouled must take the penalty shot, whereas in football the fouled team may nominate any of their players, normally, obviously, their best penalty-taker, to take the penalty, enhancing the penalising effect.[34]

I have argued that penalties strip a team of what would otherwise be 'an advantage' acquired outside the rules of the game, but we should be judicious about this idea. As in other cases of rules, we must distinguish between the justification for a rule and the requirements of the rule itself, how it applies. This will be important

[34] As Steve Smith pointed out to me, some penalties, the 'penalty shot' rules being a good example, may also have a compensatory role, restoring an opportunity to a player that was denied by a foul. But I doubt that penalties generally do so, as they are in amount and application typically insensitive to the other team's 'loss'. Where games award some advantage like a throw-in or free kick to the other team, this makes the penalty more effective along two dimensions: one, if the penalty is roughly of the right strength, the sting is provided in giving the other team an appropriate advantage; and, two, it keeps the penalty 'in the game' in the sense of not overly interfering with the flow of play.

when we consider gain-stripping in private law. In the case of penalties in games, the rules providing for them have the general justifying aim of making sure the game is played by the rules, thus ensuring that players who would gain advantages by breaking the rules do not do so, as a simple matter of fairness. But it is irrelevant that any particular infraction advantages the team. A player who attempts to pass the ball to an unmarked teammate in scoring position but sails the ball out of the pitch gains no advantage by putting the ball out of play in this case. But the other team is still awarded the throw-in. Perfectly justifiable general rules often apply to cases where their justifying purpose is not directly applicable.

VI. Punishments and Penalties in Private Law

A. The Case of Punitive Damages

Let me begin with punitive damages just to get them out of the way. The topic of punitive damages has been explored at great length in other chapters in this volume, so I can be brief. I only want to say two things.

The first is that I fully subscribe to the arguably insurmountable objections to justifying the institution of punitive damages in private law variously adumbrated by Weinrib, Stevens and Ripstein.[35] The basic idea is obvious. One cannot derive a right to punish, which is, as I have shown, a collective, public right, from a private right. A private law court cannot 'award' such a right *qua* private law court; this is not just a matter of doctrine or competence, though the worries here are severe, but a conceptual matter. Nor can the private rights of the plaintiff generate any right to the benefit of a punishment.

Second, and relatedly, is the idea that the plaintiff in such cases secures a 'windfall' unrelated either to a duty of repair she is owed for a private law breach, or to a primary private law duty of performance. This, to my mind, has nothing to do with the quantum of the award, which may tug at our 'unjust enrichment' heartstrings. Rather, as a public measure of condemnation, a punishment cannot allocate the benefit of a punishment to any private actor. In that respect punitive damages privatise punishment, and that alone brings them worryingly close to a form of private retaliation. But it gets worse. As the holder of right of action, it is up to the plaintiff to prosecute (or not) such a right. Consider settlement. As illustrated by Sharkey,[36] the power to enter into settlement can largely determine the punitive

[35] EJ Weinrib, *Corrective Justice* (Oxford, Oxford University Press, 2012) 169–83; R Stevens, *Torts and Rights* (Oxford, Oxford University Press, 2007) 85–88; A Ripstein, *Private Wrongs* (Cambridge, MA, Harvard University Press, 2016) 259–61. For a similar scepticism about allowing punitive damages against trustees, see SL Bray, 'Punitive damages against trustees?' in DG Smith and AS Gold (eds), *Research Handbook on Fiduciary Law* (Cheltenham, Edward Elgar, 2018) 201.

[36] Sharkey, ch 7 of this volume.

fate of the defendant. Far from being public, this brings the whole matter as close as can be to state-backed private retaliation for personal gain.[37]

B. The General Nature of Penalties in Private Law

The claim I am going to make here is that private, judge-made law, in its regulation of private law rights, sometimes penalises private law actors. The form of this regulation is of the second type described by Brudner, that of regulating and coordinating behaviour in an individual's pursuit of worthwhile activities. This is especially salient for what might be called 'facilitative' private law. This is the private law where, through the exercise of powers, individuals can form relationships of various kinds – contractual, agent–principal, trustee–beneficiary – relationships that advance their individual interests through these legally validated devices or mechanisms. The purpose of regulating individuals in these endeavours is to ensure that their valid purposes are advanced and, moreover, that the valuable practice of engaging in contracts, agency and trusts is protected from erosion by the law's responding to ways in which private actions can undermine them.

To get a sense of how private law might penalise someone, consider first this from Gray:

> [I]t is a good rule that a sealed bond can only be defeated by a sealed acquittance, for the rule will encourage care in business and diminish factual controversies about whether debts have been paid. If equity is permitted to undercut the rule, it is not because the rule is faulty by a moral standard above the law, but because it is not meant literally. The common law itself does not hold that careless people should always or even usually have to pay twice, but only that a *deterrent price should be attached to carelessness*. The price consists in having to bring a suit in equity, with the trouble and risk of failure any lawsuit involves; … in having … to convince the court of equity that the carelessness was in some way excusable or *the hardship of double payment an undue penalty* in the circumstances.[38]

To pursue this, let me immodestly quote something I have written elsewhere:[39]

> The thought that the law allows individuals to 'do it the easy way', such as comply with the rules about formalities, or 'do it the hard way', having to go to court and engage in a time-consuming and inefficient exploration of all the circumstances, should be given more prominence today than I think it generally has. I think the treatment of informal trusts of the family home and the application of the *Re Rose*[40] principle very much give

[37] It is beyond my purposes here to explore whether state-backed private retaliation is ever justified. For an argument that punitive damages are the private law equivalent of punishment, see SA Smith, *Rights, Wrongs, and Injustices: The Structure of Remedial Law* (Oxford, Oxford University Press, 2019) 202–06.

[38] CM Gray, 'The Boundaries of the Equitable Function' (1976) 20 *American Journal of Legal History* 192, 220 (emphasis added).

[39] JE Penner, 'Equity, Justice and Conscience' in D Klimchuk, I Samet and HE Smith (eds), *Philosophical Foundations of the Law of Equity* (Oxford, Oxford University Press, 2020) 52, 55.

[40] *Re Rose, Rose v IRC* [1952] Ch 499.

> rise to just the sort of uncertainty, and consequent likelihood of a need to resort to litigation, which in practice does amount to a penalty for failing to comply with clear rules about property transactions.

This way of thinking helps, I think, to explain equity's treatment of fiduciaries in relation to the no-profit rule, which I shall discuss shortly. But I am doubtful that all of the cases in which fiduciaries are stripped of their gains can be given a systematic treatment reflecting the same underlying principle. This is not surprising. Judge-made law is not like legislation; it develops case by case, and I shall look at several sorts of case in which I think it is fair to describe the defendants as having been penalised. But I think there is at least a theme that follows from what I noticed in the last paragraph. Equity is particularly concerned with ensuring that the fiduciary relationship is protected, not so much from *intentional abuse*, but from inappropriate transactions that simply cannot be allowed to stand. In this sense, these penalties ensure that fiduciaries are playing by the rules.

Before moving on to that, I want to reiterate and develop a point I made above. Requiring you to accounting for a gain that, if you acquire it at all, is one you must acquire for the benefit of another, is neither a penalty nor a punishment. You are not being stripped of a gain that was otherwise *yours*. The law enforces a primary obligation that flows from the nature of the relationship.[41] It is, of course, most typically distinctive of trust and agency relationships. But where liability to disgorge a gain does not flow from such a duty to account, then stripping someone of a gain *is* either a punishment or a penalty. This is a crucial point: stripping A of a gain and awarding it to B is only a punishment or a penalty if B was *not antecedently entitled* to that gain. By an antecedent entitlement I do not mean a legal entitlement in the sense that prior to an agent's entering into a contract on behalf of his principal the principal has any legal entitlement to that contract with the third-party counterparty. By entitlement I mean it is within the scope of the agent's instructions, is the kind of legal opportunity he is tasked with finding and obtaining for his principal. In this sense the 'scope of the agency relationship' question is correlative – the profit in question is one to which the principal is 'entitled' *as against the agent* because it is within the scope of the agent's instructions (leaving aside issues of apparent authority and ratification) whether the agent actually manages to acquire it or not – and the agent is (reciprocally) disentitled *as against his principal* from pursuing it for himself.

Theorists differ on where we should draw the line between genuine accounting cases and genuine gain-stripping cases,[42] but we cannot do without the distinction

[41] A clear example is *Industrial Development Consultants Ltd v Cooley* [1972] 2 All ER 162, [1972] 1 WLR 443 (AS), where the fiduciary acquired for himself the very business he was obliged to obtain for his principal. *Of course* he had to account for it.

[42] See, eg, EJ Weinrib, 'Restitutionary Damages as Corrective Justice' (2000) 1(1) *Theoretical Inquiries in Law* 1; Ripstein (n 35) 258. For my own view, see JE Penner, 'The difficult doctrinal basis for the fiduciary's proprietary liability to account for bribes' (2012) 18 *Trusts and Trustees* 1000; and JE Penner, 'Distinguishing Fiduciary, Trust, and Accounting Relationships' (2014) 8 *Journal of Equity* 202.

itself, and we see the doctrinal confusion that ignoring it leads to. Take the case of a non-fiduciary who is bribed, a case I shall return to below, like a warehouse guard who takes a bribe to admit the burglars. It is idiotic to bend the rules of private law retrospectively to impute to him a fiduciary status (which he 'undertakes' by committing the wrong – that is nonsensical) and then say he has to 'account' for his 'profit' as if the bribe was something that, within the scope of his employment, he had a liberty, power or duty to acquire for his employer. Much better to be upfront about this and acknowledge this as a private law penalty. Another way of reaching this result is by creating a private law liability of 'restitution for wrongs' or 'wrong-based unjust enrichment'.[43] For reasons I cannot get into here, I think this approach is also misguided. What is on offer here is another, independent justifying ground for legal penalties, which I hope you will find at least interesting and perhaps even persuasive.

C. Bribes

A person is bribed when he is offered a benefit to act *disloyally* in relation to another. A hitman who receives money from A to kill B is not being bribed. He is just being paid to commit a wrong against B. As I have explored in excruciating detail elsewhere,[44] a duty of loyalty is a duty not to commit a deliberate, that is bad-faith, breach of obligation owed to someone who has reposed (or has had reposed for her, in the case of a child) confidence or trust (in the colloquial, not the legal sense) in him. Such a duty is clearly held by employees, agents and trustees. I also think parents have such a duty. Where any of these take a bribe and act on it, breaching in bad faith any duty they owe to the person who entrusted them, they must disgorge that gain to that person. This is a private law penalty because, as I have stated above, bribes are not gains by the disloyal person to which the entrusting party was antecedently entitled. Bribes should never be pursued nor taken by anyone, ever. This is a clear case of gain-stripping for committing a particular kind of wrong, a disloyal breach of obligation. As between the bribee and the one to whom she owes a duty of loyalty, the latter is entitled to the value of the bribe only for the reason that the bribee is disentitled from taking or keeping it. For what it is worth, these bad-faith wrongs also allow for the summary dismissal of an employee or agent and the removal of a trustee, which, I would say, also at least penalises them, and perhaps punishes them.

[43] See, eg, Gareth Jones, 'Unjust Enrichment and the fiduciary's duty of loyalty' (1968) 84 *LQR* 472.

[44] J Penner, 'Fiduciary Law and Moral Norms' in EJ Criddle, PB Miller and RH Sitkoff (eds), *Oxford Handbook of Fiduciary Law* (Oxford, Oxford University Press, 2019) 781; J Penner, 'Trustees and Agents Behaving Badly: When and How is "Bad Faith" Relevant?' in M Harding and PB Miller (eds), *Fiduciaries and Trust: Ethics, Politics, Economics and Law* (Cambridge, Cambridge University Press, 2020) 128, 135–48.

D. Gain-stripping Rules Applying to Fiduciaries – The 'No Unauthorised Profit' Rule

Smith has done extensive work analysing the nature of the 'no unauthorised profit rule', the 'no profit rule' for short. Perhaps the most important result of that analysis is that the rule makes someone acting in a fiduciary role accountable to his principal for any gain he has acquired in that role, (i) whether or not the gain resulted from the exercise of the fiduciary's fiduciary powers, such as the power of an agent to contract upon his principal's behalf, and (ii) whether or not there was *in fact* any conflict of interest between the fiduciary and his principal. The clearest example of a case where the rule was applied where there was no exercise of fiduciary powers and no actual conflict of interest is the case of *Boardman v Phipps*, which I shall discuss shortly. Liability under the rule follows simply because the gain was acquired by the fiduciary in the course of or as a result of her acting for and on behalf of her principal, that is acting within the scope of her fiduciary–principal relationship; a fiduciary is simply disentitled, as between herself and her principal, from acquiring any such gain. As a result of this analysis, Smith concludes that the no profit rule is entirely unrelated to the no conflict principle, what might be called an umbrella principle by which any exercise of a fiduciary power by a fiduciary in conflict of interest with her principal is liable to be set aside at the instance of her principal. Such a principle explains more specific rules like the self-dealing rule.[45]

This conclusion is a point on which we differ. To see our difference, consider again what I said about the justification of a rule, and the requirements for applying a rule. In my view, although Smith rightly contends that the application of the no profit rule does not turn on whether a fiduciary power was exercised or whether there was an actual conflict in fact, I contend that the rule is justified under the no conflict principle. I contend that the rule is justified on the principle that a fiduciary is not unilaterally entitled to determine, specify or vary the scope of his fiduciary relationship with his principal, in particular to decide *which potential gains* he must pursue, if he pursues them at all, for the benefit of his principal. Let me explain.

In an ideal world, the scope of any agent–principal or trustee–beneficiary relationship would be clear and easily, objectively, determined. In the case of an express trust with a written trust instrument, this is usually mostly the case. Agents may also be given very specific instructions. I hasten to add that where an agent or a trustee has fiduciary powers, this does not mean that how those powers should be exercised can ever be objectively determined. The whole point of granting such powers is to empower the fiduciary to exercise his own best judgment about how exercising such powers will best advantage his principal, and different fiduciaries

[45] See JE Penner, *The Law of Trusts*, 11th edn (Oxford, Oxford University Press, 2019) [13.93]–[13.96].

will do so differently. Indeed the whole point of the conflict principle in respect to the exercise of fiduciary powers addresses this fact.[46] Rather, the point I am making is that it is often uncertain, in particular in agency cases, what the actual scope of the agency arrangement is, in terms of the scope or extent of what the agent ought to, and may, do for his principal. What the no profit rule basically does is deny the fiduciary the liberty or the power to decide any such uncertainty unilaterally, where the uncertainty in question concerns a gain or benefit potentially available to his principal, for having a liberty or power to do so would put him unavoidably in a situation of conflict with his principal whenever such an occasion arose. In its most stringent applications the rule applies whenever it is even arguable that the fiduciary's opportunity for gain was something that might have been within the scope of the relationship, that is, might have been an opportunity to which the principal was antecedently entitled, or at least antecedently interested in. I take it that this problem or idea was what the Lord Chancellor was getting at in *Keech v Sanford* in the passages emphasised in the following:

> *[F]or I very well see, if a trustee, on the refusal to renew, might have a lease to himself, few trust estates would be renewed to cestui que use;* … but it is very proper that rule should be strictly pursued, and not in the least relaxed; *for it is very obvious what would be the consequence of letting trustees have the lease, on refusal to renew to cestui que use.*[47]

That is, it would be obvious what would happen if a trustee could decide unilaterally whether his obligations to the beneficiary required him to renew the lease, or whether he was free to take the lease for himself. One specification of the rule is what is sometimes called the 'corporate opportunity doctrine', where the question is whether an opportunity must be pursued, if pursued at all, for the benefit of the company, or whether it is 'free' to be exploited by one or more fiduciary directors or officers of the company for their own benefit. Although the doctrine has been whittled down in various jurisdictions in some circumstances, the principle is the same: the directors are not entitled to decide this question by themselves.[48]

All of these features of the no profit rule are illustrated by the classic case of *Boardman v Phipps*.[49] Roughly, at the beginning of the story the defendants, Boardman and Tom Phipps, acted as agents[50] of some of the trustees of the Phipps

[46] Penner, 'Trustees and Agents' (n 44) 130–32.
[47] *Keech v Sandford* (1726) Sel Cas Ch 61, 62.
[48] Penner (n 45) [13.43]–[13.59].
[49] *Boardman v Phipps* [1967] 2 AC 46.
[50] There was much discussion in the various judgments of the nature of the defendants' 'agency', which is in some respects confusing. At the outset of his judgment, Wilberforce J said they 'assumed the character of self-appointed agents for the trustees' (*Phipps v Boardman* [1964] 1 WLR 993, 1007), but thereafter just referred to them as 'agents' or to their 'agency' tout court (at 1007, 1008, 1011, 1012). The first point to note is that there is no such thing as a 'self-appointed' agent. An agency only arises upon a principal's conferring authority expressly or impliedly upon an agent, either prospectively, or retrospectively under the doctrine of ratification. (See P Watts and F Reynolds, *Bowstead and Reynolds on Agency* (London, Sweet & Maxwell, 2018) 2-001 (1)). In argument before the Court of Appeal (*Phipps v Boardman* [1965] Ch 992) this point was made (at 1008D), and the reply (at 1008G) was that the defendants were 'self-appointed agents in the sense that a small boy who asks to run errands is a

family trust, acting solely on their behalf to realise the value of their shares in a private company. At some point the situation changed. Boardman got the consent from at least one of the trustees to alter their relationship to something like a joint venture, in which he and Tom Phipps would put in their own money[51] to acquire further shares in the company so that together with the trustee's shares they would have a controlling interest to their mutual benefit. If that change in the relationship, from agency to joint venture, was what actually happened, then of course the defendants would not have had to account for their personal profit under that joint venture to the trustees or the trust's beneficiaries. Indeed, reading the facts this way was roughly how Viscount Dilhorne found in the defendants' favour.[52] But the majority disagreed, holding that the defendants never got the requisite consent.[53]

self-appointed agent. The appellants asked to take on the job and the trustees assented.' But if that reply was correct, and it appears that it was, then they were not self-appointed, simply appointed at their own request. At the beginning of the story, the first thing Boardman and Phipps did was to act *as proxies* for the trustee-shareholders at a general meeting of the company, and this was no self-appointment, for the trustees had to execute the proxies. (Whilst I agree with most of the analysis of the case by Michael Bryan (M Bryan, '*Boardman v Phipps*' in C Mitchell and P Mitchell (eds), *Landmark Cases in Equity* (Oxford, Hart Publishing, 2012) 581), I disagree with his conclusion (at 585–89, 609–10) that the defendants were *self-appointed* agents in any genuine sense, or that their liability was not that of an agent, but of an 'intermeddler'. One reason Bryan gives (ibid 587–88) for this conclusion is that a true agency relationship is one in which the agent is empowered to create or affect the legal relations of her principal, and the defendants acquired no such powers. But that is not an accurate reflection of the law: see *Bowstead and Reynolds on Agency*, 1-001 (4), 1-021.) So there was no question that the defendants acted as properly appointed agents to the trustees as their principals *qua shareholders*, but it was not clear whether they were rightly regarded as agents to their principals *qua trustees*, for such an appointment would normally require a joint appointment by all trustees and that did not occur (but see Russell LJ at [1965] Ch 992, 1031G; Lord Cohen at [1967] 2 AC 46, 100E); it is in this sense that their appointment was defective, akin to a person's taking on a trusteeship but who for some reason is not properly appointed; this is the sense in which the defendants can be regarded not as self-appointed agents, but as agents *de son tort* or *de facto* agents. (See the CA judgment at 1017E–G, per Lord Denning.) There was no common finding by the various judges of who precisely the defendants' principals in law were. The point became further complicated when the widow of the testator died, so that the capital interests fell in. After that each beneficiary, including the plaintiff, was absolutely entitled to a proportionate shareholding of the company. It appears from the reasoning of the trial judge and the Court of Appeal, in requiring the defendants to get the fully informed consent of the plaintiff, essentially *ex post facto*, that this reflects the idea that when the capital interests fall in, and the trustees hold the trust assets to the order of the beneficiaries, only the beneficiaries are entitled to consent to the sort of conduct undertaken by the defendants.

[51] Or rather, money they borrowed.

[52] See Penner (n 45) [13.33]–[13.40].

[53] There was no clear, common holding by the various judges of what consent the defendants needed to obtain, but I would submit the following is correct: where there are two or more trustees, they must, unless the terms of the trust provide otherwise, *act unanimously* in the exercise of any of their fiduciary powers, those being powers over which they must exercise judgement regarding the beneficiaries' best interests in deciding to exercise them at all (eg a power to accumulate income), or powers that, even if they must be exercised, must only be exercised with judgement regarding the beneficiaries' best interests (eg a power to invest). At the start of the story in *Boardman* there were three trustees, one of whom was incapacitated. (She suffered from dementia.) The trustees therefore could not exercise any of their fiduciary powers unanimously, because one of them could not exercise any judgement at all. Thus any exercise of a fiduciary power by the other two trustees was by definition unlawful. The only solution, a solution which is of course entirely obvious, is to remove the incapacitated trustee under a power

It is important to note how the no conflict principle applied in this case. In seeking to turn the agency into a joint venture, the defendants were clearly intending to favour their own interests. There is nothing wrong with that in principle, but they could not do that on their own because of the existing agency relationship under which this opportunity came their way. They needed the fully informed explicit consent of their principal(s) to the new arrangement, and that is what they failed to get. Although the claim was completely unmeritorious – the beneficiaries would never have handsomely profited from all of the defendants' efforts if they had not put in their own money – that was irrelevant to the result. The basic regulatory lesson here is that if you proceed to act without resolving a conflict of interest, in this case by getting the fully informed explicit consent of your principal, you will be stripped of any gain you acquire, and you cannot rely upon the Viscount Dilhornes of this world to get you off the hook by sympathetically reading the facts to construct the needed consent for you. The rule applied in its full rigour despite the facts that (i) the gain was not acquired by any exercise of any fiduciary powers by the defendants – they did nothing that legally bound the trustees; (ii) as the parties' interests in their joint venture were *in fact* aligned, the defendants' gain itself was not acquired in conflict of interest; and (iii), the gain of which the defendants were stripped, the value of a large shareholding subject to reimbursement of their purchase outlays and an allowance for their efforts, was very much *not* something to which the trustees or beneficiaries of the Phipps trust were entitled under the scope of the defendants' agency.

I should also say that this result seems very intuitively to fall in the category of penalty, as opposed to punishment. At all levels the judges went out of their way to say that the application of this rule did not express any moral disapproval of the defendants. For example, Lord Cohen said[54] 'I desire to repeat that the integrity

provided by the trust terms or by application to the court. (Where the trustees have a duty not requiring the exercise of their judgement to exercise a power (eg to pay the income beneficiary the money representing the trust income) or a duty to perform some other task (eg to keep the trust accounts), the trustees must perform that duty as best they can until such time as the incapacitated trustee is removed.) (As a practical matter, this is not necessarily a problem for third parties. If the competent trustees had, for example, paid an accountant for doing the trust's tax return, an accountant with no knowledge that there was another trustee who was incompetent, he would be entitled to his payment as a bona fide purchaser.) In such circumstances, the only consent that would have made the competent trustees' acts lawful would be the unanimous consent of the beneficiaries, which consent would authorise what would otherwise be a breach of trust. On the facts, the only person who arguably gave fully informed consent to the new arrangement was one of the competent trustees, in January 1957, whilst the incompetent trustee was still alive. Moreover Boardman, who was a solicitor, and Tom Phipps, unlike the accountant in the parenthetical example above, had full knowledge that one of the trustees was incapacitated. Since the beneficiaries did not consent to the new arrangement, to the defendants' switching from acting as agents for the trustee-shareholders to joint venturers with them, the necessary consent in the circumstances was not obtained. The incompetent trustee died whilst the 'joint venture' was well underway, but Boardman did not provide significant information to the beneficiaries, who were now absolutely entitled to proportionate shares in the company, until the agreement under which the defendants were to purchase their shareholding was concluded. (See the CA decision at 1015D–G per Lord Denning.) For an indication that Boardman belatedly realised that he had not got the necessary consent, see the letter he wrote that was quoted in the House of Lords judgment at 97G–98D.

[54] *Boardman* (n 49) 104E–F.

of the appellants is not in doubt. They acted with complete honesty throughout …'. And in the Court of Appeal, Pearson LJ described their failure as a mistake: '[T]hey did disclose the facts that they were going to buy the shares on their own behalf and hoped to make a profit. Their mistake was in not fully disclosing all the material facts …'.[55] We penalise people for making mistakes; we do not punish them. Relatedly, the result here reinforces the point about 'doing it the easy way and doing it the hard way'.[56] By proceeding on an informal basis, the defendants exposed themselves to the penalty they incurred because they did not do the simple thing of sitting down with the trustees (after removing the one with dementia) and getting the proper consent to the joint venture. In consequence, they bought themselves an expensive lawsuit that went all the way to the House of Lords.

The rule also applies to the case of a trustee who votes the trust's majority holding of company shares to appoint himself to the board of directors, although the conflict principle is more apparent here. It is trite law that unless otherwise allowed by the trust instrument via the fully informed consent of the beneficiaries, he must account for his director's fees.[57] Now, in parity with the case of Mr Boardman, it is important to realise that the beneficiaries have no antecedent right to these director's fees, as if, because of the trust's majority shareholding, the beneficiaries are entitled to require the trustee to vote himself onto the board just so he can add the director's fees to the trust assets. That is a preposterous notion. The trustee has an obligation, if he thinks it is necessary to protect the beneficiaries' interests, to appoint someone to the board to look out for those interests.[58] If he identifies a third party who is in his judgement the best person for the job and at arm's length from him, say an accountant, and appoints her, she will be entitled to the director's fees, and the beneficiaries have no cause for complaint. But let us suppose that the trustee concludes that he would be best able to serve the beneficiaries' interests by appointing himself to the board. Well, now we have a clear conflict of interest because of the gain, the director's fees, he will acquire by doing so. He cannot do so unless he resolves the conflict first. He can get the fully informed consent of the beneficiaries. Strictly speaking, the beneficiaries' consent does not *remove* the conflict but simply authorises the trustee to proceed anyway. But it resolves the conflict in the sense that it is no longer an impediment to the trustee's going ahead. But as Smith would be sure to point out, *there may in fact be no actual conflict between the trustee and the beneficiaries in regard to the actual appointment* if in fact his appointment to the board would best serve their interests. But he is conflicted in exercising the power to do so because of the fees he would be able to receive. I also think that the trustee can resolve the conflict by waiving his right

[55] *Phipps* (n 50) 1031B.

[56] See the extract set out in the main text following n 39.

[57] See Penner (n 45) [13.80]–[13.82].

[58] Whether the trustee has such an obligation depends on the circumstances. See Penner (n 45) [10.15]–[10.16].

to the fees.[59] Since the beneficiaries have no antecedent right that the trustee capture these fees for the trust, they have nothing to complain about in this case either. Of course if the trustee does not resolve the conflict, he is in the same situation as Boardman. Equity penalises him for so acting by stripping him of the gain.

E. Disproportionate Penalties

Many students and teachers think that Boardman and Tom Phipps were treated too severely. Lord Upjohn felt the application of the rule in this case was 'harsh'.[60] Both a punishment and a penalty might be *disproportionate* in the circumstances. Unlike a sentencing decision, which can vary the extent of punishment according to the guilt of the defendant, penalties just apply automatically, because the penalty rule simply disentitles the wrongdoer, as between himself and his principal, to the gain, however large or small it may be. Yet in the right case the court might diminish the full force of the penalty by awarding an allowance, as in *Boardman*. More recently, Arden LJ has endorsed the award of such an allowance where the fiduciary has acted in perfect good faith.[61] In the same case Clarke LJ went further, saying that an allowance might be awarded even 'where a court of equity might well conclude that justice required that, *despite his fraud*, [a defendant] should be allowed to retain some share of the profits and not to account for them all'.[62]

Bant and Paterson,[63] relying upon Australian High Court jurisprudence, address the problem of excessive penalisation by suggesting that such awards might unjustly enrich the plaintiff.[64] I shall explain in a moment why awarding a penalty to the plaintiff, rather than the state's taking it for itself, is permissible in the case of private law penalties, whereas for the reasons given above this is never a sound idea in the case of true punishments. But in the case of penalties per se, there is no room for unjust enrichment thinking to figure in the equation. The intuition that it does seems to turn on the idea that the plaintiff gets a windfall, or on the idea that she is over-compensated for the defendant's wrong or mistake. But as we have seen, this is not a question about compensation or worrying about the extent of the 'windfall' but a simple matter of entitlement and disentitlement. The plaintiff is entitled to the gain because, as between themselves, the defendant is disentitled from taking it.

[59] A trickier case is where the trustee accepts the fees but gives them to charity. My intuitions about this case have fluctuated, but I now think the trustee must account for the value of the gains even if she has given them to charity (the charity will itself also be liable as a volunteer recipient), because having the choice of what to do with the money (by acquiring the title to it) is a gain in itself, even if the choice is realised in a non-self-serving way.

[60] *Boardman* (n 49) 123C.

[61] *Murad v Al-Saraj* [2005] EWCA Civ 959 [82]–[84].

[62] ibid [142] (emphasis added).

[63] See ch 10, section IV.D.

[64] It is not clear to me whether Bant is reporting this tactic or actually endorses it.

In the cases I have been considering, the penalty imposed upon the defendant goes to the plaintiff. I must now explain why I think that is permissible in the case of penalties, despite the fact that I think it is impermissible in the case of punishments.

As I have emphasised, but for the application of the gain-stripping rule the plaintiff would have no entitlement to the defendant's gain. So akin to the case of a punitive damages award, the result is often seen as a kind of windfall to the plaintiff. But there are significant differences between the two cases.

Because penalties are not punishments, there is no question of the plaintiff's turning a public punishment into a form of private retaliation, as arguably occurs with punitive damages. This is especially so since a principal or beneficiary can ratify or adopt a transaction that breached the rules, and in that sense can control the application of the penalty; this is one respect in which the entitlement/disentitlement application of the rule is *as between the fiduciary and her principal*. And notice, this is not like deciding not to sue for a tort or breach of contract, which does nothing to transform the tort or breach into something non-wrongful. When I ratify or adopt a fiduciary breach, this makes it the case that it was never a breach at all. It is, of course, possible to find such an *ex post facto* consent metaphysically mysterious, but the law does not seem troubled by it. Because it was in the power of your principal to allow or disallow the gain, it is, in some sense, hers – not, mind you, in the sense that she was entitled to the specific gain as something you had a duty to *get* for her, but as something over which she retained a kind of authority. By stripping you of it and allocating it to her, the penalty, to my mind at least, reinforces that point. Furthermore, there is a sense in which, as in a game, awarding the penalty to the plaintiff restores a private relationship equilibrium. The 'regulatory offence' was created to protect the plaintiff's private law interests, as a member of the class of beneficiaries, or principals, etc. As with private rule-governed activities like gains, often the most effective remedy is to award the penalty, as in football or ice hockey, to the team of the player who was fouled.

F. Penalties and Deterrence

We are almost home. The last matter I must deal with is a dispute between Conaglen and Smith about what 'deterrent' thinking is doing in the kinds of cases I have discussed. The gist of Conaglen's deterrent justification of fiduciary liability is found in the following statement:

> Fiduciary doctrine operates in a protective manner. It tries to avoid breach of non-fiduciary duties by seeking to remove incentives that may tempt a fiduciary not to perform his non-fiduciary duties properly.[65]

[65] M Conaglen, *Fiduciary Loyalty: Protecting the Due Performance of Non-Fiduciary Duties* (Oxford, Hart Publishing, 2010) 62.

I am not concerned here with whether Conaglen has properly shown that these incentives are geared only towards the right performance of non-fiduciary duties, that is, whether the class of duties that a fiduciary must *perform* is exclusively non-fiduciary.[66] The issue is whether Conaglen's view that the fiduciary rules such as the no profit rule are truly deterrent. Smith thinks they are not.

I hope I can fairly summarise Smith's objections as follows. First, he argues that if these rules are intended as deterrents, they are pretty lousy ones. So, he says:

> If a person defrauded a victim of $500, and the sanction was that the fraudster had to give the $500 back to the victim, this would be a pretty poorly-designed deterrent. Indeed, it would have the contrary effect: unless the chances of detection and litigation were 100%, there would always be more overall profit in defrauding as often as possible than in not defrauding. The same reasoning must apply in the fiduciary context, although exacerbated by the consideration that in many fiduciary relationships, detection of misconduct is very difficult indeed.
>
> Of course, the no-conflict and no-profit rules may have some deterrent effect on some people. But as we have seen, that is not relevant to explaining their function. When we are considering their function, the question is whether they can be understood to have a deterrent design. In the light of the legal consequences of their breach, this is simply implausible. No one designing a deterrent sanction would ever set the level of the sanction as the forfeiture of the precise amount of the supposedly wrongful profit.[67]

In so far as this goes, Smith is clearly right: I shall return to this point. His next argument concerns the justice of stripping a fiduciary of his profit:

> Recall that the no-conflict and no-profit rules are independent from other legal norms. If a fiduciary acquires a profit through his fiduciary role, he must give it up. It is not necessary to prove any of the things that deterrent theorists say that fiduciary obligations are supposed to deter: not harm, not misappropriation, not breach of a non-fiduciary duty. The deterrent sanction is attached only to the making of the profit. But making a profit is not inherently wrongful; on the contrary, it is generally a good thing. According to the deterrent theorists, the law takes this profit, that belongs (at common law) to the fiduciary, and assigns the benefit of it to the beneficiary, in order to deter certain conduct, without any concern for whether the fiduciary has or has not engaged in that conduct.
>
> This is profoundly unjust. We have seen that deterrence is not necessarily punishment; there can be deterrence by warning. But deterrence that takes the form of forcing a person to give up rights that he holds is harder to justify than a person's liberty to put up a sign that says 'beware of the dog'. If we are supposed to take away the rights acquired by a fiduciary, and this as a deterrent, surely it could only rightly be done in cases where the fiduciary had actually done something worthy of deterrence. Otherwise we would be using him as a means to an end. It would be no different to punishing an innocent person to deter others from crime.[68]

[66] For a contrary view, see L Smith, 'Prescriptive Fiduciary Duties' (2018) 37 *University of Queensland Law Journal* 261.
[67] Smith (n 23) 91–92, footnotes omitted.
[68] ibid 94.

But I think we can say, and not just out of an irenic disposition, that Conaglen and Smith are both right. With respect to Conaglen, this whole chapter can be seen as an attempt to elaborate on the deterrent intuitions that he and I share. But Smith is right if deterrents are to be understood as *sanctions* whose purpose is to *punish* an offender. Of course, I am now going to suggest that thinking of the fiduciary rules as penalty rules disarms Smith's objections.

As to Smith's first objection, I think the reply is found in the general theory of regulatory penalties I advanced above. We know that deterrents may not be as effective as we wish. If the number of infractions that occur in football and ice hockey are any guide, the penalties in those games are pretty lousy deterrents. But as with games, the penalties aimed at fiduciaries are not there so that they may price their conduct according to their preference scales, but to indicate that unilaterally deciding in conflict of interest to pursue a profit is to fail to give 'deliberative exclusivity'[69] to their principals. It is a gain, not wrongful in itself but one that is acquired in breach of the fully justifiable rules that operate here; therefore the fiduciary cannot keep it.

As to Smith's justice objection, the last sentence provides the short version of the answer. But we can say more. That sentence explained why it was not unjust to Boardman and Tom Phipps to strip them of their profits. They made those profits by going outside the rules that are (we are all assuming) independently justified. But leaving aside those rules for a second, Smith is right to intuit that the 'sanction' here cannot be justified because the fiduciary committed a *wrong* against her principal. Smith and I agree that merely *being* in a conflict of interest is not wrongful, nor even is *acting* in conflict of interest necessarily *wrongful*.[70] It is hard to say that as a matter of private law right Boardman acted wrongfully or unjustly. By acting in the way he did, he did not interfere with any of the rights of the trustees or beneficiaries in terms of interfering with anything they already had, or denying them a specific or crystallised gain to which they were entitled; an opportunity per se is not a legal asset. Of course he *failed* the beneficiaries (as well as himself) by not recognising that his activities were carried out without his having put them on a rightful footing by getting fully informed consent for what he did.

To conclude, then, Smith's objections are not so much refuted in the cases we have been discussing but disarmed because misplaced. His justified worries about deterrence and sanctions in this context are shown to be unwarranted if we understand that the 'sanctions' to which the fiduciary is subject are penalties, penalties for doing what would otherwise be non-wrongful but which violates the regime of regulatory rules.

[69] JE Penner, 'Is Loyalty a Virtue, and Even If It Is, Does It Really Help Explain Fiduciary Liability?' in AS Gold and PB Miller (eds), *Philosophical Foundations of Fiduciary Law* (Oxford, Oxford University Press, 2014) 159, 166–67; Penner, 'Fiduciary Law' (n 44) 791–96.

[70] Smith (n 66) 279–80; Penner, 'Is Loyalty a Virtue' (n 69) 171.

VII. Conclusion

Legal theorists struggle with the idea that private law can exact punishment, and rightly so. The aim of this chapter is to show that a much more refined inquiry can be pursued when we distinguish true punishments from penalties. I have examined the conceptual sense of the latter's being part of the law governing those with a duty of loyalty and fiduciaries, but, I would suggest, perhaps such a distinction may provide a passport to travel to other parts of private law as well.[71]

[71] For example, in the contract law doctrine that once a court determines that a 'liquidated damages' clause is found to be a penalty, it is struck out in its entirety rather than the court's reducing the amount of the agreed award to some reasonable figure. See Courtney, ch 12 of this volume. Another case is that of forfeiture where, for example, a legatee kills a testator. Recognising this to be a penalty rather than a punishment would end the discussion about whether the forfeiture exacts a civil law punishment on top of a criminal law punishment.

6

The Ultimate Sanction: The Purpose and Role of Contempt in Private Law Litigation

DAVID ROLPH

I. Introduction

The whole of private law operates in the shadow of punishment. Even if the substance of private law doctrine does not directly or indirectly serve a punitive purpose, the enforcement of private law rights and liabilities through litigation is underpinned by the ever-present threat of contempt of court as the ultimate compliance mechanism. The purpose of civil contempt, the form of contempt concerned with securing compliance with court orders and the one most commonly encountered in private law litigation, has historically been characterised as coercive or remedial. This may be contrasted with criminal contempt, the purpose of which is avowedly punitive. Attempts have also been made to justify the distinction between civil and criminal contempt on the basis that civil contempt is directed to the protection of private interests, whereas criminal contempt is directed to the protection of the public interest. Yet the distinction between civil and criminal contempt is not strict and complete; it is permeable, with some incidents of civil contempt being transformed into criminal contempt, depending upon the circumstances of the case. In addition, given that imprisonment is a well-established penalty for civil contempt, the punitive aspect of civil contempt is difficult to deny. Compounding this, there are anomalies in the attempted classification of contempts as either civil or criminal. More fundamentally, the principled bases asserted to justify the distinction may not be able to withstand scrutiny.

The purpose of this chapter is to analyse the distinction between civil and criminal contempt. It outlines the commonly advanced bases for distinguishing between these forms of contempt and provides a critique of them. It considers the principled and practical consequences of the distinction between civil and criminal contempt. The chapter then examines attempts to minimise the importance of this distinction. It then considers whether such a distinction is efficacious or desirable. However, even if it seems inefficacious or undesirable, it may be that, after such a long period of time, it is in fact ineradicable.

II. The Distinction between Civil and Criminal Contempt

The distinction between civil and criminal contempt is well-established at common law.[1] It has been sanctioned by courts of high authority in Australia,[2] Canada,[3] New Zealand,[4] the United Kingdom[5] and the United States.[6] The distinction may be simply stated. As Brennan, Deane, Toohey and Gaudron JJ observed in *Witham v Holloway*:

> In general terms, the distinction between civil and criminal contempt is that a civil contempt involves disobedience to a court order or breach of an undertaking in civil proceedings, whereas a criminal contempt is committed either when there is a contempt in the face of the court or there is an interference with the course of justice.[7]

It should be emphasised that this is an exposition of the distinction in very general terms. The true position is much more complicated.

As their Honours further observed in the same case, 'the term "civil contempt" has not always been used with enthusiasm'.[8] Civil contempt is sometimes described as a 'contempt in procedure'.[9] This description tends to minimise the importance of this type of contempt, implying that it is a formal, rather than a substantive, contempt.

[1] *Wellesley v Duke of Beaufort* (1831) 2 Russ & M 639, 665–71; 39 ER 538, 548–49 (Lord Brougham LC). See also *Witham v Holloway* (1995) 183 CLR 525 (HCA) 531 (Brennan, Deane, Toohey and Gaudron JJ); *Director of the Serious Fraud Office v O'Brien* [2014] UKSC 23, [2014] AC 1246 [37]–[39] (Lord Toulson JSC); P Londono, ATH Smith and D Eady (eds), *Arlidge, Eady and Smith on Contempt*, 5th edn (London, Sweet & Maxwell, 2017) para 3-1.

[2] *R v Metal Trades Employees' Association, ex parte Amalgamated Engineering Union, Australian Section* (1951) 82 CLR 208 (HCA) 253–54 (Dixon J); *Australasian Meat Industry Employees' Union v Mudginberri Station Pty Ltd* (1986) 161 CLR 98 (HCA) (*AMIEU*) 106 (Gibbs CJ, Mason, Wilson and Deane JJ); *Witham* (n 1) 530.

[3] See, eg, *Poje v Attorney-General of British Columbia* [1953] 1 SCR 516 (SCC), [1953] 2 DLR 785, 787 (Kellock J).

[4] See, eg, *Siemer v Solicitor-General* [2009] NZCA 62, [2009] 2 NZLR 556, 570 (*per curiam*).

[5] See, eg, *O'Brien* (n 1) [37]–[39] (Lord Toulson JSC).

[6] See, eg, *In re Nevitt* 117 Fed Rep 448, 458 (1902) (CA) (Sanborn J); *Bessette v WB Conkey Co* 194 US 324, 24 S Ct 665, 666–67 (1904) (Brewer J); *Shillitani v United States* 384 US 364, 86 S Ct 1531, 1534–35 (1966) (Clark J); *Hicks v Feiock* 485 US 632, 108 S Ct 1423, 1430, 1432 (1988) (White J); *International Union, United Mine Workers of America v Bagwell* 512 US 821, 114 S Ct 2552, 2564 (Scalia J), 2566 (Ginsburg J) (1994).

[7] *Witham* (n 1) 530. See also *In re Freston* (1883) 11 QBD 545 (CA) 552 (Brett MR).

[8] *Witham* (n 1) 531.

[9] See, eg, *Phonographic Performance Ltd v Amusement Caterers (Peckham) Ltd* [1964] 1 Ch 195 (Ch D) 199 (Cross J); *Australian Consolidated Press Ltd v Morgan* (1965) 112 CLR 483 (HCA) 489 (Barwick CJ), 494 (Windeyer J).

Whether a contempt is classified as civil or criminal does not depend upon whether the underlying proceedings in respect of which the impugned conduct occurs are civil or criminal.[10] For instance, improper pressure upon a litigant in medical negligence proceedings[11] or defamation proceedings[12] will constitute criminal contempt. The disruption of civil proceedings is just as much a contempt in the face of the court – a form of criminal contempt – as the disruption of criminal proceedings.[13] Indeed, contempt may be committed 'independently of any civil or criminal action'.[14] There are recognised forms of contempt of court arising out of interferences with the administration of justice as an ongoing process, such as scandalising the court.[15]

The distinction between civil and criminal contempt has not always existed. Indeed, it appears to have emerged in the seventeenth century.[16] It consolidated in the nineteenth century.[17] The recognition at common law of the power of a court to deal with contempt antedated the emergence of the distinction between civil and criminal contempt by several centuries. It may be argued that the distinction between civil and criminal contempt is not inherent in, or essential to, the concept of contempt. Certainly, there are jurisdictions that do not draw this distinction. For example, Scots law does not distinguish between civil and criminal contempt.[18]

Some of the most emphatic statements about the distinction between civil and criminal contempt may be found in nineteenth-century case law. There are instances in the decided cases where judges deny that imprisonment for all forms of contempt is the same and has the same incidents.[19] There are instances where judges deny that imprisonment for civil contempt serves any punitive purpose or has any punitive effect.[20] Although the distinction between civil and criminal contempt continues to be drawn, it is not asserted so emphatically, and is attended with many more doubts than in previous centuries.

The exposition of the distinction between civil and criminal contempt is often accompanied by a justification of the basis for it. The principled basis for this distinction turns upon two dichotomies. The first dichotomy is that criminal contempt serves a punitive purpose, consistent with the purpose of the criminal law more generally, whereas civil contempt serves a coercive or a remedial

[10] *Gompers v Buck's Stove & Range Co* 221 US 418, 31 S Ct 492, 498 (1911) (Lamar J).

[11] See, eg, *Attorney-General v Times Newspapers Ltd* [1974] AC 273 (HL).

[12] See, eg, *Harkianakis v Skalkos* (1997) 42 NSWLR 22 (CA).

[13] As to an example of contempt in the face of the court arising from civil proceedings, see *Re Perkins; Mesto v Gilpin* [1998] 4 VR 505 (VSC).

[14] *Bessette* (n 6) 666 (Brewer J). See also *O'Brien* (n 1) [42] (Lord Toulson JSC).

[15] This form of contempt of court was abolished in England and Wales by the Crime and Courts Act 2013, s 33.

[16] H Phillimore, *Report of the Committee on Contempt of Court* (London, HMSO, 1974) ('the Phillimore Report') para 22. See also *AMIEU* (n 2) 106 (Gibbs CJ, Mason, Wilson and Deane JJ).

[17] *Witham* (n 1) 538 (McHugh J).

[18] Phillimore Report (n 16) para 22.

[19] *Freston* (n 7) 552 (Brett MR).

[20] See, eg, *Pooley v Whetham* (1880) 15 Ch D 435 (CA) 445 (Cotton LJ).

purpose. The second dichotomy is that criminal contempt is directed towards the public interest, whereas civil contempt is concerned with private interests.

There are many judicial statements recognising the distinction between civil and criminal contempt. For instance, in *Australasian Meat Industry Employees' Union v Mudginberri Station Pty Ltd*, Gibbs CJ, Mason, Wilson and Deane JJ stated that:

> Punishment for contempt serves two functions: (a) enforcement of the process and orders of the court, disobedience to which has been described as 'civil contempt'; and (b) punishment of other acts which impede the administration of justice, such as obstructing proceedings in court while it is sitting or publishing comments on a pending case, which have both been described as 'criminal contempt' … The principal theoretical basis of the distinction is that disobedience to the process and the orders of the court in civil proceedings is said to be a civil wrong, a matter between party and party, enforcement being for the private benefit and interest of the party seeking enforcement, whereas impeding the administration of justice is a public wrong. A secondary basis for the distinction is that the main purpose of the sanction for disobedience in civil proceedings is coercive rather than punitive.[21]

One of the most influential statements in the United States of the distinction between civil and criminal contempt is found in Lamar J's judgment in *Gompers v Buck's Stove & Range Co*. His Honour observed:

> It is not the fact of punishment but rather its character and purpose that often serve to distinguish between the two classes of cases. If it is for civil contempt the punishment is remedial, and for the benefit of the complainant. But if it is for criminal contempt the sentence is punitive, to vindicate the authority of the court.[22]

The most recent consideration by the UK Supreme Court of the distinction between civil and criminal contempt defined civil contempt negatively. In *Director of the Serious Fraud Office v O'Brien*, Lord Toulson JSC defined civil contempt as 'conduct which is not itself a crime but which is punishable by the court in order to ensure that its orders are observed'.[23] Later in the judgment, his Lordship stated that '"Civil contempt" is not confined to contempt of a civil court. It simply denotes a contempt which is not itself a crime.'[24]

Notwithstanding Lord Toulson JSC's definition of a civil contempt as non-criminal conduct, his Lordship openly acknowledged the consequences of civil contempt as punishment. As Lord Toulson JSC noted:

> Breach of an order made (or undertaking obtained) in the course of legal proceedings may result in punishment of the person against whom the order was made (or from whom the undertaking was obtained) as a form of contempt … However, a contempt of

[21] *AMIEU* (n 2) 106.
[22] *Gompers* (n 10) 498.
[23] *O'Brien* (n 1) [37].
[24] ibid [42].

that kind does not constitute a criminal offence. Although the penalty contains a punitive element, its primary purpose is to make the order of the court effective. A person who commits this type of contempt does not acquire a criminal record.

A criminal contempt is conduct which goes beyond mere non-compliance with a court order or undertaking and involves a serious interference with the administration of justice. Examples include physically interfering with the course of a trial, threatening witnesses or publishing material likely to prejudice a fair trial.[25]

III. A Critique of the Principled Basis for the Distinction between Civil and Criminal Contempt

Just as the distinction between civil and criminal contempt has long been recognised, so too have the difficulties of making this distinction.[26] The principled basis for the distinction between civil and criminal contempt is more readily stated than defended. Reference has been made the 'unsatisfactory nature' of the distinction.[27] In *Australasian Meat Industry Employees' Union v Mudginberri Station Pty Ltd*, Gibbs CJ, Mason, Wilson and Deane JJ observed that 'very great difficulty has been experienced in maintaining the distinction between civil and criminal contempts and, in particular, in elaborating a precise and certain criterion which divides one class of contempt from the other'.[28]

Seeking to base the distinction between civil and criminal contempt upon a differentiation between public and private interests is self-evidently unsatisfactory. A concern to protect against interference with the administration of justice is a unifying, not a distinguishing, feature of all forms of contempt. The public interest in the proper administration of justice is not limited to criminal proceedings but extends equally to civil proceedings. The fact that civil litigation overwhelmingly involves the determination of the rights and liabilities of private parties does not mean that only private interests are engaged. The fact that private parties have recourse to a public institution, acting as a repository of public power, to determine finally their disputes clearly engages public as well as private interests. The public interest in the proper administration of justice is a unifying feature of all forms of contempt. It is not peculiar to criminal contempt. The public and private aspects of contempt are, as Salmon LJ suggested in *Jennison v Baker*, 'inextricably intermixed'.[29]

[25] ibid [38]–[39].

[26] For an early recognition of the difficulty of distinguishing between civil and criminal contempt, see *Wellesley* (n 1) 665–67, 548 (Lord Brougham LC). See also *Bessette* (n 6) 667 (Brewer J).

[27] *AMIEU* (n 2) 107 (Gibbs CJ, Mason, Wilson and Deane JJ). See also *Hearne v Street* [2008] HCA 36, (2008) 235 CLR 125 [20] (Gleeson CJ).

[28] *AMIEU* (n 2) 108.

[29] *Jennison v Baker* [1972] 2 QB 52 (CA) 64.

This point was made by the High Court of Australia in *Australasian Meat Industry Employees' Union v Mudginberri Station Pty Ltd*, Gibbs CJ, Mason, Wilson and Deane JJ observed that:

> The theoretical distinction between the two classes overlooks the underlying rationale of every exercise of the contempt power, namely that it is necessary to uphold and protect the effective administration of justice. Although the primary purpose in committing a defendant who disobeys an injunction is to enforce the injunction for the benefit of the plaintiff, another purpose is to protect the effective administration of justice by demonstrating that the court's orders will be enforced ... There is, accordingly, a public interest in the exercise of the contempt power in cases of disobedience to an order ...[30]

McHugh J reasoned to similar effect in *Witham v Holloway*, where his Honour observed:

> An order by way of fine, committal or sequestration of property for disobeying a court order cannot be regarded as a matter that concerns only the parties to the action. The fine, committal or sequestration vindicates the authority of the court and deters other suitors from disobeying the orders of the courts. Whether the object of particular civil proceedings is coercive, remedial or purely punitive, an order fining or imprisoning the contemnor or sequestrating the property of that person serves the public interest in person serves the public interest in maintaining the authority of the courts of justice.[31]

The dichotomy of privacy and publicity, as it is applied to the distinction between civil and criminal contempt, is not conceptualised purely in terms of interests. It is sometimes discussed in terms of harms or injuries. Criminal contempt, some cases suggest, deals with public harms or injuries, whereas civil contempt is concerned with private harms or injuries.[32] Thus, in the US Supreme Court decision of *Bessette v WB Conkey Co*, Brewer J, giving the opinion of the Court, distinguished forms of criminal contempt, like contempt in the face of the court, which, in his Honour's view, 'is not misconduct in which any individual suitor is specially interested', being 'more like an ordinary crime which affects the public at large', from civil contempt, which he characterises as being 'injurious to the rights of the adverse party' and consequently a 'personal injury to [that] party'.[33] Again, even civil contempt does not cause a purely private harm or injury to a particular affected litigant but tends to cause harm or injury to the administration of justice, by undermining respect for it and the efficacy of it.

The approach adopted by courts in seeking to distinguish between civil and criminal contempt is to identify the essence of the contempt or, alternatively, the primary or dominant purpose or focus of the contempt proceeding.[34] If the

[30] *AMIEU* (n 2) 107.
[31] *Witham* (n 1) 539.
[32] See, eg, *Nevitt* (n 6) 459 (Sanborn J); *AMIEU* (n 2) (Gibbs CJ, Mason, Wilson and Deane JJ).
[33] *Bessette* (n 6) 667.
[34] See, eg, *In re Armstrong, ex parte Lindsay* [1892] 1 QB 327 (QBD) 329 (Vaughan Williams J); *Bessette* (n 6) 667 (Brewer J); *Jendell Australia Pty Ltd v Kesby* [1983] 1 NSWLR 127 (SC (NSW)) 133 (McLelland J).

essential character or the primary or dominant purpose of the contempt proceeding is remedial or coercive, the contempt may be classified as a civil one. If it is punitive, the contempt will be treated as a criminal one. Often this approach will not deny that imprisonment for civil contempt has a punitive dimension but suggests that imprisonment in this context will have an additional or dominant coercive or remedial purpose.[35]

The problem with this approach is that it is entirely dependent upon characterising the conduct, applying a test that has no real content and provides no real guidance. The test appears to be subjective and impressionistic. As Lord Brougham LC suggested in *Wellesley v Duke of Beaufort*, '[i]f the contempt savours of criminality, and the sentence is penal, that according to the books appears to be enough' to distinguish a criminal contempt from a civil one.[36] This suggests that the test is instinctive, or even sensory.

Given that imprisonment is the ultimate sanction for all forms of contempt, it is artificial to characterise some forms of imprisonment as punitive and some forms of imprisonment as remedial or coercive. The deprivation of an individual's liberty is the most serious legal sanction. The idea that imprisonment may bear a different character depending upon the purpose for which it is imposed is not one that can withstand close scrutiny. Imprisonment is imprisonment, irrespective of the purpose for which it is imposed. It would be experienced by the contemnor as a form of punishment in all cases of contempt.

Even in cases in which the importance of the distinction between civil and criminal contempt is maintained, there is a recognition that the purposes of imprisonment for the different forms of contempt are not discrete but overlap. As Lamar J noted in *Gompers v Buck's Stove & Range Co*:

> It is true that either form of imprisonment has also an incidental effect. For if the case is civil and the punishment is purely remedial, there is also a vindication of the court's authority. On the other hand, if the proceeding is for criminal contempt and the imprisonment is solely punitive, to vindicate the authority of the law, the complainant may also derive some incidental benefit from the fact that such punishment tends to prevent a repetition of the disobedience.[37]

One way in which imprisonment for civil contempt is sought to be characterised as non-criminal is through the invocation of an influential metaphor. As Sanborn J famously observed in *In re Nevitt*, a contemnor imprisoned for failing to comply with a court order is 'not remediless. They are imprisoned only until they comply with the orders of the court, and this they may do at any time. They carry the keys of their prison in their own pockets.'[38]

[35] See, eg, *Gompers* (n 10) 498 (Lamar J).

[36] *Wellesley* (n 1) 667, 548.

[37] *Gompers* (n 10) 498. See also *Hicks* (n 6) 1431 (White J).

[38] *Nevitt* (n 6) 461. As to the invocation of this metaphor, see, eg, *Gompers* (n 10) 498 (Lamar J);.*Shillitani* (n 6) 1534 (Clark J); *Hicks* (n 6) 1430 (White J); *International Union* (n 6) 2556 (Ginsburg J).

According to this characterisation, imprisonment for civil contempt is not punitive but rather self-inflicted. The notion that a civil contemnor is not in truth deprived of his or her liberty by the state but is responsible for his or her own confinement may provide some solace for a court when ordering imprisonment as a sanction. Related to this is the characterisation of the civil contemnor's confinement as 'conditional imprisonment'.[39] Furthermore, in US jurisprudence in particular, the view is sometimes expressed that dealing with civil contempt 'is essentially a civil remedy designed for the benefit of other parties'.[40]

However, whether a civil contemnor in every case can unlock for himself or herself the door of the prison cell is open to question.[41] Even accepting the proposition that civil contempt is intended to serve a coercive or remedial, rather than a punitive, purpose, civil contempt may not always be effectual in achieving those purposes. For example, if a defendant is ordered to deliver up goods but fails to do so, civil contempt may be deployed to compel the defendant to comply with the order. However, if the defendant has destroyed the goods, the defendant will be unable to comply with that order. Likewise, if the defendant is ordered not to dissipate his or her assets or transfer them outside the jurisdiction, but the defendant deals with his or her assets so that the resulting judgment cannot be satisfied, a sanction for civil contempt in such circumstances cannot secure compliance with the orders, for there have already been positive acts of non-compliance and compliance has been rendered impossible. However, if a defendant is ordered not to publish confidential or private information but proceeds to do so, civil contempt cannot serve a remedial purpose for the plaintiff, because the confidential or private quality of the information the injunction was intended to preserve can never be restored but is irretrievably lost.[42] These examples illustrate the point that the asserted coercive or remedial purpose of civil contempt cannot satisfactorily account for many instances where sanctions are imposed.

IV. The Completeness of the Distinction between Civil and Criminal Contempt

Accepting that the common law has sought to draw a distinction between civil and criminal contempt, there remains an issue as to how viable this distinction is in practice. This distinction is certainly not a complete one. This is because, whilst disobedience of a court order is ordinarily classified as civil contempt, there may

[39] See, eg, *Shillitani* (n 6) 1536 (Clark J); *Hicks* (n 6) 1430 (White J); *Blakeman v Schneider* 864 SW 2d 903 (SC of Ky) 906 (1993) (Reynolds J).

[40] *Green v United States* 356 US 165, 78 S Ct 632, 650 (1958) (Black and Brennan JJ). See also *Gompers* (n 10) 498 (Lamar J);

[41] As to the way in which US law resolves this tension, see *Gompers* (n 10) (Lamar J).

[42] See, eg, *Attorney-General v Newspaper Publishing Plc* [1988] Ch 333 (CA) 358 (Sir John Donaldson MR); *Mosley v News Group Newspapers Ltd* [2008] EWHC 1777 (QB), [2008] EMLR 20 [230] (Eady J).

be circumstances in which the disobedience of a court order occurs with such contumacy or wilful defiance of the court's authority that it should be characterised as criminal contempt.[43] The fact that a civil contempt may be transformed into a criminal contempt, depending upon the quality of the contemnor's conduct and the circumstances in which that conduct occurs, suggests that the distinction is not a stark one, leading to 'arbitrary classification'.[44]

Again, this transformation is also dependent upon the court's characterisation. Slightly different approaches to this task are suggested by the decided cases. Sometimes, the approach taken involves identifying whether the contempt is really directed at the aggrieved party or to the court.[45] This approach seems to suggest that it is necessary to identify the essential character of the contempt. In other cases, the approach involves identifying the quality or aspect of conduct, in addition to the civil contempt, that would transform what would ordinarily be a civil contempt into a criminal contempt.[46] This approach seems to suggest that criminal contempt is an enhanced or superadded form of civil contempt. Whatever the proper approach is, it is clear that determining when a civil contempt should be treated as a criminal contempt turns upon the characterisation of the contemnor's conduct with the difficulties that attend such a process. In *Australasian Meat Industry Employees' Union v Mudginberri Station Pty Ltd*, Gibbs CJ, Mason, Wilson and Deane JJ justifiably described this process as 'complex and artificial'.[47]

V. Anomalies of the Distinction between Civil and Criminal Contempt

Not only is the distinction between civil and criminal contempt not stark, it is attended by anomalies. For instance, it is not only the case that a breach of a court order is transformed from a civil contempt into a criminal contempt by virtue of the quality of the defendant's conduct. There are some forms of disobedience of a court order that are treated as criminal contempt, irrespective of the quality of the defendant's conduct. A breach of a court order by a solicitor has been held to be a criminal contempt.[48] Similarly, a breach of court order by a liquidator has been held to be a criminal contempt.[49] In *Australasian Meat Industry Employees' Union v Mudginberri Station Pty Ltd*, the High Court of Australia sought to rationalise

[43] *Australian Consolidated Press Ltd* (n 9) 484 (Barwick CJ).
[44] *AMIEU* (n 2) 107 (Gibbs CJ, Mason, Wilson and Deane JJ).
[45] See, eg, *Bessette* (n 6) 667 (Brewer J).
[46] See, eg, *Witham* (n 1) 542.
[47] *AMIEU* (n 2) 108.
[48] *Freston* (n 7); *Seldon v Wilde* [1911] 1 KB 701 (CA).
[49] *In re Grantham Wholesale Fruit, Vegetable and Potato Merchants Ltd* [1972] 1 WLR 559 (Ch D) 564–66 (Megarry J) (court of its own motion entitled to act against liquidator and able to impose penalty different from, and in excess of, that sought by an aggrieved party).

the anomalous treatment of solicitors and liquidators on the basis that they were 'contempts by officers of the court and others who have a special relationship with the courts'.[50] The nature of the jurisdiction to deal with contempt by such persons is disciplinary[51] – sufficiently proximate to punishment so as to justify treating the conduct of such persons as criminal contempt.

There are further anomalies. Where a court has placed a child into the wardship of a particular person, any wrongful interference with the ward of the court is treated as a criminal contempt.[52] The failure to deliver up a child as ordered by a court is treated as a criminal contempt.[53] The breach of a non-molestation order has also been treated as a criminal contempt.[54]

The distinction between civil and criminal contempt may lead to absurd results. A case often cited to demonstrate this is *Seaward v Paterson*,[55] in which a landlord, Seaward, sued the tenant, Paterson, for breach of a covenant contained in the lease of premises that were to be used as a private club. The tenant had covenanted, inter alia, not to allow the premises to be used for anything 'noisy, noisome, offensive or inconvenient to the lessor, or the tenants or occupiers of adjoining or neighbouring premises'.[56] In the proceedings, Paterson was subject to an injunction restraining any further breach of the covenant. However, boxing matches continued to occur in the premises in violation of the covenant and the injunction. Seaward sought to have Paterson dealt with for contempt of court, as well as two other men, Sheppard and Murray, who he alleged had assisted Paterson in breaching the injunction.[57] As the master of ceremonies, Sheppard's liability for contempt was not difficult to establish.[58] Murray's liability was not so straightforward; North J did not accept that Murray was a mere spectator but was rather a principal in the club. At first instance, his Lordship found the tenant liable for contempt for breaching an injunction, and Sheppard and Murray liable for aiding and abetting the breach of the injunction.[59] The focus of the appeal was on Murray's liability for contempt. Lindley LJ held that because Murray was present in court during the proceedings and knew of the injunction, even though he was not bound by its terms, he was still liable for contempt, not because he had breached the injunction but because he interfered with the administration of justice by aiding and abetting Paterson to breach the injunction.[60] In his separate reasons for judgment, AL Smith LJ broadly

[50] *AMIEU* (n 2) 107 (Gibbs CJ, Mason, Wilson and Deane JJ).

[51] ibid 107–08 (Gibbs CJ, Mason, Wilson and Deane JJ).

[52] *Wellesley* (n 1); *Scott v Scott* [1913] AC 417 (HL) 462 (Lord Atkinson).

[53] *Corcoran v Corcoran* [1950] 1 All ER 495 496 (Willmer J) (wife unable to waive husband's contempt where husband had sent child out of jurisdiction in breach of court order). But see *R v Barnardo* (1889) 23 QBD 305 (CA) 308 (Lord Esher MR), 309 (Cotton LJ), 309 (Lindley LJ).

[54] *Stourton v Stourton* [1963] 2 WLR 397 403 (Scarman J).

[55] *Seaward v Paterson* [1897] 1 Ch 545 (CA).

[56] ibid 545.

[57] ibid 546.

[58] ibid 549.

[59] ibid 549–50.

[60] ibid 553–54.

agreed with Lindley LJ's approach to the issue.[61] Rigby LJ also agreed with the outcome and approach, but was at pains to reject the principled basis of the argument put on behalf of Murray. His Lordship rejected Murray's submission that 'the Court has no jurisdiction to commit for contempt by way of punishment; but that the jurisdiction is an ancillary or subsidiary jurisdiction in order to secure that the plaintiff in a suit shall have his rights'.[62]

Finding that the court had the power to deal with Murray for contempt, Rigby LJ stated the jurisdiction

> has been exercised for a very long time – for longer than any of us can remember – and it is a punitive jurisdiction founded upon this, that it is for the good, not of the plaintiff or of any party to the action, but of the public, that the orders of Court should not be disregarded, and that people should not be permitted to assist in the breach of those orders in what is properly called contempt of Court.[63]

This makes clear that Murray was being dealt with for criminal contempt. Paterson's contempt for breaching the injunction was civil contempt. The oddity that the person bound by the injunction was committing a civil contempt by breaching the injunction, but that the person aiding and abetting the breach of the injunction was guilty of a criminal contempt has not gone unnoticed in subsequent judgments.[64]

These anomalies relate to some basic features of contempt. The power of a court to imprison a contemnor for civil contempt was well established. The power of a court to fine a contemnor for civil contempt remained contentious, however, for a long time. There were authorities that suggested that criminal, but not civil, contempt could be dealt with by the imposition of a fine.[65] The doubt about the power of a court to impose a fine for civil contempt arose in significant part from its origins as part of the machinery by which the Court of Chancery enforced its orders.[66] The power of a court to impose a fine for civil contempt was only finally established in Australia in *Australasian Meat Industry Employees' Union v Mudginberri Station Pty Ltd*.[67] (The power of a court to impose a fine for criminal contempt was not in doubt.[68]) The fact that a person could be deprived of his or her liberty for civil contempt – the most serious sanction known to the law – but

[61] ibid 557.
[62] ibid 558.
[63] ibid.
[64] For criticisms of *Seaward v Paterson*, see, eg, *Scott* (n 52) 456–57 (Lord Atkinson) ('an absurd anomaly'); *Phonographic Performance Ltd* (n 9) 200–01 (Cross J); *AMIEU* (n 2) 108 (Gibbs CJ, Mason, Wilson and Deane JJ): '[t]he extremities to which the distinction has sometimes driven the courts is strikingly illustrated by the absurd proposition, which derives some comfort from *Seaward v Paterson* [1897] 1 Ch 545, that the defendant who disobeys an injunction granted against him commits a civil contempt whereas the stranger who aids and abets him is guilty of criminal contempt'.
[65] See, eg, *Australian Consolidated Press Ltd* (n 9) 495 (Windeyer J). See also *AMIEU* (n 2) 108 (Gibbs CJ, Mason, Wilson and Deane JJ).
[66] *Australian Consolidated Press Ltd* (n 9) 498–99 (Windeyer J).
[67] *AMIEU* (n 2).
[68] *Australian Consolidated Press Ltd* (n 9) 495 (Windeyer J).

that the power to impose a lesser sanction, such as a fine, for the same conduct was unclear, underscores the anomalous nature of the distinction between civil and criminal contempt. As McHugh J further observed in *Witham v Holloway*:

> [O]nce it is accepted that the courts do have the power in some circumstances to imprison or fine by way of punishment for civil contempt, it is difficult to maintain that civil proceedings for contempt are essentially coercive or remedial in nature and that they have a different rationale from proceedings for criminal contempt.[69]

Judicial concerns about the distinction between civil and criminal contempt have often centred on whether the established penalties for contempt, such as imprisonment and fines, serve a non-punitive purpose when applied in cases of civil contempt. The anomalous nature of contempt is further amplified by the recognition in some decided cases that damages may be awarded for contempt. In *Couling v Coxe*, Wilde CJ accepted that a witness who failed to comply with a subpoena could be sued for damages by the party who issued the subpoena.[70] Similarly, in *Fairclough & Sons v The Manchester Ship Canal Co (No 2)*, Lord Russell of Killowen CJ clearly contemplated that an inquiry as to damages could be ordered in an appropriate case, where there had been disobedience of a court order.[71] Megaw J, in *Re Mileage Conference Group of the Tyre Manufacturers' Conference Ltd's Agreement*, accepted that an award of damages may be made by a court in a case of a breach of an injunction or a breach of an undertaking.[72] In *Attorney-General v Butterworth*, Lord Denning MR observed, *obiter*, that the victimisation of a witness may constitute contempt of court, but also 'if the witness has been damnified by it, he may well have redress in a civil court for damages'.[73] In *Chapman v Honig*, the question of whether there can never be a right of action for damages for contempt of court was left open.[74] In doing so, Davies LJ, drawing upon the approach in claims for the tort of breach of statutory duty, suggested that

> the principle can, in my judgment, be applied in the present case by inquiring whether the concept of, and proceedings for, contempt of court are concerned with the preservation of the inviolability of the administration and course of justice and its proper conduct or whether, in addition, they are intended in all cases to give a remedy in damages to an individual injured by the contempt.[75]

This distinction has an equally obvious resonance with the distinction the common law has sought to draw between the respective purposes of civil and criminal contempt.

[69] *Witham* (n 1) 542.
[70] *Couling v Coxe* (1848) 6 CB 703, 717–21; 136 ER 1424, 1430–31. See also *Chapman v Honig* [1963] 2 QB 502 (CA) 525–26 (Davies LJ).
[71] *Fairclough & Sons v Manchester Ship Canal Co (No 2)* (1897) 41 Sol Jo 225 (CA) 225.
[72] *In re Mileage Conference Group of the Tyre Manufacturers' Conference Ltd's Agreement* [1966] 1 WLR 1137 (Ch D) 1162.
[73] *Attorney-General v Butterworth* [1963] 1 QB 696 (CA). See also ibid 721.
[74] *Chapman* (n 70) 522 (Pearson LJ), 527 (Davies LJ).
[75] ibid 524, citing *Phillips v Britannia Hygienic Laundry Co Ltd* [1923] 2 KB 832 (CA) 842 (Atkin LJ).

Finally, in *Astro Exito Navegacion SA v Hsu (The 'Messiniaki Tolmi)*, Mustill J held that a claim for damages resulting from contempt of court was at least arguable, such that the claim should not be struck out.[76]

On the other hand, in *Re Hudson*, Buckley J held that, because an undertaking was not an order of the court and the court could release or modify the undertaking, the undertaking conferred no person right or remedy on another party but could only be enforced by the court through the exercise of its contempt powers.[77] His Lordship did, however, consider that if the undertaking formed part of a bargain between the parties, the giver of the undertaking may owe an obligation not only to the court but also to the party to whom the undertaking is given, such that the failure to fulfil the undertaking may be enforced as a contractual debt.[78] In *Customs and Excise Commissioners v Barclays Bank Plc*, one of the reasons advanced by many of the Law Lords for rejecting the imposition of a duty of care not to inflict pure economic loss, arising from the bank's failure to prevent payments out of account in contravention of freezing orders, in circumstances where the bank had notice of the orders, was that the bank was already exposed to the risk of punishment for contempt of court for its non-compliance.[79] As Lord Hoffmann observed, 'you cannot derive a common law duty of care directly from a statutory duty. Likewise, as it seems to me, you cannot derive one from an order of court. The order carries its own remedies and its reach does not extend any further.'[80]

In its most recent consideration of the issue, in *JSC BTA Bank v Ablyazov (No 14)*, the UK Supreme Court expressly left open the question of whether an award of damages could be granted as a remedy for contempt of court.[81] The very openness of this question suggests that the compensatory impulse characteristic of many private law remedies may also manifest itself alongside the avowedly punitive purpose of much of the law of contempt of court, further complicating the distinction between civil and criminal contempt.

VI. The Consequences of the Distinction between Civil and Criminal Contempt

The distinction between civil and criminal contempt has a range of consequences. There are consequences in terms of 'procedure, onus of proof, right of appeal, mode

[76] *Astro Exito Navegacion SA v Hsu (The 'Messiniaki Tolmi')* [1983] 1 Lloyd's Rep 666 (QBD) 671.

[77] *Re Hudson* [1966] Ch 209 (Ch D) 213–14.

[78] ibid 214–15.

[79] *Customs and Excise Commissioners v Barclays Bank Plc* [2006] UKHL 28, [2007] 1 AC 181 [14]–[17] (Lord Bingham of Cornhill), [59]–[62] (Lord Rodger of Earlsferry), [101] (Lord Mance).

[80] ibid [39].

[81] *JSC BTA Bank v Ablyazov (No 14)* [2018] UKSC 19, [2018] 2 WLR 1125 [22] (Lord Sumption and Lord Lloyd-Jones JJSC). This case was principally concerned with whether contempt of court can provide the unlawful means to establish the tort of conspiracy.

of punishment, privilege from arrest, pardon and power to release an offender'.[82] The distinction between civil and criminal contempt has also proved to be important in the context of extradition. Some consequences of the distinction are more important than others. Extradition and privilege illustrate the consequences of the distinction between civil and criminal contempt.

The distinction between civil and criminal contempt remains important for the purposes of extradition. This is illustrated by the UK Supreme Court's decision in *Director of the Serious Fraud Office v O'Brien*.[83] The issue in this case was whether the defendant's non-compliance with a restraint order made against him by the Central Criminal Court, pursuant to the Proceeds of Crime Act 2002 (UK), section 412, which led to his being found guilty of contempt of court in absentia, could be dealt with as contempt following his extradition back to the United Kingdom from the United States to face fraud charges, in circumstances where the contempt was not the criminal charge that formed the basis of the extradition. Upon his return to the United Kingdom, the defendant was committed to prison for 15 months for contempt of court. Under the Extradition Act 2003 (UK), section 151A, a person who had been extradited back to the United Kingdom could only be dealt with for an offence for which the person had been extradited or that was disclosed by information provided to the extraditing country. Lord Toulson JSC, giving the judgment of the court, held that the defendant's non-compliance with the restraint order was properly characterised as a civil contempt. Consequently, the Extradition Act 2003 (UK), section 151A had no application to the defendant, with the effect that the defendant's sentence of 15 months' imprisonment for civil contempt was upheld.[84]

This position is not new. In *Pooley v Wetham*,[85] James LJ had to consider whether a person extradited from France on fraud charges could be validly served with a writ of attachment whilst in prison in England and could be detained in prison, even after he had been acquitted of the criminal charges against him, in order to secure his obedience to a court order to give up possession of a railway. Finding that the person could be validly served, James LJ stated, in relation to the writ of attachment:

> Although it assumes the form of punishment for contempt of Court, it is a mere civil process to enforce obedience to an order of a civil Court to do something on behalf of or for the benefit of a private person, which has no reference whatever to any offence committed against the State … It appears to me that it is impossible to extend the words to an attachment for a contempt which is really only a process of coercion to compel the performance of the order of the Court in what, as I have said, is a civil matter.[86]

[82] *AMIEU* (n 2) 106 (Gibbs CJ, Mason, Wilson and Deane JJ). See also E Harnon, 'Civil and Criminal Contempts of Court' (1962) 25 *MLR* 179, 179; Londono, Smith and Eady (eds) (n 1) paras 3-31–3-47.

[83] *O'Brien* (n 1).

[84] ibid 1259.

[85] *Pooley* (n 20).

[86] ibid 440.

Brett LJ agreed that the contempt in question was not an offence because, in his view, an offence had to be triable in a criminal court. The impugned conduct was 'a civil process under which [the contemnor] is detained, which he can get rid of at any time by purging his contempt'.[87]

There is a privilege against arrest for civil contempt, but not for criminal contempt. This was established by Lord Brougham LC in *Wellesley v Duke of Beaufort*, wherein his Lordship stated:

> The line, then, which I draw is this, – that against all civil process privilege protects; but that against contempt for not obeying civil process, if that contempt is in its nature of by its incidents criminal, privilege protects not …[88]

Thus, a member of parliament[89] or a peer of the realm[90] could assert privilege against arrest and commitment for civil, but not criminal, contempt. As Lord Brougham LC further pointed out in *Wellesley v Duke of Beaufort*, if a member of parliament were able to assert privilege to avoid arrest and imprisonment for criminal contempt, a member of parliament could disrupt any court proceeding with impunity, safe in the knowledge that no step could be taken to deal with his or her contempt in the face of the court, a well-established form of criminal contempt. In order to apply this settled distinction, Scarman J (as his Lordship then was) articulated the test to be 'whether the arrest is to punish a breach of the law or merely to compel performance of a civil obligation'.[91]

VII. Minimising or Abolishing the Distinction between Civil and Criminal Contempt

In recent decades, there have been a number of judicial statements minimising the importance of the distinction between civil and criminal contempt. In *Jennison v Baker*, Salmon LJ described the distinction between civil and criminal contempt as 'an unhelpful and almost meaningless classification'.[92] In *Home Office v Harman*, Lord Scarman stated that '[t]he distinction between "civil" and "criminal" contempt is no longer of much importance'.[93] In *Australasian Meat Industry Employees' Union v Mudginberri Station Pty Ltd*, Gibbs CJ, Mason, Wilson and Deane JJ, discussing the practical consequences of the distinction between civil and criminal contempt, suggested that those 'differences in approach to these matters have

[87] ibid 443.

[88] *Wellesley* (n 1) 665, 548.

[89] *Catmur v Knatchbull* (1797) 7 TR 448, 448–49; 101 ER 1069, 1069–70; *Wellesley* (n 1) 665–67, 548 (Lord Brougham LC); *Armstrong* (n 34) 328–29 (Vaughan Williams J).

[90] *Walker v Earl of Grosvenor* (1797) 7 TR 171, 101 ER 915; *Stourton* (n 54) 398–400 (Scarman J).

[91] *Stourton* (n 54) 401. See also *Armstrong* (n 34) 329 (Vaughan Williams J).

[92] *Jennison* (n 29) 61.

[93] *Home Office v Harman* [1983] 1 AC 280 (HL) 310.

largely disappeared in more recent times'.[94] Their Honours went on to suggest that there was 'much to be said for the view that all contempts should be punished as if they are quasi-criminal in character'.[95] Similarly, in *Witham v Holloway*, McHugh J observed that '[t]he case for abolishing the distinction between civil and criminal contempts is a strong one'.[96]

Law reformers have even canvassed the abolition of the distinction between civil and criminal contempt. The Phillimore Committee, in its landmark report on contempt of court, recommended the abolition of all distinctions between civil and criminal contempts.[97] This recommendation was not ultimately implemented in the Contempt of Court Act 1981, which followed seven years later.

The clearest example of the minimisation of the distinction between civil and criminal contempt is the applicable standard of proof. It is well-established that there are only two standards of proof at common law: proof on the balance of probabilities, in civil proceedings, and proof beyond reasonable doubt, in criminal proceedings.[98] It is uncontroversial that the criminal standard of proof applies in proceedings for criminal contempt. The more difficult and contentious question was whether the civil standard of proof applied to proceedings for civil contempt. On the one hand, civil contempt was, by definition, not criminal. On the other hand, a well-established sanction for civil contempt was imprisonment. That a court might deprive a person of his or her liberty on proof only of the balance of probabilities would offend contemporary notions of justice. Although there were cases in which it was suggested that civil contempt need only be proved on the civil standard of proof,[99] the High Court of Australia resolved the issue under Australian law in *Witham v Holloway*, holding that all forms of contempt must be proved to the criminal standard of proof beyond reasonable doubt.[100] As McHugh J suggested in that case:

> [C]ontemporary notions of justice are offended by a rule of law that allows a person to be imprisoned for an indefinite period to coerce him or her to comply with an order, the breach of which has only been proved on the balance of probabilities.[101]

The classification of contempt as either civil or contempt has presented difficulties for the application of human rights guarantees. This is demonstrated by the decision of the Supreme Court of New Zealand in *Siemer v Solicitor-General*.[102] Given that imprisonment is a possible outcome in proceedings for civil, as well as

[94] *AMIEU* (n 2) 106.
[95] ibid 109.
[96] *Witham* (n 1) 549.
[97] Phillimore Report (n 16) paras 72–73.
[98] *Briginshaw v Briginshaw* (1938) 60 CLR 336 (HCA) 360–62 (Dixon J).
[99] See, eg, *New South Wales Egg Corporation v Peek* (1987) 10 NSWLR 72 (CA).
[100] *Witham* (n 1) 548. The criminal standard of proof beyond reasonable doubt has been largely accepted in England and Wales since Lord Denning MR's judgment in *In re Bramblevale Ltd* [1970] Ch 128 (CA).
[101] ibid.
[102] *Siemer v Solicitor-General* [2010] NZSC 54, [2010] 3 NZLR 767.

criminal, contempt, human rights jurisprudence is less receptive to maintaining the distinction between these forms of contempt. In *Siemer v Solicitor-General*, Siemer was found guilty of contempt for breaching an injunction. Following a term of imprisonment for contempt, he persisted in his breach of the injunction, for which he was sentenced to a further term of six months' imprisonment. Siemer was tried for contempt summarily. He challenged his sentence on the basis that, under the New Zealand Bill of Rights Act 1990 (NZ), section 24(e), a person charged with an offence where the penalty includes imprisonment for more than three months was entitled to trial by jury. By majority, the Supreme Court of New Zealand reasoned that where imprisonment for more than three months was a possible outcome in a trial, the right to trial by jury was engaged. The fact that a matter could be characterised as proceedings for civil contempt did not alter this. Imprisonment was available as a possible consequence in proceedings for both civil and criminal contempt. The fact that a matter could be characterised as a civil contempt did not alter this. Blanchard J, with whom Wilson and Anderson JJ agreed, did not find 'any relevant distinction between imprisonment for criminal and civil contempts'.[103] Their Honours held that the summary procedure was well-established for contempt court.[104] They further held that it was not possible for contempt to exist as an exception to the requirements of the New Zealand Bill of Rights Act 1990 (NZ), section 24(e). Therefore, their Honours found that the maximum penalty allowed for all forms of contempt was three months' imprisonment.[105] This is another instance of the minimisation of the distinction between civil and criminal contempt.

VIII. The Ineradicable Nature of the Distinction between Civil and Criminal Contempt?

However, the distinction between civil and criminal contempt is, in some senses, ineradicable. Standing to complain about contempt is one respect in which the distinction must be maintained. Only a party to the proceeding may complain about civil contempt.[106] Standing to bring proceedings for criminal contempt is broader than this. Not only may a party to the proceedings complain about criminal contempt, but also the court of its own motion may institute such proceedings,[107] as may the Attorney-General as the first law officer, charged with the responsibility for the protection of the administration of justice.[108] It may be that a person who can demonstrate a sufficient interest in the proceedings also has standing

[103] ibid 790.
[104] ibid 790–93.
[105] ibid 798.
[106] *Gompers* (n 10) 499 (Lamar J); *Witham* (n 1) 540 (McHugh J).
[107] *Witham* (n 1) 540 (McHugh J).
[108] ibid.

to complain about criminal contempt.[109] It would be a large step, as a result of the abolition of the distinction between civil and criminal contempt, to increase the number of persons who could complain about civil contempt. It would be an unlikely consequence of any such abolition that the number of persons who had standing to complain about criminal contempt would reduce. A court would not, or arguably could not, divest itself of its power to deal with contempt – the contempt jurisdiction is part of the inherent jurisdiction of the court and is part of its defining institutional character. Similarly, the Attorney-General is unlikely to yield responsibility for instituting proceedings for criminal contempt.

The corollary of the differences in standing for the purposes of complaining about civil and criminal contempt is that civil contempt may be waived by a party to the proceedings.[110] It is a forensic matter for the party aggrieved by the civil contempt as to whether he or she wishes to complain about it. By contrast, a party to a proceeding cannot waive a criminal contempt. Because other parties have standing to complain about criminal contempt, no one party may waive a criminal contempt.

A significant obstacle to any attempted abolition of the distinction between civil and criminal contempt is that the distinction is entrenched in many statutes, directly or indirectly. This can be seen in relation to rights of appeal, which are creatures of statute. The classification of a given form of contempt as either civil or criminal has important consequences in terms of rights of appeal. At common law, no court could review a decision of another court in relation to its disposition of a contempt matter.[111] As Blackstone J stated in *Crosby's Case*, 'The sole adjudication of contempts, and the punishment thereof, in any manner, belongs exclusively, and without interfering, to each respective Court.'[112]

Given the common law later developed to recognise the supervisory jurisdiction of a superior court of record over inferior courts, so as to permit the superior courts to deal with contempts of an inferior court,[113] this proposition may need to be refined. At common law, one superior court could not review a decision of another superior court in relation to a contempt matter.

The common law position was altered by the introduction of rights of appeal under statute. Those rights of appeal under statute, though, are not always the same for all forms of contempt of court. The creation of different rights of appeal and the consequent need to classify a given contempt as either civil or criminal is demonstrated by the High Court of Australia's decision in *Hearne v Street*. In this case, a group of residents who lived near Luna Park, an amusement park located

[109] *Matthews v Seamen's Union of Australia* (1957) 1 FLR 185 (Commonwealth Industrial Court) 193–95 (Dunphy and Morgan JJ); *Witham* (n 1) 540.

[110] *Home Office* (n 93) 310 (Lord Scarman).

[111] *Bessette* (n 6) 667 (Brewer J).

[112] *Crosby's Case* (1771) 3 Wils KB 188, 204; 95 ER 1005, 1014.

[113] See, eg, *R v Parke* [1903] 2 KB 432 (KBD) 442 (Wills J); *R v Fletcher, ex parte Kisch* (1935) 52 CLR 248 (HCA) 256 (Evatt J); *Director of Public Prosecutions v Jones* (1985) 65 ACTR 11 (SC) 15 (Kelly J).

on the northern side of Sydney Harbour, commenced proceedings in the Supreme Court of New South Wales, seeking relief for private nuisance arising from the noise created by patrons. At the time, Luna Park had recently reopened following a decade's closure due to noise complaints. The proceedings were brought against two companies, Luna Park Sydney Pty Ltd and Metro Edgley Pty Ltd. Hearne was the managing director and chief executive officer of Luna Park Sydney and Tierney was the development manager and strategic advisor of Metro Edgley. Hearne and Tierney gave instructions to the solicitors conducting the litigation on behalf of Luna Park Sydney.

The residents swore and filed affidavits in the proceedings, in which they detailed the adverse impact of the noise from Luna Park on their daily lives. In mid-April 2005, the Sydney tabloid newspaper, the *Daily Telegraph*, published an article, 'The NUMBY* files'. The asterisk explained that the term, 'NUMBY', meant 'Not Under My Balcony. The city cousin of the NIMBY (Not in My Backyard)'.

The solicitors for the residents complained to Luna Park Sydney that it had released the affidavits to the media, and requested an undertaking that it not release any unread affidavits to the media or to any person not connected to the proceedings. The solicitors for Luna Park Sydney apologised for the release of the affidavits to the media and gave the undertaking sought. Subsequently, however, Hearne began to lobby the New South Wales State government to amend the Luna Park Site Act 1990 (NSW) to protect against liability for noise. Tierney sent an email to the State Minister for Tourism, Sport and Recreation, attaching a new acoustics report and a fresh affidavit, which Luna Park Sydney had received from the solicitors for the residents. In mid-October 2005, the New South Wales State government introduced the Luna Park Site Amendment (Noise Control) Bill, which sought to insulate Luna Park Sydney from liability for noise complaints dating back to its reopening. Before the parliamentary debate, Tierney sent an email to the Minister's office with a briefing note, including extracts from the residents' affidavits, but warned that the use of the quotes might constitute contempt of court. A week after its introduction, the Bill was passed, and the following day, the legislation commenced with retrospective effect. As a result of the amending legislation, the trial dates for the residents' hearing were vacated and the residents eventually abandoned their private nuisance claim against Luna Park Sydney, although they were able to amend their claim so as to seek relief under the Trade Practices Act 1974 (Cth) and the Crown Lands Act 1989 (NSW).[114] The residents' solicitors complained that Hearne and Tierney had breached the implied undertaking by providing the expert report and the affidavits to the Minister. They moved to have Hearne and Tierney dealt with for contempt of court.

At first instance, the trial judge, Gzell J, held that although their conduct was a breach of the implied undertaking owed by Luna Park Sydney, neither Hearne nor Tierney gave any undertaking to the court, nor did they have any knowledge

[114] As to the facts and the procedural history of this matter, see *Hearne* (n 27) [64]–[82] (Hayne, Heydon and Crennan JJ).

of Luna Park Sydney's implied undertaking. His Honour therefore dismissed the contempt proceedings against them. The residents appealed to the New South Wales Court of Appeal. Before the substantive issue could be reached, there was a jurisdictional issue. Under the Supreme Court Act 1970 (NSW), section 101(5), an appeal lies to the Court of Appeal in respect of any finding of the Supreme Court of contempt, whether civil or criminal. However, this right of appeal is qualified somewhat in the following subsection, which provides that no appeal lies where a person is found not to have committed criminal contempt.[115] This provision was evidently enacted to conform with the common law's aversion to appeals against acquittals. The characterisation of the contempt in question therefore became a live issue. Ipp JA, with whom Basten JA agreed, found that the breach constituted a civil contempt, such that the appeal was competent. On a further appeal to the High Court of Australia, Hayne, Heydon and Crennan JJ, giving the leading judgment, rejected the blanket proposition, derived from Deane J's judgment in *Hinch v Attorney-General for the State of Victoria*, that all contempt proceedings 'must realistically be seen as essentially criminal in nature'.[116] Their Honours accepted that such an approach might support the application of the criminal standard of proof in all contempt proceedings. However, they went on to observe that '[i]t does not affect the question of appellate rights. Section 101(6) assumes that there is a difference, in relation to appellate rights, between civil and criminal contempts.'[117]

The issue of characterisation was mandated by the legislature. Undertaking the task for themselves, Hayne, Heydon and Crennan JJ found that the conduct in question amounted to civil contempt.[118] Consequently, the appeal was competent. Courts can alter the common law to minimise the distinction between civil and criminal contempt, but it is always open to the legislature to entrench it.

The distinction between civil and criminal contempt may also be affected indirectly by statute. This is demonstrated by the issue of onus of proof. In Australia, the High Court's decision in *Witham v Holloway* settled the position at common law, requiring all contempts to be proved beyond reasonable doubt.[119] However, this was decided before the introduction of the uniform evidence legislation in Australia. In the Dictionary of the uniform evidence legislation, a 'criminal proceeding' is defined as 'a prosecution for an offence' and a 'civil proceeding' is defined negatively to mean 'a proceeding other than a criminal proceeding'. Under the Evidence Act 1995 (NSW), section 140(1), the standard of proof in a 'civil proceeding' is on the balance of probabilities, whereas under section 141(1), the standard of proof in a 'criminal proceeding' is beyond reasonable doubt.[120]

[115] Supreme Court Act 1970 (NSW), s 101(6).
[116] *Hinch v Attorney-General for the State of Victoria* (1987) 164 CLR 15 (HCA) 49.
[117] *Hearne* (n 27) [132] (Hayne, Heydon and Crennan JJ).
[118] ibid [134], [141].
[119] *Witham* (n 1).
[120] As to the position under the analogous legislation in the other jurisdictions that have adopted the uniform evidence legislation, see Evidence Act 1995 (Cth), ss 140(1), 141(1); Evidence Act 1995 (NSW), ss 140(1), 141(1); Evidence Act 2001 (Tas), ss 140(1), 141(1); Evidence Act 2008 (Vic), ss 140(1), 141(1); Evidence Act 2011 (ACT), ss 140(1), 141(1); Evidence (National Uniform Legislation) Act 2011 (NT), ss 140(1), 141(1).

An issue has arisen as to whether a proceeding for civil contempt was 'a prosecution for an offence', such that the criminal standard of proof would apply. In *Australian Securities and Investments Commission v Sigalla (No 4)*, White J (as his Honour then was) found that a civil contempt was not an offence.[121] Consequently, a proceeding dealing with a contemnor was not 'a prosecution for an offence' and was therefore a civil proceeding.[122] As a result, the standard of proof in a civil proceeding – proof on the balance of probabilities – applied by virtue of statute.[123] The rationalisation of the common law undertaken by the High Court of Australia in *Witham v Holloway* may have been displaced by statute, with the distinction between civil and criminal contempt being reasserted by statute. Even if the distinction between civil and criminal contempt were to be abolished by statute, careful consideration about the implications would need to be undertaken by the legislature, in order to avoid unintended consequences.[124]

The distinction between civil and criminal contempt has also presented difficulties for the application of constitutionally guaranteed rights. The effect of these rights is to entrench further the distinction between civil and criminal contempt. For instance, in *Turner v Rogers*, the US Supreme Court had to address the issue of whether an indigent defendant was entitled, by virtue of the Sixth Amendment to the US Constitution, to a state-appointed counsel in a civil contempt proceeding, given that such a proceeding could lead to imprisonment. The defendant had failed to pay child support.[125] Giving the opinion of the Court, Breyer J restated that the Sixth Amendment, which guarantees rights in relation to criminal prosecutions, does not apply to proceedings for civil contempt.[126] The fact that a contemnor could be imprisoned for civil contempt did not alter this position.

IX. Transcending the Distinction between Civil and Criminal Contempt

As a body of principle, contempt of court is vitally important to the administration of justice but poorly understood. Jurists cannot agree on the nature of contempt: it is variously described as 'a criminal offence', 'a common law crime', 'an offence of a criminal character',[127] 'quasi-criminal' or '*sui generis*'. Contempt has been described as 'protean'. The complexity of this area of law has been frequently noted by judges. A significant difficulty with the distinction between civil and criminal

[121] *Australian Securities and Investments Commission v Sigalla (No 4)* [2011] NSWSC 62, (2011) 80 NSWLR 113 [36].

[122] ibid [76]–[80].

[123] ibid [92]–[94].

[124] See, eg, *Broken Hill Proprietary Co Pty Ltd v Dagi* [1996] 2 VR 117, dealing with a legislative attempt to vest the sole responsibility for bringing contempt proceedings for interferences with the administration of justice in the Attorney-General of Victoria.

[125] *Turner v Rogers* 564 US 444, 131 S Ct 2507, 2515–16 (2011) (Breyer J).

[126] ibid 2516.

[127] See, eg, *Bramblevale* (n 100) 137 (Lord Denning MR).

contempt originates with the nature of the contempt jurisdiction itself. The power to punish for contempt of court is part of the inherent jurisdiction of a superior court of record.[128] The inherent jurisdiction of the court is not concerned with the taxonomical distinctions that are drawn in relation to substantive law. Contempt of court is concerned with the administration of justice generally, not public law or private law specifically. As part of the inherent jurisdiction of the court, contempt of court is part of the institutional character of the court. As a body of law, it exists to ensure that a court's orders are obeyed and a court's authority is respected, not just in private law litigation but in all litigation. It exists as a last resort to compel compliance and respect and, if necessary, to punish.

[128] *Bessette* (n 6) 666 (Brewer J).

PART III

Punitive Damages

7

Punitive Damages Transformed into Societal Damages

CATHERINE M SHARKEY*

I. Introduction

Whether termed civil penalties or statutory multiplied damages, 'supra-compensatory' damages are of increasing theoretical and practical interest not only in the United States, but also abroad, notably in France and Australia.[1] Notwithstanding criticisms directed at the controversial remedy of punitive damages and more generally at the notion of punishment within civil law,[2] there is a growing recognition that some form of supra-compensatory remedy may be necessary to deter certain forms of conduct on the part of actors, especially corporations. Around the world, 'supra-compensatory' damages seemingly arise phoenix-like from the ash heap of increasingly maligned 'punitive' damages.

There is a general consensus that punitive damages are intended 'to punish and to deter'. But this consensus masks deep and significant disagreements in terms of whether these purposes are, or should be, one and the same – namely retributive punishment whose corollary effectuates deterrence – or instead separable, with deterrence holding its own as a non-retributive purpose distinct from punishment.

Courts and commentators typically use the language of retributive punishment when describing the aims of punitive damages and the relevant features of the remedy. But at the same time, there is increasing recognition that the separate aim

* Ross Steinberg (NYU 2021) provided extraordinary research assistance. I received helpful comments from the participants at the 2019 Remedies Discussion Forum in Paris, the 2019 Punishment and Private Law Conference in Singapore, and the Duke Law Faculty Workshop. I am especially grateful to Elise Bant and Jeannie Paterson, Kit Barker, James Goudkamp and Eleni Katsampouka for providing further written comments.

[1] See, eg, Bant and Paterson, ch 10 of this volume (noting 'a significant momentum in favour of the recognition of such awards in the varied contexts of consumer law reform, intellectual property and pursuant to the common law principles of exemplary damages'); Rowan, ch 3 of this volume.

[2] See generally Penner, ch 5 of this volume (discussing the rationales and implications of civil law punishments).

of deterrence is often at play, especially in situations where the defendant's conduct has caused widespread societal harm.[3]

Courts and commentators struggle because of this alleged mismatch – namely, the awkward fit between the retributive punishment connotations of 'punitive' damages to serve societal deterrence purposes. The struggle is two-fold. First, punitive damages seem especially troubling because notions of retributive punishment, common in criminal law, seem wholly out of place in the civil sphere. For this reason, when courts award punitive damages they are inclined to place various limitations on the remedy, with the goal of avoiding 'disproportionate punishment'.

Second, notions of societal deterrence seem out of place in private law focused on bilateral interactions between the parties involved in the litigation. The notion of supra-compensatory damages for societal deterrence purposes injects a public regulatory purpose into private law. This dimension is significant where there are third-party effects or externalised harms to others stemming from bilateral interactions between defendants and plaintiffs. And it is also significant with respect to corporate wrongdoing. Statutory damages recognise this public interest element; common law courts have experienced more difficulty fashioning remedies accordingly.

My aim in this chapter is to interrogate what courts are saying – typically using the language of retributive punishment – when they might actually be doing something else – namely, effectuating societal deterrence. As a descriptive matter, I demonstrate that embedded within punitive damages is a component of damages designed to deter the tortfeasor. But my aim is also normative and aspirational – namely, what should courts be doing to effectuate societal deterrence? Building on prior work, I explore various statutory and judicial mechanisms that could transform punitive damages into societal damages. I consider whether the case for conceptualising punitive damages as a societal remedy is especially compelling in certain realms characterised by statutorily defined violations, such as in the consumer protection realm. Moreover, I explore how a reconceptualisation of punitive damages as a societal remedy could have far-reaching effects both in terms of the evolution of US doctrine, but also influencing law reform efforts in various other countries.

Sections II and III lay the necessary conceptual foundation by, first, disaggregating punitive damages by functional purpose and, second, setting forth theoretical constructs and practical factors relevant for achieving societal deterrence. Once the societal deterrence goal is acknowledged, however, the spectre of 'windfall' gains to the plaintiff looms large. It would be sheer coincidence if the amount needed to deter the defendant exactly equaled the amount of the plaintiff's losses. Section IV (the heart of the chapter) presents societal damages

[3] cf Bant and Paterson, ch 10, section I: 'Currently [in Australia], at least under statute, courts often emphasise deterrence without exploring the measures that may be most effective at achieving that goal, while also being primarily influenced by factors that mitigate the potentially harsh, overly punitive effects of such awards.'

funds – remedial funds created alternately by statute, common law courts, or private parties effectuating settlements – as an apt response to the injection of the public societal deterrence purpose within the framework of a private civil lawsuit. Finally, section V concludes by suggesting the far-reaching implications for debates regarding constitutional excessiveness review, insurability and vicarious liability for punitive damages, once punitive damages are transformed (in whole or in part) into societal damages.

II. Disaggregating Punitive Damages

Punitive damages are widely recognised as a controversial civil remedy designed to punish tortfeasors and to deter wrongdoing. All too often, however, after a quick nod to the goals of punishment and deterrence, courts and commentators dive headlong into analyses that, by and large, emphasise the notion of retributive punishment. Here, instead, I present a conceptual framework for disaggregating the purposes of punitive damages into distinct categories (notwithstanding the reality that such purposes may overlap in practice).

The two-by-two matrix in Table 7.1 disaggregates punitive damages along two significant dimensions.[4] The first (columns along the x axis) separates the retributive punishment goal from the non-retributive economic deterrence goal.[5] The second (rows along the y axis) distinguishes between individualistic and societal aims of the punitive damages remedy.

Table 7.1 Disaggregating Purposes of Punitive Damages

	Retribution	**Deterrence**
Individualistic (private interest)	I (individual punishment)	II (specific deterrence)
Societal (public interest)	III (societal punishment)	IV (general deterrence)

The individualistic, plaintiff-oriented conception of punitive damages is the more conventional and would appear to be deeply rooted in the bilateral conception of

[4] Table 7.1 is adapted from CM Sharkey, 'The Future of Classwide Punitive Damages' (2013) 46 *University of Michigan Journal of Law Reform* 1127, 1132.

[5] Here, I embrace punitive damages' primary goals of retributive punishment and economic deterrence. See, eg, *Exxon Shipping Co v Baker* 554 US 471, 492 (2008): '[T]he consensus today is that [punitive damages] are aimed not at compensation but principally at retribution and deterring harmful conduct.' In addition, I go on to discuss a closely related goal, namely the enforcement of property rights: see section III.A. Courts and commentators have discussed a variety of additional goals. See, eg, *Kemezy v Peters* 79 F3d 33, 34–35 (7th Circuit 1996) (discussing different purposes of punitive damages, including preventing under-deterrence, deterring behaviour that has no redeemable social value and expressing the moral outrage of the community).

private law, focused on doing justice between the parties to a lawsuit. This individualistic 'private' interest dimension of punitive damages focuses on the harms each particular plaintiff has suffered. In certain individual lawsuits – especially intentional torts – punitive damages are deemed an essential way to achieve retribution for particularly reprehensible conduct directed at particular individuals (Quadrant I). This individualistic conception can also accommodate a separate deterrent aim, so long as the goal is specific deterrence, namely keeping the specific defendant(s) from inflicting further harms upon the particular plaintiff(s) before the court (Quadrant II).

In sharp contrast, the societal conception of punitive damages trains its focus not on the particular plaintiff before the court but instead on the defendant's conduct, especially when it has caused widespread harms. This societal conception can address holistic harm to society caused by the defendant's conduct. Moreover, it embraces '[t]he conception of an inherent *public* interest in punitive damages that is distinct from the private individual's interest in compensatory damages'.[6]

It is not uncommon for courts to recognise that punitive damages seem like a distinct remedy in that they implicate 'societal' purposes. The Kentucky Supreme Court, for example, has recognised:

> The purpose of allowing damages of a punitive nature is to punish and discourage [the defendant] and others from similar conduct in the future. This purpose serves more of a societal interest rather than a private one as it strives to punish the wrongdoer rather than compensate the party harmed.[7]

But this recognition – that punitive damages focus on defendant's misconduct as opposed to a particular plaintiff's harm or loss, and that punitive damages thereby serve a societal punishment purpose – does not fully appreciate the ways in which punitive damages might be harnessed as a societal remedy. The societal conception can be aimed at retributive punishment: 'the punitive award can be said to constitute a punishment on behalf of society'[8] (Quadrant III). Or – as I will argue in this chapter – the societal conception can be in pursuit of non-retributive general deterrence to force an actor to internalise the full costs of the harms that it has inflicted on individuals and society, including widespread, typically diffuse harms inflicted especially by corporations (Quadrant IV).

[6] CM Sharkey, 'The BP Oil Spill Settlements, Classwide Punitive Damages, and Societal Deterrence' (2015) 64 *DePaul Law Review* 681, 682 ('BP Oil Spill'); see also CM Sharkey, 'Punitive Damages as Societal Damages' (2003) 113 *Yale Law Journal* 347, 350 (emphasis added) ('Societal Damages').

[7] *Osborne v Keeney* 399 SW3d 1, 20 (Ky 2012) (internal quotation marks omitted). cf *Harleysville Group Ins v Heritage Communities Inc* 803 SE2d 288, 306 (SC 2017) (internal quotation marks omitted): '[P]unitive damages relate not to the plaintiff, but rather to the defendant's reckless, willful, wanton, or malicious conduct.'

[8] *In re Simon II Litigation* 211 FRD 86, 104 (EDNY 2002) (Weinstein, J), *vacated* 407 F3d 125 (2nd Circuit 2005). See also EJ Cabraser, 'Unfinished Business: Reaching the Due Process Limits of Punitive Damages in Tobacco Litigation Through Unitary Classwide Adjudication' (2001) 36 *Wake Forest Law Review* 979, 980–81: 'Punitive damages stand as a civil penalty for transgression of the social compact … to penalize conduct that violates the social contract and injures society.'

Whereas the two-by-two matrix maps a fuller potential terrain of punitive damages purposes, here I will contrast the predominant individual retributive punishment goal (Quadrant I) espoused by courts and commentators with what I deem the normatively desirable goal of societal general deterrence (Quadrant IV).

A. Individual Retributive Punishment's Stranglehold

It may hardly seem surprising that individualistic notions of retributive punishment maintain a stranglehold on 'punitive' damages – the name of which connotes punishment. And retribution is at the core of most conceptions of punishment.[9] Indeed, punitive damages were historically awarded only in cases of malice or wilful and wanton conduct, a subset of intentional tort cases. The paradigmatic case was that of intentional battery or assault, including acts of physical violence, and dignitary affronts such as spitting upon one's adversary.[10] The standard verbal formulations of the doctrine require mental states ranging from 'intent to harm without lawful justification or excuse', to 'reckless disregard of the interests of others'.

The US Supreme Court, moreover, has seemingly embraced the goal of individualistic retributive punishment, all but rejecting the alternative economic deterrence rationales (whether individualistic or societal). Notwithstanding the fact that punitive damages is a State law tort remedy, the US Supreme Court 'constitutionalised' the remedy in 1996 with *BMW of North America, Inc v Gore*,[11] the first of a trio of cases (including *State Farm v Campbell* and *Philip Morris USA v Williams*) that created an edifice of federal constitutional review of punitive damages awards, setting forth a template for restrictions on punitive damages. In each of its cases, the Court has reiterated the twin purposes of punitive damages: to punish and to deter. But the Court has never specified its conception of deterrence, though it has intimated that punishment is the predominant purpose of punitive damages, with deterrence perhaps an incidental effect.[12]

In *Williams*, the Court insisted that the defendant could only be punished for the specific harms suffered by the particular plaintiff in the case; the jury could not punish the defendant for harms inflicted upon others, whom the Court characterised as 'strangers to the litigation'.[13] Somewhat cryptically, the Court elaborated that '[e]vidence of actual harm to nonparties can help to show that the conduct that harmed the plaintiff also posed a substantial risk of harm to the general public, and

[9] For an elaborated defence of this, see Barker, ch 2 of this volume.

[10] See Sharkey, 'Societal Damages' (n 6) 359, fn 23.

[11] *BMW of North America, Inc v Gore* 517 US 559 (1996).

[12] The situation is the same, moreover, in the Commonwealth, namely, the courts in England, Canada and Australia invariably stop short of offering any meaningful explanation of the concept of deterrence. I thank James Goudkamp for this observation.

[13] *Philip Morris USA v Williams* 549 US 346, 353 (2007).

so was particularly reprehensible'.[14] But the Court was nonetheless emphatic that 'a jury may not go further than this and use a punitive damages verdict to punish a defendant directly on account of harms it is alleged to have visited on nonparties'.[15] In sum, according to the Court, although evidence regarding a defendant's widespread harms could be relevant to the degree of reprehensibility of the defendant's conduct, judges have a responsibility to guard against the possibility that juries would punish the defendant for harms inflicted on those other than the named plaintiff.

Without a doubt, in *Williams*, the Court implicitly adopted the individualistic retributive conception of punitive damages. The Court did not, however, 'constitutionalise' this conception of punitive damages. To the contrary, in all of its punitive damages cases, the Court has consistently maintained that when reviewing punitive damages for excessiveness, courts should look first to 'a State's legitimate interests in punishing unlawful conduct and deterring its repetition'.[16] As I have argued, 'even as the U.S. Supreme Court intervenes to scrutinize punitive damages awarded under state law, it always begins with an opening salvo of deference to the "state interests" served by punitive damages. Nothing in *Williams* changes this key federalism point …'.[17] The individualistic retributive conception is thus not the only constitutionally permissible purpose for punitive damages.[18]

Some courts and commentators have nonetheless over-read *Williams* to claim that the Court dealt 'a crippling blow' to the entire category of societal punitive damages (wiping out Quadrants III and IV).[19] While I agree that the Court foreclosed punitive damages as societal punishment (Quadrant III), it remained silent regarding punitive damages as a vehicle for non-retributive societal deterrence

[14] ibid 355.

[15] ibid.

[16] ibid 352; *State Farm Mut Auto Ins Co v Campbell* 538 US 408, 416 (2003); *BMW of North America* (n 11) 587 (1996).

[17] CM Sharkey, 'Federal Incursions and State Defiance: Punitive Damages in the Wake of *Philip Morris v Williams*' (2010) 46 *Willamette Law Review* 449, 470. See also *Johnson v Ford Motor Co* 113 P3d 82, 92 (Cal 2005): '[W]e are not convinced the high court's precedents dictate that states take such a narrow view as to "what is to be deterred" through punitive damages as to blind state juries and courts to the state's public interest in deterring a wrongful course of conduct.'

[18] But see MP Allen, 'Of Remedy, Juries, and State Regulation of Punitive Damages: The Significance of *Philip Morris v Williams*' (2008) 63 *New York University Annual Survey of American Law* 343, 352 (arguing that the US Supreme Court 'was itself establishing the constitutionally legitimate purposes of [the] historically state-defined remedial device [of punitive damages]').

[19] Sharkey (n 4) 1137. See, eg, R Nagareda, 'Embedded Aggregation in Civil Litigation' (2010) 95 *Cornell Law Review* 1105, 1136: 'The constitutional message in *Williams* – that punitive damages are ultimately about punishment for the wrong done to the plaintiff at hand – gives a considerable nod to what [is] described as plaintiff-focused views in torts literature.'; PB Rietema, 'Reconceptualizing Split-Recovery Statutes: *Philip Morris v Williams*, 127 S Ct 1057 (2007)' (2008) 31 *Harvard Journal of Legislation and Public Policy* 1159, 1166 (suggesting *Williams* signals the demise of societal punitive damages); SB Scheuerman, 'Two Worlds Collide: How The Supreme Court's Recent Punitive Damages Decisions Affect Class Actions' (2010) 60 *Baylor Law Review* 880, 932: '[T]he Supreme Court has premised its [punitive damages] due process theory on a one-on-one model of adjudication that focuses on the parties' relationship to one another and not the impact on non-parties or larger social issues.'

(Quadrant IV). And so long as punitive damages' non-retributive societal deterrence purpose is set forth (by State legislatures and/or courts) as a legitimate State interest, it should persist as constitutionally legitimate.[20]

B. Societal General Deterrence's Emerging Influence

The nature of the legitimate State interest in the punitive damages remedy has changed and evolved over time. The historical roots of the award of punitive damages are tied to retributive punishment. As tort and criminal law emerged as distinct areas of law from an earlier historical period of undifferentiated wrongdoing, the concept of malice carried over into tort law to signify especially reprehensible conduct on the part of the tortfeasor (who acted with cruelty or the desire to wrong another) in the realm of intentional torts.[21]

But in more recent times, a newer generation of punitive damages cases has emerged that falls outside this narrow band of malicious, intentionally wrongful conduct. Such cases award punitive damages for a tortfeasor's 'reckless' conduct, performed with lack of attention to the consequences for the health and safety of others in society.[22] Cases in this category tend to involve conduct that has caused widespread harms. Policing such wrongdoing, often involving conduct that moves considerably away from punitive damages' historical roots in cruelty between individuals, may be under-enforced. An especially salient example is in the realm of mass disasters, such as oil spills, where widespread harms cannot be fully deterred (or remedied) by individual (or even classwide) compensatory awards.

Another apt paradigm centres on patterns and practices of corporate misconduct. In the United States today, for example, punitive damages are awarded frequently in widespread harm cases against corporations. It is striking that in each

[20] See, eg, *Johnson* (n 17) 92: 'California law has long endorsed the use of punitive damages to deter continuation or imitation of a corporation's course of wrongful conduct, and hence allowed consideration of that conduct's scale and profitability in determining the size of award that will vindicate the state's legitimate interests.' See also section III.B.i for further discussion of this.

[21] See generally MO DeGirolami, 'Reconstructing Malice in the Law of Punitive Damages' (2021) 14 *Journal of Tort Law* (forthcoming) (constructing a theory of malice with 'deep roots in the shared history of criminal law and tort law form the thirteenth to the nineteenth century' where '[a]t its core, malice denoted cruelty, whether the hot desire to wrong or the cold disposition of the depraved heart').

[22] Sharkey, 'Societal Damages' (n 6) 351 (noting that '[w]ith increasing frequency, punitive damages are being awarded in the kinds of cases where defendants are most likely to have inflicted harms upon individuals beyond the plaintiffs named in the complaint' – in particular, in the realms of fraud, employment discrimination and products liability); 358, fn 19; 364; 394–99 (describing hostile work environment claims as 'a useful venue for exploring the concept of distribution of societal damages to quasi-plaintiffs'). cf E Buyuksagis et al, 'Punitive Damages in Europe and Plea for the Recognition of Legal Pluralism' (2016) 27 *European Business Law Review* 137 (implying that allowing for 'compensatory' damages in Switzerland without actually having to demonstrate harm in cases of discrimination or harassment has a deterrence function). Note that punitive damages are also included in the categories of cases where there are likely to be quasi-plaintiffs, such that one might reconceptualise such damages as having a societal compensation aspect.

of the US Supreme Court trilogy of cases – *BMW v Gore*, *State Farm v Campbell* and *Williams v Philip Morris* – individual plaintiffs sued a corporate defendant, seeking punitive damages on account of the corporation's practices and policies. Indeed, in the United States, plaintiffs seek and are awarded punitive damages more often against businesses than against individuals. According to the most recent comprehensive data collected from State courts across the United States, individuals sought punitive damages in 10 per cent of cases against individuals as compared to 16 per cent against businesses.[23] And punitive damages were awarded more frequently in cases that individuals won against businesses (7 per cent) than against individuals (4 per cent).

In the United Kingdom, the situation is reversed – namely, punitive damages are sought more often against individuals than against corporations; and they are likewise awarded more frequently against persons than against corporations.[24] A similar pattern, moreover, emerges from Australia, where punitive damages are awarded more frequently against individuals than against corporations.[25] Moreover, the number of successful punitive damages claims in both the United Kingdom and Australia pales in comparison to the thousands in the United States on an annual basis.[26]

This empirical reality – namely, that in the United States plaintiffs seek (and are awarded) punitive damages against corporations proportionally more than plaintiffs in either the United Kingdom or Australia – tells us something about

[23] T Cohen and K Harbacek, 'Punitive Damage Awards in Large Counties 2005' (*Bureau of Justice Statistics*, 3 March 2011) at www.bjs.gov/content/pub/pdf/pdasc05.pdf. 'Businesses' are defined to include 'insurance companies, banks, [and] other businesses and organizations': TH Cohen, 'Punitive Damage Awards in Large Counties, 2001' (*Bureau of Justice Statistics*, 3 March 2005) at www.bjs.gov/content/pub/pdf/pdalc01.pdf. And where businesses are plaintiffs, they sought punitive damages in 7% of cases against individuals as compared to 13% of cases against businesses.

[24] See J Goudkamp and E Katsampouka, 'An Empirical Study of Punitive Damages' (2018) 38 *OJLS* 90, 106. The Goudkamp/Katsampouka study looks at all 146 cases (accessible electronically and not including appeals) in which liability was found and punitive damages awards were sought in the United Kingdom between 2000 and 2016. Of the 146 cases, punitive damages were sought from individuals in 56 (38.3%), from corporations in 30 (20.6%) and against public bodies in 60 (41.1%). Punitive damages were awarded more frequently against individuals (67.9%) than against corporations (30%) or public bodies (18.3%).

[25] F Maher, 'An Empirical Study of Exemplary Damages in Australia' (2019) 43 *Melbourne University Law Review* 1, 10, 18. The Maher study replicates the Goudkamp/Katsampouka study in Australia, looking at all 252 cases (accessible electronically and excluding appeals) in which liability was found and punitive damages awards were sought in Australia between 2000 and 2016. Punitive damages are awarded against individuals 47% of the time they are sought, as compared to 32% of the time against corporations. It may well be that a robust system of civil penalties enforced by regulators against corporations fills this gap. See Bant and Paterson, ch 10, section III.A: 'Australia's powerful and overarching statutory schemes now embrace civil penalties as a core deterrent mechanism for serious commercial misconduct.' Bant and Paterson highlight the public aspect of the Australian civil penalties jurisdiction, namely that it is enforced by regulators, with fines going into the public purse. I am grateful to Elise Bant and Jeannie Paterson for this insight.

[26] Thus, the Goudkamp/Katsampouka sample includes 146 cases of plaintiff-win cases seeking punitive damages from 2000–16; the corresponding figure for the Maher study (also from 2000–16) is 252 cases; whereas in 2005 alone, the US comprehensive sample of State cases includes thousands of such cases.

the perceived legitimate State interests in punitive damages. In the United States, where punitive damages are awarded more frequently against corporations whose conduct has led to widespread harms, the economic deterrence goal resonates,[27] whereas in the United Kingdom and Australia the aim seems more closely tethered to the historical origins in malicious, intentional bilateral conduct between individuals.[28]

This newer generation of punitive damages cases illustrates the changing nature of cases in which punitive damages are awarded. The legitimate State interest in punitive damages can therefore be seen to be both historically contingent but also evolving. States could, moreover, be more explicit about the evolving legitimate aims for punitive damages, particularly with respect to embracing a non-retributive societal deterrence goal. Because the remedy of punitive damages lies squarely within the purview of State law, State legislatures and courts possess a degree of freedom to articulate State-based goals of punitive damages – such as economic deterrence – even in the face of heavy-handed federal constitutional review imposed by the US Supreme Court.

III. Societal Deterrence

Once societal general deterrence is recognised as a legitimate purpose of punitive damages, two further challenges remain. First, as a matter of theory, general deterrence may be pursued via loss internalisation or gain elimination. Second, as a matter of practice, legislatures and courts (and juries) must be able to point to objective factors as proxies to measure societal deterrence. Whereas, at present, courts often consider 'proportionate punishment' factors, I argue that they should instead be directed to societal deterrence factors (whether premised on loss internalisation or gain elimination).

Section III.A elaborates the theoretical goals of societal deterrence, based alternatively on loss internalisation or gain elimination. At this juncture, it is worth acknowledging that, while the theoretical case for societal deterrence is sound,

[27] Sam Buell has argued persuasively that corporations cannot be retributively punished. See SW Buell, 'The Impossibility of Corporate Retribution' (2021) 83 *Law & Contemporary Problems* (forthcoming): 'Because corporations cannot experience such pain, suffering, or deprivations, they cannot be punished *on retributive grounds*.'

[28] According to Katsampouka 'the main purpose of punitive damages in England is retribution': email from Eleni Katsampouka to author (22 December 2019). See also *Rookes v Barnard* [1964] AC 1129 (HL), 1221 (punitive damages can be sought only where there is '[o]ppressive, arbitrary or unconstitutional actions by servants of government', '[w]here the defendant's conduct was "calculated" to make a profit for himself', and '[w]here a statute expressly authorises the same'). Moreover, in the United Kingdom, 'it is well established that punitive damages may not be awarded if other remedies are sufficient to achieve the goals of punishment and deterrence or if other sanctions have already been imposed on the defendant for the conduct concerned': Goudkamp and Katsampouka (n 24) 94. And similarly, in Australia, '[e]xemplary damages will not be available … where substantial punishment has been imposed on the defendant by the criminal law': Maher (n 25) 7.

its empirical validity in the real world is indeterminate. There is, at present, scant empirical evidence that imposing punitive damages in widespread harm cases affects the behaviour of individuals and companies. But given the soundness of the theory, section III.B takes up the task of identifying relevant factors. Indeed, should certain States (or countries) take the lead in setting forth such schemes, they could serve as 'laboratories' of experimentation upon which further empirical testing might be based.

A. Theoretical Goals

The primary economic rationale of optimal deterrence for supra-compensatory damages dates back to Jeremy Bentham, who set forth the loss internalisation principle, namely, that actors would internalise the future expected monetary damages awards for harms in order to weigh whether the benefits of their conduct outweighed the harms.[29] Only in recent decades, however, has this rationale been formalised in the specific context of punitive damages. Alternative economic rationales – disgorgement of ill-gotten gains and enforcement of property rights – have been proposed to align the theory with the historic and conventional focus of punitive damages on intentionally wrongful behaviour.[30]

As explained in section II, the contemporary expansion of punitive damages in the United States into reckless indifference (most prominently in products liability cases) suggests additional room for expansion of the loss internalisation rationale, with both descriptive and prescriptive payoffs.

i. Loss Internalisation

The predominant law-and-economics rationale for punitive (or supra-compensatory) damages is based upon optimal deterrence or loss internalisation and focuses on the under-enforcement problem: supra-compensatory damages are needed when under-detection of harms or other factors leads to inefficiently low expected liability, which is insufficient to induce optimal care. In other words, in situations where compensatory damages alone will not adequately deter, supra-compensatory damages (in the form of punitive damages) are necessary to force the actor to internalise the full societal costs inflicted by its conduct.

[29] See J Bowring (ed), *The Works of Jeremy Bentham*, vol 1 (New York, Russell & Russell, 1962) 365, 401–02; see also GS Becker, 'Crime and Punishment: An Economic Approach' (1968) 76 *Journal of Political Economy* 169.

[30] The Calabresi-Melamed property rule/liability rule dichotomy provides one framework for choosing between the loss internalisation (liability rule) and gain elimination/voluntary market transfer (property rule) models. For further elaboration, see CM Sharkey, 'Economic Analysis of Punitive Damages: Theory, Empirics, and Doctrine' in J Arlen (ed), *Research Handbook on the Economics of Torts* (Northampton, MA, Edward Elgar, 2013).

Mitchell Polinsky and Steven Shavell put forth a punitive damages 'multiplier' equal to the inverse of the probability of detection, highlighting the need for supra-compensatory damages where wrongdoing is not likely to be detected.[31] For example, if a tortfeasor's misconduct is likely to be detected and enforced against only one out of every 10 times, the compensatory damages (equal to the harms inflicted in the one time in which it is detected and enforced) should be multiplied by 10 (the inverse of 1/10, the probability of detection) in order to force the tortfeasor to internalise the total societal costs.[32]

In prior work, I extended this under-detection or under-enforcement rationale for supra-compensatory damages to a wider domain of situations, including those of diffuse harms inflicted on individuals and society that are not likely to be enforced by either individual or class action litigation.[33] For many reasons, tortfeasors may not internalise the full costs of the harms they inflict on people, property and publicly held resources: not only under-detection, but also under-compensation and other imperfections in the litigation system, such as false negatives in adjudication (ie where defendants erroneously get off scot-free) and the prohibitive cost of adjudication.

The domain for optimal deterrence theory is a socially productive yet externality producing (ie inflicting harms onto third parties) activity. Purely compensatory damages will not induce optimal care if negligent injurers expect to avoid liability for some of the harms they cause. The primary goal of punitive damages is to address the under-enforcement problem by increasing damages for the harms that are detected and sanctioned by a sufficient amount to ensure that injurers' expected liability equals the social cost of their harm-producing conduct. Punitive damages are warranted in all cases where under-enforcement is an issue; there is no reason to distinguish between intentional and purely negligent (or even strict liability) harms.

ii. Gain Elimination

The domain for theories of gain elimination or prevention of wrongful takings (sometimes referred to as 'complete deterrence' theories) is intentional, conscious wrongdoing. There is a distinct shift in focus away from losses suffered by the plaintiff or society and towards the defendant's wrongful conduct. In this realm, one worries about under-deterrence, but less so about over-deterrence. The primary goal of gain elimination is the complete deterrence of socially unproductive activities.

[31] AM Polinsky and S Shavell, 'Punitive Damages: An Economic Analysis' (1998) 111 *Harvard Law Review* 869, 889–90.

[32] See *Mathias v Accor Econ Lodging Inc* 347 F3d 672, 677–78 (7th Circuit 2003) (articulating this example).

[33] See generally Sharkey, 'Societal Damages' (n 6).

According to Keith Hylton, gain elimination is the primary goal of punitive damages, because complete deterrence (ie stopping the wrongful conduct altogether), rather than some form of optimal deterrence, is the goal. In other words, where punitive damages are used for disgorgement purposes (to teach that 'torts do not pay') rather than for incentive purposes (to teach that 'precautions pay'), society has implicitly chosen a goal of absolute (or complete) deterrence rather than relative (or optimal) deterrence in tort.[34] Here, the realm of 'efficient torts' is correspondingly limited; the focus instead is on eliminating the wrongful conduct altogether.

B. Relevant Factors

Once societal deterrence is recognised as a legitimate State interest or goal for the award of supra-compensatory damages, State legislatures and common law courts face the challenge of setting forth relevant factors to measure deterrence, whether premised on loss internalisation or gain elimination. State legislatures could affirmatively defend supra-compensatory damages based on under-enforcement and under-deterrence rationales. For example, they might set forth statutory multipliers for certain torts based on likelihood of under-detection. More radically, common law courts, relying on their interpretations of the underlying State law policies justifying supra-compensatory punitive damages, could develop interstitial common law standards, identifying factual situations where under-detection, under-enforcement or societal deterrence prerogatives predominate. Here, I briefly consider factors relevant to such undertakings.

i. Undetected Harms: Repeat Offenders

As a proxy for undetected harms, courts might look for the existence of repeat offenders. The US Supreme Court has maintained that 'repeated misconduct is more reprehensible than an individual instance of malfeasance'.[35] But it is also the case that repeated misconduct suggests that the penalty for the earlier misconduct did not sufficiently deter the offender.

Consider the case of the enforcement of California's 'lemon laws' for the sale of defective automobiles.[36] There is some evidence of under-enforcement of such laws.[37] Further, there is some evidence that large automobile companies proceed

[34] KN Hylton, 'Punitive Damages and the Economic Theory of Penalties' (1998) 87 *Georgetown Law Journal* 421, 452–54.

[35] *BMW of North America* (n 11) 577 (1996).

[36] See California Civil Code § 1793.2, (d)(2) (stipulating that a vehicle that cannot be repaired in a 'reasonable number' of attempts must be reacquired or replaced).

[37] R Blumenthal and E Markey, 'Blumenthal & Markey Introduce Legislation to Protect Car Shoppers from Buying, Leasing, or Loaning Unsafe Used Cars', *Senator Markey* (26 June 2019) at www.markey.senate.gov/news/press-releases/blumenthal-and-markey-introduce-legislation-to-protect-car-shoppers-from-buying-leasing-or-loaning-unsafe-used-cars: 'State laws exist that prohibit the selling of unsafe vehicles, but these laws are not being adequately enforced …'; see also Consumers for Auto Reliability and Safety at www.carconsumers.org.

by seriatim confidential settlements when caught in violation of such laws.[38] Moreover, in *Johnson v Ford Motor Co*, the California Supreme Court drew from the US Supreme Court's language in *BWM v Gore* that 'strong medicine is required to cure the defendant's disrespect for the law',[39] to hold that 'a defendant [who] has *repeatedly engaged in profitable but wrongful conduct* tends to show that "strong medicine is required" to deter the conduct's further repetition'.[40] Thus, a strong case can be made that, in an instance of successful prosecution via litigation, supra-compensatory damages should be awarded in light of the likely existence of a pattern and practice of flouting of the law, having likely caused previously under-detected harms. Indeed, as the *Johnson* court recognised:

> California has long endorsed the use of punitive damages to deter continuation or imitation of a corporation's course of wrongful conduct, and hence allowed consideration of that conduct's scale and profitability in determining the size of award that will vindicate the state's legitimate interests.[41]

ii. Widespread Harms to Other Individuals

One of the benefits of focusing the measure of supra-compensatory damages on harms to individuals other than the plaintiff(s) before the court is that it provides an objective measure (albeit likely a lower limit) of the societal harm inflicted by the defendant. Thus, just as compensatory damages that focus on quantifying the losses or harms suffered by the plaintiff(s) before the court simultaneously satisfy the loss internalisation deterrence goal of tort law, so tethering supra-compensatory damages to losses suffered by other individuals not before the court can likewise serve the societal deterrence goal.

[38] See, eg, Consumers for Auto Reliability and Safety and others, 'Auto Safety/Consumer Organizations Sue Federal Trade Commission, over Decision Allowing General Motors and Car Dealerships to Engage in False Advertising of Unrepaired Recalled "Certified" Used Cars', *Auto Safety* (6 February 2017) at www.autosafety.org/wp-content/uploads/2017/02/FTC-Release.pdf: 'State laws prohibit dealers from engaging in such practices. However, some of those laws may not be enforced until after someone has already been injured or killed. Victims of dealers who sold unrepaired recalled cars, or their surviving family members, have sued dealers for wrongs such as negligence or wrongful death, and have received confidential settlements'; MASSPIRG, 'Car Dealers Attack Massachusetts Protections Against Dangerous Recalled Used Cars', *MASSPIRG* (15 July 2019) at www.masspirg.org/news/map/car-dealers-attack-massachusetts-protections-against-dangerous-recalled-used-cars: 'Consumers in Massachusetts and other states have been suing car dealers who sold them recalled used cars … and winning in court or receiving confidential settlements'; see also Consumers for Auto Reliability and Safety at www.carconsumers.org.

[39] *BMW of North America* (n 11) 577 (1996).

[40] *Johnson* (n 17) 92 (Cal 2005) (emphasis added). In *Johnson*, the plaintiffs sued Ford Motor Co for concealing the used automobile's history of transmission repairs and replacements when reselling the car. Plaintiffs presented evidence of corporate practices by Ford amounting to a pattern and practice of similar fraud. The court reasoned that '[t]o the extent the evidence shows the defendant had a practice of engaging in, and profiting from, wrongful conduct similar to that which injured the plaintiff, such evidence may be considered on the question of how large a punitive damages award due process permits': ibid 97.

[41] ibid 93.

iii. Public Impact

Legislatures have at their disposal wider berth than courts to consider the 'public' impact of certain kinds of conduct, especially unfair or deceptive conduct that might have widespread societal impact.

Consider, for example, in the United States the proliferation of unfair and deceptive acts and practices (UDAP) statutes in each of the 50 States, where offending public policy is part and parcel of being an unfair practice. Whereas the public impact dimension is relevant under most States' statutory frameworks, it is a required prima facie element in seven States.[42] Thus, in Colorado, courts have made explicit the societal purpose underlying their UDAP statute:

> It is in the *public interest* to invoke the state's police power to prevent the use of methods that have a tendency or capacity to attract customers through deceptive trade practices … The Colorado Consumer Protection Act is an outgrowth of this conclusion …[43]

Statutes in Kentucky and Maryland, moreover, explicitly tie the public impact requirement to the 'preventive' and 'remedial' as distinct from 'punitive' purpose of the statutory damages.[44] Thus, the interest in the well-being of the community is referenced along with the desire that the statutory damages serve compensatory and deterrent functions.[45] Kentucky's statute reads:

> The General Assembly finds that the public health, welfare and interest require a strong and effective consumer protection program *to protect the public interest* and the well-being of both the consumer public and the ethical sellers of goods and services; toward this end, [the UDAP is] hereby created for the purpose of aiding in the development of preventive and remedial consumer protection programs and enforcing consumer protection statutes.[46]

[42] See *National Consumer Law Center*, 'Consumer Protection in the States: Appendix C' (*National Consumer Law Center*, 2018) at www.nclc.org/images/pdf/udap/udap-appC.pdf. These States are Colorado, Georgia, Minnesota, Nebraska, New York, South Carolina and Washington. Of these, Nebraska does not permit punitive damages. See ibid. Minnesota does not permit punitive damages to be awarded under its UDAP statute. See *In re Lutheran Bhd Variable Ins Prod Co Sales Practices Litig* 2004 WL 909741, 7 (D Minn 28 April 2004). New York sharply limits the size of a punitive award under its UDAP statute.

[43] *People ex rel Dunbar v Gym of America Inc* 493 P2d 660, 668 (Colo 1972) (emphasis added); see also *May Department Stores Co v State ex rel Woodard* 863 P2d 967, 972 (Colo 1993): 'Because the CCPA's civil penalty requirement is intended to punish and deter the wrongdoer and not to compensate the injured party, the CCPA is intended to proscribe deceptive acts and not the consequences of those acts.'

[44] For further discussion of statutory damages, see Sharkey (n 17) 471–76, which argues 'Statutory damages occupy a netherworld somewhere between compensatory and punitive damages. If statutory multiple damages are enacted for a retributive punishment purpose, then it would seem that the US Supreme Court's constitutional due process apparatus should apply, full stop. But, if instead, these legislatively enacted damages serve non-retributive, legitimate state interests – such as deterrence and compensation – then they would fall on the non-punitive side of things and outside of the Court's constitutional due process purview.'

[45] Similarly, statutes in California, Texas and Idaho reference an interest to protect consumers as a whole and to use efficient economic procedures to do so.

[46] Kentucky Revised Statutes Annotated, § 367.120 (emphasis added).

Maryland's statute lays out an equally broad public-oriented objective to 'take strong protective and preventive steps to investigate unlawful consumer practices, to assist the public in obtaining relief from these practices, and to prevent these practices from occurring in Maryland'.[47]

The public impact element offers an avenue for admission of evidence of harm to non-parties – notwithstanding the constitutional proscription against punishing a defendant for harm to non-parties in an individual case.[48] In *State ex rel Wilson v Ortho-McNeil-Janssen Pharms*, the court recognised that 'counsel for the State directly linked the elements of [South Carolina's] UTPA [Unfair Trade Practices Act] to [defendant's] misleading and deceptive practices' and explicitly approved such arguments as 'within [the] proper bounds as the State sought to establish that [defendant] acted willfully and contrary to the public interest'.[49]

Statutory multipliers exists in roughly half (25/50) of the State acts.[50] The existence of the statutory multiplier, moreover, is correlated with an express legislative statement regarding the public impact of the conduct.[51] If the legislature intends statutory multiplied damages to serve a societal compensatory purpose, it makes sense that it would be more likely to authorise such a multiplier if it could be assured it would be triggered only when there were a public impact.

Moreover, punitive damages in this context might be an apt substitute for the statutory multiplier.[52] In Idaho, supra-compensatory damages are awarded in cases of 'repeated or flagrant' violations of the relevant consumer protection act.[53] As outlined in section III.B.i, repeat offences could be an apt proxy for the existence of prior under-detected harms. Washington's UDAP statute has a public impact requirement; moreover, it allows for punitive damages under UDAP, but denies them more generally for other common law causes of action (even in cases of egregious misconduct).[54] By allowing punitive damages selectively for UDAP

[47] Maryland Code Annotated Commercial Law, § 13-102.

[48] See section II.A (discussing *Williams* and the prohibition against *punishing* a defendant for harms committed to non-parties).

[49] *State ex rel Wilson v Ortho-McNeil-Janssen Pharmaceuticals Inc* 777 SE2d 176, 190 (SC 2015).

[50] See C Carter, 'Consumer Protection in the States: A 50-State Evaluation of Unfair and Deceptive Practices Laws' (*National Consumer Law Center*, March 2018) at www.nclc.org/images/pdf/udap/udap-report.pdf.

[51] The majority of States that *require* a public impact element (5 out of 7) authorise a statutory damages multiplier; whereas slightly less than half (20 out of 43) of States without a required public impact element authorise statutory multipliers. See ibid; *National Consumer Law Center*, 'Consumer Protection in the States: Appendix C' (2018) at www.nclc.org/images/pdf/udap/udap-appC.pdf.

[52] The majority of States, though not all of them, allow punitive damages to be awarded under their consumer protection statutes. See *National Consumer Law Center* (n 42). It is worth asking whether States would continue to reject punitive damages in the UDAP context were they reconceptualised as societal compensatory damages. Indeed, the potential effects could be far-reaching, even beyond the United States, as mentioned in the text to follow above.

[53] *Mac Tools v Griffin* 879 P2d 1126, 1131 (Idaho 1994).

[54] See *McKee v AT&T Corporation* 191 P3d 845, 860 (Wash 2008): 'Washington is one of only a few states that does not provide generally for punitive damages for particularly egregious conduct.'

statutory causes of action, the Washington State legislature signals its embrace of the societal purpose for punitive damages. As one judge explained:

> If private remedies under the act are not restricted to those which arise out of the transactions which the Attorney General might sue to restrain (those affecting the public interest), the act does indeed become another remedy for purely private wrongs, and an authorization of punitive damages for such wrongs.[55]

Australia's statutory consumer protection regime (which covers commercial transactions as well) provides further illustration.[56] An option for calculating the maximum civil pecuniary penalty that may be awarded is a three-times statutory multiplier of the benefit obtained by violation of the Australian Consumer Law (ACL).[57] In Australia, unlike the United States, only public regulators can seek this remedy, whereas individuals are restricted to damages and a range of flexible court-ordered compensation orders aimed at affecting redress for loss or damage suffered. Punitive damages, however, have been ruled out. As Elise Bant and Jeannie Paterson have noted:

> [E]ven on the most generous terms, there are limits to the boundaries of orders that may be made under ss 237–8 of the ACL given the statutory direction that they must 'compensate', 'prevent or reduce' loss or damage suffered because of misleading conduct … Thus, exemplary damages, which both punish and deter contraventions of the law, are not available under the ACL.[58]

Bant and Paterson reach their conclusion given that '[o]n any view, exemplary damages are not compensatory in nature, but rather focus wholly on the egregious conduct of the defendant'.[59] Here, too, then, the reconceptualisation of punitive damages as societal damages might transform these damages into ones recognised under Australia's consumer law.

iv. *Defendant's Financial Status*

The vast majority of US States that allow punitive damages allow juries to consider a defendant's financial status when considering the amount of the punitive award.[60]

[55] *Anhold v Daniels* 614 P2d 184, 189 (Wash 1980) (Rosselini, J, concurring).

[56] Primarily the Australian Consumer Law (ACL) in *Competition and Consumer Act* (2010) (AUS), sch 2.

[57] More precisely, under ACL, s 224(3A), the maximum penalty options are the greater of: (a) $10,000,000; (b) if the court can determine the value of the benefit that the body corporate, and any body corporate related to the body corporate, have obtained directly or indirectly and that is reasonably attributable to the act or omission – 3 times the value of that benefit; (c) if the court cannot determine the value of that benefit – 10% of the annual turnover of the body corporate during the 12-month period ending at the end of the month in which the act or omission occurred or started to occur.

[58] E Bant and JM Paterson, 'Should Specifically Deterrent or Punitive Remedies Be Made Available to Victims of Misleading Conduct Under the Australian Consumer Law?' (2019) 25 *Torts Law Journal* 99, 109.

[59] ibid.

[60] The exceptions are Alabama (*In re Tylenol (Acetaminophen) Mktg Sales Practices & Prods Liab Litig* 144 F Supp3d 680, 685 (ED Pa 2015)), Colorado (Colorado Revised Statutes § 13-21-102),

In fact, juries are required to consider defendants' wealth in a sizeable number of State jurisdictions.[61] Courts typically assert that the 'defendant's financial condition is logically one of the essential factors to consider in determining an amount of punitive damages that will appropriately accomplish the goals of punishment and deterrence'.[62] The intuition is as follows:

> A punitive sanction of $1,000.00 for reprehensible conduct may be sufficient to deter an individual of modest means from subsequently engaging in similar conduct, while that sanction could be utterly ineffective to deter an individual with vast financial resources from engaging in the same conduct. Similarly, a punitive sanction of $1,000.00 may constitute a significant level of punishment for an individual of modest means, but it could amount to an inconsequential penalty for an individual with vast financial resources. Conversely, a $100,000.00 punitive sanction may sufficiently punish and deter a wealthy individual who has engaged in reprehensible conduct; yet, if that same sanction would bankrupt an individual of modest means who has engaged in the same conduct, it could therefore constitute an excessive penalty.[63]

Not only do the courts fail to distinguish the underlying retributive punishment rationale from the economic deterrence rationale, but each is applied to an individual defendant, with no appreciation for how a corporation might respond differently from an individual.

Economists are divided on the question whether the wealth of the defendant is relevant to economic deterrence (apart from the limited case of the judgment-proof tortfeasor, when all agree it is relevant). Robert Cooter argues that consideration of the defendant's wealth is 'inappropriate to deterrence of economically self-interested decisionmakers' because the 'controlling factor in a purely self-interested calculus … is the cost of compliance relative to the cost of liability'.[64] Polinsky and Shavell concur, asserting that wealth should never be taken into account for corporations as long as they can correctly balance the 'costs of precautions against the resulting reduction in harm'.[65]

By contrast, Jennifer Arlen argues that to the extent society wants to maximise social utility in the presence of risk aversion, negligence regimes must take into account wealth differences in establishing the duty of care, and further argues that both strict liability and negligence regimes should consider differences in wealth in setting the level of compensatory damages.[66] Hylton also suggests that 'the

Kentucky (*Nami Res Co LLC v Asher Land & Mineral LTD* 554 SW3d 323, 339 (Ky 2018)) and North Dakota (North Dakota Century Code § 32-03.2-11).

[61] See LC Orr, 'Making a Case for Wealth-Calibrated Punitive Damages' (2004) 37 *Loyola of Los Angeles Law Review* 1739, 1743, fn 26: 'Alaska, California, Illinois, Louisiana, Maine, Mississippi, Montana, New Jersey, New York, South Dakota, Tennessee, Utah, and West Virginia all require that a defendant's wealth be considered.'

[62] *Seltzer v Morton* 154 P3d 561, 597 (Mont 2007).

[63] ibid. See also *Mosing v Domas* 830 So 2d 967, 978 (La 2002).

[64] RD Cooter, 'Punitive Damages for Deterrence: When and How Much?' (1989) 40 *Alabama Law Review* 1143, 1176–77.

[65] Polinsky and Shavell (n 31) 910–14.

[66] JH Arlen, 'Should Defendants' Wealth Matter?' (1992) 21 *Journal of Legal Studies* 413, 428.

wealth of the defendant is relevant in the determination of a punitive award when either the victim's loss or the defendant's gain from wrongdoing is unobservable and correlated with the defendant's wealth'.[67]

Moreover, to the extent that gain elimination (as opposed to loss internalisation) is the variant of deterrence being pursued, the defendant's profits tied to its misconduct is the relevant measure. This is readily encompassed within Connecticut's 'general rule' that 'the aims of punitive damages are punishment, deterrence, and profit disgorgement'.[68]

v. Over-deterrence

Finally, to the extent that optimal deterrence (not complete deterrence) is the goal, legislatures and courts must be attuned to the risk of over-deterrence. To date, scholars have devoted insufficient attention to the interplay between punitive (or supra-compensatory) damages and other mechanisms – either regulatory or market-driven (eg reputational forces, especially in the age of the Internet) – that likewise deter wrongful conduct.[69]

IV. Societal Damages Funds

Legislatures and courts can extend their recognition of the societal deterrence purpose of punitive damages by taking creative approaches that recognise the societal nature of the harm caused by the defendant. More than 15 years ago, I published 'Punitive Damages as Societal Damages', in which I argued for a reconceptualisation of retributive, criminal-law inspired 'punitive' damages as a societal remedy designed to compensate for widespread harms and thereby force tortfeasors to internalise the full costs of the harms inflicted on people, property and publicly held resources.[70] I detailed a handful of US States with 'split-recovery'

[67] KN Hylton, 'A Theory of Wealth and Punitive Damages' (2008) 17 *Widener Law Journal* 927, 930.

[68] *Metcoff v NCT Group Inc* 50 A3d 1004, 1017 (Conn Super 2011): 'General Statutes § 42-110g (a) provides in relevant part that "[t]he court may, in its discretion, award punitive damages …" As a general rule, the aims of punitive damages are punishment, deterrence and profit disgorgement.'

[69] See, eg, Sharkey, 'BP Oil Spill' (n 6) 704: '[T]he societal economic deterrence rationale for classwide punitive damages may be blunted once one takes into account the full picture of the regulatory (and even criminal) fines and penalties that are typically assessed in widespread harm scenarios such as oil spills. But this simply means that the strength of the case for societal damages based on economic deterrence will depend heavily on how aggressively alternative cost-internalization mechanisms have been pursued and enforced; and where there is no such aggressive pursuit and enforcement, the justification has special force.' See also Bant and Paterson, ch 10, section III.B: 'The Australian Law Reform Commission has now proposed that ["adverse publicity orders"] be supplemented by other options such as disclosure orders, community service orders, probation or corrective orders, which could be awarded by the court of its own motion as part of the suite of deterrent orders, including penalties.'

[70] Sharkey, 'Societal Damages' (n 6).

statutory regimes for diverting punitive damages either to the State or a public fund. Apart from the split-recovery statutes, one of the innovative developments I highlighted was the diversion of punitive damages by a common law court, absent any authorising statute. I had one prime example: in *Dardinger v Anthem Blue Cross & Blue Shield*, the Ohio Supreme Court, in order to address the 'philosophical void between the reasons we award punitive damages and how the damages are distributed',[71] directed – on its own initiative – $20 million of a $30 million punitive award to a cancer research fund at Ohio State University.[72] The judge specifically chose a State institution as recipient because of the 'societal stake' in punitive damage awards, and chose a cancer research fund as a proxy for ameliorating the type of harm in the individual case, which involved an insurance company's mishandled request for coverage for chemotherapy treatment.[73]

Taking a page from the same playbook some 15 years later,[74] in *Sundquist v Bank of America*, a California bankruptcy judge awarded an eye-catching $45 million in punitive damages against Bank of America for egregious misconduct directed at a couple in foreclosure proceedings, but, after awarding $5 million to the couple, directed the remainder of the punitive award to entities that fight financial abuse and champion vulnerable victims.[75]

Most recently, in *Oklahoma ex rel Hunter v Purdue Pharma, LP*, the State of Oklahoma sued opioid manufacturer Purdue, seeking punitive damages for acting 'with reckless disregard for the rights of others' and penalties under Oklahoma's consumer protection statute.[76] Purdue entered into a settlement in March 2019, pursuant to which it created a fund in recognition of a broader societal remedial goal 'to improve the lives of individuals in Oklahoma and across the nation that are affected by pain and substance use disorders'.[77]

In each of these three high-profile cases, the courts and/or parties explicitly recognised that the defendant had inflicted widespread harm beyond the parties before the court, and created a fund – either from diverted punitive damages or from settlement proceeds – to acknowledge the societal harm. Punitive damages were thereby transformed into a societal remedy that simultaneously addressed the 'windfall' gains or unjust enrichment of the plaintiff and remediated the societal harm.

[71] *Dardinger v Anthem Blue Cross & Blue Shield* 781 NE2d 121, 145 (Ohio 2002).

[72] ibid.

[73] ibid.

[74] In the interim, a few courts have discussed the idea, motivated, at least in part, to address the 'windfall gains' to a plaintiff receiving a large punitive damages award. See, eg, *Payne v Jones* 711 F3d 85, 95, fn 6 (2d Circuit 2012) (discussing the fact that 'states give courts discretion to apportion awards between the plaintiff and the state').

[75] *Sundquist v Bank of America* 566 BR 563 (Bankruptcy ED Cal 2017), vacated in part by *In re Sundquist* 580 BR 536 (Bankruptcy ED Cal 2018).

[76] Before the settlement, the Oklahoma Attorney-General dropped all claims except those for equitable relief under a public nuisance theory cause of action.

[77] *Oklahoma ex rel Hunter v Purdue Pharmaceuticals LP and others* No CJ-2017-816 (Okla Dist Ct 2019) Settlement Agreement, para I(7).

A. Addressing 'Windfall' Gains or Unjust Enrichment of Plaintiff

The moment that the societal (as opposed to individual) interest in punitive damages is invoked, the windfall concern rears its head with a vengeance – namely, if punitive damages are awarded on behalf of a societal, shared interest, why should it be that the entirety of a sometimes very large award should go to an individual plaintiff?[78] One potential response is to defend such a windfall as a kind of 'bounty', compensating the plaintiff for acting as a private attorney-general.[79] But courts have not been persuaded to adopt this rationale for punitive damages. Instead, courts have used the spectre of a plaintiff's windfall gains to reduce or avoid altogether awarding punitive damages.[80]

To mitigate this concern, in prior work I canvassed developments in a handful of US States that had hitherto under-appreciated 'split-recovery' statutes directing some portion of a punitive damages award either to the State treasury or to a specified fund.[81]

B. Remediating the Societal Harm

Whereas split-recovery statutes in the United States direct a portion of punitive damages to the State or else a general fund, the normative ideal would be to create a fund whose purpose is tied to the remediation of the societal harm. This is so for three reasons. First, the establishment of such a specific fund will constrain self-dealing impulses of the State. Second, it should lend itself more readily to objectively measurable factors relevant to remedying the societal harm. Third, in addition to satisfying a general deterrence purpose, such a fund directed at remediation of societal harm would simultaneously satisfy broader corrective justice and fairness dictates.

The recent French reform proposal (Article 1266-1 of the Projet de réforme) to divert civil fines either to the state or else to a compensation fund suggests

[78] The Court of Appeals for the Second Circuit grappled with this windfall concern in *Payne v Jones*, a case in which the court vacated a punitive award as constitutionally excessive, discussing how awarding the plaintiff 100% of the award was a windfall that might be mitigated, for example, by split-recovery schemes as evoked in 'Punitive Damages as Societal Damages': *Payne v Jones* (n 74) 94–95 (citing Sharkey, 'Societal Damages' (n 6)).

[79] See *Sundquist* (n 75) vacated in part by *In re Sundquist* (n 75); see also M Rustad and T Koenig, 'The Historical Continuity of Punitive Damages Awards: Reforming the Tort Reformers' (1993) 42 *American University Law Review* 1269, 1323 (arguing that punitive damages serve as a kind of 'bounty' for plaintiffs who choose to bring the case).

[80] See, eg, *Jones* (n 74) 94–95 (noting that punitive damages are 'burdens on society' that cannot be justified by benefitting the already compensated plaintiff); *In re Collins* 233 F3d 809, 812 (3rd Circuit 2000) (holding that, due to the depleting funds available for plaintiffs in asbestos-related actions, priority should be given to compensatory claims over 'exemplary punitive damage windfalls').

[81] See Sharkey, 'Societal Damages' (n 6) 375–80 (discussing in detail the split-recovery statutes in these States).

the potential wider embrace of societal damages (albeit under the guise of civil fines).[82] The reversion of fines to the state is more consistent with a retributive punishment rationale;[83] whereas their diversion to a compensation fund is more consistent with achieving non-retributive societal deterrence.[84]

i. *Diverting Punitive Damages in Individual Litigation*

The *Dardinger* case involved a woman whose cancer death was accelerated by her insurance company's 'pervasive' corporate policy of bad faith denial of authorisation for chemotherapy treatments. The Ohio Supreme Court upheld a $30 million punitive damages award against the defendant insurance company, but conditioned its approval on the plaintiff's (spouse of the decedent) acceptance of only one-third ($10 million) of the punitive award, with the remainder (after payment of the plaintiff's attorneys) directed to a cancer research fund established by the Court.[85] The Court did not hesitate to affirm the jury's finding that 'a pervasive corporate attitude existed with the defendants to place profit over patients'. Moreover, the Court was cognisant of the fact that defendants' health insurance industry played a 'central role in the lives of so many Ohioans'; in fact, the Court explicitly relied on this fact in justifying a punitive award of significant magnitude. The Court defended its diversion of a significant portion of a punitive damages award away from the individual plaintiff and toward a court-established charity on the ground that '[a]t the punitive-damages level, it is the societal element that is most important'. The Court reasoned that the bulk of the punitive award 'should go to a place that will achieve a societal good, a good that can rationally offset the harm done by the defendants in this case'.[86] *Dardinger* caused a bit of a momentary

[82] Rowan, ch 3 of this volume. See also M Cappelletti, 'Comparative Reflections on Punishment in Tort Law' in J-S Borghetti and S Whittaker (eds), *French Civil Liability in Comparative Perspective* (Oxford, Hart Publishing, 2019) 329 (emphasis added): 'The French conception of punishment is markedly instrumental in that it sees punitive measures as serving *societal goals* such as deterrence of antisocial behaviour.'

[83] Cappelletti (n 82) 346: 'Given the ministère public's functions in criminal trials, most notably prosecuting crimes and punishing their authors in the interest of society, it is natural to consider his involvement in the operation of article 1266-1 as a strong indicator of an instrumental understanding of punishment.'

[84] ibid 347: '[B]y financing funds that shelter otherwise unprotected victims of accidents, article 1266-1 of the Projet de réforme further reinforces the ethos of social solidarity that imbues French tort law and brings tort liability one step further away from any theory of interpersonal justice.'

[85] *Dardinger v Anthem Blue Cross & Blue Shield* 781 NE2d 121 (Ohio 2002). The Ohio Supreme Court reviewed the jury's award of $2.5 million in compensatory damages and $49 million in punitive damages. The Court remitted the punitive award to $30 million on the grounds that it was excessive under Ohio (but not federal) law. The divided (4:3) Court's decision was 'historic' in that it effected a split-recovery type allocation of a punitive damages award, absent a statute directing it to do so.

[86] The Court further explained: '[A] punitive damages award is about the defendant's actions. "The purpose of punitive damages is not to compensate a plaintiff but to punish the guilty, deter future misconduct, and to demonstrate society's disapproval."' More specifically, the Court explained 'The plaintiff remains a party, but the de facto party is our society, and the jury is determining whether and to what extent we as a society should punish the defendant.' There may be much to commend this

stir but then remained largely an infrequently noted outlier.[87] That is, until *In re Sundquist*.

The opening of the California bankruptcy decision – 'Franz Kafka lives … he works at Bank of America' – foreshadowed the contents of a 107-page opinion detailing not only the abuse a couple suffered at the behest of Bank of America during a foreclosure proceeding, but also the egregiousness of the misconduct, which was characterised as illustrative of a wider pattern and practice of abuse and deceit on the part of the mega-bank, directed at vulnerable and out-classed victims, including but reaching far beyond the one couple who sued. Judge Klein did not mince words when describing the misconduct on the part of Bank of America associated with its illegal foreclosure on the Sundquists' home in Lincoln, California, nor the 'battle-fatigued demoralization' it inflicted upon the couple.[88] As reported in one news outlet, 'The couple had been in the trenches for more than eight years doing battle with the same Mega-Bank that had led thousands of homeowners down a primrose path to foreclosure.'[89] Reviewing the Kafka-esque features of the case, Judge Klein noted that the stream of loan modification applications proffered by the Sundquists 'routinely were either "lost" or declared insufficient, or incomplete, or stale and in need of resubmission, or denied without comprehensible explanation.'[90]

Judge Klein framed his discussion of punitive damages by invoking the 'governmental and societal interests' in punishing and deterring unlawful conduct.[91] But opening punitive damages to this societal lens risks bestowing a windfall on individual plaintiffs. In response, as already discussed, many courts have sharply curtailed (or even foreclosed) punitive damages. Judge Klein, however, had a different resolution in mind. Given the need for punitive damages to 'vindicate the societal interests', he rejected the idea that a defendant should avoid paying punitive damages so as to avoid bestowing a windfall upon the plaintiffs.[92] Judge Klein nonetheless recognised the existence of an asymmetry between the punitive damages the defendant ought to pay and the damages the plaintiff ought to receive.[93] To resolve this dilemma, Judge Klein proposed a punitive damages scheme whereby the plaintiffs were awarded $45 million in punitive damages,

societal punishment-based focus, at least in particular types of 'malice' torts, but alternative (possibly complementary) non-punitive rationales may exist that are more firmly rooted in civil common law, and that would apply with particular force in other kinds of 'recklessness-based' widespread-harm torts.

[87] See, eg, *Wischer v Mitsubishi Heavy Indus Am Inc* 673 NW2d 303, 322, fn 6 (Wis Ct App 2003) (Fine, J concurring) (discussing *Dardinger* but taking no stance as to whether the outcome was correct).

[88] *Sundquist* (n 75) 589 vacated in part by *In re Sundquist* (n 75).

[89] J Sucher, 'A Comeuppance for Bank of America?', *Huffpost* (5 October 2018) at www.huffpost.com/entry/a-comeuppance-for-bank-of-america_b_597d2675e4b0c69ef70528c5.

[90] *Sundquist* (n 75) 572–73.

[91] ibid 613–14.

[92] ibid 616.

[93] ibid: 'Appellate jurisprudence regarding "excessive" punitive damages tends to conflate the distinct concepts of the appropriate amount of the punitive damages award that the defendant's conduct justifies … and of the amount that the plaintiffs ought to be allowed to receive …'.

with a remittitur of the damages to $5 million if, and only if, Bank of America contributed $7.5 million to the National Consumer Law Center, $7.5 million to the National Consumer Bankruptcy Rights Center and $3 million to each University of California law school to be used for education in consumer law.[94] Judge Klein was motivated to take the total amount of legitimate punitive damages exceeding the amount that the individual plaintiffs should retain and direct those damages to a public purpose in order to serve the societal interest.[95]

Judge Klein's punitive damages scheme not only satisfied the societal purpose of punitive damages, it also simultaneously raised the stakes of the case by adding interested parties who would be motivated to defend the punitive damages award on appeal. After Judge Klein's ruling, the National Consumer Law Center, National Consumer Bankruptcy Rights Center, Regents of the University of California and the University of California Hastings College of Law (collectively, 'Intervenors') filed a motion to intervene in the case. Judge Klein ruled that the Intervenors acquired standing 'concurrent with entry of the injunction that made them third-party beneficiaries of the punitive damages award'.[96]

Judge Klein's decision in *Sundquist* made a splash. As with *Dardinger*, whose reasoning it carried forward, the question arose: would this be just a blip, or could it be said that the momentum is building in the United States for punitive damages as a societal remedy? Thus far, it seems Sundquist's influence has been largely confined to the realm of bankruptcy. In *In Re Charity*, a bankruptcy court in the Eastern District of Virginia dealt with three similar cases regarding the wilful violation of an automatic stay by NetCredit.[97] As in *Sundquist*, the court found that NetCredit's actions were egregious enough to warrant significant punitive damages due to its reckless disregard for the rights of the plaintiffs and the size of the award in similar cases (citing *Sundquist*).[98] As for the actual harm suffered, the court acknowledged that the plaintiff's actual damages were minimal, but noted that the Fourth Circuit Court of Appeals allows punitive damages to exceed single-digit ratios when the compensatory damages are nominal or minimal.[99] Further, the court discussed the need for punitive damages in order to deter future misconduct, and after mentioning that NetCredit's net worth was $233 million dollars, concluded that the company's wealth would be considered as one factor in awarding punitive damages.[100] The court awarded three of the five plaintiffs $100,000 in punitive damages.[101] Of this $100,000, the plaintiffs were ordered to deliver $37,500.00 to the National Consumer Law Center and $37,500.00 to the

[94] ibid 618–19.

[95] ibid 616.

[96] *In re Sundquist* 570 BR 92, 96 (Bankruptcy ED Cal 2017).

[97] *In Re Charity* 2017 WL 3580173, 9 (Bankruptcy ED Va 15 August 2017).

[98] ibid 19–20.

[99] ibid 19 (citing *Saunders v Equifax Info Servs* 469 F Supp 2d 343, 348 (ED Va 2007), *affirmed sub nom Saunders v Branch Banking & Trust Co of Va* 526 F3d 142 (4th Circuit 2008)).

[100] ibid 20.

[101] ibid 23.

Legal Services Corporation of Virginia.[102] However, the court indicated that there would be a remittitur of the punitive damages award to $15,000 to each plaintiff if NetCredit delivered the money to the third parties itself.[103]

The court in *Charity* relied extensively on *Sundquist* when it determined that the award should be allocated to third parties. The court echoed the concern of plaintiff windfall gains.[104] The court reasoned that the power to allocate a portion of the award was within its common law power, as was demonstrated by a Fourth Circuit case that held that Georgia's split-recovery statute was not unconstitutional under the Takings Clause because the plaintiff did not have a constitutionally protected property interest in punitive damages.[105] Finally, the court referred to Judge Klein's decision to allocate resources in a way that would address the underlying misconduct, and highlighted that, as in *Sundquist*, the plaintiffs in this case would have benefitted from better legal representation and education.[106]

ii. Classwide Punitive Damages

What happens when the notion of punitive damages as societal damages is implicated in the context of a class action? In one sense the existence of a class action would seem to be a substitute or alternative response to the societal notion of punitive damages. But there might still be limited justifications for the pursuit of a societal remedy even in the class action context.

In 2013, I published 'The Future of Classwide Punitive Damages'.[107] In that article, I discussed several high-profile cases in which courts certified punitive damages classes by focusing on the defendant's conduct. I argued that in order for a court to embrace a classwide determination of punitive damages, it must shift the focus from the plaintiff's individualised harm (or interest) to the defendant's conduct leading to widespread harm, thus highlighting the societal function of punitive damages.[108] For example, in *Palmer v Combined Insurance*, the judge

[102] ibid.

[103] ibid.

[104] ibid 22: 'The dilemma involved in achieving the goal of awarding sufficient punitive damages for automatic stay violations without simultaneously providing an individual windfall was recently confronted by Judge Klein …'.

[105] ibid (citing *Cisson v CR Bard* 810 F3d 913, 931 (4th Circuit 2016)).

[106] ibid 23: 'NetCredit's conduct in these cases reflects the need to direct additional resources to financially distressed consumers who have limited means to defend themselves against aggressive creditors.' Aside from the actual award of societal damages, there was another interesting similarity between *Sundquist* and *Charity*. In *Sundquist*, the defendant was ordered to pay a portion of the punitive award to the National Consumer Law Center and National Consumer Bankruptcy Center. As Intervenors, these two parties were represented by prominent plaintiffs' law firm Lieff Cabraser. The National Consumer Law Center was also one of the parties to which the defendant in *Charity* could deliver damages in order to reduce the plaintiff's award. It does not seem that the defendant challenged the award in *Charity*, and so the National Consumer Law Center has not needed to intervene or hire attorneys to defend its stake.

[107] Sharkey (n 4).

[108] ibid 1134.

concluded that individualised proof of a plaintiff's harm is not necessarily required when the focus is on the defendant's conduct.[109] Nor, I argued, should *Philip Morris USA, Inc v Williams* stand in the way of certifying a punitive damages class. At the time, only a couple cases had explored this issue: *Iorio v Allianz Life Ins Co of N Am*, for example, which held that *Williams* did not foreclose punitive damages on the basis of unnamed class-members, who are not equivalent to non-parties.[110]

To further explore this topic here, I examine a recent case filing that sought to certify a punitive damages class in a lawsuit filed by New Haven civil rights attorney David Rosen representing tenants of Church Street South housing complex against Northland Investment Corp of Massachusetts, the owners of the crumbling housing complex. In *Noble v Northland Investment*, Rosen filed a motion to certify the complaint as a class action, seeking damages on behalf of all present and former Church Street South tenants for damages arising from the neglected damp, mouldy conditions at the complex.[111] The putative class members are all 'low-income families or individuals who signed identical leases, resided in the same complex, and have been or will soon be relocated as a result of pervasive conditions that affected all of the residents of Church Street South'. And 'the defendants' conduct affecting each class member arose from a common motivation, the desire of Northland Investment Corporation and its affiliated entities to demolish the complex and build upscale housing in its place'.

The facts of the case do not lend themselves to the typical justifications for punitive damages as a societal remedy. To begin, given the framing of the case as a class action, there is not a significant risk of absent plaintiffs who might have been similarly affected by the alleged widespread harms inflicted by the defendant. Nor is concealment of wrongdoing an issue in the case. But the case nonetheless highlights two additional dimensions that might justify punitive damages as a societal remedy: the repeated history or pattern of wrongdoing on the part of the developer; and the fact that the claim arises under a statute that defines specific wrongdoing as an affront to the public interest.

In order to convince the court to certify a punitive damages class, the plaintiffs' attorneys attempted to disabuse the court of the conventional individualised

[109] *Palmer v Combined Insurance* 217 FRD 430, 438 (ND Ill 2003). And in *EEOC v Dial Corp* 259 F Supp 2d 710, 712, 715 (ND Ill 2003), the court reasoned that a defendant's conduct is the most important factor in determining punitive damages awards. Moreover, a jury awarding compensatory damages for an individual or small group cannot adequately determine the awards needed to deter a pattern or practice. Sharkey (n 4) 1137 (citing *Palmer*, 438 (ND Ill 2003)).

[110] *Iorio v Allianz Life Ins Co of North Am*erica 2009 WL 3415703, 5 (SD Cal 21 October 2009) ('punitive damages will be awarded based on the injury inflicted upon all class members, not individual class members … [and the] [p]unitive damages award will be based largely on the misconduct of the Defendant'); see also *Tawney v Columbia Natural Resources, LLC*, 2007 WL 5539870 (Cir Ct W Va 27 June 2007).

[111] *Personna Noble v Northland Invest Corp* No X10-UWY-CV-16-6033559-S, Plaintiffs' Corrected Memorandum in Support of Motion for Class Certification 38. The court held an all-day hearing on class certification, after which the parties engaged in a year-long mediation, culminating in a settlement. See at www.davidrosenlaw.com/_assets/images/First-Amended-Stipulation-of-Settlement-Doc-292.pdf; www.davidrosenlaw.com/church-street-south-settlement.

notion of punitive damages. The plaintiffs' attorneys did this in part by shifting the focus away from the plaintiffs' losses and onto the common nature of the defendant's conduct leading to widespread harm. In particular, the plaintiffs highlighted their engineer's findings that the widespread harms all stem from similar defective conditions in each building owned by the defendant.[112] Thus, when assessing punitive damages, a single defendant's behaviour, common to the plaintiffs, could be scrutinised.

But the plaintiffs could have bolstered their case by emphasising the societal purpose of punitive damages. *Hilao v Estate of Marcos* could be helpful support for a money damages class action centred on the societal element of punitive damages.[113] Two added dimensions (each discussed in section II.B) implicated by the *Northland* case further strengthen the case for punitive damages as societal damages. First, given a long history of housing code violations at this property, the case might be illustrative of the need for punitive damages where there is a continued pattern of misconduct. Second, the case for punitive damages is strengthened given the relationship between the societal rationale for punitive damages and the asserted public interest under Connecticut's Unfair Trade Practices Act.

C. Settlement

Equally if not more significant than the litigation arena is the extent to which private litigants might adopt a societal damages approach in negotiating settlements.[114]

i. In Recognition of Societal Damages

The May 2019 Purdue settlement provides a template that may prove to have staying power in resolving mass tort cases in the public interest, transforming a significant portion of the recovery into a form of societal damages. To settle a public nuisance lawsuit brought by the State of Oklahoma, Purdue agreed to pay $102.5 million to fund the National Center for Addiction Studies and Treatment, 'dedicated to addiction studies, treatment and education, including education to eliminate the stigma associated with addiction and treatment', housed at Oklahoma State University's Center for Health Sciences.[115] Purdue also agreed

[112] *Northland* (n 111) 7–9 (citing *Palmer* (n 110) 438.
[113] *Hilao v Estate of Marcos* 103 F3d 767, 780 (9th Circuit 1996).
[114] For a broader discussion of 'how the specter of punitive damages … influenced Gulf Coast claimants' actions, from foregoing payments from BP's private compensation fund, to the claims asserted in the BP litigation and the settlements eventually reached', see Sharkey, 'BP Oil Spill' (n 6) 691–96. It is worth noting, too, that the *Northland* case settled in the shadow of the court's hearing on the class certification motion: see n 112.
[115] *Oklahoma* (n 77) Settlement Agreement at para B(1)-(2). The National Center will be part of the OSU Center for Wellness and Recovery. The State created a foundation to receive and manage the funding directed to the National Center. Purdue agreed to supply medically assisted treatment drugs over a 5-year period with retail market value of $20 million. Purdue also agreed to pay $59.5 million

to 'use reasonable efforts to encourage the provision of additional funds for the National Center in any other settlements it may enter into regarding the sales and promotion of Purdue Opioids'.[116]

Purdue's settlement fits a pattern of what I have termed embedded societal punitive damages (even if not named as such) in the context of class action settlements. The consolidated BP oil spill lawsuits, in which plaintiffs sued BP (which leased the rig and operated the oil and gas prospect), Transocean (which owned the rig) and Halliburton (which worked the rig and poured concrete), are a case in point. In the wake of large-scale devastation to the affected communities, the environment and society at large, the plaintiffs pressed societal justifications for punitive damages based on both punishment and societal economic deterrence rationales:

> [P]iecemeal adjudications may under-deter Defendants' misconduct by failing to account for the full scope or total social costs, thereby frustrating the purpose of punitive damages – the vindication of society's interests in deterrence … that is fully and fairly proportionate to … its harm to society as a whole.[117]

After months of negotiation, the plaintiffs and BP agreed to a classwide settlement. Although the high-profile BP oil spill settlement provided in strict terms only for compensatory damages to claimants, it incorporated 'risk transfer premiums' (RTPs), or supra-compensatory multipliers applicable to certain claimants, that (I have argued previously) incorporated an embedded societal punitive damages award.[118] As is typical in mass tort settlements, the parties' attorneys negotiated a claims grid that compensated class members based on the relative strength of their claims. The RTPs are a striking feature of the compensation grid; they essentially mimic a complex multiple damages statute, providing various supra-compensatory multipliers for different types of claims. The compensation grid provides for varying RTPs based on the relative strength of claims, including eligibility for punitive damages. As my prior analysis demonstrates, the RTPs for punitive damages-eligible claimants (primarily those in commercial fishermen categories) are much higher than those for other claimant categories.[119] Moreover, the parties themselves recognised that RTPs were, in significant part, a surrogate or stand-in for punitive damages – which were not included as a separate component of the settlement. Such RTPs thus represent a form of societal damages given to classes of claimants eligible to receive punitive damages.

in attorneys' fees to the State's outside counsel; $500,000 to the Attorney-General; and $12.5 million to political subdivisions. In addition, the Sackler families agreed to contribute $75 million to the foundation over a 4-year period.

[116] ibid para I(7).

[117] *3G Fishing Charters LLC and others v Kirby Inland Marine LP and others*, No 3:14CV00107 Class Action Complaint, 9.

[118] Sharkey, 'BP Oil Spill' (n 6) 697.

[119] See ibid 699–702.

Class action settlements might readily accommodate the societal component of such punitive awards, but the possibility of settlement might just as readily thwart a court's pursuit of a societal remedy.[120]

ii. As Threat to Societal Damages

Settlement potentially threatens the viability of using punitive damages as societal damages. In 'Punitive Damages as Societal Damages', I explained that '[s]plit-recovery schemes have been criticised on the ground that they simply force more plaintiffs to settle meritorious punitive damages claims'.[121] Plaintiffs and defendants would have an added incentive to settle to cut out the State's portion of a punitive damages recovery. Courts in split-recovery regimes, moreover, have more or less sanctioned this effect. The Oregon Supreme Court has held that although the State was made a 'judgment creditor', the split-recovery statute did not 'provide that the state's consent to a settlement is required'.[122] The court reasoned that, in order for the State to prevent a settlement, the statute would have to explicitly give the State this power.[123] Similarly, although Missouri gets a 'lien for deposit into the tort victims' compensation fund to the extent of fifty percent of the punitive damages final judgment', this does not apply to cases resolved by 'compromise settlement prior to a punitive damages final judgment'.[124] Indeed, the Missouri Supreme Court reasoned that the 'legislature may have sought to encourage settlement so as to avoid the burden litigation imposes on the parties and the judicial system'.[125]

In *Weinberger v Estate of Barnes*, the Indiana Court of Appeals concluded that the State's split-recovery statute did not grant the State the right to intervene, and thus the State was unable to prevent the parties from settling in a way that cut out the State's portion of the punitive damages.[126] In its petition for direct transfer to the Supreme Court, the State of Indiana made multiple arguments as to why this outcome was incorrect. Citing 'Punitive Damages as Societal Damages', the State argued that the split-recovery statute is beneficial for achieving deterrence and simultaneously mitigating windfall gains.[127] It also noted that permitting the State

[120] ibid 682: 'Class action settlements can readily accommodate the "public law" dimension of societal damages, as demonstrated by the Halliburton class settlement and its explicit focus on punitive damages claims.'

[121] Sharkey, 'Societal Damages' (n 6) 444.

[122] *Patton v Target Corp* 242 P3d 611, 619 (Or 2010) (citing Oregon Revised Statutes Annotated § 31.735).

[123] ibid (internal quotation marks omitted): 'The court is not at liberty to give effect to any supposed intention or meaning in the legislature, unless the words to be imported into the statute are, in substance at least, contained in it.'

[124] Missouri Annotated Statutes § 537.675(3) (West 2020).

[125] *Fust v AG* 947 SW2d 424, 432 (Mo 1997).

[126] *Weinberger v Estate of Barnes* 2 NE3d 43, 50 (Ind 2013) (citing Sharkey, 'Societal Damages' (n 6)).

[127] State of Indiana's Petition for Transfer, *Weinberger v Estate of Barnes*, 2014 IN S Ct Briefs LEXIS 22 *18 (Ind 17 January 2014) (No 45A04-1107-CT-369).

to intervene would provide an incentive to settle before trial.[128] If the State cannot intervene, the plaintiff has a diminished incentive to settle before the judgment is announced, because the plaintiff can wait until the punitive damages are awarded and then settle to cut out the State's portion. Nevertheless, the Indiana Supreme Court denied the transfer, and the State was not permitted to intervene.

But in 'Punitive Damages as Societal Damages', I maintained that:

> [T]he incentive for the plaintiff and defendant to settle in order to cut out the state's portion evaporates in the realm of the societal damages theory – at least as applied to specific harms to other harmed individuals – because the plaintiff and defendant would not be able to settle and cut off recovery to the other harmed individuals.[129]

All of this, however, hinges on a court's approach to standing, intervention and, if relevant, judicial approval of settlement. Georgia's split-recovery statute, for example, is unique in that it provides that the State has an interest in the litigation as soon as the judgment is rendered.[130]

Sundquist shines a light on the role of judicial approval of settlements. Bank of America eventually settled with the Sundquists, who received more than the share of punitive damages originally allocated to them. The Sundquists voluntarily gave $300,000 post-tax to the intervening organisations.[131] Judge Klein was given the opportunity to review the settlement per the federal bankruptcy rules.[132] This process of review seems crucial for protecting societal interests. If Judge Klein did not need to sign off on the settlement, it is possible that the parties could have entirely cut out the Intervenors.

In the class action context, societal damages may be even easier to administer through settlement. Judges must approve all settlements under Federal Rule of Civil Procedure 23(e), eliminating worries of backroom settlements that cut out third parties. But there is no similar rule for judicial review of settlements in litigation.[133] Nonetheless, once a judgment is entered, the parties must move to

[128] ibid *19.

[129] Sharkey, 'Societal Damages' (n 6) 445.

[130] See Georgia Code Annotated § 51-12-5.1(e)(2) (West 2020): 'Upon issuance of judgment in such a case, the state shall have all rights due a judgment creditor until such judgment is satisfied and shall stand on equal footing with the plaintiff of the original case in securing a recovery after payment to the plaintiff of damages awarded other than as punitive damages.'

[131] See *Sundquist v Bank of Am, NA (In re Sundquist)*, 580 BR 536, 543 (Bankr ED Cal 2018).

[132] Fed R Bank P 9019(a) states, in relevant part, '[o]n motion by the trustee and after notice and a hearing, the court may approve a compromise or settlement'. Despite the fact that this language appears to be permissible, a majority of courts have held that 'compliance with the Rule is mandatory'. RA Valencia, 'The Sanctity of Settlements and the Significance of Court Approval: Discerning Clarity from Bankruptcy Rule 9019' (1999) 78 *Oregon Law Review* 425, 439. Judge Klein further noted that the court could retain jurisdiction over the settlement agreement. *In re Sundquist*, 580 BR 536, 553 (Bankruptcy ED Cal 2018) (citing *Kokkonen v Guardian Life Ins Co of Am* 511 US 375, 381 (1994)).

[133] See, eg, *Times Mirror Magazines, Inc v Field & Stream Licenses Co* 103 F Supp 2d 711, 741 (SDNY 2000): '[J]udicial review of trademark settlement agreements would undermine the policy of giving deference to the contractual agreements of business people who are in a better position than the court "to determine whether their self-interest is better served by making such contracts or not".'

vacate the judgment, as was the case in *Sundquist*, where Judge Klein agreed to vacate the damages award.[134] Judge Klein also indicated that the Intervenors could appeal the vacatur, but they had agreed not to do so. Thus, even if the judge does allow the settlement that cuts out third parties,[135] if third parties are given the right to intervene, they could appeal the decision to vacate a judgment in order to allow a settlement.

Notwithstanding approval of the settlement, Judge Klein refused to vacate the judgment because he believed that the situation had become 'bigger than the Sundquists', due in part to the fact that the Intervenors had an interest in appealing the judgment and because the opinion 'appears to have struck a chord in the development of the law'.[136] Further, Judge Klein did not want the entire settlement to remain secret because he was 'reluctant to exercise [the court's] discretion to sweep the matter under the carpet because the parties in a secret compromise are agreeing not to appeal'.[137] Judge Klein believed that the public had an interest in the final outcome. Nevertheless, the court did not disclose the amount of the settlement award; it noted only that the Sundquists received a substantial premium over their $6,074,581.50 share of the initial judgment.[138]

Finally, because Judge Klein believed the public interest component was crucial to punitive damages, he seemed to have approved the settlement only because the Sundquists elected to voluntarily donate part of their award to the Intervenors, which Judge Klein described as their 'de facto recognizing the public-interest component' of the punitive damages.[139] Thus, the court approved the settlement, vacating the damages award without vacating the opinion or the judgment.

V. Conclusion: Far-reaching Implications of Societal Damages

Because the remedy of punitive damages lies squarely within the purview of State law, State legislatures and courts possess a degree of freedom to articulate State-based goals of punitive damages – such as economic deterrence – even in the face of heavy-handed federal constitutional review imposed by the US Supreme

[134] It is entirely possible that a judge could refuse to vacate the award. Fed R Civ P 60(b) does not mandate that judges must relieve a party from a judgment – it simply permits them to vacate the judgment in certain circumstances. And in the case of a jury trial, Fed R Civ P 58(b) mandates that the clerk must enter a judgment when the jury enter a verdict, and thus the parties are prevented from settling in a gap between the verdict and judgment.

[135] This seems unlikely when the judge is the one who ordered the societal damages. This might be more likely in a State with a split-recovery statute, however, when the judge may not approve of split-recovery.

[136] *In re Sundquist* (n 75).

[137] ibid 545.

[138] ibid 553.

[139] ibid 554.

Court. Once societal deterrence is recognised as a legitimate State interest or goal for the award of supra-compensatory damages, State legislatures and common law courts face the challenge of setting forth relevant factors to measure deterrence, whether premised on loss internalisation or gain elimination.

Recognising situations where defendants (often corporations) have inflicted widespread harm, courts and litigants have created funds, from either diverted punitive damages or settlement proceeds, to acknowledge the societal harm. Punitive damages were thereby transformed into a societal remedy that simultaneously addressed the 'windfall' gains or unjust enrichment of the plaintiff and remediated the societal harm.

In closing, I hint at three significant implications of the transformation of punitive damages into societal damages, simply to indicate how far-reaching they may be. First, to the extent that societal damages are awarded for general deterrence purposes, they should not be subject to the US Supreme Court's constitutional excessiveness review, which, as mentioned earlier, is focused on the need to constrain punishment in the civil context. This is especially critical in the context of statutory damage multipliers – to the extent these are compensatory/preventative as opposed to punitive, they should fall outside the gambit of constitutional excessiveness review.

Second, societal damages should be insurable. Indeed, the gradual acceptance of insurance for punitive damages over the last 50 years stems, in part, from the evolution of punitive damages themselves. We saw earlier that punitive damages were once awarded predominantly for acts that satisfied malice aforethought or intentional wrongdoing. By contrast, now, many punitive awards arise from what was essentially accidental conduct, albeit committed recklessly. Understood as societal damages, punitive damages cannot be sequestered from other forms of compensatory damages that are legitimately the subject of litigation insurance.[140]

Third, there should be no bar for vicarious liability for societal damages. The same arguments raised against insuring punitive damages are applicable to the question whether the law should impose vicarious liability for punitive damages. That said, seen via a societal deterrence perspective, vicarious liability may, in certain contexts, serve as a substitute for punitive damages.[141] This would be the case where the risk of under-detection of harms provides the justification for an expansion of the scope of institutional or employer vicarious liability, and would correspondingly reduce the need for imposition of punitive damages on that ground.

In sum, the reconceptualisation of punitive damages as a societal remedy could have far-reaching effects in terms both of the evolution of US doctrine, but also influencing law reform efforts in various other countries.

[140] CM Sharkey, 'Revisiting the Noninsurable Costs of Accidents' (2005) 64 *Maryland Law Review* 409, 438–50.

[141] See CM Sharkey, 'Institutional Liability for Employees' Intentional Torts: Vicarious Liability as a Quasi-Substitute for Punitive Damages' (2019) 53 *Valparaiso University Law Review* 1.

8

Punitive Damages: Ten Misconceptions

JAMES GOUDKAMP AND ELENI KATSAMPOUKA*

I. Introduction

This chapter addresses 10 misconceptions regarding punitive damages.[1] In 2001, Lord Nicholls said that punitive damages 'are a controversial topic, and have been so for many years'.[2] As we shall see, some of the misconceptions discussed in this chapter have contributed to the controversies that surround the award of punitive damages, and our overall assessment is that punitive damages have often been seriously misunderstood by both the courts and commentators alike. Unless and until basic misapprehensions regarding punitive damages are corrected, judicial and academic analyses regarding punitive damages are destined to remain mired in confusion and reform efforts are likely to be misguided. Our concern is ultimately with the English law of punitive damages although we periodically touch on the law elsewhere.

The first section of this chapter offers an overview of the law of punitive damages in order to set the scene for the analysis that follows, while the second discusses the selected misconceptions. Some concluding observations are offered in the third section. The misconceptions that we target are as follows (this list is not intended to be an exhaustive catalogue of misunderstandings regarding punitive damages but rather enumerates those errors that are frequently committed or particularly pernicious):

1. Punitive damages awards are often excessive.
2. The quantum of punitive damages awards is unpredictable.

* We are grateful to the participants in the 'Punishment and Private Law' workshop for their comments on a draft of this chapter, especially Elise Bant, Kit Barker and Catherine Sharkey. María Martínez Alles also supplied us with helpful suggestions. We are indebted to the Onassis Foundation and the Foundation for Education and European Culture for providing us with financial support.

[1] In England and in certain other Commonwealth countries, punitive damages are also known as exemplary damages. According to Lord Nicholls in *Kuddus v Chief Constable of Leicestershire Constabulary* [2001] UKHL 29, [2002] 2 AC 122 [51], 'the terms are synonymous'.

[2] ibid [50].

3. Defamation cases constitute an important source of punitive damages awards.
4. Punitive damages are an anomalous remedy.
5. Punitive damages are sometimes a form of disgorgement damages.
6. Precedent establishes that prior punishment is unimportant in the decision to award punitive damages.
7. Precedent justifies the categories test.
8. Precedent justifies the unavailability of punitive damages for breach of contract.
9. Negligent conduct cannot engage the punitive damages jurisdiction.
10. Punitive damages can be reduced for contributory negligence.

The first three misconceptions are factual in the sense that they concern misunderstandings regarding the way in which the jurisdiction to award punitive damages is exercised. The fourth and fifth misconceptions concern errors regarding the relationship between punitive damages and other remedies. The sixth, seventh and eighth misconceptions relate to misreadings of the authorities regarding punitive damages. The final two misconceptions pertain to the intersection between the jurisdiction to award punitive damages and negligent conduct.

II. The Law

A. The Categories Test

Punitive damages, which can be granted only when an entitlement to them has been pleaded,[3] are awarded in order to punish the defendant for their contumelious behaviour and to deter the defendant and others from engaging in the same or similar conduct in the future.[4] Thus, although their effect, like all damages, may be to compensate the claimant for loss suffered, they are not awarded with the aim of repairing losses but for the purposes of retribution and in order to discourage persons from engaging in seriously objectionable conduct. They are available in all parts of the UK save in Scotland where the courts have steadfastly refused to recognise the remedy.[5] The law governing punitive damages in Northern Ireland

[3] 'Particulars of claim must include … if the claimant is seeking … exemplary damages, a statement to that effect and his grounds for claiming them': CPR 16.4(1)(c). See also Crime and Courts Act 2013 (UK), s 34(5) and, in the case of Northern Ireland, r 8(3) of the Rules of the Court of Judicature.

[4] 'The object of exemplary damages is to punish and deter': *Rookes v Barnard* (1964) AC 1129 (HL) 1221 (Lord Devlin). See, also, *Broome v Cassell & Co Ltd* [1972] AC 1027 (HL) 1124; *Kuddus* (n 1) [51]. The courts have also identified various subsidiary rationales, including the vindication of the claimant's rights (*A v Bottrill* [2002] UKPC 44, [2003] 1 AC 449 [29]), placating the desire for revenge (*W v W* (1999) 4 LRC 260 (PC) 264) and marking the court's disapproval of the defendant's conduct (*Kuddus* (n 1) [91]).

[5] 'I am bound to say I find no authority for any distinction between damages and "exemplary damages" in the law of Scotland. The very heading under which it is treated in our older books "Reparation" excludes the idea': *Black v North British Railway Co* 1908 SC 444 (IH) 453 (Lord President).

is the same as that in England and Wales[6] save for some relatively inconsequential differences introduced by statute.

The leading case concerning punitive damages is *Rookes v Barnard*,[7] in which Lord Devlin, in a speech with which the other members of the House of Lords agreed, famously held that punitive damages could be awarded in just three categories of case, namely: (i) cases involving arbitrary, oppressive or unconstitutional conduct by government servants acting as such; (ii) situations in which the defendant sought to profit from their wrong; and (iii) instances where statute mandates that punitive damages be available. Lord Devlin's preference would have been to abolish the remedy altogether, but he considered that precedent prevented him from doing so.

The first category focuses on wrongs committed by persons in the exercise of public power with which they have been conferred. Thus, punitive damages have been awarded under the first category in actions against the police,[8] immigration officials[9] and local authorities.[10] Although the concept of a 'government servant' has been construed liberally,[11] the mere fact that the defendant happens to be a public body or official will not bring a case within the first category. Rather, to be liable to pay punitive damages under the first category, the wrong committed by the defendant must be sufficiently connected with their public law responsibilities. Thus, a claim against a public body in respect of damage caused in carrying out commercial operations will not fall within the first category.[12]

The second category is concerned with cases in which the defendant calculated that their wrongdoing would yield a profit that would exceed the compensation payable to the claimant. In order for a case to come within this category it is unnecessary that the defendant engaged in any sort of mathematical or accounting process in this regard.[13] It suffices that they were aware that the expected benefits of their wrongdoing might outweigh the possible detriments.[14] Nor is the second category confined to cases in which the defendant was concerned with making money specifically.[15] For example, cases in which the defendant sought a general

[6] 'The modern law on exemplary damages stems from the decision of the House of Lords in *Rookes*': *Crawfordsburn Inn Ltd v Graham* (2013) NIQB 79 [6] (Weatherup J).

[7] See n 4.

[8] See, eg, *Copeland v Commissioner of Police of the Metropolis* (EWHC, 2 May 2013).

[9] See, eg, *Muuse v Secretary of State for the Home Department* [2010] EWCA Civ 453.

[10] See, eg, *Bradford City Council v Arora* [1991] 2 QB 507 (CA).

[11] See, eg, in *Broome* (n 4) 1077–78, where Lord Hailsham said that he 'would be surprised if [the first category] included only servants of the Government in the strict sense of the word. It would, in my view, obviously apply to the police … and almost as certainly to local and other officials exercising improperly rights of search or arrest without warrant, and it may be that in the future it will be held to include other abuses of power without warrant by persons purporting to exercise legal authority'. See also Lord Reid's remarks at 1087–88 and those of Lord Diplock at 1130.

[12] *AB v South West Water Services Ltd* [1993] QB 507 (CA). See also *Holden v Chief Constable of Lancashire* (1987) QB 380 (CA) 387 (holding that the mere fact that the defendant is a police officer does not bring the case within the first category).

[13] *Broome* (n 4) 1044; *John v MGN Ltd* (1997) QB 586 (CA) 618–19.

[14] *Riches v News Group Newspapers Ltd* (1986) QB 256 (CA) 269–70.

[15] 'This category is not confined to moneymaking in the strict sense': *Rookes* (n 4) 1227 (Lord Devlin).

economic advantage, such as by harassing tenants in order to obtain possession of premises,[16] incorporating the claimant's land within their own[17] and erecting scaffolding on the claimant's property in order to facilitate the construction of an adjacent building,[18] have been held to come within the second category.[19]

The third category is essentially irrelevant given that the legislature has rarely authorised the award of punitive damages (and has sometimes prohibited their award[20]). To the best of our knowledge, punitive damages have never been awarded or even claimed on the basis of statutory authorisation and there are, today, just three eclectic situations where punitive damages can be awarded under statute. The first is for breach of environmental covenants;[21] the second is for the conversion of servicemen's goods;[22] and the third is for certain wrongs committed by media defendants.[23] It had long been debated whether the award of 'additional damages' for which section 97(2) of the Copyright, Designs and Patents Act 1988 (UK) provides authorises the award of punitive damages and is hence within the third category.[24] However, the Court of Appeal recently held that such damages are sui generis and 'may be either in whole or in part' punitive damages, or 'either in whole or in part, what are now called restitutionary or disgorgement damages'.[25]

B. Other Principles Limiting the Availability of Punitive Damages

If a case falls within one (or more) of the three *Rookes* categories[26] it does not automatically follow that the court will award punitive damages, which can in

[16] See, eg, *Daley v Mahmood* (Central London County Court, 12 August 2005) [14].

[17] *Ramzan v Brookwide Ltd* [2011] EWCA Civ 985, [2012] 1 All ER 903.

[18] *Dawoodi v Zafrani* [2015] EWHC 3168 (TCC).

[19] Jason Varuhas claims that the concept of profit under the second category can also encompass non-economic gains, such as political advantages: J Varuhas, *Damages and Human Rights* (Oxford, Hart Publishing, 2016) 124.

[20] See the Law Reform (Miscellaneous Provisions) Act 1934 (UK), s 1(2)(a) and the Law Reform (Miscellaneous Provisions) Act (Northern Ireland) 1937 (NI), s 14(2)(a), which prohibit the award of punitive damages in claims on behalf of the estate of a deceased person. The Merchant Shipping Act 1995 (UK) gives effect to the Convention Relating to the Carriage of Passengers and their Luggage by Sea, and Art 3(5)(d) of that Convention precludes punitive damages from being awarded in claims to which it applies. The Competition Act 1998 (UK), s 47C and sch 8A, para 36 disallow punitive damages in claims for competition law infringements.

[21] High Speed Rail (London – West Midlands) Act 2017 (UK), s 51(10).

[22] Reserve and Auxiliary Forces (Protection of Civil Interests) Act 1951 (UK), s 13(2).

[23] Crime and Courts Act 2013 (UK), s 34.

[24] For a summary of this debate, see A Burrows, *Remedies for Torts, Breach of Contract and Equitable Wrongs*, 4th edn (Oxford, Oxford University Press, 2019) 367–68.

[25] *Phonographic Performance Ltd v Ellis* [2018] EWCA Civ 2812, [2019] Bus LR 542 [36] (Lewison LJ). Courts in other jurisdictions have taken different views in relation to equivalent statutes: see Bant and Paterson, ch 10, section II.A.

[26] There do not seem to have been any cases the facts of which fell within more than one *Rookes* category.

any event only be requested by the claimant and are not available as of right.[27] Several other conditions need to be satisfied. It is convenient to mention just three of the more important additional prerequisites here.[28] The first is that the defendant's wrongful conduct committed against the claimant must be sufficiently reprehensible.[29] The courts have not adopted a precise test that needs to be satisfied in this regard. Instead, the case law is populated by 'a whole gamut of dyslogistic judicial epithets'[30] that give a broad indication of the kind of conduct that is required to make the defendant's wrongdoing sufficiently exceptional to justify a punitive response. These epithets include 'high-handed',[31] 'outrageous',[32] 'egregious',[33] 'insulting',[34] 'cynical',[35] 'flagran[t]',[36] 'appalling'[37] and 'contumelious'.[38]

Second, the claimant must satisfy the 'if-but-only-if test'. This test is reflected in Lord Devlin's remark in *Rookes* that

> [i]n a case in which exemplary damages are appropriate, a jury should be directed that if, but only if, the sum which they have in mind to award as compensation … is inadequate to punish him for his outrageous conduct, to mark their disapproval of such conduct and to deter him from repeating it, then it can award some larger sum.[39]

Put differently, pursuant to this limiting principle punitive damages will be unavailable unless the goals of punishment and deterrence cannot be achieved by the award of compensatory damages. As such, punitive damages are 'a remedy of last resort'.[40] The 'if-but-only-if test' is important primarily because of the clear signal that it sends that judicial restraint is required in awarding punitive damages. But it also sometimes makes a practical difference to the outcomes of cases, with claims for punitive damages having been rejected on the basis of it despite satisfying the categories test.[41]

[27] *Broome* (n 4) 1060.

[28] See further J Goudkamp and D Nolan, *Winfield & Jolowicz on Tort*, 20th edn (London, Sweet & Maxwell, 2020) para 23.017.

[29] For illustrations of cases in which this requirement was decisive, see *Ministry of Defence v Fletcher* (2010) IRLR 25 (EAT) [115] (victimised army recruit not entitled to punitive damages because the conduct of the army officers, though deplorable, did not cross the high threshold of oppressive conduct); *R (Lumba) v Secretary of State for the Home Department* [2011] UKSC 12, [2012] 1 AC 245 [151]–[166] (withholding punitive damages because the misconduct by the Secretary of State and senior officials was insufficiently outrageous).

[30] *Broome* (n 4) 1129 (Lord Diplock).

[31] See, eg, *Muuse* (n 9) [74] (Thomas LJ).

[32] See, eg, *Kuddus* (n 1) [67] (Lord Mackay).

[33] See, eg, *R (ex parte Lamari) v Secretary of State for the Home Department* (2013) EWHC 3130 (QB) [85] (HHJ Cotter QC).

[34] See, eg, *Thompson v Commissioner of Police of the Metropolis* (1998) QB 498 (CA) 517 (Lord Woolf MR).

[35] *Axa Insurance UK Plc v Financial Claims Solutions Ltd* [2018] EWCA Civ 1330, [2019] RTR 1 [25] (Flaux LJ).

[36] *Bottrill* (n 4) [23] (Lord Nicholls).

[37] ibid.

[38] See, eg, *Kuddus* (n 1) [63] (Lord Mackay).

[39] *Rookes* (n 4) 1228.

[40] *Kuddus* (n 1) [63] (Lord Nicholls).

[41] See, eg, *Mohidin v Commissioner of Police of the Metropolis* (2015) EWHC 2740 (QB) [387].

Third, the claimant must sue in a cause of action that is capable of yielding punitive damages. We need to explain carefully what we mean by this. In *Kuddus v Chief Constable of Leicestershire Constabulary*[42] the House of Lords abolished the so-called 'pre-1964 test',[43] according to which punitive damages could be awarded in respect of a given cause of action only if punitive damages had been awarded in the cause of action concerned prior to the decision in *Rookes*. Despite the demise of this much reviled test,[44] the jurisdiction to award punitive damages nonetheless remains subject to numerous cause of action restrictions. For example, punitive damages cannot be awarded in a claim for breach of contract[45] or in respect of equitable wrongs.[46] Nor are they available under the Human Rights Act 1998 (UK)[47] or Consumer Protection Act 1987 (UK).[48] We have been unable to identify any instances in the UK where punitive damages have been awarded in a claim for the tort of negligence. This raises an issue (which we explore below[49]) as to whether there is an implicit bar on awards of punitive damages in respect of that wrong.

C. Quantification

Turning to the assessment of punitive damages, the starting point is that if punitive damages are to be awarded, the quantum thereof should be the amount necessary to discharge the objectives of punishment and deterrence[50] but, because awards of punitive damages must be 'moderate',[51] no more than that amount.[52] Thus, '[e]verything which aggravates or mitigates the defendant's conduct is relevant'.[53] For example, the quantum of an award should depend upon the defendant's means,[54] since a larger award is necessary to achieve the aims of punitive damages where the defendant is weathly than if they are poor (it is in view of this principle

[42] *Kuddus* (n 1).

[43] The test was recognised in *AB* (n 12).

[44] It 'committ[ed] the law to an irrational position in which the result depend[ed] not on principle but upon the accidents of litigation (or even law reporting) before 1964': WVH Rogers, *Winfield and Jolowicz on Tort*, 15th edn (London, Sweet & Maxwell, 1998) 796.

[45] See, eg, *Perera v Vandiyar* [1953] 1 WLR 672 (CA).

[46] See, eg, *Mosley v News Group Newspaper Ltd* (2008) EWHC 1777 (QB) [197]. cf Crime and Courts Act 2013 (UK), ss 34 and 42(4)(c) authorising punitive damages for breach of confidence against media defendants in respect of claims related to the publication of news-related material.

[47] *Anufrijeva* v *Southwark LBC* [2003] EWCA Civ 1406, [2004] QB 1124 [55].

[48] This, at least, is the position adopted in *Clerk & Lindsell on Torts*, 23rd edn (London, Sweet & Maxwell, 2020) para 10.85.

[49] See the text accompanying nn 264–283.

[50] *Axa* (n 35) [35].

[51] *Rookes* (n 4) 1228 (Lord Devlin).

[52] 'The sum must be sufficient to mark the Court's disapproval of the oppressive or arbitrary behaviour but should be no more than is required for this purpose': *R (ex parte Lamari)* (n 33) [90] (HHJ Cotter QC).

[53] *Rookes* (n 4) 1228 (Lord Devlin).

[54] '[T]he means of the parties … are material in the assessment of exemplary damages': ibid (Lord Devlin).

that punitive damages have sometimes been referred to as 'smart money'[55] on the basis that the award should hurt). Similarly, as a general rule, the more reprehensible the defendant's conduct the greater the award should be and vice versa.[56] Likewise, the fact that the defendant has already been punished in respect of the wrongful conduct in issue, such as by being fined,[57] subjected to disciplinary proceedings[58] or imprisoned,[59] can and usually should be taken into account in fixing the amount of punitive damages.[60]

III. Misconceptions

A. Punitive Damages Awards are Often Excessive

The jurisdiction to award punitive damages has long been criticised on various bases, but perhaps the most common complaint is that awards thereof are often excessive. For example, in 1993 the Law Commission reported that a frequent criticism is that 'exemplary awards … have reached levels which are excessive'.[61] In *Thompson v Commissioner of Police of the Metropolis*, Lord Woolf MR expressed concerns about 'excessive [punitive damages] awards … being paid out of public money'.[62] However, these grumblings about excessiveness have been made in the absence of any empirical evidence and are, accordingly, nothing more than impressionistic reactions based on anecdotes.

We recently carried out the sole empirical investigation of punitive damages awards in the UK,[63] which involved an analysis of all electronically accessible cases decided between 2000 and 2015 in which the claimant sought an award of punitive damages. In a sample containing 146 claims, the average award was just £18,181[64] and the largest, which was divided between eight claimants, was £140,896.[65]

[55] ibid 1223.

[56] *Loudon v Ryder (No 1)* [1953] 2 QB 202 (CA) 207.

[57] *Devenish Nutrition Ltd v Sanofi Aventis SA* (2007) EWHC 2394 (Ch), [2008] All ER 249 [64].

[58] *KD v Chief Constable of Hampshire* [2005] EWHC 2550 (QB), [2005] Po LR 253 [193].

[59] *Axa Insurance UK Plc v Thwaites* (Norwich County Court, 8 February 2008) [12].

[60] *Archer v Brown* [1985] QB 401 (CA) 423.

[61] Law Commission, *Aggravated Exemplary and Restitutionary Damages: A Consultation Paper* (Law Com CP No 132, 1993) 113.

[62] *Thompson* (n 34) 513.

[63] J Goudkamp and E Katsampouka, 'An Empirical Study of Punitive Damages' (2018) 38 *OJLS* 90, 107.

[64] This figure is the average sum that defendants paid rather than the average sum received by claimants, which was £12,625. The difference is attributable to the rule that where there are several claimants in the same proceedings, any award of punitive damages is to be divided equally between them: *Riches* (n 14) 261, 289. All monetary figures reported by our study that we discuss below are based on the 'as paid' measure.

[65] *Borders (UK) Ltd v Commissioner of Police for the Metropolis* [2005] EWCA Civ 197, [2005] Po LR 1 (£150,303 in today's terms). This has since been overtaken by an award of £150,000 (£152,250 in today's terms), which was divided between three claimants, in *Rees v Commissioner of Police for the Metropolis* [2019] EWHC 2339 (QB). Inflation-adjusted Sterling values have been computed via this online calculator: www.officialdata.org/, accessed 9 February 2021. The awards in *Borders* and in *Rees* are extreme outliers given that most punitive damages awards are between £588 and £38,851: Goukdamp and Katsampouka (n 63) 92.

The average award, in particular, is sufficiently modest in litigation terms that it strongly suggests that the complaints about awards of punitive damages generally being exorbitant are unfounded.

The claim that punitive damages awards are excessive can be probed further by examining the level of awards by reference to various comparators. Three obvious comparators are: (i) the level of compensatory damages awards in cases in which punitive damages were awarded; (ii) the average annual income of a full-time employee in the UK; and (iii) the size of punitive damages awards in other jurisdictions. None of those points of reference lends any support to the notion that awards of punitive damages in the UK are often excessive. In relation to the first comparator, the results of our empirical study suggest that when both punitive and compensatory damages are awarded, the amount of punitive damages is on average much lower than the amount of compensatory damages.[66] As for the second, again, the results of our study suggest that the average award of punitive damages against natural persons (which, in cases in our sample, was £8,609[67]) is not particularly high compared with the average annual income (ie, £36,952[68]). And as for the final comparator, the average award of punitive damages in the UK as reported by our study was much lower than that reported in a very substantial study of the position in the US. According to Eisenberg and Heise, the average punitive damages award in a 2005 dataset based on decisions from 156 counties across the US was US$2.4m (ie, US$3.2m in today's terms, which is equivalent to over £2.5m).[69] The average award of punitive damages in the UK as found by our investigation was also very substantially lower than that reported by a recent Australian study.[70] The average award in that study's sample was A$105,000, which equates to around £80,000. In summary, according to all three reference points that we have considered, punitive damages awards in the UK are anything but excessive.

A further potential reference point is the average fine imposed by the criminal courts.[71] After all, in *Loudon v Ryder (No 1)*, Devlin J, in his summing up to the

[66] Goudkamp and Katsampouka (n 63) 114. The average sum that defendants paid as punitive and compensatory damages in cases where both amounts were known was £21,437 and £98,826 respectively.

[67] ibid 107.

[68] This figure is the annual average earnings of a full-time employee for the period 2000–15 (ie, the temporal scope of our study): Office for National Statistics, 'Data for Earnings and Working Hours' (2015) at www.ons.gov.uk/employmentandlabourmarket/peopleinwork/earningsandworkinghours/datasets/allemployeesashetable1, accessed 9 February 2021.

[69] T Eisenberg and M Heise, 'Judge Jury Differences in Punitive Damages Awards: Who Listens to The Supreme Court?' (2011) 8 *Journal of Empirical Legal Studies* 325, 331. This and all other values in this chapter that are expressed in US dollars have been adjusted for inflation using this online calculator: https://data.bls.gov/cgi-bin/cpicalc.pl, accessed 26 March 2020.

[70] F Maher, 'An Empirical Study of Exemplary Damages in Australia' (2019) 43 *Melbourne University Law Review* 694.

[71] In *Rookes* (n 4), Lord Devlin seemed to have that comparator in mind. In urging the need for awards to be moderate, he said that '[s]ome of the awards that juries have made in the past seem to me to amount to a greater punishment than would be likely to be incurred if the conduct were criminal' (at 1227).

jury, said that 'punitive damages are rather like imposing a fine'.[72] However, we feel that criminal law fines are, in fact, a poor benchmark for gauging whether punitive damages awards are excessive for two main reasons. The first concerns the means of the person punished. It is notorious that many offenders suffer significant financial disadvantage.[73] In circumstances where the means of the offender is an important sentencing consideration,[74] this reality is bound to exert significant downward pressure on the level of fines imposed by the criminal courts. Conversely, it is equally well known that claims in tort are unlikely to be issued against defendants who do not have deep pockets or are not insured.[75] Accordingly, the means of the person paying dictates that, on average, punitive damages awards are likely to be justifiably (rather than excessively) higher than the level of fines. Second, much of the criminal behaviour that is sanctioned by way of a fine (which is how most offenders are dealt with[76]) is bound to be far too trivial to engage the jurisdiction to award punitive damages, which is reserved for cases in which the defendant has behaved exceptionally badly.[77] However, even if the level of fines were a good comparator, which it is not for the reasons we have given, it would be of no assistance for the purposes of testing the claim that punitive damages are often excessive. That is because, in what strikes us as a glaring gap in understanding regarding sentencing and a shameful failure on the part of the state to report transparently how it exercises its exceptional powers, there are no recent data available in the UK on the average fines imposed by the criminal courts.[78]

Before leaving the first misconception, it is worth briefly mentioning that the same complaint about excessiveness has been made in relation to the law governing punitive damages in several other countries, and research conducted in the jurisdictions concerned strongly suggests that these complaints are similarly unfounded. The practical operation of the law of punitive damages has been subjected to exhaustive empirical investigation in, in particular, the US.[79]

[72] *Loudon* (n 56) 208 (Singleton LJ quoting Devlin J in the first instance proceedings).

[73] 'There is substantial evidence indicating that poverty is associated with criminal activity …': P Sharkey, M Desbris and M Friedson, 'Poverty and Crime' in D Brady and L Burton (eds), *The Oxford Handbook of the Social Science of Poverty* (New York, Oxford University Press, 2016) 623.

[74] Criminal Justice Act 2003 (UK), s 164(3).

[75] Set against this, however, is the fact that contracts of insurance often exclude cover for punitive damages: see J Birds, B Lynch and S Paul, *MacGillivray on Insurance Law*, 14th edn (London, Sweet & Maxwell, 2018) para 30.009, fn 36.

[76] 'Fines remained the most common sentence, accounting for 78% of all sentences in 2019': Ministry of Justice, *Criminal Justice Statistics quarterly, England and Wales, April 2019 to March 2020* (London, Ministry of Justice, 2020) 7.

[77] Punitive 'damages [are] an exceptional remedy … reserved for the most reprehensible examples of civil wrongdoing': Law Commission (n 61) 5.

[78] The Ministry of Justice apparently collects the relevant data but does not make them publicly available. In any event, the Ministry has confirmed that, due to an error, data regarding fines between £10,000 and £99,999 imposed by the magistrates' courts were not recorded: Ministry of Justice, *A Guide to Criminal Justice Statistics* (London, Ministry of Justice, 2018) 20.

[79] See, eg, T Eisenberg et al, 'The Predictability of Punitive Damages' (1997) 26 *Journal of Legal Studies* 623; T Eisenberg, J Rachlinsky and M Wells, 'Reconciling Experimental Incoherence with Real-World Coherence in Punitive Damages' (2002) 54 *Stanford Law Review* 1239; T Eisenberg and M Wells,

Overall, the relevant studies compellingly suggest that punitive damages awards, contrary to prevailing opinion, are modest in most cases[80] and that awards are generally firmly anchored to the amounts of compensatory damages that defendants are ordered to pay.[81] As the US Supreme Court has noted, 'although some studies show the dollar amounts of punitive-damages awards growing over time, even in real terms, by most accounts the median ratio of punitive to compensatory awards has remained less than 1:1'.[82] While it is true that there have been some astronomical punitive damages awards in the US,[83] such awards do not usually remain intact but are set aside on appeal or are otherwise disturbed by settlements.[84]

Much the same story can be told in relation to Australia and Canada. It has often been asserted that punitive damages awards in Australia have spiraled out of control.[85] However, the Australian study to which we have referred found no support for that position. In particular, it reported that the average award of compensatory damages was three times higher on average than the amount of punitive damages in cases in which both types of damages were granted.[86] The only empirical investigation of punitive damages awards in Canada,[87] where it has likewise been suggested that punitive damages awards are out of control,[88] was commissioned 30 years ago by the Ontario Law Reform Commission.[89]

'The Significant Association Between Punitive and Compensatory Damages in Blockbuster Cases: A Methodological Primer' (2006) 3 *Journal of Empirical Legal Studies* 175; T Eisenberg et al, 'Judges, Juries, and Punitive Damages: Empirical Analyses Using the Civil Justice Survey of State Courts 1992, 1996, and 2001 Data' (2006) 3 *Journal of Empirical Legal Studies* 263; T Eisenberg, V Hans and M Wells, 'The Relation Between Punitive and Compensatory Awards: Combining Extreme Data with the Mass of Awards' in B Bornstein et al (eds), *Civil Juries and Civil Justice: Psychological and Legal Perspectives* (New York, Springer-Verlag, 2008) 105; T Eisenberg et al, 'The Decision to Award Punitive Damages: An Empirical Study' (2010) 2 *Journal of Legal Analysis* 577; B McMichael and K Viscusi, 'Taming Blockbuster Punitive Damages Awards' (2019) *University of Illinois Law Review* 171.

80 Although the average punitive damages award in the US is high (ie, \$3.2m in today's terms (see the text accompanying n 69)) this is because a small number of awards of more than \$1m skew the average (see Eisenberg et al, 'Judges, Juries, and Punitive Damages: Empirical Analyses Using the Civil Justice Survey of State Courts 1992, 1996, and 2001 Data' (n 79) 270).

81 ibid 273–74.

82 *Exxon Shipping v Baker* 554 US 471, 497–98 (2008) (Souter J) (footnotes omitted).

83 See, eg, *Motorola Credit Co v Uzan* 338 F 3d 39 (2nd Cir, 2004) (US\$2.1b (ie, US\$2.9b in today's terms) reduced on appeal (*Motorola Credit Co v Uzan* 509 F 3d 74 (2nd Cir, 2007)) to US\$1b (ie, US\$1.3b in today's terms). For further examples of 'blockbuster' awards, see A Del Rossi and K Viscusi, 'The Changing Landscape of Blockbuster Punitive Damages Awards' (2010) 12 *American Law and Economics Review* 116; McMichael and Viscusi (n 79).

84 Eisenberg et al, 'Reconciling Experimental Incoherence with Real-World Coherence in Punitive Damages' (n 79) 1260–61.

85 'Awards for exemplary damages are often too high': *Review of the Law of Negligence: Final Report* (Canberra, Australian Government Press, 2002) para 13.164.

86 Maher (n 70) 33.

87 N Vidmar and B Feldthusen, 'Exemplary Damages Claims in Ontario: An Empirical Profile' (1990) 16 *Canadian Business Law Journal* 262.

88 See, eg, J Gotanda, 'Punitive Damages: A Comparative Analysis' (2004) 42 *Columbia Journal of Transnational Law* 391, 435–36 (footnotes omitted): 'In recent years, punitive damages awards have increased significantly in Canada … the awards have escalated in amount.'

89 See Ontario Law Reform Commission, *Report on Exemplary Damages* (1991) 21ff.

That study, which examined reported cases and court files in Ontario, did not provide comprehensive or even certain fairly basic statistics regarding the quantum of punitive damages awards. However, on the basis of, for example, the largest award of punitive damages[90] and the size of awards of punitive damages relative to compensatory damages,[91] its authors concluded that punitive damages awards were not 'typically large'.[92] Further, lawyers who were interviewed for the study perceived punitive damages claims as 'harmless'[93] and were unconcerned by the quantum of awards.[94] While the findings of the Canadian study are dated and must consequently be treated as being of limited value as regards the contemporary position, it is debatable whether the overall picture in Canada is very different today. One of the authors of the Ontario study contends that that the relevant law in Canada has changed significantly since the study was conducted and writes that [a]wards have become more frequent and larger in the past decade'.[95] However, writing in 2017, Lewis Klar and Cameron Jefferies claim that punitive damages even for the most outrageous behaviour have been 'very moderate'[96] and most awards are 'well under C$100,000 and frequently less than C$50,000'.[97]

Given that the relevant empirical evidence regarding the level of punitive damages awards, in the UK and elsewhere, is largely all one way it is important to ask why awards of punitive damages are nonetheless frequently said to be often excessive. There are various explanations. One possibility is that the misunderstanding may be due to an availability heuristic, that is, a common cognitive error committed when the incidence of memorable incidents is overestimated.[98] Substantial punitive damages awards sometimes receive significant publicity and this may lead to the frequency of such awards being overstated. Consider, for example, *John v MGN Ltd*.[99] In this case, a jury awarded the famous singer Sir Elton John £75,000[100] in compensatory damages and £275,000[101] in punitive

[90] The largest award was C$50,000 (ie, C$113,406 in today's terms): see ibid 268. This and all other values in this chapter that are expressed in Canadian dollars have been adjusted for inflation using the Bank of Canada's inflation calculator: www.bankofcanada.ca/rates/related/inflation-calculator/, accessed 9 February 2021.

[91] The median award was found to be approximately 20% of compensatory damages: ibid 265.

[92] ibid 268.

[93] ibid 267.

[94] ibid.

[95] B Feldthusen, 'Punitive Damages: Hard Choices and High Stakes' [1998] *New Zealand Law Review* 741, 772. It is certainly the case that since the Ontario study was conducted there have been some very large awards in Canada: see, eg, *Whiten v Pilot Insurance Co* [2002] SCC 18, [2002] 1 SCR 595 (C$1m (C$1.3m in today's terms)); *Pate Estate v Galway-Cavendish and Harvey (Township)* 2013 ONCA 669, (2013) 368 DLR (4th) 193 (C$450,000 (C$503,049 in today's terms)); *Airbus Helicopters SAS v Bell Helicopter Textron Canada Ltd* 2019 FCA 29, (2019) 163 CPR (4th) 337 (C$1m, C$1.17m in today's terms).

[96] L Klar and C Jefferies, *Tort Law*, 6th edn (Toronto, Thomson Reuters, 2017) 144.

[97] ibid 144–45.

[98] See R Korobkin and T Ulen, 'Law and Behavioral Science: Removing the Rationality Assumption from Law and Economics' (2000) 88 *California Law Review* 1051, 1087.

[99] See n 13.

[100] £153,789 in today's terms.

[101] £532,161 in today's terms.

damages in respect of a defamatory newspaper article. The award attracted considerable publicity.[102] However, the Court of Appeal reduced the compensatory damages to £25,000[103] and the punitive damages to £50,000.[104] Needless to say, the initial award of punitive damages is far more headline-worthy than the award that was ultimately made.[105] A second potential explanation for the perception that punitive damages awards are often exorbitant is more cynical. It may be suggested that unsupported allegations of excessiveness have been made simply because it is hoped that the allegations will encourage the courts or the legislature further to restrict the jurisdiction to award punitive damages.

B. The Quantum of Punitive Damages Awards is Unpredictable

Concerns that punitive damages awards are often excessive are frequently ventilated in tandem with worries that the level of punitive damages awards is uncertain. For example, the Law Commission wrote that a common criticism of punitive damages awards was that they 'are indeterminate and unpredictable'[106] and Rachael Mulheron asserts that '[q]uantifying awards for exemplary damages is highly imprecise'.[107] The allegedly unpredictable level of punitive damages awards is said to be objectionable for various reasons, including that it creates uncertainty for businesses and leads to over-deterrence.[108] It is is also said to discourage 'manufacturers … from putting useful and innovative products onto the market because of fear of the potential liability'.[109]

Although concern at erratic awards is entirely understandable, and although it is true that punitive damages awards are at large,[110] it is doubtful for at least four reasons that such awards are, in fact, unpredictable (or, at least, are any more unpredictable than other types of awards that are at large). In the first place, our empirical study suggests that there is, in fact, considerable uniformity in punitive damages awards, with more than 75 per cent of awards falling within a relatively

[102] See, eg, I Katz and C Dyer, '£350,000 libel win for Elton John', *The Guardian* (5 November 1993); R Duce, 'Jury Awards £350,000 Damages to Elton John', *The Times* (5 November 1993).

[103] £51,263 in today's terms.

[104] £96,756 in today's terms.

[105] Note, however, that the Court of Appeal's decision also received substantial press coverage: see, eg, F Gibb, 'Elton John Award Cut by Libel Ruling', *The Times* (13 December 1995); C Dyer, 'Court Ruling to Slash Libel Awards', *The Guardian* (13 December 1995).

[106] Law Commission (n 61) 82.

[107] R Mulheron, *Principles of Tort Law*, 2nd edn (Cambridge, Cambridge University Press, 2020) 573.

[108] '[T]he risk of having to defend claims and to pay exemplary damages creates considerable uncertainty for business planning and … this uncertainty may produce an excessive deterrent effect which would be likely to disadvantage the national economy': Law Commission (n 61) 113.

[109] ibid.

[110] *Rookes* (n 4) 1228 (Lord Devlin). cf *Whiten* (n 95) [76].

narrow bracket (ie, £588 to £33,851).[111] The high degree of homogeneity of punitive damages awards renders it entirely possible to predict with a reasonable degree of confidence the likely award in most cases. Second, in so far as the concern about uncertainty relates to the impact on businesses and over-deterrence, it is doubtful that it is warranted given that 75 per cent of awards against corporations also fell within a fairly small band (ie, £2,806 to £63,229).[112] Third, and as to the concern that the alleged unpredictability of awards creates difficulty in the product liability context, this strikes us as baseless in circumstances where we have been unable to locate even a single product liability case in which punitive damages have been awarded.[113] According to one leading textbook, punitive damages are unavailable under the Consumer Protection Act 1987 (UK).[114] Finally, in *Thompson*[115] the Court of Appeal enunciated guidelines as to the appropriate level of punitive damages in cases of police misconduct.[116] Lord Woolf MR said:

> Where exemplary damages are appropriate they are unlikely to be less than £5,000.[117] Otherwise the case is probably not one which justifies an award of exemplary damages at all. In this class of action, the conduct must be particularly deserving of condemnation for an award of as much as £25,000[118] to be justified and the figure of £50,000[119] should be regarded as the absolute maximum, involving directly officers of at least the rank of superintendent.[120]

These guidelines, while arbitrary, ensure significant predictability in the police misconduct context, and there seem to be no instances in which the courts have departed from them.

C. Defamation Cases Constitute an Important Source of Punitive Damages Awards

The law of defamation is routinely cited as the primary example of a field in which punitive damages are awarded under the second *Rookes* category (ie, cases in which the defendant had a profit motive). For example, the Law Commission

[111] Goudkamp and Katsampouka (n 63) 115.
[112] ibid.
[113] ibid 115.
[114] See n 48.
[115] *Thompson* (n 34).
[116] However, it appears that punitive damages are awarded rather infrequently in this setting. In our empirical study, out of a total of 58 successful claims for punitive damages just seven successful claims for punitive damages were made in respect of police misconduct: see Goudkamp and Katsampouka (n 63) 112–13.
[117] £9,160 in today's terms.
[118] £45,801 in today's terms.
[119] £91,602 in today's terms.
[120] *Thompson* (n 34) 517.

referred to defamation as a wrong 'in respect of which the punitive principle has been employed most often by the courts'.[121] Similarly, according to Solène Rowan, 'Lord Devlin's second category ... targets the wrongdoer who "with a cynical disregard for a plaintiff's rights has calculated that the money to be made out of his wrongdoing will probably exceed the damages at risk". *In practice, this has most commonly been makers of defamatory statements* ...'.[122] Likewise, the authors of *Markesinis and Deakin's Tort Law* contend, but without citing any authority in support, that '[profit-seeking conduct sufficient to attract a punitive damages award] is particularly likely to happen in libel cases'.[123] These claims appear to be dramatic overstatements given that in the sample that formed our empirical study of punitive damages not a single award was made in a claim for defamation.[124]

The foregoing situation elicits two questions. The first is why the view that defamation claims are an important source of punitive damages has flourished, and the second is why punitive damages are apparently rarely awarded for defamation. As to the first question, one possible explanation is the availability heuristic that we have mentioned previously:[125] memorable awards of punitive damages in the defamation context may have encouraged the belief that the jurisdiction to award punitive damages is more important in this setting than is actually the case. Another potential explanation may be a perception that, given that defendants in defamation cases often appear to be commercial publishers, they will not infrequently have a profit motive, thereby bringing claims in this setting within the second *Rookes* category with some regularity.

As to the second question, one possible reason[126] why punitive damages awards are apparently rare in defamation claims is that awards of aggravated damages

[121] Law Commission (n 61) 26. The Law Commission also said that 'defamation cases ... represent an important source of awards of ... exemplary damages' and cited some decisions from the 1980s and 1990s to support this proposition (at 61).

[122] S Rowan, 'Comparative Observations on the Introduction of Punitive Damages in French Law' in J Cartwright, S Vogenauer and S Whittaker (eds), *Reforming the French Law of Obligations* (Oxford, Hart Publishing, 2009) 325, 331 (emphasis added). Rowan does not cite any cases in support of her claim.

[123] S Deakin and Z Adams, *Markesinis and Deakin's Tort Law*, 8th edn (Oxford, Oxford University Press, 2019) 796. See also V Wilcox, 'Punitive Damages in England' in H Koziol and V Wilcox (eds), *Punitive Damages: Common Law and Civil Law Perspectives* (Vienna, Springer-Verlag, 2009) 7, 12, who writes that 'Cases under [the second *Rookes*] category commonly come under defamation ...'. Wilcox similarly does not cite any authorities to bear out her assertion.

[124] Goudkamp and Katsampouka (n 63) 106, 111. As we explained, our study captured all claims decided between 2000 and 2015. We have been unable to identify any instances since 2015 where punitive damages were awarded in a claim in defamation. The Canadian study reported a small number of cases involving defamation: see Vidmar and Feldthusen (n 87) 265. By contrast, punitive damages awards in defamation cases seem to be far more common in the US. According to the results of a major empirical study, punitive damages were awarded in 54.7% of defamation claims in which they were sought: see Eisenberg et al, 'The Decision to Award Punitive Damages: An Empirical Study' (n 79) 598. As for Australia, punitive damages were awarded in 18.37% of the defamation claims in which they were sought: see Maher (n 70) 23 (although this result should be read in light of the fact that legislation was introduced throughout Australia during the study period that abolished the jurisdiction to award punitive damages).

[125] See the text accompanying n 98.

[126] See Law Commission (n 61) 57.

seem to be common in this setting and it has been argued that they too discharge a punitive function.[127] This is important because, if this is indeed the case, it follows that punitive damages may not need to be awarded in order to achieve the goals of punishment and deterrence (and will in such circumstances in principle be unavailable on account of the 'if-but-only-if test'). The notion that punitive damages do not have a monopoly on punishment is a theme to which we now turn.

D. Punitive Damages are an Anomalous Remedy

In *Rookes*, Lord Devlin described punitive damages as an 'anomaly'.[128] He did so not because he considered the remedy to be an outlier in terms of the rate at which punitive damages are awarded relative to other types of remedies but on account of the goal of punitive damages being, first and foremost, to punish the defendant. Lord Devlin's characterisation of punitive damages as an alien presence in private law has been, and continues to be, widely endorsed. For example, in *Axa Insurance UK Plc v Financial Claims Solutions* Flaux LJ said that punitive damages were anomalous because they were 'an exception from the normal tortious principle that damages are compensatory not penal'.[129] Similarly, in *IBM United Kingdom Holdings Ltd v Dalgleish* Warren J considered that 'exemplary damages are anomalous in that they are punitive and punishment has no part to play in the adjudication of the rights and obligations of parties in civil litigation'.[130] Allan Beever accurately summarised the position when he said that there is an 'almost universal sense' that punitive damages 'are anomalous'.[131]

In reality, however, punitive damages are not the anomaly that they are perceived to be, since private law recognises several other remedial responses that also have a decidedly punitive agenda.[132] Numerous examples are readily to hand but we will limit ourselves to mentioning just four.[133] The first concerns the rules

[127] See the text accompanying nn 153–159.

[128] *Rookes* (n 4) 1221. Lord Devlin also referred to '[t]he anomaly inherent in exemplary damages' (at 1227). See further J Goudkamp and E Katsampouka, 'Punitive Damages and the Place of Punishment in Private Law' (forthcoming).

[129] *Axa Insurance* (n 35) [19].

[130] *IBM United Kingdom Holdings Ltd v Dalgleish* (2015) EWHC 389 (Ch), [2015] Pens LR 99 [176].

[131] A Beever, 'The Structure of Aggravated and Exemplary Damages' (2003) 23 *OJLS* 87, 109, fn 91. To like effect, see S Rowan, 'Reflections on the Introduction of Punitive Damages for Breach of Contract' (2010) 30 *OJLS* 495, 507.

[132] We have been influenced here by P Cane, 'Retribution, Proportionality, and Moral Luck in Tort Law' in P Cane and J Stapleton (eds), *The Law of Obligations: Essays in Celebration of John Fleming* (Oxford, Clarendon Press, 1998) 161; and CM Sharkey, 'Crossing the Punitive-Compensation Divide' in BH Bornstein et al (eds), *Civil Juries and Civil Justice: Psychological and Legal Perspectives* (New York, Springer, 2008) 79.

[133] Other illustrations (or potential illustrations) include: (i) awards of enhanced interest (see R Chambers, 'Liability' in P Birks and A Pretto-Sakmann (eds), *Breach of Trust* (Oxford, Hart Publishing, 2002) 1, 33–37); (ii) contemptuous damages; (iii) the principles governing the imposition of trusts in respect of bribes and secret commissions received by fiduciaries (consider *FHR European Ventures LLP v Cedar Capital Partners LLC* [2014] UKSC 45, [2015] AC 250 [42]); (iv) the fraudulent claims

regarding remoteness of damage.[134] Whereas it is usually the case that damage must be of a foreseeable kind in order to be compensable,[135] where the defendant has intentionally harmed the claimant or acted dishonestly[136] or maliciously,[137] that ordinary rule is relaxed and all of the damage directly caused, whether or not it is of a foreseeable kind, is compensable. As Lord Lindley trenchantly put it in an oft-cited passage in *Quinn v Leatham*, '[t]he intention to injure the plaintiff … disposes of any question of remoteness of damage'.[138]

It has been repeatedly and explicitly said at the ultimate appellate level that punishment is the purpose of the attenunated remoteness test. The punitive agenda of the test emerges particularly clearly from Lord Nicholls's speech in *Kuwait Airways Corp v Iraqi Airways Co (No 6)*.[139] In the context of conversion, Lord Nicholls, in a passage that Lord Hoffmann[140] and Lord Hope[141] expressly endorsed, made it clear that the test for remoteness should depend on whether the defendant in converting the claimant's property acted innocently or dishonestly, on the basis that 'the more culpable the defendant the wider the area of loss for which he can fairly be held responsible'.[142] His Lordship added:

> Dishonesty is not an essential ingredient of [the tort of conversion]. The defendant may be a thief, or he may have acted wholly innocently. Both are strictly liable. But it seems to me inappropriate they should be treated alike when determining their liability for consequential loss. …
>
> [F]oreseeability, as the more restrictive test, is appropriate for those who act in good faith. …
>
> Persons who knowingly convert another's goods stand differently. Such persons are acting dishonestly. I can see no good reason why the remoteness test of 'directly and naturally' applied in cases of deceit should not apply in cases of conversion where the defendant acted dishonestly.[143]

It is axiomatic that the reason that Lord Nicholls considered that dishonest wrongdoers should be subject to more expansive liability was that such wrongdoers

rule in insurance law (consider *Versloot Dredging BV v HDI Gerling Industrie Versicherung AG* [2016] UKSC 45, [2017] AC 1 [36]); and (v) additional damages awarded under s 97(2) of the Copyright, Designs and Patents Act 1988 (UK) (consider *Phonographic Performance* (n 25) [36]).

[134] See also Rowan's contribution in this volume, where she discusses the disapplication in France of the conventional rules regarding remoteness being a disguised form of punishment: ch 3, section II.B.

[135] *Hughes v Lord Advocate* [1963] AC 837 (HL) 845; *Hadley v Baxendale* (1854) 9 Ex 341, 354; 156 ER 145, 151.

[136] Consider Lord Denning MR's remark in *Doyle v Olby (Ironmongers) Ltd* (1969) 2 QB 158 (CA) 167 that '[in a claim in deceit] all … damages can be recovered: and it does not lie in the mouth of the fraudulent person to say that they could not reasonably have been foreseen'.

[137] *Livingstone v Rawyards Coal Co* (1880) 5 App Cas 25 (HL) 39 (Lord Blackburn).

[138] *Quinn v Leatham* [1901] AC 495 (HL) 537.

[139] *Kuwait Airways Corp v Iraqi Airways Co (No 6)* [2002] UKHL 19, [2002] 2 AC 883.

[140] ibid [125].

[141] ibid [169].

[142] ibid [101].

[143] ibid [102]–[104].

deserve to be punished. Lord Nicholls' concern with whether the defendant acted 'culpably' is otherwise inexplicable.

Several points are noteworthy in this connection. One is that there is no space for any suggestion that this is a mere isolated *dictum*. It is a remark made at the ultimate appellate level that has the backing of three of the five judges who constituted the panel in issue. Further, and unsurprisingly, the foregoing passage from Lord Nicholls' speech has been endorsed in subsequent cases.[144] Another significant matter to observe is that Lord Nicholls' observations did not usher in a radical new approach. Rather, the position that he embraced reflects a long line of authority. Lord Nicholls found support for the propositions that he advanced in Lord Steyn's comments in *Smith New Court Securities Ltd v Citibank NA*,[145] who, in turn, followed the history of the attenuated approach to remoteness back over more than 100 years,[146] including to such foundational decisions in the law of obligations as *Livingstone v Rawyards Coal Co.*[147]

Beyond *Kuwait Airways* and *Smith New Court Securities* there are two other decisions at the ultimate appellate level, *SAAMCO*[148] and *Patel v Mirza*,[149] in which punishment is explicitly identified as the purpose of the diluted test for remoteness. In *SAAMCO*, Lord Hoffmann observed that the law could dispense with the usual rules regarding remoteness in order to punish defendants. Thus, he remarked that '[t]here is no reason in principle why the law should not *penalise* wrongful conduct by shifting on to the wrongdoer the whole risk of consequences which would not have happened but for the wrongful act'.[150] At one level, these remarks are puzzling in that they seem not to acknowledge that the law does indeed relax the normal remoteness rules where the defendant intentionally or dishonestly injured the claimant. However, this oddity in Lord Hoffmann's reasons is unimportant for present purposes. That which matters is that Lord Hoffmann clearly recognises that dilution of the remoteness rules falls to be explained in terms of punishment.

In *Patel*, Lord Sumption said that '[w]ith very limited exceptions, such as certain rules of causation in fraud cases or the rare occasions for awarding punitive damages, … [the] rationale [of] punishment … was no part of the rules of civil law'.[151] Although his Lordship confusingly used the language of 'causation' rather than 'remoteness', it is nevertheless obvious that he was referring to the diluted remoteness test that applies in cases of deceit. Crucially, Lord Sumption not only expressly identified the purpose of the attenuated test as being punishment but

[144] See, eg, *Essa v Laing Ltd* [2004] EWCA Civ 2, [2004] ICR 746 [34]–[39]; *Jones v Ruth* [2011] EWCA Civ 804, [2012] 1 WLR 1495 [24]–[32].
[145] *Smith New Court Securities Ltd v Citibank NA* [1997] AC 254 (HL).
[146] ibid 279–85.
[147] *Livingstone* (n 137).
[148] *South Australia Asset Management Co v York Montague Ltd* [1997] AC 191 (HL).
[149] *Patel v Mirza* [2016] UKSC 42, [2017] AC 467.
[150] *South Australia Asset Management Co* (n 148) 212 (emphasis added).
[151] *Patel* (n 149) [230].

actually saw the diluted test as being allied with the jurisdiction to award punitive damages. Lord Sumption's observations are thus explicit acknowledgement that the watered-down approach to remoteness serves a retributive agenda equivalent to that pursued by punitive damages.[152]

Our second illustration concerns aggravated damages. Although for most of their history aggravated damages were indistinguishable from punitive damages,[153] in *Rookes* they were authoritatively recast by Lord Devlin[154] as a form of compensatory damages awarded in respect of the mental distress that the claimant suffered due to the manner in which the wrong was committed. However, it has often been expressly acknowledged that punishment is among the goals of aggravated damages.[155] For example, in *KD v Chief Constable of Hampshire*,[156] which involved a claim in battery and under the Protection from Harassment Act 1997 (UK), Tugendhat J said that 'there is a penal element in aggravated damages'.[157] Further, and consistently with the fact that aggravated damages are at least sometimes awarded to punish, the courts, both in deciding whether to award aggravated damages and in quantifying them, consider broadly the same factors that they bear in mind in connection with punitive damages. As Lord Woolf MR noted in *Thompson*, 'the very circumstances which will justify an award of aggravated damages are probably the same as those which make it possible to award exemplary damages'.[158] It is true, of course, that the availability of punitive damages is restrained by various rules that do not apply to aggravated damages, such as the categories test.[159] But this is neither here nor there for present purposes, as this simply means that when punishment is merited the courts cannot always impose it via an award of punitive damages. It does not mean that punishment is not among the purposes of aggravated damages.

Our third illustration concerns general damages.[160] While the starting point is of course that general damages are compensatory, and despite the courts' occasional insistence that they should not contain any punitive element,[161] the fact

[152] Lord Sumption disagreed with a majority of the Justices in *Patel* regarding the proper approach to the doctrine of illegality. However, this disagreement is irrelevant for present purposes, and none of the other Justices cast doubt on Lord Sumption's remarks in issue.

[153] For example, the editor of the 13th edition of *Salmond on the Law of Torts* wrote that 'Damages are … distinguishable as being either compensatory or exemplary. The latter are also known as vindictive, aggravated, retributory, penal or punitive … No distinction has been taken in the authorities between "aggravated" and "exemplary" damages': R Heuston, *Salmond on the Law of Torts*, 13th edn (London, Sweet & Maxwell, 1961) 739.

[154] *Rookes* (n 4) 1221.

[155] Although see s 39(2) of the Crime and Courts Act 2013 (UK), which provides that '[a]ggravated damages may be awarded against the defendant only to compensate for mental distress and not for purposes of punishment'.

[156] *KD* (n 58).

[157] ibid [186]. To similar effect, see *Ministry of Defence v Fletcher* (n 29) [52].

[158] *Thompson* (n 34) 513.

[159] Consider also the remarks in *New South Wales v Ibbett* [2006] HCA 57, (2006) 229 CLR 638 [34].

[160] See also Rowan's contribution in this volume: ch 3, section II.B.

[161] 'Justice to the defendant also generally requires the avoidance, save in special cases, of any punitive element in the assessment of general damages': *AG of St Helena v AB* (2020) UKPC 1 [31] (Lord Briggs).

of the matter is that general damages sometimes (we put it no higher than this) have a punitive flavour to them. In particular, in at least certain circumstances general damages are inextricably linked to the wrongfulness of the defendant's conduct with the result that it misses an important part of the truth to regard such damages as purely compensatory. For example, general damages awarded in defamation cases in respect of the humiliation and distress occasioned by a defamatory statement cannot be separated from the defendant's behaviour because the nature of the statement and the manner in which it was made is centrally relevant to their assessment. Thus, it is trite law that

> the plaintiff may draw attention … when determining general damages for defamation [to] … the mode and extent of publication, the conduct of the publisher and any injury to the claimant's feelings [that is] the result of the defamation or a consequence of high-handed, oppressive or insulting behaviour by the publisher.[162]

Consistently with the foregoing, and as has often been pointed out, defamation cases can be found in which the level at which general damages were awarded can only fairly be characterised as punitive.[163] The most notorious is *Aldington v Watts*,[164] in which a jury awarded the claimant general damages of £1.5m[165] in a claim for defamation in respect of a publication that alleged that he was a war criminal. Although the trial judge directed the jury to 'leave aside any thought of punishing the defendants' and added that 'it is not your duty or your right to punish a defendant', there can be little doubt that the award was punitive, its being three times higher than any general damages award that had been previously made for defamation.[166]

Similar points to those just made about general damages awarded for defamation can also be made about mental distress damages awarded for breach of contract. Mental distress damages are notionally awarded in order to compensate the claimant for the inconvenience and annoyance occasioned by qualifying breaches of contract. However, the courts have often made remarks that perceive this type of award as being aligned with punitive damages.[167] In these circumstances, it is entirely unsurprising that the learned author of *Treitel: The Law of Contract* considers that the courts at least sometimes employ the jurisdiction to award mental distress damages to achieve much the same result as an award of punitive damages.[168]

It may be replied that the relevance of the defendant's culpability to the assessment of general damages can be explained on a loss-based account of general

[162] *Elliot v Flanagan* (2016) NIQB 8 [28] (Stephens J).

[163] eg, Cane writes that 'one suspects that there is an element of punishment in many of the larger awards of damages by juries in defamation actions': Cane (n 132) 170.

[164] *Aldington v Watts* (High Court, 30 November 1989). The case ultimately went to the European Court of Human Rights, the decision of which is reported as *Miloslavsky v UK* [1996] EMLR 152.

[165] £3,756,578 in today's terms.

[166] *Miloslavsky* (n 164) [12].

[167] See Courtney and Goudkamp, ch 1, section II.B.

[168] E Peel, *Treitel: The Law of Contract*, 15th edn (London, Sweet & Maxwell, 2020) para 20.022.

damages on the basis that the greater the defendant's culpability the greater the insult done to the claimant. The idea is that the claimant's damage is heightened by the fact that it is done deliberately.[169] However, one difficulty with this response is that it cannot explain why it is not the law that the fact that defendant was virtuously motivated does not diminish awards of general damages. More generally, this loss-based account of the relevance of the defendant's culpability is jarring. The simple fact is that it is far more plausible to explain the significance of the defendant's desert by reference to a concern with punishment in circumstances where the defendant's desert is central to whether punishment is merited and, if so, in what amount.

Our final piece of evidence concerns the account of profits remedy. Lord Burrows defines an account of profits as 'an equitable remedy by which the defendant is required to draw up an account of, and then to pay the amount of, the net profits it has acquired by particular wrongful conduct'.[170] Although it is occasionally denied that the account of profits remedy is aimed at punishment,[171] it is clear that it is so concerned, at least in some situations. Famously, in *Attorney-General v Blake*[172] the House of Lords awarded an account against a former member of the British security services who was also a Soviet spy, who, in breach of his contract, published an autobiography that revealed classified information about his work. Delivering the principal speech, Lord Nicholls emphasised that the defendant had committed grave criminal offences that 'caused untold and immeasurable damage to the public interest'[173] and that 'most of the profits from the book derive indirectly from the extremely serious and damaging breaches'[174] of his contractual undertaking. Lord Hobhouse referred to the 'punitive nature of the claim'.[175] His Lordship, although he disagreed with the majority that an account of profits should exceptionally be available for breaches of contract, also said:

> The 'just response' visualised in the present case is … that [the defendant] should be punished and deprived of any fruits of conduct connected with his former criminal and reprehensible conduct. … The policy which is being enforced is that which

[169] Consider the remarks in *Fielding v Variety Inc* (1967) 2 QB 841 (CA) 855 (Salmon LJ remarking that the defendant's blameworthiness could be taken into account not with a view to punishing the defendant but only in so far as the deliberate nature of the defendant's conduct increased the claimant's injury).

[170] Burrows (n 24) 341.

[171] See, eg, *Hollister Inc v Medik Ostomy Supplies Ltd* [2012] EWCA Civ 1419, [2013] Bus LR 428 [69] (Kitchin LJ) ('[an account of profits] ensures the infringer does not benefit from his wrong, but it contains no element of punishment'); *OOO Abbott v Design & Display Ltd* [2016] EWCA Civ 98, [2016] FSR 27 [7] (Lewison LJ) ('An account of profits is confined to profits actually made, its purpose being not to punish the defendant but to prevent his unjust enrichment'); *Tuke v Hood* (2020) EWHC 2843 (Comm) [166] (Jacobs J) ('the disgorgement compelled by the remedy is not by way of punishment').

[172] *Attorney-General v Blake* [2001] 1 AC 268 (HL).

[173] ibid 286.

[174] ibid 287.

[175] ibid 295.

> requires [the defendant] to be punished by depriving him of any benefit from anything connected with his past deplorable criminal conduct.[176]

Consistently with the fact an account of profit is at least sometimes concerned with punishment, the courts often have regard to the defendant's culpability in deciding whether to award an account and in fixing its quantum.[177] For example, the courts may withhold an account where the defendant acted inadvertently,[178] and the courts are unlikely to give a fiduciary an allowance for time and effort expended in obtaining a profit where they have acted in bad faith.[179] Similarly, and very much in line with the rules that apply to awards of punitive damages,[180] cognisance is taken of any other sanctions that have been imposed on the defendant.[181]

It may be replied that an account of profits cannot constitute punishment because its effect is simply to restore the defendant to the position in which they stood prior to the wrong by removing the profit made. As Gareth Jones contended, 'to be deprived of what you have gained can never be a penal liability'.[182] However, this line of reasoning is deeply flawed. In the first place, an account will not necessarily restore the defendant to their earlier position. For example, a defendant against whom an account is ordered will be made worse off by that fact if they are denied an allowance for their time and effort.[183] More fundamentally, even when an account does have the effect of restoring the *status quo ante*, the claim that punishment is not thereby among the remedy's goals is a *non sequitur*. The fact that a given act is not punitive in terms of its effects does not mean that the act concerned was not done for the purpose of punishment but, rather, simply that that goal was not realised in the instant case.[184] Because, as we have seen, the courts have made it explicit that an account is sometimes awarded with a view to punishing the defendant, it is irrelevant for present purposes that an account may not on occasion be punitive in terms of its outcome.

Defenders of the orthodoxy that punitive damages are anomalous may, in response to the foregoing, assert that although certain other remedies pursue the

[176] ibid 295, 299.

[177] See, further, Bant and Paterson's chapter in this volume: ch 10, section IV.

[178] Thus, in *Seager v Copydex Ltd (No 2)* [1969] 1 WLR 809 (CA), an account of profits was withheld because the defendant had used the confidential information in issue inadvertently. And in *Shaw v Holland* [1900] 2 Ch 305 (CA) 310, Webster MR said that '[i]t would … be unfair' to order an account in circumstances where 'it is not suggested that the directors were guilty of any moral fraud'. cf *Peter Pan Manufacturing Corp v Corsets Silhouette Ltd* (1964) 1 WLR 96 (Ch D) 106.

[179] *Boardman v Phipps* [1965] Ch 992 (CA) 1021; *Crown Dilmun v Sutton* (2004) EWHC 52 (Ch), [2004] 1 BCLC 468 [213].

[180] See the text accompanying nn 57–60.

[181] *Devenish Nutrition Ltd v Sanofi-Aventis SA* [2008] EWCA Civ 1086, [2009] Ch 390 [102].

[182] G Jones, 'The Recovery of Benefits Gained from a Breach of Contract' (1983) 99 *LQR* 443, 456. See also A Beever, 'Justice and Punishment in Tort: A Comparative Theoretical Analysis' in C Rickett (ed), *Justifying Private Law Remedies* (Oxford, Hart Publishing, 2008) 247, 296: '[s]tripping profits never punishes'.

[183] See the text to n 179.

[184] Regarding the difference between punishment as an aim of ϕing and punishment as an effect of ϕing, see Barker, ch 2, section II.B.

goal of punishment, punitive damages are nevertheless an aberration because they are always concerned with punishment. However, contrary to this position, and paradoxically given the remedy's name, the courts are not invariably concerned with punishment when they award punitive damages. Consider the fact that punitive damages can be awarded against deceased persons[185] and against defendants whose liability is merely vicarious.[186] Punishment, at least if understood according to HLA Hart's iconic definition,[187] is obviously impossible in these situations: in the former, the defendant cannot have pain or other unpleasantness inflicted upon them, and in the case of the latter the defendant has not committed any wrong. Thus, the better view is that that the courts are not seeking to act retributively when punitive damages are awarded against such defendants but are in fact pursuing one or more of the other acknowledged goals of the remedy, such as deterrence,[188] appeasement[189] or vindication.[190] However, even if, contrary to the foregoing, punitive damages were always concerned with punishment, that would be irrelevant for present purposes. That is because punitive damages are regarded as anomalous *not* because they are always awarded to punish *but simply* because they are concerned with punishment.

The misconception that punitive damages is an anomalous remedy is not a mere academic misunderstanding. It has had, and continues to have, very tangible practical consequences. Thus, the characterisation of punitive damages as anomalous has not only tended to encourage the courts to resist calls to liberate the punitive damages jurisdiction from the stringent restrictions to which it is subject,[191] but it induces judges to be especially (and perhaps excessively) cautious in awarding punitive damages in individual cases. It is entirely possible that judges would approach the punitive damages jurisdiction quite differently from the way in which they do at present but for the erroneous perception that the award is anomalous.

[185] 'Exemplary damages may be claimed from a deceased wrongdoer's estate': Law Commission (n 61) 90. Defamation claims are an exception to this position: Law Reform (Miscellaneous Provisions) Act 1934 (UK), s 1(1).

[186] *Rowlands v Chief Constable of Merseyside Police* [2006] EWCA Civ 1773, [2007] 1 WLR 1065 [47]–[48]. See further Morgan, ch 11 of this volume.

[187] Hart attempted to articulate a 'central case of "punishment" in terms of five elements', namely: (a) it must involve pain or other consequences normally considered unpleasant; (b) it must be for an offence against legal rules; (c) it must be of an actual or supposed offender for their offence; (d) it must be intentionally administered by persons other than the offender; and (e) it must be imposed and administered by an authority constituted by a legal system against which the offence is committed: HLA Hart, 'Prolegomenon to the Principles of Punishment' (1959–1960) 60 *Proceedings of the Aristotelian Society* 1, 4. See further Barker, ch 2, section I.

[188] *Rookes* (n 4) 1221.

[189] *W* (n 4) 264.

[190] *Bottrill* (n 4) [29].

[191] See, eg, Lord Reid in *Broome* (n 4) 1086, who contended that because punitive damages are an 'undesirable anomaly' they 'should not be permitted in any class of case where its use was not covered by authority'. Similarly, in *Axa* (n 35) [25], Flaux LJ said that because punitive damages 'are anomalous … [i]t would … be inappropriate to extend the circumstances in which they can be awarded beyond the three categories of case identified by Lord Devlin [in *Rookes*]'.

E. Punitive Damages are sometimes a Form of Disgorgement Damages

In recent years, punitive damages awarded in cases involving profit-seeking conduct (ie, cases falling within the second *Rookes* category) have increasingly been equated with disgorgement damages, that is, damages that are awarded in order to strip the defendant of gains made through wrongdoing. For example, according to Sedley LJ 'the rationale of the second category of exemplary damages is … the *confiscation* of profits which cannot be got at through the ordinary compensatory mechanisms'.[192] Likewise, in *AT v Dulghieru* Treacy J asserted that '[t]he rationale behind the second category is not the punishment of the Defendant, but the prevention of his unjust enrichment'.[193] This understanding is not confined to the judiciary. Thus Ernest Weinrib argues that punitive damages awarded under second *Rookes* category can be 'explained … in terms of unjust enrichment'.[194] It is worth observing that Weinrib's position here is clearly motivated, at least in part, by his belief that punitive damages are an anomaly in private law. In thrall to this view, which comprised the fourth misconception, he seeks to explain away what he perceives to be an intruder in private law by reimagining punitive damages awarded in the second *Rookes* category as another form of award. This, however, has led him, and others who adopt the same position, into further error since punitive damages awarded in profit-seeking conduct cases are not the same thing as disgorgement damages. That is so even if both types of damages may be awarded in order to punish since functional overlap is different from substantive equivalence.

There are at least two important points of distinction between punitive damages (including punitive damages awarded under the second *Rookes* category) and disgorgement damages. First, whereas disgorgement damages are awarded principally in order to strip the defendant of gains made as a result of wrongdoing,[195] the principal functions of punitive damages are punishment and deterrence. Consequently, punitive damages can be awarded, including under the second category in *Rookes*, in cases where the defendant failed to profit from their wrongdoing.[196] A mere aim to make a profit may support the award of punitive damages but not disgorgement damages.[197] Of course, in such a case, disgorgement damages could not be awarded, because there is no gain onto which they

[192] *Borders* (n 65) [26] (emphasis added).

[193] *AT v Dulghieru* (2009) EWHC 225 (QB) [68].

[194] E Weinrib, *The Idea of Private Law* (Oxford, Oxford University Press 2012) 135, fn 25.

[195] '[O]n the basis of restitutionary principles the object of the award [of damages is] to deprive the defendant of an unjustly acquired gain': *Morris-Garner v One Step (Support) Ltd* [2018] UKSC 20, [2019] AC 649 [58] (Lord Reed).

[196] See, eg, *Archer* (n 60) 423.

[197] N McBride and R Bagshaw, *Tort Law*, 6th edn (Harlow, Pearson, 2018) 765 (emphasis in original): 'There is no reason to think that a defendant *actually* has to have made a gain from his tort for exemplary damages to be awarded against him under the second head in *Rookes* v *Barnard*. All that has to be shown is that he *aimed* to make a gain.'

could latch. Second, different principles apply to the assessment of the two types of damages. Disgorgement damages are calculated by reference to the profit that the defendant made from their wrongful conduct. By contrast, punitive damages are assessed in view of the sum of money that it is necessary to award in order to achieve the goals of punishment and deterrence.[198] Accordingly, the level of punitive damages may differ from the quantum of the defendant's profit.[199] For these two reasons, punitive damages cannot be reduced to a species of disgorgement damages.

F. Precedent Establishes that Prior Punishment is Unimportant in the Decision to Award Punitive Damages

Traditionally, the rule prevailed that if a defendant had already been sanctioned for substantially the same conduct that formed the basis of the civil proceedings, punitive damages should not ordinarily be awarded as the need for punishment and deterrence would already have been satisfied.[200] However, this self-evidently correct principle, which only a few years ago was put onto a statutory footing in the context of wrongs committed by media defendants,[201] has been doubted in England in recent years, and judges in several cases have held, quite wrongly, that authority in fact establishes that the fact of prior punishment is unimportant. The most egregious instances of this error are *AT*[202] and *Axa*.[203] The decisions in both of these cases rely heavily on a misreading of the judgment of the Court of Appeal in *Borders (UK) Ltd v Commissioner of Police of the Metropolis*[204] and so it is sensible for us to begin with that case.

In *Borders*, eight major book retailers sued the defendant in conversion. The defendant, who was a street trader, had sold tens or hundreds of thousands of books that had been stolen from the retailers. The scheme was lucrative (when the police ultimately caught up with him, the defendant had amassed over £600,000[205] from his activities). Before damages were assessed, the defendant was convicted of

[198] See the text accompanying n 50.

[199] See, eg, *Mcmillan v Singh* (1984) 17 HLR 120 (CA), 125–26 (punitive damages awarded in excess of the amount required to achieve restitution of the unlawfully made profits); *AT* (n 193) (the amount of punitive damages less than the defendants' gain).

[200] 'A man should not be punished twice for the same offence and since the function of exemplary damages is to punish a wrongdoer … there is clearly no scope for them where the defendant has already been punished': *Archer* (n 60) 406–07 (Peter Pain J). See also the text accompanying nn 57–60.

[201] Section 35(2) of the Crime and Courts Act 2013 (UK) provides that a 'court must have regard to the principle that exemplary damages must not usually be awarded if, at any time before the decision comes to be made, the defendant has been convicted of an offence involving the conduct complained of'.

[202] See n 193.

[203] See n 35.

[204] See n 65.

[205] £901,817 in today's terms.

conspiracy to steal and to handle stolen goods, for which he received a 30-month custodial sentence. Further, confiscation proceedings had been commenced against him. It was held that neither the custodial sentence nor the prospect of a confiscation order precluded an award of punitive damages of £100,000.[206] Crucially, however, the court assumed that the punitive damages award would reduce the amount of any confiscation order pound-for-pound.[207] Because the value of any confiscation order that might ultimately have been made would be reduced by the value of the punitive damages award, there was no possibility of its resulting in the defendant being mulcted twice. And there was also no risk of double punishment being imposed on the defendant by the punitive damages award and the custodial sentence, because the award of punitive damages was an alternative to the defendant paying £100,000 under the confiscation order, and the confiscation order would have been *additional* to the custodial sentence. As such, the punitive damages award in *Borders* was wholly consistent with the principle that the fact of prior punishment should be taken into account in granting such damages.

In *AT*[208] the defendants had locked four women in a flat and coerced them into prostitution. Treacy J awarded the women punitive damages of £60,000.[209] He did so even though the defendants were subject to confiscation orders and had been sentenced to long terms of imprisonment. The judge, relying on *Borders*, considered that no issue of double punishment arose on account of the confiscation orders. He wrote:

> Since the rationale behind an award of exemplary damages is primarily one of preventing unjust enrichment, I need to consider whether the making of the confiscation orders in the criminal proceedings would in any way preclude an award of exemplary damages. For the reasons analysed in the *Borders* … case, I do not think it would.[210]

Borders, however, was a fundamentally different case. For the reasons that we have given, the spectre of double punishment did not arise in *Borders*. By contrast, in *AT* confiscation orders had already been made against the defendants who had also been imprisoned. The fact that the defendants did not have assets sufficient to satisfy the confiscation orders[211] does not alter the fact that two distinct sanctions (ie, the confiscation orders and custodial sentences) were imposed on the defendants by the criminal court. However, in addition to these sanctions, Treacy J held the defendants liable to pay punitive damages, in clear contravention of the principle against double punishment.

[206] £150,303 in today's terms.
[207] *Borders* (n 65) [17], [41], [46].
[208] See n 193.
[209] £79,817 in today's terms.
[210] *AT* (n 193) [71]–[72].
[211] ibid [71].

In *Axa*[212] the Court of Appeal awarded the claimant insurance company punitive damages of £20,000 in respect of a failed insurance scam. Punitive damages were awarded even though the defendant[213] had previously been sentenced to eight months' imprisonment in respect of the fraud.[214] Flaux LJ considered that the custodial sentence had no bearing on whether punitive damages should be awarded. He declared that 'it [was] nothing to the point that criminal proceedings could have been brought (and indeed were brought against the [defendant])'.[215] The case was analogous, Flaux LJ said, to *Borders*, in which the defendant had been both convicted and ordered to pay punitive damages. His Lordship said that in *Borders* '[t]he existence of the criminal proceedings … was not considered by this Court to affect the award of exemplary damages if appropriate and the argument of double jeopardy was rejected'.[216] While it is true that there was no threat of double punishment in *Borders* for the reasons that we have given, the factual matrix in *Axa* was fundamentally different. Whereas in *Borders* the punitive damages award was made in *substitution* for a confiscation order that would, if and when made, have been *additional* to the custodial sentence, in *Axa* the punitive damages award was simply added to the custodial sentence and, accordingly, comprised double punishment.

The judges in *AT* and *Axa* erred on account of their misunderstanding the facts in *Borders* and departing from authority that stipulates clearly that the jurisdiction to award punitive damages must be exercised subject to the principle that a person should not be punished twice for the same conduct. It is axiomatic that defendants should not be punished more than once in respect of the same or substantially the same wrongdoing, and any suggestion that *Borders* somehow countenances a contrary approach is simply incorrect. As Kirby J rightly put it in the decision of the High Court of Australia of *Gray v Motor Accident Commission*, given that punitive damages are awarded to punish and deter, 'it is impossible to contest, in the face of authority, the relevance of the fact of criminal punishment of the tortfeasor'.[217]

It is worth observing that Tracey J in *AT* appears to have reached the conclusion that he did on account of his perceiving punitive damages awarded under the second *Rookes* category to be, in reality, disgorgement damages (which is the fifth of the misconceptions that we have addressed).[218] In a clearly incorrect remark he said that the 'rationale' for punitive damages awarded in profit-motive cases is 'primarily one of preventing unjust enrichment'.[219] It is unsurprising that Tracey J,

[212] See n 35. For further discussion, see E Katsampouka, 'Exemplary Damages and Insurance Fraud' (2019) 135 *LQR* 380.

[213] There were three defendants in *Axa*. However, only one defendant had been convicted and, accordingly, our focus is on that defendant.

[214] Confiscation proceedings were also pending against the defendant, but these were irrelevant as they did not relate to the fraud, which, because it failed, did not yield any profit that could be confiscated.

[215] *Axa* (n 35) [33].

[216] ibid.

[217] *Gray v Motor Accident Commission* [1998] HCA 70, (1998) 196 CLR 1 [94].

[218] For further discussion on this point, see McBride and Bagshaw (n 197) 818–19.

[219] *AT* (n 193) [71]–[72].

having been ensnared by the fifth misconception, also found himself entrapped by the sixth. What matters, if one thinks that punitive damages are sometimes about preventing unjust enrichment, is simply whether there is a gain that falls to be removed, and on this account whether or not prior punishment was imposed on the defendant is neither here nor there. However, because punitive damages are, as has repeatedly been made clear at the ultimate appellate level,[220] first and foremost about punishment and deterrence, it is imperative to ascertain whether those goals have already been served before any award of punitive damages is made.

Is prior punishment in respect of the same or substantially the same wrongdoing an absolute bar on punitive damages or merely a factor to consider in deciding whether to award punitive damages? The High Court of Australia embraced the former view in its important decision in *Gray*,[221] at least where the prior punishment was 'substantial', which the Court considered might arguably not be the case where, for example, the criminal law imposed only a nominal sanction on the offender due to the offender's personal circumstances. The Court gave two reasons in this regard. The first was that where substantial prior punishment has been imposed on the defendant the need to punish and deter will already have been met,[222] and the second was that any other approach would violate the principle against imposing double punishment.[223] Although an automatic bar has the advantage of simplicity and guards against excessive punishment, we doubt that a bright-line rule is appropriate. One can readily envisage situations where an absolute bar may cause difficulty, such as where, for example, the sentence imposed by a criminal court was substantial but nevertheless severely limited by reason of the sentencing power of the criminal court concerned. In these circumstances, it is difficult to say that the need for punishment and deterrence will have been fully met by the prior punishment. Further, the absence of a bright-line rule is consistent with the approach that the criminal law courts would take where the civil claim is determined prior to the criminal proceedings being resolved: it could not plausibly be suggested that the award of punitive damages would automatically preclude the offender from being sentenced by the criminal court (although the existence of the prior punishment would, of course, be a matter that the sentencing judge would consider in the exercise of their discretion[224]).

G. Precedent Justifies the Categories Test

In *Rookes*, Lord Devlin limited the power to award punitive damages to just three categories of case. He sought to justify his 'categories test', or more particularly

[220] See the authorities cited in n 4.
[221] *Gray* (n 217) [40].
[222] ibid [42].
[223] ibid [43].
[224] '[T]he Court usually gives some discount to reflect the element of "double jeopardy"': A Ashworth, *Sentencing and Criminal Justice*, 5th edn (Cambridge, Cambridge University Press, 2010) 40.

the existence of the first and second categories, on the basis of precedent.[225] He contended that those categories '[were] established as part of the common law'.[226] Lord Devlin wrote:

> The … authorities convince me … that there are certain categories of cases in which an award of exemplary damages can serve a useful purpose in vindicating the strength of the law … I propose to state what these two categories are …
>
> The first category is oppressive, arbitrary or unconstitutional action by the servants of the government. …
>
> Cases in the second category are those in which the defendant's conduct has been calculated by him to make a profit for himself which may well exceed the compensation payable to the plaintiff. …
>
> To these two categories which … are established as part of the common law there must of course be added any category in which exemplary damages are expressly authorised by statute. … I must now return to the authorities I have already reviewed and make quite plain what it is that I have not accepted from them.[227]

Lord Devlin's claim that the categories are founded on precedent seems to have been accepted in most quarters. For example, according to the Law Commission, '[a]t common law [Lord Devlin] limited [the] scope [of exemplary damages] to two classes of case … where their availability was justified by precedent'.[228] Similarly, Ernest Weinrib said that '[i]n England … the House of Lords … restricted the scope [of exemplary damages] to the minimum allowed by precedent'.[229] This acceptance is particularly important given that it is generally thought that the categories test otherwise has little, if anything, to commend it. As has often been observed,[230] the test is inconsistent with the goals of awarding punitive damages because the need for punishment and deterrence can clearly arise in situations that do not fall within either of Lord Devlin's categories.[231] In short, it is on account of precedent and precedent alone by which the categories test maintains a foothold in English law (it is unsurprising that courts in other jurisdictions that are not bound by the English precedents in issue have condemned it unreservedly[232]).

[225] For further analysis, see E Katsampouka, 'A Critical Assessment of *Rookes v Barnard*' (forthcoming).

[226] *Rookes* (n 4) 1228.

[227] ibid 1225–28.

[228] Law Commission (n 61) 14–15 (emphasis added).

[229] E Weinrib, 'Punishment and Disgorgement as Contract Remedies' (2003) 78 *Chicago-Kent Law Review* 55, 84.

[230] See, eg, Law Commission, *Aggravated, Exemplary and Restitutionary Damages* (Law Com No 247, 1997) 59, 105.

[231] See, eg, *Loudon* (n 56) (expressly overruled in *Rookes* (n 4) 1229). In *Loudon*, the defendant entered the claimant's flat through a window and attacked her. Although the defendant's conduct falls outside the *Rookes* categories (because the defendant was not a public servant and did not act with a 'profit motive'), the behaviour plainly merited the award of punitive damages according to the rationales for the remedy.

[232] The categories test has been forcefully rejected elsewhere in the common law world: *Uren v John Fairfax & Son Pty Ltd* (1966) 117 CLR 118 (Australia); *Vorvis v Insurance Corp of British Columbia* (1989) 1 SCR 1085 (Supreme Court of Canada); *Taylor v Beere* (1982) 1 NZLR 81 (New Zealand Court of Appeal); *Conway v Irish National Teachers Organisation* (1991) 2 IR 305 (Supreme Court of Ireland) [324];

However, Lord Devlin's contention that the categories are based on precedent does not withstand scrutiny.[233] Lord Devlin considered that three decisions – *Wilkes v Wood*,[234] *Huckle v Money*[235] and *Benson v Frederick*[236] – demonstrated the existence of 'category 1' (oppressive, arbitrary or unconstitutional conduct by government servants). However, in none of these cases did the court in awarding punitive damages attach importance to the fact that the defendant was a public servant.[237] Rather, it was the defendant's arbitrary and outrageous conduct that justified a punitive response, and it was simply coincidental that the defendant was a government servant.

Consistently with this interpretation of the three cases on which Lord Devlin relied, commentators writing in the pre-*Rookes* era considered the defendant's conduct (rather than the defendant's capacity) as enlivening the jurisdiction to award punitive damages.[238] For example, Sir Percy Winfield, with reference to *Wilkes*, wrote:

> [I]n exemplary damages [the court] can punish the defendant for … an especially outrageous attack on the plaintiff's security … [This] is illustrated by the cases deciding against the legality of the search warrants which were issued against John Wilkes and others during the latter part of the eighteenth century.[239]

Winfield made no mention of the fact that the defendant was a public servant.

As to the second category, Lord Devlin again contended that three cases supported its existence: *Bell v Midland Railway Co*,[240] *Williams v Currie*[241] and

ACB v Thomson Medical Pte Ltd [2017] SGCA 20, [2017] 1 SLR 918 (Singapore Court of Appeal). cf *Allan v Ng & Co* [2012] HKCA 119, [2012] 2 HKLRD 160 [24] (Hong Kong Court of Appeal). Even courts in England have refused to follow the categories test. In *Broome v Cassell & Co Ltd* (1971) 2 QB 354 (CA) 380 the Court of Appeal dramatically declined to follow *Rookes*, branding it as being 'per incuriam' (at 382 (Lord Denning MR)) and 'unworkable in practice' (at 397 (Phillimore LJ)). The House of Lords allowed an appeal and, delivering a sharp rebuke to the Court of Appeal, held that the categories test had to be applied: *Broome* (n 4).

233 We are not alone in making this claim: see, eg, the remarks in *Uren v John Fairfax & Son Pty Ltd* (1966) 117 CLR 118 (HCA) 130–37; *Broome* (n 232) 386.

234 *Wilkes v Wood* (1763) Lofft 1; 98 ER 489.

235 *Huckle v Money* (1763) 2 Wils KB 205; 95 ER 768.

236 *Benson v Frederick* (1766) 3 Burr 1845; 97 ER 1130.

237 In *Huckle* (n 235) Wils KB 207; ER 769, Camden LCJ upheld an award of augmented damages for false imprisonment on the basis that there had been 'a most daring public attack made upon the liberty of the subject [and] that the 29th chapter of Magna Charta … which is pointed against arbitrary power, was violated'. In *Wilkes* (n 234) Lofft 18; ER 498, Pratt LCJ justified an award of punitive damages for trespass to land on the basis that a discretionary power to enter and search houses upon a general warrant could 'affect the person and property of every man … and [would be] totally subversive of the liberty of the subject'. Finally, in *Benson* (n 236) Burr 1846; ER 1130, Lord Mansfield upheld the award of punitive damages for battery where '[the defendant] had manifestly acted arbitrarily, unjustifiably and unreasonably'.

238 However, at least one textbook of that period refers to 'abuses by officers of the law' as a category of case in which punitive damages may be awarded: see WE Ball, *Principles of Torts and Contracts* (London, Stevens & Sons, 1880) 110 (citing *Duke of Brunswick v Slowman* (1849) 8 CB 317; 137 ER 532 in support).

239 P Winfield, *A Textbook on the Law of Torts*, 5th edn (London, Sweet & Maxwell, 1950) 150.

240 *Bell v Midland Railway Co* (1861) 10 CBNS 287; 142 ER 462.

241 *Williams v Currie* (1845) 1 CB 841; 135 ER 774.

Crouch v Great Northern Railway Co.[242] It is arguable that the last two cases were not, in fact, concerned with punitive damages but with aggravated damages.[243] However, even if those decisions did involve punitive damages, by far the better view is that the courts did not regard the existence of a profit motive as a pre-condition to an award of punitive damages but simply as reinforcing the conclusion that an award was merited. In relation to *Bell*, Lord Devlin relied on Erie CJ's remark in that case that an award of £1,000[244] for private nuisance was not excessive because the 'company [had] set up a wharf of their own, and, careless whether they were doing right or wrong, prevented all access to the plaintiff's wharf, *for the purpose of extinguishing his trade and advancing their own profit*'.[245] However, Erie CJ did not suggest that the aim of making a profit was a pre-condition to awarding punitive damages. It is far more plausible to think that the defendant's profit motive was not regarded as a *condition* that had to be satisfied in order to enliven the jurisdiction to award punitive damages but merely as an *indication* that punitive damages were warranted on the facts. Precisely the same point can be made about *Williams*[246] and *Crouch*.[247]

In summary, precedent does not support the categories test, contrary to what Lord Devlin claimed, and the development of that test must rank among one of the House of Lords' grander mistakes. Given that the sole source of support for the categories test is the belief that precedent requires its recognition, the case for abolishing the test is irresistible.

H. Precedent Justifies the Unavailability of Punitive Damages for Breach of Contract

It is widely thought that *Addis v Gramophone Co Ltd*[248] established that punitive damages are unavailable in claims for breach of contract.[249] For example, the Law Commission with reference to *Addis* said that punitive damages 'are clearly

[242] *Crouch v Great Northern Railway Co* (1856) 11 Exch 742; 156 ER 1031.

[243] Lord Devlin himself interpreted *Williams* as an aggravated damages case: *Rookes* (n 4) 1229. As for *Crouch* (n 242), only one of the three judges who decided that case, Martin B, used terminology – 'vindictive' damages – that was potentially consistent with the concept of punitive damages. However, that language is hardly decisive considering that the terms 'vindictive', 'exemplary' and 'aggravated' damages were used more or less interchangeably at the time.

[244] £119,815 in today's terms.

[245] *Bell* (n 240) CBNS 304; ER 469 (emphasis added).

[246] *Williams* (n 241) CB 848; ER 776–77. Only one of the three judges in *Williams*, Maule J, referred to the defendant's profit motive. However, he also referred to the defendant's persistence in trespassing upon the claimant's goods for several weeks in justifying the inflated damages award.

[247] In *Crouch* (n 242) Exch 759; ER 1038, Martin B provided a hypothetical scenario similar to the facts of *Crouch* in which he may have contemplated that the award of punitive damages would be justified.

[248] *Addis v Gramophone Co Ltd* [1909] AC 488 (HL).

[249] Regarding punitive damages in contract, see Barnett, ch 9 of this volume.

unavailable in a claim for breach of contract'.[250] Similarly, Ewan McKendrick writes that 'punitive damages … cannot be awarded in a purely contractual action … (*Addis v Gramophone Co Ltd* …)'.[251] However, *Addis* is exceptionally feeble authority in support of this understanding (and, arguably, no authority at all).

The defendants in *Addis* had dismissed the claimant employee from their service and the claimant sued them for breach of contract. A jury awarded the claimant, relevantly, £600.[252] The defendants challenged that sum on an appeal to the House of Lords. Lord Loreburn LC did not say anything explicit about punitive damages in his speech. His Lordship focused on the extent to which the award included a sum to compensate the claimant for injured feelings owing to the circumstances of his dismissal and a sum to reflect the difficulty that the claimant might encounter in securing employment in the future owing to his having been dismissed. The Lord Chancellor held that the award should not stand to the extent that it 'include[d] *compensation*'[253] in respect of those losses. Lord James and Lord Shaw agreed with the Lord Chancellor. Lord Atkinson, who also agreed with the Lord Chancellor that the award should be set aside, said 'I have always understood that damages for breach of contract were in the nature of compensation, not punishment'.[254] His Lordship concluded that punitive damages 'ought not to be, and are not according to any true principle of law, recoverable in such an action as the present'.[255] Conversely, Lord Collins seemed to consider that 'what are called exemplary or vindictive damages'[256] were available in contract.[257] Lord Gorell in brief reasons remarked that he could find neither 'authority nor principle for the contention that [the claimant] is entitled to have damages for the manner in which his discharge took place'.[258] The result of the decision was that the claimant could not recover damages for the manner of his dismissal.

It is plain from the foregoing that *Addis* provides only the slenderest support, if any, for the proposition that punitive damages are unavailable in a claim for breach of contract. Save for Lord Atkinson, the majority did not clearly refer to punitive damages, and it is difficult, if not impossible, to know whether the case is about punitive damages or aggravated damages (or mental distress damages), as no sharp distinction then existed between the two varieties of damages. Given that *Addis* has been treated as authority for the proposition that punitive damages cannot be awarded in respect of breaches of contract, it is ironic that *Addis*, if anything, suggests that punitive damages were once available in contract. Thus, Lord Atkinson, who drew a clear distinction between compensation and

[250] Law Commission (n 230) 63.
[251] E McKendrick, *Contract Law*, 11th edn (London, Macmillan, 2015) 341.
[252] £71,889 in today's terms.
[253] *Addis* (n 248) 491 (emphasis added).
[254] ibid 494.
[255] ibid 496.
[256] ibid 497.
[257] ibid 500.
[258] ibid 501.

punishment, recognised that although punitive damages were generally unavailable for breaches of contract, there were 'three well-known exceptions'[259] to that rule: (i) actions for breach of promise to marry; (ii) actions against a banker who refuses to pay a customer's cheque although there are sufficient funds to meet it; and (iii) actions against the vendor of real estate who fails to confer title.[260] We observe that treatise writers of the day similarly considered that breaches of contract could be met with awards of punitive damages. For example, in 1908 (the year before *Addis* was decided) Sir Frederick Pollock wrote that the availability of punitive damages in breach of promise to marry cases might lead to 'like results … in the case of other breaches of contract accompanied with circumstances of wanton injury or contumely'.[261]

In view of the foregoing, it is baffling how *Addis* came widely to be regarded as laying down the firm rule that punitive damages are unavailable in an action for breach of contract. The misreading of it by contract lawyers over the course of more than a century must be regarded as one of the more striking misunderstandings ever committed in that field. Of course, numerous intervening decisions have since confirmed that punitive damages cannot be awarded in respect of breaches of contract.[262] However, the position, in so far as it depends on a misinterpretation of *Addis*, is vulnerable to challenge, especially in view of *Kuddus*, which, by abolishing the cause of action test,[263] suggests that the availability of punitive damages should not be artificially constrained to particular causes of action but ought to be available whenever there is a need for punishment and deterrence that the award of compensatory damages has left unsatisfied.

I. Negligent Conduct cannot Engage the Punitive Damages Jurisdiction

As observed,[264] we have been unable to identify a single case in the UK in which liability in negligence attracted an award of punitive damages.[265] There are at least two explanations for this situation. First, it may be due to an unarticulated cause of action bar on punitive damages being awarded in claims based on the tort

[259] ibid 495.
[260] ibid.
[261] F Pollock, *The Law of Torts*, 8th edn (London, Stevens, 1908) 560. See also E Jenks, *The Book of English Law*, 5th edn (London, Wyman & Sons 1953) 196–97: '"Vindictive damages" … are not infrequently awarded in cases of tort, and even, though much more rarely, in cases of breach of contract. They are intended to mark the disapproval by the Court or the jury of the defendant's conduct.'
[262] See the text accompanying n 45.
[263] See the text accompanying n 43.
[264] See the text accompanying n 49.
[265] Although see *In Re Organ Retention Group Litigation* [2004] EWHC 644 (QB), [2005] QB 506 [262]–[263], where Gage J appears to assume that punitive damages may be available in a claim in the tort of negligence. In *Sharma v Noon Products Ltd* (HC, 7 April 2011) [13], HHJ Yelton declined to say that punitive damages were unavailable in a claim in respect of negligently inflicted personal injuries.

of negligence.[266] This explanation, however, sits uneasily with the the decision of the House of Lords in *Kuddus* to eliminate the cause of action test.[267] Second, the absence of negligence cases in which punitive damages were awarded may also be attributable to a belief that negligent conduct cannot, by its very nature, enliven the jurisdiction to award punitive damages. There is no doubt that this belief is held in some quarters. For example, James Edelman writes that '[i]t would not usually be expected that actions in negligence would lead to exemplary damages … since the necessary mental element is not present; and it is thought that this would be true even of gross negligence'.[268] In our view, this position is afflicted with serious confusion, and it comprises the ninth misconception.

Edelman's argument that negligent conduct lacks the qualities necessary to enliven the jurisdiction to award punitive damages depends on two propositions, both of which are false. The first is that the jurisdiction to award punitive damages requires a 'mental element' and the second is that that 'mental element' will not be 'present' where liability arises in the tort of negligence. The first proposition is erroneous because it is perfectly possible for the prerequisites to the award of punitive damages to be satisfied without the claimant establishing that the defendant had any given state of mind (and it is noteworthy that Edelman leaves the suggested 'mental element' unidentified). Thus, and by way of example, while it is accepted that the second *Rookes* category requires proof of a 'mental state' (ie, a profit motive) the first category does not, it being entirely possible to act oppressively, arbitrarily or unconstitutionally without possessing any particular state of mind.[269]

The second proposition depends on the first (because it assumes that punitive damages can only be awarded on proof of a mental state) and thus crumbles together with it. However, to the extent that the second proposition commits to the idea that negligence involves inadvertence or inattentiveness it is in any event incorrect.[270] The understanding that negligence is a state of mind was long promoted by Sir John Salmond.[271] However, the fact of the matter is that merely having a 'blank' mind with respect to a given risk of injury neither makes one negligent with respect to that risk, nor is it a prerequisite to being adjudged to have

[266] The existence of such a bar is consistent with Lord Bridge's remark in *Hicks v Chief Constable of South Yorkshire* [1992] 2 All ER 65 (HL) 68 that 'damages in a civil action for negligence … are compensatory, not punitive'.

[267] See the text accompanying n 43.

[268] J Edelman, *McGregor on Damages*, 20th edn (London, Sweet & Maxwell, 2017) para 13.015.

[269] See, eg, *Muuse* (n 9), in which punitive damages were awarded for unlawful detention even though the officers involved were unaware that they were unlawfully detaining the claimant.

[270] This understanding of the concept of negligence was famously demolished by Hart: see HLA Hart, *Punishment and Responsibility: Essays in the Philosophy of Law* (Oxford, Oxford University Press, 1968) 147–48.

[271] Negligence 'essentially consists *in the mental attitude of undue indifference with respect to one's conduct and its consequences*. … Negligence … is rightly treated as a form of *mens rea*, standing side by side with wrongful intention as a formal ground of responsibility': J Salmond, *Jurisprudence*, 7th edn (London, Sweet & Maxwell, 1924) 410 (emphasis in original).

been negligent. That is because negligence, as the authorities have long made clear, is a type of conduct, namely, taking less care than the reasonable person would have exercised in the circumstances.[272] Accordingly, there is nothing contradictory in concluding that a given defendant was both negligent and an intentional wrongdoer. As Peter Cane incisively observes:

> Negligence in tort law is failure to comply with a legally specified standard of conduct, pure and simple. … Inadvertence is not a precondition of tort liability for negligence (or under any other head). … [I]f a driver intentionally rams a pedestrian with their car in order to injure, and emotionally desiring to injure, the pedestrian, the driver could be held liable in tort for negligence on the ground that a person who does that fails to take reasonable care for the safety of another.[273]

Closely related to the two foregoing errors is a third mistake that has also wrongly led those who have committed it to the conclusion that negligent conduct cannot engage the jurisdiction to award punitive damages. That mistake is the idea that negligent behaviour is insufficiently serious to merit punishment. This understanding was endorsed by the Law Commission, which wrote:

> We do not consider that 'mere' or even 'grossly' negligent conduct should give rise to an award of punitive damages. Such conduct is not so serious that our society does or indeed should generally seek to punish such a wrongdoer, rather than, in particular, demand that he or she make reparation for the loss so caused to the plaintiff. This intuition is confirmed by a comparison with the criminal law, in which offences can only very exceptionally be satisfied by 'mere' negligent conduct.[274]

Contrary to what the Law Commission contended was 'confirmed by a comparison with the criminal law', it is perfectly plain – indeed, it is notorious – that the criminal law makes sweeping (rather than very exceptional) use of negligence-based liability. As the author of a leading criminal law textbook observes, 'there are many offences of negligence among the statutory offences regulating various commercial and other activities, often taking the form of an indictable offence'.[275] We hasten to add that it is certainly not the case that negligence-based liability is restricted to regulatory offences. So-called 'core' offences, such as manslaughter[276] and rape,[277] can be negligently committed. Indeed, very frequently the criminal

[272] 'Negligence is the omission to do something which a reasonable man, guided upon those considerations which ordinarily regulate the conduct of human affairs, would do, or doing something which a prudent and reasonable man would not do': *Blyth v Birmingham Waterworks Co* (1856) 11 Ex 781, 784; 156 ER 1047, 1049 (Alderson B).

[273] P Cane, 'Mens Rea in Tort Law' (2000) 20 *OJLS* 533, 536. See also P Handford, 'Intentional Negligence – A Contradiction in Terms?' (2010) 32 *Sydney Law Review* 29.

[274] Law Commission (n 230) 109. See also *Gray* (n 217) [22] (Gleeson CJ, McHugh, Gummow and Hayne JJ) ('exemplary damages could not properly be awarded in a case of alleged negligence in which there was no conscious wrongdoing by the defendant').

[275] J Horder, *Ashworth's Principles of Criminal Law*, 9th edn (Oxford, Oxford University Press, 2019) 205.

[276] See the text to n 281.

[277] Sexual Offences Act 2003 (UK), s 1(1) (imposing liability where D negligently believed that V consented).

law does not require fault of any variety at all. This has long been emphasised by distinguished criminal law scholars. Thus, Andrew Ashworth and Meredith Blake, in a well-known empirical study of the incidence of strict liability in offences triable in the Crown Court, reported that '45 per cent have an element of strict liability'.[278] In these circumstances, the Law Commission's stance that the criminal law 'very exceptionally' punishes wrongdoers who do not intentionally injure others betrays a fundamental misunderstanding of some of the most elementary features of the criminal law.

Further, in so far as the Law Commission suggests that negligent behaviour cannot entail significant culpability, that position must be firmly rejected.[279] The fact of the matter is that there is only a relatively loose correlation between at least certain species of fault recognised by the law and culpability.[280] Consequently, whereas some negligent defendants will be morally blameless (paradigmatically, shortcomers who were incapable of achieving the standard of the reasonable person), others will merit significant condemnation. Consider, for example, a defendant who causes the death of another through criminal negligence, that is, negligence that is so egregious that it goes 'beyond a mere matter of compensation between subjects and show[s] such disregard for the life and safety of others as to amount to a crime against the State and conduct deserving punishment'.[281] The Law Commission's commitment to the proposition that such a defendant's wrongdoing is 'not so serious' is nothing short of mystifying. It cannot explain why the criminal law holds such persons liable for manslaughter, which offence is triable only on indictment and punishable by a sentence of life imprisonment.

In summary, the absence of cases in this jurisdiction in which punitive damages have been awarded for negligent conduct appears to stem from mistaken beliefs regarding the nature of both negligence and the criminal law. None of the foregoing is meant to deny, of course, that a major conceptual distinction exists between negligence on the one hand and intentional and reckless wrongdoing on the other. Nor do we contend, needless to say, that the jurisdiction to award punitive damages should not be reserved for behaviour that evidences significant culpability (it clearly should be).[282] The modest point that we have made in this section is that there is no reason why, provided that negligent behaviour is sufficiently

[278] A Ashworth and M Blake, 'The Presumption of Innocence in English Criminal Law' [1996] *Crim LR* 306, 309.

[279] We are reminded of Hart's claim that 'if we are going in for the business at all, it does not appear unduly harsh, or a sign of archaic or unenlightened conceptions of responsibility, to include gross, unthinking carelessness among the things for which we blame and punish': Hart (n 270) 136.

[280] For discussion, see J Goldberg, 'Ten Half-Truths about Tort Law' (2008) 42 *Valparaiso Law Review* 1221, 1259–61.

[281] *R v Bateman (Percy)* (1927) 19 Cr App R 8 (CA) 11–12 (Lord Hewart CJ).

[282] 'The absence of intentional wrongdoing and conscious recklessness will always point strongly away from the case being apt for an award of exemplary damages': *Bottrill* (n 4) [37] (Lord Nicholls). See also at [43], where Lord Nicholls added that '[r]ightly, exemplary damages are associated primarily with intentional wrongdoing'.

culpable and thus creates a need for punishment and deterrence, it should not be met with an award of punitive damages.[283]

J. Punitive Damages can be Reduced for Contributory Negligence

One of the most important pieces of legislation in private law, the Law Reform Contributory Negligence Act 1945 (UK),[284] provides that:

> Where any person suffers damage as the result partly of his own fault and partly of the fault of any other person or persons, a claim in respect of that damage shall not be defeated by reason of the fault of the person suffering the damage, but the damages recoverable in respect thereof shall be reduced to such extent as the court thinks just and equitable having regard to the claimant's share in the responsibility for the damage.[285]

An interesting question arises as to whether awards of punitive damages are amenable to reduction for contributory negligence. The issue, admittedly, is more of theoretical rather than practical significance given that the doctrine of contributory negligence does not apply to torts in which punitive damages tend to be awarded with some regularity, such as trespass to the person,[286] trespass to goods[287] and deceit.[288] There does not appear to be any case law that is directly on point,[289] but the dominant view seems to be that the statute extends to punitive damages. For example, Michael Tilbury and Harold Luntz assert that the apportionment provisions 'are capable of encompassing exemplary damages'.[290] The Law Commission was more circumspect but nevertheless seemed to accept that punitive damages might be limited by the apportionment provision. It wrote that '[i]t is arguable' that the 1945 Act applies to awards of punitive damages.[291]

[283] This, rightly in our view, was the rule that the Privy Council in *Bottrill* (n 4) held was the law in New Zealand. The decision in *Couch v Attorney General (No 2)* [2010] NZSC 27, [2010] 3 NZLR 149 of a majority of the Supreme Court of New Zealand to depart from *Bottrill* was a retrograde development.

[284] See, generally, J Goudkamp and D Nolan, *Contributory Negligence: Principles and Practice* (Oxford, Oxford University Press, 2018); J Goudkamp and D Nolan, *Contributory Negligence in the Twenty-First Century* (Oxford, Oxford University Press, 2019).

[285] s 1(1).

[286] *Co-Operative Group (CWS) Ltd v Pritchard* [2011] EWCA Civ 329, [2012] QB 320.

[287] Torts (Interference with Goods) Act 1977 (UK), s 11(1).

[288] *Standard Chartered Bank v Pakistan National Shipping Corp (Nos 2 and 4)* [2002] UKHL 43, [2003] 1 AC 959. Regarding the high frequency of punitive damages awards in property torts and the tort of deceit, see Goudkamp and Katsampouka (n 63) 105–06.

[289] Punitive damages were awarded in *Ali v Hartley Poynton Ltd* [2002] VSC 113, [2002] *Aust Torts Reports* 81-665, in which the judge assumed (but without analysis) that the apportionment provision applied only to the compensatory damages.

[290] M Tilbury and H Luntz, 'Punitive Damages in Australian Law' (1995) 17 *Loyola of Los Angeles International & Comparative Law Journal* 769, 790. See also V Schwartz and C Appel, 'Two Wrongs Do Not Make a Right: Reconsidering the Application of Comparative Fault to Punitive Damages Awards' (2013) 78 *Missouri Law Review* 133, 135 (arguing that 'where punitive damages are awarded … comparative fault principles should apply').

[291] Law Commission (n 230) 81, fn 475.

The question whether punitive damages can be reduced for contributory negligence must be resolved by reference to the statutory language. The apportionment provision states that 'the damages recoverable' by the claimant shall be reduced when the claimant is contributorily negligent. The word 'damages' is, of course, capable of encompassing punitive damages. However, that word is best construed as referring only to compensatory damages. Note that reductions in the claimant's 'damages' under the apportionment provision are determined by reference to the parties' respective shares 'in the responsibility for the damage'. The term 'damage' refers, of course, to the claimant's loss. This implies that the 'damages' to which the apportionment provision refers are those relating to the harm suffered by the claimant. Those 'damages' are compensatory damages, not punitive (or other types of) damages. Reinforcing this understanding is the fact that it is well established that wrongdoing by the claimant should be considered in determining both whether punitive damages should be awarded[292] and their assessment.[293] Accordingly, cutting back punitive damages for contributory negligence would often involve impermissible double-counting.

IV. Conclusion

Sound analysis of the law governing punitive damages will remain impossible unless and until the many fundamental mistakes that afflict thinking regarding this field are corrected. The 10 misconceptions that we have addressed in this chapter have caused no end of difficulty: they have variously prompted judges and commentators to lash out at imaginary problems,[294] elicited misguided attempts to recast punitive damages as another species of award[295] (which attempts are as imaginative as they are implausible) and encouraged efforts artificially to narrow the jurisdiction to award punitive damages.[296] Thus, in this chapter we have sought to expose and debunk these erroneous claims regarding punitive damages, and in doing so hope to have cleared the way for more constructive consideration of this challenging but fascinating part of the law.

[292] 'The plaintiff's conduct may serve to exclude exemplary damages altogether': ibid 69.

[293] 'Thus provocative conduct which results in a wrongful arrest may lead to a reduced award of exemplary damages. The reason is that such conduct will usually reduce the impropriety of the defendant's reaction': ibid 81.

[294] Consider, eg, the supposed 'problem' that punitive damages awards are often excessive: see section III.A.

[295] See the text to n 194. See also R Stevens, *Torts and Rights* (Oxford, Oxford University Press, 2007) 87 (seeking to recharacterise punitive damages as 'substitutive damages').

[296] See the text to n 191.

9

Exemplary Damages in Contract Law

KATY BARNETT*

I. Introduction

In this chapter, I discuss the traditional rule that exemplary damages[1] should not be awarded in contract. I suggest that although generally speaking exemplary damages will *not* be appropriate for breach of contract, a blanket ban is not merited. This echoes the Singaporean Court of Appeal in *PH Hydraulics & Engineering Pte Ltd v Airtrust (Hong Kong) Ltd*, which stated that although generally exemplary damages should not be available for breach of contract,

> we would not rule out entirely the possibility that a case may one day come before this court, involving a particularly outrageous type of breach, which necessitates departing from the general rule. As was said in a case concerning punitive damages for negligence '"never say never" is a sound judicial admonition' (see the Privy Council decision of *A v Bottrill* [2003] 1 AC 449 at [26] *per* Lord Nicholls of Birkenhead).[2]

However, more guidance is needed: it is not enough to say that exemplary damages in contract are 'highly exceptional'. In this chapter, I suggest some guiding factors. First, it should be emphasised that if *any* other kind of award is available and adequate, including mental distress damages, reasonable fees or accounts of profit for breach of contract, these should be awarded instead. Second, it must be

* This chapter was derived from parts of a paper I presented at the Conference on Punishment and Private Law at the National University of Singapore, 16–18 December 2019. Thank you to the participants for their helpful comments at that conference, to Andy Roberts and Megan Richardson for their comments on the paper I presented there, and to Elise Bant, Wayne Courtney and James Goudkamp for their comments on a draft of the chapter.

[1] Although exemplary damages are also known as punitive damages (particularly in the United States), I will retain the Anglo-Australian nomenclature: see M Tilbury and H Luntz, 'Punitive Damages in Australian Law' (1995) 17 *Loyola of Los Angeles International and Comparative Law Journal* 769, 773–75, describing the history and differences between Australian and US law in relation to exemplary/punitive damages. cf NJ McBride, 'A Case for Awarding Punitive Damages in Response to Deliberate Breaches of Contract' (1995) 24 *Anglo-American Law Review* 369, 369, fn 1, who prefers the term 'punitive damages'.

[2] *PH Hydraulics & Engineering Pte Ltd v Airtrust (Hong Kong) Ltd* [2017] SGCA 26, [2017] 2 SLR 129 [136] (Full Court).

shown that the defendant's conduct is malicious or egregious (not just ordinary commercial brinksmanship) and that the general public would find such conduct repugnant, which links to the necessity to show that the defendant is deserving of retribution. Third, it is suggested that the plaintiff must have a legitimate interest in ensuring the contract is performed. A factor that indicates a legitimate interest may be whether there is an 'agency problem' in the economic sense, where one party agrees to act in another's interests pursuant to the contract, so that all the risk lies on the other (more vulnerable) party's side, it is in the interests of the first party to breach and it is difficult to detect the breach before it occurs. The court must also identify a broader societal reason why we wish to deter the breach in question, and the breach must be of a nature where a declaratory punishment is necessary having regard to those reasons. Some guidance can be taken from other areas of law and consumer law statutes in particular.

Because the justification for the rule against exemplary damages in contract is in part historical, in section II of this chapter I relate a short history of exemplary damages in private law and their origins in tort. In section III I consider the normative bases for exemplary damages given by courts and the main criticisms of this. In section IV I will discuss exemplary damages for breach of contract and explore the reasons why the only jurisdiction that has allowed exemplary damages for breach of contract is Canada, although as noted, Singapore has also left the possibility open in highly exceptional circumstances. In section V I suggest some criteria for the award of exemplary damages in contract, with an attempt to identify what kind of highly exceptional circumstances might give rise to an award.

II. The History of Exemplary Damages in Private Law

Others in this collection have outlined the history of exemplary damages,[3] and therefore my exposition will be brief and relate to how the history affects the availability of exemplary damages in contract. Exemplary damages are traditionally associated with the common law, not equity; and with tort, not contract.[4] In *Uren v John Fairfax & Sons Pty Ltd*, Windeyer J noted that the availability of exemplary damages in tort arises from tort law's historical kinship with crime:

> Compensation is the dominant remedy if not the purpose of the law of torts today. But fault still has a place in many forms of wrongdoing. And the roots of tort and crime in the law of England are greatly intermingled. Some things that today are seen as anomalies have roots that go deep, too deep for them to be easily uprooted.[5]

Many torts were (and still are) mirrored by criminal offences. In the past, civil wrongs were less distinct from criminal wrongs, particularly as criminal wrongs

[3] Barker, ch 2 of this volume, outlines the history in more detail.

[4] As McBride (n 1) 370 notes, it is natural to presume that longstanding rules and practices have some reasonable rationale.

[5] *Uren v John Fairfax & Sons Pty Ltd* [1966] HCA 40, (1966) 117 CLR 118, 149–50.

were also prosecuted by an individual not by the state. Punishment trickled down from the criminal law into the law of tort.

While exemplary damages have historically been available for a broad range of torts, as other chapters in this book outline, the availability of exemplary damages in England and Wales differs. The House of Lords in *Rookes v Barnard* dramatically narrowed the circumstances in which exemplary damages could be awarded to three categories: oppressive, arbitrary or unconstitutional acts by servants of the government; cynical profit-making; and where authorised by statute.[6] These categories were confirmed by the House of Lords in *Broome v Cassell & Co Ltd*.[7] The English Law Commission has said that the categories are not 'consistent with either sound principle or sound policy'[8] and that the categories should be abolished and a more principled approach taken.[9] Obviously, in any jurisdiction where these requirements are applied, it is difficult to argue for exemplary damages for breach of contract, as the categories are so narrow.[10]

In many other common law jurisdictions, the *Rookes v Barnard* categories have been resoundingly rejected on the basis that that they are arbitrary and lack logic.[11] The three categories have been rejected in Australia,[12] New Zealand,[13] Canada[14] and now Singapore,[15] although Lord Devlin's general distinction between aggravated damages as a form of compensation and exemplary damages as a form of punishment has been accepted.[16] The three categories have been inconsistently applied in Malaysia,[17] and only Hong Kong has applied them consistently outside

[6] *Rookes v Barnard* [1964] AC 1129 (HL) 1226–27 (Lord Devlin).

[7] *Broome v Cassell & Co Ltd* [1972] AC 1027 (HL).

[8] Law Commission, *Aggravated, Exemplary and Restitutionary Damages* (Law Comm No 247, 1997) para 1.2.

[9] ibid para 1.17.

[10] J Goudkamp, 'Exemplary Damages' in G Virgo and S Worthington (eds), *Commercial Remedies: Resolving Controversies* (Cambridge, Cambridge University Press, 2017) 322.

[11] See the most recent rejection in *ACB v Thomson Medical Pte Ltd* [2017] SGCA 20, [2017] 1 SLR 918 [162]–[169]. Note, however, that the division between exemplary damages and aggravated damages is generally accepted in all common law countries.

[12] *Uren* (n 5). See also *Australian Consolidated Press Ltd v Uren* [1966] HCA 37, (1967) 117 CLR 185, which was later upheld on appeal by the Privy Council: *Australian Consolidated Press Ltd v Uren* [1969] 1 AC 590 (PC).

[13] *Taylor v Beere* [1982] 1 NZLR 81 (New Zealand Court of Appeal).

[14] *Paragon Properties Ltd v Magna Envestments Ltd* (1972) 24 DLR (3d) 156 (Supreme Court of Alberta), later adopted by the Supreme Court of Canada in *Vorvis v Insurance Corporation of British Columbia* [1989] 1 SCR 1085 (Supreme Court of Canada), 1105.

[15] *ACB v Thomson Medical Pte Ltd* (n 11) [176].

[16] cf Goudkamp and Katsampouka, ch 8 in this volume, who argue that the distinction between exemplary damages and aggravated damages is not a meaningful one. Considering the way in which Australian courts have side-stepped statutory prohibitions against awarding exemplary damages in defamation by awarding aggravated damages instead, there may be something to their argument: see K Barnett and S Harder, *Remedies in Australian Private Law*, 2nd edn (Melbourne, Cambridge University Press, 2018) [14.61].

[17] The *Rookes v Barnard* categories have been applied in *Sistem Televisyen Malaysia Bhd v Nurullah bt Zawawi* [2015] 6 MLJ 703 (Malaysian Court of Appeal) [31]–[32]; *Zulkiply bin Taib v Prabakar a/l Bala Krishna* [2015] 2 MLJ 607 [14]. cf, however, *Cheong Fatt Tze Mansion Sdn Bhd v Hotel Continental Sdn Bhd* [2011] 4 MLJ 354 [53] (Malysian High Court).

the United Kingdom.[18] Australian and New Zealand courts have criticised the first category for the lack of clarity as to what constitutes a 'servant of the government', and for the lack of justification as to why oppressive and arbitrary acts by servants of government are more deserving of exemplary damages than, say, those of a contractor with government.[19] They have also criticised the second category on the basis that there seems no reason to confine awards of exemplary damages to situations where the defendant was cynically attempting to make a profit.[20]

In Australia,[21] New Zealand,[22] Canada[23] and Singapore,[24] the focus is on the quality of the defendant's conduct rather than categories. It is generally agreed that exemplary damages are only available in extraordinary situations where the defendant's conduct is particularly egregious. This leads to the next section in this chapter: the normative reasoning behind exemplary damages. Courts say that the defendant's conduct must be morally wrong before imposing liability for exemplary damages (words such as 'contumelious', 'malicious', 'outrageous' and 'egregious' are often used).

III. The Normative Bases of Exemplary Damages

Famously, in *Wilkes v Wood* Pratt LCJ said that the purpose of exemplary damages went beyond compensation and that they were awarded 'as a punishment to the guilty, to deter from any such proceeding for the future, and as proof of the detestation of the jury to the action itself'.[25] Again, others in this collection have outlined the rationales behind exemplary damages.[26] My own discussion of the bases is

[18] *China Light & Power Co Ltd v Ford* [1996] 2 HKC 23 (Hong Kong Court of Appeal); *Allan v Ng & Co* [2012] 2 HKC 266 (Hong Kong Court of Appeal).

[19] *Uren* (n 5) 132–33 (Taylor J); *Taylor v Beere* (n 13) 92 (Richardson J).

[20] *Uren* (n 5) 136–37 (Taylor J); *Taylor v Beere* (n 13) 92 (Richardson J).

[21] Australian test: whether there is 'conscious wrongdoing in contumelious disregard of another's rights': *Whitfield v De Lauret & Co Ltd* (1920) 29 CLR 71 (High Court of Australia), 77 (Knox CJ); *Australian Consolidated Press Ltd v Uren* (1967) 117 CLR 221, 232–34 (PC); *XL Petroleum (NSW) Pty Ltd v Caltex Oil (Australia) Pty Ltd* [1985] HCA 12, (1985) 155 CLR 448, 471 (Brennan J); *Gray v Motor Accident Commission* [1998] HCA 70, (1998) 196 CLR 1 [22] (Gleeson CJ, McHugh, Gummow and Hayne JJ).

[22] New Zealand test: whether there is 'truly outrageous conduct' that cannot be punished in any way except by an award of exemplary damages: *Dunlea v Attorney-General* [2000] 3 NZLR 136 (New Zealand Court of Appeal), [34] (Keith J, with whom Richardson P, Gault, and Blanchard JJ agreed).

[23] Canadian test: whether the defendant has committed 'advertent wrongful acts that are so malicious and outrageous that they are deserving of punishment on their own': see *Keays v Honda Canada Inc* [2008] 2 SCR 362 (Supreme Court of Canada) 365; and SM Waddams, *The Law of Damages*, 5th edn (Toronto, Canada Law Book, 2012) [11.210].

[24] Singaporean test: whether 'the totality of the defendant's conduct is so outrageous that it warrants punishment, deterrence, and condemnation': *ACB v Thomson Medical Pte Ltd* (n 11) [177].

[25] *Wilkes v Wood* (1763) Lofft 1, 19; 98 ER 489, 498–99. Windeyer J thought exemplary damages had even earlier origins in *Uren* (n 5) 152.

[26] Barker, ch 2, section III; Courtney, ch 12 of this volume; Penner, ch 5 of this volume.

brief. It unpacks the three elements of Pratt LCJ's statement in *Wilkes v Wood*, and focuses on punishment, deterrence and the expressive function of exemplary damages. The discussion at this point is general, but in section IV I will relate these normative bases specifically to breach of contract.

A. 'As a Punishment to the Guilty'

First, Pratt LCJ says that exemplary damages are a punishment to the guilty (and thus it follows from this that those who are liable to pay them *deserve* to be punished).

Punishment of the guilty is an aspect of the retributive rationale: that wrongful behaviour should be punished in proportion to the wrong. Retribution denotes that the victim (or the state in place of the victim in criminal law) is able to mete out unpleasant consequences upon a defendant because of his or her wrongdoing. It is a very ancient principle, enshrined in well-known principles such as 'an eye for an eye, a tooth for a tooth'.[27] While this might seem vicious, it was in fact designed to stem the spiral of retribution: once the consequences of a crime had been dealt with in the stipulated manner, there was no room for further retribution or vendettas on the part of the victim or the victim's family. In many legal systems (including our own to an extent), however, retribution does not necessarily entail physical punishment but may simply involve payment of fines.[28]

The retributive rationale looks backwards, to the past conduct of the defendant. Kant argues that it must be ascertained whether punishment is deserved by that particular person before more general aims such as the good of society are considered.[29] In speaking of whether someone *deserves* to be liable for exemplary damages, desert looks to a specific person's qualities, actions and status,[30] and considers what a person has done in the past.[31] While the specific qualities of the defendant are pivotal for questions of desert, more broadly, convention is

[27] The Code of Hammurabi, dated to around 1754 BC, states in Art 196 'If a man put out the eye of another man, they shall destroy his eye.' Art 197 states 'If a man break a man's bone, they shall break his bone.' Similar principles are expressed in the Bible in Exodus 21:24, Leviticus 24:20 and Deuteronomy 19:21. Rabbinical law moved from physical retribution to monetary payment: S Greengus, *Laws in the Bible and in Early Rabbinic Collections: The Legal Legacy of the Ancient Near East* (Eugene, OR, Wipf and Stock Publishers, 2011) 130–36.

[28] eg, Anglo-Saxon and Germanic legal systems contemplated *weregild* for injury and death rather than physical retribution.

[29] I Kant, *The Metaphysical Elements of Justice*, tr J Ladd (New York, Macmillan, 1965) 100.

[30] M Harding, 'Justifying Fiduciary Allowances' in A Robertson and TH Wu (eds), *The Goals of Private Law* (Oxford, Hart Publishing, 2009) 352; J Kleinig, 'The Concept of Desert' (1971) 8 *American Philosophical Quarterly* 71, 73; D Miller, *Social Justice* (Oxford, Clarendon Press, 1979) 85; L Becker, *Property Rights: Philosophic Foundations* (London, Routledge & Paul, 1977); SR Munzer, *A Theory of Property* (Cambridge, Cambridge University Press, 1990) 260; JW Harris, *Property and Justice* (Oxford, Clarendon Press, 1996) 205.

[31] Kleinig (n 30) 73.

also important to a decision as to whether someone is deserving: in other words, if another person has committed the same wrong previously and been liable in a particular way, the person currently before the court should be treated similarly.[32] This is why it is necessary, as a matter of justice, to be clear about the circumstances in which exemplary damages are awarded.

It may appear from this that a defendant who is liable for exemplary damages should necessarily be an intentional wrongdoer, and thus that such an award is prima facie inappropriate for breach of contract, where the wilfulness of breach is not generally scrutinised (the question of wilfulness will be discussed in greater detail in section IV.A). Generally, however, exemplary damages have not been limited to intentional torts,[33] but the defendant's actions must be deliberate or reckless before he or she will be liable for exemplary damages for a non-intentional tort.[34] Recklessness requires the defendant to have a conscious appreciation of the risk and be subjectively reckless.[35] Consequently, exemplary damages are most often available for intentional torts or torts actionable per se,[36] although some jurisdictions, including Australia, allow for the award of exemplary damages in exceptional circumstances for negligence,[37] particularly where the negligence in question in fact constitutes intentional conduct or recklessness. In the Australian case of *Gray v Motor Accident Commission*,[38] while nominally a negligence case, the tortfeasor deliberately ran his car into a group of youths because he was prejudiced against people of that particular racial background, and thus the conduct could be categorised as trespass to the person. The determinative factor seems not to be the cause of action per se but the conduct of the defendant.

[32] Harding (n 30) 353; Harris (n 30) 207–08; J Feinberg, 'Justice and Personal Desert' in J Feinberg, *Doing and Deserving: Essays in the Theory of Responsibility* (Princeton, NJ, Princeton University Press, 1970) 82; Miller (n 30) 91.

[33] See *Couch v Attorney-General (No 2)* [2010] NZSC 27, [2010] 3 NZLR 149 for an extensive discussion of the law in New Zealand, Australia, Canada and England.

[34] *Gray* (n 21) [24].

[35] *Couch* (n 33) [60], [67]–[69] (Blanchard J); [100]– [102], [114]–[117], [150] (Tipping J); [238]–[243] (McGrath J); [253]–[257] (Wilson J); [1]–[4] (Elias CJ, dissenting).

[36] Torts for which exemplary damages have been awarded in Australia include: trespass to land, nuisance, trespass to goods, trespass to the person, conversion and detinue, wrongful arrest involving trespass to land and the person, battery, false imprisonment, malicious prosecution, abuse of process, misfeasance in the public office, inducing breach of contract, interference with contractual relations, deceit, intimidation and conspiracy. Legislation has limited the availability in defamation and in some personal injury claims. See Barnett and Harder (n 16) [14.28]–[14.29].

[37] In Australia see, eg, *Gray* (n 21) (driving); *Midalco Pty Ltd v Rabenalt* [1989] VR 461 (Supreme Court of Victoria) and *Amaca Pty Ltd v Banton* [2007] NSWCA 336 (industrial injuries); *Backwell v AAA* [1997] 1 VR 182 (Victoria Court of Appeal) (medical negligence). cf *Broome v Cassell* (n 7), which doubts the availability of exemplary damages for negligence in England and Wales. The situation in New Zealand is complicated. In *A v Bottrill* [2002] UKPC 44, [2003] 1 AC 449, the Privy Council decided (on appeal from the New Zealand Court of Appeal) that 'outrageous' unintentional conduct (ie negligence) could give rise to exemplary damages, but the New Zealand Supreme Court declined to follow *A v Bottrill* in *Couch* (n 33).

[38] *Gray* (n 21).

Of course, a punitive rationale in private law is controversial, as punishment is generally seen as the realm of the criminal law. As Lord Devlin observed in *Rookes v Barnard*, damages with the aim of punishment appear to confuse or combine the criminal and civil functions, and in fact exemplary damages are peculiar to English law (and, I would add, to other common law systems).[39] Consequently, some argue that the proper party to enforce the broader regime of rights is the state, via the mechanism of the criminal law.[40] However, others have noted that retribution is used in a narrower sense than in the criminal law, as it focuses on the infringement and vindication of a private right between private individuals.[41] Similarly, it has also been argued that a retributive rationale requires the extra procedural and evidentiary constraints associated with the criminal law protections for the accused.[42] This seems overstated to me; exemplary damages do not involve the disapprobation and deprivation of liberty that criminal offences may involve. It may be suggested in response to this that many (perhaps the majority of) criminal offences involve the payment of fines, not the deprivation of liberty. As Bant and Paterson point out, there is a quasi-criminal function in some jurisdictions of pecuniary penalties.[43] The line between exemplary damages, civil penalties and fines is not entirely sharp, but the objection to procedural protections for a defendant can be dealt with by a court's exercising extreme care in awarding exemplary damages in a civil context.

Moreover, as McBride points out, there is a space where defendants might fall short of the criminal law but nonetheless deserve punishment, and it is this space that exemplary damages might fill.[44] It is clear that if the criminal law *does* punish the defendant, there is no room for 'double punishment' by the civil law.[45] The High Court of Australia has said that there are two reasons for this. First, 'the purposes of exemplary damages have been met if substantial punishment is exacted by the criminal law. The offender is punished; others are deterred.'[46] Second, the law should not punish a person twice for the same act.[47]

[39] *Rookes v Barnard* (n 6) 1221 (Lord Devlin).

[40] B Chapman and M Trebilcock, 'Punitive Damages: Divergence in Search of a Rationale' (1989) 40 *Alabama Law Rev* 741, 782.

[41] R Stevens, *Torts and Rights* (Oxford, Oxford University Press, 2007) 85; R Cunnington, 'Should Punitive Damages be Part of the Judicial Arsenal in Contract Cases?' (2006) 26 *Legal Studies* 369, 381. It has been observed that the distinction between wrongs directed against individuals and against the state is neither workable nor useful: S Smith, 'Performance, Punishment and the Nature of Contractual Obligation' (1997) 60 *MLR* 360, 366.

[42] Chapman and Trebilcock (n 40) 804–05; E Weinrib, 'Punishment and Disgorgement as Contract Remedies' (2003) 78 *Chi-Kent Law Review* 55, 100–01; P Jaffey, *The Nature and Scope of Restitution* (Oxford, Hart Publishing, 2000) 376–78; *Broome v Cassell* (n 7) 1100 (Lord Morris).

[43] Bant and Paterson, ch 10 of this volume.

[44] McBride (n 1) 373.

[45] *Gray* (n 21) [32]–[37], [80]–[83], [130].

[46] ibid [42] (Gleeson CJ, McHugh, Gummow and Hayne JJ).

[47] ibid [43] (Gleeson CJ, McHugh, Gummow and Hayne JJ).

B. 'To Deter from Any Such Proceeding for the Future'

Second, Pratt LCJ argues that exemplary damages deter others who might be tempted to commit such wrongs in the future.[48] The forward-looking and consequentialist nature of the deterrent rationale is in contrast to the backward-looking nature of the retributive rationale.[49] Deterrence has two aspects, specific and general deterrence. Specific deterrence is concerned only with deterring the specific defendant in question from repeating the wrongful conduct. The kind of deterrence that operates for exemplary damages is, by and large, general deterrence. Thus, in *Lamb v Cotogno*,[50] Lamb, a process server, attempted to serve a summons on Cotogno. In a rage, Cotogno threw himself on the bonnet of Lamb's car. Lamb sped off, in the process seriously injuring Cotogno and leaving him lying by the roadside. Cotogno sued Lamb for trespass to the person and received compensatory and exemplary damages at first instance. The court agreed that the particular defendant's conduct was required to be (and was) contumelious and deserving of punishment; however, the defendant had the benefit of compulsory third-party insurance. Consequently, the award did not specifically punish him in particular, nor did it effect specific deterrence, because the damages did not come from the defendant's pocket. However, the High Court said that the social aims of exemplary damages also extended to general deterrence and preventing plaintiffs from taking revenge,[51] and that these rationales alone could justify the imposition of exemplary damages. General deterrence can be justified by a law and economics analysis: that is, rational actors will choose not to undertake certain conduct when they know that exemplary damages will be imposed on them (and that such exemplary damages will outstrip any profits they might make). However, a generally deterrent aim presupposes that there is publicity and knowledge of such awards, and that they in fact have a deterrent effect on the populace, an assumption that may be questioned. In this collection, Kit Barker has been sceptical of the deterrent aim,[52] whereas Catherine Sharkey has argued that it may perform a socially useful aim by making legal actors internalise the cost of their wrongdoing.[53]

[48] In fact Barker notes that the deterrent rationale for exemplary damages in fact started with Pratt LCJ's statement: see Barker, ch 2, section III.E.

[49] J Berryman, 'The Case for Restitutionary Damages over Punitive Damages: Teaching the Wrongdoer that Tort does not Pay' (1994) 73 *Canadian Bar Review* 320, 322; Chapman and Trebilcock (n 40) 780.

[50] [1987] HCA 47, 164 CLR 1.

[51] ibid, 9–10, later affirmed in Gray (n 21) [32]. In Australia, the Motor Accidents Act 1988 (NSW), s 81A now precludes exemplary damages. The Transport Accident Act 1986 (Vic), s 93(7) states that damages may only be claimed for pecuniary loss and pain and suffering in the context of motor vehicle accidents. The Motor Accident Insurance Act 1994 (Qld) provides that the court may give a separate award of exemplary, punitive or aggravated damages against the insured: s 55(1). A person holding a compulsory third-party insurance policy will not be entitled to an indemnity for those damages: s 55(2).

[52] Barker, ch 2 of this volume.

[53] Sharkey, ch 7 of this volume. See also Bant and Paterson, ch 10 of this volume, who argue strongly for a deterrent view.

My own belief is that exemplary damages must have both a retributive and a generally deterrent aim. My approach follows the dissenting judgment of Mason P in *Harris v Digital Pulse Limited*:

> The various functions of exemplary damages … inhere in the single remedial act. The 'public' function is triggered on the 'private' initiative of the affected plaintiff who pockets the fruits of the award. In such a context, the distinction between deterrence and punishment is illusory. It would be entirely lost on the defendant. This is a distinction that is not drawn with regard to the award of exemplary damages generally.[54]

However, unlike Mason P, I would specify that retributive aims and deterrent aims are distinct and sometime conflicting (in that one looks at the conduct of a specific defendant in the past, and one looks at the deterrence of the general public in the future). That being said, both are parts of the act of punishment (recalling Kant's comment that punishment must be first deserved by that specific defendant, and then the social utility of that punishment must be considered). Consequently, I would doubt the correctness of *Lamb v Cotogno* because specific punishment and deterrence could not be effected, and the generally deterrent social effects of the award were not clear enough to warrant an award.

It should be noted that there are some who argue that both punitive and deterrent rationales in private law are illegitimate.[55] Ernest Weinrib argues that punishment and deterrence are aims that are incompatible with normative corrective justice, which he regards as the justification of private law, because they focus on the blameworthiness of the defendant, and that private law should not intervene on questions of desert.[56] There is some validity to the point made by corrective justice scholars that there seems no reason why the plaintiff, out of everyone, should receive exemplary damages on a correlative basis if the duty that has been breached is a societal duty.[57] Moreover, if there are multiple plaintiffs, it has been argued that legitimate claims for compensation may be impeded if one plaintiff is given a particularly generous award;[58] although on the other hand, the plaintiff who takes the risk of litigation should perhaps be rewarded.[59] Bant and Paterson have argued elsewhere that this is particularly the case if regulators are

[54] *Harris v Digital Pulse Limited* [2003] NSWCA 10, (2003) 56 NSWLR 298 [173].

[55] E Weinrib, 'The Gains and Losses of Corrective Justice' (1994) 44 *Duke Law Journal* 277; E Weinrib, 'Restitutionary Damages as Corrective Justice' (2001) 1 *Theoretical Inquiries in Law* 1; E Weinrib, 'Corrective Justice in a Nutshell' (2002) 52 *University of Toronto Law Journal* 349; E Weinrib, 'Punishment and Disgorgement as Contract Remedies' (2003) 78 *Chicago-Kent Law Review* 55; Weinrib (n 42); E Weinrib, *Corrective Justice* (Oxford, Oxford University Press, 2012).

[56] Weinrib (n 42).

[57] A Beever, 'The Structure of Aggravated and Exemplary Damages' (2003) 23 *OJLS* 87, 107; Weinrib (n 42); Weinrib, 'Restitutionary Damages' (n 55) 2–3. Kimel makes a similar point in relation to disgorgement: D Kimel, 'The Morality of Contract and Moral Culpability in Breach' (2010) 21 *King's Law Journal* 213, 229.

[58] Law Reform Commission (Ireland), *Report on Aggravated, Exemplary and Restitutionary Damages* (LRC 60-2000) [2.068].

[59] ibid [2.081].

under-resourced.[60] In *Couch*, Wilson J observed that if exemplary damages were introduced in present times, there would be a 'good argument' that they should be payable to the state, not to the plaintiff.[61] Of course, this would not be acceptable to corrective justice scholars, because such damages would still violate the principle of correlativity. In any case, it has been argued that punishment is not necessarily inconsistent with corrective justice if one accepts the theory that a breaching party deems his or her rights to be more important than those of the victim.[62] Moreover, courts do not strictly demarcate matters such that only criminal law imposes punishment and only private law compensates.[63]

C. 'As Proof of the Detestation of the Jury to the Action Itself'

The flip-side of deterring potential defendants from committing egregious wrongs is that awards of exemplary damages are also said to deter aggrieved plaintiffs from exercising self-help in violent ways by recognising the wrongdoing. Thus, in *Merest v Harvey*, it was said that exemplary damages were necessary to prevent duelling.[64] As we no longer have an 'honour culture' where duelling is prevalent, this particular concern may be less important than it was, although it is still important in understanding the history of criminal law and tort. The state has much more power than it did in days past,[65] and can act to prevent violent retribution; moreover, people tend not to carry arms or to use them lightly in most first-world societies any more.[66] The criminal law serves a 'displacement function' in Gardner's words: the law takes the heat of out disputes and stops violent retribution.[67] It may be that exemplary damages have a similar function, albeit in a civil context. The point remains that if people feel that an egregious wrong has been done to them, and this has not been adequately recognised by the legal system, they may

[60] E Bant and J Paterson, 'Should specifically deterrent or punitive remedies be made available to victims of misleading conduct under the *Australian Consumer Law*?' (2019) 25 *Torts Law Journal* 99, 125.

[61] *Couch* (n 33) [258].

[62] P-W Lee, 'Contract Damages, Corrective Justice and Punishment' (2007) 70 *MLR* 887. Lee draws on Jean Hampton's concept of 'moral injury' and the necessity of exacting retribution when a 'moral injury' occurs: J Hampton, 'The Retributive Idea' in J Murphy and J Hampton (eds), *Forgiveness and Mercy* (Cambridge, Cambridge University Press, 1988) 131–41; J Hampton, 'Correcting Harm Versus Righting Wrongs: The Goal of Retribution' (1992) 39 *UCLA Law Review* 1659.

[63] J Edelman, *Gain-Based Damages: Contract, Tort, Equity and Intellectual Property* (Oxford, Hart Publishing, 2002) 19; Cunnington (n 41) 380–81; Jaffey (n 42) 378.

[64] *Merest v Harvey* (1815) 5 Taunt 442, 444; 128 ER 761, 761 (Heath J).

[65] S Pinker, *The Better Angels of Our Nature: Why Violence Has Declined* (New York, Viking, 2011) ch 2 talks of the importance of the 'leviathan' of the state's restraining actions such as mob violence.

[66] cf the United States, which has both a Constitutional right to bear arms and a higher level of punitive damages awards than other common law jurisdictions.

[67] J Gardner, 'Crime: In Proportion and in Perspective' in J Gardner, *Offences and Defences* (Oxford, Oxford University Press, 2007) 214.

take the law into their own hands. This links to the third aspect of exemplary damages stated by Pratt LCJ: proof of detestation of the public of this conduct.

Proof of detestation of the public of the conduct links to the declaratory function of punishment, outlined by Feinberg.[68] The notion here is that by publicly recognising that the defendant has done wrong, the plaintiff will experience a vindication of his or her rights by that recognition. As Barker points out, denunciation can be understood in several different ways: as a retributive shaming of the defendant; as a general deterrent to others; and as confirming and affirming the value of our legal rights.[69] If it is either of the first two then it is folded up into retribution or general deterrence; if it is to be distinct, it must involve the confirmation and affirmation of legal rights.

It is evident that the three broad rationales of exemplary damages are a difficult fit with, and rub up against, the rationales of contract. This tension, and the extent to which is may be fatal to the application of exemplary damages to breach of contract, is the subject of the next section.

IV. Exemplary Damages in Contract: Normative Conflict

The historical bases as to why exemplary damages have not been awarded for breach of contract have been explored. But the reasons behind common law courts' reluctance to award exemplary damages go to the normative bases of contract in common law itself.[70] Stephen Waddams has noted:

> Punitive damages are not normally awarded for breach of contract. This rule is based on the assumption underlying much of contract law that a breach of contract, coupled with an offer to pay just compensation, does not harm to the plaintiff, is not morally wrong and may be desirable on the grounds of efficiency.[71]

Canada is the only common law jurisdiction that allows for punitive damages for breach of contract.[72] A precondition of the award of damages is that the defendant's conduct gives rise to an 'independent actionable wrong', but that wrong does not

[68] J Feinberg, 'The Expressive Function of Punishment' in J Feinberg (ed), *Doing and Deserving: Essays in the Theory of Responsibility* (Princeton, NJ, Princeton University Press, 1970) 104. See also Penner, ch 5 of this volume, regarding 'expressivism'.

[69] Barker, ch 2, section III.G.

[70] cf French law, which, with its emphasis on *pacta sunt servanda*, is far less averse to awarding exemplary damages for breach of contract: Rowan, ch 3 of this volume.

[71] Waddams (n 23) [11.250].

[72] *Vorvis* (n 14); *Royal Bank of Canada v W Got & Associates Electric Ltd* [1999] 3 SCR 408 (Supreme Court of Canada); and especially *Whiten v Pilot Insurance Co* [2002] 1 SCR 595 (Supreme Court of Canada). cf *Performance Industries Ltd v Sylvan Lake Golf & Tennis Club Ltd* [2002] SCR 678 (Supreme Court of Canada); *Atlantic Lottery Corp Ltd v Babstock* 2020 SCC 19, where such damages were not awarded on the facts.

have to be in tort.[73] The leading Canadian decision in *Whiten*, which recognised exemplary damages for breach of contract, has been roundly criticised.[74] It has been noted that its insurance context is an important background that may render the contract in the case different from other contracts.[75] Otherwise, exemplary damages are unavailable for breach of contract in England and Wales,[76] the United States,[77] Australia,[78] Ireland,[79] New Zealand[80] and Singapore,[81] although the Singaporean Court of Appeal has left open the possibility of exemplary damages' being available in exceptional circumstances.[82]

The Singaporean Court of Appeal in *PH Hydraulics & Engineering Pte Ltd v Airtrust (Hong Kong) Ltd* has discussed the normative basis for the rejection of exemplary damages in contract in the most detail:

> This (key) element of *agreement* in the *contractual* context militates against the availability of *punitive* damages. Since the parties to a contract have been afforded the opportunity to consider various matters that are relevant to the bargain that they have

[73] *Whiten* (n 72) 637–39. Confirmed recently in *Atlantic Lottery Corp* (n 72) [63] (Abella, Moldaver, Côté, Brown and Rowe JJ); [132]–[134] (Wagner CJ, Karakatsanis, Martin and Kasirer JJ). This requirement in *Whiten* is rightly criticised by the Singapore Court of Appeal in *PH Hydraulics* (n 2) [114]–[115].

[74] J Swan, 'Punitive Damages for Breach of Contract: A Remedy in Search of a Justification' (2003–2004) 29 *Queen's Law Journal* 596; JD McCamus, 'Prometheus Bound or Loose Cannon? Punitive Damages for Pure Breach of Contract in Canada' (2004) 41 *San Diego Law Review* 1491; S Rowan, 'Reflections on the Introduction of Punitive Damages for Breach of Contract' (2010) 30 *OJLS* 495; MP Harrington, '"A Lawless Science': Punitive Damages for Breach of Contract in Canada' (2015) 69 *Supreme Court Law Review* 185; Y Adar, '*Whiten v Pilot Insurance Co*: The Unofficial Death of the Independent Wrong Requirement and Official Birth of Punitive Damages in Contract' (2005) 41 *Canadian Business Law Journal* 247. See extensive criticism of *Whiten* in *PH Hydraulics* (n 2) [114]–[129].

[75] Waddams (n 23) [11.2579].

[76] *Addis v Gramophone Co Ltd* [1909] AC 488. Goudkamp argues that *Addis* provides weak support for the proposition that punitive damages are unavailable for breach of contract: see Goudkamp (n 10) 321–322. Law Commission (n 8) [1.71]–[1.73] recommended that exemplary damages for breach of contract should not be introduced. Goudkamp (n 10) 326 criticises this rejection.

[77] American Law Institute, *Restatement (Second) of the Law of Contracts* (1981), § 355: 'Punitive damages are not recoverable for a breach of contract unless the conduct constituting the breach is also a tort for which punitive damages are recoverable'; *Thyssen Inc v SS Fortune Star* 777 F 2d 57, 63 (2d Cir, 1985). However, punitive damages have been allowed for certain breaches of contract involving fraud or insurance contracts breached in bad faith: see A Tettenborn, 'Punitive Damages – A View from England' (2004) 41 *San Diego Law Review* 1551, 1561. The New Zealand Court of Appeal has aptly described the American position as 'confused': *Paper Reclaim Ltd v Aotearoa International* [2006] 3 NZLR 188 [174] (Chambers J, with whom Anderson P and O'Regan J agreed).

[78] *Butler v Fairclough* (1917) 23 CLR 78 (High Court of Austrailia) 89 (Griffiths CJ); *Gray* (n 21) [13] (Gleeson CJ, McHugh, Gummow and Hayne JJ); *Hospitality Group Pty Ltd v Australian Rugby Union Ltd* (2001) 110 FCR 157, 191, 197; *Digital Pulse* (n 54). Note, however, that the Victorian Civil and Administrative Tribunal is empowered by statute to award exemplary damages in respect of domestic building contracts: Domestic Building Contracts Act 1995 (Vic), s 53(2)(b)(ii). For an argument that Australia should adopt exemplary damages for breach of contract, see L Coci, 'It's Time Exemplary Damages Were Part of the Judicial Armory in Contract' (2015) 40 *University of Western Australia Law Review* 1.

[79] Law Reform Commission (Ireland) (n 58) [1.66].

[80] *Paper Reclaim* (n 77) [183].

[81] *PH Hydraulics* (n 2).

[82] ibid [136].

> entered into, and since they have decided between themselves what the terms of the contract should be, the *courts* ought to have but a *minimal* role in regulating their conduct without regard to their agreement. … [The] award of damages gives effect to the bargain struck by both parties and generally carries with it no disapproval (and, equally, no approval) of what the contract-breaker has done, regardless of whatever may have been the motive for breaching the contract. Indeed the common law has largely been 'tolerant of a certain amount of self-interested behaviour'…
>
> Looked at in this light, it would, in our view, be *anomalous or even inappropriate* for the court to *regulate the contracting parties' conduct by imposing and award of punitive damages on the party in breach by what of what is in effect an external standard.*[83]

In essence, our law of contract emphasises autonomy and rational dealing, and eschews punishment, and the motive of the defendant in breaching is irrelevant. My own view is that generally speaking, the Singaporean Court of Appeal is correct to say that in most cases contract contemplates self-interested behaviour, although this is not invariably the case, even in commercial cases, and sometimes courts will require parties to have an eye to the interests of the other.[84] In most cases, exemplary damages will be inappropriate for breach of contract, but the voluntary nature of contracting should not be overemphasised: particularly in consumer contracts, a party may not have any genuine choices if he or she wants a particular service.

A. Contract and Questions of Retributive Desert

In contract law, the 'wilfulness' of any breach of contract is said to be irrelevant.[85] For this reason, contract law does not usually consider fault or advertence or deliberateness, as these are regarded as pertaining to the wilfulness of breach. Given that questions of wilfulness help to determine retributive desert, if wilfulness is not part of contract then exemplary damages should be excluded. Kimel has argued that breach of contract 'tends to be entirely insensitive to fault',[86] and that therefore fault has no central role to play in determining the proper remedial responses to breach. For example, generally speaking, the remoteness rules applying at common law are the same regardless of whether the breach is deliberate or inadvertent; this is in stark contrast to civilian tradition.[87] However, Andrews, Clarke, Tettenborn and Virgo have argued that even if deliberate breaches are not treated differently, deliberately caused *losses* should be subject to extended liability akin to that imposed for intentional torts.[88]

[83] ibid [71]–[72] (emphasis in original). The quotation is taken from Rowan (n 74) 504.

[84] P Finn, 'Contract and The Fiduciary Principle' (1989) 12 *UNSWLJ* 76.

[85] *Butler v Fairclough* (n 78) 89 (Griffith CJ).

[86] Kimel (n 57) 225.

[87] N Andrews et al, *Contractual Duties: Performance, Breach, Termination and Remedies*, 2nd edn (London, Sweet & Maxwell, 2017) [23–052].

[88] Andrews (n 87) [23–053].

Conversely, other scholars (primarily in the United States) have also argued that 'wilfulness' or 'fault' should not be introduced into contract law because breach should not be regarded as wrongful as it may deter parties from efficiently breaching where necessary.[89] However, on the other hand, it has been argued that the wilful nature of the parties' conduct inevitably intrudes into contract law in different ways at different times.[90]

A close look at the case law suggests that the wilfulness of a breach of contract is sometimes important to the award of remedies in contract. Sometimes even awards that are compensatory on their face seem to consider the wilfulness of the breach, as in the Australian case of *Tabcorp Holdings Ltd v Bowen Investments Pty Ltd*.[91] A commercial lease of an office building contained a clause whereby the lessee agreed not to alter the foyer of the office building without the lessor's consent. The foyer was specially designed and made of particular materials. In breach of the clause, the lessee began to jackhammer and demolish the foyer. The lessor considered seeking an injunction, but by that time it was too late: the foyer lay in ruins. The lessee argued that it was liable only for the difference in value between the office building with the original foyer and the office building with the new (tasteless) foyer. The lessor argued that it was entitled to the full cost-of-cure. The High Court pointedly referred to the lessee's 'contumelious disregard' of the rights of the lessor[92] and then awarded full cost-of-cure without any betterment discount. Ordinarily some allowance would be made for the fact that the lessor was getting a 'better' foyer than it would have done once the lease ended, because it was not worn by use, but the High Court blandly said that the lessee had not sought a betterment discount, nor would it have been given if it had. It is suggested that the deliberateness of the breach in this case is front and centre.

Tabcorp may be contrasted with the English case of *Ruxley Electronics & Constructions Ltd v Forsyth*.[93] In *Ruxley*, the landowner contracted with a builder to have a pool of a particular depth constructed on his land as the pool was intended for diving. During the construction process he orally varied the depth, asking the builder to make it several inches deeper, but the builder failed to do so. The homeowner refused to pay the builder the balance of the purchase price, and the builder sued in debt. The homeowner counter claimed for cost-of-cure

[89] R Posner, 'Let Us Never Blame a Contract Breaker' (2009) 107 *Michigan Law Review* 1349. See also S Shavell, 'Why Breach of Contract May Not Be Immoral Given the Incompleteness of Contracts' (2009) 107 *Michigan Law Review* 1569.

[90] G Cohen, 'The Fault that Lies Within our Contract Law' (2009) 107 *Michigan Law Review* 1445; M Eisenberg, 'The Role of Fault in Contract Law: Unconscionability, Unexpected Circumstances, Interpretation, Mistake, and Nonperformance' (2009) 107 *Michigan Law Review* 141; S Thel and P Siegelman, 'Willfulness Versus Expectation: A Promisor-based Defense of Willful Breach Doctrine' (2009) 107 *Michigan Law Review* 1517; S Shiffrin, 'Could Breach of Contract be Immoral?' (2009) 107 *Michigan Law Review* 1551; S Grundmann, 'The Fault Principle as the Chameleon of Contract Law: A Market Function Approach' (2009) 107 *Michigan Law Review* 1583; R Kreitner, 'Fault at the Contract–Tort Interface' (2009) 107 *Michigan Law Review* 1533.

[91] *Tabcorp Holdings Ltd v Bowen Investments Pty Ltd* [2009] HCA 8, (2009) 236 CLR 272.

[92] ibid [4].

[93] *Ruxley Electronics & Constructions Ltd v Forsyth* [1996] AC 344 (HL).

damages, but was not awarded the cost of digging a replacement pool of the right depth. Although the two cases may appear inconsistent because *Tabcorp* emphasises *pacta sunt servanda*, whereas *Ruxley* seems to tolerate something less than full performance, I suggest that the wilfulness of the breach (or lack thereof) provides some explanation for the different outcomes. In *Ruxley*, the stipulation as to pool depth was changed half way through construction by an oral variation; the pool was still suitable for diving; the breach appears to have been accidental; and there seems to have been a suspicion that the property owner raised the question of rectification damages at the end of the trial as an afterthought, in order to resist the pool builder's claim in debt (the court nods to this by saying that it did not think the damages would be used for repair, and thus repair was unreasonable). Accordingly the property owner did not get full rectification costs but only a small amount for 'loss of amenity'.[94]

Another case that demonstrates the way in which contract sometimes takes into account the harmfulness of breach is *Attorney-General v Blake*,[95] which exhibits both a deterrent and punitive rationale,[96] although this was a case of an exceptional award of an account of profits for breach of contract, not exemplary damages. However it is suggested, as Bant and Paterson also argue in their chapter, that accounts of profit cases can provide guidance in this area because of the deterrent nature of that remedy.[97]

Lord Nicholls begins his speech in *Blake* with the statement, 'My Lords, George Blake is a notorious, self-confessed traitor.'[98] This suggests that retribution was one of the motivations behind the court's awarding an exceptional account of profits for breach of contract, with no allowance for the defendant's skill and effort. The facts are well known: George Blake was a spy for the British Intelligence Service and signed a contract in which he agreed (among other things) to be subject to an ongoing obligation not to publish material about his activities. However, Blake was a Soviet double-agent for many years, until he was uncovered and sentenced to 42 years' imprisonment for contravening section 1(1)(c) of the Official Secrets Act 1911. After serving five years of his sentence, in 1966, Blake escaped from Wormwood Scrubs prison and fled to Moscow. In 1990, after the fall of the Iron Curtain, he published a book called *No Other Choice*,[99] in breach of his obligation not to publish material. The British Government sought to cause Blake to disgorge his profit, but any obligation of confidence had ceased, and there was doubt as to whether any fiduciary obligation subsisted after the end of the employment relationship. Accordingly, a majority of the House of Lords held that an account of

[94] ibid 353 (Lord Bridge); 358–59 (Lord Jauncey); 359–60 (Lord Mustill), 367–71 (Lord Lloyd). Lord Keith concurred with Lords Jauncey, Mustill and Lloyd.

[95] *Attorney-General v Blake* [2000] UKHL 45, [2001] 1 AC 268.

[96] For further discussion of how *Blake* exhibits a punitive rationale in my view, see K Barnett, *Accounting for Profit for Breach of Contract: Theory and Practice* (Oxford, Hart Publishing, 2012) 32–46.

[97] Bant and Paterson, ch 10 of this volume.

[98] *Blake* (n 95) 275.

[99] G Blake, *No Other Choice* (London, Jonathan Cape, 1990).

profit could be awarded in exceptional circumstances where the plaintiff displayed a 'legitimate interest' in the defendant's profit-making activities. Although Kimel does not endorse moralised contract law, he concedes that *Blake* may be an exceptional case where the court acts in order to protect the institution of contracting itself.[100] In this way, his approach may be more consistent with a limited deterrent rationale for some contracts (discussed further below).

Turning from the cases supporting retributive considerations in contract law, it is also possible to identify theoretical arguments that endorse their application. As one of the leading academic advocates for exemplary damages for breach of contract, Pey-Woan Lee, has observed, these supporting arguments first require acceptance of the importance of performing one's contractual obligation (something that the common law does not always do wholeheartedly, discussed below). On that basis, she suggests adopting the retributive theory of Jean Hampton, which is premised on the Kantian theory of human worth, to support the principled application of exemplary damages to breach of contract.[101] Hampton proposes that a person who commits a wrong against another demeans the other, because it is implicit that he considers his rights of greater worth than those of the victim (which Hampton calls 'moral injury'). Thus, where moral injury occurs, it could be said that a retributive response is justified as it denies the wrongdoer's moral elevation and vindicates the equality of the parties. Lee concludes that punitive damages are a hybrid remedy with both compensatory and retributive elements. The victim of breach of contract is compensated for the moral injury done to her because of the violation to her liberty.[102] Lee argues that

> [a]dhering to a retributive analysis is critical in emphasising the role of private law in protecting the objective worth of the human agent, and not merely her physical or psychological well being (as the traditional emphasis on compensation is wont to do).[103]

However, it is suggested that not every breach of contract can be a moral injury deserving of exemplary damages: in fact, the very opposite is true. As Kimel has argued, for the most part, the common law of contract is *demoralised* compared to tort.[104] As a generalisation, the wilfulness of breach or the defendant's motive in breaching a contract is not relevant to liability. Indeed, as James Penner has argued in this collection (drawing on Brudner), a distinction must be drawn between moral and legal deserts.[105] Something can be morally wrong without requiring legal sanction. We shall see that this characteristic has the consequence that *most* breaches of contract will not give rise to exemplary damages, and nor should they.

[100] Kimel (n 57) 228–29.

[101] J Hampton, 'The Retributive Idea' in J Murphy and J Hampton (eds), *Forgiveness and Mercy* (Cambridge, Cambridge University Press, 1988) 111, 131–41; J Hampton, 'Correcting Harm Versus Righting Wrongs: The Goal of Retribution' (1992) 39 *UCLA Law Review* 1659.

[102] Lee (n 62) 898.

[103] ibid.

[104] Kimel (n 57) 225.

[105] Penner, ch 5, section III, citing A Brudner, *Punishment and Freedom: A Liberal Theory Of Penal Justice* (Oxford, Oxford University Press, 2009).

First, as I will discuss in section IV.B on deterrence, we tolerate some breaches as legally acceptable (subject to the obligation to pay damages). Second, there has to be something special about the breach in question. This will be discussed in section V of this chapter.

In concluding this discussion, we may observe that there are other means to compensate for the sorts of moral injuries that Lee considers justify the award of exemplary damages. Both the Singaporean Court of Appeal in *PH Hydraulics* and the New Zealand Court of Appeal in *Paper Reclaim* observe that other remedies could be utilised to redress outrageous breaches of contract,[106] including damages for mental distress. However, damages for mental distress are not readily available in contract (and particularly not for commercial contracts). In Australia, at least, damages for distress are only available for contracts the aim of which is relaxation, enjoyment and freedom from molestation.[107] Neither a commercial lease of an office building nor a home insurance contract would qualify for distress damages under that test: yet there is a sense in which we may think that the plaintiffs are justly aggrieved and distressed. Exemplary damages can be an alternative way of acknowledging that the contumelious nature of the breach caused distress that should be recognised (this will be discussed further in section IV.C in relation to the declaratory aspect of exemplary damages). It must be questioned in any given case, however, whether they are really a proper vehicle, and other vehicles like an expansion of mental distress damages or generous compensatory principles may be more appropriate.

B. Contract and Deterrence

Given that contract is self-interested, there is a question as to how much courts should allow remedies that deter breach: autonomy to bind oneself to a contract must be balanced against the autonomy to change one's mind.[108] In my view, the common law of contract leans towards allowing some level of change of mind, which is why damages are the presumptive remedy *unless* they are inadequate to compensate the plaintiff. That being said, if the plaintiff's interest in performance is to be protected, there should be some ways in which the defendant can be deterred from breaching unfairly.

Moreover, while contract is voluntary, there are entrenched limits upon the ability of parties to stipulate punitive and deterrent remedies. Thus, in *PH Hydraulics*, the Singaporean Court of Appeal held that the rule against penalties in contract is evidence that courts are not willing to accept deterrence and punishment as

[106] *PH Hydraulics* (n 2) [80]–[83]; *Paper Reclaim* (n 78) [182].

[107] *Baltic Shipping Co v Dillon* [1993] HCA 4, (1993) 176 CLR 344. Confirmed recently in *Moore v Scenic Tours Ltd* [2020] HCA 17.

[108] M Chen-Wishart, 'Specific Performance and Change of Mind' in G Virgo and S Worthington (eds), *Commercial Remedies: Resolving Controversies* (Cambridge, Cambridge University Press, 2017) 98.

legitimate aims of contract damages. Consequently, if the courts will not allow the contracting parties to stipulate punitive and deterrent remedies on their own behalf, a court should not impose unforeseen penalties *ex post facto*.[109] However, the UK Supreme Court and the Australian High Court have both narrowed the situations in which a clause may be found to be a penalty in *Cavendish Square Holding BV v Makdessi*[110] and *Paciocco v Australian and New Zealand Banking Ltd* respectively.[111] They held that where a party has a 'legitimate interest' in protecting the performance of a contract, stipulated damages may be imposed even where they are not a genuine pre-estimate of losses.[112] Consequently, in those jurisdictions, the scope for deterrent and even punitive remedies imposed by one of the parties on the other may be broader, as long as there is a 'legitimate interest' the remedy protects. Singapore, of course, is under no obligation to adopt the same approach.

By comparison with civilian jurisdictions such as France,[113] common law jurisdictions emphasise *pacta sunt servanda* to a lesser degree in the remedies awarded: breaching parties are more likely to be able to pay damages than to be compelled to perform. American scholars go further and argue that exemplary damages for breach of contract are inappropriate because they may deter 'efficient breaches' from occurring.[114] Efficient breach theory holds that if a party to an existing contract discerns a more profitable opportunity, he or she should be able to breach the contract with the first contracting party and make a more profitable contract with the second contracting party, and pay damages to the party, reflecting economic notions of 'Pareto efficiency'.[115] In my own view, 'efficient breach theory' is not a reason for rejecting remedies that deter breach.[116] It has the problems sometimes associated with economic theories, in that it makes certain over-simplifying assumptions that render its usefulness limited in explaining real world behaviour. First, it assumes that there are no transaction costs involved with breaching a contract and making it with a second party.[117] However, when it is suggested that rather than breaching, the party who wants the performance could contract with the recipient under the contract for the subject matter for the contract, efficient

[109] *PH Hydraulics* (n 2) [73], citing Rowan (n 74) 508; N Andrews et al, *Contractual Duties: Performance Breach, Termination and Remedies*, 1st edn (London, Sweet & Maxwell, 2011) [20-024]; and MP Harrington, '"A Lawless Science": Punitive Damages for Breach of Contract in Canada' (2015) 69 *Supreme Court Law Review* 185, 210. For further discussion of the operation of penalties doctrine, see Courtney, ch 12 of this volume; and Tiverios and McFarlane, ch 13 in this volume.

[110] *Cavendish Square Holding BV v Makdessi* [2015] UKSC 67, [2016] AC 1172.

[111] *Paciocco v Australian and New Zealand Banking Ltd* [2016] HCA 28, (2016) 258 CLR 252.

[112] For commentary on the likely impact of *Cavendish* on Singaporean law, see Y Goh and Y Man, 'English Reformulation of the Penalty Rule: Relevance in Singapore?' (2017) 29 *Singapore Academy of Law Journal* 257.

[113] See Rowan (n 70).

[114] *Thyssen* (n 78) 63; *Digital Pulse* (n 55) [184] (Mason P).

[115] See R Posner, *Economic Analysis of Law*, 9th edn (New York, Wolters Kluwer Law & Business, 2014) §4.10 for the classic description of 'efficient breach theory'.

[116] Barnett (n 96) 109–15.

[117] I Macneil, 'Efficient Breach of Contract: Circles in the Sky' (1982) 68 *Virginia Law Review* 947.

breach theorists object on the basis that there would be additional transaction costs. Second, it assumes that when a party chooses to breach, he or she knows the value the performance has for the other contracting party.[118] Third, it assumes that there will not be any negative relational consequences attached to breaching in this way,[119] and that the other contracting party will be indifferent between damages and performance.[120] The theory claims that it will lead to more 'efficient' outcomes in reality, in that all parties will be better off once breach has occurred, but it is not clear that this is in fact the case even on its own terms. It is also worth noting that 'efficient breach theory' has not been accepted by courts outside the United States,[121] and that indeed, in *Tabcorp*, and other cases, the High Court of Australia has disclaimed a role for 'efficient breach' in Australian law.[122] Moreover, as McBride has noted, there is room for punitive damages for the related tort of inducing breach of contract,[123] which would not be the case if courts were really concerned about efficient breach.

That being said, it is appropriate to leave room for 'tolerated breach' in many contracts;[124] if circumstances change, contractors should be able to breach and get out of a contract by paying damages if a substitute performance is readily available.[125] It is not contumelious to breach because you now find that you cannot do what you promised you could do, and in some circumstances it might actually improve the relationship between the parties to renegotiate and sort out a new deal as quickly as possible.[126] However, the kinds of circumstances in which exemplary damages for breach of contract might be available are not the kind of circumstances in which efficient breach or even tolerated breach would be relevant. They are situations where there is no reason or excuse for the breach.

[118] MA Eisenberg, 'Actual and Virtual Specific Performance, the Theory of Efficient Breach, and the Indifference Principle in Contract Law' (2005) 93 *California Law Review* 975; MA Eisenberg, 'The Disgorgement Interest in Contract Law' (2006) 105 *Michigan Law Review* 559.

[119] Macneil (n 117) 968–69.

[120] Eisenberg, 'Actual and Virtual Specific Performance' (n 118); Eisenberg, 'Disgorgement Interest' (n 118).

[121] Goudkamp (n 10) 328.

[122] *Zhu v The Treasurer of the State of New South Wales* [2004] HCA 56, (2004) 218 CLR 530 [128]; *Tabcorp* (n 91) [13].

[123] McBride (n 1) 387. In Australia see, eg, *Whitfield v De Lauret & Co Ltd* (n 21).

[124] D Friedmann, 'Economic Aspects of Damages and Specific Performance Compared' in D Saidov and R Cunnington (eds), *Contract Damages: Domestic and International Perspectives* (Oxford, Hart Publishing, 2008) 65.

[125] D Campbell and D Harris, 'In Defence of Breach: A Critique of Restitution and the Performance Interest' (2002) 22 *Journal of Legal Studies* 208, 217–21; ibid 74–83.

[126] D Campbell, 'The Relational Constitution of Remedy: Co-operation as the Implicit Second Principle of Remedies for Breach of Contract' (2005) 11 *Texas Wesleyan Law Review* 455; D Campbell, 'A Relational Critique of the Third Restatement of Restitution § 39' (2011) 68 *Washington and Lee Law Review* 1063, 1093–1109; D Campbell, 'What Do We Mean by the Non-Use of Contract?' in J Braucher, J Kidwell and WC Whitford (eds), *Revisiting the Contracts Scholarship of Stewart Macaulay: on the empirical and lyrical* (Oxford, Hart Publishing, 2013) 159, 179–81; K Barnett, 'The Performance Interest in Australian Contract Law' in J Eldridge and T Pilkington (eds), *Australian Contract Law in the 21st Century: Debates and Directions* (Alexandria, Federation Press, forthcoming 2021).

Sometimes it has been argued that exemplary damages are inappropriate for contract because contract mostly governs commercial relationships, where compensation for loss is easy to calculate by contrast to the law of tort.[127] Moreover, the assumption is that the object of contract damages (being primarily commercial) is simply to be bound by the terms of the contract, and that accordingly, a plaintiff is not entitled to be made whole as with a tort, but is simply entitled to have his or her expectation under the contract compensated.[128] It follows that there is no room for deterrence, only for efficiency. It is true to say that many contracts are commercial, and that expectation damages will be entirely adequate to compensate for breach of most such contracts. However, the argument that contractual loss is easy to calculate is dangerously overstated: in some circumstances it can be very difficult, or impossible, to work out what the expectation was.[129] Moreover, it can be argued that a highly exceptional remedy should be available for those breaches of contract (typically, but not always contracts protecting non-commercial interests) where the loss is not easy to calculate and where the breach is conscious and outrageous. Moreover, the argument as to 'commercial uncertainty' is likely also overstated.[130] As I will outline, cases in which exemplary damages have been awarded for breach of contract are rare. As Bant and Paterson have noted in their chapter, it is not commercially useful to have breaches that undermine trust in society,[131] and in fact, in the recent case of *Ancient Order of Foresters in Victoria Friendly Society Ltd v Lifeplan Australia Friendly Society Ltd*, the High Court seemed to look sideways at the doctrine of deceit in imposing a strict remoteness rule.[132]

C. Contract and the Declaratory Theory of Punishment

I do not think that exemplary damages as a mechanism to prevent vengeance or as a means of self-help by the victim has particular relevance in the area of contract (compared to the criminal law and tort). The concern in this area is not (generally) to prevent duelling or vendettas.

However, there is still a role for a declaratory aspect to exemplary damages. A declaratory award may exceptionally be appropriate because of the importance of contracting as a social practice. As Kimel has argued, contract enables deals between strangers, parties who do not trust or know each other.[133] Trust in contract as a societal institution is undermined where it is breached in a flagrant

[127] *Thyssen* (n 77) 63.

[128] *Vorvis* (n 14) 1107 (Beetz, McIntyre and Lamer JJ in the majority).

[129] See, eg, *McRae v Commonwealth Disposals Commission* [1951] HCA 79, (1951) 84 CLR 377; *Commonwealth v Amann Aviation Pty Ltd* [1991] HCA 54, (1991) 174 CLR 64.

[130] Goudkamp (n 10) 325.

[131] Bant and Paterson, ch 10, section I.

[132] *Ancient Order of Foresters in Victoria Friendly Society Ltd v Lifeplan Australia Friendly Society Ltd* [2018] HCA 43, (2018) 92 ALJR 918 ('*Lifeplan*'). See Bant and Paterson, ch 10, section IV.A.

[133] D Kimel, *From Promise to Contract: Towards a Liberal Theory of Contract* (Oxford, Hart Publishing, 2003) ch 3.

or egregious manner with no consequences for the wrongdoer. That being said, as noted earlier, Kimel is of the opinion that contract should not be overly moralised, because this goes against the liberal normative principles that underpin it.[134] He admits there are cases where the potential harm to the institution of contract that a breach may engender is independent of or exceeds harm to the contracting party, and cites *Blake* as such a case.[135] However, he issues three cautions: first, that specific relief may be the best remedy for such a breach; second, that often criminal law or tortious actions have also been committed, and these may be the best way of dealing with such actions; and, third, that there seems no reason why the plaintiff out of everyone should benefit from disgorgement or exemplary awards.[136] Taking these concerns into account, I have identified working criteria for the award of exemplary damages in contract that should not unduly undermine the norms underlying contract. In fact, they may strengthen the institution of contract *qua* contract.

V. Guidance for the Award of Exemplary Damages in Contract

I suggest that there are four elements that may (occasionally) lead to the award of exemplary damages for breach of contract. They are as follows:

1. Other remedies are unavailable or not wholly adequate: these include compensatory damages, including damages for mental distress; specific relief; reasonable fee awards (however characterised) and accounts of profits.
2. The breach must be malicious or egregious, probably to a higher degree than for other areas of private law where exemplary damages are available because contract tolerates some self-interested behaviour, but this by itself is not enough.
3. There must be a 'legitimate interest' in the performance of the contract:
   (a) One indicator of this is an 'agency problem': (i) the contract must have required the breaching party to act in the other party's best interest; (ii) it must have been in the breaching party's self-interest to breach and difficult for the other party to detect; and (iii) the risk of breach must fall disproportionately upon the other party.
   (b) Another indicator of a legitimate interest seems to be that the non-breaching party acts with outrage to the breach and displays contemporaneous and genuine distress; it is not just commercial brinksmanship. However, when this is present, it should be strongly considered whether an extension of aggravated damages is a better option.

[134] Kimel (n 57).
[135] ibid 228.
[136] ibid 229.

4. To allow breach in these circumstances must in some way undermine the institution of contract itself; and the court must also identify a public policy reason why declaratory punishment should be imposed.

In Table 9.1 I have collected several notable common law cases in which exemplary damages for breach of contract were claimed, and have attempted to draw out relevant characteristics of the cases. (I omit any consideration of US cases, because their law is different in this regard.[137]) The cases are few and far between: seven cases in superior common law courts over some 30 years.

Case	**Jurisdiction**	**Nature of dispute**	**Remedies awarded**	**Nature of breach?**	**Agency problem?**	**Mental distress caused?**
Vorvis v Insurance Corporation of British Columbia [1989] 1 SCR 108	Canada (SCC)	Employment contract (unfair dismissal)	Majority: ADs + EDs may be available but not here.[138] Minority: ADs + EDs	Malicious	Yes	Yes
Royal Bank of Canada v W Got & Associates Electric Ltd [1999] 3 SCR 408	Canada (SCC)	Commercial banking contract and conversion	CDs[139] + EDs	Dishonest and abuse of court process	Yes	Yes
Whiten v Pilot Insurance Company [2002] 1 SCR 595	Canada (SCC)	House insurance contract	CDs + EDs	Malicious and dishonest	Yes	Yes
Performance Industries Ltd v Sylvan Lake Golf & Tennis Club [2002] 1 SCR 678	Canada (SCC)	Land development contract	Rectification only	Dishonest	No. Plaintiff did not notice mistake in written contract	Unclear
Harris v Digital Pulse [2003] NSWCA 10, (2003) 56 NSWLR 298	Australia (NSWCA)	Employment contract + breach of fiduciary duty	AOP[140] for breach of fiduciary duty only	Dishonest and fraudulent	Yes	Not mentioned

(continued)

[137] Sharkey, ch 7 of this volume, discusses the prevalence of punitive awards in the United States. Exemplary damages in the United States are more common and more generous than elsewhere.
[138] 'ADs' stands for aggravated damages and 'EDs' stands for exemplary damages.
[139] 'CDs' stands for compensatory damages *simpliciter* (without any aggravated component).
[140] 'AOP' stands for account of profits.

(Continued)

Case	Jurisdiction	Nature of dispute	Remedies awarded	Nature of breach?	Agency problem?	Mental distress caused?
Paper Reclaim Ltd v Aotearoa International Ltd [2006] 3 NZLR 188	New Zealand (NZCA)	Commercial agency contract	CDs only	Not dishonest or fraudulent	Not in relation to the particular breach.	No (mental distress damages discussed but not awarded)
PH Hydraulics & Engineering Pte Ltd v Airtrust (Hong Kong) Ltd [2017] SGCA 26	Singapore (SGCA)	Commercial design, engineering and manufacturing contract	CDs only	Not fraudulent. Gross negligence at most.	Yes	No (mental distress damages discussed but not awarded)
Atlantic Lottery Corp Ltd v Babstock 2020 SCC 19	Canada (SCC)	Gaming contract class action	Majority: EDs and AOP may be available but not here. Minority: EDs and AOP may be available here.	Majority: not breach of general duty of good faith. Minority: possible breach of general duty of good faith.	Yes, but majority found no breach.	Not discussed

From a survey of the case law, it can be seen that it does not matter whether the contract is a consumer or a commercial contract (although as Bant and Paterson discuss in this collection, consumer issues are also dealt with by statute),[141] but it does matter whether or not the clause breached gives rise to an agency problem, and whether the breach was deliberate, dishonest or malicious: each of these things appear to be preconditions for an award. I discuss each of my enumerated factors in detail in this section, in reference to the cases considered in Table 9.1. *Atlantic Lottery Corp* involved the question of whether pleadings should be struck out: the majority held that the contract was not one that attracted a general duty of good faith which was then breached[142] and, accordingly, exemplary damages were not available.

[141] Bant and Paterson, ch 10 of this volume.

[142] *Atlantic Lottery Corp* (n 72) [63]–[65] (Abella, Moldaver, Côté, Brown and Rowe JJ); cf [133]–[134], (Wagner CJ, Karakatsanis, Martin and Kasirer JJ).

A. Other Remedies are Unavailable or Not Wholly Adequate

Of course generally, some other kind of other remedy is awarded before exemplary damages are awarded: usually compensatory damages and/or aggravated damages. Exemplary damages have been described as 'parasitic on compensatory damages'.[143] It is necessary to make out all elements of the host cause of action.[144] Generally (although not always) the court has already awarded compensatory damages *simpliciter* or aggravated damages, and then decides whether exemplary damages are necessary to punish or deter.[145] Therefore it follows that compensatory damages *simpliciter* or aggravated damages may already have been awarded (if they are available on the facts) but that exemplary damages have been awarded on the top of this because the court thinks the damages already awarded not adequate without more.

The Canadian cases show that sometimes, very rarely, a breach of contract can be serious enough that a court feels moved to award exemplary damages. However, it should first be emphasised that if *any* other kind of award is available and adequate, including maximum compensatory damages (as in *Tabcorp*), damages for mental distress, a reasonable fee or an accounts of profit for breach of contract (as in *Blake*), these should be awarded instead. This is because punishment is not a primary aim of contract law and does not fit well with its normative underpinnings. As the Singaporean Court of Appeal has outlined, courts are reluctant to enforce self-stipulated punitive remedies designated by the parties, let alone to impose punitive remedies *ex post facto* without the parties agreeing.

There is at least arguably an increasing tendency towards allowing other exceptional remedies in contract that deter breach. It has already been noted that the Singaporean Court of Appeal in *PH Hydraulics* and the New Zealand Court of Appeal in *Paper Reclaim* argued that cases could be dealt with by awards of damages for distress. Each of these courts, and recently the Supreme Court of Canada in *Atlantic Lottery Corp*, has noted that other deterrent and punitive remedies could be utilised to deal with outrageous breaches of contract.[146] The Singaporean Court of Appeal and the Supreme Court of Canada noted the availability of

[143] *XL Petroleum* (n 21) 468–69 (Brennan J).

[144] ibid 469 (Brennan J); *Fatimi Pty Ltd v Bryant* [2004] NSWCA 140, (2004) 59 NSWLR 678 [72] (Giles JA).

[145] *New South Wales v Ibbett* [2006] HCA 57, (2006) 229 CLR 638 [34]; *New South Wales v Radford* [2010] NSWCA 276, (2010) 79 NSWLR 327 [94] (Sackville AJA). Courts may be able to award exemplary damages in the absence of compensatory damages for torts actionable per se, or where statute bars compensation but not exemplary awards. See Barnett and Harder (n 36) [14.16]. As contract is actionable per se, this is presumably the case for contract too.

[146] *PH Hydraulics* (n 2) [80]–[83]; *Paper Reclaim* (n 78) [182]; *Atlantic Lottery Corp* (n 72) [52]–[59] (Abella, Moldaver, Côté, Brown and Rowe JJ), [107]–[128] (Wagner CJ, Karakatsanis, Martin and Kasirer JJ).

Wrotham Park damages,[147] and the Singaporean Court of Appeal, the New Zealand Court of Appeal and the Supreme Court of Canada noted the availability of accounts of profits pursuant to *Blake*.[148]

As I have also noted elsewhere, the legitimate interest test provided by *Blake* has proved notoriously difficult to apply in subsequent cases, and moreover, the English Supreme Court appeared to back away from *Blake* in *One Step (Support) Ltd v Morris-Garner*, albeit without overruling it.[149] However, I think that if the legitimate interest test is properly explained it can provide a useful guide for the award of exemplary damages in contract as well as gain-based relief. Put shortly, my argument is that accounts of profit for breach of contract should only be awarded where compensatory damages are inadequate, specific relief is unavailable, and where a profit has been made and the breach in question is wilful (or reckless). This typically only occurs in two sorts of cases: 'second sale' cases, where the subject matter of the contract is non-substitutable and unavailable on the market, and what I call 'agency problem' cases, involving breaches of negative covenant (of which *Blake* was an example). 'Agency' here is used in the economic rather than the legal sense: it denotes a relationship that is difficult to supervise. Typically, in a contractual sense, it means that Amos has made a contract with Betty to protect her interests, but there is 'moral hazard' in the sense that it is in Amos's interests to breach, Amos holds the discretion as to whether to perform and all the risks lie on Betty's side. Moreover, such contracts are typically difficult to monitor, precisely because Amos has the discretion and the power. It will be suggested in section V.C that the 'agency problem' cases may also be amenable to an exceptional award of exemplary damages if (and only if) no other remedies are adequate. However, the 'second sale' cases can be ignored for the purposes of exemplary damages, because they are cases in which an account of profits will be adequate and appropriate.

It is evident from this that I have previously argued elsewhere that accounts of profit for breach of contract should be available in exceptional circumstances,[150]

[147] Derived from *Wrotham Park Estate Co v Parkside Homes Ltd* [1974] 1 WLR 798 (Ch). This form of damages has recently been decided to be compensatory in Singapore in *Turf Club Auto Emporium Pte Ltd v Yeo Boong Hua* [2018] SGCA 44, [2018] 2 SLR 655 [179], [191], [271] and in England in *One Step (Support) Ltd v Morris-Garner* [2018] UKSC 20, [2019] AC 649 ('*Morris-Garner*'). The majority in *Atlantic Lottery Corp* (n 72) [56]–[57] also preferred a compensatory approach. The minority in *Atlantic Lottery Corp* (n 72) [121] seemed prepared to countenance a gain-based approach.

[148] *Blake* (n 95). The possibility of an account of profits for breach of contract has been left open in Singapore in *MFM Restaurants Pte Ltd v Fish & Co Restaurants Pte Ltd* [2010] SGCA 36, [2011] 1 SLR 150 [54]; and *ACES System Development Pte Ltd v Yenty Lily (trading as Access International Services)* [2013] SGCA 53, [2013] 4 SLR 1317 [53]–[55]. It has been accepted in New Zealand in *Attorney-General for England and Wales v R* [2002] 2 NZLR 91 [112]–[113], [146]–[152], and in Canada in *Amartek Inc v Canadian Commercial Corp* (2003) 229 DLR (4th) 419 (overruled in *Amartek Inc v Canadian Commercial Corp* (2005) 76 OR (3d) 241; 256 DLR (4th) 287 on different bases); *Smith v Landstar Properties Inc* [2011] BCCA 44; *NTI v Canada (Attorney-General)* [2012] NUCJ 11 [306]–[334]. It has not been accepted in Australia: see *Hospitality Group Pty Ltd v Australian Rugby Union Ltd* (2001) 110 FCR 157 [155]–[159] (Hill and Finkelstein JJ).

[149] *Morris-Garner* (n 147). See discussion in K Barnett, 'Restitution, Compensation and Disgorgement' in E Bant, K Barker and S Degeling (eds), *Research Handbook on Unjust Enrichment and Restitution* (Cheltenham, Edward Elgar, 2020) 456, 469–70.

[150] Barnett (n 96). See also Edelman (n 63).

and agree that if there is a choice between a gain-based award and exemplary damages, the courts should opt for the 'sharp axe' of disgorgement or restitution, rather than the 'blunt axe' of exemplary damages.[151]

Thus, in *Performance Industries*, a decision handed down the same day as *Whiten*, exemplary damages were not awarded even though the defendants had knowingly and dishonestly relied on a mistake in the written contract, knowing that it did not reflect the oral agreement the written agreement sought to reflect. The court contented itself with ordering rectification of the written contract. There were two reasons for this. First, rectification was adequate to meet the plaintiff's expectation. Second, as I will discuss in section V.C, the case was not one where there was an 'agency problem'.

Even if there is an agency problem and the breach was deliberate, dishonest or malicious, it does not necessary follow from this that exemplary damages will be awarded if another remedy will be adequate: thus, in *Digital Pulse*, an account of profits was awarded for breach of fiduciary duty, although the trial judge had doubted whether this was adequate in the circumstances because the defendants had destroyed evidence, and thus the losses or gains that could be quantified were minimal. The majority in *Digital Pulse* held that exemplary damages were inappropriate for breach of fiduciary duty, Heydon JA on the historical basis of equity[152] and Spiegelman CJ on the basis that exemplary damages were not available in Australia for the breach of contract in that case, and should be unavailable for the concurrent breach of fiduciary duty.[153] My own view is that the better position would be to say that exemplary damages are not *invariably* unavailable for breach of contract (or indeed breach of fiduciary duty), and that history alone is not enough to justify this conclusion, but that there may be reasons to deny exemplary damages in that particular case.[154] In any case, the recent Australian High Court case of *Lifeplan* shows that deterrence can operate very strongly in breach of fiduciary cases involving rival businesses, and that accounts of profit can be used to effect that.[155]

B. Malicious, Dishonest or Fraudulent

The case law indicates that the defendant's conduct must be malicious or egregious (not just ordinary commercial brinksmanship) and that the general public would find such conduct repugnant, which links to the necessity to show that the defendant is deserving of retribution. I see 'malicious' as importing a subjective standard, whereas 'egregious' imports a more objective standard.

[151] Edelman (n 63) 17. See also Berryman (n 49) 880; Tettenborn (n 77) 1560.
[152] *Digital Pulse* (n 54) [404]–[420].
[153] ibid [28]–[44]; cf [182]–[184] (Mason P).
[154] See A Duggan, 'Exemplary Damages in Equity: A Law and Economics Perspective' (2006) 26 *OJLS* 303, 315.
[155] *Lifeplan* (n 132).

However, it is notable that in most of the cases in which damages have been awarded, there is something objectively approaching fraud. Thus in *Whiten*, the insurance company accused the insured of fraud and arson, although their own investigators had repeatedly said this was not the case and there was no basis for claiming this: the motive appears to have been to force the insured to settle for less. In *Got*, the bank failed to inform the customer that it had called on the debt and sought to appoint receivers for failure to repay, and committed an abuse of process by informing the court that it had followed the proper procedure, whereupon the court appointed a receiver and later granted the receiver further powers.

A lack of fraud or malice seems to be fatal to a claim for exemplary damages for breach of contract, and it is relevant that in both *PH Hydraulics* and *Paper Reclaim*, the Courts of Appeal in both cases overturned the trial judge's findings that the breaches were actuated by fraud or malice. And in *Atlantic Lottery Corp*, the majority said that the Atlantic Lottery Corporation had not been criminal, nor breached a duty of good faith.[156] By contrast, the minority would have been prepared to find that there had been a possible breach of good faith or duty to render honest performance, and would have allowed the claim accordingly.[157]

However, even if it can be established, fraud or malice by itself is not enough. In *Performance Industries*, as already noted, although the defendant was fraudulent and malicious, the court simply ordered rectification of the written contract.

C. Legitimate Interest in Performance of the Contract

It is suggested that the plaintiff must have a 'legitimate interest' in ensuring the contract is performed.

An indicator of whether this is the case is whether there is an 'agency problem' in the economic sense, where one party agrees to act in another's interests pursuant to the contract, all the risk lies on the other party's side and it is in the interests of the first party to breach, and it is difficult to detect the breach before it occurs. In both *Whiten* and *Got*, the defendants pursued their own self-interest at the expense of the plaintiffs, and it was difficult for the plaintiffs to monitor that breach. Moreover, all the risks of the breach lay on the plaintiffs. Comparatively, *Performance Industries* did not involve an agency problem. The plaintiff simply failed to notice that the defendant's solicitor had recorded the oral contract incorrectly in the written version. In *Atlantic Lottery Corp*, the majority characterised the plaintiffs' complaint as 'simply that they paid to play a gambling game and did not get exactly what they paid for'.[158] On this view, it was patently obvious to anyone who entered into a gambling contract that there was a possibility of

[156] *Atlantic Lottery Corp* (n 72) [63]–[65] (Abella, Moldaver, Côté, Brown and Rowe JJ).
[157] ibid [133]–[134] (Wagner CJ, Karakatsanis, Martin and Kasirer JJ).
[158] ibid [61] (Abella, Moldaver, Côté, Brown and Rowe JJ).

losing, and there was no expectation that the Atlantic Lottery Corp would act in the plaintiffs' best interests: indeed, the very nature of a gambling contract suggests otherwise. The minority took a different view, and were prepared at least to allow the plaintiffs to argue that the Atlantic Lottery Corp 'intentionally deceived those playing members of the public by knowingly providing an unfair game and putting them at risk of gambling addiction in order to turn a profit'.[159] Their preparedness to characterise the facts thus, and to admit the existence of 'quasi-fiduciary duties',[160] shows that they considered that it was possible to argue that the gambling contracts displayed an agency problem, where the gambling provider held all the power, and ensured that the players became addicted and acted against their own self-interest.

It may be difficult for courts to ascertain whether a plaintiff has a genuine legitimate interest in the contract's being performed. It is interesting to note that in *Tabcorp*, the compensatory damages case mentioned earlier, the court emphasised that the contractual breach caused significant distress for the individuals concerned. The Court began its judgment with a vivid description of the dismay of the director of the lessor:

> She [Mrs Bergamin] was shocked and dismayed to see what remained of the floor stone work being jack hammered. A large bin was filled with the debris of the foyer. This destruction had been carried out by a tenant, Tabcorp Holdings Ltd ('the Tenant'), the appellant in this appeal.
>
> Why was Mrs Bergamin shocked and dismayed? She was a director of the respondent, Bowen Investments Pty Ltd ('the Landlord'), a company which owned the building. She had taken particular care over and interest in the construction of the foyer. It was of high quality.[161]

The distressing nature of the breach to the individual plaintiff and her protestations against the breach were brought to the fore, and while the court did not award exemplary damages, it did award the maximum level of compensatory damages, unreduced by a betterment discount. It did not matter to the court that *Tabcorp* was a commercial lease: the special subjective value of the foyer to the lessor had been protected by a contractual clause, and this had been ignored by the lessee. The immediate distress in response to the breach seems to have been taken by the court as evidence that the plaintiff had a genuine legitimate interest in the contract (compared to a case like *Ruxley*, where there seems to have been a suspicion that the home owner did not genuinely care *that* much about the depth of the pool, and it was actually a game of commercial brinksmanship).

Interestingly, in the three Canadian cases in which exemplary damages have been awarded or discussed as a possibility, mental distress of the non-breaching party has been prominent, reflecting the fact that the distress may have evidenced

[159] ibid [125] (Wagner CJ, Karakatsanis, Martin and Kasirer JJ).
[160] ibid [122] (Wagner CJ, Karakatsanis, Martin and Kasirer JJ)
[161] *Tabcorp* (n 91) [1]–[2].

some kind of legitimate interest. Exemplary damages may have been awarded perhaps because of the lack of prevalence of aggravated damages in contract: there is no other way to compensate for behaviour that has been injurious to the plaintiff because of the manner in which it has occurred. Of course, this is an aim quite different from that of exemplary damages; the aim of aggravated damages is primarily to compensate, not to punish.[162] *If* the aim of a court in awarding exemplary damages is to compensate for distress, but the problem is the lack of any adequate mechanism by which to do that, we should expand the availability of damages for mental distress or consider other compensatory measures, rather than using exemplary damages as a heavy-handed alternative mechanism.

D. Identifying a Public Policy Reason as to Why Declaratory Punishment is Necessary

The court must identify a broader societal reason why we wish to deter the breach in question, and the breach must be of a nature where a declaratory punishment is necessary having regard to that reason. I suggest that the breach must be such that it harms not just the plaintiff, but also the institution of contracting and society more generally itself. To have insurance companies attempt to fraudulently deny payouts to the insured, as in *Whiten*, is not socially advisable and has no societal benefit (quite the contrary). Similarly, to have banks fail to advise a client that they are calling on the debt and appointing receivers undermines the procedure under the contract itself. I also tentatively suggest that an award of exemplary damages in a contract case may be a 'canary in a coal mine', which suggests that Parliament should intervene to ensure that area of law is properly regulated, with pecuniary penalties of the kind outlined in Bant and Paterson's chapter;[163] this may be a more appropriate method of dealing with systemic contracting problems.

VI. Conclusion

This chapter has attempted to outline the exceptional circumstances in which exemplary damages for breach of contract might be appropriate. It has explored the historical and normative basis of exemplary damages, and then how those normative concerns may conflict with some of the normative concerns of contract. It has been suggested that generally, exemplary damages for breach of contract

[162] It is acknowledged here that the distinctions between compensatory damages *simpliciter*, aggravated damages and exemplary damages are not always easy to draw, and courts sometimes blur the boundaries, but nonetheless the formal aim of aggravated damages is different from that of exemplary damages: the plaintiff's hurt feelings are not as relevant as whether the defendant has done something that deserves punishment.

[163] Bant and Paterson, ch 10 in this volume.

will not be appropriate, simply because contract is concerned with autonomy, minimal intervention and voluntarily undertaken obligations. However, it has also been suggested that we should exceptionally consider such an award in very rare circumstances where no other remedy will suffice; where the breach is malicious, dishonest and fraudulent; where there is a legitimate interest in the performance of the contract (indicated by whether there is an 'agency problem'); and where the institution of contract is undermined and there is no other tortious or criminal law principle to deal with the problem.

10

Effecting Deterrence through Proportionate Punishment: An Assessment of Statutory and General Law Principles

ELISE BANT AND JEANNIE MARIE PATERSON*

I. Introduction

In common law jurisdictions, the domain of private law is increasingly overlaid by legislation that provides individuals with remedial rights and regulators with enforcement powers to respond to serious commercial misconduct. A comparative review of these kinds of statutes and the law reform agenda surrounding them across Australia, England, Singapore and the United States shows widespread and growing attention given to the use of civil penalties, a form of fine, to deter contravening conduct.

This focus on deterrence has been particularly evident in statutory regimes aimed at protecting consumers in markets for goods and services and for financial products. This is not surprising. Consumers classically operate in almost the paradigmatic situation of unequal bargaining power, typically with considerable information asymmetries between trader and consumer, along with limits on cognitive capacity, time and experience in making and negotiating contracts. Behaviour that distorts consumer choice by misleading, coercing or taking advantage of the inevitable information asymmetry in consumer transactions, undermines consumers' capacity to make welfare-enhancing decisions and distorts the efficiency of the market. On top of this, consumers rarely have the means to litigate over relatively small-value disputes with traders. This combination of factors

* This chapter forms part of an Australian Council Research-funded Discovery Project DP180100932 on 'Developing a Rational Law of Misleading Conduct'. Our thanks to the participants at the Punishment and Private Law conference held at NUS in December 2019 for their helpful feedback on an earlier draft of this chapter, to Calvin Collins for his excellent editing assistance, and to Kit Barker, Catherine Sharkey and James Goudkamp for their very insightful further comments and references.

presents a serious regulatory challenge for the law, governments and regulators concerned to promote efficient, free and fair markets.

However, it is not only in the field of consumer law that the role of civil penalties and deterrence has attracted serious and sustained attention. Intellectual property wrongs have long employed strongly deterrent remedial measures. Although now largely located in statutes, their doctrinal foundations are laid on economic torts[1] that also yielded forms of relief such as accounts of profit and exemplary damages,[2] which clearly aimed to discourage repeated misconduct.

Moreover, and notwithstanding *Rookes v Barnard*,[3] punitive damages continue to be accepted by common law countries as an indispensable, if exceptional, weapon in the private law remedial armoury. Where excluded by statute, it is arguable that punitive awards have tended to creep in in other guises, such as aggravated damages.[4] Certainly, strongly deterrent measures are already implicit in many wholly unexceptional, compensatory remedies. It is well known, for example, that the remoteness rules for the tort of deceit are drawn more broadly than for negligence, both to ensure full compensation of the victim and deterrence of future wrongdoing by the defendant and others similarly disposed to wrongdoing.[5] More generally, in many cases compensation will operate as a stringent deterrent measure, requiring the defendant to dig deep into his pockets in circumstances where there has been little or no profit from the wrongdoing. Equity has also long employed powerful tools to prevent and deter wrongdoing, from injunctive relief supported by contempt procedures through to requiring wrongdoers to account for and disgorge their profits from wrongdoing.

This chapter seeks to explore some lessons offered by this rich interplay between common law, equitable and statutory principles concerned to deter serious misconduct. Its principal thesis, drawing on Kit Barker's powerful insights in

[1] Consistently, in Singapore, the intellectual property wrongs are treated as any other tort: *Main-Line Corporate Holdings Ltd v United Overseas Bank Ltd* [2009] SGHC 232, [2010] 1 SLR 189 [18] (Belinda Ang Saw Ean J).

[2] See, eg, Gummow J's illuminating discussions of the tort of passing off and the account of profits in *10th Cantanae Pty Ltd v Shoshana Pty Ltd* (1987) 79 ALR 299, 319–23 and *ConAgra Inc v McCain Foods (Aust) Pty Ltd* (1992) 33 FCR 302, 363–64. It may be observed that this analysis provides further support for Justice Edelman's extra-curial statements that deceit likewise yielded and should continue to attract disgorgement damages: see J Edelman, JNE Varuhas and S Colton (eds), *McGregor on Damages*, 20th edn (London, Sweet & Maxwell, 2018) paras 15-041–15-044. In Australia, deceit is seen as the archetypal claim likely to yield the sorts of egregious facts that attract exemplary damages: *Musca v Astle Corporation Pty Ltd* (1988) 80 ALR 251, 268 (French J). Compare the tortured road taken in England, discussed in *Kuddus v Chief Constable of Leicester* [2001] UKHL 29, [2002] 2 AC 122 generally and at [122] (Lord Scott) on deceit in particular.

[3] *Rookes v Barnard* [1964] AC 1129 (HL).

[4] The English battle to re-characterise 'additional damages' for breach of copyright as compensatory is a good example: See also P Johnson, 'Compounding Uncertainty: The Need for Guidelines in the Assessment of Additional Damages for Copyright Infringement' (2019) 2 *Intellectual Property Quarterly* 136 and discussion below in the text connected to n 22.

[5] *Doyle v Olby (Ironmongers) Ltd* [1969] 2 QB 158 (CA) 167 (Lord Denning MR); *Smith New Court Securities Ltd v Citibank NA* [1997] AC 254 (HL), 264–67 (Lord Browne Wilkinson), 283 (Lord Steyn); *Palmer Bruyn & Parker Pty Limited v Parsons* [2001] HCA 69, (2001) 208 CLR 388 [78] (Gummow J).

his chapter, is that statutory and general law deterrent regimes embrace punitive concepts and elements to effect their goals. However, they also show a concern that punishment should be proportionate and not excessive. We suggest that the principles of proportionate punishment can and should be articulated. Currently, at least under statute, courts often emphasise deterrence without exploring the measures that may be most effective at achieving that goal, while also being primarily influenced by factors that mitigate the potentially harsh, overly punitive effects of such awards. The combination serves to undermine the effectiveness of the statutory schemes. Expounding the principles and role of proportionate punishment may not only address this problem, but also help support development of more consistent deterrent regulatory regimes across common law, equity and statute.

These lessons are illustrated and developed by reference to the Australian experience. There, civil pecuniary penalties regimes have been adopted in key consumer and commercial statutes, leading courts to develop a detailed jurisprudence on their operation. However, ongoing law reform efforts by the Australian Government reflect concern that the legislative strategies to date, as interpreted and applied by the courts, have not been effective in deterring significant, and, in some cases, highly culpable, breaches of the law. In many cases, penalty awards have not approached the statutory maximum, nor gone anywhere near eliminating the gain made by the contravention, yet neither have they been measured in a manner to internalise the loss suffered by consumers. We suggest that such regimes may be more effective if they explicitly recognise the role of proportionate punishment in effecting deterrence. This concept can be articulated by reference to general law principles, which render it amenable to curial oversight and consistent with the goals of civil law. In this chapter, the particular focus is on the contribution offered by equity's longstanding jurisdiction to strip profits from wrongdoers. While equity's aims here are ostensibly general and specific deterrence, it employs mechanisms that visit proportionate punishment on defendants in order to achieve those goals.

The recent High Court of Australia decision in *Ancient Order of Foresters in Victoria Friendly Society Ltd v Lifeplan Australia Friendly Society Ltd*,[6] provides a principled and staged model of effective deterrence in equity. Moreover, the case suggests that similar models of deterrence are found across the private law, including, for example, in deceit and intellectual property torts. These private law models of proportionate punishment utilised to deter unlawful conduct should be of interest to all those engaged in regulation of serious civil misconduct.

The chapter commences in section II by tracing the continued interest in statutory and general law deterrence for economic wrongs across England, New Zealand, Singapore and the United States, before turning to examine the Australian position in section III. Section IV examines the paradigm of disgorgement damages recently articulated by the High Court of Australia in the context

[6] *Ancient Order of Foresters in Victoria Friendly Society Ltd v Lifeplan Australia Friendly Society Ltd* [2018] HCA 43, (2018) 265 CLR 1 (*Lifeplan*).

of a claim for an account of profits for knowing assistance in a breach of fiduciary duty. The conclusion is that punishment is a principled response to serious civil wrongdoing as a means of effecting deterrence. Accordingly, it deserves greater jurisprudential attention than it has enjoyed to date across common law jurisdictions, to which we now turn.

II. The Role of Punishment in Deterrence

In this section, we do not seek to engage in an exhaustive account of, or assessment of the efficacy of, punitive and deterrent measures in private law seen across common law jurisdictions. Our aim is to trace what appears to be a significant momentum in favour of the recognition of such awards in the varied contexts of consumer law reform, intellectual property and pursuant to the common law principles of exemplary damages. The survey makes apparent the value placed by parliaments and courts alike on remedial and regulatory measures that aim to deter serious wrongdoing. Our observation is that as punitive considerations indubitably inform and influence these developments, a chief concern, emphasised by the courts, remains how to ensure that the awards are kept within principled boundaries.

A. The United Kingdom

In 2018, the British Government published a Green Paper on *Modernising Consumer Markets*, in which it announced its intention to 'give civil courts the power to impose financial penalties on companies for breaches of consumer law'.[7] The proposed penalties would be subject to a cap of 10 per cent of a firm's worldwide turnover. The stated aim of 'this coercive power [would be to] discourage infringements and promote prompt swift compliance with the law when a breach has been identified'.[8] On 18 June 2019, the British Government further announced that it would

> consult on giving the Competition and Markets Authority (CMA) new powers to decide itself whether consumer law has been broken, without having to go through the courts as is currently the case. New powers would enable the CMA to intervene earlier and more quickly to tackle these failings and would include being able to directly impose fines on firms for poor business behaviour.[9]

[7] Department for Business, Energy & Industrial Strategy, *Modernising Consumer Markets: Consumer Green Paper* (Cm 9595, 2018) 57.

[8] ibid.

[9] Department for Business, Energy & Industrial Strategy, 'New Powers to Fine Firms That Exploit Consumer Loyalty' (Press Release, 19 June 2019) at www.gov.uk/government/news/new-powers-to-fine-firms-that-exploit-consumer-loyalty, accessed on 7 May 2020.

These recommendations are supported by other, non-pecuniary consumer protection proposals that have a strong deterrent element, such as that the UK Regulators Network publish annual corporate 'performance score cards'.[10] As the CMA has recognised, '[r]eputational measures designed to put pressure on businesses can have a real impact'[11] in deterring serious misconduct.

This recent interest in deterrent and punitive regulatory measures in the consumer context reflects the reality, noted by the Law Commission in its 1998 report *Aggravated, Exemplary and Restitutionary Damages*, that punitive awards are required to deter sustained and egregious wrongdoing that is otherwise left without adequate sanction.[12] We will not here examine the unprincipled restrictions imposed on punitive damages by *Rookes v Barnard*,[13] which appeared to confine their award to defined categories of case.[14] It suffices to say that after a detailed review of the relevant legal and policy issues, the Commission recommended that this approach be rejected in favour of a new approach in which they would be available in exceptional cases of 'deliberate and outrageous disregard of the plaintiff's rights'.[15] In November 1999, the UK Government accepted other recommendations from the report but brusquely rejected the proposals on exemplary damages, on the grounds:

> The purpose of the civil law on damages is to provide compensation for loss, and not to punish. The function of exemplary damages is more appropriate to the criminal law, and their availability in civil proceedings blurs the distinctions between the civil and criminal law. The Government does not intend any further statutory extension of their availability.[16]

This response was demonstrably wrong on the nature of damages[17] and wholly failed to engage with the comprehensive case that had been made by the Commission, which explicitly addressed the concern over collapse of the civil and criminal divide.[18] Since then, both courts[19] and those engaged in law reform[20]

[10] *Modernising Consumer Markets* (n 7) ch 2. See also Letter from The Rt Hon Greg Clarke to Dr Andrea Coscelli (17 June 2019) at www.gov.uk/government/publications/competition-and-markets-authority-loyalty-penalty-investigation-report-government-response, accessed on 7 May 2020.

[11] Competition & Markets Authority, 'Tackling the Loyalty Penalty' (19 December 2018) recommendation 3 at www.gov.uk/government/publications/tackling-the-loyalty-penalty/tackling-the-loyalty-penalty, accessed on 7 May 2020.

[12] Law Commission, *Aggravated, Exemplary and Restitutionary Damages* (Law Comm No 247, 1997); Law Commission (Ireland), *Report on Aggravated, Exemplary and Restitutionary Damages* (LRC 60, 2000) para 1.15.

[13] *Rookes* (n 3).

[14] See *Kuddus* (n 2).

[15] Law Commission (n 12) para 1.20.

[16] Department of Constitutional Affairs, *The Law on Damages* (CP 9/07, 2007) para 198.

[17] Edelman (n 2) paras 1.001–1.003, 1.008.

[18] As the Australian High Court has long noted, this divide may be less stark than commonly appreciated: see quotation extracted below at text connected to n 79.

[19] *Kuddus* (n 2) [63].

[20] Lord Justice Leveson, *An Inquiry into the Culture, Practices and Ethics of the Press* (HC 779, vol 4, 2012) para 5.12. See also Joint Committee on Privacy and Injunctions, *Privacy and Injunctions* (HL 273,

have observed ongoing need for these measures of remedies, to fill lacunae in the law that otherwise leave victims without effective remedy and wrongdoers undeterred.[21] Thus in the statutory field of 'additional damages' permitted for breach of copyright,[22] English courts have had an unedifying history[23] of vacillating between treating them as variously compensatory,[24] punitive[25] and restitutionary.[26] In 2018, in *Phonographic Performance Ltd v Ellis (t/a Bla Bla Bar)*,[27] the English Court of Appeal held that the awards are 'sui generis'[28] but clearly include damages designed to deter or punish, as well as restitutionary and disgorgement damages. We return to the interplay between these remedial aims in sections III and IV, but for present purposes it suffices to note that the decision is consistent with a groundswell of opinion favouring recognition of the legitimacy of remedies designed to deter by utilising a punitive element, across a range of statutory and general law contexts. However, concerns also continue to be expressed that any such damages need to meet (yet to be articulated) 'tests of necessity and proportionality'.[29]

B. Singapore

Singapore has recently introduced a range of measures to strengthen its consumer protection regime.[30] The Consumer Protection (Fair Trading) Act (CPFTA) was

HC 1443, 2012) para 134. The tortured route taken by successive governments following publication of the Leveson Report is detailed in J Woodhouse, 'Press regulation after Leveson' (Briefing Paper Number 07576, 27 July 2018) at https://commonslibrary.parliament.uk/research-briefings/cbp-7576/, accessed on 7 May 2020.

[21] The steady march of cases awarding exemplary cases is laid out in Edelman (n 2) ch 13.

[22] First introduced in Copyright Act 1956 (UK), s 17(3); now see the Copyright, Designs and Patents Act 1988 (UK) (CDPA 1988), s 97(2).

[23] Powerfully recounted in Johnson (n 4). As he notes, additional damages also exist for a range of other intellectual property-style rights: eg, performers' property rights (CDPA 1988, s 191J(2)); design rights (CDPA 1988, s 229(3)); technical protection measures (CDPA 1988, ss 296(2) and 296ZD(2)); digital rights management (CDPA 1988, s 296ZG(3)); unauthorised reception of transmission (CDPA 1988, s 298(2)); publication rights (Copyright and Related Rights Regulations 1966 (SI 1996/2967), reg 17); database rights (Copyright and Rights in Database Regulations 1997 (SI 1997/3032), reg 23); and for a limited purpose relating to seed reused under patent law (Patents Act 1977, sch A1, para 12(4)). cf Patents Act 1977 (Amendment) (No 2) HC Bill (2001-02) 126, which has not been enacted.

[24] *Rank Film Distributors Ltd v Video Information Centre* [1982] AC 380 (CA), 425.

[25] *Williams v Settle* [1960] 1 WLR 1072 (CA); *Rookes* (n 3) 1225 (Lord Devlin) kept open the possibility that this form of damages was exemplary in nature. See also Board of Trade, *Report of the Copyright Committee* (Cmd 8662, 1952) para 291, examined in Johnson (n 4).

[26] Department of Constitutional Affairs (n 16) para 211, drawing on *Nottinghamshire Healthcare NHS Trust v News Group Newspapers Ltd* [2002] EWHC 409 (Ch), [2002] EMLR 33.

[27] *Phonographic Performance Ltd v Ellis (t/a Bla Bla Bar)* [2018] EWCA Civ 2812.

[28] ibid [36] and [37]. See also *O'Mara Books v Express Newspapers* [1999] FSR 49, 57.

[29] *Mosley v News Group Newspapers Ltd* [2008] EWHC 1777 (QB) [197] (Mr Justice Eady).

[30] See generally L Nottage et al, *ASEAN Consumer Law: Harmonisation and Cooperation, Achievements and Challenges* (Cambridge, Cambridge University Press, 2019) chs 4 and 7.

amended in 2016 to appoint SPRING Singapore as the administering agency for the CPFTA and to provide for investigative and enforcement powers in the interests of better consumer protection. With effect from 1 April 2018, the Competition and Consumer Commission of Singapore (CCCS) took over the administration of the CPFTA. The regulator's main enforcement powers are to enforce injunctions ordered against those in breach of CPFTA provisions. While it has powers to seek penalties against those in breach of competition law, these do not extend to consumer law, making Singapore something of an outlier amongst our comparator jurisdictions. However, courts may require wrongdoers to publicise that they are under injunction, a regulatory measure that (like the UK 'performance scorecard') has a clear expressive and reputational deterrent effect.

Singapore has seen other recent reforms that do accept a role for civil punitive and deterrent measures, in particular in relation to intellectual property statutes. The 2003 United States–Singapore Free Trade Agreement requires each party to provide civil remedies for the enforcement of intellectual property rights that should include, among other things, the opportunity for the right holder to elect between actual damages suffered (plus any profits attributable to the prohibited activity not taken into account in computing actual damages) or pre-established damages, which shall be in an amount sufficiently high 'to constitute a deterrent to future infringements'.[31] As a result, in 2004 first the Trade Marks Act 2005[32] and then the Copyright Act 2006[33] were amended to provide statutory damages awards for the proprietors of registered trade marks and copyright owners in certain circumstances.[34] These are supplementary to the existing 'additional damages'[35] provisions, which were already found in the Copyright Act but not the trade marks legislation. The additional damages provisions largely reflect their English counterparts. The new provisions, by contrast, were designed to provide more effective deterrence of counterfeit and piracy operations, where compensation in the usual measure and 'user damages', and an account of profits, are often either incalculable or inappropriate.[36] Like their US counterparts, statutory damages are said to be

[31] United States–Singapore Free Trade Agreement (6 May 2003), Art 16.9.9: Enforcement of Intellectual Property Rights.

[32] Trade Marks Act 2005 (SG), s 31(5) and (6).

[33] Copyright Act 2006 (SG), s 119(2)(d) and (5).

[34] For a very useful discussion, see D Llewellyn, 'Statutory Damages for use of a "Counterfeit Trade Mark" and for Copyright Infringement in Singapore: A Radical Remedy in The Law of Intellectual Property or One in Need of a Rethink? (2016) 28 *Singapore Academy of Law Journal* 61. As Llewellyn notes, such statutory damages are not available for owners of other registered intellectual property rights such as patents or registered designs, which may require future reforms.

[35] Copyright Act 2006 (SG), s 119.

[36] See discussion in Llewellyn (n 34) paras 8–10. For a good, albeit rare, example of its application, see *PH Hydraulics & Engineering Pte Ltd v Intrepid Offshore Construction Pte Ltd* [2012] SGHC 133, [2012] 4 SLR 36. The Australian additional damages provisions appear to be something of a hybrid in form between the UK additional and Singapore statutory damages, but clearly are considered penal in nature: see discussion and cases cited below at text connected to n 72.

compensatory in aim,[37] but the explicit statutory 'factors that the court is required to have regard to relate, respectively, to punishment due to a clear intent to infringe, compensation, restitution and deterrence'.[38] The risk of excessive awards of statutory damages is met through an aggregated damages 'cap'.[39]

Turning to the common law, in *ACB v Thomson Medical Pte Ltd*[40] the Singapore Court of Appeal undertook a sweeping review of the law of exemplary damages in the United Kingdom, Australia, New Zealand, Canada, Malaysia and Hong Kong. It observed that exemplary or punitive damages continue to form an important part of the armoury of courts in dealing with egregious civil wrongs (some citations omitted):

> [T]he award of punitive damages has a distinct and important role to play in the context of private law by filling that important interstitial space that exists between those cases where the demands of justice are served purely by the award of a compensatory sum, and those cases which properly attract criminal sanction. Among other things, it permits the private enforcement of important interests (particularly personality interests) without the need for individuals to bring a private prosecution (which is rarely done in practice, outside of cases involving intellectual property violations) and it allows for punishment to be effected without the corresponding stigma of a criminal sanction, which is not always appropriate in all cases of wrongdoing (see the Law Commission Report at para 5.23). While the terrain covered by punitive damages has been eroded somewhat by the development of other forms of redress such as judicial review and the emergence of restitutionary damages and also by the judicial recognition of other heads of damage (as has been done in this case), it has not disappeared completely. The option of awarding punitive damages still remains an important tool in the judicial toolbox.

In rejecting the categories approach of *Rookes v Barnard*, the Court considered that 'punitive damages may be awarded in tort where the totality of the defendant's conduct is so outrageous that it warrants punishment, deterrence, and condemnation'.[41] This high bar reflects the common perception that the remedy is exceptional, if not anomalous. The Court of Appeal has separately and subsequently concluded that punitive damages are not available for breach of contract.[42]

[37] A characterisation that, like the UK experience with additional damages, arguably undermines the deterrent purpose of the regime (see *Converse Inc v Ramesh Ramchandani* [2014] SGHCR 11) and may have contributed to the under-utilisation of the provisions, discussed in Llewllyn (n 34). Sharkey has noted that, in the US context, a penal characterisation attracts additional federal constitutional, due process considerations under the Fourteenth Amendment that are avoided if these forms of damages are characterised as compensatory or deterrent in nature. She argues powerfully that 'supra-compensatory' damages may be warranted to achieve 'socially optimal deterrence by forcing the defendant to internalize the full social costs of its conduct where partial enforcement is the norm' or where losses from the wrong are difficult to prove: CM Sharkey, 'Federal Incursions and State Defiance: Punitive Damages in the Wake of Phillip Morris v Williams' (2010) 46 *Willamette Law Review* 449, 471–74.

[38] Llewellyn (n 34) 75, [28].

[39] Trade Marks Act 2005 (SG), s 31(5)(c); Copyright Act 2006 (SG), s 119(2)(d).

[40] *ACB v Thomson Medical Pte Ltd* [2017] SGCA 20, [2014] 1 SLR 918 [173].

[41] *Rookes* (n 3) [175].

[42] *PH Hydraulics & Engineering Pte Ltd v Airtrust (Hong Kong) Ltd* [2017] SGCA 26 [72], [73], [84].

C. New Zealand

As with Singapore, New Zealand's approach to exemplary damages has also largely been to reject the approach adopted in *Rookes v Barnard* and, with the exception of breach of contract,[43] to see them as widely available.[44] But unlike that jurisdiction, New Zealand has a well-established, broad and deep commitment to the role of punitive damages across common law, equity and statute. Thus New Zealand has repeatedly awarded punitive damages in equity, for breach of confidence,[45] breach of charitable trust[46] and breach of fiduciary duty,[47] going well beyond the approaches of others in our comparative sample. And, as we shall see below, its statutes often expressly preserve courts' jurisdiction to award exemplary damage alongside civil penalties regimes. Yet even in this jurisdiction, concerns to limit the application of the remedy to appropriate cases have seen it experiment with various forms of restriction.

Thus in *Couch v Attorney-General (No 2)*,[48] a majority of the New Zealand Court of Appeal held that exemplary damages could only be awarded in cases of negligence where the defendant intended to cause the harm or was consciously reckless as to the risks involved. In a powerful dissent, Elias CJ considered 'Such precondition restricts the general exemplary jurisdiction to mark society's condemnation of outrageous behaviour by the defendant which is insufficiently addressed by other remedy, and is contrary to the general application of the exemplary principle recognised in *Taylor v Beere*.'[49] Elias CJ further observed that the majority's shift to curtail the application of exemplary damages was particularly surprising, given the widespread support for them in common law jurisdictions (notwithstanding *Rookes v Barnard*) and given statutory recognition of their value.[50] As she noted, the Accident Compensation Act 2001, section 319 expressly reserves the right of a court to award exemplary damages in cases of personal injury covered by the Act or its predecessors, an important carve out given the absence of compensatory damages available under the scheme.[51] This does not purport to grant a jurisdiction to award exemplary damages but preserves the courts' existing and inherent punitive jurisdiction. It might be added that the same approach is taken by the

[43] *Paper Reclaim Ltd v Aotearoa International Ltd* [2006] NZCA 27, [2006] 3 NZLR 188.

[44] *Taylor v Beere* [1982] 1 NZLR 81 (CA) 85 (Cooke J), 90 (Richardson J), 95 (Somers J). See also Cooke J in *Donselaar v Donselaar* [1982] 1 NZLR 97 (CA) 106; *Bottrill v A* [2002] UKPC 44, [2003] 2 NZLR 721 [63] per Lord Nicholls, Lord Hope and Lord Rodger; Lord Hutton and Lord Millett dissenting.

[45] *Aquaculture Corporation v New Zealand Green Mussel Co Ltd* [1990] 3 NZLR 299, affirmed in *Skids Programme Management Ltd v McNeill* [2012] NZCA 314, [2013] 1 NZLR 1 [87].

[46] *Eden Refuge Trust v Hohepa* [2011] NZHC 730, [2011] 3 NZLR 273.

[47] *Cook v Evatt (No 2)* [1992] 1 NZLR 676; but see *Paper Reclaim Ltd* (n 43) [184]. cf *Premium Real Estate Ltd v Stevens* [2009] NZSC 15; [2009] 2 NZLR 384 [110] (Tipping J).

[48] *Couch v Attorney-General (No 2)* [2010] NZSC 27, [2010] 3 NZLR 149.

[49] ibid [4].

[50] ibid [5], [31].

[51] ibid [88]–[89].

Commerce Act 1986, section 82A. Power to award exemplary damages is also conferred on the specialist tenancy tribunal under the Residential Tenancies Act 1986, section 77(2)(o), and is given as an example of an order that may be made by a court 'to any person who has suffered loss or damage' arising from a wide range of breaches of the Credit Contracts and Consumer Finance Act 2003.[52] The court's jurisdiction to award exemplary damages is assumed in the Plant Variety Rights Act 1987, section 17(c)(4).

Indeed, the sheer weight of statutory recognition of exemplary damages, available to plaintiffs under New Zealand statutes, often coupled with parallel civil pecuniary penalty regimes, available to regulators, is eloquent as to their perceived value in the law. The outlier, oddly, is New Zealand's main consumer law statute. Like its Australian counterparts (on which it was based), the New Zealand legislative landscape includes a strong statutory regime under section 9 of the Fair Trading Act 1986, prohibiting misleading or deceptive conduct, or conduct that is likely to misleading or deceive. The prohibition applies to persons 'in trade', therefore applying beyond consumer disputes to trade-to-trade transactions. This prohibition is supported by a suite of wide-ranging remedies by way of private redress for victims of misconduct.[53] Also as in Australia, this general provision is accompanied by a suite of more specific prohibitions on misleading conduct in various contexts. Section 40 of the Act makes contravention of these more specific provisions an offence and provides for penalties for natural and corporate defendants. It does not, however, impose a civil penalties regime. Under section 43, on the other hand, courts may order defendants to make public disclosure or public corrections of contravening conduct. No doubt, like the 'performance scorecard', these may be expected to give rise to reputational damage and to effect a certain level of deterrence.

Nonetheless, the omission of a civil penalties regime within the core consumer protection statute is somewhat surprising, given that civil penalties regimes have been introduced in a raft of other commercial legislation that also addresses misleading conduct in trade. For example, the Financial Markets Conduct Act 2013, section 19 contains a general prohibition on misleading conduct in the supply of financial products and services, and is followed by a number of more specific provisions to which civil penalty provisions apply.[54] The same pattern is followed in the Credit Contracts and Consumer Finance Act 2003 and the Commerce Act 1986. Under the former, exemplary damages may not be awarded under section 94(1)(c) where a penalty has already been awarded for the same conduct. By contrast, under section 86 of the Commerce Act, the civil penalties jurisdiction is cumulative to the court's right to award exemplary damages under section 82A. All this is not even to mention the ubiquitous availability of

[52] Credit Contracts and Consumer Finance Act 2003 (NZ), s 94(1)(c).
[53] See Fair Trading Act 1986 (NZ), ss 41–43.
[54] Financial Markets Conduct Act 2013 (NZ), s 489.

'additional damages' for breach of copyright, where the New Zealand jurisprudence concerning the statutory remedy has expressly been developed by reference to the law of exemplary damages.[55]

It may be concluded that while not wholly consistent in its approaches or coverage, this spread of legislation provides perhaps the clearest endorsement of the value of punitive measures in civil awards from amongst our sample jurisdictions.

D. The United States

The United States is widely regarded as the modern, common law home of punitive damages. Seminal cases such as *Grimshaw v Ford Motor Co*[56] (the Ford Pinto Case) have burned themselves into the common law collective consciousness as quintessential examples of the inherent punitive jurisdiction. However, what are possibly less well known outside its borders are the extensive range and variety of statutory measures designed to remedy and deter serious commercial misconduct.[57] State legislation to prohibit unfair or deceptive conduct is widespread, as are provisions that allow for (or sometimes mandate) double or treble damages ('multiple damages'), calculated by reference to what would otherwise be the compensatory award.[58] These are generally contingent on finding deliberate breach by the defendant. Many States also provide for the award of attorneys' fees for the winning plaintiff – a significant incentive both for plaintiffs to litigate and for defendants to settle and avoid repeated misconduct. However, it must be said that statutory practices vary wildly between States.[59] For example, some States allow extra penalties or awards where the plaintiff is a senior citizen, disabled or a veteran.[60] In others, extensive exemptions apply for particular industries, such as insurance and utilities.[61] Lenders and creditors often also attract special treatment.[62] Some US States have adopted 'split recovery' statutes under which the plaintiff is allowed to take only a proportion of the exemplary damages award, the

[55] *Skids Programme Management Ltd* (n 45) [106].

[56] *Grimshaw v Ford Motor Co* 119 Cal App 3d 757 (1981).

[57] See, eg, *International Fidelity Insurance Co v Wilson* 387 Mass 841, 857 (Mass 1983), explaining that the legislative purpose of the provisions allowing multiple damages is the imposition of a penalty that varies with the culpability of the defendant, reflecting 'the Legislature's displeasure with the proscribed conduct and its desire to deter such conduct and encourage vindictive lawsuits'.

[58] See, eg, Georgia Code, § 10-1-399; Massachusetts General Law, ch 93A, s 3.

[59] An outstandingly useful summary and critique is contained in CL Carter, 'Consumer Protection in the States: A 50-State Report on Unfair and Deceptive Acts and Practices Statutes' (National Consumer Law Center, 2009).

[60] See, eg, California Civil Code, Title 1.5 (Consumers Legal Remedies Act), § 1780.

[61] Carter (n 59) reports that '[u]tility companies in 16 states enjoy immunity from UDAP laws, as do insurance companies in 24 states'.

[62] Carter (n 59) identifies Louisiana, Michigan, New Hampshire, Rhode Island and Virginia as providing 'no or very little protection against predatory lending, mortgage fraud, and other abuses and deception in the extension of credit'.

remainder being allocated to the State or some charity.[63] Some US jurisdictions attempt to provide greater certainty through a baseline for the award – an example is Alaska's statute, which provides for 'three times the actual damages or $500, whichever is greater'.[64] Some US jurisdictions require that plaintiffs first send a letter to the defendant requesting relief before initiating litigation. Refusal to grant relief in response to the plaintiff's letter, in a clear case of breach, has been taken to justify the award of multiple damages.[65]

The US intellectual property statutes also provide influential paradigms of deterrent measures. The United States has a form of 'statutory damages'[66] that, as we have seen, has subsequently been exported to Singapore. This has come under heavy criticism by US commentators for giving rise to awards that are 'frequently arbitrary, inconsistent, unprincipled, and sometimes grossly excessive'.[67] Here, Lewellyn has noted that the conditions indigenous to the US legal landscape of no statutory 'cap', class action suits and secondary liability may combine to produce perfect conditions for excessive liability and incentives for perverse litigation behaviour.[68] On the other hand, its more general statutory strategies for stripping profits obtained in breach of copyright have been cited with approval in the High Court of Australia as a very useful paradigm of reasoning, consistent with the equitable remedy.[69] We return to this aspect of the US jurisprudence in section IV.D.

E. Conclusion of Overview

Out of this complex and varied outline some clear points emerge. The first is that, viewed as a whole, the survey demonstrates sustained, and arguably growing, recognition of the need for strongly deterrent remedial or regulatory mechanisms in order effectively to address serious and repeated commercial wrongdoing. This reflects a second point of consensus, that while traditional measures of compensation are often highly effective, requiring defendants to internalise the costs of their transgressions, they are sometimes inadequate to achieve the required specific and general deterrence. A third observation is that punitive damages continue to

[63] This option has not recommended itself to the Irish Law Reform Commission, not least because the relatively small size of exemplary awards make the significant administrative costs and complexity of introducing split recovery options impracticable: see Law Commission (Ireland) (n 12) para 2.064. On split recovery awards in the US context, see CM Sharkey, 'Punitive Damages as Societal Damages' (2003) *Yale Law Journal* 347 and her chapter in this collection (ch 7).

[64] Alaska Statutes § 45.50.531 (2016).

[65] *Heller v Silverbranch Construction Corporation* 382 NE 2d 1065 (Mass, 1978).

[66] 17 USC § 504(c)(1).

[67] P Samuelson and T Wheatland, 'Statutory Damages in Copyright Law: A Remedy in Need of Reform' (2009) 51 *William & Mary Law Review* 439, 441.

[68] A chief problem is 'copyright trolls' who game the system to extort settlements from minor or unintentional contravenors: see Llewellyn (n 34).

[69] *Lifeplan* (n 6), discussed in section IV. See also Sharkey (n 37), noting the legitimate role for such awards in achieving 'socially optimal deterrence'.

play an important role both within the private law and as a paradigm for statutory mechanisms that aim to deter wrongdoing. Finally, in all jurisdictions, a fear that punitive measures might be or become unprincipled has led to restrictions on their award. However, often those restrictions are themselves liable to criticism on the grounds of their being arbitrary or unprincipled. The ongoing challenge is how to design rules that achieve effective deterrence, without being unprincipled or disproportionate, a matter the subject of repeated and recent Australian consideration, to which we now turn.

III. Australia

A. Overview

Australia serves as an important comparator in this field, for its extensive use of strongly deterrent and punitive strategies across the field of private law.[70] Thus its intellectual property statutes provide for additional damages,[71] which are squarely recognised as containing a punitive element and subject to principles corresponding to those governing awards of exemplary damages.[72] The statutes expressly provide that one aim of additional damages is deterrence.[73] Consistently with exemplary damages,[74] both specific and general deterrence are reflected in the award.[75] It has also repeatedly been emphasised that, far from being an 'exceptional' remedy, 'an element of penalty is an accepted feature of copyright legislation'.[76]

[70] The Australian Law Reform Commission refused, for example, to follow the lead of reforms made to defamation law, which had removed exemplary damages awards, when seeking develop an effective deterrent regime for a new statutory tort of breach of privacy: Australian Law Reform Commission, *Serious Invasions of Privacy in the Digital Era* (Rep No 123, 2014) 12, Recommendations 12–13, 12–14. The defamation reforms were prompted by the jury award made in the new trial following *Carson v John Fairfax & Sons Ltd* (1993) 178 CLR 44. See, eg, Defamation Act 2005 (Vic), s 37.

[71] Copyright Act 1968 (Cth), s 115(4); Designs Act 2003 (Cth), s 75(3); Patents Act 1990 (Cth), s 122(1A); Trade Marks Act 1995 (Cth), s 126(2); Circuit Layouts Act 1989 (Cth), s 27(4).

[72] See, eg, *Bailey v Namol Pty Ltd* (1994) 53 FCR 102 [43] (Burchett, Gummow and O'Loughlin JJ), explicitly drawing on the Australian law of exemplary damages to explicate the nature of the statutory damages; *Facton Ltd v Rifai Fashions Pty Ltd* [2012] FCAFC 9, (2012) 199 FCR 569 [33], [36] (Lander and Gordon JJ) and [89] (Gilmour J)), the latter citing the *Report of the Copyright Law Review Committee 1959*, para 309, which recommended the introduction of additional damages 'equivalent to exemplary damages'. For these reasons, they cannot be awarded cumulative on an award of exemplary damages.

[73] See, eg, Copyright Act 1968 (Cth), s 115 (4)(b)(ia). See further *Aristocrat Technologies Australia Pty Ltd v DAP Services (Kempsey) Pty Limited (in liq)* [2007] FCAFC 40, (2007) 157 FCR 564 [43]–[53], noting the 'element of penalty' in effecting deterrence, as well as the need to mark the court's disapproval of the conduct.

[74] *Lamb v Cotogno* (1987) 164 CLR 1, 9–10. Exemplary damages are discussed immediately below.

[75] *Dynamic Supplies Pty Limited v Tonnex International Pty Limited (No 3)* [2014] FCA 909 [39]–[41] (Yates J).

[76] *Autodesk Inc v Yee* (1996) 68 FCR 391, 394. See also *Raben Footwear Pty Ltd v Polygram Records Inc* (1997) 75 FCR 88; *Dynamic Supplies Pty Limited* (n 75) [53] (Yates J).

Australia's powerful and overarching statutory schemes now embrace civil penalties as a core deterrent mechanism for serious commercial misconduct.[77] The jurisdiction is also notable for the fact that its civil pecuniary penalties schemes are not limited to consumer contexts but apply to wholly commercial transactions between traders and corporate commercial actors. This broader operation has meant that fair trade disputes have regularly been litigated, often through multiple levels of appeal, enabling sustained and repeated examination of the relevant principles by the courts. As a consequence, Australian courts have developed a sophisticated penalties jurisprudence aimed at both specific and general deterrence of wrongdoing.[78]

Australia's statutory landscape has also exerted a powerful influence over the award of exemplary damages in that jurisdiction, informing the High Court's rejection of the sorts of restrictive distinctions that have been so influential in English law. In the leading authority of *Gray v Motor Accident Commission*, Gleeson CJ, McHugh, Gummow and Hayne JJ observed:

> There is an appearance of tension between using civil proceedings to compensate a party who is wronged and using the same proceedings to punish the wrongdoer. But there is a tension only if it is assumed that '… a sharp cleavage between criminal law on the one hand and the law of torts and contract on the other is a cardinal principle of our legal system'. As Windeyer J points out in *Uren*, the 'roots of tort and crime' are 'greatly intermingled'. … And it is not only the roots of tort and crime that are intermingled. The increasing frequency with which civil penalty provisions are enacted, the provisions made for criminal injuries compensation, the provisions now made in some jurisdictions for the judge at a criminal trial to order restitution or compensation to a person suffering loss or damage (including pain and suffering) as a result of an offence, all deny the existence of any 'sharp cleavage' between the criminal and the civil law. The tension we have mentioned may therefore be more apparent than real.[79]

Consistently, exemplary damages are available and regularly awarded across the spectrum of torts, including negligence.[80] However, while the remedy is not considered to be 'anomalous', it is 'exceptional', in the sense that the claim must be one that involves egregious misconduct. Thus '"conscious wrongdoing in contumelious disregard of another's rights" describes at least the greater part of the relevant field'.[81] The gravity of the conduct required to justify exemplary

[77] See, eg, Australian Consumer Law (as is set out in sch 2 to the Competition and Consumer Act 2010 (Cth)), Australian Securities and Investments Commission Act 2001 (Cth) (ASIC Act) and Corporations Act 2001 (Cth) addressing various forms of misleading conduct.

[78] This is examined in detail in JM Paterson and E Bant, 'Intuitive Synthesis and Fidelity to Purpose?: Judicial Interpretation of the Discretionary Power to award Civil Penalties under the Australian Consumer Law' in P Vines and MS Donald (eds), *Statutory Interpretation in Private Law* (Leichhardt, Federation Press, 2019) 154.

[79] *Gray v Motor Accident Commission* (1998) 196 CLR 1 [16].

[80] ibid.

[81] ibid, citing *Whitfeld v De Lauret & Co Ltd* (1920) 29 CLR 71, 77 (Knox CJ). See also *XL Petroleum (NSW) Pty Ltd v Caltex Oil (Australia) Pty Ltd* (1985) 155 CLR 448, 471 (Brennan J).

damages reflects the instrumental purposes of the award. As explained in *Lamb v Cotogno*:

> The object, or at least the effect, of exemplary damages is not wholly punishment and the deterrence which is intended extends beyond the actual wrongdoer and the exact nature of his wrongdoing. … It is an aspect of exemplary damages that they serve to assuage any urge for revenge felt by victims and to discourage any temptation to engage in self-help likely to endanger the peace.[82]

In this way, both Australian courts and parliaments have identified an important role for mechanisms squarely aimed at deterrence in civil law. Moreover, the statutory context has exerted an important gravitational influence on the development and application of common law principles. However, as we shall see, courts administering the civil penalty regimes might be well served by similarly taking guidance from the general law principles of punishment and deterrence, to the extent that these are consistent with and promote the statutory language and purpose. To date, Australian courts administering the civil pecuniary penalties regime have adopted a cautious approach in setting the levels of award. Courts have identified the goals of civil penalties as specific and general deterrence, but have tended to quantify the amount imposed by reference to considerations of 'just desert' and the need to protect defendants from excessive punishment.[83] This approach potentially undermines the efficacy of the statutory regime. Our suggestion is that courts would do well to investigate with more rigour just what is needed to effect deterrence. Potentially relevant factors include not only cost internalisation, which promotes a measure driven by compensatory considerations, but also profit-stripping, as well as scholarly suggestions that any deterrent award should include a multiplier to dissuade businesses from discounting the impact of such awards by the likelihood of the contravention's going undetected by regulators.[84] To the extent that courts are concerned about the risk of over-deterrence or excessive punishment, so that businesses are unjustly crippled, they might also have regard to the success of general law principles of proportionate punishment, such as those developed in equity that operate to require wrongdoers to disgorge advantages obtained in breach of equitable obligations. These insights may support more effective use of the statutory levers designed to change commercial misconduct. They may also serve to promote a more coherent approach across the law of civil punishment.

B. The Statutory Civil Pecuniary Penalties Regime

The chief statutory point of focus in this chapter is on the prohibitions of misleading conduct under the Australian Consumer Law (ACL) and equivalent provisions

[82] *Lamb* (n 74).
[83] Paterson and Bant (n 78).
[84] See discussion in Sharkey (n 63) 367–69; Sharkey, ch 7 of this volume.

in the Australian Securities and Investments Commission Act 2001 (Cth) (ASIC Act). As we have explained elsewhere,[85] the civil penalty jurisdiction was introduced with the reforms that led to the enactment of the ACL in 2010, and has had a significant impact on the pattern of regulatory enforcement of the prohibitions on misleading and unconscionable conduct in that legislation. Criminal sanctions are available for many contraventions of the ACL/ASIC Act.[86] The reforms introduced typically parallel provisions that provided for civil penalties. This was supported on the ground that the availability of such penalties would enable a 'targeted and proportionate regulatory response' to contraventions of the regime, deterring wrongdoing without involving the more heavy-handed sanction of the criminal law.[87] The lead regulators, the Australian Competition and Consumer Commission (ACCC) and the Australian Securities and Investments Commission (ASIC), have used the possibility of pecuniary penalties' being awarded against traders as a central enforcement tool in responding to misleading conduct. This has been seen as a useful enforcement tool, particularly where the harm to consumers is difficult to quantify or disproportionate to the gain that the trader obtained through the contravention, which would suggest that a compensatory award may be ineffective to deter contraventions.

As with other jurisdictions,[88] the award for civil pecuniary penalties for contraventions of the ACL/ASIC Act is supported by a range of other orders, including corrective advertising.[89] Although expressed to be 'non-punitive', Parker has observed the 'financial and moral costs of bad publicity from noncompliance' loom particularly large in traders' thinking about the costs and gains of noncompliance.[90] Additionally, courts may, on the application of the regulator, make 'adverse publicity orders' that are considered clearly punitive in nature.[91] The Australian Law Reform Commission has now proposed that this be supplemented by other options such as disclosure orders, community service orders, probation or corrective orders, which could be awarded by the court of its own motion as part of the suite of deterrent orders, including penalties.[92]

The civil pecuniary penalty regime is found in Part 5-2 Division 1 of the ACL.[93] Under section 224, if the court is satisfied a person has contravened specified provisions of the ACL, which include the prohibition on unconscionable conduct and the prohibitions on specific forms of misleading conduct in sections 29–34

[85] Paterson and Bant (n 73) 156.

[86] See JM Paterson, *Corones' Australian Consumer Law*, 4th edn (Pyrmont, Lawbook Co, 2019).

[87] ibid 236.

[88] See UK, NZ and to a lesser degree Singapore in section II.

[89] Australian Consumer Law (n 77), s 246(2)(d).

[90] C Parker and VL Nielsen, 'How Much Does It Hurt? How Australian Businesses Think about the Costs and Gains of Compliance and Noncompliance with the Trade Practices Act' (2008) 32 *Melbourne University Law Review* 554, 563.

[91] Australian Consumer Law (n 77), s 247; ASIC Act (n 77), s 12GLB.

[92] Australian Law Reform Commission Report 136, *Corporate Criminal Responsibility* (2020) ch 8: see in particular Recommendation 12.

[93] ASIC Act (n 77), s 12GBA.

and 37, the court may order the person to pay 'such pecuniary penalty, in respect of each act or omission by the person to which this section applies, as the court determines to be appropriate'.[94] There is no precondition that any victim must have suffered loss or damage because of the contravening conduct.[95] In determining the appropriate pecuniary penalty, the court is directed to have regard to 'all relevant matters'. The legislation then specifically lists three relevant considerations: the extent of the loss or damage suffered; the circumstances of the conduct; and whether the contravening party has previously engaged in similar conduct.[96]

Courts responding to these general prompts have not embraced some unconstrained judicial discretion. Rather, they have developed a cautious, and relatively consistent, approach to the civil penalties regime.[97] This has been supported by the ubiquity of similar civil pecuniary penalty regimes found across the Australian statutory landscape,[98] encouraging productive cross-fertilisation of ideas.[99]

Courts have supplemented the statutory factors with a much richer list of considerations. The resultant guiding principles (known as the 'French factors') have been repeatedly endorsed as useful and appropriate in assisting courts in calculating civil pecuniary penalties. As summarised for the consumer protection context by Perram J in *Australian Competition and Consumer Commission v Singtel Optus Pty Ltd [No 4]*, they include:

1. the size of the contravening company;
2. the deliberateness of the contravention and the period over which it extended;
3. whether the contravention arose out of the conduct of senior management of the contravener or at some lower level;
4. whether the contravener has a corporate culture conducive to compliance with [the law] as evidenced by educational programmes and disciplinary or other corrective measures in response to an acknowledged contravention;
5. whether the contravener has shown a disposition to co-operate with the authorities responsible for the enforcement of the [statute] in relation to the contravention;

[94] Australian Consumer Law (n 77), s 224(1). Provision is also made for a penalty to be paid by persons involved in the contravention, such as by aiding and abetting the contravention or inducing the contravention.

[95] Compare Australian Consumer Law (n 77), s 236 (damages) and s 237 (compensation orders).

[96] Australian Consumer Law (n 77), s 224(2).

[97] *Trade Practices Commission v CSR Ltd* (1991) ATPR 41-076, 152, approved in *Commonwealth v Director, Fair Work Building Industry Inspectorate* [2015] HCA 46, (2015) 258 CLR 482 [59] (French CJ, Kiefel, Bell, Nettle and Gordon JJ). See also *Australian Building and Construction Commissioner v Construction, Forestry, Mining and Energy Union* [2018] HCA 3, (2018) 262 CLR 157, [44] (Keifel CJ), [87] (Keane, Nettle and Gordon JJ). *Australian Competition and Consumer Commission v TPG Internet Pty Ltd* [2013] HCA 54, 250 CLR 640 [65] (French CJ, Crennan, Bell and Keane JJ) (*ACCC v TPG*). See also *Australian Competition and Consumer Commission v Reckitt Benckiser (Australia) Pty Ltd* [2016] FCAFC 181 [58] (Jagot, Yates and Bromwich JJ).

[98] See, eg, Trade Practices Act 1974 (Cth), s 76 and Competition and Consumer Act 2010 (Cth), s 76, dealing with competition breaches. See also Environment Protection and Biodiversity Conservation Act 1999 (Cth), s 481; National Consumer Credit Protection Act 2009 (Cth), s 167; Fair Work Act 2009 (Cth), s 546.

[99] *Singtel Optus Pty Ltd v Australian Competition and Consumer Commission* [2012] FCAFC 20, (2012) 287 ALR 249 [62] (Keane CJ, Finn and Gilmour JJ).

6. whether the contravener has engaged in similar conduct in the past;
7. the financial position of the contravener;
8. whether the contravening conduct was systematic, deliberate or covert.[100]

In *Australian Competition and Consumer Commission v Woolworths Limited*, Edelman J identified four further factors as relevant to the courts' determination of the appropriate penalty:

9. the extent of contrition;
10. whether the contravening company made a profit from the contraventions;
11. the extent of the profit made by the contravening company; and
12. whether the contravening company engaged in the conduct with an intention to profit from it.[101]

The Australian Law Reform Commission has now recommended that a list of relevant factors for determining civil penalties, which builds on the French factors, be enshrined in legislation imposing criminal and civil penalties.[102] Importantly, the Law Reform Commission has elevated the factor of 'any advantage realised by the corporation as a result of the contravention' to the fourth in the list, behind only considerations of the 'nature and circumstances' of the contravention, the 'deterrent effect' of any order, and the 'injury, loss, or damage' resulting from the contravention. If accepted, this may have a significant effect on penalty jurisprudence. This is because, notwithstanding Edelman J's identification of wrongdoer profit as relevant to assessment of civil penalties, profit has yet to be adopted as a core consideration as a matter of broader judicial practice, as the following discussion explains. In any event, however, recent reforms to the consumer legislation have introduced a relinquishment award based on the profit made from the wrongdoing, which may promote considerations of gains made to a more prominent level.[103]

C. Profits, Deterrence and Punishment in the Penalties Jurisprudence

In *Trade Practices Commission v CSR Ltd*, French J identified the purpose of the penalty regime available in response to contraventions of the competition

[100] *Australian Competition and Consumer Commission v Singtel Optus Pty Ltd [No 4]* [2011] FCA 761, (2011) 282 ALR 246 [11], referred to without demurral on appeal: *Singtel Optus Pty Ltd* (n 99) [37] (Keane CJ, Finn and Gilmour JJ).

[101] *Australian Competition and Consumer Commission v Woolworths Limited* [2016] FCA 44, [2016] ATPR 42-521 [126]. See also *Australian Competition and Consumer Commission v Chrisco Hampers Australia Ltd (No 2)* [2016] FCA 144 [28].

[102] See Australian Law Reform Commission, *Principled Regulation: Federal Civil and Administrative Penalties in Australia* (ALRC Report No 95, 2002) paras 27.1 and 28.3; Australian Law Reform Commission, *Corporate Criminal Responsibility* (n 92) Recommendation 11.

[103] The reforms are discussed in the text connected to n 123.

provisions of the Trade Practices Act 1974 (Cth) as deterrence. His Honour explained:

> The principal, and I think probably the only object of the penalties imposed by s 76 is to attempt to put a price on contravention that is sufficiently high to deter repetition by the contravenor and by others who might be tempted to contravene the Act.[104]

In *ACCC v TPG*, the High Court confirmed that 'specific and general' deterrence should play a 'primary' role in assessing the appropriate penalty for contraventions of the ACL.[105]

This emphasis on deterrence to the exclusion of punitive considerations may be considered surprising, given the clear nexus Australian courts have also drawn between the statutory context and neighbouring general law principles of exemplary damages.[106] Considered from an economic perspective, deterrence is best achieved by ensuring the penalties attached to wrongdoing are not a mere 'cost of doing business'. To be effective, any award aimed at realising this aim should contain an additional amount to ensure that the effect of the possible award is not discounted by the perceived low risk of detection and prosecution of the contravention. This then would suggest a civil penalty amount that looks very like punishment, or punitive damages. However, notwithstanding the range of relevant factors, and the acknowledged need for penalties to be set at a level that removes contravening behaviour from traders' desired business model, the practice of courts has typically led to the award of modest sums as compared to the maximum available for the contravention.[107] Courts' concern not to impose 'crippling' punishment and the focus on the considerations relevant to culpability identified in the French factors have led to comparatively modest awards. This outcome is particularly stark in cases where harm is relatively small but the defendant's profit has been great, where penalties have been set at low levels that bear no relation to the benefit enjoyed by the defendant.[108] A more robust approach from courts is to be observed in cases where the contravening conduct has had a significant negative impact on consumers, for example involving people with apparent vulnerabilities,[109] a household staple[110]

[104] *Trade Practices Commission* (n 97), approved in *Fair Work Building Industry Inspectorate* (n 97). See also *Construction, Forestry, Mining and Energy Union* (n 97).

[105] *ACCC v TPG* (n 97) [65] (French CJ, Crennan, Bell and Keane JJ). See also *Reckitt Benckiser (Australia) Pty Ltd* (n 97) [58] (Jagot, Yates and Bromwich JJ).

[106] See the discussion of additional damages and exemplary damages in the text connected to n 71 and n 79.

[107] Paterson and Bant (n 78).

[108] See, eg, *Australian Competition and Consumer Commission v TPG Internet Pty Ltd (No 2)* [2012] FCA 629, [2012] ATPR 42-402; before the High Court *ACCC v TPG* (n 97) [65] (French CJ, Crennan, Bell and Keane JJ), noting that the misleading conduct generated revenue of approximately $59 million, and an estimated profit of $8 million, which meant that the penalty of $2 million could not be regarded as excessive.

[109] *Australian Competition and Consumer Commission v Acquire Learning & Careers Pty Ltd* [2017] FCA 602, [2017] ATPR 42-543 [65] (Murphy J).

[110] *Australian Competition and Consumer Commission v Coles Supermarkets Australia Pty Ltd* [2015] FCA 330, (2015) 327 ALR 540 [86].

or unsafe products.[111] This tailoring of the award to the loss to consumers might be justified as involving 'cost internalisation', but when combined with reductions in the award where the defendant, ex post, cooperates with the regulator, the approach risks undermining the effective deterrent operation of the regime. It may also reflect the courts' traditional focus in private law actions on issues of compensation, which leads to a myopic focus on plaintiff loss rather than on defendant gain. This conservative approach nonetheless remains odd, given the payment goes to the regulator not the injured consumers. In such circumstances, there can be no concern about individual plaintiffs enjoying some form of unfair windfall from the award, or the risk of creating incentives to frivolous litigation that has arguably tempered exemplary damages awards.[112]

Moreover, courts have shown themselves to be highly sensitive to considerations of the defendant's relative culpability, contrition and cooperation in setting penalties awards.[113] These factors arguably are less concerned with objectives of deterrence. Instead they seem to reflect a concern that any award is not unjustly crippling, taking account of the moral fault of the wrongdoer. They therefore seem to express conceptions of retributive justice and 'just deserts', which are most closely associated with theories of punishment. Here, the irony is that courts are only too willing to take such considerations into account as mitigating factors, while denying the role for punishment in achieving the goal of efficient deterrence. This might be unduly generous. While there are social benefits in cooperation with the regulator, there is no evidence that ex post cooperation produces a change in corporate culture such as to deter further wrongdoing by the defiant cooperation or its market peers. The problem lies in a failure to unpack the role of punishment and to understand that is possible to impose proportionate, and not crippling, punishment.

Relevantly, we observe that gain-based remedies may be a highly effective model in this context, as they both cut to the gain achieved by the wrongful conduct – thereby carrying a 'sting' that should deter – and are inherently proportionate, being capped by the amount of the pecuniary benefit enjoyed as a result of the breaching behaviour. They therefore meet the aim of setting a penalty sum that will deter companies from 'the cynical calculation involved in weighing up the risk of penalty against the profits to be made from contravention'.[114] So it would be possible for courts to emphasise profit-stripping as a key criterion within the French factors where individual harm is small but the benefits reaped from the wrongdoing are large and the degree of culpability (for example, persistent wrongdoing in

[111] *Woolworths* (n 101) [140] (Edelman J). See also *Australian Competition and Consumer Commission v Cotton On Kids Pty Ltd* [2012] FCA 1428, [2012] ATPR ¶42-427 (Tracey J); *Australian Competition and Consumer Commission v Thermomix in Australia Pty Ltd* [2018] FCA 556 [18] (Murphy J).

[112] See discussion in the text connected to n 67 and n 167. See further Sharkey (n 63) 370–71; and Llewellyn (n 34).

[113] Paterson and Bant (n 78).

[114] *Singtel Optus Pty Ltd* (n 99) [63], cited with approval in *ACCC v TPG* (n 97) [66].

the face of repeated complaints) is high.[115] Very recently, courts have started to acknowledge the relevance of profit to deterrence in such circumstances,[116] but to date this has been a marginal consideration.

In response to concerns about the relatively low levels of penalties awarded when viewed from a perspective of economic deterrence, new provisions were introduced in 2018 and 2019,[117] which provide new increased maximum measures of the civil pecuniary penalties that may be awarded under the ACL,[118] Corporations Act, ASIC Act, National Consumer Credit Protection Act 2009 and Insurance Act.[119]

The Treasury reforms display a clear legislative commitment to promoting a more effective deterrent regime through removing profit-based incentives to breach. Thus, one limb of the statutory maximum applicable to corporate wrongdoers is based on the value of 'the benefit derived and detriment avoided because of the contravention', multiplied by three.[120] The same option is also available for natural defendants.[121] This appears to endorse a clear punitive element, setting the award at a level that will inevitably 'sting'. Consistently, the reforms provide as an alternative maximum 10 per cent of the annual turnover of the body corporate,[122] an approach that is also echoed in the UK consumer law proposals,

While these new increased penalty award maximums may be seen as prompting courts to increase the penalty awarded, a significant degree of judicial discretion remains. After all, the amounts operate by way of maximum, not as a mandated award. A critical question for their future application will be how to determine 'the benefit obtained and detriment avoided because of the contravention' – questions of measure and causation on which the general law offers a range of insights. Moreover, (the ACL aside) the new provisions provide that a court may, of its own initiative or on application of a regulator, require a person to pay the Commonwealth an amount 'equal to the benefit derived and detriment avoided

[115] A common factual pattern: see, eg, *Reckitt Benckiser (Australia) Pty Ltd* (n 97).

[116] *Woolworths* (n 111).

[117] Treasury Laws Amendment (2018 Measures No 3) Act 2018 (Cth) and the Treasury Laws Amendment (Strengthening Corporate and Financial Sector Penalties) Act 2019 (Cth).

[118] Australian Consumer Law (n 77), ss 224(3) and (3A).

[119] See, eg, the new s 12GBCA in the ASIC Act (n 77) (which applies to specific misleading conduct prohibitions), which provides: '(2) The pecuniary penalty applicable to the contravention of a civil penalty provision by a body corporate is the greatest of: (a) the penalty specified for the civil penalty provision, multiplied by 10; and (b) if the Court can determine the benefit derived and detriment avoided because of the contravention – that amount multiplied by 3; and (c) either: (i) 10% of the annual turnover of the body corporate for the 12-month period ending at the end of the month in which the body corporate contravened, or began to contravene, the civil penalty provision; or (ii) if the amount worked out under subparagraph (i) is greater than an amount equal to 2.5 million penalty units – 2.5 million penalty units.'

[120] See, eg, ASIC Act (n 77), s 12GBCA(2)(b).

[121] ibid, s 12GBCA(1).

[122] cf Edelman J in *ACCC v Reckitt Benckiser (Australia) Pty Ltd (No 7)* [2016] FCA 424, (2016) 343 ALR 327 [64], noting that it would be possible for the purposes of the 'profit' component of the French factors to focus on the revenue earned from breach.

because of' a contravention of a civil penalty provision.[123] These 'relinquishment' orders may be made notwithstanding that the person has already been made the subject of a civil penalty. Again, issues of measurement and causation will be front and centre. Finally, even if the provisions do not end up being wholly applicable across the board, the legislative shift to emphasise profit-stripping may serve to highlight its relevance within the existing jurisprudence guiding the award of civil penalties, a trend we have seen is consistent with the Australian Law Reform Commission recommendations. In all respects, general law jurisprudence on these questions may be drawn into service in a manner consistent with the statutory language and purpose. Indeed, accepting guidance from these broader principles may serve not only to promote a more efficient statutory regime, but also a more coherent law of civil punishment across common law, equity and statute.

IV. Orders in Equity to Disgorge Profit Following Account

In that context, it is appropriate to consider general law principles that are consistent with and promote the statutory language and purpose.[124] Here equity comes into view, with its longstanding experience with ordering wrongdoers to disgorge profits determined following an account (compendiously known as the 'account of profits').[125] Our suggestion is that it potentially offers principles that can be used to articulate the nature and operation of proportionate punishment more broadly. This is not to say that punishment should always be reckoned by the advantage taken from the wrong: for example, deliberate breaches made (unsuccessfully) with a view to profit,[126] or non-profitable wrongdoing that causes widespread and serious harm, may also call for proportionate punishment. However, where (as is often the case in commercial misconduct) profits are enjoyed, consideration of the equitable principles may enable better and more transparent formulation of the reasons for the level of penalty awarded.

An objection to this is that, in the course of determining that exemplary damages could not be awarded for breach of fiduciary duty, a majority of the New South Wales Court of Appeal considered that the account of profits is not punitive in aim.[127] Equity and penalty are strangers.[128] However, this position has

[123] See, eg, ASIC Act (n 77), s 12GBCC.

[124] E Bant and J Paterson, 'Limitations on Defendant Liability for Misleading or Deceptive Conduct Under Statute: Some Insights from Negligent Misstatement' in K Barker, R Grantham and W Swain (eds), *The Law of Misstatements: 50 Years on from Hedley Byrne v Heller* (Oxford, Hart Publishing, 2015) 159.

[125] See the careful articulation of these two steps in *Lifeplan* (n 6) [7].

[126] *Reckitt Benckiser (Australia) Pty Ltd (No 7)* (n 122) [54] (Edelman J), citing *ACCC v TPG* (n 97) [66] (French CJ, Crennan, Bell and Keane JJ).

[127] *Harris v Digital Pulse Pty Ltd* [2003] NSWCA 10, (2003) 56 NSWLR 298.

[128] *New Zealand Green Mussel Co Ltd* (n 45) 302 (Somer J, in dissent).

been doubted[129] and, as we have seen, is not the position taken in New Zealand.[130] We might also observe a large portion of Heydon J's reasoning, which decried a role for equity in imposing punishment, rehearses the familiar dangers of punitive measures' being imposed for civil wrongs.[131] These have already been rejected by Australian courts in the common law (and statutory) context. Certainly, equity's longstanding civil enforcement mechanism of corporal internment for contempt is well understood to straddle the line between civil and criminal law.[132]

In any event, as we shall see, equity's method of assessing the relevant profits that must be disgorged adopts a range of strategies that are well calculated to make the order 'sting', in circumstances where the defendant's degree of culpability is high and other factors combine to render a generous award appropriate. Functionally, it may be said that even if punishment is not its aim, the remedy is well adapted to use proportionate punishment to effect specific and general deterrence. As Gageler J observed in *Lifeplan*:

> [A]lthough the purpose of the remedy is not to punish, consideration of what is just in the context of the equitable obligation to be vindicated by the remedy cannot exclude consideration of the severity of the breach of the fiduciary obligation and the extent of the defendant's own involvement and culpability in it.[133]

Lifeplan constitutes the most recent, and arguably the most important, contribution of the High Court of Australia to this jurisprudence. Although it follows previous High Court authority closely,[134] it very clearly articulates the staged process of reasoning involved in this remedy and clarifies that reasoning. It also points to parallel reasoning across private law that is of significant interest for current purposes.

The case involved corporate accessorial (or 'participatory') liability for 'knowing assistance' in a breach of fiduciary duty. Mr Woff and Mr Corby owed fiduciary obligations to their employer, the plaintiff Lifeplan. In concert with the defendant Foresters, a competitor of Lifeplan, they used their employer's confidential information and business opportunities in breach of their fiduciary duties to draft a five-year plan for development of a competing business for Foresters. The plan was accepted, implemented and was spectacularly successful.[135] There was no doubt on

[129] *Giller v Procopets* [2008] VSCA 236 [157] (Ashley JA: 'somewhat worrying – both as to the principle which it expresses, and the reach of the principle'). See also Neave JA at [437].

[130] Or Canada: see *M(K) v M(H)* [1992] 3 SCR 6, noted by Mason P in *Harris* (n 127) [103].

[131] *Harris* (n 127) [343]–[352]. It is arguable that this aspect of his Honour's reasoning was in the minority: see [3]–[4] (Spigelman J rejecting that analysis) and [115] (Mason P). See also discussion of equity's advertence to culpability in assessing remedies in *Hospital Products Ltd v United States Surgical Corporation* (1984) 156 CLR 41, 109–10 (Mason J).

[132] Victorian Law Reform Commission, *Contempt of Court* (Consultation Paper, May 2019) ch 6.

[133] *Lifeplan* (n 6) [94], citing *Australian Postal Corporation v Lutak* (1991) 21 NSWLR 584, 596–97.

[134] In particular, *Warman International Ltd v Dwyer* (1995) 182 CLR 544 and *Consul Development Pty Ltd v DPC Estates Pty Ltd* (1975) 132 CLR 373. See also P Ridge 'Accounting for Gains from Knowing Participation in Breach of Fiduciary Duty' (2019) 13 *Journal of Equity* 69.

[135] A graph admitted into evidence showed a striking inverse correlation between the plaintiff's and defendant's profits following breach.

appeal that Foresters was relevantly involved in the fiduciary breach. The appeal turned on issues of causation and quantification.

As Kiefel CJ, Keane and Edelman JJ explained in their joint reasons, the equitable 'liability to account and to disgorge benefits encompasses "any benefit" received by the knowing participant in a breach of fiduciary duty "as a result of" that participation'.[136] This pithy summary was then broken down into a number of key stages, examined in sections IV.A–D following.

A. Causation

Focusing first on the requirement that the profit be 'as a result of' wrongful participation, this element raises a question of 'causation or contribution'.[137] While the plurality considered that this requirement would be satisfied by 'but for' causation, it was careful not to exclude the 'a factor' test of contribution commonly used for proving decision causation at common law in cases of deceit and duress.[138] Indeed, the plurality considered that at least where dishonest conduct is involved, it will be sufficient that the misconduct was 'an inducement' (or a factor) in bringing about the profits, even if there are other factors. This is hardly accidental. In the context of considering the measure of profit obtained from contraventions of the ACL for the purposes of setting civil pecuniary penalties, Justice Edelman had previously noted that the task of assessing the relevant profit attributable to a breach becomes particularly arduous if a 'but for' test is applied to identify the precise element and quantity of profit caused by the contravention, as opposed to other factors.[139] His Honour observed (without deciding the point) that a test of contribution (that is, was the misleading conduct 'a factor' in bringing about the profit that was in fact earned) would avoid some of these difficulties.[140]

It might be added that this test is also consistent with the approach taken to statutory causation in claims for private redress for loss or damage suffered because of misleading conduct.[141] On this approach, the tests of causation or contribution for both loss and profit align.[142] The 'a factor' test also promotes the deterrent purpose

[136] *Lifeplan* (n 6) [7].
[137] ibid [9].
[138] Citing *Edgington v Fitzmaurice* (1885) 29 Ch D 459 (CA) 483; *Barton v Armstrong* [1976] AC 104 (PC) 118–19; *Gould v Vaggelas* (1984) 157 CLR 215, 236, 250–51; *San Sebastian Pty Ltd v Minister Administering Environmental Planning and Assessment Act 1979 (NSW)* (1986) 162 CLR 340, 366; *Standard Chartered Bank v Pakistan National Shipping Corpn (No 4)* [2002] UKHL 43, [2003] 1 AC 959 [16]. See also ibid [88]–[90] (Gageler J).
[139] *Reckitt Benckiser (Australia) Pty Ltd (No 7)* (n 122) [51]–[66].
[140] ibid [59].
[141] E Bant and JM Paterson, 'Statutory Causation in Cases of Misleading Conduct: Lessons from and for the Common Law' (2017) 24 *Torts Law Journal* 1.
[142] *Henville v Walker* [2001] HCA 52, (2001) 206 CLR 459.

of both the equitable remedy and the statutory penalty regime: it can hardly be conducive to their efficacy to require plaintiffs to negate, or allow wrongdoers to put up in their defence, wholly speculative iterations of 'but for' reasoning.

B. Quantification of the 'Advantage' at Large

The account of profits has repeatedly been said to be 'notoriously difficult in practice'.[143] In the case of ongoing businesses or business opportunities developed in breach, it requires courts to measure a range of complex variables, including the value of the revenue earned and potentially broader assets, consider deductible expenses, taxation liabilities, interest components, contingencies and financial risks, determine whether allowance should be made in favour of the wrongdoer and in what sum, and (in the case of ongoing profits) the period of time that should be captured by the account.[144] In some cases, a constructive trust over the profits obtained by the breach will be awarded. Although this falls outside the ambit of this discussion, we may observe that a constructive trust has the effect of capturing all consequential profits, however defined and measured. In that respect, it is the most powerful and invasive of equity's gain-based remedies. The formidable nature of the constructive trust is most apparent when the subject of the order is some going concern, such as a retail business or mining operation.[145] Here, the potential for 'collateral damage' to third parties, such as employees of, and innocent investors or partners in, the defendant's business, and indeed personal creditors of the defendant, is of particular concern. By contrast with the blunt axe of the constructive trust (and, indeed, the 'at large' award of exemplary damages), the personal award of an account of profit serves as a relatively sharp, albeit intricate, weapon to achieve deterrence.

In *Lifeplan*, the key issues on quantification were, first, whether it was open to the Court to order an account of the net present value of funeral investment contracts that had not yet matured.[146] Foresters argued that it could not be required to account for future profits not yet received. The other issue was whether the Full Court had erred in not ordering Foresters 'to account for the entire capital value of Foresters' funeral products business'.[147] The Full Court had, instead, ordered the defendant to account for the five years' head-start it had enjoyed in developing the

[143] *Dwyer* (n 134) 556.
[144] See, eg, *Dart Industries Inc v Decor Corporation Pty Ltd* (1993) 179 CLR 101.
[145] *Grimaldi v Chameleon Mining NL (No 2)* [2012] FCAFC 6, (2012) 200 FCR 296 [501]–[511], [673]–[681] (the Court). See also Nettle J in *Lifeplan* (n 6) [180], considering that a similar distinction should be drawn between business opportunities and specific assets for the purposes of the account of profits.
[146] *Lifeplan* (n 6) [61].
[147] ibid [63].

competing business, as a result of accepting Woff and Corby's business development plan.

The plurality very helpfully set out the staged framework for navigating the complex question of relevant profit (or, as they termed it – helpfully for the purposes of the statutory formula – the 'benefit' or 'advantage'). This framework simplifies considerably the otherwise complex process for the victim, largely placing the difficult issues of quantification at the feet of the wrongdoer.

First, the onus falls on the defendant wrongdoer to explain why *all* the advantage resulting from the breach should not be disgorged. Here, the concept of 'advantage' is drawn widely, consistently with the rationale of 'ensuring that the wrongdoer should not be permitted to gain from the wrongdoing'.[148] On the facts of *Lifeplan*, this meant that the actionable 'advantage' that was the subject of the account included profits that were yet to be realised, including the funeral investment contracts that had not yet matured.[149] As discussed in section IV.D, their Honours also cited a number of US cases where the approach adopted by the courts is for the plaintiff to identify all gross revenue causally connected to the breach, the onus then shifting to the defendant to apportion any profits that it says should not be attributable to the breach. As Edelman J had previously noted in the context of setting penalties for misleading conduct under the ACL, it is open to courts in sales cases to reduce very complex calculations of 'profit' by refocusing on the known revenue or earnings before interest and tax (EBIT) generated through the misleading conduct.[150] This measure can 'frame' the court's consideration of the appropriate level of penalty. That approach would be consistent with the strategy adopted for the account of profit, leaving it to the defendant (who is, after all, best placed to know its detailed financial position) to explain and justify the basis for any deductions or apportionment.

The plurality then clarified that, once the total advantage obtained from the breach is identified, there are only two ways in which the defendant may seek to reduce his scope of liability:

> The first way, which can involve notorious difficulties in attribution of costs, is by proving his or her entitlement to an allowance for costs incurred, and labour and skill employed …
>
> The second way, which was the focus of this appeal, is by demonstrating that the benefit or advantage is beyond the scope of the liability for which the wrongdoer should account for profits. A wrongdoer might prove that some profit or benefit is beyond the scope of liability for which he or she should account if the profit or benefit has no reasonable connection with the wrongdoing.[151]

We now consider these in turn.

[148] ibid [24]. See also [75] (Gageler J).
[149] Citing (among others) Millett LJ in *Potton Ltd v Yorkclose Ltd* [1990] FSR 11, 15.
[150] *Reckitt Benckiser (Australia) Pty Ltd (No 7)* (n 122) [64]–[65].
[151] *Lifeplan* (n 6) [13].

C. The Allowance for Skill and Labour

Taking seriously the numerous statements by the High Court that the account of profit should not be permitted to 'unjustly enrich' the plaintiff,[152] the allowance for skill and labour, and expenditure incurred by the defendant, can be regarded in the nature of a set-off by counter-restitution for the benefit received by the plaintiff as a result of the defendant's labours. On this approach, the obligation is of the same nature as the requirement to 'do equity' in cases of rescission:[153] it serves to recognise what is functionally a counter-claim by way on set-off on behalf of the defendant for the fair value of the defendant's services and for the expenditure incurred (and hence saved by the plaintiff) in generating the profit. Normally, a plaintiff would be entitled to deny that the defendant's unrequested labours and expenditure amounted to an enrichment to the plaintiff. However, this becomes impossible when the plaintiff seeks a disgorgement remedy: here the plaintiff clearly accepts the defendant's activities as valuable.[154]

Interestingly, this analysis suggests that it may be possible to further clarify the boundary between just deterrence and disproportionate punishment for the purposes of the account of profit. Where a defendant establishes the value of his services and that expenditure was necessarily or reasonably incurred in generating the defendant's ultimate advantage, to deny an allowance may be, without more, to engage in unjust or disproportionate punishment. There are cases where equity has denied or not ordered an allowance, in circumstances where clearly the defendant's labour was an important part of generating the end profit.[155] This suggests once more the very thin line between deterrence and unjust punishment. In most cases, the matter is dealt with as involving a failure on the part of the defendant to discharge the onus of establishing his claim to an allowance that is held in the discretion of the court.

However, it remains to be seen whether these concerns to prevent the unjust enrichment of the plaintiff apply by analogy to the statutory sphere. In the latter domain, it is regulators on behalf of the state who seek fines to deter serious misconduct, and it is the public that benefits from the award. Arguably, any fine in that context does not unjustly enrich the plaintiff regulator but may be conceptualised

[152] *Dwyer* (n 134) 561 and *Lifeplan* (n 6) [94] (Gageler J).

[153] *Plan B Trustees Ltd v Parker (No 2)* [2013] WASC 216 [89]–[91] (Edelman J).

[154] See *Guinness Plc v Saunders* [1990] 2 AC 663 (HL) 700 (Lord Goff): 'Plainly, it would be inconsistent with this long-established principle [that trustees should not be permitted to profit from their trust without consent] to award remuneration in such circumstances as of right on the basis of a quantum meruit claim. But the principle does not altogether exclude the possibility that an equitable allowance might be made in respect of services rendered. That such an allowance may be made to a trustee for work performed by him for the benefit of the trust, even though he was not in the circumstances entitled to remuneration under the terms of the trust deed, is now well established.'

[155] As in *Guinness Plc* (n 154), where Lord Goff further held that an allowance could only be permitted in 'those cases where it cannot have the effect of encouraging trustees in any way to put themselves in a position where their interests conflict with their duties as trustees'. See also *Hospital Products International Pty Ltd* (n 131) 242–43, cited with approval by Mason P in *Digital Pulse* (n 127) [164].

as redressing the broader and largely unquantifiable 'societal harm'[156] suffered as a result of serious misconduct. The statutory regime may also be concerned to set the penalty at a level that disregards the work and skills of the defendant in generating the advantage in contravention of the statute, for reasons of both general and specific deterrence.

D. Scope of Liability

On the second question of scope of liability, the plurality in *Lifeplan* expressly drew a parallel between the accounting remedy in that case and that available under US statute for breach of copyright, arguing that they both demonstrate that there must be a 'reasonable connection' or 'sufficient nexus' between the advantage gained and the breach.[157] As one of the cited authorities, *Polar Bear Productions Inc v Timex Corp*, explains:

> § 504(b) [Copyright Act] creates a two-step framework for recovery of indirect profits: 1) the copyright claimant must first show a causal nexus between the infringement and the gross revenue; and 2) once the causal nexus is shown, the infringer bears the burden of apportioning the profits that were not the result of infringement.[158]

In *Lifeplan*, the plurality indicated that the second step involves a broad assessment of the extent to which a 'profit or benefit has no reasonable connection with the wrongdoing'.

This seems a very high bar for a defendant to clear, given that the plaintiff has already established that the breach caused or contributed to the profit. One possibility, considered in the US cases, is that a defendant will be able to show that some severable portion of the profit was not caused by the breach, or the breach was a trivial cause. But we consider that the plurality is more likely to have had in mind the profit-equivalent of a compensatory remoteness rule in tort:[159] just as for deceit all *intended* loss is 'direct' loss and not too remote,[160] the plurality observed that profits intended to be generated from the breach cannot be considered as having no reasonable connection with the wrong. For this reason, they held that all profits (not simply those generated during the initial five-year period) should be recovered from Foresters: 'The advantages of the business connections appropriated from Lifeplan and FPM were to be enjoyed by Foresters for as long as those connections could be retained in its business.'

Justice Gageler, agreeing in the result in a separate, reasoned judgment, denied that the amount of the profit was circumscribed by principles akin to common law

[156] Sharkey (n 63) 367–69.
[157] *Lifeplan* (n 6) [15], citing *Frank Music Corp v Metro-Goldwyn-Mayer Inc* 886 F 2d 1545 (9th Cir 1989) and *Polar Bear Productions Inc v Timex Corp* 384 F 3d 700 (9th Cir 2004).
[158] *Polar Bear Productions Inc* (n 157) 711.
[159] cf ibid, profits may be denied where they are 'remotely or speculatively attributable' to the breach.
[160] *Palmer Bruyn* (n 5).

remoteness rules.[161] However, this appears in part to be because, as a matter of technique, the onus lies on the defendant in equity to show why his liability should be reduced, whereas at common law the plaintiff must show that the loss is not too remote.[162] Expanding on the circumstances that may limit a defendant's scope of liability, Gageler J considered that they may include: (i) disentitling conduct of the plaintiff, such as standing by while the defendant takes risks and generates profits when the plaintiff is free to act to prevent the continuing wrong; (ii) the benefit or gain is attributable in part to one or more other contributing causes by reference to which it is 'practically just' that the benefit or gain be apportioned or that some allowance be made in favour of the defendant; or (iii) 'that there is some other reason why accounting for the whole of the gain would amount to a windfall to the plaintiff of such a nature or to such a degree that the accounting would fail to vindicate the purposes underlying equity's imposition of the fiduciary obligation that has been breached'.

Gageler J emphasised that determining the amount of the profit is ultimately a normative question (a matter of evaluative judgement, not merely causation), achieved by reference to a range of factors:

> Factors which might bear on the judgment to be made in an individual case cannot be catalogued exhaustively in advance. They will include the relative extent to which other causes which might include the skill and industry of the defendant can be assessed as having contributed to the benefit or gain that is causally connected to the breach of fiduciary obligation. They will also include whether, and if so to what extent, the defendant's gain reflects uncompensated loss on the part of the plaintiff. And although the purpose of the remedy is not to punish, consideration of what is just in the context of the equitable obligation to be vindicated by the remedy cannot exclude consideration of the severity of the breach of the fiduciary obligation and the extent of the defendant's own involvement and culpability in it. The judgment to be made must accommodate the stringency of the equitable obligation to be vindicated to the need to ensure that the remedy is not 'transformed into a vehicle for the unjust enrichment of the plaintiff'.[163]

Clearly, although cautious about endorsing a remoteness-style rule in equity, his Honour's emphasis on the normative nature of the task once causation is established is not inconsistent with the plurality's 'scope of liability' style analysis.

Nettle J dissented, though not on the form of analysis adopted by the plurality;[164] his Honour considered that making the defendant account for the full advantage received from the breach, rather than only the first five years, constituted 'unwarranted punishment of Foresters and a vehicle for the unjust enrichment of Lifeplan and FPM'.[165] Again, we may observe the boundary between just deterrence and

[161] *Lifeplan* (n 6) [89].
[162] ibid [90]–[91].
[163] ibid [94].
[164] See, eg, ibid [186], discussing the arguments that may have been open to Foresters to reduce its liability, and his agreement at [203] on the treatment on future profits.
[165] ibid [183]. See also ibid [196].

disproportionate punishment is informed by considerations of unjust enrichment of the plaintiff (also expressed in Gageler J's judgment). In this case, however, the relevant enrichment was not simply the services and expenditures of the defendant but the extent to which the five-year plan developed by Woff and Corby for Foresters could properly be characterised as operating to the benefit of the defendant beyond that period. In his Honour's view, the Full Court's initial limitation of the account to the five years' head-start obtained by using Woff and Corby's business plan was entirely appropriate, reflecting as it did the inherent boundaries of their strategic influence and reflecting the real chance that they would cease to work for Foresters, leaving the company to fend for itself.[166]

In assessing the concerns regarding the potential for unjust enrichment of the plaintiff, it may be observed that similar arguments are often made in relation to exemplary damages, in terms of an 'unmerited windfall' to the plaintiff.[167] This language was also used by Gageler J to signal the outer boundaries of the account of profit.[168] We have seen that, so far as making an allowance for the defendant's services and expenditure is concerned, this can be assessed with a considerable degree of certainty. The boundary line can be policed with reasonable confidence. Where ongoing businesses are concerned, the difficulty arises in determining the ongoing influence of the initial breach as the business evolves and circumstances change. At some point, an account of profit will yield to the plaintiff benefits that cannot sensibly be attributed to the original breach. For the plurality, this issue was addressed through the concept of intended benefit: given that ongoing benefit was the aim, it could not be said to lack a 'reasonable connection' with the breach. For Gageler J, the wrongdoers' intention was also relevant in determining whether to impose a five-year time horizon on the account.[169] However, for him, the critical factor was that the evidence showed that the defendant's business gain correlated with the plaintiff's loss.[170] Accordingly, there could be no concern that disgorgement of the entirety of the value of the business would unjustly enrich the plaintiff.

V. Conclusion

This analysis has sought to identify principles of proportionate punishment that should inform the developing civil jurisdictions concerned to deter egregious

[166] ibid [187]–[189].

[167] B Chapman and M Trebilcock, 'Punitive Damages: Divergence in Search of a Rationale' (1989) 40 *Alabama Law Review* 741; A Duggan, 'Exemplary Damages in Equity: A Law and Economics Perspective' (2006) 26 *OJLS* 303; CR Sunstein, D Kahneman and D Schkade, 'Assessing Punitive Damages (with Notes on Cognition and Valuation in Law)' (1998) 107 *Yale Law Journal* 2071. See also Law Commission (n 12) para 5.165; Law Commission (Ireland) (n 12) para 1.15.

[168] *Lifeplan* (n 6) [92] and [115].

[169] ibid [117].

[170] ibid [115]–[116].

wrongdoing. We have here focused on the lessons to be learned from the equitable remedy disgorgement of profits following an account for the setting of civil pecuniary penalties in Australian consumer law, although the lessons from this interaction have wider significance, given the widespread interest in other jurisdictions in penalty and fines to deter prohibited behaviour, as opposed to relying on traditional methods of private litigation. Given the shared concepts and language of causation and advantage, and the accepted relevance of profit in settling pecuniary penalties in Australian law, equitable doctrine provides an illustration of how a punitive impact can still be balanced and principled. This should give confidence to Australian courts in their exercise of the statutory power to impose pecuniary penalties. In addition, there is considerable broader potential for other jurisdictions to draw insights from an analysis that seeks to examine and, where appropriate, synthesise common law, equitable and statutory principles concerned to deter serious misconduct. As the plurality in *Lifeplan* noted, there are lessons to be derived from the statutory principles found in intellectual property statutes, as well as the approach to remoteness rules adopted in deceit. So too the availability of exemplary damages awards reveals the legitimate role for proportionate punishment in our civil law. The challenge is to clarify and map the boundaries of what is legitimate.

11

Vicarious Punishment: Vicarious Liability for Exemplary Damages?

PHILLIP MORGAN*

I. Introduction

Given that vicarious liability has expanded in scope from its traditional territory, the question of whether there is vicarious liability for exemplary damages in English law will become of increasing importance. The major flaw in the authorities that hold that vicarious liability applies to exemplary damages is the belief that the ordinary justifications for vicarious liability for loss-based damages also justify vicarious punishment. This chapter advances the argument that since exemplary damages have a different purpose from loss-based remedies, something extra is required for vicarious punishment.

Since exemplary damages cannot be explained within a purely compensatory model and vicarious liability presently does not operate through a master's tort theory, vicarious liability for exemplary damages represents vicarious punishment. Whilst such liability anomalously punishes innocent parties, it is often assumed to be desirable based on deterrence. However, the modern theories of vicarious liability that buttress its recent expansion on models of enterprise liability and loss-spreading, reduce the importance of deterrence reasoning. These theories do not support vicarious liability for exemplary damages. Such damages are not part of the externalities that enterprise liability is designed to internalise, nor may a theory based on loss-spreading justify the spreading of non-loss-based damages.

With vicarious liability there is difference between the three *Rookes v Barnard*[1] categories. Vicarious punishment is a historic and powerful tool against state oppression, and to eliminate it (even in the era of human rights legislation) would be to diminish the defensive arms of the citizen against egregious abuses of the

* I would like to thank participants at the 2019 Punishment and Private Law Conference at the National University of Singapore, and participants at a work-in-progress seminar at the University of York for their helpful comments and advice. I am also grateful to Jenny Steele and James Goudkamp for their written comments on this piece.

[1] *Rookes v Barnard* [1964] AC 1129 (HL).

state's power. Further, the state has a special ability to avoid justice, in that it has the primary role in the investigation and prosecution of crimes. The exceptional remedy of vicarious liability for exemplary damages helps to counter any incentive of the state not to pursue its own agents. It is these extra elements that justify vicarious liability for category one exemplary damages, a factor not available for the other categories – for which vicarious liability is unjustifiable.

II. The Vicarious Liability Revolution

Vicarious liability makes one party, A, strictly liable for the torts of another, B. By multiplying the number of possible defendants it increases the probability of finding a solvent or insured defendant.[2] Vicarious liability is such a core feature of tort litigation that in most cases where it is deployed it goes without saying.

There are two stages to establishing vicarious liability. First, there must be a relationship between A and B that is sufficient to trigger the doctrine; second, the tort committed by B must be sufficiently connected with that relationship to render A vicariously liable for the tort.[3]

As declared by Lord Phillips in *Various Claimants v Catholic Child Welfare Society*,[4] '[t]he law of vicarious liability is on the move'. In reply, Lord Reed in *Cox v Ministry of Justice*[5] noted that '[i]t has not yet come to a stop'. This expansionary movement has continued post-*Cox*, and is evident in all of the recent higher appellate court decisions on the doctrine until *Various Claimants v Barclays Bank plc* and *WM Morrison Supermarkets plc v Various Claimants*,[6] where the Supreme Court attempted to draw a new line in the sand over which the doctrine should not pass. In doing so the Supreme Court appeared to accept the previous expansion of the doctrine up to this point, and did not seek to overturn previous case law. Only time will tell if this new line proves to be a temporary one, but it should be noted that the current doctrine has expanded considerably beyond its historic parameters. Previously, limits to vicarious liability rendered the question of whether there was vicarious liability for exemplary damages a niche, if not esoteric, point, since many cases that would trigger exemplary damages would not be within the scope of vicarious liability. However, as vicarious liability has expanded in scope, this question becomes of increasing importance.

[2] P Cane and J Goudkamp, *Atiyah's Accidents, Compensation and the Law*, 9th edn (Cambridge, Cambridge University Press, 2018) 217.

[3] P Morgan, 'Vicarious Liability on the Move' (2013) 129 *LQR* 139, approved: *Allen v The Chief Constable of the Hampshire Constabulary* [2013] EWCA Civ 967 [17]; approach also adopted in *Various Claimants v Catholic Child Welfare Society* [2012] UKSC 56, [2013] 2 AC 1 (*CCWS*) [21].

[4] *CCWS* (n 3) [19].

[5] *Cox v Ministry of Justice* [2016] UKSC 10, [2016] AC 660 [1].

[6] *Various Claimants v Barclays Bank plc* [2020] UKSC 13, [2020] 2 WLR 960; *WM Morrison Supermarkets plc v Various Claimants* [2020] UKSC 12, [2020] 2 WLR 941; *Mohamud v Wm Morrison Supermarkets plc* [2016] UKSC 11, [2016] AC 677; *Bellman v Northampton Recruitment Ltd* [2018] EWCA Civ 2214, [2019] 1 All ER 1133; *Armes v Nottinghamshire County Council* [2017] UKSC 60, [2018] AC 355.

The vicarious liability revolution can be traced to judicial responses to institutionalised sexual abuse. However, where abuse cases led, other cases followed. The first wave of such cases occurred in an employment context and concerned the sufficiency of connection stage (the second stage). Influenced by the Supreme Court of Canada in *Bazley v Curry*,[7] the House of Lords in *Lister v Hesley Hall*[8] and *Dubai Aluminium Co Ltd v Salaam*[9] expanded the remit of vicarious liability by adopting the 'close connection' test at the second stage.[10] This expansion was facilitated through the adoption of enterprise liability and loss-spreading reasoning. The Supreme Court further expanded the approach to the second stage in *Mohamud v Wm Morrison Supermarkets plc*.[11] Now a wide range of torts are deemed sufficiently connected at this second stage for vicarious liability to apply: for instance sexual abuse committed by a school housemaster, violent assault committed on a customer by a petrol station attendant, an assault committed by a managing director on an employee at a separate drinking session after the works Christmas party, and the facilitation of fraud committed by a solicitor. However, there are limits to this expansion, for example the deliberate mass release of employee personal data onto the Internet by an IT auditor, in order to harm his employer and to frame a fellow employee, is not sufficiently connected for vicarious liability to apply.[12]

As with stage two, there has been a significant broadening at stage one – the relationships between A and B that may trigger vicarious liability. The development of the 'akin to employment' category of vicarious liability,[13] and vicarious liability within unincorporated associations,[14] means that vicarious liability is now applicable to a range of relationships to which it would not previously have applied. Again, there are limits to this expansion. Whilst there have been attempts to extend vicarious liability to independent contractors, the Supreme Court has recently upheld the traditional position that vicarious liability does not apply to independent contractors who carry out business on their own account.[15]

Given the categories of exemplary damages, it is worth remembering that vicarious liability is not just a common law topic. That there is vicarious liability for the torts of police officers results from statutory intervention.[16] Such intervention was necessary when the common law approach to stage one of vicarious liability was narrower than it is at the present day.

[7] *Bazley v Curry* [1999] 2 SCR 534 (SCC).

[8] *Lister v Hesley Hall Ltd* [2001] UKHL 22, [2002] 1 AC 215.

[9] *Dubai Aluminium Co Ltd v Salaam* [2002] UKHL 48, [2003] 2 AC 366.

[10] ibid [23].

[11] *Mohamud* (n 6).

[12] *Morrison* (n 6); see also *Shelbourne v Cancer Research UK* [2019] EWHC 842, [2019] PIQR P16; *Brayshaw v The Partners of Apsley Surgery* [2018] EWHC 3286, [2019] 2 All ER 997. Compare *TPKN v Ministry of Defence* [2019] EWHC 1488.

[13] *JGE v Portsmouth Roman Catholic Diocesan Trust* [2012] EWCA Civ 938, [2013] QB 722; *CCWS* (n 3); *Cox* (n 5); *Armes* (n 6).

[14] *CCWS* (n 3).

[15] *Barclays Bank* (n 6).

[16] Police Act 1996, s 88(1). Note that immunity from vicarious liability for the torts of state agents is waived by the Crown Proceedings Act 1947, s 2(1)(a).

It is not the role of this chapter to question the current position of vicarious liability generally. That is for other work. However, as more and more remote connections between the relationship and the tort appear to trigger the doctrine, and looser connections between the parties are sufficient, the time is ripe to reconsider the position of exemplary damages within vicarious liability. The realm of vicarious liability is increasingly likely to overlap with the sphere of exemplary damages.

III. Exemplary Damages

Exemplary damages are designed to punish tortfeasors for their wrongdoing, and to deter tortfeasors and others from committing torts. Within the English common law, exemplary damages in tort are typically traced[17] to *Wilkes v Wood*[18] (trespass) and *Huckle v Money*[19] (assault and false imprisonment). Both cases arose from the unlawful actions of officials during government attempts to shut down the *North Britain* newspaper. In *Wilkes*, Pratt CJ stated that damages alongside providing satisfaction to the claimant could be used as 'a punishment to the guilty, to deter from any such proceeding for the future, and as a proof of the detestation of the jury to the action itself'.[20] From this point on, 'exemplary damages became a familiar feature of tort'.[21]

Rookes[22] is the defining point of the modern English law of exemplary damages, representing a shift that rendered the previous law obsolete. Although the House of Lords considered exemplary damages to be an anomaly, they felt that previous authority prevented them from eliminating the doctrine, and that it played an important role in a limited number of cases in 'vindicating the strength of the law',[23] filling gaps where existing remedies are inadequate.[24]

Lord Devlin introduced a new category of damages, aggravated damages, which were distinct from exemplary damages.[25] Aggravated damages, unlike exemplary damages, are compensatory. They are available where the conduct of the defendant aggravates the claimant's injuries,[26] and they represent additional compensation

[17] *Rookes* (n 1) 1221–22. However, there are earlier roots: *BMW of North America Inc v Gore* 517 US 559, 581, 116 S Ct 1589, 1602 (1996).

[18] *Wilkes v Wood* (1763) Lofft 1 19; 98 ER 489.

[19] *Huckle v Money* (1763) 2 Wils KB 206; 95 ER 768.

[20] *Wilkes* (n 18) 19, 498–99.

[21] J Edelman, J Varuhas and S Colton (eds), *McGregor on Damages*, 20th edn (London, Sweet & Maxwell, 2019) para 13-002.

[22] *Rookes* (n 1).

[23] ibid 1226 (Lord Devlin).

[24] Law Commission, *Aggravated, Exemplary and Restitutionary Damages* (Law Com No 247, 1997) pt I, para 1.15.

[25] *Broome v Cassell & Co Ltd* [1972] AC 1027 (HL) 1111 (Viscount Dilhorne); Law Commission (n 24) pt II, para 1.2.

[26] *Kuddus v Chief Constable of Leicestershire* [2001] UKHL 29, [2002] 2 AC 122 [50].

for injuries to the victim's feelings or dignity caused by the defendant's spite, malevolence or manner of committing the tort.[27] His Lordship re-categorised case law previously regarded as exemplary damages as aggravated damages where it was explicable in such compensatory terms. This new category was declared by Lord Devlin to be able to 'do most, if not all, of the work' of exemplary damages,[28] and could explain most (but not all) of the then existing case law.[29]

Lord Devlin narrowed the application of exemplary damages to three categories: (i) 'oppressive, arbitrary or unconstitutional action by the servants of the government'; (ii) where 'the defendant's conduct has been calculated by him to make a profit for himself which may well exceed the compensation payable to the plaintiff'; and (iii) where 'exemplary damages are expressly authorised by statute'.[30] Merely falling within these categories is not enough. Exemplary damages are discretionary. They are available only when the claimant himself is the victim of the punishable behaviour, and they are awarded only if the sum awarded in compensation (including any aggravated damages) is inadequate to punish the defendant and deter and mark disapproval of the conduct.[31] Exemplary damages potentially apply to all torts.[32] It is the defendant's conduct, not the cause of action, that determines if they are available.[33]

IV. Categories

Whilst restricting exemplary damages to the three *Rookes* categories has been rejected by other common law jurisdictions, which apply exemplary damages more widely,[34] this chapter does not seek to challenge the categorised approach in English law. Instead this chapter asks whether there should be vicarious liability for the *existing* doctrine. Since the nature of the categories is key to this chapter's arguments on vicarious liability, we need to examine them in detail.

Since category three only concerns two clear statutory examples of authorisation to award exemplary damages, which apply in highly restrictive circumstances,[35] it need not detain us.

[27] *Rookes* (n 1) 1221.

[28] ibid 1230.

[29] Edelman, Varuhas and Colton (eds) (n 21) para 13-004.

[30] *Rookes* (n 1) 1226–27.

[31] ibid 1221; *Broome* (n 25) 1060.

[32] *Kuddus* (n 26).

[33] Edelman, Varuhas and Colton (eds) (n 21) paras 13-011–13-014.

[34] *Australian Consolidated Press Ltd v Uren* [1969] 1 AC 590 (PC); *A v Bottrill* [2002] UKPC 44, [2003] 1 AC 449; *Lamb v Cotogno* (1987) 164 CLR 1 (HCA); *Whiten v Pilot Insurance Co* 2002 SCC 18, [2002] 1 SCR 5; H McGregor, 'In Defence of Lord Devlin' (1971) 34 *MLR* 520.

[35] Reserve and Auxiliary Forces (Protection of Civil Interests) Act 1951, s 13(2); Crime and Courts Act 2013, ss 34–38. See also Law Commission (n 24) pt IV, para 1.105. Note that it is possible that statutory exemplary damages may also apply to copyright protection.

A. Category One

Category one damages apply to the unlawful use of executive power, and are reserved to the worst abuses of this power.[36] Lord Devlin stated that they serve 'a valuable purpose in restraining the arbitrary and outrageous use of executive power'[37] and are also a 'weapon that … can be used in defence of liberty'.[38] Whilst large multinationals may also use their size to oppress,[39] category one damages only apply to government agents. This is since it is deemed that it is a special wrong to abuse state power – servants of the government are also servants of the people. We also expect more from state agents.[40] This power is also different from the power exercised by large corporations since it is an exercise of sovereign power.

Executive power is interpreted broadly. This category applies to agents of the central government, local authorities and the police.[41] Not all oppressive, arbitrary or unconstitutional uses of state power trigger such damages. The latter needs 'aggravating features'.[42] Further, the defendant needs to be exercising a government function when the tort is committed.[43] Such damages should also apply to contractors acting on behalf of the state where they exercise state power, for instance in the case of a private prison, or with custody staff provided by an outsourcing company to work in a police station. Here it is the nature of the power used that is significant; mere overlap in the type of services delivered by a contractor is insufficient for category one to be potentially in play.[44]

This category represents the earliest form of exemplary damages. It emerged to protect the civil liberties of citizens against the state. It retains this function today, enjoying a renaissance from the 1980s onwards alongside increased public criticisms of abuses of police power.[45] Today it is typically deployed in actions against the police and immigration authorities.[46]

Cases in the last few decades in which such damages have been awarded include where police officers tortured a suspect to extract a confession,[47] where a police

[36] *Ministry of Defence v Fletcher* [2010] IRLR 25 (EAT).

[37] *Rookes* (n 1) 1223.

[38] ibid 1227.

[39] *Kuddus* (n 26) [66].

[40] *Ashby v White* (1703) 2 Ld Raym 938, 956; 92 ER 126, 1373 (Holt CJ).

[41] *Broome* (n 25).

[42] Edelman, Varuhas and Colton (eds) (n 21) para 13-019.

[43] *AB v South West Water Services Ltd* [1993] QB 507 (CA); Edelman, Varuhas and Colton (eds) (n 21) para 13-019.

[44] Overlaps noted in *Uren v John Fairfax & Sons Pty Ltd* (1966) 117 CLR 118 (HCA). Note also that for the purposes of the Human Rights Act 1998 (UK), contractors are treated as public authorities when they carry out public functions.

[45] A Burrows, *Remedies for Torts, Breach of Contract, and Equitable Wrongs*, 4th edn (Oxford, Oxford University Press, 2019) 362–63.

[46] J Goudkamp and E Katsampouka, 'An Empirical Study of Punitive Damages' (2018) 38 *OJLS* 90, 91–113.

[47] *Treadaway v Chief Constable of the West Midlands*, *The Times* (QB, 25 October 1994).

officer hit an innocent bystander,[48] where police officers fabricated evidence and gave false evidence at trial,[49] and where police officers fabricated evidence to justify their violent assault and false imprisonment of the claimants.[50] In a Northern Irish context, such awards have been granted where police officers colluded with UVF terrorists, leading a state agent to attempt to murder the claimant.[51]

In a liberal democratic country without a written constitution, the freedom of individuals is often protected through torts such as false imprisonment, battery, assault and malicious prosecution. Exemplary damages give such claims more teeth in relation to the state. Lord Nicholls in *Kuddus v Chief Constable of Leicestershire*[52] argued that '[t]he availability of exemplary damages has played a significant role in buttressing civil liberties, in claims for false imprisonment and wrongful arrest'. This claim is also made by the Law Commission.[53] Given their role in protecting civil liberties, category one exemplary damages may be awarded (unlike with category two) where the defendant does not appreciate that what he was doing was wrongful.[54]

Despite strong statements of support for the continuation of category one damages, Lord Diplock and Lord Scott have advanced that such a remedy has been superseded by judicial review.[55] This is a flawed position, which fails to take into account the significant costs of judicial review, its extremely short limitation periods and that such proceedings cannot be brought in the County Court. Many category one claimants will be vulnerable people who will not be able to act in sufficient time, nor be able to raise sufficient funds to bring their claim within the three-month judicial review limitation period.[56] Tort claims, on the other hand, provide claimants with significantly longer limitation periods, and significantly greater opportunities to fund the litigation through conditional fee agreements or damages-based agreements. Further, damages are not the primary remedy in judicial review.

With the enactment of the Human Rights Act 1998 (UK), many category one claims will overlap with the statutory claim, but given the low level of Human Rights Act damages, the fact that the damages provide only for 'just satisfaction' (and do not contain a punishment element), and the fact that in some situations English common law rights are more extensive than Convention rights,[57] category one may still be seen as having a distinctive role in relation to claims relating to civil liberties. Even in the era of human rights legislation the common law of tort

[48] *Connor v Chief Constable of Cambridgeshire*, *The Times* (QB, 11 April 1984).

[49] *Manley v Commissioner of Police of the Metropolis* [2006] EWCA Civ 879, [2006] Po LR 117; *Rowlands v Chief Constable of Merseyside Police* [2006] EWCA Civ 1773, [2007] 1 WLR 1065.

[50] *Thompson v Commissioner of Police of the Metropolis* [1998] QB 498 (CA).

[51] *John Flynn v The Chief Constable of the Police Service of Northern Ireland* [2016] NIQB 24.

[52] *Kuddus* (n 26) [63].

[53] Law Commission (n 24) pt IV, para 1.92.

[54] ibid para 1.134.

[55] *Kuddus* (n 26) [104]–[108]; *Broome* (n 25) 1130.

[56] Civil Procedures Rules (CPR) r 54.5(1).

[57] *R (Jalloh) v Secretary of State for the Home Department* [2020] UKSC 4, [2020] 2 WLR 418.

is still used to protect fundamental rights. Common lawyers should also be wary of allowing the statutory claim to lead to the elimination of category one damages given recent political pressures to repeal the statute.

B. Category Two

Category two exemplary damages apply where the defendant's conduct is calculated to make a profit for him, notwithstanding his need to pay compensation.[58] Profit is viewed broadly; it is not simply money making, and other gains may suffice.[59] What is needed is knowledge that the act is unlawful or recklessness as to its legality, and a decision to carry out the act because the potential material advantages of doing so outweigh the potential losses.[60] Such cases have primarily related to the wrongful eviction and harassment of tenants.[61]

The case for exemplary damages in this category is that disgorgement of profits is not enough to discourage torts. Since disgorgement only removes the gain, it leaves the defendant with having nothing to lose with which to balance up against the possibility of the claimant's failing to sue him, or the claimant's case failing due to litigation hazards. Lord Diplock noted '[i]t is only if there is a prospect that the damages may exceed the defendant's gain that the social purpose of this category is achieved – to teach a wrong-doer that tort does not pay'.[62]

It is odd that this category does not apply where the defendant acted out of malice, particularly since in a positive economic sense this must also represent a gain in utility for the claimant.

V. Exemplary Damages in Practice

Although exemplary damages are at large, and take into account factors such as the means of the defendant, suggested tariffs exist for certain types of case.[63] Whilst large exemplary damages have been awarded, an empirical study in England and Wales showed that typically such awards are modest, and fairly uniform,[64] sums awarded against companies being higher than sums awarded against individuals or public bodies.

Nevertheless, as demonstrated by *Mohidin v Commissioner of Police of the Metropolis*,[65] a case in which the employer brought a claim for an indemnity against

[58] *Rookes* (n 1) 1226–27.
[59] *Broome* (n 25) 1094.
[60] ibid 1079.
[61] Law Commission (n 24) pt IV, para 1.99; Goudkamp and Katsampouka (n 46) 91–113.
[62] *Broome* (n 25) 1130.
[63] *Thompson* (n 50) 517, 520.
[64] Goudkamp and Katsampouka (n 46) 90–92, 103, 115.
[65] *Mohidin v Commissioner of Police of the Metropolis* [2016] EWHC 105, [2016] 1 Costs LR 71.

the tortfeasing employees, the means of an employee, particularly if his conduct has led to the loss of his job or he has now retired, may be minimal. The employer of the tortfeasor(s) may be the only potential defendant able to satisfy judgment for exemplary damages, even for small awards. Further, where an employee has sufficient assets to meet the judgment, it may be more difficult to sue the employee compared to his employer, perhaps due to the increased likelihood of resistance to the claim, or enhanced costs to enforce judgment.[66] For instance, where the defendant has sizable equity in his house, obtaining possession of the defendant's house may prove difficult.[67] Likewise, attachments to the employee's earnings may mean that the claimant waits a very long time, if not indefinitely, to receive full damages. Further, in addition, awards against corporate or organisational defendants are often larger (since such claims take into account their means), making such defendants more attractive to claimants.

VI. Exemplary?

Although vicarious punishment is prima facie objectionable, if exemplary damages in fact *compensate* claimants for the infringement of a right, vicarious liability for exemplary damages should follow where the defendant is vicariously liable for its agent's tort. Since aggravated damages *are* compensatory, vicarious liability includes such damages.[68] This section advances, contrary to the claims of some scholars, that exemplary damages are a species of damages different from compensatory damages. This means that the answers to whether there can be vicarious liability for compensatory damages and vicarious liability for exemplary damages may differ.

A. Compensatory?

Concerns that punishment and deterrence are out of place within tort law[69] have led to attempts to redefine exemplary damages as compensatory,[70] and also to calls for their abolition.[71] If exemplary damages are in fact compensatory (and it must be remembered that in *Rookes* Lord Devlin already reclassified much of their original territory as aggravated damages, and thus compensatory), this will

[66] See, eg, T Baker, 'Blood Money, New Money, and the Moral Economy of Tort Law in Action' (2001) 35 *Law & Society Review* 275.

[67] Cane and Goudkamp (n 2) 212.

[68] PS Atiyah, *Vicarious Liability in the Law of Torts* (London, Butterworths, 1967) 433.

[69] *Broome* (n 25) 1086. See also *Rookes* (n 1) 1221.

[70] See, eg, V Janecek, 'Exemplary Damages: A Genuine Concept' (2013) 6 *European Journal of Legal Studies* 243, 244.

[71] *Kuddus* (n 26) [121]; A Beever, 'The Structure of Aggravated and Exemplary Damages' (2003) 23 *OJLS* 87, 105.

impact on vicarious liability. It is true that there are some features that suggest a compensatory function; however, this is to ignore the authorities that consistently explain and justify the doctrine on punishment and deterrence grounds, and many significant features that demonstrate an overriding concern for punishment and deterrence.

Stevens attempts to convert them into a form of compensation for violation of right, although he acknowledges that the evidence is not all one way. He advances that exemplary damages relate to the level of infringement of a claimant's right, and that they are an 'emphatic vindication of the claimant's rights',[72] which explains why they are due to the claimant and why only the victim may claim them. He argues that once we consider that they are substitutive damages for a claimant's rights, objections to them drop away.[73]

There are indeed features of exemplary damages that best fit with a compensatory narrative. For example, the fact that the damages are given to the claimant, and not to the state or to other worthy causes where the state is the defendant. This appears to be a windfall to the claimant, since it is not due to him. Likewise the requirement that the claimant himself must be the tort victim sits oddly with a punishment rationale. That where there are multiple defendants does not add to the exemplary damages due, even though there may be more wrongdoers to punish (indeed it lightens the load for the defendants), again appears to be explicable on the basis of compensating the victim for a wrong. Their insurability (although the authorities only cover insurability for vicarious liability) also suggests a non-punitive foundation.[74] Further, that claims for exemplary damages are extinguished on the claimant's death[75] is an oddity if punishment and deterrence are key. Neither rationale would lead to an extinction of the claim. Extinction on death implies that the claimant is in fact being compensated for some form of dignitary loss.

It is possible to explain away some of these problematic elements to the punishment narrative. That the claimant receives the award may be necessary to encourage claimants to bring such claims and to incur the additional costs of proving the elements needed for such an award over and above a compensatory award. That the claimant, and not the state, brings the claim is explicable by the fact that a core role of exemplary damages is controlling state agents, and that such claims are often brought due to the state's failure to prosecute its own agents. Further, that only the claimant may bring suit may prevent a litigation free-for-all, and prevent the emergence of a class of bounty-hunting litigants unassociated with the wrong. Other problematic aspects may simply emerge from incorrect policy calls, and date to a time where they were less clearly defined and separated from

[72] R Stevens, *Torts and Rights* (Oxford, Oxford University Press, 2009) 86.
[73] ibid 87.
[74] ibid.
[75] Law Reform (Miscellaneous Provisions) Act 1934, s 1(2)(a).

compensatory aggravated damages. Further, not all aspects of the rules surrounding exemplary damages are logical.

However, there are strong objections to the compensatory thesis. Exemplary damages have been consistently explained by the highest courts in non-compensatory terms. For instance, Lord Devlin in *Rookes* declared that their purpose is to 'punish and deter',[76] and Lord Hoffmann, in *W v W*,[77] stated that their main purpose was to punish.[78] The standard jury directions also make it very clear that compensation is limited to the primary award, as uplifted for aggravated damages, and that exemplary damages are distinct and based solely on punishment.[79]

Many features point towards these damages' not being based on compensatory principles. For instance, where there are multiple claimants the relevant exemplary damages are divided between the claimants. They do not each receive separate exemplary damages.[80] This focuses on the defendant's wrong and the need to punish the defendant, and not on compensating the claimants. The existence of other claimants should not reduce the wrong to any individual claimant, nor the compensation due to him. A large number of potential claimants has also been given as a reason for not awarding exemplary damages;[81] again this points to a defendant-centric punishment and deterrence approach, and not compensation.

Further, where there are joint tortfeasors, concerns for tortfeasor rights are such that only the lowest sum necessary to punish either of the two tortfeasors is awarded,[82] even if one of the tortfeasors if sued alone would be liable to pay a higher sum. The involvement of a less guilty tortfeasor lessens the sum the claimant receives, which makes sense only if the purpose of the award is to punish and deter, and not to compensate. The courts do not wish to over-punish any tortfeasor.

Core to the argument that the award is not compensatory is the method of its calculation. The calculation of exemplary damages is at the discretion of the court or jury. It is fundamentally different from compensatory awards, being the sum necessary to punish and deter the defendant and others.[83] In arriving at this sum the defendant's means are considered.[84] This is not relevant to compensation. It appears that where an employer is sued for an employee's wrongs, it is the means of the former, not those of the latter, that are considered.[85] Again, this should not be relevant for a compensatory award. Further, to prevent double punishment if the

[76] *Rookes* (n 1) 1221. These two different justifications for exemplary damages may each point towards a different amount of damages. This could be resolved by split awards: see Sharkey, ch 7 of this volume.

[77] *W v W* [1999] 2 NZLR 1 (PC) 2.

[78] See also *Mafo v Adams* [1970] 1 QB 548 (CA) 558.

[79] *Thompson* (n 50) 514–17.

[80] *Riches v News Group Newspapers Ltd* [1986] QB 256 (CA).

[81] *R (Lumba) v Secretary of State for the Home Department* [2011] UKSC 12, [2012] 1 AC 245.

[82] *Broome* (n 25).

[83] Burrows (n 45) 372.

[84] *Rookes* (n 1) 1228.

[85] *Rowlands* (n 49); Edelman, Varuhas, Colton (eds) (n 21) para 13-038.

defendant has already been punished, for instance by the criminal law, this is taken into account in making the determination as to whether exemplary damages are due, and their quantum. This is since to punish twice would offend against natural justice.[86] Again, that a defendant has been punished should have no impact on the compensation due to a claimant.

The name given to the damages also points away from any compensatory purpose. Whilst exemplary damages is the name primarily used within the case law, they have also been referred to as punitive damages.[87] The former name emphasises the example made of the defendant, focusing on their deterrent role and not on their punishment feature. The latter name better encapsulates this punishment feature. However, both names describe non-compensatory purposes. To avoid confusion, this chapter uses the name found within the authorities. Further, the special treatment of these damages, and the desire of the courts to confine them to very narrow categories, again evidences their punitive role.

That these damages may not be explained in compensatory terms need not trouble us. To explain tort as solely compensatory is an oversimplification.[88] As Lord Wilberforce noted in *Broome v Cassell*:

> It cannot lightly be taken for granted, even as a matter of theory, that the purpose of the law of tort is compensation, still less that it ought to be … or that there is something inappropriate or illogical or anomalous (a question-begging word) in including a punitive element in civil damages …[89]

This chapter concurs with Burrows that there is 'no logical reason why punishment should not be a response available to the civil law'.[90] As disgorgement damages and nominal damages show, tort damages extend beyond the merely compensatory.[91] In addition, punishment and deterrence are present in other private law contexts, for instance with breaches of fiduciary duty, and with disgorgement in contract law. Likewise, deterrence has a long pedigree in tort law,[92] and it is sometimes used in leading cases as a factor in determining the existence and parameters of a duty of care.[93]

[86] *Archer v Brown* [1985] QB 401 (QB); *AB* (n 43) 527 (overruled on other grounds); *Gray v Motor Accident Commission* [1998] HCA 70, (1998) 196 CLR 1. Compare *Borders (UK) Ltd v Commissioner of Police of the Metropolis* [2005] EWCA Civ 197, [2005] Po LR 1; *Axa Insurance UK plc v Financial Claims Solutions Ltd* [2018] EWCA Civ 1330, [2019] RTR 1.

[87] Punitive damages, see eg, *Broome* (n 25) 1121 (Lord Diplock); Law Commission (n 24) pt V, para 1.39; Burrows (n 45) 360; exemplary damages, see eg, *Broome* (n 25) (Lord Hailsham LC) 1073; Edelman, Varuhas, Colton (eds) (n 21) para 13-001.

[88] RW Hodgin and E Veitch, 'Punitive Damages – Reassessed' (1972) 21 *ICLQ* 119, 130.

[89] *Broome* (n 25) 1114.

[90] Burrows (n 45) 376.

[91] Law Commission (n 24) pt I, para 1.1; pt V, para 1.142.

[92] J Edelman, 'In Defence of Exemplary Damages' in CEF Rickett (ed), *Justifying Private Law Remedies* (Oxford, Hart Publishing, 2008) 225.

[93] See, eg, *Yuen Kun Yeu v Attorney-General of Hong Kong* [1988] AC 175 (PC); *Hill v Chief Constable of West Yorkshire* [1989] AC 53 (HL); *X (Minors) v Bedfordshire CC* [1995] 2 AC 633 (HL); *Harris v Evans* [1998] 1 WLR 1285 (CA); *Van Colle v Chief Constable of Hertfordshire* [2008] UKHL 50,

Since exemplary damages are not a form of compensation, the issue of vicarious liability is more complex, and requires an examination of the justifications for the doctrine.

VII. Justifying Vicarious Deterrence and Punishment?

Where the employer is liable as a secondary party, for instance where it authorises or procures the tort, if the tortfeasing employee is liable for exemplary damages, the secondary party is also held liable for such damages.[94] However, here we are concerned with employers who are innocent of any involvement with the tort.

Given that the overlap between vicarious liability and exemplary damages was until recently fairly small,[95] there is little authority on the issue. There appears to be a long-standing assumption of vicarious liability for exemplary damages; they have been awarded against employers for some time, with their level being calculated in accordance with the employer's, not the employee's, resources – leading to larger damages.[96] Even in a number of classic cases the sums awarded were such that juries must have considered that the employer was the real defendant.[97] Although this issue was spotted earlier in other common law jurisdictions,[98] it is only recently that English courts have started to consider why an innocent party should be punished.[99] Given the rejection of the master's tort theory in English law, it cannot be said that the employer is being punished for its own tort.[100]

That the defendant is not the tortfeasor, which makes exemplary damages harder to justify, was first judicially noticed in an English context by Lord Woolf MR in *Thompson v Commissioner*.[101] However, the issue of vicarious liability was first discussed in the English courts by Lords Scott and Hutton in *Kuddus*,[102] although since the point was not an issue in the appeal and was not argued by counsel, their discussion is strictly obiter.[103] The only English authority on this point

[2009] 1 AC 225; *Mitchell v Glasgow City Council* [2009] UKHL 11, [2009] 1 AC 874; *Robinson v Chief Constable of West Yorkshire Police* [2014] EWCA Civ 15, [2014] PIQR P14.

[94] Atiyah (n 68) 434.

[95] See, eg, *Makanjuola v Commissioner of Police of the Metropolis* (1990) 2 Admin LR 214 (QB), where the police officer used his status to gain access to the claimant's flat and coerce her into sex under threat of reporting her to the immigration authorities, which did not at the time lead to vicarious liability.

[96] *Thompson* (n 50); Edelman, Varuhas and Colton (eds) (n 21) para 13-045.

[97] Atiyah (n 68) 434 (see, eg, the *North Britain* cases).

[98] Hodgin and Veitch (n 88) 122.

[99] P Giliker, *Vicarious Liability in Tort: A Comparative Perspective* (Cambridge, Cambridge University Press, 2010) 18.

[100] *Staveley Iron and Chemical Co v Jones* [1956] AC 627 (HL); *Imperial Chemical Industries Ltd v Shatwell* [1965] AC 656 (HL); M Jones, A Dugdale and M Simpson, *Clerk & Lindsell on Torts*, 22nd edn (London, Sweet & Maxwell, 2017) para 6-60; W Swain, 'A Historical Examination of Vicarious Liability: a "Veritable Upas Tree"?' (2019) 78 *CLJ* 640. Compare Stevens (n 72) ch 11.

[101] *Thompson* (n 50) 512–13.

[102] *Kuddus* (n 26).

[103] ibid [27] (Lord Slynn), [47]–[48] (Lord Mackay), [69] (Lord Nicholls).

is *Rowlands v Chief Constable of Merseyside*,[104] the Court of Appeal holding that the defendant Chief Constable was vicariously liable for the exemplary damages flowing from a police officer's tort. Whilst this decision concerns a category one exemplary damages case in a statutory vicarious liability context, its reasoning appears to establish vicarious liability for all classes of exemplary damages. Indeed, whilst Eady J in *Mosley v News Group Newspapers Ltd*[105] expressed disquiet in relation to vicarious liability for exemplary damages, he stated (obiter) that in light of *Rowlands* a lower court judge would be unable to limit vicarious liability to the first category only.

Other first instance cases have placed a question mark over vicarious liability for exemplary damages. For instance, in *Parabola Investments Ltd v Browallia Cal Ltd*,[106] Flaux J noted *Kuddus* but questioned the applicability of vicarious liability for exemplary damages in the case of fraud; but this comment is undermined by his failure to note the binding authority on the Court of *Rowlands*.

VIII. An Odd Fit with Vicarious Liability

Various features of exemplary damages fit oddly with vicarious liability. Prima facie it seems inconsistent with the rationale of exemplary damages to make an innocent employer liable for damages specifically designed to punish and deter the employee tortfeasor.[107] It seems odd in principle to punish those other than the malefactor.[108]

There has been significant concern, when dealing with exemplary damages, for the rights of defendants, particularly with punishing them for amorphous wrongs that are insufficiently crystallised and with lower standards of proof and safeguards than in a criminal trial. Here, with vicarious liability, an individual is being punished for behaviour that is not even wrongful. The safeguard of even needing to commit a wrong has been eliminated. Further, setting the level of exemplary damages is a personalised approach based on the defendant's conduct and means. In the absence of applying the master's tort theory, it is extremely odd to calculate the penalty due from the employer. The employer may have greater means than the employee, but its conduct may have been faultless. The master's tort theory (with the acts attributable to the employer) would make calculation

[104] *Rowlands* (n 49).

[105] *Mosley v News Group Newspapers Ltd* [2008] EWHC 1777, [2008] EMLR 20 [199]–[203].

[106] *Parabola Investments Ltd v Browallia Cal Ltd* [2009] EWHC 901, [2009] 2 All ER (Comm) 589 [208]. See also *Benjamin Pell v Express Newspapers* [2009] EWHC 118 [83]–[85]; again *Rowlands* is not noted.

[107] Giliker (n 99) 40.

[108] *S v Attorney-General* [2003] NZCA 149, [2003] 3 NZLR 450; Law Commission (n 24) pt V, para 1.188; Atiyah (n 68) 435. Compare J Rawls, 'Two Concepts of Rules' (1955) 64 *The Philosophical Review* 3 (who uses the term 'telishment').

less perverse in this context.[109] Lord Scott in *Kuddus* considered that the objections to vicarious liability for exemplary damages were fundamental, since their purpose is to punish, and there is thus no room to award such damages against one whose behaviour is not punishable. He considered that the fact that only the perpetrator of the punishable behaviour should be punished was the natural converse of the fact that only the victim of the punishable behaviour can recover.[110]

Vicarious liability means that the actual wrongdoer remains unpunished. It can have the practical effect of acting as a protective mechanism for tortfeasors,[111] by diverting the liability to their employer. This is perfectly proper when dealing with compensatory damages: many employees will be expecting their employer to pay for and insure such losses, do not hold personal policies of insurance and have not bargained for additional remuneration to allow them to absorb such losses. However, by establishing vicarious liability for exemplary damages we are in fact protecting those most deserving of punishment, specifically in the circumstances where the law has designed a penalty to punish them for *their* wrong. Instead others have to absorb these damages.[112] It does not seem legitimate for such an employee to look to his employer to protect him from the penal consequences of his behaviour. It would also seem to undermine the deterrent rationale for such damages if vicarious liability allows such wrongdoers in practical terms to escape liability. The view that this will lead to indirect punishment of the wrongdoer, in that the employer will discipline its employee if it is held so liable or seek contribution,[113] is arbitrary and not based on any evidence of how employees are disciplined for torts, and how this differs in the case of vicarious liability for exemplary damages combined with compensatory damages, when compared to just the latter. Further, given the inevitably long period of time from the tort to final judgment, in many cases an employee will already have changed employers, or may even have retired.

To make an employer vicariously liable also sits oddly[114] with the principle that where there are two joint tortfeasors, only the lowest sum of exemplary damages that may be awarded against either of them can be awarded; and if one of the tortfeasors does not merit such a penalty, exemplary damages cannot be awarded. This protects the less culpable tortfeasor against being punished for the other's guilt. The Law Commission attempts to distinguish joint tortfeasors from employers, arguing that the unfairness is less clear with the latter.[115] This appears to be

[109] A Gray, *Vicarious Liability Critique and Reform* (Oxford, Hart Publishing, 2018) 264.
[110] *Kuddus* (n 26) [131].
[111] P Morgan, 'Recasting Vicarious Liability' (2012) 71 *CLJ* 615, 616. See also Irish Law Reform Commission, *Civil Liability of Good Samaritans and Volunteers* (Irish Law Reform Commission No 93-2009) paras 3.88, 4.12.
[112] See, eg, Law Commission (n 24) pt V, para 1.211.
[113] ibid para 1.266.
[114] ibid para 1.210.
[115] ibid para 1.213; E Taylor, 'Vicarious Punishment: An Employer's Vicarious Liability for Exemplary Damages' (2009) 1 *King's Student Law Review* 1.

based on the idea of deterrence, that an employer has power over an employee and can use this to prevent torts, whereas joint tortfeasors may not necessarily have such power over one another. However, this is not clear-cut. Further, deterrence might lead to liability for the larger sum in both cases – with joint tortfeasors it would discourage participation in the wrong, indeed the deterrence case for higher damages may be stronger with joint tortfeasors. After all, in some cases the vicariously liable employer will have followed all of the proper practices for selecting, training and disciplining its employees, and could in fact be a market leader in these areas. A joint tortfeasor, on the other hand, by definition has acted improperly, and without his involvement, in many cases the tort would not have been committed.

Vicarious liability for exemplary damages may lead to indemnification problems. An employer who is held liable for its employee's tort may in turn sue the employee for an indemnity.[116] If an employer was originally sued without the tortfeasing employee being joined to the action, since in such a case damages are determined by the employer's assets,[117] the size of the exemplary damages is likely to be greater than if the two parties were both sued in the same action. Where both are sued, the exemplary damages would be the lesser of the two sums appropriate to either defendant. The action for an indemnity may therefore lead to greater punishment of the tortfeasor then a court would deem just.[118] However, it may be possible to deal with this problem via section 2 of the Civil Liability (Contribution) Act 1978 (UK), to prevent the exemplary damages from being fully reimbursed where they are disproportionate to the employee's wrong and his means.[119] It may also be resolved by determining the level of the damages by reference to the employee's guilt and resources.

The Law Commission appears to answer the question as to the unfairness of making an innocent party vicariously liable for exemplary damages with the odd view that vicarious liability is already unfair by making innocent employers liable for their employee's torts.[120] This flawed argument is that injustice in one context justifies injustice elsewhere. Further, this fails to consider the complex matrix of factors invoked by the courts to justify the imposition of vicarious liability for compensatory damages, some of which (as we shall see) do not apply to exemplary damages. Thus, it can be said that to the extent that vicarious liability is generally 'unfair' (which this current author rejects), vicarious liability for exemplary damages has a *greater* level of unfairness.

Exemplary damages are ordinarily tailored to the guilt of the defendant; this is to ensure that it is neither disproportionate nor unfair.[121] However, assessing the 'guilt' of a party wholly innocent of a wrong seems problematic. Whilst the

[116] A problem alluded to by Atiyah (n 68) 436, fn 12.
[117] Which seems an odd resurrection of the master's tort theory.
[118] Giliker (n 99) 41.
[119] *Thompson* (n 50) 517.
[120] Law Commission (n 24) pt V, paras 1.215–1.216.
[121] P Ghandhi, 'Exemplary Damages in the English Law of Tort' (1990) 10 *Legal Studies* 182, 200.

employer is innocent, the exemplary damages are assessed with regards to the employer's assets. This means that the punishment is a personal one, rather than vicarious. To that extent vicarious liability for exemplary damages actually goes beyond vicarious punishment, since the employer itself is personally punished, with the punishment set by the employer's own resources. The employer is not just simply paying for its employee's wrong.

IX. Deterrence and Deep Pockets

Despite the odd fit between the two doctrines, the case for vicarious liability for exemplary damages that has been made is primarily based on both deterrence and deep-pockets reasoning. However, it is also possible to detect justifications based on identification, and on punishment of institutional wrongs.

A. Deterrence

In *Kuddus*, Lord Hutton gave a number of examples of cases concerning violations of civil liberties committed by police and security forces in Northern Ireland,[122] and considered (obiter) that vicarious liability for exemplary damages would uphold the rule of law by exerting a deterrent effect on those in command to ensure that discipline is maintained. The idea is that vicarious liability will encourage employers to select, educate and control their employees properly.[123]

There has been much support for the deterrence justification for vicarious liability for exemplary damages, and it has proved to be the key justification in the academic literature. For instance, McGregor's support for such liability for exemplary damages is primarily based on the deterrent effect's incentivisation of employers to control their employees.[124]

Atiyah (in the context of category one damages) likewise supports a case for liability based on deterrence, arguing that deterrence is more effective, particularly at preventing repetition of tortious behaviour, if it is aimed at the employer not the employee.[125] This is also the primary argument given by the Law Commission, which adds an additional punishment rationale, arguing that employer liability enhances the employer's incentive to control and educate its workforce, and that the employer's disciplinary powers have greater punishment and deterrence potential upon employees than exemplary damages.[126] However, in the context of exemplary damages many of the torts will also be criminal offences, and it is

[122] *Kuddus* (n 26) [76]–[79].
[123] Giliker (n 99) 41.
[124] Edelman, Varuhas and Colton (eds) (n 21) para 13-047; cf Gray (n 109) 266.
[125] Atiyah (n 68) 435.
[126] Law Commission (n 24) pt V, para 1.220.

difficult to see how the possible application of employer's disciplinary measures will make much difference when the conduct is already criminalised.[127] The cases and literature have also failed to notice that with vicarious liability for exemplary damages, we are looking at double deterrence. That is *if* vicarious liability for compensatory damages is partly justified on grounds of employer deterrence, and exemplary damages against tortfeasors are partly justified by deterrence, then to combine vicarious liability with exemplary damages leads to double deterrence, and thus the potential for overdeterrence.[128]

Whilst the deterrent effect of exemplary damages has been questioned, particularly in the light of their low sums,[129] there is good evidence that tort asserts a deterrent effect at an organisation level,[130] and that vicarious liability asserts a deterrent effect on employers.[131] It is also reasonable to assume that the greater the extent of liability to which an organisation is exposed, the greater the deterrent effect.

Nevertheless, to rest the case of vicarious liability for exemplary damages on deterrence has significant flaws. It is not widely accepted as a theory for vicarious liability,[132] although it may be a by-product of the doctrine. As Lord Reed noted in *Armes v Nottinghamshire County Council*,[133] deterrence is not prominent amongst the justifications for vicarious liability used in English case law.[134] A deterrence-based theory of vicarious liability as noted by Stevens fails to explain why an employer may be liable even where it has taken due care,[135] or where it has taken all possible precautions. It also fails to explain the parameters of the doctrine, which, if based on deterrence encouraging the exercise of control over potential tortfeasors, would also catch parent–child, and teacher–child relationships.[136]

[127] See, eg, JW Neyers, 'A Theory of Vicarious Liability' (2005) 43 *Alberta Law Review* 287, 293–96.

[128] C Sharkey, 'Institutional Liability for Employees' Intentional Torts: Vicarious Liability as a Quasi-Substitute for Punitive Damages' (2019) 53 *Valparaiso University Law Review* 1, also suggests overdeterrence but for different reasons: they are quasi-substitutes that both target the problem of under-detection.

[129] Goudkamp and Katsampouka (n 46) 113.

[130] See, eg, G Schwartz, 'Reality in the Economic Analysis of Tort Law: Does Tort Law Really Deter?' (1994–1995) 42 *UCLA Law Review* 377; D Dewees, D Duff and M Trebilcock, *Exploring the Domain of Accident Law: Taking the Facts Seriously* (Oxford, Oxford University Press, 1996); B van Velthoven, 'Empirics of Tort' in M Faure (ed), *Tort Law and Economics* (Cheltenham, Edward Elgar Publishing, 2009) 453; J Schwartz, 'A Dose of Reality for Medical Malpractice Reform' (2013) 88 *New York University Law Review* 1224.

[131] R Kraakman, 'Vicarious and Corporate Civil Liability' in Faure (ed) (n 130) 135; A Sykes, 'The Economics of Vicarious Liability' (1984) 93 *Yale Law Journal* 1231, 1241–50; W Landes and R Posner, *The Economic Structure of Tort Law* (Cambridge, MA, Harvard University Press, 1987) 120–21.

[132] Giliker (n 99) 241–43; Atiyah (n 68) 15–17.

[133] *Armes* (n 6); cf *Bazley* (n 7).

[134] *Armes* (n 6) [67].

[135] Stevens (n 72) 258. See also S Todd, 'A New Zealand Perspective on Exemplary Damages' (2004) 33 *Common Law World Review* 255, 273.

[136] Stevens (n 72) 258.

Atiyah's support for vicarious liability for exemplary damages on a deterrence basis pre-dated their insurability. The deterrence case has been considerably weakened in the light of *Lancashire CC v Municipal Mutual Insurance Ltd*,[137] which held that an employer could insure for vicarious liability for exemplary damages. Atiyah questioned the value of deterrence as a theory for vicarious liability generally in the light of insurance. For Atiyah, the change in premiums for a good or bad accident record is insufficient to play a significant role in tort prevention.[138] This is a moral hazard point,[139] that there are insufficient incentives to guard against risk. In *Lancashire*, Simon Brown LJ acknowledged that insurability would reduce deterrence and punishment in this context, but his focus was on the recoverability of the damages for the victim. He argued that such an effect would remain in some form given the limits of liability and deductibles often found within insurance policies.[140]

The insurance field has developed since Atiyah's book. Insurers work to reduce moral hazards using a number of devices, not just deductibles, exclusions and premium ratings, but also devices such as bundled loss-control services with mandatory conditions to ensure compliance. The insurance policy may also require the organisation to monitor its workforce, with a refusal to cover vicarious liability if there is inadequate supervision.[141] It may also require a minimum spend on risk reduction.[142] The moral hazard problem is thus often overstated.[143] However, in the light of insurance, the deterrent effect of vicarious liability for exemplary damages will undoubtedly have decreased.

Gray advances that vicarious liability for exemplary damages is the wrong tool to assert deterrence over employers. He argues that strict liability, no matter how the employer acts, does not incentivise the desired behaviour, and that this role is better carried out by fault-based liability. Gray states that where an organisation knows that *its* behaviour will be examined in determining whether or not it is liable, this better deters and promotes the type of behaviour desired than strict liability. This appears to contradict his earlier rejection of the deterrent justification of vicarious liability, and its deterrent effect, which he argues is speculative and untested,[144] since his comparative deterrence argument is also an assertion without recourse to empirical evidence, or law and economics.

[137] *Lancashire CC v Municipal Mutual Insurance Ltd* [1997] QB 897 (CA). See also Beever (n 71) 95.
[138] Atiyah (n 68) 16–17. See also Gray (n 109) 263–66.
[139] See, eg, M Clarke, *Policies and Perceptions of Insurance: An Introduction to Insurance Law*, 1st edn (Oxford, Oxford University Press, 1997) 216–26.
[140] *Lancashire CC* (n 137) 909.
[141] R Merkin and J Steele, *Insurance and the Law of Obligations* (Oxford, Oxford University Press, 2013) 322.
[142] RI McEwin, 'No-Fault and Road Accidents: Some Australasian Evidence' (1989) 9 *International Review of Law and Economics* 13, 18.
[143] T Baker and P Siegelman, 'The Law and Economics of Liability Insurance: A Theoretical and Empirical Review' in J Arlen (ed), *Research Handbook on the Economics of Torts* (Cheltenham, Edward Elgar, 2013).
[144] Gray (n 109) 129, 146, 262.

Deterrence seems an insufficient foundation upon which to establish vicarious liability for exemplary damages.[145]

B. Deep Pockets

In *Rowlands*,[146] Moore-Bick LJ recognised that whilst there were strong arguments of principle in limiting exemplary damages to those personally at fault, 'since the power to award exemplary damages rests on policy rather than principle … whether awards can be made against persons whose liability is vicarious only must also be answered by resort to considerations of policy rather than strict principle'.[147] The policy reasons he advanced are that few employees have the means to pay exemplary damages, and that since the damages take into account the defendant's means, permitting vicarious liability allows awards of an adequate amount to be made.[148] This is a deep-pockets argument – the employer can pay more, so it should be made liable. Whilst the example discussed is in dealing with lower-ranked police officers of limited means,[149] and it is possible to detect a liberty issue in the tenor of Moore-Bick LJ's argument, his argument is not so limited.

Deep pockets is a flawed argument to use to impose vicarious liability for exemplary damages. Whilst it has been invoked as a justification for vicarious liability,[150] mere wealth, by itself, is insufficient to justify the imposition of vicarious liability.[151] The deep-pockets argument cannot explain many of the features of tort, or vicarious liability, since it ultimately collapses into state liability.[152] Given that category one damages are in fact a form of state liability, these are less problematic in this context than categories two or three.

The deep-pockets argument in this context is also flawed in that it focuses on the claimant and his entitlement to damages – a compensatory approach. Instead exemplary damages should focus on the defendant, and punishment. Simply because a defendant who deserves punishment does not have sufficient resources to be punished, should not lead to his punishment's being transferred to an innocent who does have such resources, in order to provide a windfall to the claimant.[153]

[145] Giliker (n 99) 43. Whilst Giliker does not come to a firm conclusion on exemplary damages, she notes that the effectiveness of deterrence as a rationale for vicarious liability should raise the question whether *Rowlands* struck the correct balance.

[146] *Rowlands* (n 49).

[147] ibid [47].

[148] ibid.

[149] ibid [39].

[150] *CCWS* (n 3) [35].

[151] *Cox* (n 5) [20]; G Williams, 'Vicarious Liability and the Master's Indemnity' (1957) 20 *MLR* 220, 232; Gray (n 109) 152.

[152] Stevens (n 72) 258.

[153] See, eg, Beever (n 71) 95.

C. Institutional Disapproval

The second argument raised by Moore-Bick LJ for vicarious liability in *Rowlands* is one of institutional disapproval. The award permits a court to express disapproval for the conduct of an institution.[154] This appears to be a resurrection of an old justification for vicarious liability, based on the employer's fault in permitting the tort to occur. This is a flawed fiction if the institution itself is not at fault. We already have a fault-based direct duty of care regime to encourage the proper selection, training and monitoring of employees,[155] which incentivises due employer care, and this is the proper place to express such disapproval for an employer's acts. There is, however, an exception in the situation of category one damages (see section XII), where the disapproval relates to the employer's failure to prosecute its own employees.

D. Identification/Evidence

Lord Hutton's second argument in *Kuddus* was evidential: with vicarious liability, such damages may still be awarded even where the individual wrongdoer cannot be identified. Indeed identification has proved difficult in some exemplary damages cases.[156] However, whilst this explanation may make sense in a compensatory situation (particularly alongside enterprise liability), with exemplary damages the claimant has no right to compensation. Here the identification argument is a disguised deterrence argument.

X. Modern Justifications

It is problematic to primarily base vicarious liability for exemplary damages on deep pockets and deterrence. Both are highly criticised as vicarious liability theories and do not form the core of its modern justifications. Instead, we must examine enterprise liability, and loss-spreading.

A. Enterprise Liability

The basic tenet of enterprise liability is that where an enterprise introduces characteristic risks into society, it should pay for them if they materialise.[157] It requires

[154] *Rowlands* (n 49) [42].
[155] *Mattis v Pollock* [2003] EWCA Civ 887, [2003] 1 WLR 2158.
[156] Law Commission (n 24) pt V, para 1.221, fn 766.
[157] *Bazley* (n 7) [31]; Atiyah (n 68) 22–28. *Both* a fairness and economic rationale: G Keating, 'The Idea of Fairness in the Law of Enterprise Liability' (1997) 95 *Michigan Law Review* 1266.

enterprises to internalise their negative externalities. That is, they must pay for the losses that they cause to other members of society, such that the enterprise pays for its true costs to society.[158]

This concept has significantly influenced tort,[159] and has found a special role within vicarious liability. In *Armes* it was referred to as the most influential of the modern vicarious liability justifications.[160] Enterprise liability is not limited to profit-making activities and organisations.[161] *Bazley*, the seminal case that invoked enterprise liability to expand vicarious liability, concerned a non-profit organisation, as do many leading English vicarious liability cases that rely on the doctrine.[162] In *Cox*,[163] Lord Reed, referring to 'business' activity in an enterprise liability context, stressed that it need not be commercial or profit-making. Thus, the concept could justify the Ministry of Justice's vicarious liability for prisoners working in a prison kitchen. Likewise in *Armes*,[164] Lord Reed invoked enterprise liability[165] to justify holding the local authority vicariously liable for foster parents, again stressing that the word 'business' did not mean that enterprise liability was confined to commercial activities.

The Law Commission appears to invoke enterprise liability to justify vicarious liability for exemplary damages, by stating that 'one who derives a benefit – in particular a financial profit – from certain acts, should also bear the risk of loss therefrom', and arguing that this also applies to exemplary damages.[166]

Enterprise liability requires enterprises to compensate victims for the torts of their employees that are characteristic of the enterprise. With exemplary damages, however, vicarious liability requires the enterprise to internalise the employee's punishment, and not the victim's loss. Once compensatory damages have been paid, the victim has no loss to compensate. A model of liability based on the internalisation of the victim's loss would not result in liability for exemplary damages. Punishment does not form part of the harm or costs that the enterprise generates for society. The cost is only generated for the tortfeasing employee, and given its punishment rationale there is no good reason for an enterprise to protect its employee by sustaining this loss in his place.

Exemplary damages also purport to deter future harms by other enterprises. It is possible to argue that the need for future deterrence is a cost that is generated by the existence of enterprises, and that this should be internalised by them. However, this appears to advance that an enterprise should internalise the cost of

[158] See generally D Brodie, *Enterprise Liability and the Common Law* (Cambridge, Cambridge University Press, 2010).

[159] ibid 1–10; G Keating, 'The Theory of Enterprise Liability and Common Law Strict Liability' (2001) 54 *Vanderbilt Law Review* 1285.

[160] *Armes* (n 6) [67].

[161] Brodie (n 158) 11.

[162] See, eg, *CCWS* (n 3); *JGE* (n 13); cf Stevens (n 72) ch 11; Gray (n 109) ch 6.

[163] *Cox* (n 5).

[164] *Armes* (n 6).

[165] ibid [67].

[166] Law Commission (n 24) pt V, para 1.223.

regulating *another* enterprise, a future potential tortfeasor, and not itself. Further, this argument only leads to the internalisation of the costs of operating a sector regulator, or the costs of litigation in relation to the enterprise itself, and not the exemplary damages.[167]

Enterprise liability does not support vicarious liability for exemplary damages. However, whilst it has been highly influential within vicarious liability, it does not entirely explain the doctrine. Presently, harm may result to a victim from a defendant's activities that are not tortious, and in such cases the loss lies where it falls. Harm without a tort does not lead to compensation. However, enterprise liability would point to liability in such circumstances.

B. Loss-spreading

Loss-spreading is often linked to enterprise liability, and has been influential as a doctrine within vicarious liability,[168] although it cannot explain vicarious liability, since if loss-spreading took primacy, it would be difficult to see why vicarious liability requires a tort and why we have a system of tort law rather than a no-fault accident scheme organised at the level of the state.[169]

Loss-spreading allows an injury's cost to be spread amongst a broad group, over time,[170] minimising the impact on any one individual. Compensatory costs are spread by passing them on to consumers or distributing them through insurance. However, it is more complex than typically suggested by torts scholars, with reinsurance, investment and risk management playing a part. As noted, employers may insure for vicarious liability for exemplary damages, and thus the cost of the penalty may be distributed. It is key to note that word; exemplary damages represent a *penalty*, not a loss. Loss-spreading therefore does not properly apply to exemplary damages.[171]

XI. Approaches from Other Common Law Jurisdictions

Given the limited English case law on this issue, it is worth examining other jurisdictions. However, other Commonwealth common law jurisdictions add little to this debate. Commonwealth jurisdictions generally take a more expansive approach towards exemplary damages than the English courts. However, in

[167] Unless such damages are necessary to encourage claimants to sue – this being the 'cost' of tort regulation. In England this seems unlikely since compensatory damages tend to be larger in comparison to exemplary damages (and thus more of an incentive) (unlike the US model of punitive damages).

[168] See, eg, *Jacobi v Griffiths* [1999] 2 SCR 570 (SCC) [69].

[169] Morgan (n 111). See also Stevens (n 72) 258.

[170] Cane and Goudkamp (n 2) 397.

[171] *S* (n 108) [90].

Blackwater v Plint,[172] in the context of an abuse case, the Supreme Court of Canada refused to find the employer vicariously liable for exemplary damages, on the basis that the employer did not behave reprehensibly. Unfortunately a single paragraph dealt with the issue, and no reasoning was given other than the need for specific misconduct on the part of the employer.[173] Likewise in *S v Attorney-General*,[174] the Court of Appeal of New Zealand refused to hold the principal of the foster carers – in this case the Crown – vicariously liable for exemplary damages.

Similar arguments were raised by the claimant's counsel in *S* to those made for such liability in England, for instance deterrence, identification, deep pockets, that it is better for the principal to pay than for the claimant not to be awarded exemplary damages, and opportunities for institutional disapproval.[175] In rejecting these arguments the Court discussed *Kuddus*. Core to their reasoning is that in this case the Crown was already vicariously liable for the compensatory award, that this fully compensated the victim's loss[176] and that

> when it is appreciated that the primary purpose of such damages is to punish a flagrant wrongdoer, not to provide additional compensation … it might seem to be quite unfair to inflict a punishment upon someone who has been found not to have been complicit in the wrongdoing. Exemplary or punitive damages would not then be a reflection of the culpability of the defendant. Any 'message of disapproval' would be delivered to the wrong person. It is one thing to require a principal who has without neglect created a situation leading to injury to compensate the injured person; it is quite another to punish the principal for the sins of the agent.[177]

The Court also rejected loss-spreading arguments on the basis that exemplary damages do not represent a loss, alongside rejecting the argument that they are of therapeutic value to mitigate the offence, since here their value is reduced given that the person punished is not the wrongdoer.[178]

The New Zealand accident compensation scheme arguably makes the deterrence argument in this context stronger than in England, since without this remedy it may be that claimants are otherwise unable to hold organisations to account through litigation. However, it must be noted that the employer may be liable for increased levies under the scheme in future years. Nevertheless, the Court rejected the deterrence argument, considering that it was doubtful that such liability would add additional deterrence where the employer was not at fault; in such situations employers are already doing their duty, and it is unlikely that such liability would provide additional incentives on an 'economically sensible basis'[179] for greater precautions. Given the infrequency and unpredictability

[172] *Blackwater v Plint* 2005 SCC 58, [2005] 3 SCR 3.
[173] ibid [91].
[174] *S* (n 108).
[175] ibid [82].
[176] ibid [89].
[177] ibid [88].
[178] ibid [90].
[179] ibid [91].

of such claims (outside of the category one context), this may indeed be the case. Tipping J was also concerned with the risk of overdeterrence.[180]

However, in New Zealand vicarious liability for exemplary damages has been permitted in what in England would be a category one claim,[181] where damages were awarded against the police department for assaults committed by unidentifiable police officers. The basis of this award was to discourage the closing of ranks, and to prevent the employer from failing to identify the tortfeasor. In rejecting vicarious liability for exemplary damages in *S*, the Court refused to answer the question as to whether the situation would be the same where a state agent such as a police officer had deliberately or recklessly, or with gross negligence, inflicted personal injury on the claimant.[182]

The Australian position is unclear: whilst such damages were awarded in the context of police misconduct in *New South Wales v Ibbett*,[183] the case related to a statutory vicarious liability claim,[184] where the statute's provisions were predominant in the Court's reasoning. The statute also prevented a claim from being made against the wrongdoers and replaced this with a claim against the state. The High Court of Australia made it clear that its judgment did not necessarily apply to exemplary damages outside of the state defendant context.[185] It is difficult to draw upon this authority outside of the statutory context since the statute adopted a form of master's tort theory, which eliminates some of the criticisms of vicarious punishment, in that the employer is being punished for its own wrong, and in this statutory context the employee cannot be so punished. However, Australian case law appears to assume vicarious liability for exemplary damages.[186]

The United States has a rich jurisprudence on the issue of vicarious liability for punitive damages (which share a history with English exemplary damages). This is understandable given that punitive damages play a much more important role in US tort law than in English law. Vicarious liability has been described as one of the most divisive issues within the law of US punitive damages.[187] A full range of approaches is detectable across different US jurisdictions, including vicarious liability for punitive damages,[188] no vicarious liability for punitive damages and a compromise approach, found in the *Restatement (Second) of Torts*, § 909 (1979), which is a complicity approach where the damages are granted 'primarily because

[180] ibid [123].

[181] *Monroe v Attorney-General* (High Court of New Zealand, 27 March 1985).

[182] *S* (n 108) [93].

[183] *New South Wales v Ibbett* [2006] HCA 57, (2006) 229 CLR 638.

[184] Law Reform (Vicarious Liability) Act 1983 (NSW), ss 6–8; Police Legislation Amendment (Civil Liability) Act 2003 (NSW).

[185] *New South Wales* (n 183) [46].

[186] Gray (n 109) 256; D McGill, 'Exemplary Damages and Vicarious Liability' (Queensland Law Society Symposium, Brisbane, 30 March 2012) at www.austlii.edu.au/au/journals/QldJSchol/2012/11.pdf, accessed 13 April 2020, 17–19.

[187] S Speiser, C Krause and A Gans (eds), *American Law of Torts*, vol 2A (New York, Clark Boardman Callaghan, 2012–20) § 8:52.

[188] See, eg, *Miller v Blanton* 213 Ark 246, 210 SW 2d 293 (1948) (Supreme Court of Arkansas).

of the principal's own wrongful conduct'.[189] The last of these is more along the lines of liability where the employer would be a secondary party, or personally at fault in English law, in that it applies in the case of authorisation of the tort, ratification of the act and/or fault in employing the agent. However, it extends beyond a secondary participation approach in that it also applies where the agent is acting in a managerial capacity.

Nevertheless, there are problems in drawing on this rich jurisprudence. United States punitive damages have become a very different institution from English exemplary damages. In the United States they have become a device used to indemnify a successful claimant for his legal costs, since costs are not typically awarded in US civil litigation, and with contingent fees a claimant's compensatory damages will otherwise be eroded by legal costs,[190] whereas in English civil litigation such costs are normally awarded to the successful party.[191] Further, such awards in the United States are much more strongly influenced by a deterrence theory of tort, and the policing of corporate misconduct, whereby claims are encouraged against corporate miscreants by providing for greater rewards for claimants and lawyers through large, punitive damages.[192] In addition, from a deterrence perspective, the English costs rules already enhance deterrence over that produced by compensatory damages alone; US law, on the other hand, enhances deterrence through punitive awards.

Most importantly, tort plays a different role in England in protecting civil liberties compared to the United States. In the United States, given the significantly more extensive tort immunities held by State and federal governments and officials when compared to those under English law,[193] and the existence of alternative constitutional and civil rights claims, tort (and punitive/exemplary damages) is less significant in this context. This may explain the extreme hostility in the United States towards awarding exemplary damages against State defendants.

The Federal Tort Claims Act 1946, which waives elements of the Federal Government's immunity to tort claims, retains immunity in relation to punitive damages.[194] Further, in *City of Newport v Fact Concerts Inc*,[195] the US Supreme Court noted a traditional common law rule against awarding punitive damages against municipal authorities for the acts of their officials, on the basis that punishment is proper only to the offending officials, and that such damages would only punish the taxpayer, and would result in an increase in taxation or a decrease in

[189] *Restatement (Second) of Torts*, § 909. See also M Sturley, 'Vicarious Liability for Punitive Damages' (2010) 70 *Louisiana Law Review* 501.

[190] See, eg, McGregor (n 34) 526; J Fleming, *The American Tort Process* (Oxford, Oxford University Press, 1991) 214.

[191] CPR r 44.2(2)(a).

[192] Fleming (n 190) 214–21.

[193] See, eg, P Cane, *Controlling Administrative Power: An Historical Comparison* (Cambridge, Cambridge University Press, 2016) 368–98.

[194] Federal Tort Claims Act 1946, 28 US Code § 2674.

[195] *City of Newport v Fact Concerts Inc* 453 US 247, 101 S Ct 2748 (1981).

public services.[196] In the English common law context such damages are seen as part of the necessary costs of maintaining the rule of law and holding the executive to account. The US experience is therefore distinguishable.

XII. The Exceptional Case for Category One

Vicarious liability for exemplary damages represents punishment without fault. It therefore requires additional justification over and above that required for vicarious liability for compensatory damages. That the core modern justifications for vicarious liability do not point towards such liability for exemplary damages, and the fact that vicarious liability for exemplary damages merely rests on highly criticised justifications insufficient to justify the doctrine of vicarious liability itself, even for compensatory awards, means that generally vicarious liability should not apply to exemplary damages.

Situations in which category two damages arise where the employer is not also implicated will be unusual.[197] If the employer is not a secondary participant in the tort but has made a profit by it, that profit may be targeted.[198] However, with vicarious liability's expansion there will be circumstances in which the employee's tort does not implicate his employer, and vicarious liability remains the only avenue of claim against the employer. Whilst Atiyah's arguments for vicarious liability for exemplary damages appear to apply to all of the categories, he cryptically suggests that with category two the employer should not be so liable, but gives no reasons for this.[199] As we have seen, there have also been suggestions in the New Zealand case law that category one may be different. Gray, on the other hand, rejects vicarious liability for exemplary damages on the basis of rejecting deterrence, but he fails to consider if there is any difference between the categories of damages. This is perhaps due to his only briefly footnoting the *Rookes* categories[200] and not considering their significance, which means that his account fails to appreciate the diversity of the phenomenon and the distinctiveness of the different forms of exemplary damages in English law.

This chapter argues that whilst generally there should be no vicarious liability for exemplary damages, with category one damages the additional justifications sufficient to justify vicarious punishment are present. That is: (i) the state is special; (ii) there is a need to protect the citizen from the state's potentially overwhelming power; and (iii) the state's special role in prosecuting crimes. As we have seen,

[196] ibid 267. See also *McCandless v State* 6 Misc 2d 391, 166 NYS 2d 272 (1997) (New York Court of Claims) ('[t]he State is not subject to punitive damages'); *Restatement (Second) of Torts*, § 908 Commentary.

[197] See, eg, *Mehta v Royal Bank of Scotland* (2000) 32 HLR 45 (QB); although the Court appears to use vicarious liability, this could also be a case of secondary participation.

[198] Atiyah (n 68) 435.

[199] ibid.

[200] Gray (n 109) 252, fn 23.

remedies under the Human Rights Act 1998 (UK) are low. There is a long history of exemplary damages claims being brought against the state,[201] and it is only recently that the vicarious liability issue has been raised and challenged. To eliminate vicarious liability for category one damages would be to reduce the rights of the citizen vis-à-vis the state, and is thus undesirable. The power to bring such a claim is also arguably of greater significance (notwithstanding the development of judicial review) as the size of the state and its powers have grown.

Unlike the other two categories, category one exemplary damages almost invariably involve criminal acts. Given that exemplary damages may be reduced or eliminated by prior punishment, when category one claims are brought, the state has chosen not to prosecute its own agents. The state, unlike any other employer, is the primary prosecuting authority. It has the power to decide whether or not to prosecute at public expense those accused of crimes, and state prosecutorial authorities determine whether or not it is in the public interest to do so. Likewise, prosecutions that are commenced may fail due to inadequacies, or to a failure adequately to pursue them. The state thus has a unique power to cover up the matter or stymie any investigation into itself or its own agents. Indeed, it may benefit from failing to pursue its own agents by maintaining good employment relations with its agents, and by reducing its exposure or the exposure of its operations to negative publicity. The ability for a victim to commence a private prosecution does not overcome this.[202] There is thus a need for extra protection against the state via exemplary damages, given the risk that in making these prosecutorial decisions the state is acting as a judge in its own cause. Such a claim permits the claimant publicly to vindicate his own account of state oppression.[203]

With vicarious liability for exemplary damages, the state is being punished for its own wrong, in this case the failure properly to investigate and prosecute its own servants.[204] Non-state employers do not have the same incentives, or power, to prevent investigation or stymie criminal proceedings against their own agents. Where the Crown Prosecution Service fails to prosecute a private employee, apart from in situations where the employer itself has perverted the course of justice (and is thus liable for prosecution), generally this is not the fault of the employer. In this context deterrence operates directly, to deter the state from failing to prosecute its own agents, and this is not a case of double deterrence – deterrence of

[201] In the era of wider Crown immunity, although actions were brought against the offending official himself, the convention was that the state would stand behind its agent and pay the damages: TT Arvind, 'Restraining the State Through Tort? The Crown Proceedings Act in Retrospect' in TT Arvind and J Steele (eds), *Tort Law and the Legislature: Common Law, Statute and the Dynamics of Legal Change* (Oxford, Hart Publishing, 2013) 407.

[202] See, eg, Law Commission (n 24) pt V, para 1.12: victims have little control over public prosecutions.

[203] *W v W* (n 77). See also Beever (n 71) 98, who considers that this should lead to greater involvement of the victim in the criminal process. However, this would require a revolution in criminal procedure, and vicarious liability for exemplary damages in this context provides a neater solution.

[204] See, eg, *Michael Quinn v Ministry of Defence* [2018] NIQB 82, where the fact that the state had set up the Saville Inquiry and the Prime Minister had made a public apology were factors in the Court's refusing to grant exemplary damages.

the tort is already covered by compensatory damages. Whilst it may be advanced that some parts of the state apparatus do not have investigation and prosecution powers, and thus are not at fault in this situation, most category one cases in fact concern police and immigration authorities, the latter being an emanation of the Home Office. Further, given the unitary nature of the state, there may be an incentive for one arm of the state not to prosecute agents of another arm of the state (or its contractors), even where they are from separate departments. For instance, if an official from a department without prosecutorial functions commits misfeasance in public office, the state may still have an incentive not to prosecute that official, for example so as to prevent 'dirty laundry' from being aired in public. This incentive will be particularly pronounced when dealing with the highest levels of administration, or where it may cause serious embarrassment to the Government.

Whilst the vast majority of category one torts will also be crimes, and given the definition of category one it is difficult to imagine one that will not be, there is the possibility that in very rare cases the tort may not be a crime. This may, for instance, result from the application of different defences, or from the defences diverging over time between the relevant crime and the tort, such that an official is not guilty of the former but liable for the latter. This chapter advances that if a category one tort is prima facie a criminal act, or potentially subject to criminal prosecution, and/or it is not criminal only due to the application of a potential defence, and the state decides not to prosecute its agent, the category one tort should still trigger vicarious liability for exemplary damages, otherwise the state could argue in all category one cases that it is not vicariously liable since its agent may have had a defence to the otherwise criminal act. Although it is hypothetically possible that there may be a category one tort that is not prima facie criminal, and which instead is only worthy of disciplinary action, rather than carve out a hypothetical exemption to vicarious liability in such cases where the state fails to investigate or discipline its agent (which if carried out may eliminate exemplary damages), vicarious liability should still apply for the reason that state power is special, and the state should act with great care to restrain its agents from abusing this unique authority.

Category one is different as it provides tort victims with greater power vis-à-vis the state. Such liability is an important redress against abuse of state power against citizens. The state cannot complain of being oppressed or punished using state power (which can be the situation in category two or three vicarious liability claims). The state deserves special censure when it allows its special powers to be abused vis-à-vis the citizen. As noted in *Rookes*, exemplary damages can be both a defence of liberty and a potential danger to liberty. Again, this is another reason to limit vicarious liability for exemplary damages to category one damages. With the state we need not be concerned with constraining the state's liberty. Restricting the liberty of the state is often highly legitimate, and necessary in maintaining the rule of law, but much greater care needs to be taken over potential restrictions to the liberty of individuals (who may be employers) and, to a lesser extent, legal persons. This distinction is reflected in the fact that the state acts unlawfully unless it acts within the powers granted to it, whereas the actions of individuals are prima facie lawful unless they are expressly prohibited by law. In the case of unidentified tortfeasing agents, the employer's difficulty in defending such exemplary damages vicarious liability claims may lead to a significant imbalance in the litigation such as to undermine the defendant's rights under Article 6 of the European Convention on Human Rights (ECHR). The state, on the other hand, has no such rights.[205]

How category one cases are tried reflects their constitutional function, and their difference from ordinary tort claims. In English civil cases, trial by a single judge is the norm. However, the torts with which category one exemplary damages are primarily concerned – malicious prosecution and false imprisonment – are still tried by jury on application of either party.[206] This role is also reflected in the requirements of a category one claim, when compared to a category two claim. This constitutional function makes category one different from other forms of exemplary damages, which in turn justifies vicarious liability for this category.

XIII. Conclusion

As vicarious liability has expanded in scope, the question of vicarious liability for exemplary damages has become more important. Employers' vicarious liability for compensatory damages (including aggravated damages) is the norm for torts closely connected with an employee's role. Despite some features of exemplary damages that appear compensatory, exemplary damages are designed to punish and deter wrongdoers. This means that vicarious liability for exemplary damages represents the punishment of an innocent, and also perversely shields the guilty from punishment.

Vicarious liability fits oddly with a number of features within exemplary damages. Whilst English law seems currently to permit vicarious liability for all categories of exemplary damages, the case for such liability rests on older, discredited vicarious liability justifications and is not rooted in the modern justifications for the doctrine. The primary case for vicarious liability for such damages is based on deterrence. The argument is that such liability encourages employers to properly select, monitor and control their employees, and that the employer's power to discipline its employees is of greater impact than the effect of exemplary damages on employees. However, deterrence is a weak foundation on which to base vicarious liability for exemplary damages. Deterrence is a highly criticised rationale for vicarious liability that fails to explain the parameters of the

[205] ECHR, Art 6, Art 34; *Holy Monasteries v Greece* (1994) 20 EHRR 1; *Aston Cantlow and Wilmcote with Billesley Parochial Church Council v Wallbank* [2003] UKHL 37, [2004] 1 AC 546.
[206] Senior Courts Act 1981, s 69(1).

doctrine, and here it is being used to justify double deterrence and not simply the liability for compensatory damages to which the employer is already subjected. The insurability of such damages also significantly reduces the deterrent rationale in this context.

The secondary reason typically given for vicarious liability for exemplary damages is deep pockets: the employer can pay, the employee cannot. But mere wealth alone can never justify liability. This rationale also improperly focuses on the claimant, when the award is made actually to deter and punish the defendant and should focus on the latter. Just because a wrongdoer cannot pay does not by itself mean that punishment should be transferred to a richer party. Arguments used to justify the doctrine relating to institutional disapproval are also flawed when the institution itself is not at fault. This is instead properly the sphere of the direct duty of care.

The modern justifications that have driven the recent vicarious liability revolution do not point towards such liability for exemplary damages. Enterprise liability concerns the internalisation of negative externalities, by requiring an enterprise to pay for the losses it causes to other members of society. Whilst this may justify vicarious liability for compensatory damages, once compensation has been paid victims have no further losses to be compensated. Here the only person who may actually suffer financial harm (in this case in the form of a penalty) is the tortfeasor, who is deemed worthy of punishment by exemplary damages. There is no good reason for the employer to pay for this (unless it is a secondary participant). Despite the fact that such damages are insurable, loss-spreading models of vicarious liability do not justify vicarious liability for exemplary damages, since here there is no loss on the part of the victim to spread.

Within English law exemplary damages are split into three categories. This chapter argues that vicarious liability should apply only to category one exemplary damages. Category one damages have a special rule in protecting the rights of the citizen vis-à-vis the state. The long history of exemplary damages in this context demonstrates that they were introduced to protect, and that there is a need to protect, citizens from abuses of state power through exemplary damages, and this is still the case even in the era of human rights legislation. Most torts within category one cases are also crimes. With category one vicarious liability the state is in special position, and such cases are only brought where the state has failed to prosecute its own agents. Given the state's primary role in prosecution and criminal investigation, vicarious liability for exemplary damages ensures that the state is encouraged to sufficiently pursue the wrongs of its agents, and to properly discharge its prosecutorial functions. Given this role, there is a need for additional recourse against the state in this context, which is not present in the other categories of exemplary damages.

Vicarious liability for exemplary damages has the power to protect liberty, as well as to oppress. It is important that it is not used for the latter purpose. However, we should have no such concerns as to the defendant's being oppressed where the defendant is the state. Even within jurisdictions with long-standing commitments to the rule of law, history demonstrates egregious abuses of state power. England is no exception. In a liberal democratic society there is a good in restraining the excesses of state power. The state and its agents must only act within its lawful powers, while an individual's liberty should only be restricted where absolutely required.

PART IV

Limiting Punishment

12

Agreed Punishment

WAYNE COURTNEY*

I. Introduction

Freedom of contract remains the dominant philosophy of the common law institution of contract. Freedom includes the liberty of parties to choose the terms of their agreement. Such terms may relate to primary or secondary obligations, to use the Austinian concept championed in contract by Lord Diplock.[1] Thus, the default position is that parties can agree in advance the sanctions to be applied against the contract-breaker upon a breach of contract. I use the expression 'agreed sanction' to describe a response to breach (or termination for breach), expressly agreed by the parties, that imposes some detriment or disadvantage upon the contract-breaker. The expression embraces sanctions whether they are duties, liabilities or no-rights for the contract-breaker; whether they are self-executing or only enforceable by the innocent party through legal process; and whether they affect primary or secondary obligations in contract. Nor are sanctions limited to dealing with rights and obligations sourced in contract. They may affect other private law rights and obligations, such as the contract-breaker's restitutionary right to recover payments made before termination of contract.

While very broad, the parties' freedom to define their own sanctions is curtailed by an assortment of principles and construction techniques. These are seen as exceptional.[2] The rule against penalties, for example, is often cast as an 'interference' with freedom of contract.[3] Such limitations, being exceptional,

* I thank Emeritus Professor JW Carter for his comments on an earlier draft, and the participants at the *Punishment and Private Law* workshop for their helpful insights. I also acknowledge the assistance of the NUS Start-up Grant, project R-241-000-154-133.

[1] *Photo Production Ltd v Securicor Transport Ltd* [1980] AC 827 (HL), 848–49.

[2] But see I Macneil, 'Power of Contract and Agreed Remedies' (1962) 47 *Cornell Law Quarterly* 495.

[3] *Dunlop Pneumatic Tyre Co Ltd v New Garage and Motor Co Ltd* [1915] AC 79 (HL), 100–01 (Lord Parmoor); *Clydebank Engineering and Shipbuilding Co Ltd v Don Jose Ramos Yzquierdo y Castaneda* [1905] AC 6 (HL), 10 (Earl of Halsbury LC); *Elsley v JG Collins Insurance Agencies Ltd* [1978] 2 SCR 916 (SCC), 937; *Esanda Finance Corp Ltd v Plessnig* (1989) 166 CLR 131 (HCA), 140 (Wilson and Toohey JJ); *Cavendish Square Holding BV v Makdessi* [2015] UKSC 67, [2016] AC 1172 [33] (Lord Neuberger and Lord Sumption).

are assumed to need justification. This chapter considers whether prevention of punishment is part of that justification. That is, to what extent is contract law's control of agreed sanctions based on the norm that parties to a contract cannot agree to punish each other?

My answer is that contract doctrine has little to do with preventing agreed punishment. The rationale, most evident in the cases on penalties, is misguided. Contract law even tolerates punishment in limited situations where one party is seen to have the authority to punish and a legitimate interest in so doing. Looking over the range of restrictions on agreed sanctions, the law is primarily concerned with two matters. First, it regulates some kinds of hard treatment (not amounting to punishment) imposed as a response to breach. Second, where an agreed sanction genuinely punishes and punishment is acceptable in context, the law scrutinises the proportionality between the wrong and the sanction.

Agreed sanctions for breach come in an infinite variety of forms. The correspondence between the form of sanction and the restrictions placed upon it by the law of contract is not always tidy. My approach in this chapter is, accordingly, thematic. I consider three significant sets of principles. The first is the rule against penalties. The second is relief against forfeiture in its various incarnations. The third set is more nebulous. It comprises principles and techniques that govern one party's exercise of a power, upon breach, to alter the terms of the parties' future contractual relationship, or to end it.

The discussion is based on English law, with substantial reference to supporting and contrasting decisions in Australia. Section II adopts a working definition of punishment and then explains why the law in principle might object to parties' privately agreeing to punish each other. Sections III to V examine the rationale of preventing punishment so far as it underpins the three areas mentioned above. Section III deals with the rule against penalties, section IV with relief against forfeiture, and section V with control of contractual powers. Section VI contains concluding remarks.

II. Objections to Agreed Punishment

A. Defining Punishment

HLA Hart's definition of punishment provides a useful starting point.[4] The definition, developed from prior work by Benn and Flew,[5] specifies five elements: (i) punishment must involve pain or other consequences ordinarily considered

[4] HLA Hart, *Punishment and Responsibility: Essays in the Philosophy of Law*, 2nd edn (Oxford, Oxford University Press, 2008) 4–5. Of course, other definitions exist.

[5] A Flew, 'The Justification of Punishment' (1954) 29 *Philosophy* 291; SI Benn, 'An Approach to the Problems of Punishment' (1958) 33 *Philosophy* 325.

unpleasant; (ii) it must be for an offence against legal rules; (iii) it must be of an actual or supposed offender for the offence; (iv) it must intentionally be administered by human agency; and (v) it must be imposed and administered by an authority constituted by the legal system against which the offence is committed. These elements are coloured by Hart's assumption that legal punishment in the criminal law represents the paradigm. While he accepted that punishment could take other forms, these were relegated to being 'secondary' or 'sub-standard' instances. Adapting the definition to contract, 'offence against legal rules' becomes 'breach of contract'; 'offender' becomes 'contract-breaker'.

This definition omits an important characteristic. Punishment performs an expressive function, which is to manifest condemnation, reprobation or censure of the wrong. HM Hart wrote that '[w]hat distinguishes a criminal from a civil sanction and all that distinguishes it … is the judgment of community condemnation which accompanies and justifies its imposition'.[6] In an influential essay, Feinberg offered a more sophisticated rendering of the same concept.[7] He drew a distinction between 'penalties' and 'punishments'. Both possess the character of being hard treatment in response to a wrong, yet only punishment expresses 'attitudes of resentment or indignation, and … judgments of disapproval and reprobation'.[8]

For Feinberg, the administering agent punishes by selecting a symbol that is conventionally understood to represent condemnation.[9] The punishment itself is that symbol. A term of imprisonment signifies condemnation.[10] Liability to pay a sum of money for wrongdoing, without more, is neutral: it may be only a penalty. This part of Feinberg's argument strays into more controversial territory. It could be argued, for example, that some hard treatment naturally embodies – not merely symbolises – condemnation.[11] The implicit claim that the form of hard treatment alone manifests condemnation also raises challenges. It neglects other means of expression, such as a declaration of responsibility (verdict rather than sentence or award), or some explanatory act accompanying the imposition of the hard treatment.[12] Leaving those out of the account necessitates qualitative distinctions between forms of hard treatment. Since Feinberg sees punitive damages as punishment,[13] he must draw a distinction between payment of money, and payment of money *as punitive damages*. In what follows, I accept Feinberg's insights about

[6] HM Hart, 'The Aims of the Criminal Law' (1958) 23 *Law and Contemporary Problems* 401, 404.

[7] J Feinberg, 'The Expressive Function of Punishment' (1965) 49 *The Monist* 397, 400.

[8] Compare BE Harcourt, 'Joel Feinberg on Crime and Punishment: Exploring the Relationship between *The Moral Limits of the Criminal Law* and *The Expressive Function of Punishment*' (2001) 5 *Buffalo Criminal Law Review* 145, 168–69.

[9] It is implicit in Feinberg's argument that the selection process is intentional. The agent chooses the symbol with the aim of punishing. See also Barker, ch 2, section II.B.

[10] Feinberg (n 7) 402.

[11] AJ Skillen, 'How to Say Things with Walls' (1980) 55 *Philosophy* 509, 516–18; I Primoratz, 'Punishment as Language' (1989) 64 *Philosophy* 187, 199.

[12] Compare Primoratz (n 11) 199 (mere verbal condemnation usually insufficient).

[13] Feinberg (n 7) 407–08.

the distinction between penalty and punishment, and that the form of punishment itself can express condemnation. I need not resolve the other debates.

B. The Objections

i. Objections to Punishment

In *Cavendish Square Holding BV v Makdessi*,[14] Lord Neuberger and Lord Sumption remarked that '[t]he innocent party can have no proper interest in simply punishing the defaulter'. Such statements are ambiguous because public policy can be rationalised at varying levels of generality. The broadest claim is that punishment is properly the province of the criminal law, whereas the civil law is concerned with redress, usually in the form of compensation.[15] The correctness of this claim would be enough to seal the fate of a punitive agreed damages clause. I will proceed on the basis that this claim is disputable in theory and is contradicted by the law in practice.

A more specific claim is that punishment is a legitimate function of some areas of private law, such as tort, but not contract. In *Cooperative Insurance Society Ltd v Argyll Stores (Holdings) Ltd*,[16] Lord Hoffmann said that 'the purpose of the law of contract is not to punish wrongdoing but to satisfy the expectations of the party entitled to performance'. Other contributions to this volume address this question.[17] Acceptance of the claim greatly strengthens the case against agreeing punishment by contract. It also provides a straightforward and plausible rationale for those rules of contract that place limits on agreed sanctions. It is not necessarily conclusive, though, as there can be concurrent liability for breach of contract and another civil wrong. Negligence in tort is the obvious instance. Non-delivery of goods under a sale contract may amount to a conversion.[18] Had the operating arrangements for the car park in *ParkingEye Ltd v Beavis*[19] been different,

[14] *Cavendish* (n 3) [32]. See also ibid [148] (Lord Mance), [243], [253] (Lord Hodge); *Paciocco v Australia & New Zealand Banking Group Ltd* [2016] HCA 28, (2016) 258 CLR 525 [22], [32] (Kiefel J), [131] (Gageler J), [253]–[254] (Keane J).

[15] *Broome v Cassell & Co Ltd* [1972] AC 1027 (HL), 1086–87 (Lord Reid), against 1114 (Lord Wilberforce). See also *Patel v Mirza* [2016] UKSC 42, [2017] AC 467 [108] (Lord Toulson, with whom Lady Hale and Lords Kerr, Wilson and Hodge agreed), [230] (Lord Sumption, with whom Lord Clarke agreed). Compare A Ashworth, 'Punishment and Compensation: Victims, Offenders and the State' (1986) 6 *OJLS* 86 (criminal compensation).

[16] *Cooperative Insurance Society Ltd v Argyll Stores (Holdings) Ltd* [1998] AC 1 (HL), 15.

[17] See Barnett, ch 9 of this volume. See also N McBride, 'A Case for Awarding Punitive Damages in Response to Deliberate Breaches of Contract' (1995) 24 *Anglo-American Law Review* 369; A Tettenborn, 'Punitive Damages – A View from England' (2004) 41 *San Diego Law Review* 1551, 1561–65; R Cunnington, 'Should Punitive Damages Be Part of the Judicial Arsenal in Contract Cases?' (2006) 26 *Legal Studies* 369; S Rowan, 'Reflections on the Introduction of Punitive Damages for Breach of Contract' (2010) 30 *OJLS* 495. The American literature is vast.

[18] *The Arpad (No 2)* [1934] P 189 (CA).

[19] The appeal conjoined with *Cavendish* (n 3).

Mr Beavis' delay could have constituted a breach of contract and trespass against the same party.[20]

It is well established that a contractual exclusion clause can address events or bases of liability, such as a failure to exercise reasonable care, whatever the underlying cause of action. The same exhaustive statement of responsibility ought to be achievable for an agreed damages clause by appropriate drafting, subject to the rule against penalties. Parties could draft the trigger event narrowly, to cover egregious misconduct that constitutes a tort for which punitive damages would be likely to be awarded. Suppose that the stipulated sum included compensatory and punitive elements, as a reasonable forecast of the outcome at law. Would the clause be valid?

Traditional statements of the test for a penalty contemplate liability in contract only. While *Cavendish* develops the 'legitimate interest' concept, it still treats compensation as the touchstone for testing validity in ordinary cases.[21] Denying that punishment is a legitimate interest[22] seems to rule out agreed punitive damages for a non-contractual wrong. It is doubtful, however, that any of the Court had concurrent liability squarely in mind. Lord Mance in passing did remark that there was 'little doubt' that the rule against penalties would extend to cover a liability in trespass or another tort.[23] The decision also leaves open the possibility that a party, with an appropriate interest, might fix a measure of loss that falls somewhere between compensation and punishment, such as an account of profits.[24] In Australia, the answer depends upon which judgment in *Paciocco v Australia & New Zealand Banking Group Ltd* is applied.[25] A clause liquidating damages for a non-contractual wrong, with mixed compensatory and punitive elements, might be upheld for one of several reasons. Either the sole purpose is not to punish;[26] or the predominant purpose is not to punish;[27] or, punishment being irrelevant, the clause is not disproportionate to the 'foreseeable consequences' of breach.[28]

ii. Objections to Contractual Agreement

There is a still narrower claim. The law of contract could permit punishment, depending upon its nature and by whom it is administered. Public policy,

[20] See also *Penarth Dock Engineering Co Ltd v Pounds* [1963] 1 Lloyd's Rep 359 (QBD).
[21] *Cavendish* (n 3) [32] (Lord Neuberger and Lord Sumption), [255] (Lord Hodge).
[22] *Cavendish* arguably went too far in this respect: see text following n 118.
[23] *Cavendish* (n 3) [192].
[24] Compare S Rowan, 'For the Recognition of Remedial Terms Agreed Inter Partes' (2010) 126 *LQR* 448, 458–59; S Rowan, 'The "Legitimate Interest in Performance" in the Law of Penalties' (2019) 78 *CLJ* 148, 161–64.
[25] *Paciocco v Australia & New Zealand Banking Group Ltd* [2016] HCA 28, (2016) 258 CLR 525.
[26] ibid [165]–[166] (Gageler J).
[27] ibid [221] (Keane J).
[28] ibid [330] (Nettle J).

no doubt, provides some limits on consensual corporal punishment, humiliating or degrading activities and so forth. Element (v) in Hart's definition (see section II.A) takes punishment by the state to be the paradigm. Punishment by others, for example by parents or schools, is a sub-standard case, in respect both of the rules (non-legal) infringed and of the agent who administers the punishment. Assuming that contractual promises with institutional backing qualify as 'legal rules', punishment in contract might be acceptable when imposed by the state but not when imposed by private actors. This was Frankfurter J's rationale in *Priebe & Sons Inc v United States*.[29] He explained that penal provisions in contracts were not enforced for the 'basic reason … that the infliction of punishment through courts is a function of society, and should not insure [*sic*] to the benefit of individuals'.

The reservation to the state of the power to punish breach of contract can be justified on several grounds. Two of them can be noted briefly, as punishment is only incidental. Some law-and-economics scholarship objects to agreed damages clauses (*a fortiori* punitive ones) as being economically inefficient, though there is considerable debate over the circumstances in which, if at all, this is true.[30] A corresponding argument for lawyers is that a severe agreed sanction effectively compels specific performance.[31] This is objectionable either because the law should preserve personal autonomy, or because courts should retain for themselves the power to dispense the exceptional remedies of specific performance and injunction.[32]

Turning to punishment, one justification considers the authority of an actor to decide upon and then exact punishment. The starting proposition is negative. Individuals do not normally possess the authority to punish others of their own motion. Being a victim of a breach of contract does not confer authority. Nor, even, does a prior agreement to this effect by the contract-breaker (though

[29] *Priebe & Sons Inc v United States* 332 US 407 (1947) (SC) 418.

[30] See, eg, C Goetz and R Scott, 'Liquidated Damages, Penalties and the Just Compensation Principle: Some Notes on an Enforcement Model and a Theory of Efficient Breach' (1977) 77 *Columbia Law Review* 554; P Rubin, 'Unenforceable Contracts: Penalty Clauses and Specific Performance' (1981) 10 *Journal of Legal Studies* 237; S Rea, 'Efficiency Implications of Penalties and Liquidated Damages' (1984) 13 *Journal of Legal Studies* 147; A Schwartz, 'The Myth that Promisees Prefer Supracompensatory Remedies: An Analysis of Contracting for Damage Measures' (1990) 100 *Yale Law Journal* 369; A Edlin and A Schwartz, 'Optimal Penalties in Contract' (2003) 78 *Chicago-Kent Law Review* 33. See also in this volume Courtney and Goudkamp, ch 1, section I.D. Equally, the spectre of state-imposed punitive damages may interfere with efficient breach.

[31] M Chen-Wishart, 'Controlling the Power to Agree Damages' in P Birks (ed), *Wrongs and Remedies in the Twenty-First Century* (Oxford, Clarendon Press, 1996) 271, 281. Compare S Smith, 'Performance, Punishment and the Nature of Contractual Obligation' (1997) 60 *MLR* 360, 374.

[32] An even wider argument is made by S Shiffrin, 'Remedial Clauses: The Overprivatization of Private Law' (2016) 67 *Hastings Law Journal* 407. See also *127 Hobson Street Ltd v Honey Bees Preschool Ltd* [2019] NZCA 122, [2019] 2 NZLR 790 [40]; *Denka Advantech Pte Ltd v Seraya Energy Pte Ltd* [2020] SGCA 119 [93]. Compare Rowan, 'For the Recognition of Remedial Terms' (n 24) 450–53.

this rather begs the question). Authority may be derived from positive legal rules or from societal practices and conventions that are given legal recognition. The latter span a range of relationships. Some forms of authority exist outside contract (eg, parent–child[33]) while others (eg, in employment) can coincide with contract.

All that this argument establishes is that one contracting party *usually* has no authority to punish another. Where authority coincides with a contractual relationship, the argument reveals nothing about the propriety of using contract law as an instrument to effect punishment. It seems that the source of authority is more fundamental than contractual agreement. What the parties can achieve by agreement is to enliven or exercise an authority to punish that is already recognised. This explains, for example, why some sanctions in an employment contract can have a punitive element, yet the employer's power to apply them must generally be conferred expressly.[34]

In *Priebe*, Frankfurter J expressed concern that agreed punishment would allow one party to unjustly enrich itself at the other's expense, by obtaining extra-compensatory damages. But the innocent party obtains the same windfall when a court awards punitive damages for other wrongs. Nor is compensation any longer the sole basis for a valid agreement on damages. A more compelling argument is that procedural imbalance or oppression can lead to substantive unfairness in agreeing punishment. Institutional processes for imposing civil punishment provide basic safeguards. Most obviously, the arbiter is disinterested in the outcome. The wrongdoer is entitled to procedural fairness and there are rules about evidence, onus of proof and so forth. Substantive principles require a minimum degree of gravity for the award of punitive damages.[35] While these civil safeguards are less rigorous than those applied in the criminal law,[36] they afford minimum protections, many of which are lacking in an open pre-contractual negotiation. Leaving matters to the parties, the innocent party has an incentive to punish, and the measure of punishment may be excessive.

A related objection looks to substantive consistency in determining punishment. A potential contract-breaker's exposure to sanctions will depend upon its information and bargaining power relative to the innocent party at the time of contract. Desert should not be determined by these factors, whether one has a

[33] One manifestation of which is the 'reasonable chastisement' defence to battery: *R v Hopley* (1860) 2 F & F 202; 175 ER 1024; *R v Brown* [1994] 1 AC 212 (HL), 266–67 (Lord Mustill). See also Children Act 2004, s 58.

[34] See text to n 193.

[35] *Rookes v Barnard* [1964] AC 1129 (HL), 1226–27 (Lord Devlin); *Gray v Motor Accident Commission* [1998] HCA 70, (1998) 196 CLR 1 [14] (Gleeson CJ, McHugh, Gummow and Hayne JJ), [85] (Kirby J), [122] (Callinan J); *Whiten v Pilot Insurance Co* 2002 SCC 18, [2002] 1 SCR 595 [78], [94] (Binnie J, with whom McLachlin CJ, L'Heureux-Dubé, Gonthier, Major and Arbour JJ agreed).

[36] A Burrows, 'Reforming Exemplary Damages: Expansion or Abolition?' in Birks (n 31) 153, 160–62.

retributivist or consequentialist orientation. A centralised system aims to treat like cases alike; decentralised negotiation leads to differentiated treatment, at the expense of weaker parties. Similar arguments about consistency could, however, be made with respect to agreements on compensatory damages. Sceptics might also point to the arbitrariness of punitive awards imposed by legal process, particularly in cases where the sum is determined by jury.[37] And the law, if it so chose, could regulate rather than proscribe agreed punishment. The consistency objection must therefore be underpinned by a view that punishment is a more serious phenomenon and so the conditions for it ought to be more stringent than those for compensation. A complementary perspective is that punishment, compared to compensation, is more firmly bound by public reason.[38] Legal institutions can be called upon to enforce punishment only by reference to norms reasonably acceptable to the community at large and not by reference to the shared norms of private actors.[39]

The exaction of a sanction agreed in contract can occur in two ways. Some sanctions are self-executing. Termination of contract, or forfeiture of money already paid to the innocent party are examples. Other sanctions, such as agreed damages, are executory. They cannot be enforced against an unwilling contract-breaker without resort to legal process. The law sometimes appears to treat self-executing sanctions more favourably, despite the greater potential for abuse. For example, forfeiture of a deposit may be allowed even though the quantum exceeds a genuine pre-estimate of loss, the traditional requirement for an agreed damages provision.[40] Relief against forfeiture is, certain routine situations aside, available relatively rarely to restrain termination of contract; and to recover payments the forfeiture has to be unconscionable as well as penal.[41]

In truth, the distinction is unreliable. Whether a sanction is self-executing or executory may be an accident of the circumstances, and its treatment a product of technical boundaries of contract law doctrine. So, a vendor can sue for an unpaid deposit after terminating for the purchaser's default:[42] the sanction is, at that time, practically executory. The validity of the sum is tested in the same way as a paid

[37] Law Commission, *Aggravated, Exemplary and Restitutionary Damages* (Law Com No 247, 1997) pt V, paras 1.81–1.90. But see J Goudkamp and E Katsampouka, 'An Empirical Study of Punitive Damages' (2018) 38 *OJLS* 90, 115–17.

[38] See generally J Rawls, *Political Liberalism*, expanded edn (New York, Columbia University Press, 2005) 212–54, 437–90; J Quong, 'On the Idea of Public Reason' in J Mandle and D Reidy (eds), *The Blackwell Companion to Rawls* (Oxford, John Wiley & Sons Ltd, 2013) 265.

[39] See, eg, Shiffrin (n 32) 422–24; C Flanders, 'Punishment, Liberalism and Public Reason' (2017) 36 *Criminal Justice Ethics* 61, 68.

[40] *Workers Trust & Merchant Bank Ltd v Dojap Investments Ltd* [1993] AC 573 (PC); *Cavendish* (n 3) [35] (Lord Neuberger and Lord Sumption), [235], [238] (Lord Hodge). See also Law Commission, *Penalty Clauses and Forfeiture of Monies Paid* (Working Paper 61, 1975) para 53.

[41] See text to n 168.

[42] *Griffon Shipping LLC v Firodi Shipping Ltd (The Griffon)* [2013] EWCA Civ 1567, [2014] 1 Lloyd's Rep 471 [15]. See also JW Carter, *Carter's Breach of Contract*, 2nd edn (Oxford, Hart Publishing, 2018) para 13–43.

deposit forfeited upon termination. Further, *Cavendish* now makes clear that both situations are governed by the rule against penalties and that some other forfeitures of money also fall within the rule. Any generosity shown towards self-executing sanctions probably says more about the courts' reluctance to help a contract-breaker upset the status quo,[43] than it does about an appetite for particular kinds of agreed sanction or punishment.

III. The Rule Against Penalties

A. The Scope of the Rule

The rule against penalties generally applies to clauses that impose a different or additional executory obligation upon breach. That obligation, which is secondary in character, is typically to pay a fixed sum or sum calculated by reference to a formula, by way of compensation. Non-monetary obligations, such as to transfer possession[44] or ownership[45] of property free or at undervalue, are within the scope of the rule. The rule also catches some clauses that forfeit the contract-breaker's right to a sum that has, at the time of breach, already been earned by[46] or otherwise accrued due to[47] the contract-breaker.

Forfeiture of deposits was for a long time thought to be beyond the rule against penalties.[48] This is partly for historical reasons: deposits have a far longer pedigree in the common law than penalties. The nature of a deposit differs from a typical agreed damages clause. A deposit serves the additional function of being an earnest of performance; it is payable in performance of the contract and not in consequence of default. Title to the deposit money when paid ordinarily[49] vests in the vendor, whereas one rationalisation of the rule against penalties has been that

[43] Compare AL Corbin, 'The Right of a Defaulting Vendee to the Restitution of Instalments Paid' (1931) 40 *Yale Law Journal* 1013, 1029.

[44] *Forestry Commission of NSW v Stefanetto* (1975) 133 CLR 507, 519, 521 (Mason J), 523–24 (Jacobs J), but cf 515 (Barwick CJ).

[45] See, eg, *Jobson v Johnson* [1989] 1 WLR 1026 (CA); *Ringrow Pty Ltd v BP Australia Pty Ltd* [2005] HCA 71, (2005) 224 CLR 656.

[46] *Commissioner of Public Works v Hills* [1906] AC 368 (PC); *Gilbert-Ash (Northern) Ltd v Modern Engineering (Bristol) Ltd* [1974] AC 689 (HL).

[47] *Socony Mobil Oil Co Inc v West of England Ship Owners Mutual Insurance Association Ltd (The Padre Island) (No 2)* [1989] 1 Lloyd's Rep 239 (CA), 262 (Stuart-Smith LJ), 265 (O'Connor LJ), cf 254–55 (Bingham LJ). Compare *Nutting v Baldwin* [1995] 1 WLR 201 (Ch D).

[48] *Hinton v Sparkes* (1868) LR 3 CP 161 (Court of Common Pleas); *Wallis v Smith* (1882) 21 Ch D 243 (CA), 258 (Jessel MR); *Lock v Bell* [1931] 1 Ch 35 (Ch D); *Linggi Plantations* v *Jagatheesan* [1972] 1 MLJ 89 (PC) 91; *Aribisala v St James' Homes (Grosvenor Dock) Ltd* [2008] EWHC 456, [2009] 1 WLR 1089 [14]; *Amble Assets LLP (in Administration) v Longbenton Foods Ltd (in Administration)* [2011] EWHC 1943, [2012] 1 All ER (Comm) 764 [75]. See also Law Commission (n 40) paras 57–60. Compare *Pye v British Automobile Commercial Syndicate Ltd* [1906] 1 KB 425 (KBD).

[49] But see, eg, *Masters v Cameron* (1954) 91 CLR 353 (HCA), 364–65.

it controls forfeiture or withholding of sums that 'belong to' the contract-breaker.[50] In some contexts, most notably sale of land, the general law position has been less important due to the existence of statutory relief.[51]

The Supreme Court in *Cavendish*, following the lead set by the Privy Council in *Workers Trust & Merchant Bank Ltd v Dojap Investments Ltd*,[52] brought deposits under the rule against penalties.[53] Lord Neuberger and Lord Sumption did this directly.[54] Lord Hodge excluded 'reasonable' deposits from the scope of the rule against penalties.[55] His statement conflates the scope of the rule with its substantive application to determine reasonableness, but the thrust of his reasoning is clear enough. Lord Mance was more equivocal.[56]

Australian law diverges from the law in the United Kingdom in two notable respects. First, there is an expanded jurisdiction, which controls some sanctions that are not dependent upon breach.[57] Second, deposits are not subject to the rule against penalties.[58] Relief against forfeiture may, however, be available in analogous circumstances where the deposit is excessive and 'penal'.[59] As the basis of the jurisdiction in both situations is equitable, the form of relief may be more flexible. In the case of deposits, for example, Lord Browne-Wilkinson said in *Workers Trust* that the purchaser was to be repaid the whole amount of the deposit, less a deduction for any damages of the vendor. On the logic accepted in *Cavendish*, the deduction must be by way of set-off.[60] In Australia, relief may be given on terms.[61] Scaling down to a reasonable sum[62] or making a deduction[63] for proven damages ought to be possible.

[50] *Stockloser v Johnson* [1954] 1 QB 476 (CA), 488–89 (Denning LJ); *Else (1982) Ltd v Parkland Holdings Ltd* [1994] 1 BCLC 130 (CA), 138–39 (Evans LJ), 146 (Hoffmann LJ).

[51] Law of Property Act 1925, s 49(2). See also Consumer Rights Act 2015, s 63 (unfair terms) and sch 2, items 4–6.

[52] *Workers Trust* (n 40). See also H Beale, 'Unreasonable Deposits' (1993) 109 *LQR* 524; JW Carter, 'Two Privy Council Cases' (1993) 6 *Journal of Contract Law* 266.

[53] See, eg, C Conte, 'Deposit Clauses' in G Virgo and S Worthington (eds), *Commercial Remedies: Resolving Controversies* (Cambridge, Cambridge University Press, 2017) 390.

[54] *Cavendish* (n 3) [16].

[55] ibid [237]–[238].

[56] ibid [156], [170].

[57] See text to n 66. Singapore and New Zealand, like the United Kingdom, have retained the breach requirement: *Denka Advantech* (n 32); *127 Hobson Street* (n 32) [42] (dicta, point not addressed on appeal: [2020] NZSC 53 [41]–[42]).

[58] *Legione v Hateley* (1983) 152 CLR 406 (HCA) 445 (Mason and Deane JJ); *Federal Commissioner of Taxation v Reliance Carpet Co Pty Ltd* [2008] HCA 22, (2008) 236 CLR 342 [26]; *Andrews v Australia and New Zealand Banking Group Ltd* [2012] HCA 30, (2012) 247 CLR 205 [43]. See also *NLS Pty Ltd v Hughes* (1966) 120 CLR 583 (HCA), 588–89 (Barwick CJ, with whom McTiernan J agreed).

[59] See, eg, *Smyth v Jessep* [1956] VLR 230 (VSC), 232; *Re Hoobin (decd)* [1957] VR 341 (VSC); *Coates v Sarich* [1964] WAR 2 (FC), 14–15 (Hale J); *Yardley v Saunders* [1982] WAR 231 (WASC); *Fiorelli Properties Pty Ltd v Professional Fencemakers Pty Ltd* [2011] VSC 661, (2011) 34 VR 257 [66], cf [61]–[62].

[60] Either equitable, or procedural based on netting off competing claims brought to judgment: see Civil Procedure Rules, r 40.13.

[61] See, eg, *Pitt v Curotta* (1931) 31 SR (NSW) 477 (Eq Div) (relief against forfeiture of instalments).

[62] Compare *Freedom v AHR Constructions Pty Ltd* [1987] 1 Qd R 59 (QSC), 70 (large prepayment recharacterised as a 10% deposit plus instalment payment).

[63] *Smyth* (n 59) 234. See also *Amble Assets* (n 48) [81].

B. The Rationale

i. Punishment or Security?

Cavendish confirms that the rule against penalties in the United Kingdom is a matter of public policy. The outer boundaries of the rule are marked by a prohibition against punishment for breach. Lord Neuberger and Lord Sumption gave qualified approval[64] to this statement by Mason and Deane JJ in *Legione v Hateley*:

> A penalty, as its name suggests, is in the nature of a punishment for non-observance of a contractual stipulation; it consists of the imposition of an additional or different liability upon breach of the contractual stipulation …[65]

The penalties jurisdiction in Australia is not limited to sanctions triggered by breach. It extends to a term that 'is collateral (or accessory) to a primary stipulation in favour of a second party' and which, 'upon the failure of the primary stipulation, imposes upon the first party an additional detriment, the penalty, to the benefit of the second party'.[66] This brings the scope of the doctrine closer to the reform proposed by the English Law Commission over 40 years ago.[67]

The rationale for this compound jurisdiction remains a matter of debate. In *Andrews v Australia and New Zealand Banking Group Ltd*,[68] the High Court cited Mason and Deane JJ's remarks about punishment and then went on to present the equitable jurisdiction for penalties in rather different terms. Relief is available for an excessive collateral stipulation because the stipulation is seen as being merely *in terrorem* of, and security for, fulfilment of the primary stipulation. This description of the rule highlights its similarity to relief against forfeiture.[69] Lord Neuberger and Lord Sumption directly rejected this rationalisation in *Cavendish*,[70] which is consistent with their views about punishment. So far as the penalties jurisdiction in Australia applies to sanctions triggered by breach, the sanction agreed by the parties possesses one essential quality of punishment: it is for a wrong (Hart's element (ii)). The punishment rationale for the expanded jurisdiction is a non-starter because there is no wrong.

The uncertainty was magnified in *Paciocco*, where the clause was activated by breach. Nettle J alone thought that the rule against penalties was not concerned with punishment 'as such'; it was instead addressed to grossly

[64] *Cavendish* (n 3) [31].
[65] *Legione* (n 58) 445. See also *Esanda Finance* (n 3) 153 (Deane J) ('additional or different financial obligation … in the nature of a disincentive or punishment').
[66] *Andrews* (n 58) [10].
[67] Law Commission (n 40) paras 26, 68.
[68] *Andrews* (n 58) [9]–[10].
[69] See text to n 153.
[70] *Cavendish* (n 3) [8].

disproportionate obligations.[71] Keane J saw different aspects of the jurisdiction as being supported by different rationales. Where the sanction was triggered by breach, the correct rationale was avoidance of punishment rather than the security characterisation embraced by equity.[72] Kiefel J and Gageler J attempted a synthesis. Kiefel J saw 'threats and punishment' as 'essential characteristics of a penalty'.[73] Since in equity the purpose of bonds was compensatory, the sanction was regarded only as a security. The obligor could obtain relief upon payment of appropriate compensation for the 'default'. In this way, equity promoted compensation and prevented the obligee 'exacting punishment'.[74] There is a clash of priorities in this account. If punishment is the essential quality then avoiding it must be the reason for, not the consequence of, equity's compensatory predisposition.

Gageler J was clearer that punishment is the driving force behind the rule.[75] For him, the security characterisation is merely another way of stating a conclusion, namely, that 'the only purpose of the stipulation was to punish: to impose a detriment … in order to deter non-observance' of the principal term.[76] Neither Kiefel J nor Gageler J explained how a sanction can be regarded as punishment in the absence of a wrong. Both judgments attached significance to the role of deterrence. And neither identified any genuinely condemnatory element, beyond the sanction amounting to hard or oppressive treatment. This is problematic for the reasons discussed next.

ii. Deterrence

The *in terrorem* concept came to prominence in connection with penalties as part of Lord Dunedin's famous judgment in *Dunlop Pneumatic Tyre Co Ltd v New Garage and Motor Ltd*,[77] though usage pre-dates that decision. Lord Dunedin used it in his proposition (2) to describe the 'essence' of a penalty, in contradistinction to a genuine pre-estimate of loss.[78] The concept is unhelpful and the *coup de grâce* delivered in *Cavendish* was long overdue. Lord Radcliffe pointed out in *Bridge v Campbell Discount Co Ltd*[79] that 'penalties may quite readily be undertaken by parties who are not in the least terrorised by the prospect of having to pay them'. The $35 or $20 late payment fees in *Paciocco* and the £85 parking fee in *ParkingEye* might irritate the average customer but they were hardly frightening. Whether they even deterred breach would depend upon each customer's

[71] *Paciocco* (n 25) [330]. See also *Denka Advantech* (n 32) [90] ('to prevent … the imposition of a remedy that is clearly disproportionate to the loss suffered as a result of the breach').
[72] ibid [221], [252]–[254].
[73] ibid [17] (French CJ agreed).
[74] ibid [21].
[75] ibid [130].
[76] ibid [158].
[77] *Dunlop* (n 3).
[78] ibid 86.
[79] *Bridge v Campbell Discount Co* Ltd [1962] AC 600 (HL) 622.

personal circumstances. Singling out the deterrent quality of a term overlooks the fact that contracts establish a finely-balanced system of rewards and disincentives, whether as primary or secondary obligations.[80] There is nothing inherently objectionable in a contract's presenting more or less desirable alternatives to the performing party.

As Lord Radcliffe also explained in *Bridge*, the description *in terrorem* adds nothing 'of substance to the idea conveyed by the word "penalty" itself'.[81] Like the label 'punishment',[82] *in terrorem* describes a prior conclusion that a clause is invalid as a penalty. If the rule against penalties really were about sanctions operating *in terrorem*, the law would look very different. The rationale underpinning the rule would be to prevent compulsion of performance rather than to prevent punishment. Lord Dunedin's guidelines set out in his proposition (4)[83] would require revision because they are ill-suited to evaluating deterrence.

For an agreed sanction to function as a deterrent, the contract-breaker must have a genuine opportunity to choose between performing the contract and suffering the sanction. This is not always so. Accepting the premise, the effectiveness of the sanction as a deterrent can be assessed by comparing two quantities: (i) the net cost of performance (accounting for benefits obtained through performance) to the contract-breaker; and (ii) the net cost of non-performance, being the cost of the sanction less net benefits obtained through non-performance. This comparison is only approximate since, as orthodoxy requires, it must be based on circumstances at the time of contract rather than the latest time at which the contract-breaker can decide to perform. It could be further refined by adjusting (ii) to account for the chance of breach going undetected, haggling for a lower settlement afterwards and so on.

The greatest conceivable loss test, which appears as Lord Dunedin's proposition (4)(a) in *Dunlop*,[84] measures the wrong quantities. It compares the first part of (ii) with: (iii) the greatest conceivable loss that could be proved to have followed from breach. The sum that might be awarded as common law damages is usually taken as a guide,[85] though the test is one of genuine pre-estimation not accuracy. At best, the test is a crude attempt to measure 'increase' in deterrence. The test disregards the fact that the threat of a common law damages award can be an effective deterrent where (iii) exceeds (i). Lord Dunedin's greater money sum test – proposition (4)(b)[86] – is a better illustration but it is not irrefutable.

[80] Compare *Cavendish* (n 3) [31] (Lord Neuberger and Lord Sumption).

[81] *Bridge* (n 79) 622.

[82] See section III.C.i.

[83] *Dunlop* (n 3) 87–88.

[84] *Dunlop* (n 3) 87.

[85] *Robophone Facilities Ltd v Blank* [1966] 1 WLR 1428 (CA), 1447 (Diplock LJ); *Ringrow* (n 45) [21]; *Murray v Leisureplay Plc* [2005] EWCA Civ 963, [2005] IRLR 946 [42] (Arden LJ), but see [113] (Buxton LJ, with whom Clarke LJ agreed). Compare *Paciocco* (n 25) [145] (Gageler J), [282]–[283] (Keane J).

[86] *Dunlop* (n 3) 87.

It is possible that the payer's benefit in holding on to the money after the due date outweighs the amount by which the sum payable upon breach exceeds the sum originally payable. Then (ii) is reduced below (i) and the sanction does not effectively deter. Or, if the payee's cash flow is critical, so that late payment would foreseeably cause catastrophic harm, the estimated greatest loss (iii) may again exceed (i). The common law alone could effectively deter.

Kiefel J and Gageler J in *Paciocco* disagreed with Lord Radcliffe and insisted on the element of deterrence.[87] For Gageler J, the question was whether the 'negative incentive to perform' was so far out of proportion to the innocent party's 'positive interest in performance' that the negative incentive 'amounts to deterrence by threat of punishment'.[88] The test compares some version of (ii) with something new: (iv) the innocent party's interest in performance. It is not obvious that these are directly commensurable. In any event this test, like the greatest conceivable loss test, compares the wrong quantities to evaluate deterrence. Since Gageler J accepted that valid agreed damages clauses, and even awards of common law damages, can create strong disincentives,[89] the quality of deterrence is ultimately beside the point. What matters is that the sanction is so disproportionate as to conclude that it can only serve to punish. Kiefel J's analysis reduces in the same manner. She conceded that the bank's customers would not have been terrified by the late fee. The critical question was whether the sum to be paid could be accounted for on some basis other than as punishment.[90]

A rationale of preventing deterrence would also change the nature of the courts' role in invalidating an agreed sanction. According to the punishment rationale, the court either refuses its aid to the innocent party to exact punishment, or assists the contract-breaker to reverse a punishment already exacted. The effect of the court's involvement conforms to the rationale. Under the deterrence rationale the starting position is that the deterrent has failed on this occasion. Unless the contract is ongoing, or the parties are repeat players, arguments based on future deterrence are weak. The sanction is not upheld or invalidated on the basis of its deterrent effect but, rather, on the basis that parties should be kept to their agreement where the deterrent was justifiable or proportionate at the time of contract. It is not clear how proportionality would be assessed. There must be a break-even point at which, all things considered, the expected cost of (ii) exceeds (i), so that the sanction becomes an effective deterrent for a rational actor. It is hard to imagine courts welcoming a quantitative, fact-intensive and speculative approach to resolve a narrow issue.

[87] *Paciocco* (n 25) [17], [165], cf [259] (Keane J) (concept 'may not be unhelpful').
[88] ibid [164].
[89] ibid.
[90] ibid [17].

C. Discerning Punishment

i. Description or Substance?

The conclusion that a clause punishes the contract-breaker has traditionally been drawn as an inference of law.[91] It is simply another way of saying that a clause is 'penal' because it fails the test for validity. This is apparent from Mason and Deane JJ's statement in *Legione*, which was quoted in *Cavendish*.[92] Diplock LJ in *Robophone Facilities Ltd v Blank*[93] was careful to refer to a sanction 'in the nature of a penalty *or* punishment' imposed upon the contract-breaker. It is also consistent with other features of the rule against penalties. The rule is applied by construction, which in turn involves a process of characterisation.[94] The label applied by the parties is not conclusive, nor is direct evidence of the parties' intentions relevant. The contract-breaker does not prove that the clause is penal by showing that the innocent party had an intention to punish at the time of contract or enforcement. Equally, the test is not based on upon whether a reasonable person in the parties' position would infer, as a matter of fact, an intention to punish.

These features provide a strong clue that the rule against penalties is not truly concerned with preventing punishment. *Cavendish* is orthodox in method, while clinging to the punishment rationale. Notwithstanding Kiefel J's assertions in *Paciocco* about the essentiality of punishment, it plays no direct role in the balance of her judgment.[95] This seems to be broadly consistent with orthodox method. Gageler J inverted the normal sequence. Punishment did not follow from invalidity. Instead, the usual guidelines became tools for discerning a punitive element in the sanction.[96] Keane J accepted the punitive rationale but was ambivalent about method. Some of his judgment is consistent with orthodoxy, that punishment merely describes invalidity.[97] He strays in other passages, suggesting that a punitive objective is paramount and that this can be established separately as a matter of fact.[98]

Once a punitive element has been identified, the question is then one of degree. Gageler J said that a clause is invalid if the only purpose is to punish,[99] whereas for

[91] See JW Carter, W Courtney and GJ Tolhurst, 'Assessment of Contractual Penalties: *Dunlop* Deflated' (2017) 34 *Journal of Contract Law* 4, 18–19.

[92] See above (n 65).

[93] *Robophone Facilities Ltd v Blank* [1966] 1 WLR 1428 (CA), 1446 (emphasis added).

[94] *Dunlop* (n 3) 86–87 (Lord Dunedin) (proposition (3)); *O'Dea v Allstates Leasing System (WA) Pty Ltd* (1983) 152 CLR 359 (HCA), 400 (Deane J); *Cavendish* (n 3) [28] (Lord Neuberger and Lord Sumption), [243] (Lord Hodge); *Paciocco* (n 25) [31] (Kiefel J), [146] (Gageler J), [243] (Keane J).

[95] Compare *Paciocco* (n 25) [32].

[96] ibid [159]–[161], [164]–[165]. See also text to n 75.

[97] ibid [242]–[243], [253]–[256].

[98] ibid [217], [221], [267].

[99] ibid [165]–[166].

Keane J a predominantly punitive purpose is enough.[100] Gageler J's test must be nigh impossible to fail [101] An agreed sanction that requires the contract-breaker to confer some benefit upon the innocent party can almost always be seen to possess a compensatory aspect, whatever its other purposes.

ii. The Dunlop *Tests*

To qualify as punishment, the sanction for breach must inflict hard treatment upon the contract-breaker and manifest condemnation. The *Dunlop* tests are a relatively good indicator of the former. Hard treatment in this context means something more than adverse treatment. Anticipated common law entitlements provide a rough benchmark.[102] A clause that substantially under-liquidates damages still imposes a detriment upon the contract-breaker but it does not amount to hard treatment. It is consistent with the punishment rationale that such clauses are generally not invalidated by the rule against penalties.[103]

One situation is apparently difficult to square with this analysis. It occurs when the innocent party's actual loss exceeds the sum fixed by contract and yet the clause is struck down as being penal.[104] That result is not self-contradictory. Agreed sanctions are necessarily predictive and their validity is not tested by reference to the innocent party's actual loss. The most likely reasons are that circumstances have markedly worsened for the innocent party between time of contract and time of breach, so that what seemed like an extravagant sum initially is not so later; or that the parties have fallen foul of the technicalities of the *Dunlop* tests.[105] Another possibility is that the agreed damages formula is arbitrary or patently erroneous and so overcompensates or undercompensates depending upon the circumstances.[106]

The *Dunlop* tests fare much worse in identifying the condemnatory aspect of the sanction. The sanction itself can symbolise (or embody) denunciation by the innocent party. Typical agreed sanctions, for the payment of money as liquidated damages or for the transfer of property, do not ordinarily possess that significance. Attaching the label 'penalty' to the agreed sanction expressly conveys disapproval. The presumption in favour of the parties' classification[107] then points the right way. The label is not decisive, however, and the word 'penalty' in ordinary usage may denote a milder reproach than condemnation.

[100] ibid [221].

[101] See, eg, Carter, Courtney and Tolhurst (n 91) 19.

[102] See n 85).

[103] *Cellulose Acetate Silk Co Ltd v Widnes Foundry (1925) Ltd* [1933] AC 20 (HL); *Tullett Prebon Group Ltd v El-Hajjali* [2008] EWHC 1924, [2008] IRLR 760 [83].

[104] See, eg, *Dingwall v Burnett* 1912 SC 1097 (Court of Session); *Wall v Rederiaktiebolaget Luggude* [1915] 3 KB 66 (KBD).

[105] In particular, the 'same sum for varying events' test: *Dunlop* (n 3) 87 (proposition (4)(c)). See also E Peel, *Treitel: The Law of Contract*, 14th edn (London, Sweet & Maxwell, 2015) para 20-141.

[106] See, eg, *Bridge* (n 79).

[107] *Dunlop* (n 3) 86 (Lord Dunedin) (proposition (1)).

Another course is to infer condemnation from the severity of the sanction. Although 'punishments' are usually harsher than 'penalties', this criterion is specious. It leads to thorny questions about the interplay between the criminal and civil law, and between compensation and punishment.[108] If, for example, a large award of compensatory damages financially ruins the defendant, is that punishment? Does an award of compensatory damages punish the defendant when it exceeds the criminal fine, or amount of punitive damages, payable in the same event? In *ParkingEye*, Mr Beavis was liable to pay a charge of £85 (reducible to £50 if paid promptly) for staying in the car park beyond two hours. This was greater than the statutory fine for overstaying an allotted time in a public street or in a local authority car park. If the statutory fine punished Mr Beavis then, looking only at quantum,[109] a greater private parking charge also did so. The Supreme Court's approach was more sophisticated and it was untroubled by the excess.[110] Feinberg would reach the same conclusion by a different route. For him, parking fines are the archetypal penalty – not punishment – because they lack any condemnatory quality.[111] The same must be true of a contractual charge imposed by a private car park operator. The fact that the charge is higher than a statutory fine does not change its character.

iii. The Legitimate Interest Test

The various tests formulated in *Cavendish* describe the sanction as being 'extravagant', 'exorbitant', 'unconscionable' or 'out of all proportion' with respect to the innocent party's interest in performance of the contract.[112] The connection between the test and the contract-breaker's punishment was asserted most directly by Lord Neuberger and Lord Sumption,[113] who referred to punishment immediately after stating the test. Lord Hodge's judgment is to similar effect, though less explicit about their relationship.[114] Lord Mance said little about it in *Cavendish*; he had emphasised it in the past.[115]

The leap to punishment is a non sequitur. It involves a Holmesian logical fallacy:[116] if no acceptable and proportionate reason for the clause can be found then it must have been intended to punish. A far more likely explanation,

[108] See, eg, Burrows (n 36) 156, 165.

[109] But see *Cavendish* (n 3) [196] (Lord Mance) (statutory scheme 'in no way analogous' to the private parking fees).

[110] ibid [100] (Lord Neuberger and Lord Sumption), [196] (Lord Mance), [287] (Lord Hodge).

[111] Feinberg (n 7) 398.

[112] *Cavendish* (n 3) [32] (Lord Neuberger and Lord Sumption), [152] (Lord Mance), [255] (Lord Hodge), [293] (Lord Toulson).

[113] ibid [32].

[114] ibid [223], [253]–[255].

[115] *Cine Bes Filmcilik Ve Yapimcilik AS v United International Pictures* [2003] EWCA Civ 1669, [2004] 1 CLC 401 [33] (Mance LJ).

[116] AC Doyle, *The Sign of the Four* (London, Spencer Blackett, 1890) 93 ('when you have eliminated the impossible, whatever remains, *however improbable*, must be the truth').

in commercial cases at least, is that the innocent party was seeking to profiteer from breach,[117] or to coerce performance by threat of a devastating sanction. There must be reasons, other than punishment, that cannot be legitimate. While the judgments in *Paciocco* are less uniform, all bar Nettle J's converge on punishment or deterrence, and nothing else, as being illegitimate.[118] The other difficulty with the punishment rationale in both *Cavendish* and *Paciocco* is that it is too absolute. It overlooks the fact that punishment between contracting parties is sometimes accepted.

D. Tolerating Punishment

Organised sport[119] and employment are familiar contexts in which punitive sanctions seem to be tolerated. Fining players and clubs for misconduct is commonplace, as are suspensions. At the extreme end of the scale, participants may be permanently banned. I will assume that the legal basis of these disciplinary procedures is, at least to some extent, contractual. Employees are commonly subjected to disciplinary sanctions in the form of warnings, deductions, demotions, suspensions or dismissal. The existence and likely success of extra-curial disciplinary proceedings against a wrongdoer may be a factor affecting the award of punitive damages in tort.[120]

The following discussion only considers sanctions that are clearly within the scope of the rule against penalties, such as fixed fines and other fixed deductions from remuneration.[121] The boundaries of the rule present an issue of consistency that should be mentioned at the outset. If, as I argue below, the law tolerates some punitive sanctions in contract that are beyond the reach of the rule, the supposed punishment rationale for the rule looks peculiar. That the sanction is fixed by agreement in advance hardly seems to justify more stringent control than, say, a discretionary sanction; indeed, the reverse is more plausible.

There is scant English or Australian case law on fines in organised sport. Many fines would bear no relation to the sporting organisation's loss caused by the contract-breaker's default. The conventional justification based on *Dunlop* must be that the loss from any single breach would be indirect and near impossible

[117] See also A Summers, 'Unresolved Issues in the Law of Penalties' [2017] *LMCLQ* 95, 115.

[118] See generally E Peden, 'Penalties after *Paciocco* – the Enigma of "Legitimate Interests"' (2019) 35 *Journal of Contract Law* 263. By contrast, New Zealand has adopted the 'legitimate interests' test while rejecting an additional inquiry as to punitive purpose: *127 Hobson Street* (SC) (n 57) [58].

[119] See generally JY Kim and MJ Parlow, 'Off-Court Misbehavior: Sports Leagues and Private Punishment' (2009) 99 *Journal of Criminal Law and Criminology* 573; RC Ellickson, 'When Civil Society Uses an Iron Fist: The Roles of Private Associations in Rulemaking and Adjudication' (2016) 18 *American Law and Economics Review* 235.

[120] *Thompson v Commissioner of Police of the Metropolis* [1998] QB 498 (CA) 518 (Lord Woolf MR for the Court); Law Commission (n 37) pt IV, paras 1.44–1.46.

[121] Discretionary sanctions are discussed in section V.

to forecast;[122] it could also be difficult or practically impossible to prove afterwards. This argument glosses over the fact that sporting fines can have a punitive character. To be clear, I am not suggesting that all sanctions imposed upon sporting participants constitute punishment; merely that those towards the more severe end of the spectrum for serious wrongdoing may do so. Some are calculated to denounce, perhaps publicly, the contract-breaker's misconduct and are severe enough to sting. Fines may also perform some of the functions typically associated with punishment, such as specific and general deterrence, authoritative disavowal of the misconduct and vindication of the rules governing the sporting enterprise.

This punitive aspect ought to be acknowledged, contrary to *Cavendish*, and justified by other legitimate interests of the sporting organisation. Maintaining certain standards of conduct or performance among all participants, reducing the risk of personal injury, ensuring the integrity of the competition and upholding the sport's public image are all plausible interests. In *R v Barnes*,[123] Lord Woolf recognised the legitimacy of internal disciplinary procedures to punish misconduct on the sporting field. For that reason, he remarked, the criminal law ought to be reserved for the minority of serious cases where the conduct was properly categorised as criminal.

In the employment context, some clauses are routinely subjected to the rule against penalties. 'Bad leaver' provisions are reviewable when they are triggered by breach, though the rule can be evaded with careful drafting.[124] The rule is also applied to agreed damages for failing to commence work[125] or to serve out a notice period.[126] On that basis, *Cavendish* would proscribe punishment. A backwards glance at history, to the Truck Act 1896 in particular, paints a more complex picture. There were many Truck Acts, stretching back to around the mid-fifteenth century. The Acts were principally concerned with ensuring that workers in certain trades were paid in money and not in kind. The Truck Act 1896 went further. Sections 1 and 2 regulated fines levied on workers, and other deductions or payments for bad work or damage to the employer's property. These controls lasted for most of the twentieth century until replaced by diluted requirements, which continue in the present day.[127]

Fines in the form of fixed tariffs for defaults are ripe to be attacked under the rule against penalties. The lack of reported cases challenging fines on this common

[122] *Dunlop* (n 3) 87–88 (Lord Dunedin) (proposition (4)(d)). See also *Clydebank* (n 3) 11 (Earl of Halsbury LC).

[123] *R v Barnes* [2004] EWCA Crim 3246, [2005] 1 WLR 910 [5].

[124] *Imam-Sadeque v Bluebay Asset Management (Services) Ltd* [2012] EWHC 3511, [2013] IRLR 344 [203]–[209]. Compare *Richards v IP Solutions Group Ltd* [2016] EWHC 1835, [2017] IRLR 133 [84]–[85]. See also Zou and Liu, ch 14, section III.

[125] *Tullett Prebon Group Ltd v El-Hajjali* [2008] EWHC 1924, [2008] IRLR 760.

[126] *Giraud UK Ltd v Smith* [2000] IRLR 763 (EAT).

[127] By the Wages Act 1986, pt I and then by the Employment Rights Act 1996, pt II.

law basis is, therefore, 'striking'.[128] The prohibitive cost of legal action for an affected worker was, no doubt, one reason.[129] Another explanation might be that the safeguards in section 1 covered the same ground as the rule against penalties. For example, sanctions for non-attendance at work could be dealt with under the Act,[130] whereas nowadays the rule against penalties is invoked.[131] This explanation is not convincing. To begin with, the Act did not cover all workers. So far as the Act applied, sections 1 and 2 were regulatory, not enabling, provisions.[132] They operated on the basis that contractual fines and other deductions from wages were lawful (to some extent) at the time the Act was passed.[133] And this was not long before the quartet of leading penalty cases decided in the early twentieth century.[134]

Section 1 established procedural and substantive controls. The employer of a worker[135] was not permitted to impose a fine unless prior notice had been given of the relevant defaults and tariff for each default.[136] The default was one that would cause, or be likely to cause, harm to the employer, and the amount of the fine had to be fair and reasonable. These substantive controls were more generous than the rule against penalties as described in *Dunlop* or *Cavendish*. A default only had to be 'likely' to cause harm This, in addition to 'damage' or 'loss', included 'interruption' or 'hindrance' of the employer's business. It appears that considerable latitude was allowed when the Act was applied in practice. In *Squire v Bayer & Co*,[137] a fine of 2*d* for an employee's breach of a provision requiring good order and decorum was upheld. Her wrongful act was to play a harp during dinner time; the dust raised by other employees' dancing to the music had the potential to harm machinery and materials. 'Fine' in section 1 embraced sanctions of a punitive nature. The controversy was whether section 1 extended to non-punitive or mixed sanctions. In *Bristow v City Petroleum Ltd*[138] the House of Lords held that it did. Lord Ackner explained:

> 5 … [T]he fine which the Act permitted to be imposed, would almost always contain an element of *retribution*, recompense or compensation. 6. The purpose of the imposition of the fine might be *to deter or denounce* the act or omission or to obtain *retribution*,

[128] M Freedland, *The Personal Employment Contract* (Oxford, Oxford University Press, 2005) 209.

[129] Enforcement of the Truck legislation in practice rested with the Factory Inspectorate.

[130] *Buxton Lime Firms Co Ltd v Howe* [1900] 2 QB 232 (DC).

[131] See, eg, *Giraud* (n 126); *Tullett Prebon Group* (n 125).

[132] *Hart v Riversdale Mill Co Ltd* [1928] 1 KB 176 (CA), 190 (Scrutton LJ); *Sagar v H Ridehalgh and Son Ltd* [1931] 1 Ch 310 (CA), 338 (Lawrence LJ). See also HC Deb 4 May 1896, vol 40, col 523; HC Deb 30 July 1896, vol 43, col 1078.

[133] See also *Redgrave v Kelly* (1889) 5 TLR 477 (QBD).

[134] *Clydebank* (n 3); *Hills* (n 46); *Webster v Bosanquet* [1912] AC 394 (PC); *Dunlop* (n 3).

[135] Section 1 applied to workmen and shop assistants.

[136] There may be a parallel with Diplock LJ's analysis in *Robophone* (n 93) 1448.

[137] *Squire v Bayer & Co* [1901] 2 KB 299 (DC).

[138] *Bristow v City Petroleum Ltd* [1987] 1 WLR 529 (HL). See also *Sealand Petroleum Co Ltd v Barratt* [1986] 1 WLR 700 (QBD); D Howarth, 'The Truck Act 1986 – Last Rites' (1986) 45 *CLJ* 30.

> recompense or compensation for the loss or damage it occasioned or a mixture of these aims.[139]

The employer's contractual right to fine was regarded as being separate from, and additional to, the right to damages for breach.[140] Further, the financial limit on fines in section 1 was framed differently from that for deductions or payments in section 2. A 'fair and reasonable' fine under section 1 could take account of repeated defaults and provide 'more than financial compensation' to the employer.[141] In contrast, deductions or payments for poor work under section 2 could not exceed the 'actual or estimated damage or loss'. This is much closer to the rule against penalties.

This brief sketch shows that the law openly tolerated punishment in employment contracts, and at a time when the rule against penalties was relatively well established. Community expectations of labour relations are, of course, radically different today compared with a century ago. The practice of fining has largely disappeared. This does not necessarily entail outright proscription of punishment. Rather, contemporary values should shape the circumstances in which the employer is recognised as having a legitimate interest in punishing the employee. These may be very limited. Sanctions designed to preserve the employment relationship or to reform the employee are, perhaps, more easily justified than those operating upon, or after, termination of employment.

IV. Relief Against Forfeiture

A. Completing the Transaction

Relief against forfeiture has two distinct orientations. Relief can be directed towards completion ('perfection'[142]) of the transaction after a forfeiture triggered by breach or termination for breach.[143] The jurisdiction is ancient. One branch encompasses the traditional equitable grounds of fraud, mistake, accident and surprise.[144] Another branch looks to the substance of the transaction and may be engaged where the forfeiture merely stands as security for the achievement of an important object of the parties' bargain. Its origins lie in mortgages and leases,

[139] *Bristow* (n 138) 536 (emphasis added).

[140] *Buxton* (n 130) 237 (Ridley J), 239 (Darling J).

[141] *Bristow* (n 138) 537 (Lord Ackner).

[142] L Smith, 'Relief Against Forfeiture: A Restatement' (2001) 60 *CLJ* 178, 184.

[143] Relief is not, however, limited to instances of breach: J McGhee and S Elliott (eds), *Snell's Equity*, 34th edn (London, Sweet & Maxwell, 2020) para 13-025.

[144] *Shiloh Spinners Ltd v Harding* [1973] AC 691 (HL) 722 (Lord Wilberforce); *Tanwar Enterprises Pty Ltd v Cauchi* [2003] HCA 57, (2003) 217 CLR 315 [58] (Gleeson CJ, McHugh, Gummow, Hayne and Heydon JJ).

though these instances are now mostly addressed by statute.[145] In *Shiloh Spinners Ltd v Harding*,[146] Lord Wilberforce reviewed this branch of the jurisdiction in relation to securities for the payment of money and securities for non-monetary obligations. He reaffirmed

> the right of courts of equity in appropriate and limited cases to relieve against forfeiture for breach of covenant or condition where the primary object of the bargain is to secure a stated result which can effectively be attained when the matter comes before the court, and where the forfeiture provision is added by way of security for the production of that result.[147]

The party seeking relief generally must be ready and willing to perform and to pay compensation for its default, for example interest and costs. Whether relief is granted depends upon consideration of all the circumstances.[148] Substantive relief has the effect of preventing or reversing the forfeiture. An element not mentioned in this key passage,[149] but which has assumed prominence in later cases, is that the subject matter of forfeiture must be a proprietary or possessory right; mere contractual rights are not protected.[150]

Relief against forfeiture in this form is concerned with preventing an unconscionable exercise of strict legal rights.[151] There is nothing distinctively punitive involved in the branch of the jurisdiction addressing fraud, mistake, accident or surprise. Where the jurisdiction is founded upon characterising the forfeiture as a security, the penal nature of the forfeiture is sometimes emphasised.[152] 'Penal' has various senses. It may be a vestige of a time when Chancery judges saw penalties and forfeitures as being governed by similar principles.[153] It may indicate that, like some penalties, the forfeiture is designed to ensure performance of the associated

[145] See, eg, Law of Property Act 1925, s 146(2); Senior Courts Act 1981, s 38; County Courts Act 1984, s 138.

[146] *Shiloh Spinners* (n 144).

[147] ibid 723 (Viscount Dilhorne, Lord Pearson and Lord Kilbrandon agreed).

[148] ibid 723–24 (Lord Wilberforce).

[149] Compare ibid 722 (courts of equity asserting the right 'to relieve against forfeitures of property').

[150] *Scandinavian Trading Tanker Co AB v Flota Petrolera Ecuatoriana (The Scaptrade)* [1983] 2 AC 694 (HL); *Sport Internationaal Bussum BV v Inter-Footwear Ltd* [1984] 1 WLR 776 (HL); *Çukurova Finance International Ltd v Alfa Telecom Turkey Ltd (Nos 3 to 5)* [2013] UKPC 2, [2016] AC 923 [94]; *Vauxhall Motors Ltd v Manchester Ship Canal Co Ltd* [2019] UKSC 46, [2019] 3 WLR 852.

[151] *Vauxhall Motors* (n 150) [2] (Lord Briggs, with whom Lord Carnwath, Lady Black and Lord Kitchin agreed).

[152] *Re Dagenham (Thames) Dock Co, ex parte Hulse* (1873) LR 8 Ch App 1022; *Kilmer v British Columbia Orchard Lands Ltd* [1913] AC 319 (PC); *Shiloh* (n 144) 722 (Lord Wilberforce).

[153] *Peachy v Duke of Somerset* (1720) 1 Str 447; 93 ER 626; *Sloman v Walter* (1783) 1 Bro CC 418; 28 ER 1213; *Kreglinger (G & C) v New Patagonia Meat and Cold Storage Co Ltd* [1914] AC 25 (HL), 35 (Viscount Haldane LC), 49–50 (Lord Parker). See also C Rossiter, *Penalties and Forfeiture* (Sydney, Law Book Co, 1992) 20, 155; N Tiverios, *Contractual Penalties in Australia and the United Kingdom: History, Theory and Practice* (Sydney, Federation Press, 2019) 25–29.

primary obligation.[154] Or it may reflect the fact that the forfeiture inflicts hardship upon the contract-breaker.[155]

If there is any penal element nowadays, it is probably[156] just a factor going to discretion rather than the existence of jurisdiction.[157] In *Cavendish*, the relationship between the rule against penalties and relief against forfeiture was clouded by a failure consistently to distinguish forfeitures of the present kind from forfeitures of money. Lord Mance, and perhaps Lord Hodge, thought that some forfeitures of the present kind could be subject to the rule against penalties and also relief against forfeiture, the principles being applied in that order.[158] This only makes sense if relief against forfeiture can operate in respect of non-penal sanctions.

An element of hard treatment may be found in the circumstances that justify the grant of relief. Harshness is not measured only by comparing the value of the forfeiture against the amount of the innocent party's loss from breach or the contract-breaker's liability for it. Matters such as the wilfulness of the breach, and whether belated performance and compensation are an adequate remedy for the innocent party, are relevant.[159] Similarly, although controversial, the fact that the innocent party terminated for breach of an essential time stipulation is not always fatal to the contract-breaker's claim for relief.[160]

The critical point is that there is no suggestion that the forfeiture must condemn or denounce the contract-breaker. Losing a proprietary or possessory right is not ordinarily symbolic of condemnation. And so long as the innocent party is genuinely enforcing the forfeiture as a remedy for the default, additional or collateral purposes are irrelevant.[161] The jurisdiction therefore cannot be concerned with preventing punishment. The artificiality of a punitive rationale is plain from Gibbs CJ and Murphy J's judgment in *Legione*. The vendors terminated a contract for the sale of land for the purchasers' failure to complete. Gibbs CJ and Murphy J were prepared to hold, if it were necessary to invoke the jurisdiction, that the forfeiture

[154] *Legione* (n 58) 445 (Mason and Deane JJ).

[155] *Sanders v Pope* (1806) 12 Ves Jun 282, 289; 33 ER 108, 110; *Kilmer* (n 152) 325.

[156] This is not the occasion to examine the proper basis of the decisions in *Re Dagenham* (n 152) and *Kilmer* (n 152).

[157] *Legione* (n 58) 425 (Gibbs CJ and Murphy J), 444 (Mason and Deane JJ); *Stern v McArthur* (1988) 165 CLR 489, 524 (Deane and Dawson JJ).

[158] *Cavendish* (n 3) [160]–[161] (Lord Mance), [226]–[227] (Lord Hodge) (referring to money but also citing *BICC Plc v Burndy Corp* [1985] Ch 232 (CA)); cf [17]–[18] (Lord Neuberger and Lord Sumption).

[159] *Shiloh* (n 144) 723–24 (Lord Wilberforce).

[160] Compare *Steedman v Drinkle* [1916] 1 AC 275 (PC); *Brickles v Snell* [1916] 2 AC 599 (PC); *Union Eagle Ltd v Golden Achievement Ltd* [1997] AC 514 (PC) with *Kilmer* (n 152); *Legione* (n 58); *Stern* (n 157) (failure to comply with notice to complete); *Else* (n 50) 145 (Hoffmann LJ); *Celestial Aviation Trading 71 Ltd v Paramount Airways Private Ltd* [2010] EWHC 185, [2011] 1 All ER (Comm) 259 [78] (essentiality does not oust jurisdiction). See also C Harpum, 'Relief against Forfeiture and the Purchaser of Land' (1984) 43 *CLJ* 134, 146–56.

[161] *Çukurova* (n 150) [77]–[78].

'punished' the purchasers.[162] That description was catachrestic. The real concern was the severity of the consequences of forfeiture. The purchasers would lose the benefit of improvements they had made on the land while in possession, a 'harsh and excessive penalty for a comparatively trivial breach'.[163]

B. Enabling Restitution

Relief against forfeiture in this form facilitates restitution for monetary and non-monetary[164] benefits conferred by the contract-breaker prior to discharge of the contract. Typically, relief overrides a clause that expressly or impliedly forfeits money paid – deposits or part-payments of the contract price – by the contract-breaker in performance of the contract. This form of relief has prompted many debates that need not be resolved presently. I will assume for the sake of argument that relief exists;[165] that it does not depend upon the contract-breaker's being ready and willing to perform;[166] and that the substantive requirements are those accepted by the majority in *Stockloser v Johnson*.[167] Denning LJ described two conditions: 'first, the forfeiture clause must be of a penal nature, in this sense, that the sum forfeited must be out of all proportion to the damage, and, secondly, it must be unconscionable for the seller to retain the money'.[168] The former requirement is probably assessed at time of contract,[169] the latter at the time relief is sought.[170]

The quality of hard treatment in Denning LJ's test is to be found in a mix of considerations. The penal condition looks to the innocent party's expected loss and so, presumably, the contract-breaker's liability for it. The condition of unconscionability may concentrate or temper the perception of harshness by reference to the circumstances after contract. The relative magnitude of the sum forfeited, compared with what would otherwise have been the contract-breaker's restitutionary entitlement at law, is relevant though not decisive. So far as the jurisdiction

[162] *Legione* (n 58) 425.

[163] ibid 429. The underlying assumption may have been wrong: *Lexane Pty Ltd v Highfern Pty Ltd* [1985] 1 Qd R 446 (QSC) 455.

[164] *PC Developments Pty Ltd v Revell* (1991) 22 NSWLR 615 (CA), 645–46 (Clarke JA).

[165] *Steedman* (n 160); *Brickles* (n 160) 604; *McDonald v Dennys Lascelles Ltd* (1933) 48 CLR 457 (HCA) 478 (Dixon J); *Stockloser v Johnson* [1954] 1 QB 476 (CA) 484–85 (Somervell LJ), 490 (Denning LJ), but see 499–501 (Romer LJ); *Union Eagle* (n 160) 520. Compare *Cadogan Petroleum Holdings Ltd v Global Process Systems LLC* [2013] EWHC 214, [2013] 2 Lloyd's Rep 26 [38].

[166] *Stockloser* (n 165) 487–88 (Somervell LJ), 491 (Denning LJ), but see 501–02 (Romer LJ). Compare *Mussen v Van Diemen's Land Co* [1938] Ch 253 (Ch D), 265–66; *Galbraith v Mitchenall Estates Ltd* [1965] 2 QB 473 (QBD), 481 and cf *Legione* (n 58) 443–44 (Mason and Deane JJ) (point left open). See also Harpum (n 160) 158–61.

[167] *Stockloser* (n 165).

[168] ibid 490. See also ibid 484–85 (Somervell LJ).

[169] *Smyth* (n 59) 232; *PC Developments* (n 164) 645 (Clarke JA).

[170] *Stockloser* (n 165) 492 (Denning LJ); *Else* (n 50) 140 (Evans LJ), 145–46 (Hoffmann LJ).

applies to deposits,[171] a sum that exceeds a reasonable earnest[172] could qualify as harsh. For part payments of the contract price, harshness may be found in a combination of factors. Unlike deposits, there is no generally recognised right to retain a 'reasonable' part payment.[173] Also, the forfeiture operates in the wrong direction with no relation to the innocent party's loss: the greater the contract-breaker's performance, the more severe the effect of the forfeiture and the greater the potential advantage for the innocent party.[174]

Even so, neither of the two conditions mentioned in *Stockloser* depends upon the sanction's condemning or denouncing the contract-breaker. This branch of the jurisdiction is not concerned with preventing punishment. Deane and Dawson JJ, in *Stern v McArthur*,[175] discussing contracts for the sale of land, remarked that forfeiture of instalments paid by a purchaser 'could only be by way of punishment' for the purchaser's default. This, again, is a misnomer. The most obvious objective of the vendor is to snatch a windfall, not to punish the purchaser. Deane and Dawson JJ were only describing harsh treatment, that is, a penalty in the Feinbergian sense.

V. Other Controls Upon Sanctions

A. Nature of Sanctions

The sanctions considered here are produced by the innocent party's exercising a power, upon breach, to change the parties' contractual relationship in the future in a manner adverse to the contract-breaker's interests. The most drastic sanction is termination. Contract lawyers are accustomed to thinking of commercial contracts, where the usual instance is an express power to terminate the contract for breach by the other party. In contracts with a personal dimension, powers to expel (from an association or partnership) or to dismiss (from employment) for misconduct perform an equivalent role. Less extreme sanctions may alter the terms of the contract or the performance rendered under it. Breaches of contract can be taken into account in other ways, for example in exercising a discretion to award a performance bonus for the relevant period. I exclude discretionary

[171] It may have been substantially eroded in the United Kingdom by the development of the rule against penalties in *Cavendish*: see n 54.

[172] *Smyth* (n 59) 233; *Linggi Plantations* (n 48) 94; *Workers Trust* (n 40); *Amble Assets* (n 48) [43]. Compare *Cavendish* (n 3) [16] (Lord Neuberger and Lord Sumption), [156] (Lord Mance), [237]–[238] (Lord Hodge).

[173] *Mayson v Clouet* [1924] AC 980 (PC); *Pitt v Curotta* (1931) 31 SR (NSW) 477 (Eq Div); *McDonald* (n165) 478 (Dixon J); *Dies v British and International Mining and Finance Corp Ltd* [1939] 1 KB 724 (KBD).

[174] *Kilmer* (n 152) 325.

[175] *Stern* (n 157) 524.

bonuses and the like from consideration. The discretion does not depend upon breach and an unfavourable outcome is better understood as reflecting a lack of desert for reward.

Termination and lesser sanctions are considered in sections V.B and V.C. The discussion establishes two points. First, the exercise of an express right to terminate for breach will rarely constitute punishment. Even if it does so, the law has no objection to it. Second, there are some lesser sanctions that are distinctly punitive in character. These are not necessarily objectionable per se; the law regulates the proportionality between breach and punishment.

B. Express Rights to Terminate for Breach

Controls on termination may be sourced in the common law or in statute. Statutes do not follow any pattern amenable to systematic analysis. This is not to deny, however, that statutory restrictions or regulation can have a tremendous impact in practice, as in the case of unfair dismissal in employment.[176] Common law controls are various. The rule against penalties is not applied to a provision conferring an express right to terminate,[177] though a clause fixing compensation upon termination for breach is subject to review.[178] Relief against forfeiture may restrict termination for breach pursuant to a common law or contractual right. The conditions for relief make it relevant only in limited circumstances. Certainty in commercial dealings has been seen as an added reason for keeping a tight rein on the class of qualifying rights and on the award of relief in commercial cases.[179]

Common law rights to terminate for breach need not be exercised reasonably or in 'good faith'.[180] English law treats express rights to terminate for breach in the same way, in the absence of any express restriction.[181] Some Australian decisions, by contrast, have attached a 'good faith' requirement to an express right to terminate as a matter of general principle.[182] This has not gained

[176] Employment Rights Act 1996, pt X. See also text to n 145.

[177] See, eg, *Queensland Nickel Sales Pty Ltd v Mount Isa Mines Ltd* [2019] QCA 32 [121]–[122]. Nor does it apply to a provision expressly designating a non-essential term to be a condition: *Lombard North Central Plc v Butterworth* [1987] QB 527 (CA).

[178] *Financings Ltd v Baldock* [1963] 2 QB 104 (CA); *AMEV-UDC Finance Ltd v Austin* (1986) 162 CLR 170 (HCA); *Esanda Finance* (n 3).

[179] *The Scaptrade* [1983] QB 529 (CA), 540–41 (Robert Goff LJ); *The Scaptrade* (n 150) 703–04 (Lord Diplock); *Sport Internationaal* (n 150); *Vauxhall Motors* (n 150) [78]–[82] (Lady Arden).

[180] See, eg, *MSC Mediterranean Shipping Co SA v Cottonex Anstalt* [2016] EWCA Civ 789, [2016] 2 Lloyd's Rep 494 [45] (Moore-Bick LJ, with whom Tomlinson LJ and Keehan J agreed) rebuffing the suggestion by Leggatt J below: [2015] EWHC 283 (Comm), [2015] 1 Lloyd's Rep 359 [97].

[181] *Lomas v JFB Firth Rixson Inc* [2012] EWCA Civ 419, [2012] 2 Lloyd's Rep 548 [46]; *ENE Kos 1 Ltd v Petroleo Brasileiro SA (The Kos) (No 2)* [2012] UKSC 17, [2012] 2 AC 164 [7] (Lord Sumption, with whom Lord Walker and Lord Phillips agreed), [77] (Lord Clarke).

[182] *Renard Constructions (ME) Pty Ltd v Minister for Public Works* (1992) 26 NSWLR 234 (CA) is the seminal authority. See also *Burger King Corp v Hungry Jack's Pty Ltd* [2001] NSWCA 187, (2001) 69

universal acceptance[183] and a compelling justification remains elusive. The content of the 'good faith' requirement is also unsettled.

What does this mean for punishment? Taking common law rights to terminate as the yardstick,[184] it cannot be said that termination pursuant to an express right is necessarily harsher upon the contract-breaker. Much depends upon the particular breach, the conditions prescribed to activate the right and the consequences of its exercise. An express right has the potential to operate harshly when it is used to terminate for a breach that is not sufficiently serious to sustain termination at law. Contract law addresses this concern obliquely in several ways. The scope of a clause may be whittled down by construction, to confine it to serious breaches.[185] In Australia, 'good faith' may regulate the existence or exercise of the right to terminate for breach. It is often said that a party acting in good faith must have due regard to the other party's interests, though it need not put them ahead of its own.

The default consequences of termination for breach pursuant to an express right are, in both England and Australia, less severe in principle than those at common law. Although the contract-breaker is still denied the benefit of the bargain in the future, it is only liable for the innocent party's losses accrued up to the point of termination and not beyond.[186] Whether there is any practical difference thus turns on whether the innocent party suffers a loss by premature termination. Australian law permits parties, by express agreement, to override this exclusion of loss of bargain damages.[187] The rule against penalties has been applied more strictly in English law to shut out this possibility;[188] that stance may have softened after *Cavendish*.[189]

The symbolism of the act of termination depends upon context. Withdrawal of a vessel under charter for non-payment of hire says more about the shipowner's desire to capture a rising market, or to break free of an insolvent charterer, than it does about condemnation. An employer's dismissal of an employee for misconduct is consistent with self-protection, a desire to punish, or a mix of both. In a

NSWLR 558 [163], [186]; *Pacific Brands Sport & Leisure Pty Ltd v Underworks Pty Ltd* [2005] FCA 288, (2005) Aust Contract R 90-213 [64]–[66] (point not addressed on appeal: [2006] FCAFC 40, (2006) 149 FCR 395); *Bundanoon Sandstone Pty Ltd v Cenric Group Pty Ltd* [2019] NSWCA 87 [154]–[156] (Gleeson JA, with whom Meagher and McCallum JJA agreed).

183 See, eg, *Androvitsaneas v Members First Broker Network* [2013] VSCA 212 [108]–[109].

184 *Mann v Paterson Constructions Pty Ltd* [2019] HCA 32, (2019) 373 ALR 1 [39] ('termination for repudiation or breach is not an occasion for … inflicting a punishment').

185 *Antaios Compania Naviera SA v Salen Rederierna AB (The Antaios)* [1985] AC 191 (HL); *Rice v Great Yarmouth BC* (2001) 3 LGLR 4 (CA) [20]–[24].

186 *Overstone Ltd v Shipway* [1962] 1 WLR 117 (CA); *Shevill v Builders Licensing Board* (1982) 149 CLR 620 (HCA).

187 *Shevill* (n 186) 628 (Gibbs CJ, with whom Murphy and Brennan JJ agreed), 637 (Wilson J); *AMEV-UDC Finance* (n 178) 194 (Mason and Wilson JJ), 204–05 (Deane J), 210, 217 (Dawson J); *Esanda Finance* (n 3).

188 See, eg, *Baldock* (n 178).

189 See, eg, JW Carter and W Courtney, 'Breach of Condition and Express Termination Right: A Distinction with a Difference' (2017) 133 *LQR* 395, 414.

different context, a decision to disqualify a professional from practice is usually protective, not punitive, in character.[190] Feinberg's analysis cannot establish any general rule.

An additional quality of condemnation may have to be found in some expressed intention by the innocent party to punish, or in the manner of termination. Neither of these is relevant to the exercise of common law rights to terminate. Indeed, so long as the common law disregards harsh and humiliating treatment in the case of a wrongful dismissal,[191] it would be perverse to pay any regard to punitive intention in a *lawful* dismissal. The position is the same for express rights to terminate for breach. Even at its highest, the 'good faith' requirement recognised in some Australian decisions goes no further. It is sufficient that breach be a genuine reason for the innocent party's decision to terminate; additional motives are irrelevant.[192] Thus, a genuine decision to terminate for breach is valid even if accompanied by an intention to punish for that breach.

C. Lesser Sanctions

Discretionary sanctions appear in many forms. Contracts with a personal aspect may contain disciplinary procedures that call for the exercise of a discretion in response to breach. Short of dismissal, an employee may be issued with a warning, given a disciplinary suspension or demoted. Likewise, many sanctions applied in organised sport are not fixed in advance but depend upon determinations made by an arbiter. As above,[193] I do not claim that every discretionary sanction imposed in sport or employment is punitive in nature, merely that some can be.

It is natural to think in terms of the conditions for the exercise of the relevant contractual power and any express or implied restrictions upon it. Sanctions used in employment provide an illustration. The employer's power to suspend or demote must, in general, be conferred expressly.[194] There are many cases about observing procedural fairness before imposing a sanction. Disciplinary procedures are, nowadays, often written comprehensively, with an eye on dismissal as the ultimate sanction. The law on unfair dismissal under statute is, therefore, influential in this process. Of most interest is the sanction ultimately chosen by the employer and any limits on its severity. Suspensions and demotions

[190] *New South Wales Bar Association v Evatt* (1968) 117 CLR 177 (HCA), 183–84. Compare *Thompson v British Medical Association (NSW Branch)* [1924] AC 764 (PC), 769.

[191] *Addis v Gramophone Co Ltd* [1909] AC 488 (HL). But see *Johnson v Unisys Ltd* [2001] UKHL 13, [2003] 1 AC 518 [21], [24] (Lord Steyn), [43]–[46] (Lord Hoffmann, with whom Lord Bingham and Lord Millett agreed).

[192] *Asia Television Ltd v Yau's Entertainment Pty Ltd* [2000] FCA 254, (2000) 48 IPR 283 [76]–[77]; *Mangrove Mountain Quarries Pty Ltd v Barlow* [2007] NSWSC 492, (2007) 23 BCL 448 [28].

[193] See text following n 122.

[194] *Hanley v Pease & Partners Ltd* [1915] 1 KB 698 (KBD). Compare *Theedom v British Railways Board* [1976] IRLR 137 (IT) (power to demote implied by custom and usage).

can inflict hard treatment upon the employee, by loss of status, implications of incompetence,[195] and temporary or ongoing reduction in pay. A formal warning may entail the first two consequences and expose the employee to a greater risk of dismissal for misconduct in the future.

The striking feature of such sanctions is that they have been regarded as 'punishment'. The employer's power to punish is restricted, not proscribed. The 'punishment' must not be 'grossly out of proportion to the offence', nor 'imposed from improper motives'.[196] This test was developed originally for demotions; it has also been applied to warnings,[197] and would be equally apt for disciplinary suspensions.[198]

VI. Conclusion

As the law stands in England, the plainest objection to contracting parties agreeing to punish each other is doctrinal coherence. If punishment is not a function of contract law, and punitive damages are unavailable for breach of contract, parties should not circumvent that policy by express agreement. Were the law to change, as it has in Canada, other objections come to the fore. These include: that the innocent party lacks authority to punish; that there are insufficient procedural protections for the contract-breaker; and that, for substantive consistency or deeper policy reasons, punishment must be determined by an agent acting on behalf of the state. The last two objections are general; the first objection admits exceptions.

For all of that, the policy that parties cannot agree to punish each other has relatively little traction in the law of contract. It is not the principal rationale of the rule against penalties, despite frequent statements to the contrary. Nor does it figure in relief against forfeiture or restrictions upon termination for breach. Indeed, in limited circumstances, punitive sanctions are tolerated. The law is then concerned to regulate the proportionality between breach and sanction. *Cavendish* overstates the proscription of punishment. Given the boundaries of the rule against penalties, it also encourages uneven treatment of fixed and discretionary sanctions.

The faint relevance of punishment is not surprising. It would be peculiar for major contract doctrines to be constructed around atypical considerations. With

[195] *Mezey v South West London and St George's Mental Health NHS Trust* [2007] EWCA Civ 106, [2007] IRLR 244 [12] (Sedley LJ, with whom Dyson LJ and Sir Peter Gibson agreed) (precautionary suspension).

[196] *Theedom* (n 194); *British Broadcasting Corp v Beckett* [1983] IRLR 43 (EAT). See also *Cawley v South Wales Electricity Board* [1985] IRLR 89 (EAT).

[197] *Stanley Cole (Wainfleet) Ltd v Sheridan* [2003] ICR 297 (EAT) [68] (appeal on procedural grounds dismissed: [2003] EWCA Civ 1046, [2003] ICR 1449).

[198] The implied term of mutual trust and confidence may place other limits on the exercise of the power: *Gogay v Hertfordshire County Council* [2000] EWCA Civ 228, [2000] IRLR 703; *London Borough of Lambeth v Agoreyo* [2019] EWCA Civ 322, [2019] ICR 1572 (precautionary suspensions).

the exception of contracts with a personal element, it must be relatively rare for a party to want to punish another for breach of contract. Self-interest is far more important. Peeling away the punishment rationale from contract doctrine exposes more fundamental concerns. Other justifications must be found, particularly for the rule against penalties. And if punishment is occasionally permitted, the law of contract must develop a better understanding of when this is so, and what limits are placed upon it.

13

Controlling Private Punishment in Three Dimensions: Penalties and Forfeiture in England and Australia

NICHOLAS A TIVERIOS AND BEN McFARLANE

I. Introduction and Overview

In *Union Eagle Ltd v Golden Achievement Ltd*, Lord Hoffmann observed that the 'boundaries of the equitable jurisdiction to relieve against contractual penalties and forfeitures are in some places imprecise'.[1] This chapter considers those two non-statutory means by which private law controls parties' attempts to build the possibility of punishment into their private dealings: the rule against penalties (the rule) and the doctrine of relief against forfeiture (the doctrine). It examines them by considering three contrasts: between the rule and the doctrine; between common law and equity; and between English and Australian law. We suggest that a careful examination of the operation of the rule and the doctrine provides valuable broader lessons not only about private law's attitude to punishment, but also about the relationship of common law and equity, and of the differences between the English and Australian approaches. Such an examination is also timely, as recent decisions of the Supreme Court of the United Kingdom and of the High Court of Australia have raised as many questions about the rule and the doctrine as they have answered.[2]

The key distinction made in this chapter is between two basic forms of intervention that courts may employ in order to deal with parties' attempts to create rights which are regarded, for some reason, as objectionable. When considering the rule and the doctrine, the objection is related to the punitive effect of the planned rights, but the same responses are available to deal with rights that are objectionable for different reasons. The first response consists of a court holding

[1] *Union Eagle Ltd v Golden Achievement Ltd* [1997] AC 514 (PC), 518.

[2] Indeed, in its still more recent examination of the rule, the Court of Appeal of Singapore adopted an approach that varies from each of the current English and Australian positions. See *Denka Advantech Pte Ltd v Seraya Energy Pte Ltd* [2020] SGCA 119, referred to here at n 72 and n 114.

that the parties did not have the power to create the purported objectionable right. The most direct means of doing so is to say that the purported right is void: it was never brought into being or acquired by either party. The second response consists instead of recognising that that the right does exist, but limiting the extent to which it can be enforced or asserted. Some subtle but potentially practically important differences turn on which of these two sub-forms is employed. In the context of dealing with a right of A that A and B agreed to create but which is regarded as punishing B, the similarities of these two sub-forms are more significant than those differences: they share the feature that, even though A and B agreed that A should have a particular right, the punitive effect of that right means that private law prevents A's enforcing it as agreed.

The English version of the rule against penalties, as set out by the Supreme Court in its decisions in *Cavendish Square Holding BV v Makdessi*[3] and *ParkingEye Ltd v Beavis*,[4] is an example of the first form of response. The most obvious reason for such a response, expressed in the joint judgment of Lord Sumption and Lord Neuberger when hearing those conjoined appeals, is that the parties' agreement is 'by its nature contrary to the policy of the law'.[5] The policy goal in this context must be linked to the courts' insistence, seen in the general law of remedies, that a response to B's civil wrong against A must not aim to punish B.[6] The parties' general power to determine the substantive content of the rights arising from their agreement is thereby limited: a punitive remedial right is one which the parties have no competence to create.

The second response has a different form and instead consists of the court restraining A's attempt to enforce an admittedly existing right against B. In such a case, there is no denial that A and B had the power to create that right, and indeed the right may still have some important practical effects. It cannot therefore be said that the right was, from the outset, either void or wholly unenforceable. Rather, given the particular circumstances which exist at the time of A's attempted enforcement of the right, a court can at that point limit A's use of the right against B. This form of intervention, like the first, thus has a disabling effect, but the power denied to A is a power of A to enforce the right in a particular way, rather than the power of A to create or enforce the right at all. Such intervention is therefore more limited than the first form in two, interconnected ways. First, there is no attempt

[3] *Cavendish Square Holding BV v Makdessi* [2015] UKSC 67, [2016] AC 1172.

[4] ibid.

[5] ibid [9] (Lord Neuberger and Lord Sumption). See also *Pencil Hill Ltd v US Citta Di Palermo SpA* (HC, 19 January 2016) [24] (Bird J); *TK (Hong Kong) Ltd v Diamond Milk Formulas Ltd* [2016] NZHC 2642 [39] (Doogue J); *Wilaci Pty Ltd v Torchlight Fund No 1 LP (in receivership)* [2017] NZCA 152, [2017] 3 NZLR 293 [55] (Kós P); *Holyoake v Candy* [2017] EWHC 3397 (Ch) [467] (Nugee J): 'In English law the doctrine of penalties applies only to contractual provisions operating on a breach of contract; the penalty rule regulates only the remedies available for breach of a party's primary obligations, not the primary obligations themselves.'

[6] *Cavendish* (n 3) [7]–[14] (Lord Neuberger and Lord Sumption), [129]–[130] (Lord Mance), [239]–[241], [243] (Lord Hodge). See also *Export Credits Guarantee Department v Universal Oil Products Co* [1983] 1 WLR 399 (HL).

to deny that A and B did validly create the right and so that right may still have an impact: the court can place conditions on the circumstances in which B can resist enforcement, for example by allowing A to enforce the right in part, or by allowing B to resist enforcement, in whole or in part, only if B meets certain conditions. Second, a court can, indeed must, take into account the circumstances at the time when A attempts to enforce the right, and not only those that existed at the point when the right was created. In some cases, this may assist A, by allowing A to show that, given a change in circumstances, the reasons for preventing A's full enforcement of the right do not now obtain.

In each of England[7] and Australia,[8] the doctrine of relief against forfeiture is an example of this second form of response. Given its form, such a response cannot simply be based on a policy that denies parties the power to create particular rights. In the case of the doctrine, we argue, this type of response is explained by, and tailored to, a broader concern to prevent A's making use of a right in a way that is, as regards B, unconscientious. We focus here on the particular strand of the doctrine that deals with rights created by A and B for the purpose of providing A with security for the non-occurrence of a particular event, which may or may not involve breach by B of a contractual duty owed to A.[9] In that strand, the doctrine prevents a use of a right by A that would be unconscientious, as against B, in a specific way: it would involve using a security right for a purpose other than as security.[10] The principal reason for controlling such use by A is that it would be inconsistent with the substantive purpose for which the right was created, and thus the basis on which B agreed to its creation. This strand of the doctrine thus provides an example of a broader idea: where a right is created by A and B for a specific shared purpose, it may then be unconscientious, as against B, for A to use that right against B for a different purpose.

The Australian version of the rule (against penalties) is, in our view, also an example of this second form of response, and shares the rationale of the doctrine (of relief against forfeiture) as applied to security rights. We also argue that this understanding of the rule against penalties is consistent with the historical origins

[7] See, eg, *Shiloh Spinners Ltd v Harding* [1973] AC 691 (HL), 722 (Lord Wilberforce); *Manchester Ship Canal Company Ltd v Vauxhall Motors Ltd (formerly General Motors UK Ltd)* [2019] UKSC 46, [2019] 3 WLR 852 [35]–[50] (Lord Briggs).

[8] See, eg, *Stern v Mcarthur* (1988) 165 CLR 489 (HCA); *Tanwar Enterprises Pty Ltd v Cauchi* [2003] HCA 57, (2003) 217 CLR 315 [58] (Gleeson CJ, McHugh, Gummow, Hayne and Heydon JJ); *Mineralogy Pty Ltd v Sino Iron Pty Ltd (No 6)* [2015] FCA 825, (2015) 329 ALR 1 [987] (Edelman J).

[9] The other strand of the doctrine concerns circumstances where A's enforcement of the impugned right or power as against B can be limited instead on the grounds of 'fraud, accident, mistake or surprise': *Shiloh Spinners* (n 7) 722–23 (Lord Wilberforce). Such circumstances are beyond the scope of this chapter as they transcend the idea of controlling for private punishment. See further text at n 32 and n 33.

[10] We note that there is a fundamental tension here about the extent to which equity can identify a right as a security right, and thus limit its enforcement, even if, on the face of the transaction, the right does not take the form of a security right. Such a tension is as old as the equitable maxim that 'once a mortgage always a mortgage'. See, eg, NA Tiverios, *Contractual Penalties in Australia and the United Kingdom: History, Theory and Practice* (Sydney, Federation Press, 2019) 25–39, 45–67, 104–09.

of the English rule,[11] and indeed with its operation until late in the twentieth century. This analysis has consequences for how best to understand the differences between English and Australian law in this area, and also for the difficult questions arising in each of English and Australian law as to the scope of the doctrine (of relief against forfeiture) and its relationship with the rule (against penalties). We argue that Australian law, by sticking more closely to the historical basis of both the doctrine and the rule, now faces a situation in which it is rationally very difficult to maintain the distinction between the doctrine and the rule. As a result, there is a strong case for the Australian courts now taking a unified approach to forfeiture and penalties. There would be two chief practical consequences of such an approach. The first would be to confirm the removal, foreshadowed by Edelman J in *Mineralogy Pty Ltd v Sino Iron Pty Ltd (No 6)*,[12] of the limit of relief against forfeiture to cases where B loses a proprietary or possessory right; the second, which would require overruling some existing authority in relation to the rule against penalties, would be to apply the relevant tests not at the time when the impugned term was agreed, but rather at the point when A seeks to enforce it against B.[13]

Our prescription for English law is different. In *Manchester Ship Canal Company Ltd v Vauxhall Motors Ltd (formerly General Motors UK Ltd)*,[14] a majority[15] of the Supreme Court rejected an argument, based in part on suggestions in the Australian authorities, that English law should give up the proprietary or possessory right requirement in order to engage the doctrine (of relief against forfeiture).[16] Whilst some powerful arguments can be made against this limit,[17] it cannot be said to be inconsistent with the English courts' current approach to penalties. Indeed, maintaining the proprietary or possessory right requirement may be necessary in order to support the position, confirmed in *Cavendish*, that the English rule against penalties, unlike its Australian counterpart, applies only to terms that seek to regulate the consequences of B's breach of a contract with A.

[11] See the discussion below, text at nn 35–39.

[12] *Mineralogy (No 6)* (n 8) [981] (Edelman J). See also *Mineralogy Pty Ltd v Sino Iron Pty Ltd* [2017] FCAFC 55 [421]; *Auburn Shopping Village Pty Ltd v Nelmeer Hoteliers Pty Ltd* [2018] NSWCA 114, 19 BPR 38569 [25] (Bathurst CJ); *Ayers Rock SkyShip Pty Ltd v Voyages Indigenous Tourism Australia Pty Ltd* [2019] NSWSC 828 19 BPR 39541 [106]–[107] (Drake J); *JPA Finance Pty Ltd v Gordon Nominees Pty Ltd* [2019] VSCA 159, 58 VR 393 [82]. But see *Kay v Playup Australia Pty Ltd* [2020] NSWCA 33 [100]–[123], where Brereton JA favoured the English approach and took a more restrictive reading of Australian law to conclude obiter that 'the doctrine [of relief against forfeiture] is confined to proprietary or possessory rights, and does not extend to mere contractual rights' (Macfarlan JA and Simpson AJA not deciding this point).

[13] But see the discussion at n 110.

[14] *Manchester Ship Canal* (n 7).

[15] Lord Briggs, with whom Lord Carnwath, Lady Black and Lord Kitchin agreed. Lady Arden concurred in the result but took a different view on the specific question of whether the doctrine is limited to cases where B loses a proprietary or possessory right.

[16] *Manchester Ship Canal* (n 7) [35]–[50] (Lord Briggs).

[17] ibid [69], [83]–[89] (Lady Arden). This case has been noted by one of the authors: NA Tiverios, 'The Forfeiture of Contractual Rights' (2020) 79 *CLJ* 17.

If the doctrine of relief against forfeiture were allowed to operate more widely in English law, there is a risk that it would then remove the freedom *Cavendish* confers on the parties to impose a punitive burden on B on the happening of an event other than B's breach of a contract with A. Arguments can of course also be made against that limit on the scope of the penalties rule, but its existence provides a clear reason for English law also to differ from Australian law as to the scope of relief against forfeiture.

Our analysis also has implications for understanding the role of equity in each of England and Australia. In our view, it is no coincidence that the determination by the Supreme Court in *Cavendish* that the English rule rests on public policy, and operates to deny the parties' creation a particular type of right, was accompanied by an analysis of the rule as operating at common law rather than in equity. That is because the distinction between the two general forms of response identified above has been reflected in the distinction between common law and equity, with the first form of response (rendering a purported term void or wholly unenforceable) the preserve of common law and the second type of response (controlling the enforcement of a valid right) characteristic instead of equity.[18] In *Cavendish*, the sequential consideration of the rule (against penalties) and then the doctrine (of relief against forfeiture) was contemplated, in cases involving a breach by B of B's contract with A.[19] This is consistent with our argument that the former, common law rule asks if A's right against B exists at all, whereas the latter, equitable doctrine answers the different question of whether A can be prevented from enforcing an admittedly valid right. More broadly, the formal difference between a rule that determines the validity of a right and a doctrine that instead controls the enforcement of such a right, is often crucial to justifying the continued existence of a distinct equitable doctrine. For example, where, following a promise by A to B in relation to an existing contractual right of A against B, promissory estoppel operates to restrain A's assertion of a contractual right against B, equity does not purport to amend the doctrine of consideration and find that A's contractual right has been varied; rather, equity recognises the validity of A's right but limits its enforcement. Recognising the distinct form of equity's intervention can show why equity does not undermine – indeed, it may even support – an existing common law rule.[20]

This does not mean, however, that equity is always welcome: the fact of a formal difference does not necessarily prevent a substantive clash. This can be seen, for example, in relation to common mistake in the law of contract. As the common

[18] But not exclusive to equity; for example, the common law vitiating factor of duress renders a contract voidable: *Pao On v Lau Yiu Long* [1980] AC 614 (PC), 636 (Lord Scarman); *Crescendo Management Pty Ltd v Westpac Banking Corporation* (1988) 19 NSWLR 40 (CA), 45–46 (McHugh JA). See also the discussion at n 47.

[19] *Cavendish* (n 3) [160] (Lord Mance).

[20] For a broader discussion of this point, see B McFarlane, 'Form and Substance in Equity' in A Robertson and J Goudkamp (eds), *Form and Substance in the Law of Obligations* (Oxford, Hart Publishing, 2019) 197.

law rules regulate the initial question of whether or not a contract has been made at all, there is formal space for an equitable rule that instead controls the parties' powers to enforce rights under the contract, perhaps allowing them to do so only if certain conditions imposed by the court are met. Yet, as recognised by the Court of Appeal in *Great Peace Shipping v Tsavliris*,[21] there is not substantive space for such an equitable doctrine of common mistake if there are no circumstances in which the common mistake is *not* of a type serious enough to make the contract void at common law but is sufficiently serious otherwise to justify limiting A's enforcement of A's rights under the admittedly valid contract. This lack of substantive space for equitable intervention may now also be the position in English law in cases where a term imposes a burden on B on the occurrence of an event other than B's breach of a contract with A: the freedom of the parties to impose such burdens, recognised in *Cavendish*, also overrides any attempt to limit A's power to enforce such a right by reference to the substantive burden imposed on B.[22] At the moment, of course, that freedom *is* limited by English law in cases where the burden imposed is B's loss of a proprietary or possessory right. The operation of the doctrine (of relief against forfeiture) in those cases is seen as sufficiently well-established as to be beyond question; in other cases, though, the need to preserve the parties' freedom of contract is seen as decisive and, as a result, the doctrine is allowed to go no further.[23]

This analysis is consistent with, and indeed depends on, the secondary nature of equity as a system that can control the acquisition and enforcement of primary rights recognised at common law.[24] On this view, a key part of the function of equity is to mitigate unwelcome effects of those primary rules, and thus to assist in their justification.[25] This has consequences for comparing equitable doctrines in

[21] *Great Peace Shipping v Tsavliris Salvage (International) Ltd* [2002] EWCA Civ 1407, [2003] QB 679 (CA), 724. But see *Solle v Butcher* [1950] 1 KB 671 (CA) 690, where Denning LJ (in the context of common mistake) said '[i]n order to see whether [a contract] can be avoided for this mistake it is necessary to remember that mistake is of two kinds: first, mistake which renders the contract void, that is, a nullity from the beginning, which is the kind of mistake which was dealt with by the courts of common law; and, secondly, mistake which renders the contract not void, but voidable, that is, liable to be set aside on such terms as the court thinks fit, which is the kind of mistake which was dealt with by the courts of equity'.

[22] Of course, other reasons recognised in equity as general bases for preventing A's enforcement of a valid right (eg a pre-contractual misrepresentation, or undue influence) would continue to apply if relevant on the facts, as these do not undermine the parties' freedom as to the substance of their contract.

[23] *Manchester Ship Canal* (n 7) [50] (Lord Briggs).

[24] FW Maitland, *Equity: A Course of Lectures*, revised edn (Cambridge, Cambridge University Press, 1936) 16–19; V Windeyer, *Lectures on Legal History*, 2nd revised edn (Sydney, Law Book Co, 1957) 259.

[25] See, eg, B McFarlane, 'Equitable Estoppel as a Cause of Action: Neither One Thing Nor One Other' in S Degeling, J Edelman and J Goudkamp (eds), *Contract in Commercial Law* (Sydney, Law Book Co, 2016) 359; McFarlane (n 20); B McFarlane and R Stevens, 'What's Special about Equity?' in D Klimchuk, I Samet and H E Smith (eds), *Philosophical Foundations of the Law of Equity* (Oxford, Oxford University Press, 2020) 191; HE Smith, 'Equitable Defences as Meta-Law' in PS Davies, S Douglas and J Goudkamp (eds), *Defences in Equity* (Oxford, Hart Publishing, 2018) 17; HE Smith, 'Equity as Meta-Law' (*Yale Law Journal*, forthcoming); Nicholas A Tiverios and Michael JR Crawford, 'Equitable property and the law of the horse: Assignment, intermediated securities, and data trusts' (2020) 14 *Journal of Equity* 272.

different jurisdictions. Even if those doctrines have a common origin in the courts of Chancery, divergence is likely as differences develop in the primary rights in each jurisdiction, set not only by common law but also by statute. Indeed, the area of penalties and forfeiture is not the first one in which English and Australian judges have taken different views of the permitted scope of equitable intervention; given continued differences in the common law and statutory rules of each jurisdiction, it is unlikely to be the last. This, however, should come as no surprise, and any desire for a global law of equity is misplaced as it overlooks the key equitable function of regulating the enforcement, and thus mitigating the effects, of rights set by common law and statute.

II. Shared Origins: Penalties and Forfeiture; England and Australia

Notwithstanding the modern differences between them outlined in section I, the four areas considered in this chapter (each of the rule against penalties and the doctrine of forfeiture in English law; and each of those two in Australia) have a common origin. The equitable doctrine (of relief against forfeiture) concerns the long-established[26] principle under which B will be prevented from losing a proprietary or possessory right[27] to A on an event of default, even where the strict legal effect of a transaction between A and B is to produce such a result.[28]

There are two separate grounds on which equity will grant relief from forfeiture.[29] The first operates where A has a right against B that was intended, as a matter of substance, to secure some other primary result (eg, B's payment of money or B's performance of some contractual duty) and does so by stipulating that B will lose a proprietary or possessory right if the secured result does not occur. Equity will relieve B from the forfeiture of that right on the condition that B compensates A (including interest and costs) for the failure of the secured result.[30] The second

[26] Which, as noted, shares its origins with the penalties doctrine. See also *Jobson v Johnson* [1989] 1 WLR 1026 (CA).

[27] On the importance of a property right to engage the doctrine, see especially *Shiloh Spinners* (n 7) 722 (Lord Wilberforce); *Scandinavian Trading Tanker Co AB v Flota Petrolera Ecuatoriana ('The Scaptrade')* [1983] 2 AC 694 (HL); *Sport Internationaal Bussum BV v Inter-Footwear Ltd* [1984] 1 WLR 776 (HL); *BICC Plc v Burndy Corporation* [1984] 1 Ch 232 (CA), 252 (Dillon LJ); *Manchester Ship Canal* (n 7) [35]–[50] (Lord Briggs).

[28] *Peachy v Duke of Somerset* (1721) 1 Str 447, 452–53; 93 ER 626, 630 (Lord Macclesfield); *Cukurova Finance International Ltd v Alfa Telecom Turkey Ltd* [2013] UKPC 25, [2016] AC 923 [90] (Lord Neuberger); JD Heydon, MJ Leeming and PG Turner, *Meagher, Gummow & Lehane's Equity: Doctrines & Remedies*, 5th edn (Sydney, Butterworths, 2015) para 18-210.

[29] *Shiloh Spinners* (n 7) 722 (Lord Wilberforce); *Legione v Hateley* (1983) 152 CLR 406 (HCA), 424–25 (Gibbs CJ and Murphy J); Heydon, Leeming and Turner (n 28) para 18-250; *Australia Capital Financial Management Pty Ltd v Linfield Developments Pty Ltd* [2017] NSWCA 99, (2017) 18 BPR 36683 [357] (Ward JA).

[30] *G&C Kreglinger v New Patagonia Meat and Cold Storage Co Ltd* [1914] AC 25 (HL), 49–50 (Lord Parker); *Shiloh Spinners* (n 7) 722–23 (Lord Wilberforce); S Worthington, 'What is Left of Equity's Relief Against Forfeiture' in E Bant and M Harding (eds), *Exploring Private Law* (Cambridge,

ground applies beyond the context of security rights and involves circumstances where A has engaged in an unconscientious exercise of a legal right or legal power.[31] That is, B may be entitled to retain her proprietary or possessory right in circumstances where A's acquisition of B's right is affected by 'fraud, accident, mistake or surprise'[32] and where A has sufficient notice of the impugned circumstances such that A's insistence on the forfeiture is unconscionable.[33] For the purposes of this chapter, relief on the unconscionability basis can be put to one side for the simple reason that it has nothing to do with the regulation of civil punishment.[34]

The law of penalties developed into a relatively settled and identifiable equitable rule by around the time of the Restoration (1660).[35] At that point, the rule against penalties took the form of an exclusively equitable rule that was indistinguishable from the equitable doctrine to provide relief against forfeiture in relation to security rights. Accordingly, penalties and forfeitures were both captured by a broad-based equitable jurisdiction applicable to control (or disable) A's assertion of an otherwise valid legal term as against B, provided that the impugned legal term was 'in the nature of a security'[36] designed to ensure that B brought about a particular primary result. If a legal term was in the nature of a security then, if the matter before the Lord Chancellor[37] involved B's failure to bring about that

Cambridge University Press, 2010) 249, 254; L Smith, 'Relief Against Forfeiture: A Restatement' (2001) 60 *CLJ* 178, 195–97.

[31] *Shiloh Spinners* (n 7) 722; *Legione* (n 29) 424, 447 (Mason and Deane JJ); *Stern* (n 8); *Tanwar* (n 8) [58] (Gleeson CJ, McHugh, Gummow, Hayne and Heydon JJ); *Mineralogy (No 6)* (n 8) [981], [987].

[32] *Shiloh Spinners* (n 7) 722–23 (Lord Wilberforce).

[33] For example, relief is often refused under this head on the basis that A has done nothing unconscionable: *ACCC v CG Berbatis Holdings Pty Ltd* [2003] HCA 18, (2003) 214 CLR 51 [42] (Gummow and Hayne JJ); *Tanwar* (n 8) [63] (Gleeson CJ, McHugh, Gummow, Hayne and Heydon JJ); *Auburn* (n 12) [60]–[65] (Bathurst CJ).

[34] In this connection it was correctly observed by Gibbs CJ and Murphy J in *Legione* (n 29) 425 that, 'except in the sense that a provision for forfeiture can be described as a penalty it is unnecessary that the condition which provides for forfeiture should be a penal one before the jurisdiction of equity [to relieve against a forfeiture] can be invoked'. See also the similar observations of Mason and Deane JJ, ibid at 444–45, which illustrate that the unconscionability basis for relief against forfeiture is wider than the need to prevent punishment.

[35] WH Loyd, 'Penalties and Forfeitures: Before *Peachy v The Duke of Somerset*' (1915) 29 *Harvard Law Review* 117, 125; DEC Yale, 'An Essay on Mortgages and Trusts and Allied Topics in Equity' in DEC Yale (ed), *Lord Nottingham's Chancery Cases*, vol 2 (London, B Quaritch, 1957–61) 15; AWB Simpson, 'The Penal Bond with Conditional Defeasance' (1966) 82 *LQR* 392, 417. See also *Hall v Higham* (1663) Ch Rep 5; 21 ER 711; *Wilson v Barton* (1671) Nels 148; 21 ER 812; *Friend v Burgh* (1679) Rep T Finch 437; 23 ER 238. The fact that such relief was common is illustrated by a 1675 case in which a plaintiff first sought to enforce a conditional bond in the Court of Chancery, given that the defendant would likely seek equitable relief had the plaintiff sought to enforce the bond in the Court of Common Pleas: *Finch v Finch* in DEC Yale (ed), *Lord Nottingham's Chancery Cases*, vol 1 (London, B Quaritch, 1957–61) 403. See also H Potter, *An Introduction to the History of Equity and its Courts* (London, Sweet & Maxwell, 1931), regarding the equivalent development of the equity of redemption. On the wider history in this area (including an overview of progenitor rules to the modern penalties doctrine), see Tiverios (n 10) 9–44.

[36] Yale (n 35) 24–25. See also *Sloman v Walter* (1783) 1 Bro CC 418, 419; 28 ER 1213, 1214 (Lord Thurlow); JL Barton, 'Penalties and Damages' (1976) 92 *LQR* 20, 23.

[37] Or Lord Keepers, as sometimes the monarch appointed a Lord Keeper of the Great Seal. Insofar as the functions of Chancery as a court of equity are concerned, the functions of a Lord Chancellor

underlying primary result, provided that A could be compensated for the failure, the strict legal enforcement of the impugned term would be disabled so that it would 'not be allowed generally to work a forfeiture or inflict a penalty'.[38] Indeed, as late as 1914, Viscount Haldane was able to say that equitable control of the powers of a mortgagee was 'merely a special application of a more general power to relieve against penalties and to mould them into mere securities'.[39]

On this equitable conception of the rule against penalties, it clearly falls, like the doctrine of relief against forfeiture, into the second of the two basic forms of intervention discussed in section I: it does not deny A and B the power to create a particular type of right, it rather disables the strict enforcement of an otherwise valid legal right, by ensuring that the enforcement of the right is consistent with its nature as a security right, created by A and B for the purpose of securing a particular primary result (which may, but need not, be B's performance of a particular contractual duty or condition).[40] At a high level of generality, if A's right is acquired on that basis, it would be against conscience for A then to take advantage of that right by using it to gain a benefit, or to impose a punishment on B, that is 'extravagant' in the sense that it clearly exceeds the benefit or the burden that would have resulted to A, or have been imposed on B, had the underlying secured primary result occurred.[41] Lord Macclesfield, for example, stated in the seminal case of

and Lord Keeper were not materially different: Windeyer (n 24) 253. Note too that other courts had an equitable jurisdiction, such as the London Mayoral Court and the Court of Exchequer.

[38] Yale (n 35) 24–25.

[39] *Kreglinger* (n 30) 35 (Viscount Haldane). See also *Thompson v Hudson* (1869) LR 4 HL 1 (HL), 15 (Lord Hatherley); *Forestry Commission of NSW v Stefanetto* (1976) 133 CLR 507 (HCA), 519 (Mason J). The first English edition of *Story's Commentaries*, published in 1884, notes, albeit critically, an emerging distinction between penalties in the nature of a security and punitive forfeitures in the nature of a security. The distinction being that relief against forfeiture was then being applied more narrowly, ie only in circumstances where the secured default was the failure to pay a sum certain and not where 'the forfeiture arises from the breach of any other covenants of a collateral nature; as for example, of a covenant to repair'. Importantly, the author of *Story* notes that this was a mere arbitrary distinction rather than a positive justification for differing treatment between penalties and forfeitures. In an observation that fits the central thesis of this chapter, 'in the case of a penalty, such a distinction is wholly repudiated; because the penalty is treated as a security. The forfeiture is also treated as a security, in the cases of non-payment of rent. And in other cases of covenant, if the damages are capable of being ascertained, and will, in a legal and equitable sense, be an adequate compensation, the reason is not very clear why, under such circumstances, the forfeiture may not be equally treated as a security for such damages.': WE Grigsby, *Story's Commentaries on Equity Jurisprudence,* 1st English edn (London, Stevens and Haynes, 1884) 912. For discussion of the 19th-century judicial debate as to the scope of forfeiture, see, eg, *Shiloh Spinners* (n 7) 724–25 (Lord Wilberforce).

[40] Note there is the potential for relief against forfeiture and the equitable penalties rule to apply absent a breach of duty by B, and instead on the fulfilment (or non-fulfilment) of a contractual stipulation within B's power to control. On relief against forfeiture absent a breach of duty, see *UK Housing Alliance (North West) Ltd v Francis* [2010] EWCA Civ 117, [2010] 3 All ER 519 [10]–[15] (Longmore LJ); JD Heydon, MJ Leeming and PG Turner (n 28) paras 18-010, 18-315. On relief against penalties absent a breach of duty in Australia, see Tiverios (n 10) 103–20.

[41] See, eg, *Marks v Marks* (1718) Prec Ch 486, 488–89; 24 ER 218, 219 (Sir Thomas Powis and Sir Robert Raymond); *Peachy* (n 28) 452–53; 630 (Lord Macclesfield); *Roy v Duke of Beaufort* (1741) 2 Atk 190, 192–93; 26 ER 519, 520 (Lord Hardwicke); *Lowe v Peers* (1768) 4 Burr 2225, 2228–29; 98 ER 160, 162 (Lord Mansfield); *Sloman* (n 36) 419; 1214 (Lord Thurlow); *Clark v Watkins* (1863) 1 New Rep 227

Peachy v Duke of Somerset that '[t]he true ground of relief against penalties is from the original intent of the case, where the penalty is designed only to secure money, and the Court gives him all that he expected or desired'.[42]

III. Divergence: Penalties and Forfeiture; England and Australia

A. The Current Position: Penalties

Notwithstanding the clear equitable starting point of the English rule against penalties, this area of law was significantly reformed over the course of the twentieth century, as was confirmed by the Supreme Court's decisions in the conjoined 2015 appeals of *Cavendish*[43] and *ParkingEye*.[44] In deciding those two cases, the Supreme Court held that the English rule against penalties, whatever its historical origins, is now properly characterised as a rule of common law[45] and not a rule of equity. As noted in section I, the rule now clearly has the first of the general forms set out there: it operates to deny A and B the power to create a valid legal right. Its scope of operation is limited to cases where the term imposes a burden on B as a result of B's breach of a contractual duty to A, and does so in such a way that it imposes a 'secondary obligation'.[46] The Supreme Court also reformulated the test for determining whether such a term is 'penal': this will be the case only if it 'imposes a detriment on the contract-breaker out of all proportion to any legitimate interest of the innocent party in the enforcement of the primary obligation'. Where an agreed remedy clause fails this test, the consequence is that the term is void (or wholly unenforceable)[47] and imposes no duty on B, so that A is left to

(Ch D) 228 (Stuart VC); *Thompson* (n 39) 15 (Lord Hatherley); *Protector Endowment Loan and Annuity Co v Grice* (1880) 5 QBD 592 (CA) 595 (Baggallay LJ); *ACCC* (n 33) [42] (Gummow and Hayne JJ); *Tanwar* (n 8) [58] (Gleeson CJ, McHugh, Gummow, Hayne and Heydon JJ); *Andrews v Australia and New Zealand Banking Group Ltd* [2012] HCA 30, (2012) 247 CLR 205 [10] (French CJ, Gummow, Crennan, Kiefel and Bell JJ); *Cukurova* (n 28) [90] (Lord Neuberger); Several Gentlemen of the Respective Branches of Law, *A Supplement to Viner's Abridgement*, vol V (London, A Strahan, 1805) 375.

[42] *Peachy* (n 28) 453; 630.

[43] *Cavendish* (n 3).

[44] ibid.

[45] On the academic historical debate concerning the extent to which the common law developed an independent rule against penalties, see the authorities collected in Tiverios (n 10) 30–31.

[46] *Cavendish* (n 3) [32] (Lord Neuberger and Lord Sumption).

[47] For convenience we will simply refer to a penalty clause as being 'void' under the English approach. However, it may be possible for an otherwise void penalty clause to have some potentially valid applications under English law. For example, it is possible for a clause to be a penalty at English law where it hinges on multiple events of default, some of which constitute a breach of contract and other events that would not constitute a breach, provided the matter before the court involves a breach event. Accordingly, the same clause would not be a penalty (and thus valid) if the matter before the court involved a non-breach event: *Cooden Engineering Co Ltd v Stanford* [1953] 1 QB 86 (CA), 96–97 (Somerwell LJ); *Wright v Prudential Assurance Co Ltd* [2018] EWHC 402 (Ch), [2018] Bus LR 1173 [23] (Pymont QC).

seek a remedy pursuant to general law principles governing relief for breach of contract.[48]

In defining the rule against penalties as a product of common law, the Supreme Court consciously rejected the more historically-orientated approach of the High Court of Australia in *Andrews v Australia and New Zealand Banking Group Ltd*.[49] That decision reaffirmed the equitable basis of the rule and set out the penalties doctrine in a manner that is conceptually similar to the security rights basis of relief against forfeiture and can therefore apply to any such right, whether or not it is triggered by a B's breach of a contractual duty owed to A.[50] The test applied to see if a term falling within the scope of the rule is penal is materially identical to the English test, but the influence of the equitable characterisation can be seen in the Australian view of the consequences of terms failing that test. The purpose of intervention is to restrain the exercise of A's security right in order to ensure that it is only enforced to the extent necessary to secure to A performance of the related primary condition (or the monetised equivalent of performance). As a result, where partial enforcement of A's security right may be all that is required to achieve the substance of the underlying secured primary condition, the court may provide for a scaled down or *pro tanto* enforcement of A's security.

B. The Current Position: Forfeiture

In each of England and Australia, there has been little change in the basis of the doctrine of relief against forfeiture, as applied to security rights. In *Cukurova Finance International Ltd v Alfa Telecom Turkey Ltd*,[51] for example, Lord Neuberger described the 'paradigm case for relief' against forfeiture in a way that Lord Macclesfield[52] or Viscount Haldane[53] would have recognised:

> [T]he primary object of the bargain is to secure a stated result which can be effectively attained when the matter comes before the court, and where the forfeiture provision is added by way of security for the production of that result.[54]

Likewise, there is a contentious issue regarding whether a punitive agreed remedy creates a cap on liability: E Peel, *Treitel's Law of Contract*, 14th edn (London, Sweet & Maxwell, 2015) para 20-141; Tiverios (n 10) 195–200. Note also that there are limited contexts in which a 'wholly unenforceable' clause with respect to one party may still be enforceable by the other contracting party in certain circumstances: P Atiyah, '*Couturier v Hastie* and the Sale of Non-Existent Goods' (1957) 73 *LQR* 340, 345. Likewise, 'self-induced frustration' is relevant only against a party alleging frustration, and thus a frustrated contract may still be enforceable by one party: *Shepherd (FC) & Co Ltd v Jerrom* [1987] QB 301 (CA).

[48] *Cavendish* (n 3) [84]–[87] (Lord Neuberger and Lord Sumption) [230], [283] (Lord Hodge).

[49] *Andrews* (n 41).

[50] ibid [10] (French CJ, Gummow, Crennan, Kiefel and Bell JJ).

[51] *Cukurova* (n 28).

[52] *Peachy* (n 28) 453; 630.

[53] *Kreglinger* (n 30) 35.

[54] *Cukurova* (n 28) [90].

The chief debate surrounding the scope of the doctrine is whether it is limited to cases where the contractual power or right A wishes to assert has the effect of causing B to lose a right that can be defined as either possessory or proprietary. As noted in section I, that limit was recently confirmed in English law by the Supreme Court's decision in *Manchester Ship Canal*, whereas in Australia, an important impetus to challenging the restriction was provided by the reasoning of Edelman J (then a judge of the Federal Court of Australia) in *Mineralogy Pty Ltd v Sino Iron Pty Ltd (No 6)*,[55] which raised the critical question of *why* there should be such a limit to the doctrine. In the *Manchester Ship Canal* case, for example, it was fortunate for B that the contractual licence A sought to terminate was one that conferred on B unusually broad rights in relation to A's land. The licence conferred on B the liberty to discharge water (comprising both surface water from rainfall and trade effluent created by B's manufacturing plant) into the Manchester Ship Canal. The water would pass over A's land through a drainage system to be constructed and maintained by B. The terms of the licence specified that only B could use the drainage system, and that B would be obliged to maintain and repair the system even though part of the drainage system was situated on (and indeed acceded to) A's land. As a result, B was regarded as having a right to possession of the land, and it was only the lack of an agreed term of years (the licence was granted in perpetuity) that prevented B's having a lease of A's land. The Supreme Court considered, but rejected, B's contention that, even if B had not been able to establish such possession, relief against forfeiture would still have been possible. Lord Briggs (with whom Lord Carnwath, Lady Black and Lord Kitchin agreed) was reluctant to interfere with what his Lordship described as the 'careful development of the principled limitation of the jurisdiction to the forfeiture of proprietary or possessory rights, worked out over many years in a succession of broadly coherent authorities'.[56] In her concurring judgment, in contrast, Lady Arden was less sanguine about applying a limit on relief based on the type of right B holds, preferring instead to identify other restrictions on relief, based on, for example, the nature of the parties' dealings.[57] As a result, in her view, the denial of relief in the earlier House of Lords authority *The Scaptrade*, seen by the other members of the Court as supporting the possessory or proprietary limit, is better explained as a consequence of the fact that A simply sought to enforce 'an ordinary and lawful commercial bargain'.[58]

[55] *Mineralogy (No 6)* (n 8) [981] (Edelman J). See also *Auburn* (n 12) [25] (Bathurst CJ); *Ayers* (n 12) [106]–[107] (Drake J).

[56] *Manchester Ship Canal* (n 7) [50] (Lord Briggs).

[57] ibid [69], [83]–[89] (Lady Arden).

[58] ibid [78]. For more on justifying the decision in *The Scaptrade* without recourse to the possessory or proprietary right requirement, see NA Tiverios, 'Property, Therefore: Justifying Relief Against the Forfeiture of Personal Rights' in S Degeling, M Crawford and NA Tiverios (eds), *Justifying Private Rights* (Oxford, Hart Publishing, 2021) 247.

IV. Justifying Divergence?

A. England

As suggested in section I, in England, the rule against penalties and the doctrine of relief against forfeiture both have the effect of limiting the power of one private party to impose a punishment on another, but each has a distinct form and a different basis. The limit of the former rule to 'secondary obligations'[59] is linked to its justification. Whilst the primary contractual rights are created by the parties' agreement, secondary rights, on the other hand, are generally imposed by the state as a sanction or remedy for a breach of a primary right.[60] This analytical structure can be found in JL Austin's influential nineteenth-century *Lectures on Jurisprudence*[61] and has been given judicial support,[62] including penalties decisions prior to *Cavendish*.[63]

The essential observation to be derived from the use of the primary and secondary rights dichotomy in the English law of penalties is that the causative event that gives rise to a secondary right must be a breach of duty (ie a wrong). This indicates that the purpose of the rule against penalties is to preserve the state's capacity to impose a secondary right for the breach of a primary obligation (here, a breach of a contract): the common law will not allow the creation of an agreed remedy that would go too far in stultifying the general remedial policies

[59] *Cavendish* (n 3) [22], [28], [31]–[32] (Lord Neuberger and Lord Sumption). See also [151]–[153] (Lord Mance), [255] (Lord Hodge).

[60] This is most often done by means of a court order, giving rise, for example, to a duty to pay damages. It should not be forgotten, however, that a secondary right can arise independently of the curial process. An example is provided by the privileges of self-help and self-defence, which arise in response to the wrongs of trespass to land and trespass to the person: J Austin, *Lectures on Jurisprudence*, 5th edn (London, James Cockcroft and Co, 1885) vol II; WN Hohfeld, 'The Relations between Equity and Law' (1913) 6 *Michigan Law Review* 537, 554.

[61] Austin (n 60) para 1031, 1037–40. On the primary and secondary right distinction, see also Hohfeld (n 60) 556; W Anson and A Corbin, *Principles of the Law of Contract*, 3rd edn (New York, Oxford University Press, 1919) para 401; P Birks, 'Obligations: One Tier or Two?' in PG Stein and ADE Lewis (eds), *Studies in Justinian's Institutes in Memory of JAC Thomas* (London, Sweet & Maxwell, 1983) 21; P Birks, 'Personal Property: Property Rights and Remedies' (2000) 11 *King's College Law Journal* 1, 8; J Edelman, 'Gain-Based Damages and Compensation' in A Burrows and Lord Rodger of Earlsferry (eds), *Mapping the Law: Essays in Memory of Peter Birks* (Oxford, Oxford University Press, 2006) 141, 142–46; R Stevens, 'Damages and the Right to Performance: A Golden Victory or Not?' in J Neyers, R Bronaugh and S Pitel (eds), *Exploring Contract Law* (Oxford, Hart Publishing, 2009) 172; S Smith, 'Remedies for Breach of Contract: One Principle or Two?' in G Klass, G Letsas and P Saprari (eds), *Philosophical Foundations of Contract Law* (Oxford, Oxford University Press, 2014) 341, 354–61.

[62] *Robophone Facilities Ltd v Blank* [1966] 1 WLR 1428 (CA), 1446–47 (Diplock LJ); *Moschi v Lep Air Services Ltd* [1973] AC 331 (HL), 346–47 (Lord Diplock); *Photo Production Ltd v Securicor Transport Ltd* [1980] AC 827 (HL), 848–49 (Lord Diplock); *Morris-Garner v One Step (Support) Ltd* [2018] UKSC 20, [2018] WLR 1353 [34]–[35].

[63] See, eg, *The Angelic Star* [1988] 1 Lloyd's Rep 122 (CA) 127; *Lombard North Central Plc v Butterworth* [1987] QB 527 (CA), 538 (Mustill LJ); *Jobson* (n 26) 1032 (Dillon LJ). See also Tiverios (n 10) 57–61.

otherwise applicable on a breach of contract.[64] The typical state-provided remedies for breach of contract seek to respond to the injustice of B's breach by correcting it and not punishing B for her default.[65] This is achieved by providing A with either (i) the monetary value of B's promised performance,[66] or (ii) actual performance (or the closest equivalent) by compelling B to specifically perform the contract. In addition, as punitive damages are not available for a breach of contract,[67] the penalties doctrine ensures that an agreed remedy clause will not result in a party being unduly 'punished' for the related breach of the primary obligation.[68] The point is not so much that A can never punish B by means of a contractual term; it is rather that seeking to punish B *as a result of* B's breach of contract is inconsistent with the values the courts have developed in asking precisely the same question of what consequences should befall B as a result of B's breach of contract.

Reasonable minds will, however, differ regarding the point at which an impugned agreed remedy clause goes too far, and it is therefore no surprise that, in adopting a test of whether a term is out of all proportion to any legitimate interest of A in B's performance, the courts have given A a relatively large margin for error.[69] It is important to note that given that the parties are seeking to create an agreed remedy prior to any event of default, they cannot be required, ahead of time, to create a perfect facsimile of the court award of damages that would

[64] *Robophone* (n 62) 1446–47 (Diplock LJ).

[65] See, eg, J Gardner, *Torts and Other Wrongs* (Oxford, Oxford University Press, 2019) 336–41, noting that legal responses to a breach of contract, like those to a tort, are 'primarily reparative' and attempt to achieve 'primarily corrective justice'.

[66] *Robinson v Harman* (1848) 1 Ex 850, 855; 154 ER 363, 365 (Parke B); *Commonwealth v Amann Aviation Pty Ltd* (1991) 174 CLR 64 (HCA), 80 (Mason CJ and Dawson J). Such damages can be calculated on a substitutive basis. See, eg, *Williams Bros v Ed T Agius Ltd* [1914] AC 510 (HL); *Clark v Macourt* [2013] HCA 56, (2013) 253 CLR 1. In England the additional remedies of restitutionary or disgorgement damages are recoverable but only in very limited exceptional circumstances, see, eg, *Attorney-General v Blake* [2001] 1 AC 268 (HL).

[67] *Perera v Vandiyar* [1953] 1 WLR 672 (CA); *Kenny v Preen* [1963] 1 QB 499 (CA). See also *Morris-Garner* (n 62) [34], [91] (Lord Reed), which also confirms the compensatory focus of damages available on a breach of contract. For academic arguments that punitive damages should be available for breach of contract, see N McBride, 'A Case for Awarding Punitive Damages in Response to Deliberate Breaches of Contract' (1995) *Anglo-American Law Review* 369; N McBride, 'Punitive Damages' in P Birks (ed), *Wrongs and Remedies in the Twenty-First Century* (Oxford, Clarendon Press, 1996) 175; J Edelman, 'Exemplary Damages for Breach of Contract' (2001) 117 *LQR* 53; J Edelman, 'A "Fusion Fallacy" Fallacy?' (2003) 119 *LQR* 375; A Tettenborn, 'Punitive Damages – A View from England' (2004) 41 *San Diego Law Review* 1551; J Edelman, 'In Defence of Exemplary Damages' in CEF Rickett (ed), *Justifying Private Law Remedies* (Oxford, Hart Publishing, 2008) 225; S Rowan, 'Reflections on the Introduction of Punitive Damages for Breach of Contract' (2010) 30 *OJLS* 495. On the view presented in this chapter, it would be possible to reconcile punitive damages with the penalties doctrine on the basis that punitive damages for breach of contract would be an exceptional remedy (akin to gain-based damages, the rare availability of which has not destroyed the penalties doctrine); see also Tiverios (n 10) 69–70.

[68] *Cavendish* (n 3) [31] (Lord Neuberger and Lord Sumption), [243] (Lord Hodge).

[69] Note also that the general rule is that the party seeking to avail itself of the penalties doctrine bears the evidential and persuasive onus of proving that the impugned clause constitutes a penalty: *Robophone* (n 62) 1447 (Diplock LJ); *Murray v Leisureplay plc* [2005] EWCA Civ 963, [2005] IRLR 946 [55] (Arden LJ), [106] (Clarke LJ); *General Trading Co (Holdings) Ltd v Richmond Corp Ltd* [2008] EWHC 1479 (Comm), [2008] 2 Lloyd's Rep 475 [123] (Beatson J).

otherwise be awarded.[70] Perfect symmetry between an agreed remedy and what the court would do cannot realistically be expected. In this connection, the law of penalties seeks to balance considerations of keeping the parties to their promises and the utility of agreed remedies with ensuring proportionality between an agreed remedy and the underlying wrong. Accordingly, the rule requires an agreed remedy to be either (i) referable to the value (albeit loosely) of the relevant primary obligation breached,[71] or (ii) inserted into the contract as a proportionate means of achieving some other legitimate non-punitive function.[72] When the agreed remedy clause fails this test, the doctrine applies wholly to invalidate the impugned term and the parties are then left to avail themselves of the remedial regime at common law. Thus there is a symmetry between the area of operation of the English rule against penalties (hinging the rule on breach of contract) and the common law's remedial response (the clause is void), because the common law is only voiding an impugned term where it can provide an effective substitute by means of a court-ordered remedy for breach of contract. As such, A may not get his bespoke suit (ie the agreed remedy is void), but he is still provided with a standardised off-the-rack substitute (ie A can avail himself of the remedy the general law will provide for the underlying breach of contract).

The extent to which an impugned non-compensatory agreed remedy can pass muster under the penalties doctrine where the remedy is nonetheless characterised as a proportionate means of achieving some other legitimate non-punitive function warrants a brief comment. It is true that the 'legitimate interest' standard[73] was endorsed, and articulated clearly, in the relatively recent 2015 decision of the Supreme Court of the United Kingdom in *Cavendish* (and likewise this approach has been recently adopted at final appellate level in Australia).[74] But it is important to appreciate that this 'legitimate function' approach was not cut from whole cloth.[75] Importantly, whilst A can have no legitimate interest in punishing B for

[70] Tiverios (n 10) 171–72.

[71] *Dunlop Pneumatic Tyre Co Ltd v New Garage & Motor Co Ltd* [1915] AC 79 (HL), 86–88 (Lord Dunedin).

[72] *Cavendish* (n 3) [22], [28], [31]–[32] (Lord Neuberger and Lord Sumption), [151]–[153] (Lord Mance), [255] (Lord Hodge); *Paciocco v Australia and New Zealand Banking Group Ltd* [2016] HCA 28, (2016) 258 CLR 525 [31], [66] (Kiefel J), [148] (Gageler J), [273] (Keane J). This legitimate function approach has also been adopted by the Supreme Court of New Zealand: *127 Hobson Street Ltd v Honey Bees Preschool Ltd* [2020] NZSC 53, [56] (Winkelmann CJ) (noted by one of the authors in (2020) 29 New Zealand Universities Law Review 385). However, the legitimate function approach was rejected by the Court of Appeal of Singapore: *Denka Advantech* (n 2) [151]. The judge-made law in Singapore instead adopts the *Dunlop* (n 71) approach.

[73] On this standard, see also S Rowan, 'The "Legitimate Interest in Performance" in the Law on Penalties' (2019) 78 *CLJ* 148; Courtney, ch 12, section III.C.iii. On the debate about the non-syllogistic nature of this standard, see Tiveiros (n 10) 174.

[74] See, eg, *Paciocco* (n 72) [31], [66] (Kiefel J), [148] (Gageler J), [273] (Keane J).

[75] For example, in England the legitimate function standard can be traced back to the decision of the House of Lords in *Clydebank Engineering and Shipbuilding Co Ltd v Yzquierdo E Castaneda* [1905] AC 6 (HL), 19–20 (Lord Robertson). This approach also fits comfortably with cases reasoned on the basis that an impugned clause had a commercial justification: *Lordsvale Finance plc v Bank of Zambia* [1996] QB 752 (QBD); *Cine Bes Filmcilik ve Yapimcilik v United International Pictures* [2003]

a breach of contract, it is now recognised that A can have a legitimate interest in *deterring* B (and others in the same position as B) from a breach of contract, particularly where such deterrence facilitates a wider lawful scheme or protects third parties who will suffer loss on an event of default.[76] On the other hand, prior to the decision in *Cavendish* it was often said that a potential rationale for the existence of the penalties doctrine was that non-compensatory agreed remedies are 'likely to be regarded as penal because their function is to act as a deterrent' for B's breach of contract.[77] However, such a view overlooks the fact that deterrence has long been an inherent feature of many valid agreed remedy clauses, even prior to the decision in *Cavendish*.[78] This feature of the penalties doctrine was appreciated in the response to the House of Lords decisions in *Clydebank Engineering and Shipbuilding Co Ltd v Yzquierdo E Castaneda*[79] and also *Dunlop Pneumatic Tyre Co Ltd v New Garage and Motor Company Limited*.[80] For example, Professor Williams and Sir John Salmond observed that '[i]t is not, indeed, to be supposed that a term in a contract providing for the payment of a fixed sum upon default in performing some other obligation is to be regarded as providing for a penalty merely because it operates as a deterrent to such a default'.[81]

The best example is the agreed remedy clause upheld in *Dunlop Pneumatic Tyre Co Ltd* itself,[82] the leading authority in this area for almost a century.[83]

EWCA Civ 1669, [2004] 1 CLC 401; *Murray* (n 69); *Lancore Services Ltd v Barclays Bank plc* [2008] EWHC 1264 (Ch), [2008] 1 CLC 1039. In Australia the legitimate function was previously cited with approval in *Lamson Store Service Co Ltd v Russell Wilkins & Sons Ltd* (1906) 4 CLR 672 (HCA), 681–83 (Griffith CJ); *Hamilton v Lethbridge* (1912) 14 CLR 236 (HCA), 264 (Isaacs J); *O'Dea v Allstates Leasing System* (1983) 152 CLR 359 (HCA), 383 (Wilson J). It also fits with the majority reasoning and outcome in *Forestry Commission* (n 39), and appears to have been applied in *Egan v South Australian Railway Commissioner* (1979) 25 SASR 5, 18 (Mitchell J), 24 (Hogarth and Zelling JJ).

[76] See, eg, *ParkingEye* (n 3) (see also text at n 86), where deterrence of over-staying parking was required for the operation of the overall parking scheme, which included two hours' free parking (note that the legitimate interests in this case included protecting the landowner of a related retail park who was not a party to the contract between A and B). See also *Australia Capital* (n 29); *Guan v Linfield Developments Pty Ltd* [2017] NSWCA 99, 18 BPR 36683 [311], [336]–[339], [358], [371] (Ward JA), where a contractual power in favour of one joint venture party (A) to force the other (B) to transfer land the parties were developing (exercisable on, inter alia, B's insolvency) was held to be non-punitive. One reason given by Ward JA was that A had a legitimate interest in ensuring that it did not lose the benefit of the proposed commercial and residential development project on the event of B's insolvency (particularly given that A had invested significant capital, time and labour into the project and expected to profit at a future date).

[77] See, eg, *Murray* (n 69) [111] (Buxton LJ); *Makdessi v Cavendish Square Holding BV* [2013] EWCA Civ 1539, [2014] 2 All ER (Comm) 125 [120] (Clarke LJ) (revd *Cavendish* (n 3)). The position that a penalty clause is an ineffective deterrent is implicit in the view expressed in PS Atiyah, *Essays on Contract* (Oxford, Oxford University Press, 1988) 369–74.

[78] *Cavendish* (n 3) [28]–[31] (Lord Neuberger and Lord Sumption).

[79] *Clydebank* (n 75) 19–20 (Lord Robertson).

[80] *Dunlop* (n 71).

[81] J Salmond and J Williams, *Principles of the Law of Contracts*, 2nd edn (London, Sweet & Maxwell, 1945) 580–81. Note that the 2nd edn of the text was published posthumously after the death of Sir John Salmond.

[82] *Dunlop* (n 71).

[83] As noted in *Ringrow Pty Ltd v BP Australia Pty Ltd* [2005] HCA 71, (2005) 224 CLR 656 [12] (Gleeson CJ, Gummow, Kirby Hayne, Callinan and Heydon JJ).

The impugned clause reviewed by the House of Lords stipulated that B (a retailer) must pay an agreed sum of £5 to A (a wholesaler) for every item supplied by A that B sold below the price prescribed by a retail price maintenance scheme, thereby *deterring* B from undermining the scheme. The speeches in the House of Lords make clear that preventing 'deterrence' was never the universal concern of the penalties doctrine. This is because one reason why the agreed remedy was not a penalty was that the impugned clause had a legitimate function in preserving the integrity of A's wholesale distribution system *in globo* by giving effect to the retail price maintenance scheme (which, although anticompetitive when viewed through modern spectacles, was unobjectionable in 1915).[84] In *Cavendish*, the Supreme Court picked up on this often overlooked aspect of the reasoning in *Dunlop Pneumatic Tyre Co* and observed that it was a clear example of an early manifestation of the 'legitimate function' standard to uphold an agreed remedy even if it is not a genuine pre-estimate of A's loss.[85] Similar reasoning was deployed by the Supreme Court of the United Kingdom in *ParkingEye v Beavis*.[86] In that case, the Court held that a parking fee levied on B (motorists) by A (a car park services operator) when vehicles, in breach of a contractual obligation, were parked beyond two hours in an otherwise free car park was held to be valid. Deterrence of overstaying was necessary to support the free parking scheme, both by: (i) facilitating the turnover of vehicles for the related retail facility; and (ii) creating a revenue stream from which to administer an otherwise free car park. Likewise, the High Court of Australia in *Paciocco v Australia and New Zealand Banking Group Ltd*[87] pointed to the existence of several legitimate functions in order to uphold a non-compensatory late payment fee on credit card accounts, notwithstanding that such fees could be seen as deterring B from failing, in breach of a contractual duty, to make an obliged monthly minimum repayment.

In contrast to the rule against penalties, the doctrine of relief against forfeiture, whilst most commonly invoked in practice in cases where B is in breach of a contractual duty owed to A, is not limited to such cases. Its operation remains consistent with its historical basis as set out in section II. The justification for equity's disabling A's strict exercise of a valid legal right lies in the circumstances in which that right was created, and the purposes it was designed by the parties

[84] See, eg, *Dunlop* (n 71) 88 (Lord Dunedin), 91–93 (Lord Atkinson), 97–99 (Lord Parker). The other reason why the clause was upheld was that the court was unable to determine the damage A would suffer if B departed from the prescribed prices, and therefore it was appropriate to defer to the agreed sum: ibid 88–89 (Lord Dunedin), 91 (Lord Atkinson), 103 (Lord Parmoor).

[85] *Cavendish* (n 3) (Lord Neuberger and Lord Sumption).

[86] ibid. The same result should follow under the Australian law of penalties.

[87] *Paciocco* (n 72) [58], [69] (Kiefel J), [141]–[143], [172]–[177] (Gageler J), [271]–[279] (Keane J). See also *Paciocco v Australia and New Zealand Banking Group Ltd* [2015] FCAFC 50, (2015) 321 ALR 584 [163]–[165], [176]–[170], [177] (Allsop CJ); his Honour also referred to the difficulty of assessing damages that would result from B's breach of contract (ibid [183]). Similar reasoning, focusing on provisioning costs and regulatory capital costs, was adopted in upholding a similar clause in *Arab Bank Australia Ltd v Sayde Developments Pty Ltd* [2016] NSWCA 328, (2016) 93 NSWLR 231 [23], [26], [29], [90]–[95] (McDougall J) (special leave refused: [2017] HCASL 29).

to serve. Where the parties' intentions, as objectively manifested, are that a right is to provide security for the performance of a primary or principal right, it would be an abuse of that right for A to use it, against B, for a different purpose. The point is not so much that A can never punish B by means of enforcing a contractual term; it is rather that seeking to punish B is prevented as the term has a substantive purpose, and that purpose does not involve punishment.[88] This rationale does not require regarding the impugned term as void; rather, equity needs only to restrain the exercise of A's security right in order to ensure that it is enforced only to the extent necessary to secure performance of the related primary condition (or the condition's monetised equivalent).

The limitation of the doctrine at English law to cases where B stands to lose a possessory or proprietary right is relatively recent.[89] Whilst the language of 'possessory or proprietary right' is familiar, it is generally used when determining the effects on a third party of a right created by A and B: if, for example, B acquires a possessory or proprietary right in a physical asset, third parties come under a prima facie duty to B not to interfere, carelessly or deliberately, with that asset; whereas if B's right is merely contractual, no such general duty arises.[90] The puzzle in relation to forfeiture is why a test used to determine the third-party effect of a right should be relevant when instead considering a question that relates solely to A's rights as against B.

Lord Briggs in *Manchester Ship Canal* places great store on the certainty provided, in particular to commercial parties, of maintaining the limit, but it is easy to come up with examples (real or fictitious) of sufficiently 'certain' legal rules that are otherwise morally difficult to justify. As stated by Glanville Williams,[91] 'it is to the interest of legal certainty that, *other things being equal*, the rules of law should be as clear of application as possible'. As a matter of legal history and logic, the security basis for relief could apply beyond the context of the loss of proprietary and possessory rights. The most obvious example is relief against the strict enforcement of conditional bonds (a form of personal right) in the same circumstances in which the English law relating to relief against forfeiture now applies.[92] As John Barton observed, 'In the year 1700, the statement that a penalty

[88] The question is whether A's right is, as a matter of substance, in the nature of a security. Indeed, whether the court is construing a contract, penal clause, licence, lease, trust or security instrument, the labels used by the parties to describe the legal effect of the impugned provisions are never determinative: *Re Universal Management* [1983] NZLR 462 (CA), 470 (Cooke J); *Street v Mountford* [1985] AC 809 (HL); *Welsh Development Agency v Export Finance Co Ltd* [1992] BCC 270 (CA), 278 (Dillon LJ), 300 (Staughton LJ).

[89] See, eg, PG Turner, 'What Delimits Equitable Relief From Forfeiture?' (2019) 78 *CLJ* 276. Also note the authorities at n 35.

[90] See, eg, *Cattle v Stockton Waterworks Co* (1874–75) LR 10 QB 453 (QBD); *Leigh & Sillivan Ltd v Aliakmon Shipping Co Ltd* [1986] AC 785 (HL); *OBG Ltd v Allan* [2007] UKHL 21, [2008] 1 AC 1.

[91] G Williams, 'Law and Language – II' (1945) 61 *LQR* 179, 185 (emphasis added).

[92] *Anonymous* (1602) Cary 2; 21 ER 1; various cases listed in Toth 131–33; 21 ER 145; Yale (n 35) 24–25; Several Gentlemen of the Respective Branches of Law (n 41). See also the authorities listed at (n 35).

is intended merely as security for the performance of an agreement expressed a well-understood fact of commercial life.'[93] Indeed, this historical and analytical point was accepted by Lady Arden in her concurring judgment in *Manchester Ship Canal*.[94] The options of maintaining or rejecting the possessory or proprietary limit cannot be considered as 'equal', with the certainty of the former providing the tie-break, if there is a clear argument of principle for the latter option. In the *Manchester Ship Canal* case, for example, even if B had no possession of any part of A's land and instead had simply a personal liberty against A under the contractual licence to drain water through the infrastructure, there would still be good reason to prevent A from using the termination clause, intended merely to serve as an incentive for B to pay the annual rent of £50, to deprive B of a contractual right worth at least £300,000 per annum.[95] Moreover, the certainty of the current limit can be doubted. For example, hallmarks of modern commerce, such as charges over book debts or bank accounts, merely impose an equitable encumbrance over wholly personal rights. Nonetheless, equity's jurisdiction to relieve against forfeiture on the basis of security rights applies in such contexts.[96]

The justification for limiting the security-based strand of relief against forfeiture, in English law, to possessory or proprietary rights may lie in pragmatism rather than principle. As suggested in section I, it can be linked to the limit on the English rule against penalties. It is important to note that whilst most usually applied to secondary obligations of B to pay a sum of money to A, that rule can extend to other agreed sanctions triggered by a breach of contract, such as a duty of B to transfer a right to A,[97] or a power of A to retain a sum of money, or right, already transferred by B to A.[98] If the security-based strand of relief against forfeiture were not limited to the loss of possessory or proprietary rights, it could apply to limit A's ability to enforce a right in cases (such as where the right is not triggered by B's breach of contract) where, following the Supreme Court's decision in *Cavendish*, the courts have expressly decided not to intervene in the context of the rule against penalties. Put simply, any removal of the 'proprietary or possessory' right threshold in the context of the doctrine of relief against forfeiture will blur the distinction between the scope of operation of the rule against penalties and the doctrine of relief against forfeiture, and undermine the unanimous view

[93] Barton (n 36) 23.

[94] *Manchester Ship Canal* (n 7) [70]–[71] (Lady Arden).

[95] The estimated value of B's right per annum was between £300,000 and £440,000, and this value seems to be attributable to the discharge of surface water and trade effluent over A's land, rather than to the possessory aspects of B's right.

[96] See, eg, *Re Kent & Sussex Sawmills* [1947] Ch 177 (Ch D), 181–82 (Wynn-Parry J), where an equity of redemption is recognised with respect to a charge over book debts.

[97] See, eg, *Cavendish* (n 3) [84] (Lord Neuberger and Lord Sumption), [157] (Lord Mance), [230] (Lord Hodge).

[98] See, eg, *Signia Wealth Ltd v Vector Trustees Ltd* [2018] EWHC 1040 (Ch) [653], where Marcus Smith J stated that 'it is clear that the penalty doctrine extends to deposits, forfeiture clauses and provisions that require a party in breach of contract to transfer property to the other party at less than its full value'.

in *Cavendish* that the rule applies only to regulate agreed remedies payable on breach of contract.[99]

B. Australia

The crucial difference between English and Australian law, on our analysis, is the centrality in the latter of a security-based understanding of the rule against penalties. That understanding maintains the historic basis of the rule and is consistent with the Australian law as to both its scope (its ability to operate even where the secured event is not B's breach of a contract with A) and its effect (it does not invalidate A's right, but rather allows a court to control A's enforcement of that right). The relationship between that rule and the doctrine of relief against forfeiture has not yet been made clear, but we would argue that it is now possible to unite those two aspects of the courts' response to agreed rights that may operate punitively. Indeed, the doubts expressed in the Australian case law as to the justification of the possessory or proprietary rights limit to relief against forfeiture are consistent with such a unification.[100] If the general need to control A's enforcement of a security right is acknowledged in the rule against penalties, without any limit to the means by which that right imposes a burden on B, there is no need to maintain a distinct doctrine of relief against forfeiture simply for the purposes of giving effect to that general need in cases where B's burden consists of losing a right.

The current position of Australian law is thus much more amenable to such unification than that of English law. This does not mean, however, that such a move could occur without any substantive changes. In *Else (1982) Ltd v Parkland Holdings Ltd*,[101] for example, Hoffmann LJ noted the 'common equitable origin' of the rule against penalties and of relief against forfeiture, but distinguished them on the basis that the former 'looks at the position when the contract is made' and is 'mechanical in effect and involves no exercise of discretion at all', whereas the latter looks at the position when A is enforcing the forfeiture and 'asks whether in all the circumstances it would be unconscionable to allow the forfeiture to take effect. This is an exercise of discretion to grant equitable relief.'[102] To some extent, this distinction is based on the then prevailing, but now discredited,[103] view that the

[99] *Cavendish* (n 3) [7]–[14], [43] (Lord Neuberger and Lord Sumption), [129]–[130] (Lord Mance), [241], [258] (Lord Hodge), [291] (Lord Clarke), [292] (Lord Toulson).

[100] See the authorities listed at n 12.

[101] *Else (1982) Ltd v Parkland Holdings Ltd* [1994] 1 BCLC 130 (CA).

[102] ibid 144. A view that has recently been restated in the Court of Appeal of the Supreme Court of New South Wales, see, eg, *Australia Capital* (n 29) [326] (Ward JA). However, Smith (n 30) 198, observes that one response to the idea that relief against forfeiture involves too much discretion would be for this area of law to 'settle down to a predictable doctrine that rights by way of security are just that and no more … [thus] one might expect that the case in which forfeiture is not granted will be the exceptional case'.

[103] See, eg, *Cavendish* (n 3) [31] (Lord Neuberger and Lord Sumption).

rule against penalties simply involves distinguishing between a clause 'intended to operate in terrorem' and one that is instead a 'genuine pre-estimate of damage'.[104] The different test applied in *Cavendish*, and essentially adopted by the High Court of Australia in *Paciocco v Australia and New Zealand Banking Group Ltd*,[105] is clearly not mechanical, and involves an assessment of both A's legitimate interests in B's performance and whether the agreed remedy is out of all proportion to such interests. Such a test, in our view, is essentially identical to that applied when considering if the security-based strand of relief against forfeiture should be granted. The key question in such a case is whether B can show it would be unconscionable for A to insist on enforcing a clause intended to operate as security. As in the penalties context, this depends on whether the clause imposes a burden on B, or confers a benefit on A, which is excessive when compared to that which would arise had the secured event occurred. Indeed, it may be that the concept of A's legitimate interest in B's performance, whilst it has emerged in the context of penalties, is useful in determining the availability of relief against forfeiture (ie as a general test for ascertaining whether the impugned clause has a legitimate function or purpose beyond merely standing as a security). In *The Scaptrade*,[106] for example, A required payment from B in order to meet the expense of providing a crew and ship to B, and the power to terminate the contract, and thus end B's hire of the ship, simply had the legitimate function of protecting A from exposure to those expenses.

Hoffmann LJ's analysis in *Else*, therefore, cannot be justified on the basis that the application of the rule against penalties is mechanical and does not require the court to exercise its judgment. It is nonetheless significant, as it suggests that even if there is no real difference in the substance of the test applied when deciding if a clause is penal and when deciding whether to grant relief against forfeiture, a difference as to timing remains.[107] This idea has persisted in Australian law, with a penalty clause to be judged according to the circumstances at the time of its making[108] and, in contrast to relief against forfeiture, not at the point when A seeks to enforce it. This distinction makes sense in England, where a penal clause

[104] *Else* (n 101).

[105] *Paciocco* (n 72). See also *Paciocco* (n 87) [99]–[103] (Allsop CJ).

[106] *Scandinavian Trading Tanker* (n 27). See also Turner (n 89) 279, who has made the similar observation that certainty can then be achieved by a detailed consideration of whether or not the impugned right has some other legitimate non-security function such that relief will only be afforded 'where the security purpose stands ahead of any other', cited with approval by Lady Arden in *Manchester Ship Canal* (n 7) [70].

[107] Note that, in this way, Hoffmann LJ's analysis is consistent with a more general point that also applies to other equitable doctrines: in the words of Hoffmann LJ, in the context of equitable estoppel, in *Walton v Walton* (CA, 14 April 1994) such doctrines often 'look backwards' and ask 'whether, in the circumstances which have actually happened' it would be unconscionable for A to act in a particular way as regards B. See also McFarlane (n 20) 212–17.

[108] *Paciocco* (n 87) [95], [200] (Allsop CJ); *Australia Capital* (n 29) [329]–[331], [336], [371] (Ward JA). For the position in England see, eg, *Dunlop* (n 71) 86–87 (Lord Dunedin); *Cavendish* (n 3) [99] (Lord Neuberger and Lord Sumption): 'the question whether a contractual provision is a penalty turns on the construction of the contract'.

is void at common law as a matter of public policy, but it is harder to justify in Australia, where the equitable characterisation of the rule against penalties has been retained.[109] In our view, then, even if Australian law can usefully draw on English law as to the substance of the test to be applied to a potential penalty, it need not follow it as regards the point at which that test is to be applied.[110]

V. Conclusion

In this chapter, we have sought to explain the relationship between relief against penalties and relief against forfeitures. The explanations differ between England and Australia. Under English law the position is clear: the two doctrines are analytically distinct. This is because the English penalties doctrine (which is now characterised as being a 'common law' rule) involves ascertaining whether or not A has acquired a valid legal right against B to an agreed remedy. The English law concerning relief against forfeiture instead involves circumstances under which A has a valid legal right against B but equity subsequently controls, in B's favour, the assertion of that right. The key analytical difference between the equitable relief against forfeiture principle and the common law penalties doctrine in English law is therefore that the equitable rule limits the assertion of a legal right, whereas the common law rule concerns the valid acquisition of such a right in the first place. Once the salient analytical features of relief against penalties and forfeitures are properly understood, the borders between the two doctrines become easier to map, and the manner in which each doctrine deals with the problem of potentially punitive private agreements becomes clearer. The position under Australian law is, however, distinct. This is because the law in Australia concerning relief against penalties has maintained key characteristics from the doctrine's equitable origins. The Australian penalties doctrine operates to disable A from exercising a punitive contractual right, and so concerns the extent to which A can enforce her legal right to an agreed remedy against B. Given the analytical similarities between penalties and forfeitures in Australia, it is argued that it is possible (and desirable) to harmonise the Australian penalties doctrine with certain aspects of relief against forfeiture.

It may be useful to reflect on the contingency of the comparative analysis. There was a point in time, following the decision of the High Court of Australia

[109] C Rossiter, *Penalties and Forfeiture* (Sydney, Law Book Co, 1992) 153–54.

[110] Although more generally on the questions of timing concerning (i) whether A's right is in the nature of security (in both the context of relief against forfeiture and penalties in Australia), being a question of construction determined at the point of entry into the contract; and (ii) the ex post factors pertaining to relief once a right is characterised as such, see Tiverios (n 10) 225. For example, as a matter of coherence, Australian law can take the position that issue (i) is determined at the point of entry into the contract, whereas issue (ii) can be determined at the date of trial. See also *Stern* (n 8) 540 (Gaudron J).

in *AMEV-UDC Finance Ltd v Austin*,[111] when it could be stated that, in the words of Mason and Wilson JJ, 'the equitable jurisdiction to relieve against penalties withered on the vine for the simple reason that, except perhaps in very unusual circumstances, it offered no prospect of relief which was not ordinarily available in proceedings to recover a stipulated sum or, alternatively, damages'.[112] Similarly, there was a point when two members of the House of Lords, in an obiter discussion of the point, pointed to the absurdity of limiting the rule against penalties to cases where B had breached a contract with A, as this gave B greater protection in a case of breach than in a case where B had simply failed to meet a non-promissory condition.[113] In the end, of course, each jurisdiction took a different path, and the equitable characterisation of the rule in Australia has now opened the way to its re-unification with the doctrine of relief against forfeiture; whereas in England, confirmation of the need for a breach of contract has not only supported a common law analysis of the rule but, in our view, has also led to the maintenance of limits on the scope of relief against forfeiture that, as a matter of principle, are difficult to defend. So whilst it is clear that each of English and Australian law shares a broad aim, evident in the rule against penalties and the doctrine of relief against forfeiture, to prevent private agreements having punitive effect, the forms by which each jurisdiction gives effect to that aim have diverged, and so the scope of the relevant principles differs as between the two countries.[114]

[111] *AMEV-UDC Finance Ltd v Austin* (1986) 162 CLR 170 (HCA).

[112] ibid 191.

[113] *Bridge v Campbell Discount Co Ltd* [1962] AC 600 (HL) 630 (Lord Denning), 633 (Lord Devlin).

[114] Note of course that the current English and Australian positions do not between them exhaust the list of possible approaches: in *Denka Advantech* (n 2) the Singapore Court of Appeal affirmed the restriction of the rule against penalties to terms dealing with the effect of a breach of contract, but rejected the 'legitimate function' test applied in each of England and Australia: see further n 72.

14

Penalty in the Contract of Employment: The Good, the Bad (Leavers) and the Ugly

MIMI ZOU AND HIN LIU

I. Introduction

An employer may wish to restrain a key employee from leaving a company. The employer may attempt to do so by imposing certain negative consequences on the employee through a range of contractual mechanisms. A common mechanism is a post-termination restrictive covenant, which seeks to prevent employees from working in the same business or industry for a certain duration (or perhaps indefinitely) after they have parted from the employer. There may also be contractual provisions that require repayments by departing employees for relocation allowances, training costs and other benefits connected with their employment. In addition, contractual clauses may entail the withholding or reduction of a substantial bonus, or of other payments deemed to be 'unearned' by the departing employee. On the one hand, it would seem reasonable for an employer to have in place such arrangements to recoup its investment in hiring and training the departing employee and protect other legitimate business interests in holding on to its key employees. On the other hand, there are instances where the disincentives created by these contractual mechanisms can become so onerous that the employee's basic freedom to quit her job is severely undermined.

A 'good leaver' or 'bad leaver' clause is commonly found in a company's articles of association, shareholders' agreements and employees' share schemes. 'Bad leaver' clauses frequently entail the compulsory transfer of the employee's shares for (often substantially) less than the shares' market value upon her departure from the company. The clauses are triggered depending on the event or circumstances surrounding the employee's departure, which are usually defined (but not always explicitly) in the applicable contractual document. For example, an employee may be defined by the company as a 'good leaver' if the employment relationship ended because of retirement, redundancy, death, illness or injury.

Meanwhile, a 'bad leaver' could be defined as an employee who is dismissed for misconduct or consistently poor performance. However, a 'bad leaver' could also be defined as an employee leaving voluntarily for whatever reason. It has been known that 'bad leaver' clauses have been triggered 'merely because the individual concerned was not taken to be a "Good Leaver"'.[1] In other words, if an employee wants to leave her employer for reasons aside from normal retirement, redundancy, death, illness or injury (or other circumstances as defined within the scope of a 'good leaver'), the 'bad leaver' clause can become operative. As such, an employee may quit her job in accordance with the terms of her employment contract but nevertheless be deemed a 'bad leaver'.

As we show in this chapter, the regulation of 'bad leaver' clauses at common law is manifestly inadequate in light of the current law controlling penalty clauses. The penalty rule, as it stands post-*Cavendish v Makdessi*,[2] does not furnish adequate protection for employees who are subject to 'bad leaver' clauses. This is especially the case for employees whose salary is constituted in large part by share entitlements, as we examine in a number of cases involving (all unsuccessful) challenges to 'bad leaver' clauses. As noted by the Scottish Law Commission, employees (even those on relatively high-value employment contracts) often have little opportunity to negotiate or take independent legal advice in relation to such clauses.[3] We adopt a labour law perspective to identify what we believe is the most objectionable aspect of these provisions: that an employee's freedom to exit an employment relationship can be severely constrained by the operation of 'bad leaver' clauses. The right to quit is considered a critical freedom that protects an individual worker's autonomy and serves as a bulwark against abusive employment relationships.[4]

Adding a unique perspective to the debates in this book, our primary normative concern here is the *effect* of these contractual provisions on an employee's basic freedom to leave an employment relationship. We argue that framing 'bad leaver' clauses as a form of 'punishment' in private law, as the jurisprudence on penalties currently stands, does not go to the root of this concern. At the same time, we recognise that the concept of punishment itself has a variety of meanings within private law.[5] We agree with Barker on the importance of identifying the *purpose* of punishment, and that deterrence is commonly viewed as a core purpose in discussions of punitive damages and civil penalties.[6] From this perspective,

[1] Scottish Law Commission, *Review of Contract Law Discussion Paper on Penalty Clauses* (Discussion Paper No 162, 2016) para 5.8.

[2] *Cavendish Square Holding BV v Makdessi and Beavis v Parking Eye* [2015] UKSC 67, [2016] AC 1172.

[3] Scottish Law Commission (n 1) para 4.34.

[4] Our underlying concern about the inequality of bargaining power and protection of fundamental rights in the employment context is also reflected in Bant and Paterson, ch 10 of this volume on consumer protection. Consumer law is another area of private law, like employment law, that has been subject to considerable statutory interventions in light of inherent power asymmetries between the parties.

[5] Barker, ch 2 of this volume.

[6] ibid.

a possible argument is that 'bad leaver' clauses have a deterrent aim: they are used by employers to prevent employees from acting in a 'bad' way, such as engaging in misconduct or other breaches of their contractual obligations. However, it is extremely problematic when such clauses apply to an employee who merely resigns without any breach of contract. This is because our general understanding of deterrence in the punishment context applies only to preventing some form of *wrongdoing*. As we argue in this chapter, leaving an employment relationship per se cannot be 'wrongdoing', and an employee who does so cannot possibly be viewed as a 'wrongdoer' or a 'contract-breaker'. This is because, from a contemporary labour law perspective, the right to quit is a fundamental freedom of an employee. As we examine in this chapter, attempts to challenge 'bad leaver' clauses based on the penalty doctrine have been futile. Courts have largely found that the operation of these clauses (in the way they were drafted) did not require a breach of contractual obligations.

In comparison with the extensive body of practitioners' writings on 'bad leaver' clauses, there has been, astonishingly, very little, if any, scholarly analysis of this topic. This chapter may be the first of its kind. Section II expounds our main normative concern regarding the operation of some 'bad leaver' clauses: an employee's right to quit. In section III we review recent cases before UK courts and tribunals involving (all) unsuccessful challenges to 'bad leaver' clauses. These cases reveal how 'bad leaver' clauses can be drafted and deployed in a variety of ways by employers to avoid the application of the penalty doctrine as it currently stands. This analysis sheds light on the inadequate protection at common law in respect of employees who can suffer significant financial detriment a result of these provisions. In section IV we offer suggestions for statutory reform that address our normative concerns. We conclude that it is more appropriate to regulate 'bad leaver' clauses based on protecting an employee's right to exit an employment relationship instead of attempting to bring these provisions within 'the paradigm of a penalty'.[7]

II. The Right to Quit and 'Bad Leaver' Clauses

A. The Main Mischief

Before we examine the current limitations of the penalty doctrine in addressing the potentially significant detriment for employees who are subject to 'bad leaver' clauses, we set out the normative basis for our objection to what we see as the principal mischief of such clauses. Here, our key argument is that a lack of common law or statutory controls over 'bad leaver' clauses can undermine a person's freedom to exit an employment relationship: in other words, her right to quit.

[7] *Signia Wealth Limited v Vector Trustees Ltd* [2018] EWHC 1040 (Ch D) [653].

The idea of a 'right to quit' was explored by sociologist Julius Roth, who argued that 'the decision about staying with or quitting a given relationship or membership should be in the hands of the individual concerned as much as possible'.[8] This places prime importance on the employee's decision to choose whether or not a particular course of action (staying or quitting) is advantageous to the employee. Roth argues that not only is this choice intrinsically valuable, insofar as it allows 'greater control over [one's] own life', but it also confers on the employee a 'crucial bargaining element in his relationship with authorities [including employers]'.[9]

In addition to legal rights that may restrict the right to quit, Roth also draws attention to 'the *social* conditions which increase or decrease the prospect of quitting'.[10] If an individual encounters *social circumstances* that render it extremely difficult to quit, she ought to have a proper avenue of exit. He provides the example of where economic depression and inadequate social protection can undermine the right to quit (which, he argues, 'becomes the right to starve').[11] In other words, without adequate alternatives such as other jobs or means of support, the right to quit cannot be meaningfully realised.

A conceptual framework that may be helpful for understanding the constraints on leaving an employment relationship is a 'continuous' (as opposed to bifurcated) approach to understanding labour freedom. Steinfeld argues that there is no natural line existing between unfree and free labour: 'the distinction itself serves as a proxy for … a moral/political judgement about the kinds of pressures to enter and remain at work that are considered legitimate and those that are not'.[12] Labour freedom and unfreedom should not be viewed as binary opposites but as 'a combined scale of pressures, legal, physical, economic, social, psychological all running along a continuum from severe to mild'.[13] Such a continuum directs us to

> see that the real focus of inquiry should be upon the choice sets with which individuals are confronted as they make their decisions about conducting their lives, and the ways in which these choice sets may be altered by changing legal arrangements.[14]

Roth draws the line as to 'illegitimate pressures' at the point where the 'clear-cut protection of society is … imperative',[15] and as such, where such protection is not imperative, the 'regulatory restrictions against quitting [should] be removed entirely'.[16]

[8] JA Roth, 'The Right to Quit' (1973) 21 *The Sociological Review* 381, 395.
[9] ibid.
[10] ibid 392.
[11] ibid.
[12] R Steinfeld, 'Coercion/ Consent in Labour', COMPAS Working Paper No 66 (Annual Conference of the Centre on Migration, Policy and Society on 'Theorising Key Migration Debates', Oxford University, 30 June 2009) 13 at www.compas.ox.ac.uk/wp-content/uploads/WP-2009-066-Steinfeld_Coercion_Consent_Labour.pdf, accessed 23 June 2020.
[13] ibid.
[14] ibid.
[15] Roth (n 8) 395.
[16] ibid.

How, then, does the above discussion apply in the context of 'bad leaver' clauses? The most important impact to note is that the operation of 'bad leaver' clauses can prevent people from leaving their existing jobs and employers and moving to more productive, efficient, well-paying, and satisfying jobs and employers. This is because they must weigh up the detriment imposed by the 'bad leaver' clause alongside other factors, such as continued mistreatment in the workplace.

B. Types of Objections

There are three types of normative objections to this kind of constraint on the right to change one's employer and job. The first type is generally focused on preserving individual freedom, which reflects courts' longstanding reluctance to award specific performance in cases involving breach of contracts for personal services and contract of employment so as to avoid excessive or undue interference with personal liberty.[17] To compel a person, against her will, to work for another would turn such contracts into 'contracts of slavery'.[18] As Parks puts it, '[t]he court will not become a slave-driver in this sense of the word'.[19] Legislation also forbids court orders of specific performance against an employee,[20] though the court or tribunal can order specific performance (reinstatement or re-engagement of the employee) against an employer in cases of unfair dismissals.[21] In tethering the employee to a particular employer for a period of time, the *de facto* effect of a 'bad leaver' clause may not be too far off (in terms of *degree*) from the effect of awarding specific performance in contracts of personal services on the employee's freedom to quit.

Another objection of this type is the deontological argument that such a constraint on an employee's freedom to quit would constitute an inherent violation of the employee's right to choose what is good for herself. As Roth argues:

> [T]here is the point of view of each individual involved in a particular relationship that he might like to terminate. If we value the feeling that we can make choices for ourselves rather than having them forced upon us, the right to quit any kind of relationship is essential.[22]

Indeed, given the centrality of employment to one's well-being and self-esteem, prime regard must be had to a person's freedom to be 'the final arbiter'[23] of whether she should remain in a particular employment relationship.

[17] This idea was raised by Professor Jeannie Paterson in discussions relating to an earlier draft of this chapter, which was presented at the Conference on Punishment and Private Law, 16–18 December 2019, National University of Singapore. See also *Lumley v Wagner* (1852) 5 De G & Sm 485; 64 ER 1209.

[18] *De Francesco v Barnum* (1890) 45 Ch D 430.

[19] JL Parks, 'Equitable Relief in Contracts Involving Personal Services' (1918) 66 *University of Pennsylvania Law Review* 251, 253.

[20] Trade Union Act 1992, s 236.

[21] Employment Rights Act 1996, s 113.

[22] Roth (n 8) 381.

[23] ibid 387.

A second type of objection concerns unfair and/or oppressive imbalances in the employment relationship. A central objective of labour law has been to address the substantial inequality in bargaining power inherent in such a relationship.[24] As Roth argues, where there is no right to leave a particular relationship, persons in a position of authority can perpetrate oppressive or violent conduct without being properly held to account: 'If persons in authority know that a person over whom they have control cannot quit, they may very well treat him differently from the way they would if he *could* quit.'[25] Beyond employment, Roth discusses the tendency for this to occur in other contexts of life and society, such as marriage, prisons and hospitals.

There is a third category of objections, which can be characterised as 'utilitarian' in nature. 'Bad leaver' clauses, in serving as a potentially powerful disincentive against leaving one's employer, limit the employee's ability to work for another employer and in other jobs that would be more efficient in terms of productivity and output (at an individual and a macro-labour market level). Existing legal doctrines that may help address restraints on an employee's labour mobility are underpinned primarily by this kind of objection. The prime example is the striking down of contractual clauses based on unlawful restraint of trade, in which the test focuses on the employer's legitimate business interests and certain kinds of public policy considerations. The court is to assess whether the *employer* has a legitimate interest to protect, and whether the clause is reasonable in light of such interest. Public policy tends to emphasise the need to maintain free market competition and ensure the productive and efficient use of one's trade. In this sense, the vindication of the employee's freedom to leave an employer is treated as the collateral consequence of the primary aims of skill utilisation and market competition.

C. 'Punishment' and the Freedom to Leave

How does our argument relate to 'punishment'? It is important to ascertain what is meant by 'punishment' in a particular context. As Barker eloquently puts it in his contribution to this volume, 'some of the meanings and purposes attributed to punishment … in the modern day are now so highly diluted that it is probably better to abandon the principal term altogether in favour of more precise, less atavistic terminology'.[26] Furthermore, is it a concept understood by reference to its *aim*, or to its *effect*? One could describe the *effect* of 'bad leaver' clause on employees as 'punitive', in the sense that the detriment suffered by the employee was disproportionate to the seriousness of her 'wrongdoing'. For Barker, it is the *purpose* of punishment in private law that really matters.

[24] See, eg, O Kahn-Freud, *Labour and the Law*, 1st edn (London, Stevens & Sons Ltd, 1972) 8.
[25] Roth (n 8).
[26] Barker, ch 2, section I.

Moreover, the deterrence rationale seems to be a widely propounded purpose underlying punitive damages.[27]

In the employment relationship, Courtney has argued that it is one of 'familiar contexts in which punitive sanctions seem to be tolerated', since 'one party is seen to have the authority to punish and a legitimate interest in so doing'.[28] He points out that employee disciplinary sanctions, which include warnings, wage deductions, demotions, suspensions or dismissal, are regarded as 'punishment', and the power of the employer to punish is 'restricted, not proscribed' by the law.[29] This analysis reveals the difficulties highlighted by Barker of defining 'punishment', and the need to distinguish between purpose and effect. As Courtney notes, dismissal could be symbolically viewed as the 'ultimate' sanction in the employment relationship. He adds that an employer's objective in dismissing an employee for misconduct may be the protection of the employer's reputation or other commercial interests, or a desire to punish the employee or both. However, statutory controls such as unfair dismissal legislation could enormously restrict the employer's unilateral exercise of this sanction.[30]

What about contractual mechanisms aimed at disincentivising an employee from leaving the employer? It cannot be said that these mechanisms constitute a 'tolerated' form of sanction in contemporary employment relationships, given the outright legal and moral condemnation of labour practices that 'tie' an employee to a particular employer.[31] The International Labour Organization (ILO) has pointed out that there should be no 'penalty' or the 'threat of penalty' (including the loss of rights or privileges) that constrains the ability of the worker to leave the employment at any time. The existence of such constraints may constitute forced labour.[32] Being able to enter and exit an employment relationship voluntarily and freely is seen as a fundamental right. This is the premise of our main objection to 'bad leaver' clauses, which, we argue, is a stronger normative foundation than other private law objections such as the penalties doctrine.

Even if we consider the role of deterrence in the operation of 'bad leaver' clauses and recognise that they indeed have a deterrent *aim*, it is hard to normatively justify their underlying purpose. Our concern here is with the nature of the 'wrongdoing' that the employer is trying to deter, that is, an employee's seeking to leave an employment relationship. Given that a worker's freedom to quit is a fundamental right, the purpose of deterrence in this context cannot be normatively justified. In other words, there is no 'wrongdoing' to be deterred. Quitting a

[27] Barker, ch 2, section III.E.

[28] Courtney, ch 12, section III.D and section I respectively.

[29] Courtney, ch 12, section V.

[30] Courtney, ch 12, section V.B.

[31] See also M Zou, 'The Legal Construction of Hyper-Dependence and Hyper-Precarity in Migrant Work Relations' (2015) 31 *International Journal of Comparative Labour Law and Industrial Relations* 141.

[32] International Labour Organization, *Combating Forced Labour: A Handbook for Employers & Businesses*, 2nd edn (Geneva, International Labour Organization, 2015) 4, 7, 18.

job (provided certain procedures are followed) is neither misconduct nor breach of contractual obligations on the part of the employee. What we should be really concerned about is how 'bad leaver' clauses operate to constrain this fundamental right. As we examine in section III, the penalty doctrine, which is commonly used by departing employees to challenge these clauses, does not get to the heart of this issue. The English rules pertaining to this doctrine effectively exclude the prima facie review of these clauses as potential penalties.[33]

III. Cases Involving 'Bad Leaver' Clauses and the Penalty Doctrine

Under the penalty rule set out in *Cavendish*, the contractual provision in question would generally be unenforceable if 'the impugned provision is a secondary obligation which imposes a detriment on the contract-breaker out of all proportion to any legitimate interest of the innocent party in the enforcement of the primary obligation'.[34] To put it another way, such a provision may be enforceable if the innocent party can show that: (i) she has a legitimate interest in the contract-breaker's performance of the primary obligation; and (ii) the sanction for breach by the contract-breaker is not out of all proportion (or 'extravagant, exorbitant or unconscionable'[35] in relation) to such an interest. Even before the court considers these two conditions, it must first embark on an inquiry in ascertaining whether the penalty rule is engaged in the first place.

'Bad leaver' clauses, like any other contractual clauses, can be subject to the penalty doctrine. In our analysis of cases involving these clauses, we find that the doctrine can be easily avoided at the initial stage of the inquiry, that is, in ascertaining whether the penalty rule is triggered at all. There are three main ways for an employer to avoid the rule's application in this context. First, the 'bad leaver event' can be framed in the relevant contractual document as a primary obligation instead of a breach of contract. Second, the 'bad leaver event' can be construed as a 'conditional primary obligation'. Third, the applicable contractual clause can stipulate that the employee has no entitlement to a bonus or payment in question in the first place, such that nothing is to be 'forfeited' upon a breach of contract.

[33] Compare the Australian approach, which takes a broader view of the penalty doctrine. See, eg, *Andrews v Australia and New Zealand Banking Group Ltd* [2012] HCA 30, (2012) 247 CLR 205: 'In general terms, a stipulation prima facie imposes a penalty on a party ("the first party") if, as a matter of substance, it is collateral (or accessory) to a primary stipulation in favour of a second party and this collateral stipulation, upon the failure of the primary stipulation, imposes upon the first party an additional detriment, the penalty, to the benefit of the second party.' Importantly, a contractual clause that imposes an obligation to pay an agreed sum, even where there is no breach of contract, can still be a penalty.

[34] *Cavendish* (n 2) [32] (Lord Neuberger and Lord Sumption).

[35] ibid [152] (Lord Mance).

A. Ways of Avoiding the Penalty Doctrine

i. Primary Obligation Triggered by a Non-breach Event

The first and most obvious way of evading the application of the penalty doctrine is by drafting a clause as being triggered by a condition other than a breach of contract. This has recently been used in the context of 'bad leaver' clauses against employees whose equity share constitutes a large part of their total remuneration packages. There are two cases in particular we shall examine: *Signia Wealth v Vector Trustees Ltd and Others*[36] and *Nosworthy v Instinctif Partners Ltd.*[37]

In *Signia*, the company's articles of association provided that departing employees (including directors) had to transfer their shares to the company. The price of those shares was to be calculated based on whether the employee was a 'good leaver' or 'bad leaver'. If the employee was a 'bad leaver', she would receive an amount significantly lower than market value. The 'bad leaver' in this case was the managing director, who held a 49 per cent shareholding in the company. The relationship between the employee and the company deteriorated over time, with the latter commencing disciplinary proceedings against the former in relation to an expense claim. The employee resigned during the disciplinary proceedings and was deemed a 'bad leaver' under the company's articles. On this basis, her shares were acquired by the company far below market value in accordance with the articles.

The definition of a 'Bad Leaver' in the company articles was defined as 'any Leaver who is not a Good Leaver or an Incapacitated Good Leaver',[38] which the court acknowledged as an 'entirely negative "catch all" definition'.[39] In other words, in order to find the employee a 'Bad Leaver', the court had to determine if the employee was *not* a Good Leaver or Incapacitated Good Leaver. There were two classes of a 'Good Leaver' in the company's articles: (i) where the employee left the company by giving notice (and where such notice of termination would expire five years or more after the employment start date) and was not in breach of her terms of employment; or (ii) where the employee left the company as a result of summary dismissal when the employer had no right to dismiss the employee without notice. An 'Incapacitated Good Leaver' was an employee who left the company due to death, serious illness or disability, or on summary dismissal based on mental incapacity or long-term absence. Applying these definitions to the circumstances of the employee's resignation, the court found her to be a 'Bad Leaver'.[40]

When the employee challenged the 'bad leaver' provision on the basis of the penalty rule, the court held that the doctrine did not apply. The court

[36] *Signia* (n 7).
[37] *Nosworthy v Instinctif Partners Ltd* [2019] UKEAT/0100/18.
[38] *Signia* (n 7) [512].
[39] ibid.
[40] ibid [650].

acknowledged that '[it] must be astute to detect disguised penalties, and it is clear that the penalty doctrine extends to deposits, forfeiture clauses and provisions that require a party in breach of contract to transfer property to the other party at less than its full value'.[41] Nevertheless, the doctrine did not apply because of the nature of the compulsory transfer process in the company's articles, which did not 'have anything to do with the shareholder's breach of contract'.[42] Moreover, although a breach of the employment contract was a pertinent factor in determining whether an employee was a good or bad leaver, the court pointed out that these provisions were 'triggered by events other than a breach of contract'.[43] Here, the employee's departure did not entail a breach of her employment contract.

In another unsuccessful attempt to challenge 'bad leaver' provisions, the claimant in *Nosworthy* signed an employment contract initially with a company that the respondent later acquired. Upon the company's acquisition, the claimant was given some shares and loan notes by the respondent's company as deferred consideration on the share sale. The claimant agreed to forfeit her deferred earn-out shares and loan notes if she were to be classified as a 'Bad Leaver' under the respondent's articles of association. A 'Bad Leaver' was defined in the articles as including a shareholder who ceased to be employed by the respondent due to voluntary resignation. When the claimant resigned, the 'bad leaver' provision became operative and she was required to sell her shares to the respondent at the acquisition cost of £1 per share, and her loan notes were also forfeited. The claimant challenged the 'bad leaver' provision as an unenforceable penalty.

The employment tribunal held that the 'Bad Leaver' provision in the company's articles fell outside the scope of the penalty doctrine since it operated independently of any breach of contract by the claimant.[44] The Employment Appeals Tribunal (EAT) upheld the employment tribunal's decision. As the EAT noted, 'The definition of "Bad Leaver" in Article 15.9.2(a) does not depend on a breach of contract. Its effect is not the consequence of a breach of a primary obligation.'[45] While the claimant's act of resignation made her a 'Bad Leaver' as defined in the principal agreement between the parties, the act itself did not constitute a breach of contract.

Fundamentally, in England, the threshold for the penalty doctrine to apply is a breach of contract. As the above two cases demonstrate, by adopting 'bad leaver' clauses within the company's articles as being triggered independently of a breach of the employment contract (or other relevant contracts), an employer can enforce such clauses that can have significantly detrimental financial effects on the departing employee.

[41] ibid [653].
[42] ibid.
[43] ibid.
[44] *Nosworthy* (n 37).
[45] ibid [67].

ii. 'Conditional Primary Obligation'

Even if a contract provides for a sum payable upon a breach of contract, the penalty rule may nevertheless be avoided if the court characterises the obligation in question as a primary obligation of the contract. In *Cavendish*, the clause in question provided that if the seller was in breach of its restrictive covenants on non-competition, he would not receive the last two instalments of the purchase price. Lord Neuberger and Lord Sumption (with the agreement of Lord Carnwath) held that this clause was a primary obligation instead of a secondary obligation, despite being triggered by a breach of contract. The clause was 'not a contractual alternative to damages' or 'concerned with regulating the measure of compensation for breach'.[46] Instead, the nature of the clause was 'in reality a price adjustment clause',[47] which regulated the parties' primary bargain by adjusting the purchase price on the (non-)occurrence of certain event(s). The characterisation of this clause was what the court called a 'conditional primary obligation'. This is because the extra sum could only be earned upon the non-occurrence of certain events, of which breach of the non-compete covenant was one. The court emphasised that a conditional primary obligation could not be a penalty.[48]

Such analysis in *Cavendish* was applied in the case of *Richards v IP Solutions Group Ltd*.[49] In this case, a 'bad leaver' provision was included in a company's articles of association, whereby shareholder-employees would be subject to a compulsory transfer of their existing shares in the event of a summary dismissal by the company. In this case, the two claimants worked for the respondent company as CEO and Sales Director respectively. The claimants each held a 30 per cent shareholding in the company. The claimants were summarily dismissed by the respondent on the basis that they had (purportedly) seriously breached their statutory duties as directors and duties as employees of the company. The respondent sought to invoke the 'bad leaver' provision in the company's articles, which stated that a bad leaver would be paid £1 for the aggregate shareholding he was required to transfer.

The High Court in *Richards* found that the claimants were wrongfully dismissed as their breach of statutory duties was not material. The respondent was therefore not entitled to summarily dismiss the claimants and invoke the 'bad leaver' provision. The court proceeded to discuss the hypothetical legal position in a situation where the respondent was entitled to summarily dismiss the claimants (summary dismissal being consequent on the claimants' breach of contract).[50] Drawing on the reasoning in *Cavendish*, the court's tentative conclusion was that the 'bad leaver provision' in the respondent's articles of association was more akin

[46] *Cavendish* (n 2) [74].
[47] ibid.
[48] ibid [14].
[49] *Richards v IP Solutions Group Ltd* [2016] EWHC 1835, [2017] IRLR 133.
[50] ibid [76], [79].

to a primary obligation between the parties that was backed by sound commercial reasons related to a shareholder's leaving the company. As such, the fact that only £1 was payable upon the summary dismissal of a 'bad leaver' needed to be read against the background context that such a sum was merely the agreed price for the share transfer.

Cavendish and *Richards* show how an employer can avoid the application of the penalty rule by framing a provision requiring payment of a sum on breach of contract as part of the primary bargain between the parties. This is, of course, subject to the 'substance and reality' test articulated in *Dunlop* and referred to in *Cavendish*, insofar as the penalty rule would catch a provision that *in substance* is a secondary obligation. However, with careful drafting, an employer can still structure a transaction and related contractual documents in such a way that a 'bad leaver' clause would escape the reach of the penalty doctrine, even if the clause was triggered by a breach of contract. Once again, it can be seen that the doctrine is of little avail to employees attempting to challenge the operation of these clauses.

iii. No Entitlement to Asset, thus Nothing to Forfeit

Another way to avoid the penalty rule when it comes to 'bad leaver' provisions that are triggered by a breach of contract is to stipulate in the relevant contract that the employee has no entitlement to shares, a sum of money or other property in the first place, such that nothing is to be 'payable', 'forgone', or 'forfeited' upon a breach. In *Imam-Sadeque v Bluebay Asset Management (Services) Ltd*,[51] the employee sought, following the termination of his employment, to claim his 'entitlement' to unvested fund units as part of employee bonus plans from the respondent. The respondent resisted the claim on the ground of the claimant's breach of his obligation not to compete (in working for a rival company). Under the terms of the bonus plans, only a 'good leaver' would be entitled to the fund units.

The court held that the claimant did not come within the respondent's definition of a 'good leaver', which was an employee who ceased employment due to retirement, redundancy, injury or termination by the company for reasons other than the employee's serious misconduct. Furthermore, the claimant was deemed a 'Bad Leaver', which, as defined by the company, was 'a person who: (A) ceases to hold employment with the Group in any circumstances not covered by the definition of Good Leaver'.[52]

The court reasoned that the employee's being a 'good leaver' was a condition precedent for the acquisition of any rights to the restricted shares that were invested in the fund units. As the claimant was deemed a 'bad leaver' who did not satisfy this condition precedent, the fund units never belonged to the claimant. As the court put it, the restricted shares were merely 'contingent future interests'.[53]

[51] *Imam-Sadeque v Bluebay Asset Management (Services) Ltd* [2012] EWHC 3511, [2013] IRLR 344.
[52] ibid [17].
[53] ibid [210].

The nature of these shares was not the same as a sum of money payable upon breach, whereby the employee would have had a prima facie entitlement to the sum (that would then be forfeited upon a breach of contract). In this case, the court found that there was no entitlement on the part of the employee to begin with, since his rights to the restricted shares were conditional on his being a 'good leaver'.

B. Legitimate Interest

Even if a 'bad leaver' clause prima facie falls within the penalty doctrine, the requirement of a 'legitimate interest' is often established in a commercial setting. The relevant cases we examine below all highlight two considerations in this regard. The first is concerned with whether the parties received extensive professional or legal advice. The second is whether there was a sound commercial justification for structuring the arrangement in question in a certain way.

In a Scottish case, *Gray v Braid Group (Holdings) Ltd*,[54] the claimant was found guilty of gross misconduct arising from being implicated in bribery offences involving the respondent company's business. The issue concerning the valuation of the claimant's shares arose in the context of a successful unfair prejudice petition, and specifically whether the respondent could rely on a 'bad leaver' clause in its Articles of Association that required the transfer of the claimant's shares back to the company at subscription price.

In *Gray*, Lord Menzies reasoned that on a proper construction of the contract, there was a primary obligation that the employee would not commit gross misconduct or consistently underperform. In turn, Lord Menzies and Lord Brodie agreed that the 'bad leaver' provision (and the negative consequences flowing therefrom) was to be construed as a secondary obligation. As to whether the negative consequence of the provision was out of all proportion to the legitimate interest(s) of the respondent, Lords Brodie and Malcolm reasoned that because the basis for dismissal was fraud or gross misconduct, the 'bad leaver' consequence was a proportionate and legitimate response, especially given that the transaction in question was a commercial transaction agreed on the basis of professional legal advice.[55] Lord Malcolm also seemed to have in mind the lack of a common law 'fall-back' arrangement in the event of the clause's being unenforceable, in eventually deciding that the clause was enforceable.[56]

The same reasoning regarding 'legitimate interest' is also seen in *Richards*, where the court discussed obiter the consequence of the 'bad leaver' provision's being a secondary obligation. The court held that there was nothing 'unconscionable' in the transfer and pricing clause, as the parties had dealt with each other at

[54] *Gray v Braid Group (Holdings) Ltd* [2016] CSIH 68, 2017 SC 409 (Court of Session).
[55] ibid [109]–[113] (Lord Brodie), [124]–[125] (Lord Malcolm).
[56] ibid [125].

arm's length and received considerable expert advice.[57] Again, in *Signia*, the judge noted obiter that the 'bad leaver' provisions in that case would have been enforceable even if they had been caught by the penalty rule. In reaching this conclusion, Smith J placed special emphasis on two factors. First, he noted the commercial justification and contextual background behind such a clause: in particular, the importance of concentrating the shareholdings in a start-up venture such that they would 'not be too diffuse and remain vested in those directly concerned with the development of the company'.[58] Second, he noted that the provisions performed the legitimate function of 'incentivising employees to stay'[59] or employee loyalty, by connecting the measure of an employee's 'reward' with the duration of time over which she stayed in the company. However, we argue here that the court failed to recognise a countervailing consideration regarding the normative legitimacy of these clauses in terms of limiting an employee's freedom to *leave* the company, especially where there is no contractual breach by the employee and where significant inequality of bargaining power exists. Overall, it can be seen that the scope of what counts as a 'legitimate' justification for an employer vis-à-vis the 'bad leaver' is rather wide. Thus, arguments at the 'legitimate interest' stage often lead to the conclusion that a clause falling within the penalty doctrine is nonetheless enforceable.

C. Other Possible Judicial Controls on 'Bad Leaver' Clauses

Given the limitations of the penalty doctrine, employees challenging 'bad leaver' clauses have turned to other (sometimes creative) legal arguments, such as the restraint of trade doctrine. In *20:20 London Ltd v Riley*,[60] a case cited in *Nosworthy*, the respondent sold his company to the claimant for around £2.2 million in shares and cash. The terms of the sale were set out in a share purchase agreement (SPA). At the same time, the respondent entered into a contract of employment with the claimant, which allowed the respondent to resign on six months' notice. However, under a provision in the SPA, if the respondent ceased to be an employee for any reason within the first three years of the company's purchase, he would be obliged to repay the £1.5 million consideration (in some circumstances, the repayment would be reduced on a sliding scale during the third year). The respondent ceased his employment with the company after two years. The claimant sought repayment of a large part of the £1.5 million cash consideration. The respondent defended the claim on four bases, including a defence based on restraint of trade. He argued that the repayment provision on which the claimant relied was a provision that effectively prevented him from resigning for three years.

[57] *Richards* (n 50) [85].
[58] *Signia* (n 7) [653].
[59] ibid.
[60] *20:20 London Ltd v Riley* [2012] EWHC 1912 (Ch D).

As such, the respondent claimed it was an unlawful restraint of trade and therefore should be struck out.

The argument that a 'bad leaver' clause constitutes an unenforceable 'restraint of trade' clause can be rebutted by an employer who can show that it has a legitimate interest in restricting the activities of a departing employee and that the clause is reasonable in protecting such interest.[61] This burden is relatively easy to discharge by an employer in relation to 'bad leaver' clauses. The main objective of having a restraint of trade clause in place is to constrain the employee's ability to work for a competitor in the same industry *after termination of the employment relationship*. In comparison, a 'bad leaver' clause has no such legal consequence. The core concern of restraint of trade is to 'neuter' disproportionately long or onerous legal constraints[62] on employment post-termination. This is because the law needs to balance the employer's interest in maintaining confidential information and trade secrets against the employee's interest in using her skills and expertise in the most productive and efficient way.[63] In any event, as the focus of the restraint of trade doctrine is on assessing whether the clause protects the *employer*'s legitimate interest to a reasonable (as opposed to disproportionate) extent, as well as public policy, insufficient regard is being paid to the perspective of employees, as will be shown further in section III.D.

Other areas of contract law have been raised in the above cases, seeking to challenge the enforceability of 'bad leaver' clauses, including contractual construction, implied terms, rectification, unilateral mistake and unconscionability. All these arguments have failed before the courts. In *Nosworthy*, for example, the claimant tried to argue that 'good faith' required a constraint on the employer's contractual discretion to withhold the 'good leaver' sum. This did not succeed in the face of clear express terms.[64] Furthermore, it is extremely difficult to challenge such clauses under the extremely narrow doctrine of unconscionability, as is evident from *Nosworthy*, where the argument was raised but roundly rejected by the court.[65]

D. The Limits of the 'Paradigm of Penalty'

Based on the current rules under the penalty doctrine, our analysis of relevant cases has shown that it is relatively easy for an employer to draft 'bad leaver' clauses

[61] *Marion White Ltd v Francis* [1972] 1 WLR 1423 (CA); *Lucas (T) & Co Ltd v Mitchell* [1972] 3 WLR 934 (CA).

[62] Regarding the 'reasonableness' of a restraint of trade clause, the two most important factors are the operative duration of the clause and the scope of work being prohibited. These are legal restraints that can continue for a significant duration post-employment.

[63] H Collins, KD Ewing and A McColgan, *Labour Law* (Cambridge, Cambridge University Press, 2012) 153–54, 156.

[64] *Nosworthy* (n 38) [54]–[62].

[65] ibid [50].

to avoid the doctrine's application altogether. It is also evident that other contract law doctrines and rules offer hardly any protection for employees who are subject to these clauses. Notably, as those cases on compulsory share transfers illustrate, employees whose total remuneration package may be constituted in large part by equity shares can easily find their shares substantially devalued (and sometimes, practically 'expropriated'). While one might assume that these clauses tend to apply to key (and therefore presumably the most skilled and valued) employees who have a relatively high degree of bargaining power vis-à-vis the employer, cases like *Nosworthy* demonstrate the prevalent use of such mechanisms across different remuneration grades within a company.

As we have argued, our main concern arising from these cases relates to how 'bad leaver' clauses can affect an employee's basic freedom to leave her job and employer, which has received little (if any) attention from labour law or contract law scholars alike. It is somewhat surprising that given the concern of labour law regimes in correcting the imbalance in bargaining power inherent within an employment relationship, there is little protection for employees in respect of 'bad leaver clauses'. For example, in *Nosworthy*, both the employment tribunal and the EAT rejected the claimant's argument under section 27 of the Employment Rights Act in relation to the 'deduction of wages' arising from the operation of the 'bad leaver' clause. This is because section 27(2)(e) excludes 'any payment to the worker otherwise than in his capacity as a worker' from the meaning of 'wages'. Both tribunals held that the claim was being brought in Ms Nosworthy's capacity as vendor rather than worker.[66]

The claimant in *Nosworthy* also sought to argue that the contract was illegal on the basis that the relevant agreement entailing the 'bad leaver' clause comprised forced or compulsory labour, hence contravening the Modern Slavery Act 2015. Again, this argument did not find favour before the EAT, as it held that the claimant 'took up employment as a volunteer and when she was no longer wishing to continue working for the Respondent she resigned'.[67] Nevertheless, it is notable that the employment tribunal had commented that

> reasons that may have operated on her mind that could have discouraged an earlier resignation would be applicable to any employment and any employee who was considering resigning. One of those factors that might encourage them not to resign would be the loss of salary and benefits.[68]

It may be objected that there is no violation of a 'right to exit' if, under a particular contract, the 'good leaver' clauses are always conditional upon 'good leaver behaviour'. In other words, the essence of the employer–employee bargain is that the rewards for being a 'good leaver' are only available in defined circumstances (for example, where the employee is not summarily dismissed for a period of

[66] ibid [52].
[67] ibid [23].
[68] ibid.

five years). Following this line of this argument, the fact is that employees simply do not gain such 'good leaver' entitlements if they exit the employment relationship as 'bad leavers', for *ex hypothesi* they do not fulfil the conditions precedent for such 'good leaver' entitlements to arise in the first place.

However, if we situate such an objection within the framework of an employee's basic freedom to choose whether and when to remain or leave an employment relationship, it is clear that this objection does not affect the fact that 'unaccrued' 'good leaver' entitlements can act as a disincentive for an employee to quit. There may still be an unacceptable intrusion into the employee's freedom to exit, based on the idea that the 'good leaver' entitlements can serve as a 'reference point' (vis-à-vis the consequences of being a 'bad leaver') for the employee. The incentive to stay with the employer can be particularly strong, given that (as well-documented in psychology[69]) individuals are more averse to avoiding losses than to acquiring equivalent gains. Where a 'bad leaver' clause exists, the employee may believe that she has a lot to lose if she quits, especially if there is a considerable difference between the pay-outs to good leavers and bad leavers. Given the psychological tendency, an employee may be anxious to avoid such a 'loss'. As such, she may adjust her behaviour to comply with the employer's every demand, which provides fertile ground for opportunistic exploitation.

IV. Proposal for Legislative Reform

The Scottish Law Commission report deliberately left open the question of regulating penalty clauses in the employment law context, recognising that there are special considerations at play specifically in this context.[70] In our chapter, we have argued that one such special and fundamental consideration is the right to leave an employment relationship. Considering the inadequacies of the penalty doctrine in regulating 'bad leaver' clauses, we propose that the regulation of such clauses should not be within the 'paradigm' of penalty but instead be subject to statutory control that would sufficiently vindicate an employee's right to quit. We acknowledge that in some cases, such statutory control may strike down carefully considered and negotiated bargains between parties whereby the asymmetry of bargaining power between the employer and employee may not be so significant. What, then, should the appropriate normative balance be?

We could draw an analogy with the context of minority shareholder protection, where the courts have given a right of exit in the form of the typical buy-out remedy following a successful unfair prejudice petition.[71] The archetypal petition

[69] SM Tom, CR Fox, C Trepel and RA Poldrack, 'The Neural Basis of Loss Aversion in Decision-Making Under Risk' (2007) 315 *Science* 515.

[70] Scottish Law Commission (n 1) para 4.34.

[71] In the UK, the 'unfair prejudice' rule under the Companies Act 2006, s 994 affords remedies to a minority shareholder where there is a breach of a 'legitimate expectation(s)' held by that shareholder.

involves a minority shareholder in a closely-held company, who has a legitimate expectation of conduct on the part of the company's owner-managers, only to have this expectation defeated by the prejudicial conduct of the company. A common remedy awarded by the court following a successful petition is a share buy-out, generally based on a fair valuation, which provides a right of exit for the minority shareholder.

This situation parallels that of an employee who is subject to 'bad leaver' clauses. The employer has considerable discretion to deem the employee a 'bad leaver' under the company's articles and deprive the employee of substantial financial rewards, just as majority shareholders can exercise their powers to exclude the minority shareholder or otherwise create unfair prejudice to the latter's interests (which are not restricted to her legal rights but also her legitimate expectations). Just as courts can grant a right of exit to the minority shareholder in this situation, an employee's right of exit in the context of 'bad leaver' clauses should also be vindicated, for example, by a fair valuation of the shares transferred.

As we have highlighted earlier, protecting an employee's right to quit is a vindication of her personal liberty, and also serves to prevent unilateral oppression and abuse by the employer. It was established in section III that the penalty doctrine and other common law doctrines do not offer adequate protection for employees when it comes to 'bad leaver' provisions. Moreover, there is a tendency to prioritise a utilitarian concern of promoting market freedom and competition in the case of restraint of trade. The task of reform, as we suggest, is to have the law focus on protecting an employee's freedom to change jobs and curbing opportunistic exploitation by employers. Substantively, therefore, the scope of statutory regulation should be dictated by the need to vindicate the employee's right to quit. The appropriate legal test may be as follows:

> If a worker or employee's freedom to exit an employment relationship is constrained by a 'bad leaver clause', the employer will be prevented from relying on such a clause to the extent that the constraint excessively interferes with this freedom.

Unlike the restraint of trade analysis, the proposed test would focus the court's attention on the impact of the 'bad leaver' clause on the employee's freedom to leave an employment relationship (in whatever form such a clause may be drafted). Furthermore, our test draws a balance between the interests of the employer and the employee, because judicial scrutiny will only be attracted where there is an 'excessive' interference with the employee's right to quit. Indeed, our suggested test tracks the Scottish Law Commission's proposal in relation to penalty clauses, namely, that such clauses should be struck down only when they are 'excessively penal' in their effects.[72] In ascertaining whether such an interference is 'excessive', we suggest that the primary concern of an employee's right to exit is weighed up

[72] Scottish Law Commission (n 1) para 5.13. In fact, the proposal specifically mentions 'bad leaver' clauses.

against other considerations such as the employer's legitimate business interests (including those mentioned in the cases analysed in section III). The primacy of protecting a fundamental right is the crucial factor that distinguishes our proposed test from the test associated with restraint of trade.

Another merit of this test is to overcome attempts to use formalistic arguments to escape review of 'bad leaver' clauses. Two such arguments were raised in *Nosworthy*. The first argument was that the claimant's status as a vendor of shares should be distinguished from her status as an employee, which excluded the application of labour law rules in that case.[73] The second argument was that the agreement for the sale of the claimant's shares (in return for upfront and deferred consideration in the form of loan notes and shares) was not a condition of her entering into an employment contract with the respondent, and so the 'bad leaver' clauses (which resulted from the respondent's articles of association as opposed to the employment contract) could escape judicial scrutiny due to the absence of a breach of the main (employment) contract.[74]

Under the proposed test, these arguments would only gain traction if the employer were to succeed in demonstrating that the constraint on the employee's freedom to exit an employment relationship was not 'excessive'. It may well be that the company's articles (or shareholders agreement) and one's employment contract have no connection in strict legal terms, but they may be so closely connected that it leads to the imposition of an excessive constraint on this freedom. To put it another way, if the two 'capacities' of employee and shareholder are so intrinsically connected that enforcing a 'bad leaver' provision will necessarily 'infect' the claimant's capacity as an employee by excessively constraining her right to quit, the 'bad leaver' provision should attract judicial scrutiny.

V. Conclusion

A 'bad leaver' clause can be an insidious type of contractual provision that strikes at the heart of an employee's right to quit. As we have shown, the current law on penalties does not protect this basic right. An analysis of recent cases suggests that an employer can avoid the application of the penalty doctrine to 'bad leaver' clauses with relative ease, and that it is difficult to invoke other contractual doctrines to challenge a potentially major impediment to an employee's leaving a particular employer.

Given the shortcomings of the existing penalty 'paradigm', we have argued that some statutory intervention is necessary to specifically formulate controls on the enforceability of bad leaver clauses. Yet the law should be mindful not to take this to the extreme and strike down legitimate bargains. In drawing the appropriate

[73] *Nosworthy* (n 38) [52].
[74] ibid [67]–[71].

balance, we have suggested that judicial intervention only be attracted in cases where 'bad leaver' clauses impose an excessive constraint on the employee's freedom to exit an employment relationship. In so doing, the law would align itself with the key concerns of protecting a person's autonomy in a field as central to human flourishing as her employment, and preventing unilateral oppression by a significantly more powerful party in such a relationship.

PART V

Conclusion

15

Punishment and Private Law: Future Themes and Perspectives

ELISE BANT AND JEANNIE MARIE PATERSON

In this brief, concluding chapter, we seek to identify some key themes and perspectives that we consider should inform future research and developments in private law with respect to conceptions of punishment. As will become apparent, many of these themes are identified or articulated in the contributions to this collection of essays. However, it also seems apparent that much remains to be done to develop a coherent theory of punishment and private law. As the following reflections reveal, future work will benefit from drawing liberally upon the rich materials found at common law, in equity and pursuant to statute, informed by insights from fields such as criminal and comparative law, legal and economic theory, and based upon solid empirical foundations, to inform understanding about patterns, trends and consequences of legal approaches and doctrine.

I. The Role of Punishment in Achieving Private Law Aims

The first theme that we identify arises from the assumption that punishment is foreign to the civil law, being a conception essentially grounded in criminal law.[1] While views on this differ,[2] we consider that there is great force in Kit Barker's insight that it is necessary and helpful to distinguish between punishment as an aim of the law and as an incident of other purposes or outcomes being pursued by the law.[3] In particular, punishment may be a consequence of doctrine or

[1] This issue is the subject of particular examination in Courtney and Goudkamp, ch 1, sections I.A and I.E; Barker, ch 2, section I.

[2] Goudkamp and Courtney (ch 1, section II), Goudkamp and Katsampouka (ch 8), as well as Courtney (ch 12), for example, favour the view that the private law does aim squarely to punish in some scenarios.

[3] Barker, ch 2, section II.B.

interventions that have a primary purpose of deterring or expressing condemnation of wrongful conduct.[4]

This role for punishment is hardly a stranger to the common law. Even in England, where the environment appears to have been most hostile to its reception,[5] it is arguable that courts have evidenced grudging and even growing recognition of the necessity for legal responses to misconduct that punish in effect, if not in aim, in the interests of deterrence.[6] The modest and highly predictable measures of punitive damages in that jurisdiction are noted by Goudkamp and Katsampouka.[7] It is plausible that this judicial constraint suggests an emphasis on the expressive role of punitive damages, as well as keen appreciation of the need to avoid undue punishment. This interpretation is consistent with Barker's thesis on the ancillary role of punitive damages. Beyond England, it is apparent that many common law jurisdictions have been far more transparent and ready in accepting punitive awards made to support or effect private law aims, such as deterrence.[8]

The ongoing role of punitive (or exemplary) damages is but one aspect of the private law's nuanced use of punitive measures. The highly differential measures of compensation awarded by courts for varying forms of civil wrongdoing are another example of this ancillary use of punitive measures.[9] Here, awards are calibrated to reflect degrees of culpability, leading to potentially significant differences in the measure of compensation. Thus, at one end of the spectrum, egregious wrongs like deceit typically attract generous remoteness rules[10] and largely deny the relevance of contributory negligence considerations,[11] and while mitigation principles apply, they appear to be applied charitably, with full credit given to the victim's difficulties as the victim of fraud.[12] These liberal recovery principles

[4] It may also be appropriate in other circumstances, discussed at text accompanying n 33.

[5] The range of arguments against the award of punitive damages commonly employed in that jurisdiction is well-examined and criticised in Goudkamp and Katsampouka, ch 8.

[6] Bant and Paterson, ch 10, section II.A.

[7] Goudkamp and Katsampouka, ch 8, section III.A.

[8] A general review is contained in Bant and Paterson, ch 10, section II.

[9] Bant and Paterson, ch 10, section I; Goudkamp and Katsampouka, ch 8, section III.D; see also Rowan, ch 3, section II.B, discussed later in this section.

[10] *Doyle v Olby (Ironmongers) Ltd* [1969] 2 QB 158 (CA) 167 (Lord Denning MR); *Smith New Court Securities Ltd v Citibank NA* [1997] AC 254 (HL) 264–67 (Lord Browne-Wilkinson), 283 (Lord Steyn); *Palmer Bruyn & Parker Pty Limited v Parsons* [2001] HCA 69, (2001) 208 CLR 388 [78] (Gummow J).

[11] *Standard Chartered Bank v Pakistan Shipping Corporation* [2002] UKHL 43, [2003] 1 AC 959, approved in *Ancient Order of Foresters in Victoria Friendly Society Ltd v Lifeplan Australia Friendly Society Ltd* [2018] HCA 43, (2018) 265 CLR 1 ('*Lifeplan*') [9] (Kiefel CJ, Keane and Edelman JJ); *Jamieson v Westpac* [2014] QSC 32, [166] (Jackson CJ).

[12] See, eg, the generous approach adopted in *Doyle v Olby (Ironmongers) Ltd* [1969] 2 QB 158 (CA) 166 (Lord Denning MR), allowing recovery with respect to 'the expense and loss in trying to run a business [for three years] which has turned out to be a disaster for him … There is nothing to be taken off in mitigation …'; and the application of deceit measures in a statutory context in *Henville v Walker* (2001) 206 CLR 459. Courts often frame the enquiry as to whether the plaintiff's fault was such as to constitute an 'intervening cause' or was 'extrinsic' to the transaction, for example because of the plaintiff's foolishness, ineptitude or gross negligence: see, eg, *Gould v Vaggelas* (1984) 157 CLR 215, 221–22 (Gibbs CJ) 267 (Dawson J). At general law, the degree of unreasonableness required to break the chain of causation

operate in addition to deceit's being regarded, at least in some jurisdictions, as the paradigm case to which punitive damages should apply.[13] By contrast, the law of negligence draws more limited boundaries to the defendant's scope of liability for compensatory awards,[14] while leaving open (in some jurisdictions at least) the possibility of award of punitive damages to mark particularly egregious defendant misconduct.[15]

At the other end of the spectrum, the non-wrong of innocent misrepresentation yields only restitutionary relief, which is then subject to additional defensive considerations such as good faith change of position on the part of the defendant.[16] Revealingly, these defensive considerations also fall away in the face of bad-faith conduct. Some statutory doctrines and remedies permit courts to draw similar, if not wholly equivalent lines to reflect relative defendant culpability.[17] Where they do not, they are subject to considerable criticism as unprincipled responses that require reform.[18]

Beyond these subtle adjustments to compensatory and restitutionary relief, there is also significant (albeit far from universal)[19] support for the view that the equitable remedy of disgorgement following an account of profits aims to deter misconduct.[20] Indeed, on one view, the equitable remedy (particularly as developed by the Australian High Court) provides an outstanding and principled

is 'very high': *Emeh v Kensington etc AHA* [1984] 3 All ER 1044, 1049 per Waller LJ. Taking a generous approach to the mitigation principle aligns entirely with the position taken in respect of contributory negligence in cases of deceit. However, this does not entitle a plaintiff simply to sit and accumulate losses: see, eg, in a related statutory context, *Henjo Investments Pty Ltd v Collins Marrickville Pty Ltd (No 2)* (1989) 40 FCR 76.

[13] *Musca v Astle Corporation Pty Ltd* (1988) 80 ALR 251, 268 (French J). cf *Kuddus v Chief Constable of Leicester* [2001] UKHL 29, [2002] 2 AC 122 [43] (Lord Mackay) [50]–[56], [62]–[68] (Lord Nicholls) and at [122] (Lord Scott), suggesting that cases of deceit may properly give rise to punitive damages.

[14] *Palmer Bruyn & Parker Pty Limited v Parsons* [2001] HCA 69, (2001) 208 CLR 388.

[15] *Gray v Motor Accident Commission* (1998) 196 CLR 1; *Couch v Attorney-General (No 2)* [2010] NZSC 27, [2010] 3 NZLR 149. See also Goudkamp and Katsampouka, ch 8, section III.I; and Bant and Paterson, ch 10, sections II.C and III.A.

[16] E Bant, 'Rescission, Restitution and Compensation' in S Degeling and J Varuhas (eds), *Equitable Compensation and Disgorgement of Profit* (Oxford, Hart Publishing, 2017) 277.

[17] E Bant and J Paterson, 'Limitations on Defendant Liability for Misleading or Deceptive Conduct under Statute: Some Insights from Negligent Misstatement' in K Barker, R Grantham and W Swain (eds), *Law of Misstatements: 50 Years on from Hedley Byrne v Heller* (Oxford, Hart Publishing, 2015) 159.

[18] eg Misrepresentation Act 1967 (UK). For a discussion of the issues and main authorities, see JM Paterson and E Bant, 'Misrepresentation, Misleading Conduct and Statute through the Lens of Form and Substance' in A Robertson and J Goudkamp (eds), *Form and Substance in the Law of Obligations* (Oxford, Hart Publishing, 2019) ch 17.

[19] eg L Smith, 'Deterrence, prophylaxis, and punishment in fiduciary obligations' (2013) 7 *Journal of Equity* 87. Smith's important contributions to understanding equity's fiduciary principles, and their implications for punishment in private law, are discussed in detail in Penner, ch 5, sections VI.D and VI.F.

[20] Importantly, Penner argues that the account of profits involves neither punishment nor penalty, in that it simply requires the defendant to give up a gain owed to the plaintiff as a necessary incident of their relationship. By contrast, profit-stripping remedies that fall outside those accounting relationships have the quality of penalty: see Penner, ch 5, sections III and VI.

model of proportionate punishment.[21] Additionally to these remedial indicators signalling private law's ongoing engagement with punitive concerns, we may observe growing statutory recognition of the central regulatory role for civil penalties or fines.[22]

In the field of contract, the position regarding punitive considerations is more nuanced and unstable, warranting both the sustained attention of scholars such as the contributors in this volume, as well as future, further examination. On the one hand, some contractual doctrines, in particular the rule against penalties, operate to exclude a demand by one party that is 'excessive' in its punitive effect.[23] Thus, as Tiverios and McFarlane note, one party to a contract 'can have no legitimate interest in punishing [the other] for a breach of contract'.[24] The converse is that an agreed remedies clause will not be invalid as a penalty where it is not out of proportion to 'any legitimate interest of the innocent party in the enforcement of the primary obligation',[25] including through deterring a breach of contract.[26] Consistently, Barnett powerfully argues that contract law may properly draw on or engage with punitive measures in some defined contexts, for legitimate expressive and deterrent purposes.[27] Her analysis provides a framework for the further development of contractual remedial principles to these ends.

On the other hand, Courtney posits that, when viewed against a broad landscape of contractual and statutory history, contract law tolerates punishment, provided that there is some level of proportionality between the agreed sanction and the wrong.[28] As he further notes, however, this view still leaves open for future clarification what justifications lie for contract's rule against agreed penalties, including whether the apparent wariness around punishment is justified, as well as the justifications for, and limitations on, punishment within contract. We observe here that contract's apparent normative and doctrinal limitations when it comes to policing the boundaries of acceptable contracting behaviour are well illustrated

[21] *Lifeplan* (n 11), discussed in Bant and Paterson, ch 10, section IV.

[22] Rowan, ch 3; Bant and Paterson, ch 10.

[23] The authorities are gathered and fully discussed, with quite distinct interpretations, in Courtney, ch 12, section III and Tiverios and McFarlane, ch 13 sections II, III and IV; see also Courtney and Goudkamp, ch 1, section II.D.

[24] Tiverios and McFarlane, ch 13, section IV.A; see also their outline of analysis at ch 13, section II. On their analysis, the rule against penalties is best understood in terms of preserving courts' capacity to impose secondary rights for the breach of contract: the common law will not allow agreed remedies that will stultify the law's remedial policies, as determined by courts. Relief against forfeiture has a different justification, in ensuring the contractual right is not subverted or abused through being used for a punitive, as opposed to security, purpose. The relationship between the doctrines is a subject of ongoing debate: see also Courtney, ch 12, section IV.

[25] *Cavendish Square Holding BV v Makdessi* [2015] UKSC 67, [2016] AC 1172 [32] (Lord Neuberger and Lord Sumption) [152] (Lord Mance) [255] (Lord Hodge) [293] (Lord Toulson), discussed in Tiverios and McFarlane, ch 13, section II.A. Also see also S Rowan, 'The "Legitimate Interest in Performance" in the Law on Penalties' (2019) 78 *CLJ* 148.

[26] *Cavendish Square Holding BV v Makdessi* [2015] UKSC 67, [2016] AC 1172, [31], [82].

[27] Barnett, ch 9, section V.

[28] Courtney, ch 12, sections I, III.D and V.C.

by the 'bad leaver' clauses examined by Zou and Liu.[29] These often have strongly punitive effects on employees who quit their employment in circumstances that fall within, or do not clearly fall outside, the relevant provision. On their analysis, such punitive measures cannot plausibly be argued to operate in support of legitimate deterrent objectives, given that in many cases, employees have engaged in no 'wrongdoing'.

Finally, the foundational (if controversial) role of the doctrine(s) of contempt is yet another of the many areas that betray the civil law's close and necessary relationship with punishment. As Rolph strikingly puts it, from the perspective of the law's enforcement procedures and its foundational concern to protect the administration of justice, '[t]he whole of private law operates in the shadow of punishment'.[30]

Viewed against this backdrop of sporadic yet ubiquitous operation, punishment has a clear, if incidental, role to support or effect the distinctive aims of private law. Nor is this simply a common law oddity. As Rowan demonstrates, notwithstanding its supposed aversion to punishment and private law, French civil law also evinces an abiding, and now deepening, interest in the role of punishment in core private law fields, such as contract and tort.[31] And (as we discuss further, immediately below) it manifests that interest through strikingly similar mechanisms to those found at common law.[32]

But, as the essays in this collection further reveal, the relationship between civil doctrines and punishment is necessarily and properly guided by the distinctive aims of the civil law. Here, compensation, declaration and deterrence are chief aims – and punitive considerations can and do have a role to play in promoting and supporting each. As Sharkey observes, punitive damages may serve to ensure that wrongdoers pay for the undifferentiated and incalculable harms they cause, forcing defendants to internalise those losses while sending a powerful message about the law's demands.[33] That is, (and against initial intuitions, perhaps) punitive damages may sensibly and on a principled basis serve compensatory, as well as expressive, objectives of the civil law. Beyond compensatory objectives, equity contains further subtle and detailed guidance on how to effect deterrent and expressive objectives through monetary awards that strip a defendant of all advantage enjoyed from the breach.[34] The contempt jurisdiction is another striking example of the length to which courts will and do go to ensure compliance with the civil law, and the fine (indefinable) line that courts straddle between criminal and civil sanction in so

[29] Zou and Liu, ch 14.

[30] Rolph, ch 6, section I.

[31] Rowan, ch 3, sections II and III.

[32] Her discussion of agreed penalties, remoteness rules and what appears to be a civil form of contempt mechanism closely track the common law issues, as does more recent focus on the role of disgorgement, or profit-stripping remedies.

[33] Sharkey, ch 7, section III.

[34] Compare Penner, ch 5, section VI and Bant and Paterson, ch 10, section IV.

doing: a matter of ongoing debate and concern.[35] Nor is this sensitivity to proper and proportionate use of punishment in civil fields of regulation, to ensure it operates consistently with and promotes distinctly civil aims, confined to common law jurisdictions. French reform proposals to introduce civil penalties for egregious tortious misconduct, the subject of Rowan's analysis, seek to find novel and appropriate measures to deter profitable wrongdoing. These reforms come off the back of proposals variously to introduce punitive damages, or disgorgement damages, and longstanding academic calls for remedial measures that go beyond compensation. The current reforms found in Draft Article 1266-1 emphasise the need to strip profits from wrongdoing, but they have provoked heated debates over what appear to be excessively punitive penalty ceilings. Rowan's essay also demonstrates how these reform efforts must be understood in light of existing private law mechanisms, such as tolerance of punitive contractual damages clauses, the graduated approaches to measurement of compensation adopted by courts to reflect varying degrees of culpability, as well as the *astreinte*, which engage punitive means to enforce compensatory orders.[36]

In all aspects, we might conclude, a key challenge remains to determine how to ensure that punitive measures are proportionate and well-adapted to achieve distinctly civil aims.[37] The mirror enquiry is to interrogate further why subtle and targeted remedies, which do seem well-adapted to achieve proportionate punishment in appropriate cases, such as equity's disgorgement of profits following an account, are not available more broadly and consistently in respect of egregious common law wrongs.[38] As Barnett's work both within and outside of this collection shows, it is entirely possible for the general law to articulate principled bases for their award.[39] We shall see in section IV that this view is only fortified once statutory principles and trends are taken into account.

II. Fluid and Interlocking Boundaries

As this first theme demonstrates, a second major issue for better understanding of punishment and private law is the need carefully to map and untangle

[35] Rolph, ch 6.

[36] Rowan, ch 3.

[37] Morgan's chapter well demonstrates the sort of subtle and targeted examination that may be required to determine the role of punitive damages in specific contexts, in his case, vicarious liability scenarios: see ch 11. See also Tiverios and McFarlane, ch 13, section IV.A on the relationship between courts' role in creating secondary rights arising from breach of contract and parties' capacity to agree remedies that might operate to subvert courts' remedial choices.

[38] Barnett's chapter is eloquent on the spectrum of approaches; see ch 9, sections IV and V. Justice Edelman's extra-curial statements that deceit has yielded and should yield disgorgement damages are of particular interest in light of *Lifeplan* (n 11), which similarly draws threads across equitable, statutory and common law wrongs: see J Edelman, JNE Varuhas, and S Colton (eds), *McGregor on Damages*, 20th edn (London, Sweet & Maxwell, 2018) paras 15-041–15-044.

[39] Barnett, ch 9. K Barnett, *Accounting for Profit for Breach of Contract: Theory and Practice* (Oxford, Hart Publishing, 2012).

the intertwined threads of criminal and civil law, (here including interlocking statutory principles), and in particular the roles of punishment and deterrence.[40] Criminal and civil prohibitions and remedies, including civil fines,[41] sit along a spectrum of doctrinal and legislative tools,[42] supported by courts' own inherent enforcement mechanisms and procedures.[43] But it remains the case that criminal liability exerts a profound and distinctive force, denouncing conduct, with personal, financial and societal consequences for the defendant that are not properly found in civil law.[44] Penner further argues, powerfully, that punishment serves not only to condemn criminal acts, but also to provide public assurance that the community has 'taken the side' of the victim and takes their rights seriously.[45] Key to just punishment of this sort is, again, ensuring that it is proportionate and that it does not stray into unjustifiable forms of (state-backed) private retaliation, the latter of which is (in Penner's assessment) perilously in view with punitive damages.[46]

It is clearly appropriate that courts and legislatures are cautious about unwittingly collapsing this divide, and that scholars are astute both to distil the lessons from one jurisdiction for the other and to recognise where the potential for exchange properly ends. Here we consider that Roberts and Richardson's chapter is an exemplar of how this may be done.[47] As they show, the boundaries between private and public law, between civil and criminal liability, are fluid, evolving and context-specific.[48] Proper navigation of these borders requires significant collaboration and coordination of theoretical and practical elements and understandings. However, the end product may be a more integrated and harmonious system of law overall – a possibility to which we return in section IV.

[40] See Barker, ch 2, sections II and III generally and section III.E in particular. Penner's analysis of deterrence as providing prudent reasons for conduct, as opposed to punishment as 'assurance', provides one cogent account of how this may be done. He would notably separate out punishment from penalties, the latter of which may be appropriate in the civil law context: see Penner, ch 5, sections IV and VI.

[41] Rowan, ch 3; Penner, ch 5; Bant and Paterson, ch 10; Courtney, ch 12.

[42] The rich spectrum of potential regulatory mechanisms, including administrative arrangements such as voluntary undertakings, is well-surveyed in the Australian Law Reform Commission Report 136, *Corporate Criminal Responsibility* (2020) ch 5.

[43] Rolph, ch 6.

[44] eg J Feinberg, 'The Expressive Function of Punishment' (1965) 49(3) *Monist* 397. This and the expressive account of punishment is closely analysed by Penner, ch 5, sections II and III. It is for this reason that the ALRC has recommended that corporate criminalisation only occur where 'denunciation and condemnation of the conduct constituting the offence is warranted': Australian Law Reform Commission Report 136, *Corporate Criminal Responsibility* (2020) Recommendation 2.

[45] Penner, ch 5, sections I and II.

[46] Penner, ch 5, section VI.A.

[47] Roberts and Richardson, ch 4.

[48] cf Rolph, ch 6, section I: '[T]he distinction between civil and criminal contempt is not strict and complete; it is permeable …'. While Rolph questions whether the distinction is either efficacious or desirable, or indeed capable of elucidation in a rational way, he considers that it may be too deeply ingrained to be removed. One reason for the last is the integration of the distinction into statutes, as to which see the fourth theme, in section IV of this chapter.

III. Testing Deterrence: Fact and Fit

A third theme is the need to explore more fully the role and effectiveness of the central concept of deterrence in private law, including through further quantitative and qualitative empirical work. As Goudkamp and Katsampouka observe, there is little empirical analysis in the United Kingdom of the incidence and award of punitive damages, although some important early steps have been taken.[49] We may add that there is still less research into the basal question of whether civil deterrent remedies work and, if so, what essential features characterise that success.[50] Does a punitive award at the sorts of meagre levels identified in the UK studies to date[51] nonetheless have a stronger deterrent effect because of the expressive value of the award, in comparison to a (potentially) much greater disgorgement remedy in equity? How are these alternative approaches to be reconciled, if at all? When no advantage is enjoyed, how can we best frame compensatory measures to ensure general and specific deterrence?[52] Conversely, do punitive measures have deleterious broader effects? Courtney, for example, notes that the oft-made law-and-economics claim that agreed damages clauses, particularly punitive ones, are inefficient, is subject to 'considerable debate over the circumstances in which, if at all, this is true'.[53] And how do civil penalties (or fines) and other statutory awards relate to the general law's remedial scheme? Here, civil penalties might be seen as filling a regulatory gap in the private law by providing a deterrent response to bad behaviour even where there is no loss suffered or, indeed, profit gained. On this understanding, core tasks for future examination include charting and assessing their effectiveness in this role.[54]

[49] Goudkamp and Katsampouka, ch 8, section III.A. As they explain, the sole UK analysis is J Goudkamp and E Katsampouka, 'An Empirical Study of Punitive Damages' (2018) 38 *OJLS* 90; in Australia, F Maher, 'An Empirical Study of Exemplary Damages in Australia' (2019) 43 *Melbourne University Law Review* 694; and in Canada, N Vidmar and B Feldthusen, 'Exemplary Damages Claims in Ontario: An Empirical Profile' (1990) 16 *Canadian Business Law Journal* 262. By contrast, in the US, 'the law of punitive damages has been subjected to exhaustive empirical investigation': Goudkamp and Katsampouka, ch 8, section III.A, text accompanying n 79.

[50] Lionel Smith (n 19), for example, has doubted the deterrent effect of the equitable account of profits, but this is premised on the basis that the account strips only the net profit: for the far more wide-reaching approach taken in Australia, see *Lifeplan* (n 11), examined in detail in Bant and Paterson, ch 10, section IV. No empirical work, to our knowledge, exists in relation to the deterrent potency of the equitable remedy, nor are there more concrete insights from legislative adoption of advantage-stripping pecuniary fines: see discussion in section IV.

[51] Rowan, ch 3, section V.B observes that the authors of the draft French civil penalties bill would regard the modest English punitive measures as 'toothless'.

[52] Here Sharkey's groundbreaking work, including in ch 7, provides valuable foundations. See also C Parker and VL Nielsen, 'How Much Does It Hurt? How Australian Businesses Think about the Costs and Gains of Compliance and Noncompliance with the Trade Practices Act' (2008) 32 *Melbourne University Law Review* 554.

[53] Courtney, ch 12, section II.A.ii; see also Courtney and Goudkamp, ch 1, section I.D.

[54] The Australian Law Reform Commission's Report 136 into Corporate Criminal Responsibility (2020) ch 3 notes that the lack of accessible and complete quantitative data, including on enforcement action (and hence on penalties), presents a major hurdle to the assessment and principled

These empirical enquiries stand separate from the ongoing and important questions of theory, doctrine and practice that challenge the 'fit' between punitive measures and awards on the one hand, and deterrent objectives on the other. Chapters in this collection exemplify the kinds of enquiries that demand further attention. For example, Morgan's analysis of punitive damages and vicarious liability suggests that a deterrence objective struggles to justify 'vicarious punishment' in most cases.[55] The exception is the role of punitive damages to deter egregious abuses of state power. Yet other jurisdictions with less constrained approaches to the award of punitive damages have seen a wider role for 'general deterrence' in their award, beyond state authorities.[56] Whether this provides a more principled basis for vicarious punishment will also depend on the (contested) juridical basis for vicarious liability. In the field of contract law, Zou and Liu's criticisms of 'bad leaver' clauses identify their punitive operation but also lack of fit with deterrent objectives.[57] That analysis informs their call for statutory intervention. Penner's chapter, by contrast, draws a number of careful distinctions that are critical to understanding the operation of allegedly deterrent aims in fiduciary law.[58] He distinguishes (for example) between profit-stripping remedies that simply enforce a fiduciary's primary obligation, and remedies that, while superficially similar, operate as true private law penalties. His analysis also posits a novel distinction between punishment and penalty, showing how the latter may operate in a principled way to achieve deterrent objectives in private law. Much work clearly remains to be done, building from such foundations.

IV. Statute and Coherence

A fourth, related theme is the need to take seriously statutory developments affecting the common law, when seeking both to describe and map its future development.[59] Statutes need not constitute unwelcome and unprincipled

development of corporate criminal law. It has accordingly recommended (Recommendation 1) the development of 'national principles and policies for the collection, maintenance and dissemination of criminal justice data'.

[55] Morgan, ch 11, sections I, IV.A and XII.

[56] See, eg, *Uren v John Fairfax & Sons Pty Ltd* (1966) 117 CLR 118; *Lamb v Cotogno* (1987) 164 CLR 1.

[57] Zou and Liu, ch 14, section I.

[58] Penner, ch 5, sections III and IV.

[59] The growing interest in the interaction between statute and general law is now considerable, but for some influential examples, see P Finn, 'Statutes and the Common Law' (1992) 22 *University of Western Australia Law Review* 7; J Beatson, 'Has the Common Law a Future?' (1997) 56 *CLJ* 300; W Gummow, *Change and Continuity: Statute, Equity and Federalism* (Oxford, Oxford University Press, 1999); J Beatson, 'The Role of Statute in the Development of Common Law Doctrine' (2001) 117 *LQR* 247; P Finn, 'Statutes and the Common Law: The Continuing Story' in S Corcoran and S Bottomley (eds), *Interpreting Statutes* (Annandale, Federation Press, 2005) 52; R French, 'Torts in Commercial Law: Promiscuous Entanglement or Blessed Union?' in S Degeling, J Edelman and J Goudkamp (eds), *Torts in Commercial Law* (Pyrmont,Thomson Reuters, 2011) 17; A Burrows, 'The Relationship of Common

incursions into the law (although that may, of course, be true in some cases).[60] Rather, they may well express or manifest important statutory principles, which provide guidance for development of a more rational and integrated treatment of punishment in private law, across related common law, equitable and statutory fields.[61] In our chapter, we sought to show some of the valuable insights to be obtained from considering civil penalties in light of equitable principles. The converse is also true. Civil penalty regimes, which impose fines for civil misconduct, constitute a clear and undeniable acknowledgement of the central role of deterrence in modern market societies. Their widespread adoption arguably undermines any 'a priori' argument that punitive measures are foreign to private law objectives. Their search to identify relevant criteria effective to achieve deterrence may also underline the legitimacy of general law principles that remain themselves controversial. For example, growing statutory (across common law and civilian law traditions)[62] recognition of the value of taking the advantage enjoyed by the defendant from the breach into account for deterrence objectives both highlights the utility of equity's disgorgement remedies and raises penetrating questions over courts' caution to award these in respect of serious common law wrongs, such as deceit.[63]

Courtney's chapter also examines the revealing intersections between statutory and general law principles. It draws on historic statutory schemes that imposed fines on workers for breach of their employment contracts to support Courtney's interpretation of the common law penalties doctrine.[64] While law and society may have evolved considerably since those times, his point is that these statutes reveal longstanding tolerance of punitive measures in contract, at least in some contexts. Rowan's discussion of the French reforms to introduce civil penalties for tort

Law and Statute in the Law of Obligations' (2012) 128 *LQR* 231; M Leeming, 'Theories and Principles Underlying the Development of the Common Law: The Statutory Elephant in the Room' (2013) 36 *University of New South Wales Law Journal* 1002; D Wright, *Common Law in the Age of Statutes: The Equity of the Statute* (Chatswood, LexisNexis Butterworths, 2015); E Bant, 'Statute and Common Law: Interaction and Influence in Light of the Principle of Coherence' (2015) 38(1) *University of New South Wales Law Review* 367; A Mason, 'A Judicial Perspective on the Development of Common Law Doctrine in the Light of Statute Law' in A Robertson and M Tilbury (eds), *The Common Law of Obligations: Divergence and Unity* (Oxford, Hart Publishing, 2016) 119; R Grantham and D Jensen, 'Coherence in the Age of Statutes' (2016) 42 *Monash University Law Review* 360. Collections such as those edited by TT Arvind and Jenny Steele show what is possible through applying this statutory lens: TT Arvind and J Steele (eds), *Tort Law and the Legislature: Common Law, Statute and the Dynamics of Legal Change* (Oxford, Hart Publishing 2020); and TT Arvind and J Steele (eds), *Contract Law and the Legislature: Autonomy, Expectations, and the Making of Legal Doctrine* (Oxford, Hart Publishing 2020).

[60] The Australian civil liability acts are generally a case in point, but even these show occasionally flashes of principle, for example on their divisions of factual causation from scope of liability enquiries: see, eg, Civil Liability Act 2002 (WA), s 5C; Civil Liability Act 2002 (NSW), s 5D; Civil Liability Act 2003 (Qld), s 11; Civil Liability Act 1936 (SA), s 34; Wrongs Act 1958 (Vic), s 51; Civil Liability Act 2002 (Tas), s 13; Civil Law (Wrongs) Act 2002 (ACT), s 45.

[61] See, eg, Finn, 'Statutes and the Common Law' (n 59) 52; French (n 59) 18–10; Bant (n 59).

[62] See Rowan, ch 3, section III; Bant and Paterson, ch 10, sections II and III.B.

[63] Edelman (n 38).

[64] Courtney, ch 12, section III.D. Contrast Tiverios and McFarlane, ch 13, section II.

suggests that this tolerance of punishment in private law fields is also increasingly the case, in at least some civilian jurisdictions. The reforms emphasise the necessity for proportionality in the assessment of the level of fine, which must be 'proportionate to the seriousness of the fault, the financial means of the wrongdoer and the profit gained from the wrongful conduct'.[65] Rowan notes the resemblances, as well as distinctions, between these statutory principles and their English common law counterparts relating to punitive and disgorgement damages.

Yet despite these interconnections, statutory penalties also represent a distinct regulatory mechanism from their general law cousins, being sought through proceedings brought by regulators in the public interest. Thus, they avoid the commonly expressed concerns about punitive damages' effecting a plaintiff windfall.[66] Rather, any fine is directed to the public purse.[67] Statutory fines hence occupy a position that straddles the public–private divide and operate beyond strictly private disputes. It seems, therefore, that they can be more blunt and overtly punitive in their operation and effect.

Equally, statutory regimes often pursue different protective and instrumental goals, which may at times require them to cut across private law rules and principles. Thus, in Courtney's opening words, 'Freedom of contract remains the dominant philosophy of the common law institution of contract'.[68] Yet the freedoms of contract may legitimately be subject to restriction for protective purposes, for example (as Zou and Liu argue) where the contractual freedom to deter breach becomes oppressive in its operation.[69] The tension between resilient private law values, such as contractual themes of freedom of contract, and countervailing trends in legislation aimed at protecting other rights, such as human rights, the position of employees and other vulnerable parties such as consumers, remains a key and ongoing challenge to development of a more coherent and integrated legal system.

V. The Way Forward

This last point brings us squarely to the issue of legal development and reform. If, as we assert, it is highly desirable to promote the development of a more coherent

[65] Rowan, ch 3, section III.B.iii.

[66] See also Rowan, ch 3, section V.A; Courtney and Goudkamp, ch 1, section I.C; Sharkey, ch 7, section IV.A.

[67] Sharkey's analysis (ch 7, section IV) raises the intriguing possibility of directed fines, that is, fines that are paid to appropriate third party bodies, such as community legal centres, universities or other appropriate bodies. Interestingly, while these sorts of community awards are commonly agreed between regulator and defendant pursuant to enforceable undertakings in the Australian context, their formal adoption as part of an expanded judicial armoury was not considered by the Australian Law Reform Commission Report 136 Corporate Criminal Responsibility (2020). This merits further examination.

[68] Courtney, ch 12, section I.

[69] Zou and Liu, ch 14, section IV.

legal system, it remains the case that the system must be not only rational, but also just and (desirably) efficient. Here we simply observe that this requires not only close attention to patterns of doctrine and rules developed across and within civil and criminal spheres, but also that we take advantage of the considerable insights offered from theoretical, economic, political, historic, comparative and broader perspectives. This collection gives testament to the value of adopting multiple perspectives and the potential they offer for development of concrete principles or pathways to better regulation of egregious misconduct. As will be already apparent, Rowan engages deeply with civilian viewpoints and insights, Barker and Penner with legal theory, Rolph, Tiverious and McFarlane with legal history, Roberts and Richardson with political theory and criminal law understandings, Sharkey with economic analysis drawing on the distinctive US experience, Morgan with implications of state power, and so it goes on. This sort of multifaceted survey provides a richness against which the original, doctrinal analyses of contributors such as Barnett, Zou and Liu, which seek to provide roadmaps for judicial and legislative reform, may be appreciated, contested and further developed.

INDEX

accessorial liability 277–8
account of profits 18, 206–7, 402
assurance theory 25, 119–26
Australia 225, 239, 245, 249–50, 276–85, 399–400
causation 28, 278–9, 283
definition 206
deterrence 28, 53, 74–6, 239–40, 276–85, 399, 406–7
fiduciaries 250, 276–8, 283
France, proposal for civil penalty in 74–6, 407
gain-based damages 74
gain-stripping rules 119–26
intellectual property rights 74
legitimate interest requirement 75–6, 240, 249
no unauthorised profit rule 119, 121–6
proportionality 300
quantification 279–80
retribution 239–40
scope of liability 282–3
Singapore 261–2
agency
assurance theory 25, 109, 111–13, 115, 118–25
principal, relationship with 121–2
aggravated damages
breach of contract, unavailability for 217
Australia 227, 245, 248, 253
compensatory, as 290–1, 295–7
defamation 200–1
deterrence 256
feelings or dignity of victim 291
vicarious liability 290–1, 295–7
agreed punishment 321–50, 406
agreed damages/remedies clauses 22, 324–5, 328, 334, 336, 360, 363–7, 370, 400, 404
authority to punish 327, 349
Cavendish v Makdessi 324–5, 329–32, 337–40, 343, 347, 349
common law 321, 329, 333–6, 346–8, 406–7
deposit, forfeiture of 328–9
disciplinary sanctions 348–9
employment 347–9
executory sanctions 328–9
express rights to terminate for breach 346–8, 349
forfeiture, relief against 29, 322, 328, 341–5, 349
freedom of contract 321–2, 407
hard treatment 348–9
inequality of bargaining power 327–8
legitimate interest concept 325, 400
objections 324–9, 349
contractual agreement, to 325–9
punishment, to 324–5
other controls upon sanctions 345–9
penalties, rule against 22, 29, 321–5, 329–41, 346, 349–50
primary obligations 321, 400
procedural safeguards, insufficiency of 29, 327, 349
proportionality 30, 322, 325, 349, 400
public policy 324, 325–6
punishment, definition of 29, 322–4
restitution 321, 344–5
secondary obligations 321
self-executing sanctions 328–9
termination 321, 328–9, 341, 343, 345–9
windfalls 29, 327
aims of punishment *see* **punishment, meaning and aims of**
appeasement 15–16, 24, 55–6, 60, 208
arbitrary, oppressive or unconstitutional conduct by government servants 29, 189, 213–15, 227–8, 291–7, 311–18, 405
assurance theory of prohibition and punishment 105–30
account of profits 25, 119–26
agency 25, 109, 111–13, 115, 118–25
bribes 25, 120
conflict of interests 121–3, 128–9
criminal law 106–15, 126–7, 403
desert 111–12

deterrence 25, 113–15, 127–9
expressivist theory 25, 105–13
facilitative regimes 115–17, 118
fiduciaries 25, 105, 119–29, 130, 405
gain-stripping rules 119–27, 405
penalties, rule against 105, 114–29, 405
proportionality 114, 126–7, 403
punitive damages 117–18
regulatory offences 114–15, 127, 129
responding to wrongdoers 106–9
retaliation 109, 118, 127, 403
retribution 105, 109–11
teleology or purpose of punishment 112
windfalls 25, 117, 126–7

attorneys' fees, awards of 265

Australia
civil pecuniary penalties 170, 257, 264, 268–7, 406
Consumer Law 170, 263–71, 275, 285
contempt 132, 134–5, 145–50
deposits, forfeiture against 330
excessive, awards as often 194, 196
fines 141
good faith 346–8
mental distress damages 17
prior punishment 213
privacy 83–5, 91–2, 101
solicitors, breach of court orders by 139–40
vicarious liability 54, 311

autonomy
bad leaver clauses and rule against penalties 31, 376, 394
corrective justice 47
penalties, rule against 21, 31, 376, 394
privacy 89–91, 94, 96, 102–3

bad leaver clauses and rule against penalties 339, 375–94
abusive employment relationships 376, 380
autonomy 31, 376, 394
avoidance of penalties 383–7
bad leaver, definition of 376, 383–4, 386
bonuses, withholding or reduction in 31, 375, 382
Cavendish v Makdessi 376, 382, 385–6
deductions from wages 381, 390
deterrence 22, 376–7, 381, 401, 405, 407
drafting 31, 377
efficiency 31, 379–80, 389
financial detriment 375–7, 381, 390, 392
freedom to leave and punishment 380–2
good faith 389
inequality in bargaining power 380, 388, 390–1, 394
judicial controls 388–9
legitimate interest requirement 382, 387–9, 393
limits on the paradigm of penalty 389–91, 393
minority shareholder protection and right to exit 391–2
misconduct, dismissal for 31, 376–7, 382, 387
oppressive conduct by stronger parties, control of 31
poor performance, dismissal for 376
reason for termination 31, 375–6
reform proposals 31, 391–3
regulation of penalty clauses 391
repayment provisions 375, 388–9
restraint of trade 380, 388–9, 392–3
restrictive covenants 375, 385
right/freedom to quit 31, 376–82, 388, 390–4
secondary obligations 385, 387–8
shareholders' agreements 375
social conditions for leaving 378
specific performance 379
statutory controls 31, 377, 391–2
substance and reality test 386
summary dismissal 385–6
triggers 375, 383–4
unconscionability 387–8, 389
unfair and/or oppressive imbalances in employment relationship 380
utilitarianism 31, 380, 392

bribes 25, 120

burden of proof 10–11, 150, 327

Canada
contempt 132
deterrence 53–4
employment 310
excessive awards 196–7
exemplary damages in contract law 236, 248–9, 252–3
mental distress damages 17
punitive damages 17, 76, 228, 235–6
Quebec Charter of Human Rights 54
retribution, egregious or outrageous conduct in 14
Rookes categories 227

causation 28, 203–4, 278–9, 283, 363

causes of action 13–14, 192, 218–19, 226–8, 248, 255–6
civil and criminal contempt, distinction between 131–52, 401–2
administration of justice (criminal), interference with 26, 133, 135, 140–1
anomalies 139–43
appeals 148–50
Australia 132, 134–5, 145–50
breaches of orders (civil) 25–6, 138–9
burden of proof 150
classification 131, 133, 137–9, 145–7
coercive, civil contempt as 26, 131, 133–4, 137–8
common law 131, 138, 146, 148–9
damages 142–3
extradition 144
human rights guarantees 146–7
imprisonment 131, 133, 137–8, 141–2, 144, 146–7, 151
injunctions 140–1, 147
institution of proceedings by court of its own motion 147
judicial statements 134
justification for distinction 131, 133–4
primary or dominant purpose 136–7
privilege 144–5
punitive, criminal contempt as 26, 131, 133–4
reform 146
remedial, civil contempt as 26, 131, 133–4, 137–8
scandalising the court 133
standard of proof 146, 150
standing 147–8
statutes 148–50
transformation of civil contempt into criminal contempt 139
undertakings 143
civil penalties
Australia 42, 257, 264, 268–76, 406
burden of proof 10–11
commercial misconduct 268
deterrence 52, 61, 264, 267–8, 270–9, 404
double or treble damages in civil actions 39
equity 276, 406
France 71–2, 77, 80
'French factors' in setting awards 271–4
injunctions 52
procedural safeguards 9–11
profit 272–6
rehabilitation 51–2
standard of proof 10–11
class actions 49, 181
common law
civil law, separation from 23
contempt 131, 138, 146, 148–9
corrective justice 48
deposits, forfeiture against 329
deterrence 28, 256, 258, 265, 269, 276–8, 282–3, 333–4, 398, 407
equity 256–7, 355–7
forfeiture, rule against 30, 351, 355–6
freedom of contract 321
mistake 355–6
penalties, rule against 30, 329, 333–4, 336, 351, 355–6, 360–5, 372–3
punitive damages 12, 48, 73, 93, 189, 235, 236, 262–8, 290, 309–13, 338, 364, 398–9
retribution 26–7
standard of proof 146
statute 405–6
vicarious liability 289, 293–4, 299, 309–13
compensation fund, diversion of penalties to 77–8, 172–84
compensatory damages 4, 6, 17
account of profits 249
aggravated damages 290–1, 295–7
agreed punishment 325
capping of compensatory awards to high-earners 60
deterrence 256
excessive, awards as 194, 196–7
negligence 399
punitive damages 6–7, 194, 196–7, 204–5
vicarious liability 295–301, 307, 309–10, 315–16
concurrent liability 324
confiscation orders 210–11
conflicts of interest 25, 121–6, 128–9
consumer law
Australia 170, 236, 237, 247
Consumer Protection Act 1987 (UK) 192
deterrence 26, 156, 255–6, 258–9, 269–74, 285
inequality of bargaining power 255
market efficiency 255–6
statute 192, 226, 257

contempt of court *see* **civil and criminal contempt, distinction between**
civil contempt 131, 133 137–8, 141–2, 151
definition 132
disobedience to court orders 138–9
imprisonment 131, 133, 137–8, 141–2, 151
criminal contempt 133–4, 139–40, 147–8
Attorney-General, institution of proceedings by 148
definition 134
deterrence 256
disobedience to court orders 138–9
fines 141–2
formal contempt 131
imprisonment 131, 133, 137–8, 141–2, 151
procedure, contempt in 131
proximity 140
public interest 134
punishment, as 134–5, 137–8
solicitors, breach of court orders by 139–40
standing 147–8
contract law *see also* **agreed punishment; bad leaver clauses and rule against penalties**
certainty 13
concurrent liability 324
deterrence 232–4, 241–4, 400
efficient breach thesis in contract law 7–9, 13, 242–3
exclusion clauses 66, 325
expressive function 400
France, proposal for civil penalty in 75–7, 401
information, duty to provide 77
mere contractual rights, loss of 30
negotiations 77
profitable wrongs, remedies for 75–7
punitive damages 13, 17, 75–7, 235, 240, 248, 349, 400
damages inadequate 248–50
declaratory function and 234–5, 244–5
deterrence and 232–4, 241–4
guiding factors 245–8
history 226–8
legitimate interest 251–3
maliciousness 250–1
normative bases 228
public policy 253
punishment and 229–31
retributive desert and 237–41
contribution 302
contributory negligence 188, 222–3, 398
copyright 260–1, 264–5, 267
corporations
accessorial or participatory liability 277–8
corporate opportunity doctrine 122
deterrence 80, 155, 158, 161–3, 185, 275, 277–8
France, proposal for civil penalty in 80
corrective justice 4, 22, 36, 47–50, 55–6, 59–61, 233
corruption 101–3
costs 6, 47, 312
criminal law *see also* **civil and criminal contempt, distinction between; sentencing**
arbitrary, oppressive or unconstitutional conduct by government servants 314, 317
assurance theory 106–15, 126–7, 403
burden of proof 10–11
civil and criminal law, boundaries between 37, 259–60, 403
compensation orders 3
contempt of court 133–4, 139–40, 147–8
corrective justice 50
criminalisation
assurance theory 108
privacy 84–5, 94, 100–2
deterrence 161
displacement function 108–9
hearsay rule 11
malicious prosecution 293, 316
negligence 12, 220–1
parsimony, principle of 12, 98–9
privacy 24–5, 83–7, 92–3, 96–7, 101–3
private prosecutions 39, 314
procedural safeguards 9–10
prosecutorial indifference, overcoming 101–3
punishment, definition of 35, 43, 323
purposes of punishment 35, 56, 61, 38
regulatory offences 114–15, 127
repeat offenders 114
retribution 45–7
standard of proof 10–11
state's role in prosecutions 313–14
tort 38
vengeance 45–6
vicarious liability 298, 303–4, 314, 317
victimless crimes 108
culpability 16, 27, 398–9
deterrence 274–7
punitive damages 5, 14, 205–6, 221–2

damages *see also* **compensatory damages; excessive damages; mental distress damages; punitive damages; quantum of damages**
additional damages 261–2, 265, 267
assurance theory 113
contempt 142–3
cost-of-cure damages 238–9
disgorgement damages 27, 188, 190, 209–13, 276–84, 402, 407
double or treble damages in civil actions 39
expectation damages 244
loss-based damages 287
multiple damages 265–6
multipliers 169–70
nominal damages 298
reasonable fee awards 225, 245
restitutionary damages 4–5, 74, 120, 260, 281, 321, 344–5, 399
societal damages/remedial funds 172–84
statutory damages 156, 168–71, 262, 266
vindicatory damages 57
Wrotham Park damages 249
data protection 24, 92–4, 99–100
deceit 244, 256–7, 285, 398–9
declaratory theory of punishment 60–1, 235, 244–6, 253
deep pockets reasoning 303, 306, 310, 317
defamation
absolute privilege defence 40
aggravated damages 200–1
availability heuristic 200
deterrence 201
excessive, awards as 197–8
profit motive 199–200
punitive damages 188, 199–201, 205
deposits, forfeiture of 329–30, 344–5
deserts
agreed punishment 327–8
assurance theory 111–12
consequentialism 328
deterrence 269
moral and legal deserts, distinction between 240–1
punishment, definition of 16
retribution 237–41, 328
wilfulness 237–8
deterrence 39, 52–5
accessorial liability 277–8
account of profit 53, 239–40, 260, 276–84
additional damages 261–2, 265, 267
adverse publicity orders 259, 261, 270
aggravated damages 256
assurance theory 25, 113–15, 127–9
bad leaver clauses and rule against penalties 22, 376–7, 381, 401, 405, 407
civil and criminal law, boundaries between 259–60, 403
civil penalties 52, 163–5, 166–72, 267–8, 270–9, 404
common law 28, 256, 258, 265, 269, 276–8, 282–3, 333–4, 398, 407
compensatory damages 256, 401
Competitions and Markets Authority 258–9
consumer law 28, 255–9, 266, 269–74, 285
contempt 256
contract law 400
copyright 256, 260, 261, 265, 267, 282
corporations 155, 275, 277–8
deceit 256–7, 282, 285, 398, 399, 402, 406
deep pockets reasoning 303, 306, 310, 317
defamation 201
disgorgement damages 209–10, 276–84
double deterrence 304, 314–17
effectiveness 53, 257, 267, 333–4, 404
employment 303–4
equity 28, 256–7, 276–7, 283, 401
excessive damages 27, 47, 65, 79, 114, 126, 160, 171, 185, 262, 266
expressive functions of awards 404
fiduciaries 60, 127–9
fines 115, 174–5, 258–9, 281, 285, 337–8
general deterrence 232, 257, 266, 267, 269, 273, 276–7, 282, 404
intellectual property rights 28, 256, 258, 261, 264–5, 267, 285
misleading conduct 264, 269–72
negative incentive to perform 334
negligence 222, 247, 256, 263, 268, 399
over-deterrence 165, 172, 198–9, 269
penalties, rule against 22, 65, 76, 127–9, 257, 265, 332–4, 338, 366–7
prior punishment 210, 212–13
privacy 85, 101
proportionality 28, 156, 163, 255–85
punitive damages 16, 26, 52–4, 60, 71, 192, 193–8, 208–13, 218, 222, 226, 229, 231–4, 239–44, 248, 401
punishment, definition of 42, 52–5, 60–1, 232–3, 255, 267–76, 281
reform 156, 259–60, 272, 275–6, 402, 407–8

remoteness principles and 15, 65, 66, 77, 244, 256, 282–3, 285, 398
rescission and 281, 399
retribution 55, 60, 155, 233, 274
Rookes v Barnard 214, 256, 259
societal damages/remedial funds 172, 176–7, 181–3
specific deterrence 266, 267, 273, 277, 282, 404
statutory law 28, 255–67, 268–76, 405–7
tort 60, 156, 158–9, 161, 165–6, 268
trust, undermining 244
unconscionable conduct 270–1
under-deterrence 9, 165–6
unjust enrichment and 126, 174, 185, 209, 213, 281–4, 327
vicarious liability 54, 287, 290, 296–300, 303–17, 405
deep pockets reasoning 303, 306, 310, 317
double deterrence 304, 314–17
digital technologies 24, 83, 96–8, 101–2
disciplinary sanctions 338, 348–9
disgorgement *see also* **account of profits**
assurance theory 25
damages 27, 188, 209–10, 212–13, 245, 260
deterrence 164, 166, 172, 256
vicarious liability 294, 298
dishonesty 202–3, 250–1
distributive justice 22–3, 44–5, 50–1, 60
double punishment 92–3, 101, 211–12, 231, 297–8
duelling 234, 244

efficiency 7–9, 166, 242–3, 408
agreed punishment 326
bad leaver clauses and rule against penalties 31, 379–80, 389
compensation fund, diversion of penalties to 78
deterrence 28, 52, 274
efficient breach thesis in contract law 7–9, 13, 242–3
Kaldor-Hicks efficiency 8
Pareto efficiency 8, 242
employment
arbitrary, oppressive or unconstitutional conduct by government servants 314
bad leaver clauses and rule against penalties 22, 31, 339, 375–94
deductions from salary 338
deterrence 303–4
disciplinary sanctions 348–9
failure to prosecute employees 314
fines 338–41
incentives 303, 307
indemnities 302
procedural fairness 348–9
termination/dismissal 31, 338–41, 375–6, 381–7, 389
vicarious liability 288, 294–5, 300–7, 310, 313–16
enterprise liability 287, 307–9
equity *see also* **account of profits**
Australia 226
civil penalties 406
common law 256–7, 355–7
deterrence 28, 256–7, 276–7, 283, 401
forfeiture, rule against 30, 351, 355–8, 369, 372
New Zealand 263
penalties, rule against 331, 361, 370–3
promissory estoppel 355
punitive damages 13, 192, 401
excessive damages
deterrence 65, 79, 262, 266
due process 47
punitive damages 27, 29, 187, 193–8
exclusion clauses 66, 325
executory sanctions 328–9
exemplary damages *see* **punitive damages**
expressivist theory 25, 105–13, 119–25, 229, 323, 398, 401, 404

fairness 22, 316, 348–9, 380
false imprisonment 290, 293, 316
fault 70–1, 73, 80, 82, 237–4, 274, 305, 307
fiduciaries
account of profits 250
assurance theory 15, 105, 119–29, 130, 405
conflict of interests 121–3, 128–9
contract law 400
corporate opportunity doctrine 122
deterrence 60, 127–9
gain-stripping rules 119–26, 405
loyalty, duty of 130
no unauthorised profit rule 119, 121–6, 128
penalties 128–9
punishment, definition of 323
restitution for wrongs 120
self-dealing rule 121
trusts 119, 121–2, 125–6
unjust enrichment 120

financial status of defendants 170–2
fines *see also* **civil penalties**
- data protection 92
- deterrence 115, 174–5, 258–9, 281, 285, 337–8
- employment 338–41
- excessive, awards as 194–5
- means of offenders 195
- retribution 175

foreseeability 66, 325
forfeiture 21, 30, 329, 386–7 *see also* **forfeiture, relief against**
forfeiture, relief against
- *Cavendish v Makdessi* 30, 354–6, 360
- deposits 344–5
- equity 30, 351, 355–8, 369, 372
- historical background 353–4, 357, 367–9
- leases 341–2
- mere contractual rights, loss of 30
- money distinguished, forfeiture of 343
- mortgages 341–2
- penalties, rule against 329–30, 342–3, 351–73
  - current position 361–2
  - shared origins 357–60
- proprietary or possessory rights, need for 30, 342–3, 354, 357–8, 362, 368–9
- termination 30, 328, 341, 362, 369–71
- unconscionability 342, 344, 358
- windfalls 345

fraud
- insurance 19, 212
- mitigation 398

freedom of contract 321–2, 407
French law, proposal for civil penalty to deter and punish in
- account of profits 74–6, 407
- Article 1266-1 Civil Code 63–82, 174, 402, 406–7
- *astreinte* 24, 67, 402
- beneficiary of the punitive sanction 77–8
- Catala proposals 69–70, 71
- *Champagne* case 69
- Civil Code 63–81
- compensation fund, diversion of penalty to 77–8
- disparate and informal manifestations of punishment in civil law 65–7
- draft bill for reform of civil liability 63–4
- fault with a view to making a gain or saving 70–1, 73, 80, 82
- foreseeability 66
- formal and general introduction of punishment in civil law 67–72
- gain-based damages 65, 67, 71–2, 74, 76, 81–2
- inflated damages awards 66
- information, duty to provide 77
- insurance 66, 67, 72, 81
- level of the penal award 79–80
- *ministère public*, claims by 78
- moral gap 64–5, 69
- non-compliance with court orders, punishment of 24, 67
- non-pecuniary losses 24, 66
- objection to profitable wrongs 67–9
- objective of French law, punishment as 64
- penalty clauses 24, 65, 76–7
- personality rights 73
- privacy 68, 73
- profitable wrongs 67–82
- proportionality 71, 79–80, 407
- punitive damages 65–72, 74–81
- quantum of damages 66, 79–80
- remedies for profitable wrongs 72–7
- remoteness 15, 24, 66, 77
- tort 63–4, 72–5, 76, 81–2, 401
- windfalls 70, 77–8
- wrongful eviction, punitive damages for 73–4

future themes and perspectives 397–408
- deterrence, testing 404–5
- fluid and interlocking boundaries 402–3
- private law aims, role of punishment in achieving 397–402
- statute and coherence 405–7

good faith 19, 247, 251, 346–8, 389, 399

hearsay rule 11
historical background
- civil and common law, separation of 23
- contempt 133
- forfeiture, rule against 353–4, 357, 367–8
- penalties, rule against 353–4, 357–8, 361, 368–70
- public/private law 37–9
- punitive damages 226–8, 235
- retribution in Medieval England 45

human rights *see also* **privacy**
contempt 146–7
double punishment 92–3
fair hearing, right to a 316
Human Rights Act 1998 (UK) 40, 192, 293–4, 314
just satisfaction 293–4

illegality doctrine 19–21, 40
inducing breach of contract 243
inequality of bargaining power 255, 327–8, 380, 388, 390–1, 394
injunctions 52, 256
insurance/insurability
deterrence 54, 232, 236, 275
France, proposal for civil penalty in 66, 67, 72, 81
fraud 19, 212
health insurance 175–6
liability insurance 46, 54
punitive damages 15, 46, 72, 81, 157
retribution 22, 46
intellectual property rights
account of profits 74
additional damages 267
copyright 260–1, 264–5, 267
deterrence 28, 256, 258, 261, 264–5, 267, 285
economic torts 256
intention 14, 100–1, 159, 230, 236, 335, 348

joint tortfeasors 297, 301–2
judicial review 293
just deserts *see* **deserts**

law-and-economics movement 7, 164, 232, 305, 326, 404
Law Commission 78, 81, 227
breach of contract, unavailability of punitive damages for 215–17
civil liberties 293
contributory negligence 222
defamation 200
deterrence 259–60
enterprise liability 308
excessive, awards as 193
illegality 20–1
limitation periods 293
negligence 220–1
penalties, rule against 331
Rookes categories 214
vicarious liability 301–4, 308

leases
eviction and harassment of tenants, wrongful 294
forfeiture, relief against 341–2
wrongful eviction, punitive damages for 73–4
limitation clauses 66
loss-spreading 287, 309–10

malicious prosecution 293, 316
meanings and aims of punishment *see* **punishment, meaning and aims of**
mental distress damages 16–18, 47, 225, 241, 245, 248, 252–3
misrepresentation 399
mistake 341–2, 358
misuse of executive power 29
misuse of private information, tort of 83, 94
mitigation 60, 103, 398
morality
assurance theory 25, 106–9, 112–13
deserts 240–1
fault 274
France, proposal for civil penalty in 64–5, 69
privacy 85–7, 99–100
retribution 111
vengeance 39

natural justice 298
negligence
compensatory damages 399
contributory negligence 188, 222–3, 398
criminal law 12
deterrence 256, 268
financial status of defendants 171
gross negligence 24, 66
privacy 100–1
punitive damages 192, 324–5, 399
recklessness 14
New Zealand
accident compensation scheme 310–11
Bill of Rights Act 1990 (NZ) 147
contempt 146–7
copyright, additional damages for breach of 264–5
deterrence 263–5, 310–11
mental distress damages 241
negligence 14
penalties 264–5
personal injury covered by Accident Compensation Act 2001 (NZ) 263

punitive damages 95, 228, 236, 241, 248–9, 311, 313
Rookes v Barnard 227–8, 263
vicarious liability 310–11, 313
non-molestation orders 140
non-pecuniary losses 24, 66, 329

overt and convert punishment 16–19

parsimony, principle of 12, 98–9
penalties, rule against *see* **rule against penalties**
police 199, 289, 292–3
prevention of harm 51–2
prevention of punishment 51–2, 322, 335, 342
prior punishment 27, 188, 210–13
privacy 83–103, 403
autonomy 89–91, 94, 96, 102–3
corruption 101–3
criminal law 24–5, 83–7, 92–3, 96–9, 101–3
criminalisation 84–5, 94, 100–2
data protection 24, 92–4, 99–100
deterrence 85, 101
digital technologies 24, 83, 96–8, 101–2
disclosure of information as injury 98
double punishment 92–3, 101
economic value of data 98
elections, manipulating 97–8
emerging problems 96–8, 101–2
English law 83, 94–5
exemplary damages 85, 91–3, 95–102
France, proposal for civil penalty in 68, 73
identity theft 98
intentional harm 100–1
justification for punishment 84–9, 96
misuse of private information, tort of 83, 94
morality 85–7, 99–100
negligence 100–1
political participation 84
political philosophy 24, 87–8
prosecutorial indifference, overcoming 101–3
public harm, prevention of 85–7, 91
public interest 24, 83–4, 86–8, 90, 96, 99
reciprocity 88, 90, 97
republican liberalism 84, 87–98, 102–3
revenge porn 102
social relationships 89–90
tort 100, 103
private law, definition of 40–1
private prosecutions 39, 314
procedure
burden of proof 10–11, 143, 150, 280, 283
certainty 10
civil liability 9–11
contempt 131, 143, 150
fairness 348–9
insufficiency 9–12
retribution 47, 59
safeguards 9–12, 47, 59, 231
profitable wrongs 67–82
French law, proposal for civil penalty to deter and punish in 67–82
profit from wrong, where defendant sought to 28–9, 189–90, 199–200, 213–15, 294, 313
profits, account of *see* **account of profits**
proportionality
agreed punishment 30, 322, 325, 349, 400
assurance theory 114, 126–7, 403
deterrence 28, 156, 163, 255–85
distributive justice 50–1
France, proposal for civil penalty in 71, 79–80, 407
penalties, rule against 126–7, 331–2, 334, 337, 360, 365
punitive damages 71
sentencing 114, 126
protection as aim of punishment 51–2
public harm, prevention of 85–7, 91
public interest *see also* **societal deterrence in United States, punitive damages as**
contempt 134
corrective justice 47–8
privacy 24, 83–4, 86–8, 90, 96, 99
settlements 184
statutory damages 156
public policy
agreed punishment 324, 325–6
declaratory theory of punishment 246, 253
penalties, rule against 352, 355, 372
retribution 46
punishment, meaning and aims of 16, 35–7, 43–62 *see also* **deserts; deterrence; retribution**
abolitionists 35
acts and purpose, combination of 23
appeasement 15–16, 24, 55–6, 60, 208
assurance theory 110
corrective justice 4, 22, 36, 47–50, 55–6, 59–61, 233
criminal law 35, 43, 56, 61, 323
declaratory function 60–1, 235, 244–6, 253

denunciation 60–1
distributive justice 22–3, 44–5, 50–1, 60
expressive function 25, 105–13, 119–25, 229, 323, 398, 401, 404
functional purpose 156, 157–63
harm prevention 61
instrumentalism 23
judicial acts/orders 23, 41–3
multiple aims and meanings 59
pragmatism 23
prevention (prophylaxis) 51–2
protection 51–2
rehabilitation 22, 51–2, 61
restorative justice 56, 107
social messaging 24, 56–9
symbolism 323
terminology 44, 61–2
vengeance 38–9
punitive damages 4
account of profits 206–7, 225, 239–40, 245, 249–50
aggravated damages 204, 217, 227, 245, 248, 253
anomalous, punitive damages as 27, 188, 201–8
ancillary role 74, 398
arbitrary, oppressive or unconstitutional conduct by government servants 227–8
assurance theory 117–18
breach of contract, unavailability for 188, 192, 216–18
causes of action 13–14, 192, 218–19
classwide damages 178–81
common law 12, 48, 75, 93, 189, 226, 235–6, 241–2, 246, 262–8, 290, 309–13, 338, 364, 398–9
compensatory damages 6, 155–6, 164–9, 204–5, 248, 252
compensation fund, diversion of penalties to 77–8
consumer law 226, 236, 237, 247, 259, 264, 268, 273
contract and 13, 17, 75–7, 235, 240, 248, 349, 400
damages inadequate 248–50
declaratory function and 234–5, 244–5
deterrence and 232–4, 241–4
guiding factors 245–8
history 226–8
legitimate interest 251–3
maliciousness 250–1
normative bases 228
public policy 253
punishment and 229–31
retributive desert and 237–41
corrective justice 48–50
criminal law 220–1, 226–7, 231, 234
culpability 5, 14, 205–6, 221–2
deceit 244, 256–7, 285, 398–9
deserts 229–30, 233, 237–41
deterrence 16, 26, 52–4, 60, 71, 192, 208–13, 218, 222, 226, 229, 231–44, 248, 401
disgorgement damages 27, 188, 190, 209–13, 276–84, 402, 407
distributive justice 60
double punishment 211–12, 231
equity 13, 192, 276–84, 401
excessive, awards as 27, 29, 187, 193–8
exemplary damages, terminology of 16, 52, 226, 298
expressive role 398, 401
France, proposal for civil penalty in 65, 67, 74–6
general damages 204–6
history of 37–40, 48, 159, 161, 163, 226–8, 235, 311, 314, 317
Human Rights Act 1998 (UK) 192
inducing breach of contract 243
'if but only if' test 12, 191
insurance 15, 46, 72, 81, 212, 236, 275
intention 68, 159, 161, 164, 165, 230, 236, 253, 272
justification 13
last resort, as 12, 27, 191, 245, 248–50
legitimate interest requirement 27, 226, 245, 249, 251–4
limiting availability of punitive damages, principles limiting the 190–2
litigation boom 70
mental distress damages 16–18, 47, 205, 225, 241, 245, 248, 252–3
mental element 219, 226, 230, 245, 249, 251–4
misconceptions 27, 187–223, 398
negligence 27, 188, 192, 218–23, 230, 247, 263, 268, 311, 399
other responses, relationship with 14–15, 225, 245, 249–50
pre-1964 test 192
precedent 210–13, 216–18
prior punishment, irrelevance of 27, 188, 210–13

privacy 85, 91–3, 95–102
profitable wrongs 70–1, 74, 227–8
quantum 54, 66, 79–80, 192–3
rationale 26–9, 401
remoteness 202–4, 237, 244, 282, 285, 398
retribution 4, 5, 14, 26, 45–6, 155–6, 208, 226, 229–31, 233–4, 237–41, 250
Rookes v Barnard 188–92, 199–201, 204, 212–16, 219, 227–8, 231
social messaging 57
societal harm 15
societal damages and 26–7, 156–7, 161–172, 252
statutory offences 219, 227–8, 263–265
substitutive, as 49
supra-compensatory damages, as 155–6, 164–9, 172, 181, 185
tort 13–14, 17, 226–7, 230, 262–3, 268–9, 299–304
unpredictability 8, 187, 198–9
vindication 16, 57–8, 176, 208, 231, 235, 240, 283, 290, 296, 314
windfall objection 6–7, 70, 77–8, 117, 283–4
wrongful eviction, for 73–4

purposes of punishment *see* **punishment, meaning and aims of**

quantum of damages; *see also* **remoteness**
aggravating factors 192
deterrence 170–2, 192, 2
disgorgement damages 210, 276–84
France, proposal for civil penalty in 66, 79–80
mitigating factors 192
punitive damages 66, 79–80, 187, 192–3, 198–9
statutory factors 271–6
unpredictability 187, 198–9
vicarious liability 294–5, 298

reasonable fee awards 225, 245
recklessness 14, 159, 161, 164, 230
rectification 250–1
reform *see also* **French law, proposal for civil penalty to deter and punish in; Law Commission**
bad leaver clauses and rule against penalties 31, 391–3
civil penalties 257, 264, 268–76, 406
consumer law 258–62, 264, 272, 275–6
contempt 146
deterrence 156, 259–60, 275
Law Commission 78, 81, 227, 259–60
privacy 96
Scottish Law Commission 376, 391–2
Singapore 261

regulatory offences 114–15, 127, 129
rehabilitation 24, 51–2, 61
relief against forfeiture *see* **forfeiture, relief against**
remoteness
attenuated approach 202–4
causation 203–4
deceit 244, 282, 285, 398
deterrence 283, 285
diluted test 203–4
dishonesty 202–3
France, proposal for civil penalty in 15, 24, 66, 77
vicarious liability 290

repeat offenders 166–70
republican liberalism 84, 87–98, 102–3
rescission 19, 281
restorative justice 56, 107
restraint of trade 380, 388–9, 392–3
restitution 4–5, 74, 120, 260, 281, 321, 344–5, 399
restrictive covenants 375, 385
retaliation 109, 118, 127, 403
retribution 35, 39, 59–62
account of profits 239–40
assurance theory 105, 109–11
corrective justice 44–5
criminal law 45–7
definition 59
deserts 237–41, 328
deterrence 26–7, 55, 60, 155, 157–61, 233, 274
distributive justice 44–5
excusing the victim 47
fines 175
legal retribution 111
moral retribution 111
procedural safeguards 47, 59
punitive damages 4, 5, 14, 26, 45–6, 155–6, 208
punishment, definition of 16, 42–7, 56, 59–62
sentencing 99
social duty 46
social messaging 56–7
vengeance 44–6
vicarious liability 22, 46
victims, personal rights of 45–6

risk transfer premiums 181
Roman law 37–8
***Rookes* categories** *see also* **arbitrary, oppressive or unconstitutional conduct by government servants**
arbitrary, oppressive or unconstitutional conduct by government servants 29, 189 213–15, 227–8, 291–7, 311–18, 405
common law 214
deterrence 214
irrationality 29
precedent 213–16
profit from wrong, where defendant sought to 28–9, 189–90, 199–200, 213–15, 294, 313
punitive damages 188–91, 199–200, 213–16
Singapore 262
statutory authorisation 189, 190, 213–15, 291
vicarious liability 28–9, 287–8, 291–7, 311, 313–18, 405
rule against penalties 329–41
agreed punishment 22, 29, 321–5, 329–41, 349–50, 360, 363–7, 370
assurance theory 105, 114–29
Cavendish v Makdessi 30, 352–6, 360, 363, 365–7, 369–71
common law 30, 329, 333–4, 336, 351, 355–6, 360–5, 372–3
deposits, forfeiture against 329–30
deterrence 22, 65, 76, 127–9, 257, 265, 332–4, 338, 366–7
Dunlop tests 336–9
deterrence 366–7
efficiency 8–9
enforcement 355, 358–60
equity 30, 331, 351, 355–61, 370–3
facilitative regimes 115–17, 118
forfeiture of money 329
forfeiture, relief from 60, 329–30, 342–3, 351–73
current position 361–2
divergence 30, 360–72
reunification of doctrines 30–1
shared origins 357–60
France, proposal for civil penalty in 24, 65, 76–7
freedom of contract 321–2
general nature of penalties in private law 118–20
historical origins 353–4, 357–8, 361, 368–9, 370
justifications 22, 350
legitimate interest requirement 21, 242, 325, 337–8, 365–6, 400
New Zealand 264–5
non-compensatory agreed remedies 365–6
non-monetary obligations 329
penal, penalties as 360, 366, 371–2
pre-estimates of loss 332–3
prevention of punishment 335
proportionality 126–7, 331–2, 334, 337, 360, 365
proprietary or possessory rights requirement 254, 357–8, 369–70
public policy 352, 355, 372
punishment distinguished 29, 114, 124, 127–8, 323–4, 405
scope of the rule 329–30
secondary obligations 360, 363–4, 369
security rights 331–2, 353–4, 358–61, 369–70
termination 346

Scotland
contempt 133
Scottish Law Commission 376, 391–2
security rights
forfeiture, rule against 358–9, 361, 368, 371
penalties, rule against 353–4, 358–61, 369–70
self-dealing rule 121
self-executing sanctions 328–9
self-help 234, 244
sentencing
assurance theory 114, 126
fixed maximum sentences 10
proportionality 114, 126
rehabilitation 52
retribution 99
settlements 78, 117–18, 157, 180–4
shame 56
shares
bad leaver clauses and rule against penalties 31, 375–6, 383–8
compulsory transfer of shares 31, 375, 383–7, 390, 393
minority shareholder protection 391–2
unfair prejudice 391–2
Singapore
account of profits 261–2
deterrence 260–2
intellectual property statutes, additional damages in 261–2

penalties, rule against 241–2
punitive damages 225, 227, 236–7, 241–2, 248–9
Rookes categories 227
statutory damages 261–2

social messaging 24, 56–9

societal damages/remedial funds 77–8, 172–84
classwide punitive damages 178–81
common law courts, creation by 157
deterrence 172, 176–7, 181–3
fines 175
individual litigation 175–9
recognition of societal damages 180–2
remediating the societal harm 174–5
risk transfer premiums 181
settlements by private parties 157, 180–4
threat to societal damages 182–4
windfall objection 26–7, 156–7, 173–4, 177–8, 182–3

societal deterrence in United States, punitive damages as 59, 155–85, 401
bilateral concept of private law 156–8, 163
California's 'lemon laws' 166–7
classwide punitive damages 178–80
complete deterrence 163–4, 165–6
constitutional excessiveness review 158–60, 185
corporate misconduct 158, 161–3, 185
damages 168–71
multipliers 169–70
statutory 168–71
disaggregation of punitive damages 156, 157–63
disgorgement 164, 166, 172
diverting punitive damages to individual litigation 175–8
economic deterrence 157, 159, 163, 184–5
financial status of defendants 170–2
functional purpose of punitive damages 156, 157–63
gain elimination 163–4, 165–6, 172
general deterrence 157, 159, 161–3, 185
individualistic (private) interests 157–61
insurability 15, 157
loss internalisation 163–7, 172
malice 159, 161
objective factors 163, 167
optimal deterrence 164–6
over-deterrence 165, 172
property rights, enforcement of 164
proportionality 156, 163
public impact 168–70
quantum of damages 170–2
recklessness 159, 161, 164
relevant factors 166–72
remediation of societal harm 174–80
repeat offenders 166–70
retribution 26–7, 155–61
settlement 157, 180–4
specific deterrence 157–8
statutory damages 156, 261, 266
supra-compensatory damages 155–6, 164–9
theory 156, 163–6
tort 156, 158–9, 161, 165–6
under-detection/under-enforcement 164–7
unfair and deceptive acts and practices 168
unjust enrichment 174, 185
vicarious liability for punitive damages 157, 185
windfall objection 26–7, 156–7, 185

specific performance 22, 27, 77, 326, 364, 379

standard of proof 10–11, 47, 59, 146, 150, 300

statute
bad leaver clauses and rule against penalties 31, 377, 391–2
civil contempt and criminal contempt, distinction between 148–50
commercial law 257
common law 405–6
consumer law 226, 257
damages 156, 168–71
deterrence 28, 157, 255–76
vicarious liability 291

stigma 9–10, 56, 77

strict liability 171

termination
as form of punishment 321, 328–9, 341, 343, 345–9
good faith requirement in 345–9
deposits, forfeiture of 329
employment 31, 338, 341, 375–6, 381–7, 389
punitive sanctions 217, 381
summary dismissal 120, 383, 385–6
unfair dismissal 346, 379
forfeiture, relief against 30, 328, 341, 362, 369–71

tort *see also* **negligence; vicarious liability for exemplary damages**
Australia 226–7, 230, 244
concurrent liability 324

corrective justice 48
criminal law 39
deterrence 156, 158–9, 161, 165–6, 268
economic torts 256
efficiency 9, 166
France, proposal for civil penalty in 63–4, 72–5, 76, 81–2, 401
immunities 312–13
malice 161
master's tort theory 28
privacy 100, 103
profitable wrongs, remedies for 72–5, 76
punitive damages 13–14, 17, 226–7, 230, 299–304
purposes of punishment 38
retribution 46
trespass 290, 325
trusts 25, 119, 121–2, 125–6

unconscionability
bad leaver clauses and rule against penalties 387–8, 389
deterrence 270–1
forfeiture, relief against 342, 344, 358, 370–1
inequality of bargaining power 328
unincorporated associations 289
United States *see also* **societal deterrence in United States, punitive damages as**
attorneys' fees, awards of 265
compensatory damages 196
complicity approach 311–12
contempt 132, 134, 136, 151
contingency fees 312
costs 6, 312
deterrence 53, 265–6, 282, 312
due process 47
efficient breach 7–8, 242
excessive, awards as 195–6
Federal Tort Claims Act 1946 312–13
foreclosure 176
health insurance 175–6
insurance 46, 175–6, 265
mental distress damages 18
multiple damages 53, 255–6
private law, definition of 41
punitive damages 265
Restatement (Second) of Torts 311–12
retribution 46–7
settlements 180–1
split recovery regimes 172–4, 178, 182–3, 265–6
statutory damages 266
tort immunities 312–13
vicarious liability 311–13
wilful breach 14
unjust enrichment 49, 120, 126, 174, 209, 213, 281–4, 327
utilitarianism 31, 380, 392

vengeance 38–9, 44–6
vicarious liability for exemplary damages 208, 287–318
aggravated damages 290–1, 295–7
arbitrary, oppressive or unconstitutional conduct by government servants 29, 291, 292–4, 296–7, 313–18, 405
assault 290, 293
Australia 54, 311
close connection test 288–90
common law 289, 293–4, 299, 309–13
Commonwealth jurisdictions 309–10
compensatory damages 295–301, 307, 309–10, 315–16
contribution 302
costs 312
criminal law 298, 303–4, 314, 317
deep pockets reasoning 303, 306, 310, 317
deterrence 54, 287, 290, 296–300, 303–17, 405
deep pockets reasoning 303, 306, 310, 317
double deterrence 304, 314–17
detestation of the jury to the action 290
discretion 291, 297
disgorgement 294, 298
double punishment 297–8
employment 288, 294–5, 300–7, 310, 313–16
enterprise liability 287, 307–9
exemplary, meaning of 295–9
expansion of doctrine 288
extinction on death 296
fair hearing, right to a 316
false imprisonment 290, 293, 316
fault 305, 307
Human Rights Act 1998 (UK) 293–4, 314
identification/evidence 307
immigration 292
indemnities 302
independent contractors 289
institutional disapproval 307, 310
joint tortfeasors 297, 301–2

justifications 287, 291–4, 296–300, 304, 307–9, 313–17
Law Commission 301–4, 308
loss-based damages 287
loss-spreading 287, 309–10
malicious prosecution 293, 316
master's tort theory 28
misuse of executive power 29
natural justice 298
objections 28
other common law jurisdictions 309–13
police 289, 292–3
practice, exemplary damages in 294–5
profit from wrong, where defendant sought to 28–9, 294, 313
punishment 28–9, 287–318
quantification 294–5, 298
relationships triggering liability 288–9
remoteness 290
retribution 22, 46
Rookes categories 28–9, 287–8, 291–7, 311–17
sexual abuse in institutions 289
standard of proof 300
State, power of the 21, 287–8, 291, 292–7, 313–18
trespass 290
unincorporated associations 289
United States 311–13
windfalls 306

victims
excusing the victim 47
moral duty to take side of victims 25, 106–13, 403
personal rights 45–6
retribution 45–6
victim impact statements 56
victimless crimes 108

vindication of rights 16, 57, 208, 235

windfall objection
agreed punishment 29, 327
assurance theory 25, 117, 126–7
deterrence 283–4
forfeiture, relief against 345
France, proposal for civil penalty in 70, 77–8
future losses 6
punitive damages 6–7, 70, 77–8, 117
societal damages/remedial funds 26–7, 156–7, 173–4, 177–8, 182–3
under-compensation 6
vicarious liability 306

www.ingramcontent.com/pod-product-compliance
Ingram Content Group UK Ltd.
Pitfield, Milton Keynes, MK11 3LW, UK
UKHW020226290926
15470UKWH00001B/407

9 781509 93915